Advanced Graphics Programming Using OpenGL

The Morgan Kaufmann Series in Computer Graphics and Geometric Modeling

Series Editor: Brian A. Barsky University of California, Berkeley

This series publishes the finest works for the accomplished and aspiring graphics professional. The series includes intermediate and advanced textbooks, graphics programming books, surveys of important new areas and methods, and reference works.

Advanced Graphics Programming Using OpenGL

TOM McREYNOLDS

DAVID BLYTHE

AMSTERDAM • BOSTON • HEIDELBERG • LONDON
NEW YORK • OXFORD • PARIS • SAN DIEGO
SAN FRANCISCO • SINGAPORE • SYDNEY • TOKYO
MORGAN KAUFMANN PUBLISHERS IS AN IMPRINT OF ELSEVIER

Publishing Director: Diane Cerra
Publishing Services Manager: Simon Crump
Project Manager: Brandy Lilly
Editorial Coordinator: Mona Buehler
Cover Design: Dutton & Sherman Design
Text Design: Julio Esperas
Composition: Cepha Imaging Pvt. Ltd.
Illustrations: Dartmouth Publishing, Inc.
Copyeditor: Daril Bentley; Graphic World
Proofreader: Graphic World
Indexer: Graphic World
Interior printer: China Translation & Printing Services, Ltd.
Cover printer: China Tranalation & Printing Services, Ltd.

Morgan Kaufmann Publishers is an imprint of Elsevier.
500 Sansome Street, Suite 400, San Francisco, CA 94111

This book is printed on acid-free paper.

Library of Congress Cataloging-in-Publication Data
Application Submitted

ISBN: 1-55860-659-9

For information on all Morgan Kaufmann publications,
visit our Web site at *www.mkp.com or www.books.elsevier.com*

Printed in China
10 9 8 7 6 5 4 3 2 1

To my friends and colleagues from Silicon Graphics; it was a fabulous time and place to learn about 3D graphics. – DB

To Ede Forney and Harry McGinnis; you were there when it counted. – TM

Contents

CHAPTER 6

Rasterization and Fragment Processing   103

CHAPTER 7

Window System and Platform Integration   119

CHAPTER 8

OpenGL Implementations   129

PART III

Advanced Techniques   361

CHAPTER 16

CAD and Modeling Techniques   363

CHAPTER 21

Structuring Applications for Performance   571

Preface

Overview

Computer graphics has come a long way from the early days of line drawings and light pens. Today anyone can run interactive and realistic graphics applications on the hardware available on an affordable personal computer. While hardware progress has been impressive, widespread gains in software expertise has been more elusive. There are many computer graphics professionals and enthusiasts out there, but a comprehensive understanding of the accelerated graphics pipeline and how to exploit it is less widespread.

This book attempts to bring the computer graphics enthusiast, whether professional or amateur, beyond the basics covered in computer graphics texts, and introduce them to a mix of more intense practical and theoretical discussion that is hard to obtain outside of a professional computer graphics environment.

We emphasize the algorithmic side of computer graphics, with a practical application focus. We try to strike a balance between useful examples and approachable theory. We present usable techniques for real world problems, but support them with enough theory and background so the reader can extend and modify the ideas presented here.

This book is about graphics techniques, techniques that don't require esoteric hardware or custom graphics libraries, that are written in a comprehensible style, and do useful things. This book will teach you some graphics, especially areas that are sometimes underrepresented in graphics texts. But it also goes further, showing you how to apply those techniques in real world applications, filling real world needs.

Since there are already a number of excellent books that provide an introduction to computer graphics (Foley, 1994; Watt, 1989; Rogers, 1997; Angel, 1997; Newman, 1973) and to OpenGL programming (Neider, 1997; Angel, 1997) we have been necessarily brief in these areas. We assume that the reader is comfortable with these fundamentals; however, we have included extra introductory material where we thought it would improve understanding of later sections.

We also note that the computer graphics field has a lot of competing notation and vocabulary. We have tried to be consistent with terminology and notation used in the OpenGL specification and the "standard" OpenGL books while at the same time providing some mention of alternative terminology when it is relevent.

OpenGL

We chose OpenGL as our base graphics language for a number of reasons. It is designed to be full featured, to run efficiently on a wide range of graphics architectures, and is clean and straightforward to use. It also dictates very little policy. It is easy to mix and match graphics features in OpenGL to get new effects that may not have even been considered when the language was designed. Its clear specification gives the application programmer confidence that applications written in OpenGL will act predictably on many different graphics hardware and driver implementations.

OpenGL is also widely available. It can be obtained for free on all the important architectures today: Apple Machintosh, all flavors of Microsoft Windows, nearly all Unix variants including Linux, and OS/2. Most commercial system and graphics hardware vendors support OpenGL as well, and support for hardware accelerated implementations has grown rapidly, especially in the personal computer space. OpenGL runs on a wide range of graphics hardware; from "big iron" compute clusters, to OpenGL ES, which is designed to provide 3D graphics on embedded devices as small as a cell phone.

Given the broad applicability, scalability, and wide availability, OpenGL is an easy choice as the basis for describing graphics algorithms. However, even if you don't use OpenGL, the graphics APIs in common use are conceptually similar enough that you will still find this book useful. OpenGL remains an evolving specification. Throughout the book we make references to various revisions of the specification (versions 1.0–1.5) and discuss both OpenGL architecture review board (ARB) extensions and various vendor-specific extensions when we believe they enhance the discussion of a particular subject. Rather than focus on the feature set of the most advanced versions of OpenGL, we have included a broad range of algorithms with varying requirements. For many techniques we describe algorithm variations that cover a range of earlier and more advanced versions of OpenGL. We have followed this path since a wide range of OpenGL versions are deployed across various environments including the burgeoning embedded space.

Book Organization

This book is divided into three parts. We start with a conceptual overview of computer graphics, emphasizing areas important to the techniques in this book, with extra attention in some overlooked areas. Hand in hand with our introduction to computer graphics, we'll describe the OpenGL pipeline, with extra detail on the parts of the pipeline most techniques rely on heavily: lighting, texture mapping, rasterization, and depth buffering. We also use this opportunity to describe OpenGL system deployment, including the platform embedding layer and an overview of common hardware acceleration techniques for the pipeline.

With this foundation in place, Part II introduces a set of important basic techniques. Useful by themselves, they help re-enforce the insights gleaned from the overview. These sequences are also used as building blocks for more complex and sophisticated techniques. To help tie them more tightly to the graphics concepts described in the previous part, these techniques are presented and organized with respect to the OpenGL architecture.

The third and final part covers more sophisticated and complex techniques. These techniques are categorized into application areas to help organize the material. The start of each application section has an introduction to the problems and issues important for that area, making these sections more interesting and useful to readers not well versed in that particular field.

The book is heavily cross-referenced. Complex techniques reference the simple ones they build upon, and both levels of technique reference the conceptual overview. This allows the reader to use the book as a self-guided tutorial, learning more about techniques and concepts of interest in greater depth.

Example Code

To avoid cluttering the text with large fragments of example code, code fragments are used sparingly. Algorithms are usually described as a sequence of steps. However, since details are often the difference between a working program and a black screen, we have tried to include full blown example programs for most algorithms. This example code is available for internet download from www.mkp.com/opengl.

Conventions

We use conventions and terminology similar to that found in the OpenGL specification and in the "red-blue-green-white" series of OpenGL books. In addition, we use the following conventions:

- Equations involving matrices, vectors, and points use single uppercase letters for most variables. Vectors are emboldened (**V**), whereas points and matrices are not (*M*, *P*). In rare occasions vectors or points are in lower case.

- Occasionally symbols are context specific, but generally the following meanings hold:

  – **N** - normal vector

  – **L** - light vector

- **R** - reflection vector

- **T** - tangent vector

- **B** - binormal vector

- s, t, r, q - texture coordinates

- x, y, z, w - vertex coordinates

- θ, φ - spherical coordinate angles

- $RGBA$ - red, green, blue, and alpha components

- I - intensity

- C - color (usually RGB or RGBA)

- $\|V\|$ - length of vector V

- $[n, m]$ a number between n and m including the end points

- $\mathbf{A} \cdot \mathbf{B}$ - inner product of vectors $\mathbf{A}$ and $\mathbf{B}$

- $\mathbf{A} \odot \mathbf{B}$ - $\max\{0, \mathbf{A} \cdot \mathbf{B}\}$ – the clamped inner product

- $\mathbf{A} \times \mathbf{B}$ - cross product of vectors $\mathbf{A}$ and $\mathbf{B}$

Acknowledgments

This book reflects a significant part of our collective experience in working with OpenGL applications for the past 13 years. While the book couldn't possibly cover everything known about using OpenGL, we are pleased to provide this useful subset. Of course, we didn't figure it out all on our own; we are indebted to the many people that helped us one way or the other: either by providing ideas, correcting misconceptions, prototyping early algorithms, teasing us about taking so long to complete the book, or providing the occasional encouraging word. Many people contributed to this effort: any omissions from the list below are inadvertent.

The following people contributed directly to the original 1996–2000 SIGGRAPH course notes that were the genesis for this book: Celeste Fowler, Brad Grantham, Mark Kilgard, Scott Nelson, Simon Hui, and Paula Womack.

We had invaluable production help with the course notes over the years from Dany Galgani (illustrations), Linda Rae Sande (production editing), Bob Brown, and Chris Everett.

Bowen 'Cheetah' Goletz helped with the logistics of sharing the source material over the internet. We are also indebted to those who have made tools such as TeX/LaTeX, GhostScript/Ghostview, and cvs freely available on the three different computing platforms that we used for preparing the original course notes.

The original notes benefited from the patient attention of an army of reviewers. They include Dave Shreiner, Paul Strauss, David Yu, Hansong Zhang, Sharon Clay, Robert Grzeszczuk, Phil Lacroute, Mark Peercy, Lena Petrovic, Allan Schaffer, Mark Stadler, John Airey, Allen Akin, Brian Cabral, Tom Davis, Bob Drebin, Ben Garlick, Michael Gold, Paul Haeberli, Michael Jones, Phil Keslin, Erik Lindholm, Mark Young, and Mark Segal.

This book would not exist without the wealth of experience, cool ideas, tricks, hacks, and wisdom generously provided to us. It is hard to acknowledge everyone properly. Here is our attempt to do so: Kurt Akeley, Brian Cabral, Amy Gooch, Wolfgang Heidrich, Detlev Stalling, Hansong Zhang, Luis Barcena, Angus Dorbie, Bob Drebin, Mark Peercy, Nacho Sanz-Pastor Revorio, Chris Tanner, David Yu, John Airey, Remi Arnaud, Greg Ward, Phil Lacroute, and Peter-Pike Sloan. We would also like to acknowledge Atul Narkhede, Rob Wheeler, Nate Robbins, and Chris McCue for coding prototype algorithms.

A number of people helped refine the raw material from the course notes into this manuscript and have earned our gratitude: Ben Luna, Jeff Somers, Brandy Lilly, and Jessica Meehan in particular. We are also greatly indebted to our reviewers: Ian Ashdown, Dave Shreiner, Noah Gibbs, Brian Paul, and Clay Budin.

Biographies

David Blythe

David Blythe has worked in the 3D graphics field professionally for the last 14 years, including serving as Chief Engineer at Silicon Graphics, a representative on the OpenGL Architecture Review Board, editor for the OpenGL ES 1.0 specification, and a frequent SIGGRAPH course presenter. While at Silicon Graphics, David contributed to the development of the RealityEngine and InfiniteReality graphics systems. He has worked extensively on implementations of the OpenGL graphics library, OpenGL extension specifications, and high-level toolkits built on top of OpenGL. David's other industry experience includes embedded and system-on-a-chip design, mobile devices, and wireless networking. David is currently a graphics architect in the Windows Graphics and Gaming Technologies division at Microsoft working on DirectX and OpenGL graphics technologies.

Tom McReynolds

Tom McReynolds has worked on 3D graphics at Sun Microsystems, Silicon Graphics, Gigapixel, 3Dfx, and NVIDIA. He has worked in software organizations, writing graphics libraries and drivers, and on the hardware side, writing simulators and verification software for 3D hardware. He presented 3D graphics courses at a number of SIGGRAPH conferences, as well as at a number of Silicon Graphics Developer conferences, an X technical conference, and at Linux World. Tom is currently managing a development team that writes 3D graphics drivers for embedded GPUs at NVIDIA, and contributing to the evolution of OpenGL ES by participating in the Khronos working group.

Concepts

Geometry Representation and Modeling

Two principal tasks are required to create an image of a three-dimensional scene: modeling and rendering. The modeling task generates a *model*, which is the description of an object that is going to be used by the graphics system. Models must be created for every object in a scene; they should accurately capture the geometric shape and appearance of the object. Some or all of this task commonly occurs when the application is being developed, by creating and storing model descriptions as part of the application's data.

The second task, rendering, takes models as input and generates pixel values for the final image. OpenGL is principally concerned with object rendering; it does not provide explicit support for creating object models. The model input data is left to the application to provide. The OpenGL architecture is focused primarily on rendering polygonal models; it doesn't directly support more complex object descriptions, such as implicit surfaces. Because polygonal models are the central manner in which to define an object with OpenGL, it is useful to review the basic ideas behind polygonal modeling and how they relate to it.

1.1 Polygonal Representation

OpenGL supports a handful of primitive types for modeling two-dimensional (2D) and three-dimensional (3D) objects: points, lines, triangles, quadrilaterals, and (convex) polygons. In addition, OpenGL includes support for rendering higher-order surface patches using evaluators. A simple object, such as a box, can be represented using a polygon for each *face* in the object. Part of the modeling task consists of determining the 3D coordinates of each vertex in each polygon that makes up a model. To provide accurate rendering of a model's appearance or surface shading, the modeler may also have to determine color values, shading normals, and texture coordinates for the model's vertices and faces.

Complex objects with curved surfaces can also be modeled using polygons. A curved surface is represented by a gridwork or *mesh* of polygons in which each polygon vertex is placed on a location on the surface. Even if its vertices closely follow the shape of the curved surface, the interior of the polygon won't necessarily lie on the surface. If a larger number of smaller polygons are used, the disparity between the true surface and the polygonal representation will be reduced. As the number of polygons increases, the approximation improves, leading to a trade-off between model accuracy and rendering overhead.

When an object is modeled using polygons, adjacent polygons may share edges. To ensure that shared edges are rendered without creating gaps between them, polygons that share an edge should use identical coordinate values at the edge's endpoints. The limited precision arithmetic used during rendering means edges will not necessarily stay aligned when their vertex coordinates are transformed unless their initial values are identical. Many data structures used in modeling ensure this (and save space) by using the same data structure to represent the coincident vertices defining the shared edges.

1.2 Decomposition and Tessellation

Tessellation refers to the process of decomposing a complex surface, such as a sphere, into simpler primitives such as triangles or quadrilaterals. Most OpenGL implementations are tuned to process triangles (strips, fans, and independents) efficiently. Triangles are desirable because they are planar and easy to rasterize unambiguously. When an OpenGL implementation is optimized for processing triangles, more complex primitives such as quad strips, quads, and polygons are decomposed into triangles early in the pipeline.

If the underlying implementation is performing this decomposition, there is a performance benefit in performing it *a priori*, either when the database is created or at application initialization time, rather than each time the primitive is issued. Another advantage of having the application decompose primitives is that it can be done consistently and independently of the OpenGL implementation. OpenGL does not specify a decomposition algorithm, so different implementations may decompose a given quadrilateral or polygon differently. This can result in an image that is shaded differently and has different silhouette edges when drawn on two different OpenGL implementations. Most OpenGL implementations have simple decomposition algorithms. Polygons are trivially converted to triangle fans using the same vertex order and quadrilaterals are divided into two triangles; one triangle using the first three vertices and the second using the first plus the last two vertices.

These simple decomposition algorithms are chosen to minimize computation over-head. An alternative is to choose decompositions that improve the rendering quality. Since shading computations assume that a primitive is flat, choosing a decomposition that creates triangles with the best match of the surface curvature may result in better shading. Decomposing a quad to two triangles requires introducing a new edge along one of the two diagonals.

A method to find the diagonal that results in more faithful curvature is to compare the angles formed between the surface normals at diagonally opposing vertices. The angle measures the change in surface normal from one corner to its opposite. The pair of opposites forming the smallest angle between them (closest to flat) is the best candidate diagonal; it will produce the flattest possible edge between the resulting triangles, as shown in Figure 1.1. This algorithm may be implemented by computing the dot product between normal pairs, then choosing the pair with the largest dot product (smallest angle). If surface normals are not available, then normals for a vertex may be computed by taking the cross products of the two vectors with origins at that vertex. Surface curvature isn't the only quality metric to use when decomposing quads. Another one splits the quadrilateral into triangles that are closest to equal in size.

Tessellation of simple surfaces such as spheres and cylinders is not difficult. Most implementations of the OpenGL Utility (GLU) library use a straightforward latitude-longitude tessellation for a sphere. While this algorithm is easy to implement, it has the disadvantage that the quads produced from the tessellation have widely

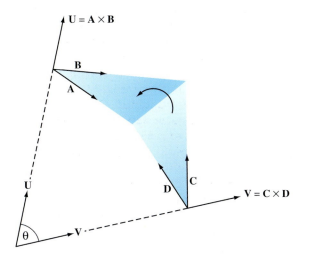

Figure 1.1 Quadrilateral decomposition.

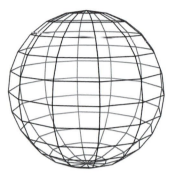

Figure 1.2 Latitude-longitude tessellation of a sphere.

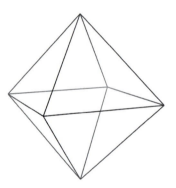

Figure 1.3 Triangle subdivision: starting octahedron.

varying sizes, as shown in Figure 1.2. The different sized quads can cause noticeable artifacts, particularly if the object is lighted and rotating.

A better algorithm generates triangles with sizes that are more consistent. Octahedral and icosahedral tessellations work well and are not very difficult to implement. An octahedral tessellation starts by approximating a sphere with a single octahedron whose vertices are all on the unit sphere, as shown in Figure 1.3. Since each face of the octahedron is a triangle, they can each be easily split into four new triangles.

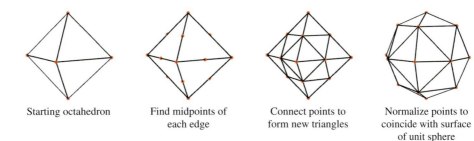

Starting octahedron · Find midpoints of each edge · Connect points to form new triangles · Normalize points to coincide with surface of unit sphere

Figure 1.4 Octahedron with each triangle being subdivided into four.

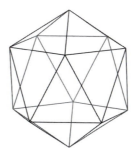

Figure 1.5 Triangle subdivision: starting icosahedron.

Each triangle is split by creating a new vertex in the middle of each of the triangle's existing edges, then connecting them, forming three new edges. The result is that four new triangles are created from the original one; the process is shown in Figure 1.4. The coordinates of each new vertex are divided by the vertex's distance from the origin, normalizing them. This process scales the new vertex so that it lies on the surface of the unit sphere. These two steps can be repeated as desired, recursively dividing all of the triangles generated in each iteration.

The same algorithm can be used with an icosahedron as the base object, as shown in Figure 1.5, by recursively dividing all 20 sides. With either algorithm, it may not be optimal to split the triangle edges in half when tesselating. Splitting the triangle by other amounts, such as by thirds, or even an arbitrary number, may be necessary to produce a uniform triangle size when the tessellation is complete. Both the icosahedral and octahedral algorithms can be coded so that triangle strips are generated instead of independent triangles, maximizing rendering performance. Alternatively, indexed independent triangle lists can be generated instead. This type of primitive may be processed more efficiently on some graphics hardware.

1.3 Shading Normals

OpenGL computes surface shading by evaluating lighting equations at polygon vertices. The most general form of the lighting equation uses both the vertex position and a vector that is normal to the object's surface at that position; this is called the normal vector. Ideally, these normal vectors are captured or computed with the original model data, but in practice there are many models that do not include normal vectors.

Given an arbitrary polygonal model without precomputed normals, it is easy to generate polygon normals for faceted shading, but a bit more difficult to create correct vertex normals when smooth shading is desired. Computing the cross-product of two edges,

$$\mathbf{U} = V_0 - V_1$$

$$\mathbf{V} = V_2 - V_1$$

$$\mathbf{N} = \mathbf{U} \times \mathbf{V} = \begin{pmatrix} U_y V_z - U_z V_y \\ U_z V_x - U_x V_z \\ U_x V_y - U_y V_x \end{pmatrix}$$

then normalizing the result,

$$\mathbf{N}' = \frac{\mathbf{N}}{\|\mathbf{N}\|} = \frac{\mathbf{N}}{\sqrt{N_x^2 + N_y^2 + N_z^2}}$$

yields a unit-length vector, $\mathbf{N}'$, called a *facet normal*. Figure 1.6 shows the vectors to use for generating a triangle's cross product (assuming counterclockwise winding for a front-facing surface).

Computing the facet normal of a polygon with more than three vertices is more difficult. Often such polygons are not perfectly planar, so the result may vary depending on which three vertices are used. If the polygon is a quadrilateral, one good method is to take the cross product of the vectors between opposing vertices. The two diagonal vectors $\mathbf{U} = V0 - V2$ and $\mathbf{V} = V3 - V1$ used for the cross product are shown in Figure 1.7.

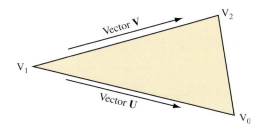

Figure 1.6 Computing a surface normal from edge cross-product.

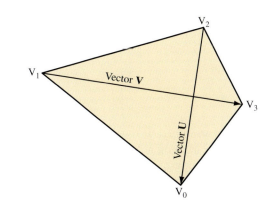

Figure 1.7 Computing quadrilateral surface normal from vertex cross-product.

For polygons with more than four vertices it can be difficult to choose the best vertices to use for the cross product. One method is to to choose vertices that are the furthest apart from each other, or to average the result of several vertex cross products.

1.3.1 Smooth Shading

To smoothly shade an object, a given vertex normal should be used by all polygons that share that vertex. Ideally, this vertex normal is the same as the surface normal at the corresponding point on the original surface. However, if the true surface normal isn't available, the simplest way to approximate one is to add all (normalized) normals from the common facets then renormalize the result (Gouraud, 1971). This provides reasonable results for surfaces that are fairly smooth, but does not look good for surfaces with sharp edges.

In general, the polygonal nature of models can be hidden by smoothing the transition between adjacent polygons. However, an object that should have *hard edges*, such as a

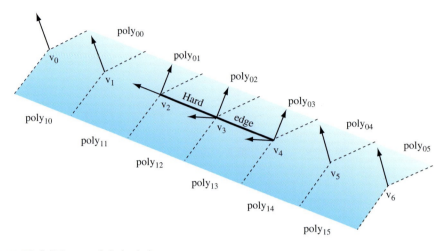

Figure 1.8 Splitting normals for hard edges.

cube, should not have its edges smoothed. If the model doesn't specify which edges are hard, the angle between polygons defining an edge, called the *crease angle*, may be used to distinguish hard edges from soft ones.

The value of the angle that distinguishes hard edges from soft can vary from model to model. It is fairly clear that a 90-degree angle nearly always defines a hard edge, but the best edge type for a 45-degree crease angle is less clear. The transition angle can be defined by the application for tuning to a particular model; using 45 degrees as a default value usually produces good results.

The angle between polygons is determined using the dot product of the unit-length facet normals. The value of the dot product is equal to the cosine of the angle between the vectors. If the dot product of the two normals is greater than the cosine of the desired crease angle, the edge is considered soft, otherwise it is considered hard. A hard edge is created by generating separate normals for each side of the edge. Models commonly have a mixture of both hard and soft edges, and a single edge may transition from hard to soft. The remaining normals common to soft edges should not be split to ensure that those soft edges retain their smoothness.

Figure 1.8 shows an example of a mesh with two hard edges in it. The three vertices making up these hard edges, v_2, v_3, and v_4, need to be split using two separate normals. In the case of vertex v_4, one normal would be applied to *poly02* and *poly03* while a different normal would apply to *poly12* and *poly13*. This ensures that the edge between *poly02* and *poly03* looks smooth while the edge between *poly03* and *poly13* has a distinct crease. Since v_5 is not split, the edge between *poly04* and *poly14* will look sharper near v_4 and will become smoother as it gets closer to v_5. The edge between v_5 and v_6 would then be completely smooth. This is the desired effect.

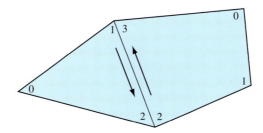

Figure 1.9 Proper winding for shared edge of adjoining facets.

For an object such as a cube, three hard edges will share one common vertex. In this case the edge-splitting algorithm needs to be repeated for the third edge to achieve the correct results.

1.3.2 Vertex Winding Order

Some 3D models come with polygons that are not all wound in a clockwise or counter-clockwise direction, but are a mixture of both. Since the polygon winding may be used to cull back or front-facing triangles, for performance reasons it is important that models are made consistent; a polygon wound inconsistently with its neighbors should have its vertex order reversed. A good way to accomplish this is to find all common edges and verify that neighboring polygon edges are drawn in the opposite order (Figure 1.9).

To rewind an entire model, one polygon is chosen as the seed. All neighboring polygons are then found and made consistent with it. This process is repeated recursively for each reoriented polygon until no more neighboring polygons are found. If the model is a single closed object, all polygons will now be consistent. However, if the model has multiple unconnected pieces, another polygon that has not yet been tested is chosen and the process repeats until all polygons are tested and made consistent.

To ensure that the rewound model is oriented properly (i.e., all polygons are wound so that their front faces are on the outside surface of the object), the algorithm begins by choosing and properly orienting the seed polygon. One way to do this is to find the geometric center of the object: compute the object's bounding box, then compute its mid-point. Next, select a vertex that is the maximum distance from the center point and compute a (normalized) *out* vector from the center point to this vertex. One of the polygons using that vertex is chosen as the seed. Compute the normal of the seed polygon, then compute the dot product of the normal with the out vector. A positive result indicates that seed is oriented correctly. A negative result indicates the polygon's normal is facing inward. If the seed polygon is backward, reverse its winding before using it to rewind the rest of the model.

1.4 Triangle Stripping

One of the simplest ways to speed up an OpenGL program while simultaneously saving storage space is to convert independent triangles or polygons into triangle strips. If the model is generated directly from NURBS data or from some other regular geometry, it is straightforward to connect the triangles together into longer strips. Decide whether the first triangle should have a clockwise or counterclockwise winding, then ensure all subsequent triangles in the list alternate windings (as shown in Figure 1.10). Triangle fans must also be started with the correct winding, but all subsequent triangles are wound in the same direction (Figure 1.11).

Since OpenGL does not have a way to specify generalized triangle strips, the user must choose between GL_TRIANGLE_STRIP and GL_TRIANGLE_FAN. In general, the triangle strip is the more versatile primitive. While triangle fans are ideal for large convex polygons that need to be converted to triangles or for triangulating geometry that is cone-shaped, most other cases are best converted to triangle strips.

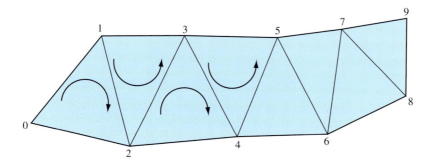

Figure 1.10 Triangle strip winding.

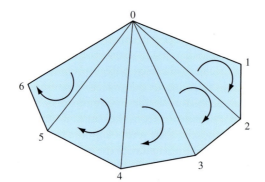

Figure 1.11 Triangle fan winding.

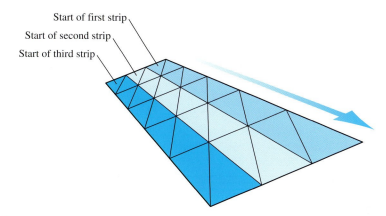

Figure 1.12 A mesh made up of multiple triangle strips.

For regular meshes, triangle strips should be lined up side by side as shown in Figure 1.12. The goal here is to minimize the number of total strips and try to avoid "orphan" triangles (also known as *singleton strips*) that cannot be made part of a longer strip. It is possible to turn a corner in a triangle strip by using redundant vertices and degenerate triangles, as described in Evans et al. (1996).

1.4.1 Greedy Tri-stripping

A fairly simple method of converting a model into triangle strips is often known as *greedy tri-stripping*. One of the early greedy algorithms, developed for IRIS GL,[1] allowed swapping of vertices to create direction changes to the facet with the least neighbors. In OpenGL, however, the only way to get behavior equivalent to swapping vertices is to repeat a vertex and create a degenerate triangle, which is more expensive than the original vertex swap operation was.

For OpenGL, a better algorithm is to choose a polygon, convert it to triangles, then move to the polygon which has an edge that is shared with the last edge of the previous polygon. A given starting polygon and starting edge determines the strip path. The strip grows until it runs off the edge of the model or reaches a polygon that is already part of another strip (Figure 1.13). To maximize the number of triangles per strip, grow the strip in both directions from starting polygon and edge as far as possible.

A triangle strip should not cross a hard edge, since the vertices on that edge must be repeated redundantly. A hard edge requires different normals for the two triangles on either side of that edge. Once one strip is complete, the best polygon to choose for the next strip is often a neighbor to the polygon at one end or the other of the previous strip. More advanced triangulation methods do not try to keep all triangles of a polygon together. For more information on such a method refer to Evans et al. (1996).

---

1. Silicon Graphics' predecessor to OpenGL.

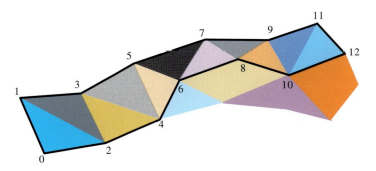

Figure 1.13 "Greedy" triangle strip generation.

1.5 Vertices and Vertex Arrays

In addition to providing several different modeling primitives, OpenGL provides multiple ways to specify the vertices and vertex attributes for each of the primitive types. There are two reasons for this. The first is to provide flexibility, making it easier to match the way the model data is transferred to the OpenGL pipeline with the application's representation of the model (data structure). The second reason is to create a more compact representation, reducing the amount of data sent to the graphics accelerator to generate the image — less data means better performance.

For example, an application can render a sphere tessellated into individual (independent) triangles. For each triangle vertex, the application can specify a vertex position, color, normal vector, and one or more texture coordinates. Furthermore, for each of these attributes, the application chooses how many components to send (2 (x, y), 3 (x, y, z), or 4 (x, y, z, w) positions, 3 (r, g, b), or 4 (r, g, b, a) colors, and so on) and the representation for each component: short integer, integer, single-precision floating-point, double-precision floating-point.

If the application writer is not concerned about performance, they may always specify all attributes, using the largest number of components (3 component vertices, 4 component colors, 3 component texture coordinates, etc.), and the most general component representation. Excess vertex data is not a problem; in OpenGL it is relatively straightforward to ignore unnecessary attributes and components. For example, if lighting is disabled (and texture generation isn't using normals), then the normal vectors are ignored. If three component texture coordinates are specified, but only two component texture maps are enabled, then the r coordinate is effectively ignored. Similarly, effects such as faceted shading can be achieved by enabling flat shading mode, effectively ignoring the extra vertex normals.

However, such a strategy hurts performance in several ways. First, it increases the amount of memory needed to store the model data, since the application may be storing attributes that are never used. Second, it can limit the efficiency of the pipeline, since the application must send these unused attributes and some amount of processing must be performed on them, if only to ultimately discard them. As a result, well written and tuned applications try to eliminate any unused or redundant data.

In the 1.1 release of the OpenGL specification, an additional mechanism for specifying vertices and vertex attributes, called *vertex arrays*, was introduced. The reason for adding this additional mechanism was to improve performance; vertex arrays reduce the number of function calls required by an application to specify a vertex and its attributes. Instead of calling a function to issue each vertex and attribute in a primitive, the application specifies a pointer to an array of attributes for each attribute type (position, color, normal, etc.). It can then issue a single function call to send the attributes to the pipeline. To render a cube as 12 triangles (2 triangles × 6 faces) with a position, color, and normal vector requires 108 (12 triangles × 3 vertices/triangle × 3 attributes/vertex) function calls. Using vertex arrays, only 4 function calls are needed, 3 to set the vertex, color, and normal array addresses and 1 to draw the array (2 more if calls to enable the color and normal arrays are also included). Alternatively, the cube can be drawn as 6 triangle strips, reducing the number of function calls to 72 for the separate attribute commands, while increasing the number of calls to 6 for vertex arrays.

There is a catch, however. Vertex arrays require all attributes to be specified for each vertex. For the cube example, if each face of the cube is a different color, using the the function-per-attribute style (called the *fine grain* calls) results in 6 calls to the color function (one for each face). For vertex arrays, 36 color values must be specified, since color must be specified for each vertex. Furthermore, if the number of vertices in the primitive is small, the overhead in setting up the array pointers and enabling and disabling individual arrays may outweigh the savings in the individual function calls (for example, if four vertex billboards are being drawn). For this reason, some applications go to great lengths to pack multiple objects into a single large array to minimize the number of array pointer changes. While such an approach may be reasonable for applications that simply draw the data, it may be unreasonable for applications that make frequent changes to it. For example, inserting or removing vertices from an object may require extra operations to shuffle data within the array.

1.5.1 Vertex Buffer Objects

The mechanisms for moving geometry and texture data to the rendering pipeline continue to be an area of active development. One of the perennial difficulties in achieving good performance on modern accelerators is moving geometry data into the accelerator. Usually the accelerator is attached to the host system via a high speed bus. Each time a vertex array is drawn, the vertex data is retrieved from application memory and processed by the pipeline. Display lists offer an advantage in that the opaque representation allows the data to be moved closer to the accelerator, including into memory that is on the same side of the bus as the accelerator itself. This allows implementations to achieve high-performance display list processing by exploiting this advantage.

Unfortunately with vertex arrays it is nearly impossible to use the same technique, since the vertex data is created and managed in memory in the application's address space (client memory). In OpenGL 1.5, *vertex buffer objects* were added to the specification to enable the same *server placement* optimizations that are used with display lists. Vertex buffer objects allow the application to allocate vertex data storage that is managed by the OpenGL implementation and can be allocated from accelerator memory. The application can store vertex data to the buffer using an explicit transfer command (`glBufferData`), or by *mapping* the buffer (`glMapBuffer`). The vertex buffer data can also be examined by the application allowing dynamic modification of the data, though it may be slower if the buffer storage is now in the accelerator. Having dynamic read-write access allows geometric data to be modified each frame, without requiring the application to maintain a separate copy of the data or explicitly copy it to and from the accelerator. Vertex buffer objects are used with the vertex array drawing commands by binding a vertex buffer object to the appropriate array binding point (vertex, color, normal, texture coordinate) using the array point commands (for example, `glNormalPointer`). When an array has a bound buffer object, the array pointer is interpreted relative to the buffer object storage rather than application memory addresses.

Vertex buffer objects do create additional complexity for applications, but they are needed in order to achieve maximum rendering performance on very fast hardware accelerators. Chapter 21 discusses additional techniques and issues in achieving maximum rendering performance from an OpenGL implementation.

1.5.2 Triangle Lists

Most of this chapter has emphasized triangle strips and fans as the optimal performing primitive. It is worth noting that in some OpenGL implementations there are other triangle-based representations that perform well and have their own distinct advantages. Using the `glDrawElements` command with independent triangle primitives (GL_TRIANGLES), an application can define lists of triangles in which vertices are shared. A vertex is shared by reusing the index that refers to it. Triangle lists have the advantage that they are simple to use and promote the sharing of vertex data; the index is duplicated in the index list, rather than the actual triangle.

In the past, hardware accelerators did not process triangle lists well. They often transformed and lit a vertex each time it was encountered in the index list, even if it had been processed earlier. Modern desktop accelerators can cache transformed vertices and reuse them if the indices that refer to them are "close together" in the array. More details of the underlying implementation are described in Section 8.2. With these improvements in implementations, triangle lists are a viable high-performance representation. It is often still advantageous to use strip and fan structures, however, to provide more optimization opportunities to the accelerator.

1.6 Modeling vs. Rendering Revisited

This chapter began by asserting that OpenGL is primarily concerned with rendering, not modeling. The interactivity of an application, however, can range from displaying a single static image, to interactively creating objects and changing their attributes dynamically. The characteristics of the application have a fundamental influence on how their geometric data is represented, and how OpenGL is used to render the data. When speed is paramount, the application writer may go to extreme lengths to optimize the data representation for efficient rendering. Such optimizations may include the use of display lists and vertex arrays, pre-computing the lighted color values at each vertex, and so forth. However, a modeling application, such as a mechanical design program, may use a more general representation of the model data: double-precision coordinate representation, full sets of colors and normals for each vertex. Furthermore, the application may re-use the model representation for non-rendering purposes, such as collision detection or finite element computations.

There are other possibilities. Many applications use multiple representations: they start with a single "master" representation, then generate subordinate representations tuned for other purposes, including rendering, collision detection, and physical model simulations. The creation of these subordinate representations may be scheduled using a number of different techniques. They may be generated on demand then cached, incrementally rebuilt as needed, or constructed over time as a background task. The method chosen depends on the needs of the application.

The key point is that there isn't a "one size fits all" recipe for representing model data in an application. One must have a thorough understanding of all of the requirements of the application to find the representation and rendering strategy that best suits it.

3D Transformations

OpenGL has a simple and powerful transformation model. Vertices can be created with position, normal direction, and sets of texture coordinates. These values are manipulated by a series of affine transformations (a linear combinations of translation, rotation, scaling, and shearing) that are set by the application. The fundamental transformation representation in OpenGL is the 4×4 matrix. Application-controlled transforms, along with the perspective division functionality available in both positional and texture coordinate pipelines, offer substantial control to the application program. This chapter describes the OpenGL transformation pipeline, providing insights needed to use it effectively, and discusses the transformation issues that can affect visual accuracy.

2.1 Data Representation

Before describing the transformation mechanisms, it is helpful to discuss some details about representations of the transformed data. OpenGL represents vertex coordinates, texture coordinates, normal vectors, and colors generically as *tuples*. Tuples can be thought of as 4-component vectors. When working with the 1D, 2D, and 3D forms of commands the tuples are implicitly expanded to fill in unspecified components (e.g., for vertex coordinates, an unspecified z coordinate is set to 0 and an unspecified w is set to 1, etc.). OpenGL represents transforms as 4×4 matrices, plane equations as 4-component tuples, etc. When thinking about matrix and vector operations on these tuples, it's helpful to treat them as column vectors, so a point p is transformed by a matrix M by writing it as Mp.

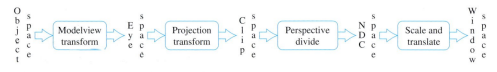

Figure 2.1 OpenGL transformation pipeline.

2.2 Overview of the Transformation Pipeline

The OpenGL transformation pipeline can be thought of as a series of cartesian coordinate spaces connected by transformations that can be directly set by the application (Figure 2.1). Five spaces are used: *object space*, which starts with the application's coordinates, *eye space*, where the scene is assembled, *clip space*, which defines the geometry that will be visible in the scene, *NDC space*, the canonical space resulting from perspective division, and *window space*, which maps to the framebuffer's pixel locations. The following sections describe each space in the pipeline, along with its controlling transform, in the order in which they appear in the pipeline.

2.2.1 Object Space and the Modelview Transform

The pipeline begins with texture, vertex, and light position coordinates, along with normal vectors, sent down from the application. These untransformed values are said to be in *object space*. If the application has enabled the generation of object space texture coordinates, they are created here from untransformed vertex positions.

Object space coordinates are transformed into eye space by transforming them with the current contents of the *modelview matrix*; it is typically used to assemble a series of objects into a coherent scene viewed from a particular vantage. As suggested by its name, the modelview matrix performs both viewing and modeling transformations.

A modeling transform positions and orients objects in the scene. It transforms all of the primitives comprising an object as a group. In general, each object in the scene may require a different modeling transform to correctly position it. This is done, object by object, by setting the transform then drawing the corresponding objects. To animate an object, its modeling transformation is updated each time the scene is redrawn.

A viewing transform positions and orients the entire collection of objects as a single entity with respect to the "camera position" of the scene. The transformed scene is said to be in eye space. The viewing part of the transformation only changes when the camera position does, typically once per frame.

Since the modelview matrix contains both a viewing transform and a modeling transform, it must be updated when either transform needs to be changed. The modelview matrix is created by multiplying the modeling transform (M) by the viewing transform (V), yielding VM. Typically the application uses OpenGL to do the multiplication of transforms by first loading the viewing transform, then multiplying by a modeling transform. To avoid reloading the viewing transform each time the composite transform needs to be computed, the application can use OpenGL matrix stack operations. The stack can be used to push a copy of the current model matrix or to remove it. To avoid reloading the viewing matrix, the application can load it onto the stack, then duplicate it with a push stack operation before issuing any modeling transforms.

The net result is that modeling transforms are being applied to a copy of the viewing transform. After drawing the corresponding geometry, the composite matrix is popped from the stack, leaving the original viewing matrix on the stack ready for another push, transform, draw, pop sequence.

An important use of the modelview matrix is modifying the parameters of OpenGL light sources. When a light position is issued using the `glLight` command, the position or direction of the light is transformed by the current modelview matrix before being stored. The transformed position is used in the lighting computations until it's updated with a new call to `glLight`. If the position of the light is fixed in the scene (a lamp in a room, for example) then its position must be re-specified each time the viewing transform changes. On the other hand, the light may be fixed relative to the viewpoint (a car's headlights as seen from the driver's viewpoint, for example). In this case, the position of the light is specified before a viewing transform is loaded (i.e., while the current transform is the identity matrix).

2.2.2 Eye Space and Projection Transform

The *eye space* coordinate system is where object lighting is applied and eye-space texture coordinate generation occurs. OpenGL makes certain assumptions about eye space. The viewer position is defined to be at the origin of the eye-space coordinate system. The direction of view is assumed to be the negative z-axis, and the viewer's up position is the y-axis (Figure 2.2).

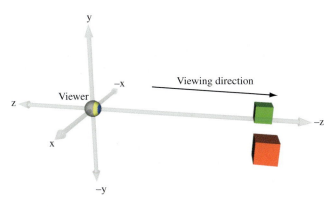

Figure 2.2 Eye space orientation.

Normals are consumed by the pipeline in eye space. If lighting is enabled, they are used by the lighting equation — along with eye position and light positions — to modify the current vertex color. The *projection transform* transforms the remaining vertex and texture coordinates into clip space. If the projection transform has perspective elements in it, the w values of the transformed vertices are modified.

2.2.3 Clip Space and Perspective Divide

Clip space is where all objects or parts of objects that are outside the view volume are clipped away, such that

$$-w_{clip} \leq x_{clip} \leq w_{clip}$$

$$-w_{clip} \leq y_{clip} \leq w_{clip}$$

$$-w_{clip} \leq z_{clip} \leq w_{clip}$$

If new vertices are generated as a result of clipping, the new vertices will have texture coordinates and colors interpolated to match the new vertex positions. The exact shape of the view volume depends on the type of projection transform; a perspective transformation results in a frustum (a pyramid with the tip cut off), while an orthographic projection will create a parallelepiped volume.

A perspective divide — dividing the clip space x, y, and z coordinate of each point by its w value — is used to transform the clipped primitives into normalized device coordinate (NDC) space. The effect of a perspective divide on a point depends on whether the clip space w component is 1 or not. If the untransformed positions have a w of one (the common case), the value of w depends on the projection transform. An orthographic transform leaves the w value unmodified; typically the incoming w coordinate is one, so the post-transform w is also one. In this case, the perspective divide has no effect.

A perspective transform scales the w value as a function of the position's z value; a perspective divide on the resulting point will scale, x y, and z as a function of the untransformed z. This produces the perspective *foreshortening* effect, where objects become smaller with increasing distance from the viewer. This transform can also produce an undesirable non-linear mapping of z values. The effects of perspective divide on depth buffering and texture coordinate interpolation are discussed in Section 2.8 and Section 6.1.4, respectively.

2.2.4 NDC Space and the Viewport Transform

Normalized device coordinate or NDC space is a screen independent display coordinate system; it encompasses a cube where the x, y, and z components range from -1 to 1. Although clipping to the view volume is specified to happen in clip space, NDC space can be thought of as the space that *defines* the view volume. The view volume is effectively the result of reversing the divide by w_{clip} operation on the corners of the NDC cube.

The current viewport transform is applied to each vertex coordinate to generate window space coordinates. The viewport transform scales and biases x_{ndc} and y_{ndc} components to fit within the currently defined viewport, while the z_{ndc} component is scaled and biased to the currently defined depth range. By convention, this transformed z value is referred to as *depth* rather than z. The viewport is defined by integral origin, width, and height values measured in pixels.

2.2.5 Window Space

Window coordinates map primitives to pixel positions in the framebuffer. The integral x and y coordinates correspond to the lower left corner of a corresponding pixel in the window; the z coordinate corresponds to the distance from the viewer into the screen. All z values are retained for visibility testing. Each z coordinate is scaled to fall within the range 0 (closest to the viewer) to 1 (farthest from the viewer), abstracting away the details of depth buffer resolution. The application can modify the z scale and bias so that z values fall within a subset of this range, or reverse the mapping between increasing z distance and increasing depth.

The term *screen coordinates* is also used to describe this space. The distinction is that screen coordinates are pixel coordinates relative to the entire display screen, while window coordinates are pixel coordinates relative to a window on the screen (assuming a window system is present on the host computer).

2.3 Normal Transformation

OpenGL uses normal vectors for lighting computations and to generate texture coordinates when environment mapping is enabled. Like vertices, normal vectors are transformed from object space to eye space before being used. However, normal vectors are different from vertex positions; they are *covectors* and are transformed differently (Figure 2.3). Vertex positions are specified in OpenGL as column vectors; normals and some other direction tuples are row vectors. Mathematically, the first is left-multiplied

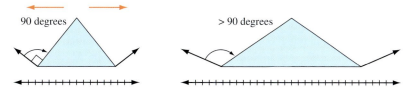

Non-Uniform Scaling affects vectors and vertices differently; normal vectors are no longer normal to surface after scaling by Sx = 2, Sy = 1

Figure 2.3 Preserving vector and vertex orientation.

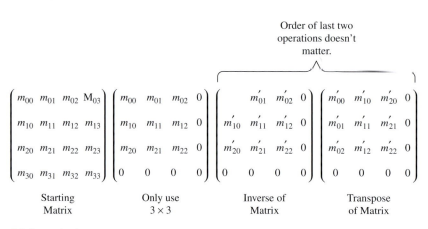

Figure 2.4 Generating inverse transpose.

by a matrix, the other has the matrix on the right. If they are both to be transformed the same way (which is commonly done to simplify the implementation code), the matrix must be transposed before being used to transform normals.

$$\begin{pmatrix} m_{11} & m_{12} & m_{13} & m_{14} \\ m_{21} & m_{22} & m_{23} & m_{24} \\ m_{31} & m_{32} & m_{33} & m_{34} \\ m_{41} & m_{42} & m_{43} & m_{44} \end{pmatrix} \begin{pmatrix} v_1 \\ v_2 \\ v_3 \\ v_4 \end{pmatrix} = \left(v_1 v_2 v_3 v_4 \right) \begin{pmatrix} m_{11} & m_{12} & m_{13} & m_{14} \\ m_{21} & m_{22} & m_{23} & m_{24} \\ m_{31} & m_{32} & m_{33} & m_{34} \\ m_{41} & m_{42} & m_{43} & m_{44} \end{pmatrix}^T$$

When transforming normals, it's not enough to simply transpose the matrix. The transform that preserves the relationship between a normal and its surface is created by taking the transpose of the inverse of the modelview matrix $(M^{-1})^T$, sometimes called the *adjoint transpose* of M (Figure 2.4). That is, the transformed normal $\mathbf{N}'$ is:

$$\mathbf{N}' = \mathbf{N}M^{-1} = \left((M^{-1})^T \mathbf{N}^T \right)^T$$

For a "well-behaved" set of transforms consisting of rotations and translations, the resulting modelview matrix is *orthonormal*.[1] In this case, the adjoint transpose of M is M and no work needs to be done.

However, if the modelview matrix contains scaling transforms then more is required. If a single *uniform* scale s is included in the transform, then $M = sI$. Therefore $M^{-1} = (1/s)I$ and the transformed normal vector will be scaled by $1/s$, losing its important unit length property ($\mathbf{N} \cdot \mathbf{N} = 1$). If the scale factor is non-uniform, then the scale factor computation becomes more complicated (figure 2.3). If the scaling factor

---

1. Orthnormal means that $MM^T = I$.

is uniform, and the incoming normals started out with unit lengths, then they can be restored to unit length by enabling GL_RESCALE_NORMAL. This option instructs the OpenGL transformation pipeline to compute s and scale the transformed normal. This is opposed to GL_NORMALIZE, which has OpenGL compute the length of each transformed normal in order to normalize them to unit length. Normalize is more costly, but can handle incoming vectors that aren't of length one.

2.4 Texture Coordinate Generation and Transformation

Texture coordinates have their own transformation pipeline (Figure 2.5), simpler than the one used for geometry transformations. Coordinates are either provided by the application directly, or generated from vertex coordinates or normal vectors. In either case, the texture coordinates are transformed by a 4×4 *texture transform matrix*. Like vertex coordinates, texture coordinates always have four components, even if only one, two, or three components are specified by the application. The missing components are assigned default values; 0 for s, t, and r values (these coordinates can be thought of as x, y, and z equivalents in texture coordinate space) while the q coordinate (the equivalent of w) is assigned the default value of 1.

2.4.1 Texture Matrix

After being transformed by the texture matrix, the transformed coordinates undergo their own perspective divide, using q to divide the other components. Since texture maps may use anywhere from one to four components, texture coordinate components that aren't needed to index a texture map are discarded at this stage. The remaining components are scaled and wrapped (or clamped) appropriately before being used to index the texture map. This full 4×4 transform with perspective divide applied to the coordinates for 1D or 2D textures will be used as the basis of a number of techniques, such as projected textures (Section 14.9) and volume texturing (Section 20.5.8), described later in the book.

2.4.2 Texture Coordinate Generation

The texture coordinate pipeline can generate texture coordinates that are a function of vertex attributes. This functionality, called *texture coordinate generation* (texgen), is useful for establishing a relationship between geometry and its associated textures. It can also be used to improve an application's triangle rate performance, since explicit texture coordinates don't have to be sent with each vertex. The source (x, y, z, w) values can be untransformed vertices (object space), or vertices transformed by the modelview matrix (eye space).

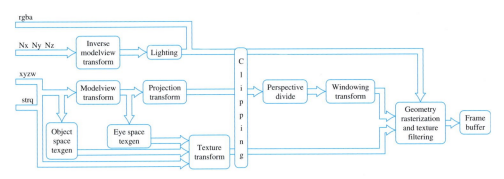

Figure 2.5 Texture coordinate transformation pipeline.

A great deal of flexibility is available for choosing how vertex coordinates are mapped into texture coordinates. There are several categories of mapping functions in core OpenGL; two forms of linear mapping, a version based on vertex normals, and two based on reflection vectors (the last two are used in environment mapping). Linear mapping generates each texture coordinate from the dot product of the vertex and an application-supplied coefficient vector (which can be thought of as a plane equation). Normal mapping copies the vertex normal vector components to s, t, and r. Reflection mapping computes the reflection vector based on the eye position and the vertex and its normal, assigning the vector components to texture coordinates. Sphere mapping also calculates the reflection vector, but then projects it into two dimensions, assigning the result to texture coordinates s and t.

There are two flavors of linear texgen; they differ on where the texture coordinates are computed. Object space linear texgen uses the x, y, z, and w components of untransformed vertices in object space as its source. Eye-space linear texgen uses the positional components of vertices as its source also, but doesn't use them until after they have been transformed by the modelview matrix.

Textures mapped with object-space linear texgen appear fixed to their objects; eye-space linear textures are fixed relative to the viewpoint and appear fixed in the scene. Object space mappings are typically used to apply textures to the surface of an object to create a specific surface appearance, whereas eye-space mappings are used to apply texturing effects to all or part of the environment containing the object.

One of OpenGL's more important texture generation modes is environment mapping. Environment mapping derives texture coordinate values from vectors (such as normals or reflection vectors) rather than points. The applied textures simulate effects that are a function of one or more vectors. Examples include specular and diffuse reflections, and specular lighting effects. OpenGL directly supports two forms of environment mapping; sphere mapping and cube mapping. Details on these features and their use are found in Section 5.4.

2.5 Modeling Transforms

Modeling transforms are used to place objects within the scene. Modeling transforms can position objects, orient them, change their size and shape through scaling and shearing, assemble complex objects by proper placement and orientation of their components, and animate objects by changing these attributes from frame to frame.

Modeling transforms can be thought of as part of an object's description (Figure 2.6). When an application defines a geometric primitive, it can include modeling transforms to modify the coordinates of the primitive's vertices. This is useful since it allows re-use of objects. The same object can be used in another part of the scene, with a different size, shape, position, or orientation. This technique can reduce the amount of geometry that

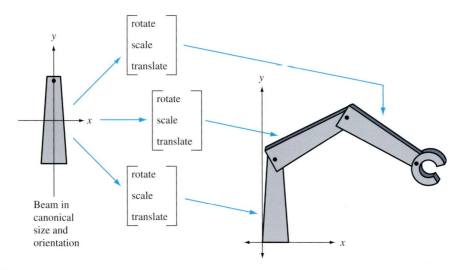

Figure 2.6 Modeling transform as part of model description.

the application has to store and send to the graphics pipeline, and can make the modeling process simpler.

Modeling transforms are even more important if an object needs to be animated. A modeling transform can be updated each frame to change the position, orientation, and other properties of an object, animating it without requiring the application to compute and generate new vertex positions each frame. The application can describe a modeling transform parametrically (for example, the angle through which a wheel should be rotated), update the parameter appropriately each frame, then generate a new transform from the parametric description. Note that generating a new transform each frame is generally better than incrementally updating a particular transformation, since the latter approach can lead to large accumulation of arithmetic errors over time.

2.6 Visualizing Transform Sequences

Using transformations to build complex objects from simpler ones, then placing and orienting them in the scene can result in long sequences of transformations concatenated together. Taking full advantage of transform functionality requires being able to understand and accurately visualize the effect of transform combinations.

There are a number of ways to visualize a transformation sequence. The most basic paradigm is the mathematical one. Each transformation is represented as a 4×4 matrix. A vertex is represented as a 4×1 column vector. When a vertex is sent through the transformation pipeline, the vertex components are transformed by multiplying the column vector v by the current transformation M, resulting in a modified vector v' that is equal to Mv. An OpenGL command stream is composed of updates to the transformation matrix, followed by a sequence of vertices that are modified by the current transform. This process alternates back and forth until the entire scene is rendered.

Instead of applying a single transformation to each vertex, a sequence of transformations can be created and combined into a single 4×4 matrix. An ordered set of matrices, representing the desired transform sequence, is multiplied together, and the result is multiplied with the vertices to be transformed. OpenGL provides applications with the means to multiply a new matrix into the current one, growing a sequence of transformations one by one.

In OpenGL, adding a matrix to a sequence means *right multiplying* the new matrix with the current transformation. If the current transformation is matrix C, and the new matrix is N, the result of applying the matrix will be a new matrix containing CN. The matrices can be thought of acting from right to left: matrix N can be thought of as acting on the vertex *before* matrix C. If the sequence of transforms should act in the order A, then B, then C, they should be concatenated together as CBA, and issued to OpenGL in the order C, then B, then A (Figure 2.7).

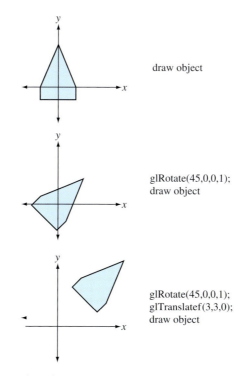

Figure 2.7 Transform concatenation order.

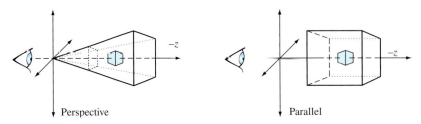

Figure 2.8 Perspective and parallel projections.

2.7 Projection Transform

The projection transform establishes which part of the modeled scene will be visible, and what sort of projection will be applied. Although any transformation that can be represented with a 4×4 matrix and a perspective divide can be modeled, most applications will use either a parallel (orthographic) or a perspective projection (Figure 2.8).

The view volume of a parallel projection is parallelepiped (box shape). The viewer position establishes the front and back of the viewing volume by setting the front and back clipping planes. Objects both in front of and behind the viewer will be visible, as long as they are within the view volume. The glOrtho command establishes a parallel projection, or alternatively, a sequence of translations and scales can be concatenated directly by the application.

A perspective projection changes the value of vertex coordinates being transformed, so the perspective divide step will modify the vertex x, y, and z values. As mentioned in the viewing section, the view volume is now a frustum (truncated pyramid), and the view position relative to the objects in the scene is very important. The degree to which the sides of the frustum diverge will determine how quickly objects change in size as a function of their z coordinate. This translates into a more "wide angle" or "telephoto" view.

2.8 The Z Coordinate and Perspective Projection

The depth buffer is used to determine which portions of objects are visible within the scene. When two objects cover the same x and y positions but have different z values, the depth buffer ensures that only the closer object is visible.

Depth buffering can fail to resolve objects whose z values are nearly the same value. Since the depth buffer stores z values with limited precision, z values are rounded as they are stored. The z values may round to the same number, causing depth buffering artifacts.

Since the application can exactly specify the desired perspective transformation, it can specify transforms that maximize the performance of the depth buffer. This can

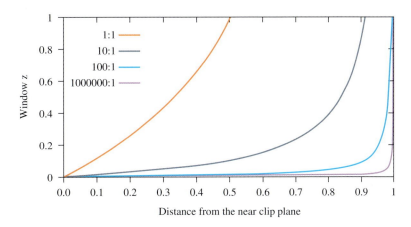

Figure 2.9 Window *z* to eye *z* relationship for near/far ratios.

reduce the chance of depth buffer artifacts. For example, if the `glFrustum` call is used to set the perspective transform, the properties of the *z* values can be tuned by changing the ratio of the near and far clipping planes. This is done by adjusting the *near* and *far* parameters of the function. The same can be done with the `gluPerspective` command, by changing the values of *zNear* and *zFar*.

To set these values correctly, it is important to understand the characteristics of the window *z* coordinate. The *z* value specifies the distance from the fragment to the plane of the eye. The relationship between distance and *z* is linear in an orthographic projection, but not in a perspective one. Figure 2.9 plots the window coordinate *z* value vs. the eye-to-pixel distance for several ratios of far to near. The non-linearity increases the resolution of the *z* values when they are close to the near clipping plane, increasing the resolving power of the depth buffer, but decreasing the precision throughout the rest of the viewing frustum. As a result, the accuracy of the depth buffer in the back part of the viewing volume is decreased.

For an object a given distance from the eye, however, the depth precision is not as bad as it looks in Figure 2.9. No matter how distant the far clip plane is, at least half of the available depth range is present in the first "unit" of distance. In other words, if the distance from the eye to the near clip plane is one unit, at least half of the *z* range is used up traveling the same distance from the near clip plane toward the far clip plane. Figure 2.10 plots the *z* range for the first unit distance for various ranges. With a million to one ratio, the *z* value is approximately 0.5 at one unit of distance. As long as the data is mostly drawn close to the near plane, the *z* precision is good. The far plane could be set to infinity without significantly changing the accuracy of the depth buffer near the viewer.

To achieve the best depth buffer precision, the near plane should be moved as far from the eye as possible without touching the object of interest (which would cause part or all of it to be clipped away). The position of the near clipping plane has no effect

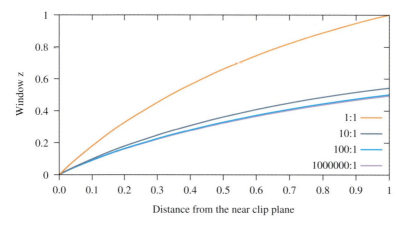

Figure 2.10 Available window *z* depth values near/far ratios.

on the projection of the *x* and *y* coordinates, so moving it has only a minimal effect on the image. As a result, readjusting the near plane dynamically shouldn't cause noticeable artifacts while animating. On the other hand, allowing the near clip plane to be closer to the eye than to the object will result in loss of depth buffer precision.

2.8.1 Z Coordinates and Fog

In addition to depth buffering, the *z* coordinate is also used for fog computations. Some implementations may perform the fog computation on a per-vertex basis, using the eye-space *z* value at each vertex, then interpolate the resulting vertex colors. Other implementations may perform fog computations per fragment. In the latter case, the implementation may choose to use the window *z* coordinate to perform the fog computation. Implementations may also choose to convert the fog computations into a table lookup operation to save computation overhead. This shortcut can lead to difficulties due to the non-linear nature of window *z* under perspective projections. For example, if the implementation uses a linearly indexed table, large far to near ratios will leave few table entries for the large eye *z* values. This can cause noticeable Mach bands in fogged scenes.

2.9 Vertex Programs

Vertex programs, sometimes known as "Vertex Shaders"[2] provide additional flexibility and programmability to per-vertex operations. OpenGL provides a fixed sequence of

---

2. The name comes from the "shader" construct used in the RenderMan shading language.

operations to perform transform, coordinate generation, lighting and clipping operations on vertex data. This fixed sequence of operations is called the *fixed-function pipeline*. The OpenGL 1.4 specification includes the `ARB_vertex_program` extension which provides a restricted programming language for performing these operations and variations on them, sending the results as vertex components to the rest of the pipeline. This programmable functionality is called the *programmable pipeline*. While vertex programs provide an assembly language like interface, there are also a number of more "C"-like languages. The OpenGL Shading Language[3] (GLSL) [KBR03] and Cg [NVI04] are two examples. Vertex programs not only provide much more control and generality when generating vertex position, normal, texture, and color components per-vertex, but also allow micropass sequences to be defined to implement per-vertex shading algorithms.

In implementations that support vertex programs, part of the transformation pipeline can be switched between conventional transform mode and vertex program mode. Switching between the two modes is controlled by enabling or disabling the `GL_VERTEX_PROGRAM_ARB` state value. When enabled, vertex programs bypass the traditional vertex and normal transform functionality, texture coordinate generation and transformation, normal processing (such as renormalization) and lighting, clipping by user-defined clip planes, and per-vertex fog computations. Transform and light extensions, such as vertex weighting and separate specular color, are also replaced by vertex program functionality when it is enabled. Figure 2.11 shows how the two modes are related.

The vertex programming language capabilities are limited to allow efficient hardware implementations: for example, there is no ability to control the flow of the vertex program; it is a linear sequence of commands. The number and type of intermediate results and input and output parameters are also strictly defined and limited. Nevertheless, vertex programming provides a powerful tool further augmenting OpenGL's use as a graphics assembly language.

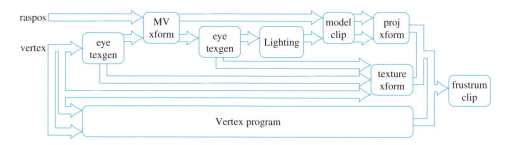

Figure 2.11 Vertex program and conventional transform modes.

---

3. An ARB extension in OpenGL 1.5.

2.10 Summary

This chapter only provides an overview of vertex, normal, and texture coordinate transformations and related OpenGL functionality. There are a number of texts that go into these topics in significantly more depth. Beyond the classic computer graphics texts such as that by Foley et al. (1990), there a number of more specialized texts that focus on transformation topics, as well as many excellent linear algebra texts.

Color, Shading, and Lighting

In this chapter we cover the basics of color representation, lighting models, and shading objects. Geometric modeling operations are responsible for accurately reproducing shape, size, position, and orientation. Knowledge of the basics of color, lighting, and shading are the next step in reproducing the visual appearance of an object.

3.1 Representing Color

To produce more realistic images, objects being rendered must be shaded with accurate colors. Modern graphics accelerators can faithfully generate colors from a large, but finite palette. In OpenGL, color values are specified to be represented with a triple of floating-point numbers in the range [0, 1]. These values specify the amount of red, green, and blue (RGB) primaries in the color. RGB triples are also used to store pixel colors in the framebuffer, and are used by the video display hardware to drive a cathode ray tube (CRT) or liquid crystal display (LCD) display.

A given color representation scheme is referred to as a *color space*. The RGB space used by OpenGL is a cartesian space well suited for describing colors for display devices that emit light, such as color monitors. The addition of the three primary colors mimics the mixing of three light sources. Other examples of color spaces include:

Hue Saturation Value (HSV) model is a polar color space that is often used by artists and designers to describe colors in a more intuitive fashion. Hue specifies the spectral wavelength, saturation the proportion of the color present (higher saturation means the color is more vivid and less gray), while value specifies the overall brightness of the color.

Cyan Magenta Yellow blacK (CMYK) is a subtractive color space which mimics the process of mixing paints. Subtractive color spaces are used in publishing, since the production of colors on a printed medium involves applying ink to a substrate, which is a subtractive process. Printing colors using a mixture of four inks is called *process color*. In contrast, printing tasks that involve a small number of different colors may use a separate ink for each color. These are referred to as *spot colors*. Spot colors are frequently specified using individual codes from a color matching system such as Pantone (2003).

YCbCr is an additive color space that models colors using a brightness (Y) component and two chrominance components (Cb and Cr). Often the luminance signal is encoded with more precision than the chrominance components. YCbCr[1] is used in digital video processing [Jac96].

sRGB is a non-linear color space that better matches the visual perception of brightness. sRGB serves as a standard for displaying colors on monitors (CRT and LCD) with the goal of having the same image display identically on different devices [Pac01]. Since it also matches human sensitivity to intensity, it allows colors to be more compactly or efficiently represented without introducing perceptual errors. For example, 8-bit sRGB values require 12-bit linear values to preserve accuracy across the full range of values.

The choice of an RGB color space is not critical to the functioning of the OpenGL pipeline; an application can use the rendering pipeline to perform processing on data from other color spaces if done carefully.

3.1.1 Resolution and Dynamic Range

The number of colors that can be represented, or palette size, is determined by the number of bits used to represent each of the R, G, and B color components. An accelerator that uses 8 bits per component can represent 2^{24} (about 16 million) different colors. Color components are typically normalized to the range [0, 1], so an 8-bit color component

---

1. The term *YCrCb* is also used and means the same thing except the order of the two color difference signals Cb and Cr is exchanged. The name may or may not imply something about the order of the components in a pixel stream.

can represent or resolve changes in [0, 1] colors by as little as 1/256. For some types of rendering algorithms it is useful to represent colors beyond the normal [0, 1] range. In particular, colors in the range [−1, 1] are useful for subtractive operations. Natively representing color values beyond the [−1, 1] range is becoming increasingly useful to support algorithms that use high dynamic range intermediate results. Such algorithms are used to achieve more realistic lighting and for algorithms that go beyond traditional rendering.

An OpenGL implementation may represent color components with different numbers of bits in different parts of the pipeline, varying both the resolution and the range. For example, the colorbuffer may store 8 bits of data per component, but for performance reasons, a texture map might store only 4 bits per component. Over time, the bit resolution has increased; ultimately most computations may well be performed with the equivalent of standard IEEE-754 32-bit floating-point arithmetic. Today, however, contemporary consumer graphics accelerators typically support 32-bit float values when operating on vertex colors and use 8 bits per component while operating on fragment (pixel) colors. Higher end hardware increases the resolution (and range) to 10, 12, or 16 bits per component for framebuffer and texture storage and as much as 32-bit floating-point for intermediate fragment computations.

Opinions vary on the subject of how much resolution is necessary, but the human eye can resolve somewhere between 10 and 14 bits per component. The sRGB representation provides a means to use fewer bits per component without adding visual artifacts. It accomplishes this using a non-linear representation related to the concept of *gamma*.

3.1.2 Gamma

Gamma describes the relationship between a color value and its brightness on a particular device. For images described in an RGB color space to appear visually correct, the display device should generate an output brightness directly proportional (linearly related) to the input color value. Most display devices do not have this property. Gamma correction is a technique used to compensate for the non-linear display characteristics of a device.

Gamma correction is achieved by mapping the input values through a correction function, tailored to the characteristics of the display device, before sending them to the display device. The mapping function is often implemented using a lookup table, typically using a separate table for each of the RGB color components. For a CRT display, the relationship between the input and displayed signal is approximately[2] $D = I^\gamma$, as shown in Figure 3.1. Gamma correction is accomplished by sending the signal through the inverse function $I^{1/\gamma}$ as shown in Figure 3.2.

The gamma value for a CRT display is somewhat dependent on the exact characteristics of the device, but the nominal value is 2.5. The story is somewhat more complicated though, as there is a subjective aspect to the human perception of brightness (actually *lightness*), that is influenced by the viewing environment. CRTs are frequently used for

---

2. More correctly, the relationship is $D = (I + \epsilon)^\gamma$, where ϵ is a black level offset. The black level is adjusted using the *brightness* control on a CRT. The gamma value is adjusted using the *contrast* control.

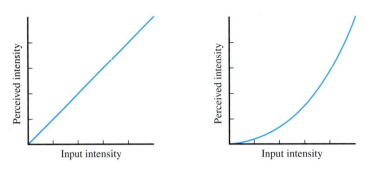

Figure 3.1 Displayed ramp intensity without gamma correction.

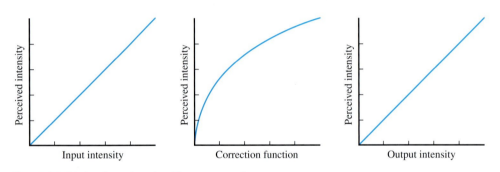

Figure 3.2 Displayed ramp intensity with gamma correction.

viewing video in a dim environment. To provide a correct subjective response in this environment, video signals are typically precompensated, treating the CRT as if it has a gamma value of 2.2. Thus, the well-known 2.2 gamma value has a built-in *dim viewing environment* assumption [Poy98]. The sRGB space represents color values in an approximate gamma 2.2 space.

Other types of display devices have non-linear display characteristics as well, but the manufacturers typically include compensation circuits so that they appear to have a gamma of 2.5. Printers and other devices also have non-linear characteristics and these may or may not include compensation circuitry to make them compatible with monitor displays. Color management systems (CMS) attempt to solve problems with variation using transfer functions. They are controlled by a system of profiles that describes the characteristics of a device. Application or driver software uses these profiles to appropriately adjust image color values as part of the display process.

Gamma correction is not directly addressed by the OpenGL specification; it is usually part of the native windowing system in which OpenGL is embedded. Even though gamma correction isn't part of OpenGL, it is essential to understand that the OpenGL pipeline computations work best in a linear color space, and that gamma correction typically takes place between the framebuffer and the display device. Care must be taken when importing image data into OpenGL applications, such as texture maps. If the image data has already been gamma corrected for a particular display device, then the linear computations performed in the pipeline and a second application of gamma correction may result in poorer quality images.

There are two problems that typically arise with gamma correction: not enough correction and too much correction. The first occurs when working with older graphics cards that do not provide gamma correction on framebuffer display. Uncorrected scenes will appear dark on such displays. To address this, many applications perform gamma correction themselves in an *ad hoc* fashion; brightening the input colors and using compensated texture maps. If the application does not compensate, then the only recourse for the user is to adjust the monitor brightness and contrast controls to brighten the image. Both of these lead to examples of the second problem, too much gamma correction. If the application has pre-compensated its colors, then the subsequent application of gamma correction by graphics hardware with gamma correction support results in overly bright images. The same problem occurs if the user has previously increased the monitor brightness to compensate for a non-gamma-aware application. This can be corrected by disabling the gamma correction in the graphics display hardware, but of course, there are still errors resulting from computations such as blending and texture filtering that assume a linear space.

In either case, the mixture of gamma-aware and unaware hardware has given rise to a set of applications and texture maps that are mismatched to hardware and leads to a great deal of confusion. While not all graphics accelerators contain gamma correction hardware, for the purposes of this book we shall assume that input colors are in a linear space and gamma correction is provided in the display subsystem.

3.1.3 Alpha

In addition to the red, green, and blue color components, OpenGL uses a fourth component called *alpha* in many of its color computations. Alpha is mainly used to perform blending operations between two different colors (for example, a foreground and a background color) or for modeling transparency. The role of alpha in those computations is described in Section 11.8 . The alpha component also shares most of the computations of the RGB color components, so when advantageous, alpha can also be treated as an additional color component.

3.1.4 Color Index

In addition to operating on colors as RGBA tuples (usually referred to as *RGB mode*), OpenGL also allows applications to operate in *color index mode* (also called pseudo-color mode, or ramp mode). In index mode, the application supplies index values instead of

RGBA tuples to OpenGL. The indexes represent colors as references into a color lookup table (also called a color map or palette). These index values are operated on by the OpenGL pipeline and stored in the framebuffer. The conversion from index to RGB color values is performed as part of display processing. Color index mode is principally used to support legacy applications written for older graphics hardware. Older hardware avoided a substantial cost burden by performing computations on and saving in framebuffer memory a single index value rather than three color components per-pixel. Of course, the savings comes at the cost of a greatly reduced color palette.

Today there are a very few reasons for applications to use color index mode. There are a few performance tricks that can be achieved by manipulating the color map rather than redrawing the scene, but for the most part the functionality of color index mode can be emulated by texture mapping with 1D texture maps. The main reason index mode is still present on modern hardware is that the native window system traditionally required it and the incremental work necessary to support it in an OpenGL implementation is usually minor.

3.2 Shading

Shading is the term used to describe the assignment of a color value to a pixel. For photo-realistic applications—applications that strive to generate images that look as good as photographs of a real scene—the goal is to choose a color value that most accurately captures the color of the light reflected from the object to the viewer. Photorealistic rendering attempts to take into account the real world interactions between objects, light sources, and the environment. It describes the interactions as a set of equations that can be evaluated at each surface point on the object. For some applications, photorealistic shading is not the objective. For instance, technical illustration, cartoon rendering, and image processing all have different objectives, but still need to perform shading computations at each pixel and arrive at a color value.

The shading computation is by definition a *per-pixel-fragment* operation, but portions of the computation may not be performed per-pixel. Avoiding per-pixel computations is done to reduce the amount of processing power required to render a scene. Figure 3.3 illustrates schematically the places in the OpenGL pipeline where the color for a pixel fragment may be modified by parts of the shading computation.

There are five fundamental places where the fragment color can be affected: input color, vertex lighting, texturing, fog, and blending. OpenGL maintains the concept of a current color (with the caveat that it is undefined after a vertex array drawing command has been issued), so if a new color is not issued with the vertex primitive, then the current color is used. If lighting is enabled, then the vertex color is replaced with the result of the vertex lighting computation.

There is some subtlety in the vertex lighting computation. While lighting uses the current material definition to provide the color attributes for the vertex, if

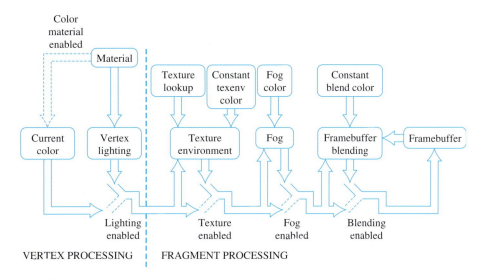

Figure 3.3 Color-processing path.

GL_COLOR_MATERIAL is enabled, then the current color updates the current material definition before being used in the lighting computation.[3]

After vertex lighting, the primitive is rasterized. Depending on the shading model (GL_FLAT or GL_SMOOTH), the resulting pixel fragments will have the color associated with the vertex or a color interpolated from multiple vertex colors. If texturing is enabled, then the color value is further modified, or even replaced altogether by texture environment processing. If fog is enabled, then the fragment color is mixed with the fog color, where the proportions of the mix are controlled by the distance of the fragment from the viewer. Finally, if blending is enabled, then the fragment color value is modified according to the enabled blending mode.

By controlling which parts of the pipeline are enabled and disabled, some simple shading models can be implemented:

Constant Shading If the OpenGL shading model is set to GL_FLAT and all other parts of the shading pipeline disabled, then each generated pixel of a primitive has the color of the *provoking vertex* of the primitive. The provoking vertex is a term that describes which vertex is used to define a primitive, or to delineate the individual triangles, quads, or lines within a compound primitive. In general it is the last vertex of a line, triangle, or quadrilateral (for strips and fans, the last vertex to

---

3. Note that when color material is enabled, the current color updates the material definition. In hindsight, it would have been cleaner and less confusing to simply use the current color in the lighting computation, but not replace the current material definition as a side effect.

define each line, triangle or quadrilateral within the primitive). For polygons it is the first vertex. Constant shading is also called flat or faceted shading.

Smooth Shading If the shading model is set to GL_SMOOTH, then the colors of each vertex are interpolated to produce the fragment color. This results in smooth transitions between polygons of different colors. If all of the vertex colors are the same, then smooth shading produces the same result as constant shading. If vertex lighting is combined with smooth shading, then the polygons are Gouraud shaded [Gou71].

Texture Shading If the input color and vertex lighting calculations are ignored or disabled, and the pixel color comes from simply replacing the vertex color with a color determined from a texture map, we have texture shading. With texture shading, the appearance of a polygon is determined entirely by the texture map applied to the polygon including the effects from light sources. It is quite common to decouple lighting from the texture map, for example, by combining vertex lighting with texture shading by using a GL_MODULATE texture environment with the result of computing lighting values for *white* vertices. In effect, the lighting computation is used to perform intensity or *Lambertian* shading that modulates the color from the texture map.

Phong Shading Early computer graphics papers and books have occasionally confused the definition of the lighting model (lighting) from how the lighting model is evaluated (shading). The original description of Gouraud shading applies a particular lighting model to each vertex and linearly interpolates the colors computed for each vertex to produce fragment colors. We prefer to generalize that idea to two orthogonal concepts *per-vertex lighting* and *smooth shading*. Similarly, Phong describes a more advanced lighting model that includes the effects of specular reflection. This model is evaluated at each pixel fragment to avoid artifacts that can result from evaluating the model at vertices and interpolating the colors. Again, we separate the concept of *per-pixel lighting* from the Phong lighting model.

In general, when Phong shading is discussed, it often means per-pixel lighting, or, for OpenGL, it is more correctly termed *per-fragment lighting*. The OpenGL specification does not define support for per-fragment lighting in the fixed-function pipeline, but provides several features and OpenGL Architectural Review Board (ARB) extensions, notably fragment programs, that can be used to evaluate lighting equations at each fragment. Lighting techniques using these features are described in Chapter 15.

In principle, an arbitrary computation may be performed at each pixel to find the pixel value. Later chapters will show that it is possible to use OpenGL to efficiently perform a wide range of computations at each pixel. It is still useful, at least for the photorealistic rendering case, to separate the concept of a light source and lighting model as distinct classes of shading computation.

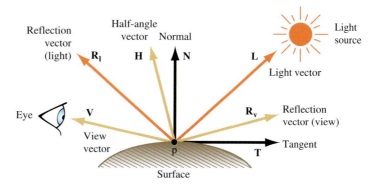

Figure 3.4 Lighting model components.

3.3 Lighting

In real-world environments, the appearance of objects is affected by light sources. These effects can be simulated using a lighting model. A lighting model is a set of equations that approximates (models) the effect of light sources on an object. The lighting model may include reflection, absorption, and transmission of a light source. The lighting model computes the color at one point on the surface of an object, using information about the light sources, the object position and surface characteristics, and perhaps information about the location of the viewer and the rest of the environment containing the object (such as other reflective objects in the scene, atmospheric properties, and so on) (Figure 3.4).

Computer graphics and physics research have resulted in a number of lighting models (Cook and Torrance, 1981; Phong, 1975; Blinn, 1977; Ward, 1994; Ashikhmin et al., 2000). These models typically differ in how well they approximate reality, how much information is required to evaluate the model, and the amount of computational power required to evaluate the model. Some models may make very simple assumptions about the surface characteristics of the object, for example, whether the object is smooth or rough, while others may require much more detailed information, such as the index of refraction or spectral response curves.

OpenGL provides direct support for a relatively simple lighting model called *Phong lighting* [Pho75].[4] This lighting model separates the contributions from the light sources reflecting off the object into four intensity contributions—ambient, diffuse, specular, and emissive ($I_{tot} = I_{am} + I_{di} + I_{sp} + I_{em}$)—that are combined with surface properties to produce the shaded color.

The ambient term models directionless illumination coming from inter-object reflections in the environment. The ambient term is typically expressed as a constant value for

---

4. The name Phong lighting is a misnomer, the equations used in the OpenGL specification are from Blinn [Bli77].

the scene, independent of the number of light sources, though OpenGL provides both scene ambient and light source ambient contributions.

The diffuse term models the reflection of a light source from a rough surface. The intensity at a point on the object's surface is proportional to the cosine of the angle made by a unit vector from the point to the light source, **L**, and the surface normal vector at that point, **N**,

$$I_{di} = \mathbf{N} \cdot \mathbf{L}.$$

If the surface normal is pointing away from the light source, then the dot product is negative. To avoid including a negative intensity contribution, the dot product is clamped to zero. In the OpenGL specification, the clamped dot product expression $\max(\mathbf{N} \cdot \mathbf{L}, 0)$ is written as $\mathbf{N} \odot \mathbf{L}$. This notation is used throughout the text.

As the discussion of a clamped dot product illustrates, considering lighting equations brings up the notion of *sideness* to a surface. If the object is a closed surface (a sphere, for example), then it seems clear that a light shining onto the top of the sphere should not illuminate the bottom of the sphere. However, if the object is not a closed surface (a hemisphere, for example), then the exterior should be illuminated when the light source points at it, and the interior should be illuminated when the light source points inside. If the hemisphere is modeled as a single layer of polygons tiling the surface of the hemisphere, then the normal vector at each vertex can either be directed inward or outward, with the consequence that only one side of the surface is lighted regardless of the location of the light source.

Arguably, the solution to the problem is to not model objects with open surfaces, but rather to force everything to be a closed surface as in Figure 3.5. This is, in fact, the rule used by CAD programs to solve this and a number of related problems. However, since this may adversely complicate modeling for some applications, OpenGL also includes the notion of *two-sided lighting*. With two-sided lighting, different surface properties are used and the direction of the surface normal is flipped during the lighting computation depending on which side of a polygon is visible. To determine which side is visible, the *signed area* of the polygon is computed using the polygon's window coordinates. The orientation of the polygon is give by the sign of the area computation.

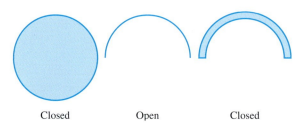

Closed   Open   Closed

Figure 3.5 Closed and open surface cross-sections.

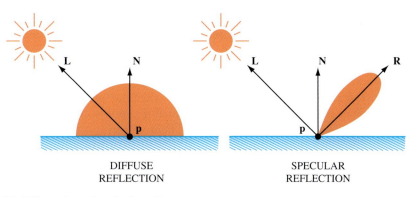

DIFFUSE
REFLECTION

SPECULAR
REFLECTION

Figure 3.6 Diffuse and specular reflection patterns.

The specular term models the reflection of a light source from a smooth surface, producing a *highlight* focused in the direction of the reflection vector. This behavior is much different than the diffuse term, which reflects light equally in all directions, as shown in Figure 3.6. Things get a little more complicated when light isn't equally reflected in all directions; the location of the viewer needs to be included in the equation. In the original Phong formulation, the angle between the reflection of the light vector, $\mathbf{R}_l$, and viewing vector (a unit vector between the surface point and the viewer position, $\mathbf{V}$) determines amount of specular reflection in the direction of the viewer.[5]

In the Blinn formulation used in OpenGL, however, the angle between the surface normal, and the *unit bisector*, $\mathbf{H}$, of the light vector $\mathbf{L}$, and the view vector $\mathbf{V}$, is used. This bisector is also called the *half-angle* vector. It produces an effect similar to $\mathbf{V} \cdot \mathbf{R}_l$, but Blinn argues that it more closely matches observed behavior, and in some circumstances is less expensive to compute.

To model surfaces of differing smoothness, this cosine term is raised to a power:

$$I_{sp} = \left(\frac{(\mathbf{V} + \mathbf{L})}{\|\mathbf{V} + \mathbf{L}\|} \odot \mathbf{N} \right)^n$$

The larger this *shininess* exponent, n, the more polished the surface appears, and the more rapidly the contribution falls off as the reflection angle diverges from the reflection of the light vector. In OpenGL the exponent is limited to the range $[0, 128]$, but there is least one vendor extension to allow a larger range.[6]

The specular term is also called the power function. OpenGL supports two different positions for the viewer: at the origin of eye space and infinitely far away along the positive

---

5. $\mathbf{V} \cdot \mathbf{R}_l$ can equivalently be written as $\mathbf{L} \cdot \mathbf{R}_v$, where $\mathbf{R}_v$ is the reflection of the view vector $\mathbf{V}$.

6. `NV_light_max_exponent`

z-axis. If the viewer is at infinity, $(0, 0, 1)^T$ is used for the view vector. These two viewing variations are referred to as *local viewer* and *infinite viewer*. The latter model makes the specular computation independent of the position of the surface point, thereby making it more efficient to compute. Note that this approximation is not really correct for large objects in the foreground of the scene.

To ensure that the specular contribution is zero when the surface normal is pointing away from the light source, the specular term is gated (multiplied) by a function derived from the inner product of the surface normal and light vector: $f_{gate} = (0 \text{ if } \mathbf{N} \odot \mathbf{L} = 0; 1$ otherwise).

The specular term is an example of a *bidirectional reflectance distribution function* or BRDF — a function that is described by both the angle of incidence (the light direction) and angle of reflection (the view direction) $\rho(\theta_i, \phi_i, \theta_r, \phi_r)$. The angles are typically defined using spherical coordinates with θ, the angle with the normal vector, and ϕ, the angle in the plane tangent to the normal vector. The function is also written as $\rho(\omega_i, \omega_r)$. The BRDF represents the amount of light (in inverse steradians) that is scattered in each outgoing angle, for each incoming angle.

The emissive term models the emission of light from an object in cases where the object itself acts as a light source. An example is an object that fluoresces. In OpenGL, emission is a property of the object being shaded and does not depend on any light source. Since neither the emissive or ambient terms are dependent on the location of the light source, they don't use a gating function the way the diffuse and specular terms do (note that the diffuse term gates itself).

3.3.1 Intensities, Colors, and Materials

So far, we have described the lighting model in terms of producing intensity values for each contribution. These intensity values are used to scale color values to produce a set of color contributions. In OpenGL, both the object and light have an RGBA color, which are multiplied together to get the final color value:

$$
\begin{aligned}
C_{final} \quad = \quad & Material_{am} * Scene_{am} \\
+ \quad & Material_{am} * Light_{am} * I_{am} \\
+ \quad & Material_{di} * Light_{di} * I_{di} \\
+ \quad & Material_{sp} * Light_{sp} * I_{sp} \\
+ \quad & Material_{em}
\end{aligned}
$$

The colors associated with the object are referred to as *reflectance* values or reflectance coefficients. They represent the amount of light reflected (rather than absorbed or transmitted) from the surface. The set of reflectance values and the specular exponent are collectively called *material properties*. The color values associated with light sources are intensity values for each of the R, G, and B components. OpenGL also stores alpha component values for reflectances and intensities, though they aren't really used in the lighting computation. They are stored largely to keep the application programming interface (API) simple and regular, and perhaps so they are available in case there's a use for them in the future. The alpha component may seem odd, since one doesn't normally think of objects reflecting alpha, but the alpha component of the diffuse reflectance is used as the alpha value of the final color. Here alpha is typically used to model transparency of the surface. For conciseness, the abbreviations a_m, d_m, s_m, a_l, d_l, and s_l are used to represent the ambient, diffuse, specular material reflectances and light intensities; e_m represents the emissive reflectance (intensity), while a_{sc} represents the scene ambient intensity.

The interaction of up to 8 different light sources with the object's material are evaluated and combined (by summing them) to produce a final color.

3.3.2 Light Source Properties

In addition to intensity values, OpenGL also defines additional properties of the light sources. Both directional (*infinite lights*) and positional (*local lights*) light sources can be emulated. The directional model simulates light sources, such as the sun, that are so distant that the lighting vector doesn't change direction over the surface of the primitive. Since the light vector doesn't change, directional lights are the simplest to compute. If both an infinite light source and an infinite viewer model are set, the half-angle vector used in the specular computation is constant for each light source.

Positional light sources can show two effects not seen with directional lights. The first derives from the fact that a vector drawn from each point on the surface to the light source changes as lighting is computed across the surface. This leads to changes in intensity that depend on light source position. For example, a light source located between two objects will illuminate the areas that face the light source. A directional light, on the other hand, illuminates the same regions on both objects (Figure 3.7). Positional lights also include an attenuation factor, modeling the falloff in intensity for objects that are further away from the light source:

$$attenuation = \frac{1}{k_c + k_l d + k_q d^2}$$

OpenGL distinguishes between directional and positional lights with the w coordinate of the light position. If w is 0, then then the light source is at infinity, if it is non-zero then it is not. Typically, only values of 0 and 1 are used. Since the light position is transformed from object space to eye space before the lighting computation is performed (when a light position is specified), applications can easily specify the positions of light sources relative to other objects in the scene.

In addition to omnidirectional lights radiating uniformly in all directions (sometimes called *point lights*), OpenGL also models spotlight sources. Spotlights are light sources that have a cone-shaped radiation pattern: the illumination is brightest along the the axis of the cone, decreases from the center to the edge of the cone, and drops to zero outside

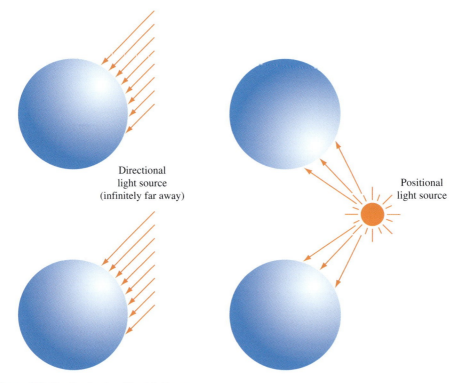

Figure 3.7 Directional and positional light sources.

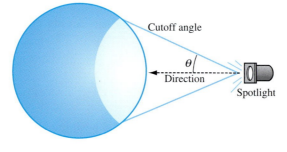

Figure 3.8 Spotlight sources.

the cone (as shown in Figure 3.8). This radiation pattern is parameterized by the spotlight direction (**sd**), cutoff angle (*co*), and spotlight exponent (*se*), controlling how rapidly the illumination falls off between the center and the edge of the cone:

$$spot = (\mathbf{L} \odot \mathbf{sd})^{se}$$

If the angle between the light vector and spot direction is greater than the cutoff angle (dot product is less than the cosine of the cutoff angle), then the spot attenuation is set to zero.

3.3.3 Material Properties

OpenGL provides great flexibility for setting material reflectance coefficients, light intensities, and other lighting mode parameters, but doesn't specify how to choose the proper values for these parameters.

Material properties are modeled with four groups of reflectance coefficients (ambient, diffuse, specular, and emissive) and a specular exponent. In practice, the emissive term doesn't play a significant role in modeling normal materials, so it will be ignored in this discussion.

For lighting purposes, materials can be described by the type of material, and the smoothness of its surface. Surface smoothness is simulated by the overall magnitude of the three reflectances, and the value of the specular exponent. As the magnitude of the reflectances get closer to one, and the specular exponent value increases, the material appears to have a smoother surface.

Material type is simulated by the relationship between three of the reflectances (ambient, diffuse, and specular). For classification purposes, simulated materials can be divided into four categories: dielectrics, metals, composites, and other materials.

Dielectrics This is the most common category. Dielectrics are non-conductive materials, such as plastic or wood, which don't have free electrons. As a result, dielectrics have relatively low reflectivity; what reflectivity they do have is independent of light color. Because they don't strongly interact with light, some dielectrics are transparent. The ambient, diffuse, and specular colors tend to have similar values in dielectric materials.

Powdered dielectrics tend to look white because of the high surface area between the powdered dielectric and the surrounding air. Because of this high surface area, they also tend to reflect diffusely.

Metals Metals are conductive and have free electrons. As a result, metals are opaque and tend to be very reflective, and their ambient, diffuse, and specular colors tend to be the same. The way free electrons react to light can be a function of the light's wavelength, determining the color of the metal. Materials like steel and nickel have nearly the same response over all visible wavelengths, resulting in a grayish reflection. Copper and gold, on the other hand, reflect long wavelengths more strongly than short ones, giving them their reddish and yellowish colors.

The color of light reflected from metals is also a function angle between the incident or reflected light directions and the surface normal. This effect can't be modeled accurately with the OpenGL lighting model, compromising the appearance of metallic objects. However, a modified form of environment mapping (such as the OpenGL sphere mapping) can be used to approximate the angle dependency. Additional details are described in Section 15.9.1.

Composite Materials Common composites, like plastic and paint, are composed of a dielectric binder with metal pigments suspended in them. As a result, they combine the reflective properties of metals and dielectrics. Their specular reflection is dielectric, while their diffuse reflection is like metal.

Other Materials Other materials that don't fit into the above categories are materials such as thin films and other exotics. These materials are described further in Chapter 15.

As mentioned previously, the apparent smoothness of a material is a function of how strongly it reflects and the size of the specular highlight. This is affected by the overall magnitude of the GL_AMBIENT, GL_DIFFUSE, and GL_SPECULAR parameters, and the value of GL_SHININESS. Here are some heuristics that describe useful relationships between the magnitudes of these parameters:

1. The spectral color of the ambient and diffuse reflectance parameters should be the same.

2. The magnitudes of diffuse and specular reflectance should sum to a value close to 1. This helps prevent color value overflow.

3. The value of the specular exponent should increase as the magnitude of specular reflectance approaches 1.

Using these relationships, or the values in Table 3.1, will not result in a perfect imitation of a given material. The empirical model used by OpenGL emphasizes performance, not physical exactness. Improving material accuracy requires going beyond the OpenGL lighting model to more sophisticated multipass techniques or use of the programmable pipeline. For an excellent description of material properties see Hall (1989).

3.3.4 Vertex and Fragment Lighting

Ideally the lighting model should be evaluated at each point on the object's surface. When rendering to a framebuffer, the computation should be recalculated at each pixel. At the time the OpenGL specification was written, however, the amount of processing power required to perform these computations at each pixel was deemed too expensive to be widely available. Instead the specification uses a basic vertex lighting model.

This lighting model can provide visually appealing results with modest computation requirements, but it does suffer from a number of drawbacks. One drawback related to color representation occurs when combining lighting with texture mapping. To texture a lighted surface, the intent is to use texture samples as reflectances for the surface. This can be done by using vertex lighting to compute an intensity value at the vertex color (by setting all of the material reflectance values to 1.0) then multiplying by the

Table 3.1 Parameters for Common Materials

Material	GL_AMBIENT	GL_DIFFUSE	GL_SPECULAR	GL_SHININESS
Brass	0.329412 0.223529 0.027451 1.0	0.780392 0.568627 0.113725 1.0	0.992157 0.941176 0.807843 1.0	27.8974
Bronze	0.2125 0.1275 0.054 1.0	0.714 0.4284 0.18144 1.0	0.393548 0.271906 0.166721 1.0	25.6
Polished Bronze	0.25 0.148 0.06475 1.0	0.4 0.2368 0.1036 1.0	0.774597 0.458561 0.200621 1.0	76.8
Chrome	0.25 0.25 0.25 1.0	0.4 0.4 0.4 1.0	0.774597 0.774597 0.774597 1.0	76.8
Copper	0.19125 0.0735 0.0225 1.0	0.7038 0.27048 0.0828 1.0	0.256777 0.137622 0.086014 1.0	12.8
Polished Copper	0.2295 0.08825 0.0275 1.0	0.5508 0.2118 0.066 1.0	0.580594 0.223257 0.0695701 1.0	51.2
Gold	0.24725 0.1995 0.0745 1.0	0.75164 0.60648 0.22648 1.0	0.628281 0.555802 0.366065 1.0	51.2
Polished Gold	0.24725 0.2245 0.0645 1.0	0.34615 0.3143 0.0903 1.0	0.797357 0.723991 0.208006 1.0	83.2
Pewter	0.105882 0.058824 0.113725 1.0	0.427451 0.470588 0.541176 1.0	0.333333 0.333333 0.521569 1.0	9.84615

continued

Table 3.1 Parameters for Common Materials (Continued)

Material	GL_AMBIENT	GL_DIFFUSE	GL_SPECULAR	GL_SHININESS
Silver	0.19225	0.50754	0.508273	51.2
	0.19225	0.50754	0.508273	
	0.19225	0.50754	0.508273	
	1.0	1.0	1.0	
Polished Silver	0.23125	0.2775	0.773911	89.6
	0.23125	0.2775	0.773911	
	0.23125	0.2775	0.773911	
	1.0	1.0	1.0	
Emerald	0.0215	0.07568	0.633	76.8
	0.1745	0.61424	0.727811	
	0.0215	0.07568	0.633	
	0.55	0.55	0.55	
Jade	0.135	0.54	0.316228	12.8
	0.2225	0.89	0.316228	
	0.1575	0.63	0.316228	
	0.95	0.95	0.95	
Obsidian	0.05375	0.18275	0.332741	38.4
	0.05	0.17	0.328634	
	0.06625	0.22525	0.346435	
	0.82	0.82	0.82	
Pearl	0.25	1.0	0.296648	11.264
	0.20725	0.829	0.296648	
	0.20725	0.829	0.296648	
	0.922	0.922	0.922	
Ruby	0.1745	0.61424	0.727811	76.8
	0.01175	0.04136	0.626959	
	0.01175	0.04136	0.626959	
	0.55	0.55	0.55	
Turquoise	0.1	0.396	0.297254	12.8
	0.18725	0.74151	0.30829	
	0.1745	0.69102	0.306678	
	0.8	0.8	0.8	
Black Plastic	0.0	0.01	0.50	32
	0.0	0.01	0.50	
	0.0	0.01	0.50	
	1.0	1.0	1.0	
Black Rubber	0.02	0.01	0.4	10
	0.02	0.01	0.4	
	0.02	0.01	0.4	
	1.0	1.0	1.0	

reflectance value from the texture map, using the GL_MODULATE texture environment. This approach can have problems with specular surfaces, however. Only a single intensity and reflectance value can be simulated, since texturing is applied only after the lighting equation has been evaluated to a single intensity. Texture should be applied separately to compute diffuse and specular terms.

To work around this problem, OpenGL 1.2 adds a mode to the vertex lighting model, GL_SEPARATE_SPECULAR_COLOR, to generate two final color values—*primary* and *secondary*. The first color contains the sum of all of the terms except for the specular term, the second contains just the specular color. These two colors are passed into the rasterization stage, but only the primary color is modified by texturing. The secondary color is added to the primary after the texturing stage. This allows the application to use the texture as the diffuse reflectance and to use the material's specular reflectance settings to define the object's specular properties.

This mode and other enhancements to the lighting model are described in detail in Chapter 15.

3.4 Fixed-Point and Floating-Point Arithmetic

There is more to color representation than the number of bits per color component. Typically the transformation pipeline represents colors using some form of floating-point, often a streamlined IEEE single-precision representation. This isn't much of a burden since the need for floating-point representation already exists for vertex, normal, and texture coordinate processing. In the transformation pipeline, RGB colors can be represented in the range $[-1, 1]$. The negative part of the range can be used to perform a limited amount of subtractive processing in the lighting stage, but as the colors are passed to the rasterization pipeline, toward their framebuffer destination (usually composed of unsigned integers), they are clamped to the $[0, 1]$ range.

Traditionally, the rasterization pipeline uses a fixed-point representation with the requisite reduction in range and precision. The fixed-point representation requires careful implementation of arithmetic operations to avoid artifacts. The principal complexity comes from the difficulty in representing the number 1.0. A traditional fixed-point representation using 8 bits might use the most significant bit as the integer part and the remaining 7 bits as fraction. This straightforward interpretation can represent numbers in the range $[0, 1.9921875]$, which is $[0, 1 + \frac{127}{128}]$.

This representation wastes 1 bit, since it represents numbers almost up to 2, when only 1 is required. Most rasterization implementations don't use any integer bits, instead they use a somewhat more complicated representation in which 1.0 is represented with the "all ones" bit pattern. This means that an 8-bit number x in the range $[0, 1]$ converts to this representation using the formula $f = x255$. The complexity enters when implementing multiplication. For example, the identity $a * 1 = a$ should be preserved, but the naive implementation, using a multiplication and a shift, will not do so.

For example multiplying $(255 * 255)$ and shifting right produces 254. The correct operation is $(255 * 255)/255$, but the expensive division operation is often replaced with a faster, but less accurate approximation.

Later revisions to OpenGL added the ability to perform subtractions at various stages of rasterization and framebuffer processing (subtractive blend[7], subtractive texture environment[8]) using fixed-point signed values. Accurate fixed-point representation of signed values is difficult. A signed representation should preserve three identities: $a * 1 = a$, $a * 0 = 0$, and $a * -1 = -a$. Fixed step sizes in value should result in equal step sizes in the representation, and resolution should be maximized.

One approach is to divide the set of fixed-point values into three pieces: a 0 value, positive values increasing to 1, and negative values decreasing to negative one. Unfortunately, this can't be done symmetrically for a representation with 2^n bits. OpenGL compromises, using the representation $(2^n \times value - 1)/2$. This provides a 0, 1, and negative one value, but does so asymmetrically; there is an extra value in the negative range.

3.4.1 Biased Arithmetic

Although the accumulation buffer is the only part of the OpenGL framebuffer that directly represents negative colors, it is possible for an application to subtract color values in the framebuffer by scaling and biasing the colors and using subtractive operations. For example, numbers in the range $[-1, 1]$ can be mapped to the $[0, 1]$ range by scaling by 0.5 and biasing by 0.5. This effectively converts the fixed-point representation into a *sign and magnitude* representation.[9]

Working with biased numbers requires modifying the arithmetic rules (Figure 3.9). Assume a and b are numbers in the original representation and $\hat{a}$ and $\hat{b}$ are in the biased

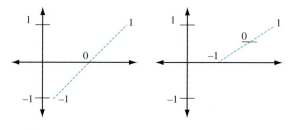

Figure 3.9 Biased representation.

---

7. In the OpenGL 1.2 ARB imaging subset.

8. OpenGL 1.3.

9. In traditional sign and magnitude representation, the sign bit is 1 for a negative number; in ours a sign bit of 0 represents a negative number.

representation. The two representations can be converted back and forth with the following equations:

$$\widehat{a} = a/2 + 1/2$$
$$a = 2(\widehat{a} - 1/2)$$

When converting between representations, the order of operations must be controlled to avoid losing information when OpenGL clamps colors to $[0, 1]$. For example, when converting from $\widehat{a}$ to a, the value of 1/2 should be subtracted first, then the result should be scaled by 2, rather than rewriting the equation as $2\widehat{a} - 1$. Biased arithmetic can be derived from these equations using substitution. Note that biased arithmetic values require special treatment before they can be operated on with regular (2's complement) computer arithmetic; they can't just be added and subtracted:

$$\widehat{a + b} = \widehat{a} + (\widehat{b} - 1/2)$$
$$\widehat{a - b} = \widehat{a} - (\widehat{b} - 1/2)$$

The equation $\widehat{a} + (\widehat{b} - 1/2)$ is supported directly by the GL_COMBINE texture function GL_ ADD_SIGNED.[10]

The following equations add or subtract a regular number with a biased number, reducing the computational overhead of converting both numbers first:

$$\widehat{a + b} = \widehat{a} + b/2$$
$$\widehat{a - b} = \widehat{a} - b/2$$

This representation allows us to represent numbers in the range $[-1, 1]$. We can extend the technique to allow us to increase the range. For example, to represent a number in the range $[-n, n]$, we use the equations:

$$\widehat{a} = \frac{a}{2n} + 1/2$$
$$a = 2n(\widehat{a} - 1/2)$$

---

10. OpenGL 1.3.

and alter the arithmetic as above. The extended range need not be symmetric. We can represent a number in the range $[-m, n]$ with the formula:

$$\widehat{a} = \frac{a}{n+m} + \frac{m}{n+m}$$

$$a = (n+m)\left(\widehat{a} - \frac{m}{n+m}\right)$$

and modify the the equations for addition and subtraction as before.

With appropriate choices of scale and bias, the dynamic range can be increased, but this comes at the cost of precision. For each factor of 2 increase in range, 1 bit of precision is lost. In addition, some error is introduced when converting back and forth between representations. For an 8-bit framebuffer it isn't really practical to go beyond $[-1, 1]$ before losing too much precision. With higher precision framebuffers, a little more range can be obtained, but the extent to which the lost precision is tolerable depends on the application. As the rendering pipeline evolves and becomes more programmable and floating-point computation becomes pervasive in the rasterization stage of the pipeline, many of these problems will disappear. However, the expansion of OpenGL implementations to an ever-increasing set of devices means that these same problems will remain on smaller, less costly devices for some time.

3.5 Summary

This chapter provided an overview of the representation and manipulation of color values in the OpenGL pipeline. It also described some of the computational models used to shade an object, focusing on the vertex lighting model built into OpenGL. The next chapter covers some of the principles and complications involved in representing an image as an array of discrete color values.

Digital Images and Image Manipulation

Geometric rendering is, at best, half of a good graphics library. Modern rendering techniques combine both geometric and image-based rendering. Texture mapping is only the simplest example of this concept; later chapters in this book cover more sophisticated techniques that rely both on geometry rendering and image processing. This chapter reviews the characteristics of a *digital image* and outlines OpenGL's image manipulation capabilities. These capabilities are traditionally encompassed by the pipeline's "pixel path", and the blend functionality in the "fragment operations" part of the OpenGL pipeline.

Even if an application doesn't make use of sophisticated image processing, familiarity with the basics of image representation and sampling theory guides the crafting of good quality images and helps when fixing many problems encountered when rendering and texture mapping.

4.1 Image Representation

The output of the rendering process is a digital image stored as a rectangular array of pixels in the color buffer. These pixels may be displayed on a CRT or LCD display device, copied to application memory to be stored or further manipulated, or re-used as a texture map in another rendering task. Each pixel value may be a single scalar component, or a vector containing a separate scalar value for each color component.

Details on how a geometric primitive is converted to pixels are given in Chapter 6; for now assume that each pixel accurately represents the average color value of the geometric primitives that cover it. The process of converting a continuous function into a series of discrete values is called *sampling*. A geometric primitive, projected into 2D, can be thought of as defining a continuous function of its spatial coordinates x and y.

For example, a triangle can be represented by a function $f_{continuous}(x, y)$. It returns the color of the triangle when evaluated within the triangle's extent, then drops to zero if evaluated outside of the triangle. Note that an ideal function has an abrupt change of value at the triangle boundaries. This instantaneous drop-off is what leads to problems when representing geometry as a sampled image. The output of the function isn't limited to a color; it can be any of the primitive attributes: intensity (color), depth, or texture coordinates; these values may also vary across the primitive. To avoid overcomplicating matters, we can limit the discussion to intensity values without losing any generality.

A straightforward approach to sampling the geometric function is to evaluate the function at the center of each pixel in window coordinates. The result of this process is a pixel image; a rectangular array of intensity samples taken uniformly across the projected geometry, with the sample grid aligned to the x and y axes. The number of samples per unit length in each direction defines the *sample rate*.

When the pixel values are used to display the image, a reproduction of the original function is *reconstructed* from the set of sample values. The reconstruction process produces a new continuous function. The reconstruction function may vary in complexity; for example, it may simply repeat the sample value across the sample period

$$f_{reconstructed}(x, y) = pixel[\lfloor x \rfloor][\lfloor y \rfloor]$$

or compute a weighted sum of pixel values that bracket the reconstruction point. Figure 4.1 shows an example of image reconstruction.

When displaying a graphics image, the reconstruction phase is often implicit; the reconstruction is part of the video display circuitry and the physics of the pixel display. For example, in a CRT display, the display circuitry uses each pixel intensity value to adjust the intensity of the electron beam striking a set of phosphors on the screen. This reconstruction function is complex, involving not only properties of the video circuitry, but also the shape, pattern, and physics of the phosphor on the screen. The accuracy of a

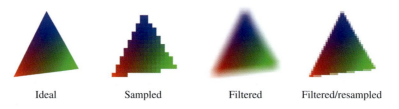

| Ideal | Sampled | Filtered | Filtered/resampled |

Figure 4.1 Example of image reconstruction.

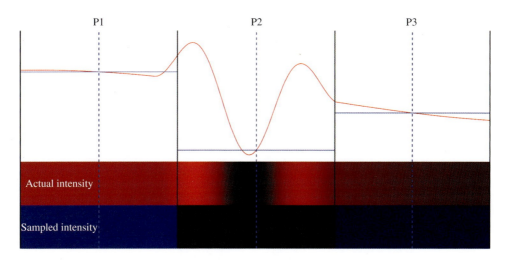

Figure 4.2 Undersampling: Intensity varies wildly between sample points P_1 and P_2.

reconstructed triangle may depend on the alignment of phosphors to pixels, how abruptly the electron beam can change intensity, the linearity of the analog control circuitry, and the design of the digital to analog circuitry. Each type of output device has a different reconstruction process. However, the objective is always the same, to faithfully reproduce the original image from a set of samples.

The fidelity of the reproduction is a critical aspect of using digital images. A fundamental concern of sampling is ensuring that there are enough samples to accurately reproduce the desired function. The problem is that a set of discrete sample points cannot capture arbitrarily complicated detail, even if we use the most sophisticated reconstruction function. This is illustrated by considering an intensity function that has the similar values at two sample points P_1 and P_3, but between these points P_2 the intensity varies significantly, as shown in Figure 4.2. The result is that the reconstructed function doesn't reproduce the original function very well. Using too few sample points is called *undersampling*; the effects on a rendered image can be severe, so it is useful to understand the issue in more detail.

To understand sampling, it helps to rely on some signal processing theory, in particular, *Fourier analysis* (Heidrich and Seidel, 1998; Gonzalez and Wintz, 1987). In signal processing, the continuous intensity function is called a *signal*. This signal is traditionally represented in the *spatial domain* as a function of spatial coordinates. Fourier analysis states that the signal can be equivalently represented as a weighted sum of sine waves of different frequencies and phase offsets. This is a bit of an oversimplification, but it doesn't affect the result. The corresponding *frequency domain* representation of a signal describes the magnitude and phase offset of each sine wave component. The frequency domain representation describes the *spectral composition* of the signal.

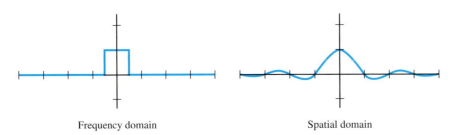

Frequency domain   Spatial domain

Figure 4.3 Ideal reconstruction function.

The sine wave decomposition and frequency domain representation are tools that help simplify the characterization of the sampling process. From sine wave decomposition, it becomes clear that the number of samples required to reproduce a sine wave must be twice its frequency, assuming ideal reconstruction. This requirement is called the *Nyquist limit*. Generalizing from this result, to accurately reconstruct a signal, the sample rate must be at least twice the rate of the maximum frequency in the original signal. Reconstructing an undersampled sine wave results in a *different* sine wave of a lower frequency. This low-frequency version is called an *alias*. An aliased signal stands in for the original, since at the lower sampling frequency, the original signal and its aliases are indistinguishable. Aliased signals in digital images give rise to the familiar artifacts of *jaggies*, or staircasing at object boundaries. Techniques for avoiding aliasing artifacts during rasterization are described in Chapter 10.

Frequency domain analysis also points to a technique for building a reconstruction function. The desired function can be found by converting its frequency domain representation to one in the spatial domain. In the frequency domain, the ideal function is straightforward; the function that captures the frequency spectrum of the original image is a *comb* function. Each "tooth" of the comb encloses the frequencies in the original spectrum; in the interests of simplicity, the comb is usually replaced with a single "wide tooth" or box that encloses all of the original frequencies (Figure 4.3). Converting this box function to the spatial domain results in the *sinc* function. Signal processing theory provides a framework for evaluating the fidelity of sampling and reconstruction in both the spatial and frequency domain. Often it is more useful to look at the frequency domain analysis since it determines how individual spectral components (frequencies) are affected by the reconstruction function.

4.2 Digital Filtering

Consider again the original continuous function representing a primitive. The function drops to zero abruptly at the edge of the polyon, representing a step function at the polygon boundaries. Representing a *step function* in the frequency domain results in frequency components with non-zero values at infinite frequencies. Avoiding creating undersampling artifacts when reconstructing a sampled step function requires changing the input function, or the way it is sampled. In essence, the boundaries of the polygon must be "smoothed" so that the transition can be represented by a bounded frequency representation. The frequency bound is chosen so that it can be captured by the samples. This process is an application of *filtering*.

As alluded to in the discussion above, filtering goes hand in hand with the concept of sampling and reconstruction. Conceptually, filtering applies a function to an input signal to produce a new one. The filter modifies some of the properties of the original signal, such as removing frequency components above or below some threshold (low- and high-pass filters). With digital images, filtering is often combined with reconstruction followed by *resampling*. Reconstruction produces a continuous signal for the filter to operate on and resampling produces a set of sample values from the filtered signal, possibly at a different sample rate. The term *filter* is frequently used to mean all three parts: reconstruction, filtering, and resampling. The objective of applying the filter is most often to transform the spectral composition of the signal.

As an example, consider the steps to produce a new version of an image that is half the size in the *x* and *y* dimensions. One way to generate the new image is to copy every second pixel into the new image. This process can be viewed as a reconstruction and resampling process. By skipping every other pixel (which represents a sample of the original image), we are sampling at half the rate used to capture the original image. Reducing the rate is a form of undersampling, and will introduces new signal aliases.

These aliased signals can be avoided by eliminating the frequency components that cannot be represented at the new, lower sampling rate. This is done by applying a *low-pass* filter during signal reconstruction, before the new samples are computed. There are many useful low-pass filter functions; one of the simplest is the *box* filter. The 2×2-box filter computes a new sample by taking an equally weighted average of four adjacent samples. The effect of the box filter on the spectrum of the signal can be evaluated by converting it to the frequency domain. Although simple, the box filter isn't a terrific low-pass filter, it corresponds to multiplying the spectrum by a sinc function in the frequency domain (Figure 4.4). This function doesn't cut off the high frequencies very cleanly, and leads to its own set of artifacts.

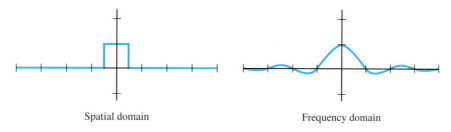

Spatial domain   Frequency domain

Figure 4.4 Box filter in spatial and frequency domain.

4.3 Convolution

Both the reconstruction and spectrum-shaping filter functions compute weighted sums of surrounding sample values. These weights are values from a second function and the computation of the weighted sum is called *convolution*. In one dimension, the convolution of two continuous functions $f(x)$ and $g(x)$ produces a third function:

$$h(x) = f(x) \circledast g(x) = \int_{-\infty}^{+\infty} f(\tau)g(x - \tau)d\tau \qquad (4.1)$$

$g(x)$ is referred to as the *filter*. The integral only needs to be evaluated over the range where $g(x - \tau)$ is non-zero, called the *support* of the filter.

The discrete form of convolution operates on two arrays, the discretized signal $F[x]$ and the *convolution kernel* $G[0...(width - 1)]$. The value of *width* defines the support of the filter and Equation 4.1 becomes:

$$H[x] = \sum_{i=0}^{width-1} F[x + i]G[i] \qquad (4.2)$$

The 1D discrete form is extended to two dimensions as:

$$H[x][y] = \sum_{j=0}^{height-1} \sum_{i=0}^{width-1} F[x + i][y + j]G[i][j] \qquad (4.3)$$

As shown in Figure 4.5, a convolution kernel is positioned over each pixel in an image to be convolved, and an output pixel is generated. The kernel can be thought of as an array of data values; these values are applied to the input pixels that the convolution kernel covers. Multiplying and summing the kernel against its footprint in the image creates a new pixel value, which is used to update the convolved image. Note that the

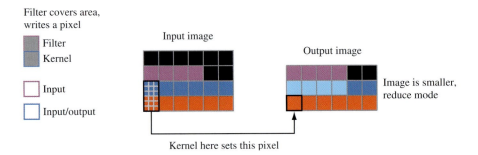

Figure 4.5 Convolution.

results of a previous convolution step don't affect any subsequent steps; each output pixel is independent of the surrounding output pixels.

The formalization and use of the convolution operation isn't accidental; it relates back to Fourier analysis. The significance of convolution in the spatial domain is that it is equivalent to multiplying the frequency domain representations of the two functions. This means that a filter with some desired properties can be constructed in the frequency domain and then converted to the spatial domain to perform the filtering. In some cases it is more efficient to transform the signal to the frequency domain, perform the multiplication, and convert back to the spatial domain. Discussion of techniques for implementing filters and of different types of filters is in Chapter 12. For the rest of this chapter we shall describe the basic mechanisms OpenGL provides for operating on images.

4.4 Images in OpenGL

The OpenGL API contains a pixel pipeline for performing many traditional image processing operations, such as scaling or rotating an image. The use of hybrid 3D rasterization and image processing techniques has increased over recent years, giving rise to the term *image-based rendering* [MB95, LH96, GGSC96] . More recent versions of OpenGL have increased the power and sophistication of the pixel pipeline to match the demand for these capabilities.

Image processing operations can be applied while loading pixel images and textures into OpenGL, reading them back to the host, or copying them. The ability to modify textures during loading operations and to modify framebuffer contents during copy operations provides high-performance paths for image processing operations. These operations may be performed entirely within the graphics accelerator, so they can be independent of the performance of the host.

OpenGL distinguishes between several types of images. Pixel images, or *pixmaps* are transferred using the `glDrawPixels` command. Pixmaps can represent index or RGB color values, depth values, or stencil values. Bitmap images are a special case of pixmaps consisting of single-bit per-pixel images. When bitmaps are drawn they are expanded into constant index or RGB colors. The `glBitmap` command is used to draw bitmaps and includes extra support for adjusting the current drawing position so that text strings can be efficiently rendered and positioned as bitmap glyphs. A third image type is texture images. Texture images are virtually identical to pixmap images, but special commands are used to transfer texture image data to texture objects. Texture maps are specialized to support 1D, 2D and 3D images as well as 6-sided cube maps. Texture maps also include support for *image pyramids* (also called mipmaps), used to provide additional filtering support.

Figure 4.6 shows a block diagram of the base OpenGL pixel pipeline. The pipeline is divided into two major blocks of operations: *pixel storage* operations that control how pixels are read or written to application memory, and *pixel transfer* operations that operate on streams of pixels in a uniform format inside the pipeline. At the end of the

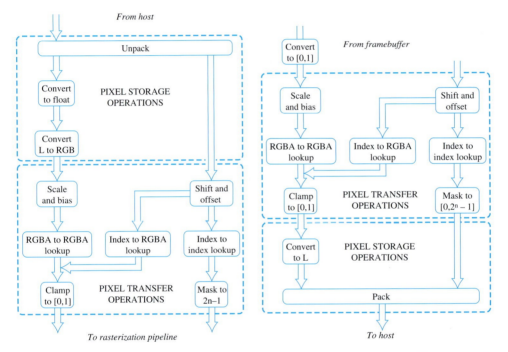

From host

To rasterization pipeline

From framebuffer

To host

TRANSFERING PIXELS FROM THE HOST (DRAWPIXELS) TRANSFERING PIXELS TO THE HOST (READPIXELS)

Figure 4.6 Basic pixel pipeline.

pixel pipeline is a pixel zoom operation that allow simple (unfiltered) scaling of images. After the zoom operation, pixel images are converted into individual fragments, where the fragments are processed in exactly the same way as fragments generated from geometry.

4.5 Positioning Images

Each of the image types (pixmaps, bitmaps, and textures) has slight variations in how they are specified to the pipeline. Both pixmaps and bitmaps share the notion of the current raster position defining the window coordinates of the bottom left corner of the image. The raster position is specified and transformed as a 3D homogeneous point similar to the vertices of other geometric primitives. The raster position also undergoes frustum clip testing and the entire primitive is discarded if the raster position is outside the frustum. The window coordinate raster position can be manipulated directly using the `glWindowPos`[1] or `glBitmap` commands. Neither the absolute position of the window position command or the result of adding the relative adjustment from the bitmap command are clip tested, so they can be used to position images partially outside the viewport.

The texture image commands have undergone some evolution since OpenGL 1.0 to allow incremental update to individual images. The necessary changes include commands that include offsets within the texture map and the ability to use a null image to initialize texture map with a size but no actual data.

4.6 Pixel Store Operations

OpenGL can read and write images with varying numbers, sizes, packings, and orderings of pixel components into system memory. This diversity in storage formats provides a great deal of control, allowing applications to fine tune storage formats to match external representations and maximize performance or compactness. Inside the pipeline, images are converted to a stream of RGBA pixels at an implementation-specific component resolution. There are few exceptions: depth, stencil, color index, and bitmap images are treated differently since they don't represent RGBA color values. OpenGL also distinguishes intensity and luminance images from RGBA ones. Intensity images are single component images that are expanded to RGBA images by copying the intensity to each of the R, G, B, and A components.[2] Luminance images are also single component images, but are expanded to RGB in the pipeline by copying the luminance to the R component while setting the G and B components to zero.

---

1. OpenGL 1.4.

2. Intensity images are only used during texture mapping.

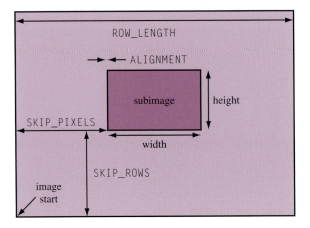

Figure 4.7 2D image memory layout.

Pixel storage operations process an image as it is read or written into host memory, converting to and from OpenGL's internal representation and the application's memory format. The storage operations do not affect how the image is stored in the framebuffer; that information is implementation-dependent. Pixel storage operations are divided into two symmetric groups: the *pack* group, controlling how data is stored to host memory, and the *unpack* group, controlling how image data is read from host memory.

2D images are stored in application memory as regularly spaced arrays, ordered so they can be transfered one row at a time to form rectangular regions. The first row starts at the lowest memory address and the first pixel corresponds to the bottom left pixel of the image when rendered (assuming no geometric transforms). A 3D image is stored as a series of these rectangles, stacked together to form a block of image data starting with the *slice* nearest to the image pointer, progressively moving to the furthest.

In addition to component ordering and size, the pixel storage modes provide some additional control over the layout of images in memory, including the ability to address a subrectangle within a memory image. Figure 4.7 shows the layout of an image in memory and the effect of the alignment and spacing parameters. Additional parameters facilitate portability between different platforms: byte swapping within individual component representations and bit ordering for bitmaps.

From an application writer's point of view, the pixel store operations provide an opportunity for the OpenGL pipeline to efficiently accelerate common conversion operations, rather than performing the operations on the host. For example, if a storage format operates with 16-bit (unsigned short) components, OpenGL can read and write those directly. Similarly, if a very large image is to be operated on in pieces, OpenGL's ability to transfer a subrectangle can be exploited, avoiding the need to extract and transfer individual rows of the subrectangle.

One feature that OpenGL does *not* provide is support for reading images directly from files. There are several reasons for this: it would be difficult to support all the existing image file formats, and keep up with their changes. Providing a simple file access format for all PC architectures would probably not result in the maximum performance implementation. It is also generally better for an application to control the I/O operations themselves. Having no file format also keeps OpenGL cleanly separated from operating system dependencies such as file I/O.

Even if a file interface was implemented, it wouldn't be sufficient for some applications. In some cases, it can be advantageous to stream image data directly to the graphics pipeline without first transferring the data into application memory. An example is streaming live video from a video capture device. Some vendors have supported this by creating an additional window-like resource that acts as a proxy for the video stream as part of the OpenGL embedding layer. The video source is bound as a read-only window and pixel copy operations are used to read from the video source and push the stream through the pixel pipeline. More details on the platform embedding layer are covered in Chapter 7.

For these reasons OpenGL has no native texture image format, external display list format, or any entrenched dependency on platform capabilities beyond display resource management.

4.7 Pixel Transfer Operations

Pixel transfer operations provide ways of operating on pixel values as they are moved to, read from, or copied within the framebuffer; or as pixels are moved to texture maps. In the base pipeline there are two types of transfer operations: scale and bias and pixel mapping.

4.7.1 Scale and Bias

Scale operations multiply each pixel component by a constant scale factor. The bias operation follows the scale and adds a constant value. RGBA and depth components are operated on with floating-point scales and biases. Analogous operations for indexed components (color index and stencil) use signed integer shift and offset values. Scale and bias operations allow simple affine remapping of pixel components. One example of scale and bias is changing the range of pixel values from [0, 1] to [0.5, 1] for later computations using biased arithmetic. Pixel operations are performed using signed arithmetic and the pixel storage modes support signed component representations; however, at the end of the transfer pipeline component values are clamped to the [0, 1] range.

4.7.2 Pixel Mapping Operations

Pixel mapping operations apply a set of one-dimensional lookup tables to each pixel, making it possible to remap its color components. There are multiple lookup tables, each handling a specific color component. For RGBA colors, there are four maps for converting each color component independently. For indexed colors, there is only one map. Four maps are available for converting indexed colors to RGBA.

A lookup table group applies an application-defined, non-linear transform to image pixels at a specific point in the pixel pipeline. The contents of the lookup tables describe the function; the size of the tables, also application-specified, sets the resolution of the transform operation. Some useful lookup table transforms are: gamma correction, image thresholding, and color inversion. Unfortunately, this feature has an important limitation: a lookup applied to one component cannot change the value of any other component in the pixel.

4.8 ARB Imaging Subset

The OpenGL ARB has defined an additional set of features to significantly enhance OpenGL's basic image processing capabilities. To preserve OpenGL's role as an API that can run well on a wide range of graphics hardware, these resource-intensive imaging features are not part of core OpenGL, but grouped into an imaging extension, with the label GL_ARB_imaging.

The imaging subset adds convolution, color matrix transform, histogram, and min-max statistics to the pixel transfer block, connecting them with additional color lookup tables. It also adds some additional color buffer blending functionality. Figure 4.8 shows a block diagram of the extended pixel processing pipeline.

4.8.1 Convolution

The imaging subset defines 1D and 2D convolution operations, applied individually to each color component. The maximum kernel width is implementation-dependent but is typically in the range of 7 to 11 pixels. Convolution support includes additional modes for separable 2D filters allowing the filter to be processed as two 1D filters. It also provides different *border modes* allowing the application different ways of handling the image boundary. Convolution operations, including methods for implementing them without using the imaging subset, are described in more detail in Chapter 12.

A convolution filter is treated similarly to an OpenGL pixel image, except for implementation-specific limitations on the maximum filter dimensions. A filter is loaded by transferring an image to a special OpenGL target. Only pixel storage operations are available to process a filter image while it is being loaded.

4.8.2 Color Matrix Transform

OpenGL's color matrix provides a 4×4 matrix transform that operates on pixel color components. Each color component can be modified as a linear function of the other components in the pixel. This can't be done with color lookup tables, since they operate independently on each color component. The matrix is manipulated using the same commands available for manipulating the modelview, texture, and projection matrices.

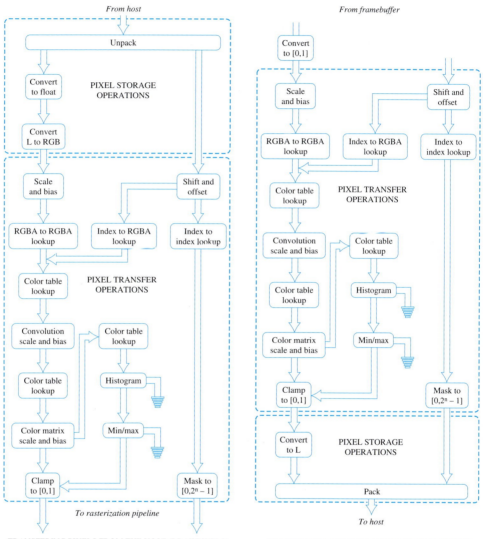

Figure 4.8 Pixel pipeline with imaging extensions.

4.8.3 Histogram

The histogram operation divides each RGBA pixel in the image into four separate color components. Each color component is categorized by its intensity and a counter in the corresponding *bin* for that component is incremented. The results are kept in four arrays, one for each color component. Effectively, the arrays record the number of occurrences of each intensity range. The size of each range or bin is determined by the length of the application-specified array. For example, a 2-element array stores separate counts for intensity ranges $0 \leq i < 0.5$ and $0.5 < i \leq 1$. The maximum size of the array is implementation-dependent and can be determined using the proxy mechanism.

Histogram operations are useful for analyzing an image by measuring the distribution of its component intensity values. The results can also be used as parameters for other pixel operations. The image may be discarded after the histogram operation is performed, if the image itself is not of interest.

4.8.4 MinMax

The minmax operation looks through all the pixels in an image, finding the largest and smallest intensity value for each color component. The results are saved in a set of two-element arrays, each array corresponding to a different color component. The application can also specify that the image be discarded after minmax information is generated.

4.8.5 Color Tables

Color tables provide additional lookup tables in the OpenGL pixel transfer pipeline. Although the capabilities of color tables and pixel maps are similar, color tables reflect an evolutionary improvement over pixel maps, making them easier to use. Color tables only operate on color components, including luminance and intensity (not color indices, stencil, or depth). Color tables can be defined that affect only a subset of the color components, leaving the rest unmodified.

Color tables are specified as images (like convolution filters). Specifying the complete table at once enables better performance when updating tables often, compared to specifying pixel maps one component at a time. The capability to leave selected components unchanged parallels a similar capability in texturing; this design is simpler than the corresponding functionality in pixel maps, which requires loading an identity map to leave a component unmodified. Color tables don't operate on depth, stencil, or color index values since those operations don't occur frequently in applications; the existing pixel map functionality is adequate for these cases.

The additional tables are defined at places in the pipeline where a *component normalization* operation is likely to be required: before convolution (GL_COLOR_TABLE), after convolution (GL_POST_CONVOLUTION_COLOR_TABLE), and after the color matrix operations (GL_POST_COLOR_MATRIX_COLOR_TABLE). Sometimes normalization operation can be implemented more efficiently using scale and bias operations. To support this, the latter two color tables are preceded by scale and bias operators which may be used in conjunction with, or instead of, the corresponding color tables.

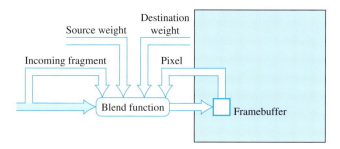

Figure 4.9 Blend inputs and outputs.

4.8.6 Blend Equation and Constant Color Blending

Beyond the pixel path, OpenGL provides an opportunity for the application to manipulate the image in the fragment operations path. OpenGL's blending function supports additive operations, where scaled versions of the source and destination pixel are added together:

$$C = C_s S + C_d D$$

In the equation above, S and D are the source and destination scale factors. Figure 4.9 shows the relationships between the source fragment, target pixel, and source and destination weighting factors. If the `glBlendEquation` command is supported,[3] OpenGL defines additional equations for generating the final pixel value from the source and destination pixels. The new equations are:

$$\begin{aligned} subtract \qquad & C = C_s S - C_d D \\ reverse\ subtract \quad & C = C_d D - C_s S \\ min \qquad & C = \min(C_s, C_d) \\ max \qquad & C = \max(C_s, C_d) \end{aligned}$$

The ARB imaging extension includes an additional blending feature, *constant color blending*, providing more ways to manipulate the image being blended. Constant color blending adds an additional constant blending factor specified by the application. It is usable as either a source or destination blending factor. This functionality makes it possible for the application to introduce an additional color, set by `glBlendColor`, that can be used to scale the source or destination image during blending.

Both the blend equation and constant color blending functionality were promoted to the base standard in OpenGL 1.4, since they are useful in many other algorithms besides those for image processing. As with texture mapping (see Section 5.14), OpenGL provides

---

3. `glBlendEquation` is an extension in OpenGL implementations before version 1.4.

proxy support on convolution filters and lookup tables in the pixel pipeline. These are needed to help applications work within the limits an implementation may impose for these images.

4.9 Off-Screen Processing

Image processing or rendering operations don't always have to produce a transient image for display as part of an application. Some applications may generate images and save them to secondary storage for later use. Batches of images may be efficiently processed without need for operator intervention, for example, filtering an image sequence captured from some other source. Also, some image processing operations may use multiple images to generate the final one. For situations such as these, off-screen storage is useful for holding intermediate images or for accumulating the final result. Support for off-screen rendering is part of the *platform embedding layer* and is described in Section 7.4.

4.10 Summary

The OpenGL image pipeline is still undergoing evolution. With the transition to a more programmable pipeline, some image manipulation operations can be readily expressed in fragment processing, but many sophisticated operations still require specialized support or more complex algorithms that will be described in Chapter 12.

Image representation and manipulation are essential to the rendering pipeline, not only for generating the final image for viewing, but as part of the rendering process itself. In the next chapter, we will describe the role of images in the texture mapping process. All of the representation issues and the pipeline mechanisms for manipulating images play an important part in the correct application of texture mapping.

Texture Mapping

Texture mapping is a fundamental method for controlling the appearance of rendered objects. A common use of texturing is to provide surface detail to geometry by modifying surface color on a per-pixel basis. A digital image is used as a source of surface color information. Texture mapping can do much more than this, however. It is a powerful and general technique for combining images and geometry. To take advantage of its capabilities, the application designer should understand texturing in depth. This chapter reviews OpenGL's texture mapping abilities with an emphasis on features important to more complex rendering techniques.

5.1 Loading Texture Images

At the heart of a texture map are the map images, each an n-dimensional array of color values. The individual elements of the array are called *texels*. The texture image array has one, two, or three dimensions. Core OpenGL requires that the texture image have power-of-two dimensions. The main reason for this is to simplify the computations required to map texture coordinates to addresses of individual texels. This simplification comes at a cost; non-power-of-two sized images need to be padded to a power-of-two size before they can be used as a texture map. There are OpenGL extensions that remove this limit, usually at the expense of some functionality; for example, there is an extension that allows the creation of textures with arbitrary sizes, but restricts the parameter values that can be bound to it, and prohibits mipmapped versions of the texture.[1]

---

1. `ARB_texture_non_power_of_two`.

The `glTexImage1D`, `glTexImage2D`, and `glTexImage3D` commands load a complete texture image, referencing the data in system memory that should be used to create it. These commands copy the texture image data from the application's address space into texture memory. OpenGL pixel store unpack state describes how the texture image is arranged in memory. Other OpenGL commands update rectangular subregions of an existing texture image (subimage loads). These are useful for dynamically updating an existing texture; in many implementations re-using an existing texture instead of creating a new one can save significant overhead.

The OpenGL pixel transfer pipeline processes the texture image data when texture images are specified. Operations such as color space conversions can be performed during texture image load. If optimized by the OpenGL implementation, the pixel transfer operations can significantly accelerate common image processing operations applied to texture data. Image processing operations are described in Chapter 12.

Texture images are referenced using texture coordinates. The coordinates of a texture map, no matter what the image resolution, range from 0 to 1. Individual texels are referenced by scaling the coordinate values by the texture dimensions. When a texture coordinate is outside the [0, 1] range, OpenGL can be set to wrap the coordinate (use the fractional part of the number), or clamp to the boundaries, based on the value of the texture wrap mode.

5.1.1 Texture Borders

A useful (and sometimes misunderstood) feature of OpenGL is the texture border (Figure 5.1). The border is used by certain wrapping modes to compute texel colors

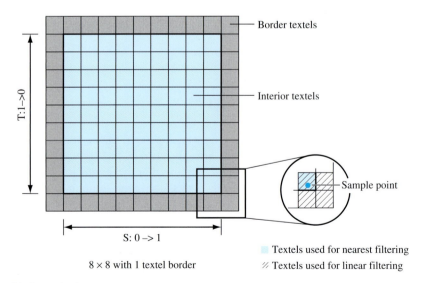

Figure 5.1 Texture borders.

needed by linear filtering when the edge of a texture image is sampled. By definition, the texture border is outside the texture coordinate range of [0, 1]. Texture borders come into play when a texture is sampled near the boundaries of the [0,1] range and the texture wrap mode is set to GL_CLAMP. Textures using GL_NEAREST filtering never sample the border, since this filtering method always uses the nearest texel to the sample point, which is always in the range of [0,1].

When the texture filter is GL_LINEAR, however, texture coordinates near the extremes of 0 or 1 will generate texture colors which are a mix of the border and edge texels of the texture image. This is because linear filtering samples the four texels closest to the sample point. Depending on sample position, up to 3 of these texels may be in the texture border.

The texture border can be specified as a one texel-wide ring of texels surrounding the texture image or as a single color. Individual texels are supplied as part of a slightly bigger texture image; the glTexImage command provides a *border* parameter to indicate that a border is being supplied. If a border consisting of a single constant color is needed, no border is specified with glTexImage, instead GL_TEXTURE_BORDER_COLOR is specified with the glTexParameter command.

Texture borders are very useful if multiple textures are being tiled together to form a larger one. Without borders, the texture color at the edge of textures using GL_LINEAR filtering would be improperly sampled, forming visible edges. This problem is solved by using edge texels from adjacent textures in the border; each texture is then seamlessly sampling its neighbor's texels at the edges.

The texture border is one way of ensuring that there are no filtering artifacts at texture boundaries. Another way to avoid filtering artifacts at the tile edges is to use a different clamping mode, called *clamp to edge*. This mode, added in OpenGL 1.2 and set using the texture parameter GL_CLAMP_TO_EDGE, restricts the sampled texture coordinates so that the texture border is never sampled. The sample is displaced away from the edge so that linear filtering only uses texels that are part of the texture image.

Unlike OpenGL's standard texture clamping, the clamp to edge behavior is unable to guarantee a consistent border appearance when used with mipmapping, because the clamping range changes with each mipmap level. The clamping range is defined in terms of the texture's dimensions, which are different at each mipmap level. The clamp to edge behavior is easier to implement in hardware than texture borders because the texture dimensions are not augmented by additional border texels, so the dimensions are always efficient powers of two. As a result, there are OpenGL implementations that support clamp to edge well, but texture border poorly.

5.1.2 Internal Texture Formats

An application can make trade-offs between texel resolution, texture size, and load bandwidth requirements by choosing the appropriate texture format. For example, choosing a GL_LUMINANCE format instead of GL_RGB reduces texture memory usage to one third.

A size-specific internal format such as GL_RGBA8 or GL_RGBA4 directs the OpenGL implementation to store the texture with the specified resolution, if it's supported. The more general internal formats, such as GL_RGBA, leave the implementation free to pick the "most appropriate" format for the particular implementation. If maintaining a particular level of format resolution is important, select a size-specific internal format.

Not all OpenGL implementations support all the available internal texture formats. Requesting GL_LUMINANCE12_ALPHA4, for example, does not guarantee that the texture will be stored in this format. The size-specific internal texture formats are merely hints. The application can exercise more control by querying the OpenGL implementation for supported formats using proxy textures, and picking the most appropriate one.

When choosing lower resolution color formats, some reduction in image quality is unavoidable. Choosing the right trade-off between color resolution and size is not a simple matter. Since textures are applied to particular surfaces, there is more flexibility trading quality for size and load speed than when choosing framebuffer resolutions. For example, a surface texture on an object that will never be close to the viewer, or whose image is composed of similar, low contrast colors, will suffer less if the texture uses a compact texel format. Even texture size is not the dominant issue when and how often the texture will be loaded are also factors to consider. If the texture is static, and its load time doesn't affect overall performance, then there's little motivation to improve load bandwidth performance by going to a smaller texel format.

All of these trade-offs are necessarily highly dependent on the details of the application. The best approach is to carefully analyze the use of texture in the application, and use more texel resolution where it has the most impact and the fewest drawbacks. In come cases, re-designing the layout of textures on the objects in the scene makes it possible to get more leverage out of compact texel formats.

5.1.3 Compressed Textures

As another way to reduce the size of texture images, OpenGL includes infrastructure to load texture images using more elaborate compression schemes.[2] Reducing the resolution of components can be thought of as one type of compression technique, but other image compression algorithms also exist. The characteristics of a good texture compression algorithm are that it does not reduce the fidelity of an image too much and that individual texels can be easily retrieved from the compressed representation. The glCompressedTexImage commands allow other forms of compressed images to be loaded as texture maps. The core OpenGL specification doesn't actually define or require any specific compression formats, largely because there isn't a suitable publicly-available standard format. However, there are some popular vendor-specific formats available as extensions, for example, EXT_texture_compression_s3tc.

---

2. Added in OpenGL 1.3.

5.1.4 Proxy Textures

Texture memory is a limited resource on most graphics hardware; it is possible to run out of it. It is not a trivial task for the application to manage it; the amount of texture memory a particular texture will use is hard to predict and very implementation-dependent. Many graphics applications are also very sensitive to texture load performance; there may be an unacceptable performance penalty if the application simply tries to load the textures that it needs, and executes a recovery scheme when the load fails.

To make it possible for an application to see if a texture will fit before it is loaded, OpenGL provides a *proxy texture* scheme. The same texture load commands are used, the difference is in the texture target: GL_PROXY_TEXTURE_1D is used in place of GL_TEXTURE_1D, GL_PROXY_TEXTURE_2D in place of GL_TEXTURE_2D, and so on. If these targets are used, the implementation doesn't load any texture data. Instead it does a "dry run", indicating to the application whether the texture load *would have been* successful. This approach may appear awkward, but upon close examination it is actually a superior approach. It works well because of its flexibility; it can accurately report back whether space is available for the texture specified regardless of the number of texture loads that have already happened, what internal texture format the OpenGL implementation has chosen, or details of the underlying graphics hardware.

If the load would not have succeeded, OpenGL doesn't signal an error, but instead sets all the texture state to zero. The application can read back any element of this state to determine the success of the load request. A simple way to check for success is to call glGetTexLevelParameter, again using the proxy texture target, the appropriate level, and a state parameter that shouldn't be zero, such as GL_TEXTURE_WIDTH. If the width is zero, the texture load would have failed.

Determining whether there is space for a full mipmap array requires a subtle change. Rather than loading the base image level, normally zero, a level greater than the base level is loaded. This indicates to the proxy mechanism whether to calculate space for just the base level or to compute it for the entire array, starting from the base level and ending at the maximum array level.

Proxy texture requests don't simply check for available space; they check the entire texture state. A proxy texture command will fail if an invalid state is specified, even if there is enough room for the texture. However, this type of failure shouldn't occur for debugged production programs.

5.2 Texture Coordinates

Texture coordinates associate positions on the texture image to the textured primitive's vertices. The per-vertex assignment of texture coordinates provide an overall mapping of a texture image to rendered geometry. During rasterization, the texture coordinates of a primitive's vertices are interpolated over the primitive, assigning each rasterized fragment its own texture coordinates.

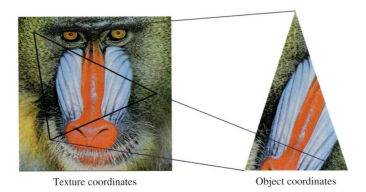

Texture coordinates   Object coordinates

Figure 5.2 Vertices with texture coordinates. Texture coordinates determine how a texture maps to the triangle.

In OpenGL, a vertex of any primitive (and the raster position of pixel images) can have texture coordinates associated with it. Figure 5.2 shows how a primitive's position and texture coordinate values at each vertex establish a relationship between a texture image and the primitive.

OpenGL generalizes the notion of a two-component texture coordinate (s,t) into a four-component homogeneous texture coordinate (s,t,r,q). The q coordinate is analogous to the w component found in vertex coordinates, making texture coordinates homogeneous. Homogeneous coordinates make correct texturing possible even if the texture coordinates are perspectively projected. The r coordinate allows for 3D texturing in implementations that support it.[3] The r coordinate is interpolated in a manner similar to s and t. OpenGL provides default values for both r (0) and q (1).

A primitive being rasterized may have w values that aren't unity. This commonly occurs when the projection matrix is loaded with a perspective projection. To apply a texture map on such a primitive without perspective artifacts, the texture coordinates must be interpolated with a method that works correctly with perspective projection. A well-known method is to divide the texture coordinates at each vertex by the vertex's w component, interpolate the resulting values for each fragment, then divide the resulting values by a $1/w$ component that has also been interpolated from $1/w$ values computed at the vertices (Blinn, 1992). For a more detailed discussion of perspective correct vertex interpolation see Section 6.1.4.

Since OpenGL supports a texture transform matrix, the texture coordinates themselves can be projected through a perspective transform. To avoid artifacts created by projected *texture coordinates*, the texture values should also be scaled by the interpolated q value. So rather than interpolating $(s/w,t/w,r/w)$ at each fragment, then dividing by $1/w$, the division step becomes a division by q/w, where q/w is also interpolated to

---

3. 3D textures were available as an extension and later became part of the core standard in OpenGL 1.2.

the fragment position. Thus, in implementations that perform perspective correction, there is no extra rasterization burden associated with processing q (Segal and Akeley, 2003).

OpenGL can apply a general 4×4 transformation matrix followed by a perspective divide to texture coordinates before using them to apply the texture map. This transform capability allows textures to be rotated, scaled, and translated on the geometry. It also allows texture coordinates to be projected onto an arbitrary plane before being used to map texture to geometry. Although the texture pipeline only has a single transform matrix compared to the geometry pipeline's two, the distinction can still be made between modelview and projective transforms. The difference is now conceptual, however, since all transforms must share a single matrix.

5.2.1 Texture Coordinate Generation and Transformation

An alternative to assigning texture coordinates explicitly is to have OpenGL generate them. OpenGL texture coordinate generation (called *texgen* for short) generates texture coordinates from other components in the vertex. Sources include position, normal vector, or reflection vector (computed from the texture position and its normal). Texture coordinates computed from vertex positions are created from a linear function of eye-space or object-space coordinates. Texture coordinates computed from reflection vectors can have three components, or be two-component coordinates produced from a projection formula.

OpenGL provides a 4×4 *texture matrix* used to transform the texture coordinates, whether supplied explicitly with each vertex, or implicitly through texture coordinate generation. The texture matrix provides a means to rescale, translate, or even project texture coordinates before the texture is applied during rasterization.

Figure 5.3 shows where texture coordinates are generated in the transformation pipeline and how they are processed by the texture transform matrix. Only `GL_OBJECT_LINEAR` and `GL_EYE_LINEAR` modes are shown here. Note that the texture transformation matrix transforms the results, just like it does if texture coordinates are sent explicitly.

5.3 Loading Texture Images from the Frame Buffer

Texture map images are created by storing bitmaps into a texture. The direct approach is for the application to supply the image, then load it with `glTexImage2D`. A less obvious but powerful approach is to create the texture dynamically instead; rendering an image into the framebuffer, then copying it into a texture. Transferring an image from the color buffer to a texture is a simple procedure in OpenGL. The image is rendered, then the resulting image is read back into system memory buffer using `glReadPixels`. The application can then use the buffer to load a texture with `glTexImage2D`.

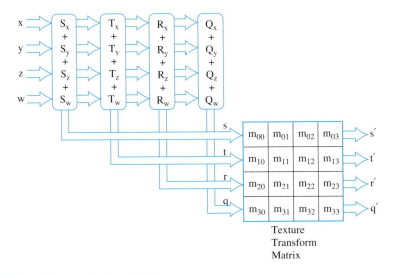

Figure 5.3 Linear texture coordinate generation.

In later versions of OpenGL,[4] the process was streamlined. A region of a framebuffer image can now be copied directly into a texture using `glCopyTexImage`, bypassing the `glReadPixels` step and improving performance. This technique is so useful that a WGL extension, `ARB_render_texture`, makes the method even more efficient. It does away with the copy step entirely, making it possible to render an image directly into a texture. The new feature is not an extension of core OpenGL. It is an extension of the OpenGL embedding layer (described in Chapter 7), adding the ability to configure a texture map as a rendering target. OpenGL can be used to render to it, just as if it was a color buffer. See Section 14.1 for more information on transferring images between textures and framebuffers, and how it can be a useful building block for graphics techniques.

5.4 Environment Mapping

Scene realism can be improved by modeling the lighting effects that result from inter-object reflections. OpenGL provides an ambient light term in its lighting equation, but this is only the crudest approximation to the lighting environment that results from light reflecting off of other objects. A more sophisticated approach is available through the use of OpenGL texturing functionality. The term *environment mapping* describes a texturing technique used to model some of the influences of the surrounding environment on an object's appearance.

---

4. Introduced in OpenGL 1.1.

Environment mapping, like regular surface texturing, changes an object's appearance by applying a texture map to its surface. An environment texture map, however, takes into account the surrounding view of the object's environment. If the object's surface has high specularity, the texture map shows surrounding objects reflected off of the surface. Objects with low specularity can be textured with an image approximating the radiance coming from the surrounding environment.

The environment map, once created, must be properly applied to an object's surface. Since it is simulating a lighting effect, texels are selected as a function of the normal vector or reflection vector at each point on the surface. These vectors are converted into texture coordinates at each vertex, then interpolated to each point on the surface, as they would for a regular surface texture. Using these vectors as inputs to the texture generation function makes it possible to simulate the behavior of diffuse and specular lighting artifacts.

5.4.1 Generating Environment Map Texture Coordinates

The OpenGL environment mapping functionality is divided into two parts: a set of texture coordinate generation functions, and an additional texture map type called a *cube map*. To maximize flexibility, the two groups are orthogonal; texture generation functions can be used with any type of texture map, and cube map textures can be indexed normally with three texture coordinates. There are three texture generation functions designed for environment mapping; normal mapping, reflection vector mapping, and sphere mapping. A function can be selected by setting the appropriate parameter to `glTexGen` command: `GL_NORMAL_MAP`, `GL_REFLECTION_MAP`, or `GL_SPHERE_MAP`.

Normal vector texture generation makes it possible to apply a texture map onto a surface based on the direction of the surface normals. It uses the three component vertex normals as texture coordinates, mapping N_x, N_y, and N_z into s, t, and r, respectively. Normal vectors are assumed to be unit length, so the generated texture coordinates range from -1 to 1. This technique is useful for environment mapping an object's diffuse reflections; the surface color becomes a function of the surface's orientation relative to the light sources of its surroundings.

Reflection texture generation indexes a surface texture based on the component values of the reflection vector. The reflection vector is computed using the vertex normal and an eye vector. The eye vector is of unit length, pointing from the eye position toward the vertex. Both the eye vector $\mathbf{U}$, and the reflection vector $\mathbf{R}$, are computed in eye space. The reflection vector is generated by applying the equation $\mathbf{R} = \mathbf{U} - 2\mathbf{N}^T(\mathbf{U} \cdot \mathbf{N})$, where $\mathbf{N}$ is the vertex normal transformed into eye space. The reflection equation used is the standard for computing the reflection vector given a surface normal and incident vector.[5]

---

5. Many texts (Foley et al., 1990; Foley et al., 1994; Rogers, 1997) present this reflection vector formula with a sign reversed, but it is the same fundamental formula. The difference is simply one of convention: the OpenGL U vector points from the eye to the surface vertex (an eye-space position), while many texts use a light vector pointing from the surface to the light.

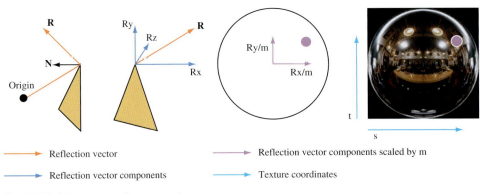

Figure 5.4 Sphere map coordinate generation.

Once the reflection vector is computed, its components are converted to texture coordinates, mapping R_x, R_y, and R_z to s, t, and r, respectively. Because **N** and **U** are normalized, the resulting **R** is normalized as well, so the texture coordinates will range from -1 to 1. This function is useful for modeling specular objects, whose lighting depends on both object and viewer position.

Sphere map texture generation has been supported by OpenGL since version 1.0. While the other two texture generation modes create three texture coordinates, sphere map generation only produces two; s and t. It does this by generating a reflection vector, as defined previously, then scaling the R_x and R_y components by a modified reflection vector length, called m. The m length is computed as $2\sqrt{R_x^2 + R_y^2 + (R_z + 1)^2}$. Dividing the R_x and R_y by this m length projects the two components into a vector describing a unit circle in the $R_z = 0$ plane. When these scaled R_x and R_y vectors are scaled by $\frac{1}{2}$ and biased by $\frac{1}{2}$, they are bounded to a [0,1] range and can be used as s and t coordinates. While the other texture generation modes create three texture coordinates, requiring a texture map that can index them (usually a cube map), the sphere map generation function can be used with a normal 2D texture (Figure 5.4).

5.4.2 Texture Maps Used in Environment Mapping

The following sections describe the two basic OpenGL environment mapping techniques: sphere mapping and cube mapping (for a description of another environment mapping method, dual paraboloid mapping, see Section 14.8).

We'll consider the creation and application of environment textures, as well as the limitations associated with their usage. In both cases, sampling issues are paramount. Any functionality that converts normal vectors into texture coordinates will have sampling issues. Since texture maps themselves are not spherical, any coordinate generation method will produce sampling rates that vary across the texture. Another important consideration when evaluating environment maps is the effort required to create an environment map texture. This issue looms larger when environment maps must be created dynamically, or if the environment mapping technique is not view-independent.

5.4.3 Cube Mapping

From its first specification, OpenGL supported environment mapping, but only through sphere map texture generation. With OpenGL 1.3, cube map textures, partnered with normal and reflection texture coordinate generation, have been added to augment OpenGL's environment mapping capabilities. A cube map texture is composed of six 2D texture maps, which can be thought of as covering the six faces of an axis-aligned cube. The *s*, *t*, and *r* texture coordinates form the components of a normalized vector emanating from the cube's center. Each component of the vector is bound to the range $[-1, 1]$. The vector's *major axis*, the axis of the vector's largest magnitude component, is used to select the texture map (cube face). The remaining two components index the texels used for filtering. Since the components range from -1 to 1, the filtering step scales and biases the values into the normal 0 to 1 range so they can be used to index into the cube face's 2D texture.

Cube map functionality has been added to the OpenGL in a very orthogonal manner, so the OpenGL commands and methodology needed to use them should be familiar. To use a cube map, the cube map textures must be loaded, configured, and enabled. The appropriate texture coordinates must be set or generated (the latter is the more common case) for each vertex. A cube map texture can be loaded with the usual OpenGL functions, including `glTexImage2D` and `glCopyTexImage2D`. The target must be set to one of the six cube map faces, listed in Table 5.1.

The OpenGL enumeration values are consecutive, and increase from the top to the bottom of the table. This enumerant ordering makes it easier to load the images using a loop construct in the application code. Cube map texturing is enabled using `glEnable` with an argument of `GL_TEXTURE_CUBE_MAP`.

Each cube map face can be a single 2D texture level or a mipmap. The usual procedures apply; the only difference is in the texture target name. The appropriate texture

Table 5.1 Cube Map Texture Targets

GL_TEXTURE_CUBE_MAP_POSITIVE_X
GL_TEXTURE_CUBE_MAP_NEGATIVE_X
GL_TEXTURE_CUBE_MAP_POSITIVE_Y
GL_TEXTURE_CUBE_MAP_NEGATIVE_Y
GL_TEXTURE_CUBE_MAP_POSITIVE_Z
GL_TEXTURE_CUBE_MAP_NEGATIVE_Z

target shown in Table 5.1 must be used in the place of GL_TEXTURE_2D. The same caveats and limitations also apply; if the cube map does not have mipmapped faces, its minification filter must be set to an appropriate type, such as GL_LINEAR. The minification filter of GL_LINEAR_MIPMAP_LINEAR is the default minification value, just as it is for 2D textures.

If the application enables multiple texture maps at the same time, cube map textures take precedence over 1D, 2D, or 3D texture maps. If multitexturing is used, cube map textures can be bound to one or more texture units. Multiple cube maps can also be managed with texture objects.

As noted previously, a cube map can be indexed directly using texture coordinates. A 3D set of texture coordinates must be applied to each vertex, using a command such as glTexCoord3f. Although setting texture coordinates directly can be useful, especially for debugging, the most common way to index cube map textures is with a texture generation function. In this case, the texture generation function should create s, t, and r components. To set the s coordinate to reflection texture generation, the glTexGen function is set with the GL_S coordinate, the GL_TEXTURE_GEN_MODE parameter, and the GL_REFLECTION_MAP value.

The combination of a texture generation function and a cube map can be thought of as a programmable function that can take as input one of two types of 3D vectors.; the texture map provides the filtered table lookup, while the texture coordinate generation provides the input vector. The GL_EYE_LINEAR texgen provides the eye vector to the vertex, GL_NORMAL_MAP provides the vertex's normal, and GL_REFLECTION_MAP provides its reflection vector.

Cube Map Texture Limitations

Although very powerful, cube map texturing has a number of important limitations. Since the textures aren't spherical, the sampling rate varies across each texture face. The sample rate is best at the center of each texture face; a fixed angular change in direction cuts through the smallest number of texels at this point. The ratio between the best and worst sampling rates is signficant; although better than sphere maps, it is worse than dual paraboloid maps.

Sampling across cube face boundaries can also be an issue. Since a cube texture is composed of six non-overlapping pieces, creating textures that provide good border sampling isn't trivial. Cube map textures with borders must correctly sample texel values from their neighbors; because of the cube geometry, simply using a strip of texels from adjacent textures will result in slightly inaccurate sampling. The border texels must be projected back along the line to the cube center to find the adjacent cube samples that provide their colors.

Things get more complex if mipmapped textures with borders are used. Border texels cover different areas, depending on the coarseness of the mipmap level. Mipmap textures with borders handle texture coordinates generated from rapidly changing vertex vectors. An example is a small triangle, covering only a few pixels on the screen, containing

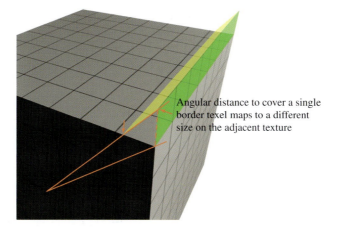

Angular distance to cover a single
border texel maps to a different
size on the adjacent texture

Figure 5.5 Cube map texture border calculations.

three highly divergent vertex normals. Normal or reflection vector interpolation leads to adjacent pixels sampled from different faces of the cube map; only good texture generation will avoid aliasing artifacts in these conditions.

If a geometry primitive with antiparallel vectors is interpolated, the interpolated vector may become degenerate. In this case, the sampled texel will be arbitrary. A cube map with mipmapped face textures will reduce the chance of aliasing in this case. Such interpolations have a large derivative value, and the coarse mipmap levels of the cube faces tend to have similar texel colors. Cube map textures also consume lots of texture memory. For any given texture resolution (which because of the sampling rate variations, tend to be large to maintain quality), the texture memory usage must be multipled by six to take into account all of the cube faces.

5.4.4 Sphere Mapping

Sphere mapping is the original environment mapping method for OpenGL; it has been a core feature since OpenGL 1.0. A sphere map texture is a normal 2D texture with a specially distorted image on it. The sphere map image is inscribed in the interior of a circle in the texture map with radius $\frac{1}{2}$ centered at $(\frac{1}{2}, \frac{1}{2})$ in texture coordinates. The image within the circle can be visualized as the image of a chrome sphere reflecting its surroundings. The silhouette edge of the sphere is seen as an extreme grazing reflection of whatever is directly behind the sphere. Visualize the sphere as infinitely small; it doesn't obscure any objects, and its grazing reflection is of only one point behind it. This implies that, ignoring sampling issues, every point on the circle's edge of a properly generated sphere map should be the same color. Properly normalized reflection vectors are guaranteed to fall within the sphere map's circle, so texels outside the circle will never be filtered.

Since sphere mapping requires only a single texture, configuring OpenGL for sphere mapping is straightforward. The desired sphere map texture is made current, then texturing is done in the usual manner. The sphere map texture image is designed to map texture coordinates derived from reflection vectors at each vertex. Although regular texture coordinates can be used, OpenGL provides a special texture coordinate generation mode that can be used to map texture coordinates from reflection vectors. Since a sphere map texture is 2D, only the *s* and *t* coordinates need to be generated:

```
glTexGeni(GL_S, GL_TEXTURE_GEN_MODE, GL_SPHERE_MAP);
glTexGeni(GL_T, GL_TEXTURE_GEN_MODE, GL_SPHERE_MAP);

glEnable(GL_TEXTURE_GEN_S);
glEnable(GL_TEXTURE_GEN_T);
```

As with any environment mapping technique, the combination of sphere map texture and sphere map texture coordinate generation can be thought of as a 2D mapping function converting reflection vector directions into color values.

Sphere Map Limitations

Although sphere mapping can be used to create convincing environment mapped objects, sphere-mapped reflections are not physically correct. Most of the artifacts come from the discrepancy between a sphere map image generation and its application onto textured geometry. A sphere map image is mapped as if its reflection vectors originate from a single location. On the other hand, a sphere map texture is often applied over the extended area of an object's surface. As a result, sphere-mapped objects can't accurately reproduce the optical effect of reflecting a nearby object, or represent a reflective object that is self-reflecting. Sphere mapping results are only completely accurate when the assumption is made that all of the reflected surroundings are infinitely far from the reflective object.

The variable sampling rate of sphere map can also lead to sampling artifacts. The computed texture coordinates are perspective correct at the vertices, but linearly interpolated across each polygon. Unfortunately, a sphere map image is highly non-linear, so this interpolation is not correct. This can lead to poor sampling rates for the parts of the textured primitive that sample near the edge of the sphere map circle, with the usual aliasing artifacts.

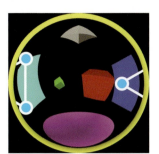

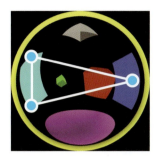

Reasonably sampled polygons that do not cross behind the spere map

Reasonable: Intended environment wrap through the sphere map perimeter

Wrong: But 2D texturing hardware simply crosses the environment instead of wrapping

Figure 5.6 The source of sphere mapping sparkles.

Additionally, the points at the edge of the sphere-map circle all map to the same location. This can lead to multiple valid but varying interpolations for the same set of vertex texture coordinates; interpolating within the sphere map circle, or interpolating the "long way around," across the sphere-map circle boundary. This type of interpolation is necessary when the reflecting primitive is nearly edge on to the viewer. In these cases, sphere map coordinates will be interpolated incorrectly, since they always interpolate within the sphere map circle. Figure 5.6 illustrates this ambiguity.

The failure to wrap around the sphere map edge is responsible for an unsightly artifact that appears as random "sparkles" or "dirt" at the silhouette edge of a sphere-mapped object. The wrong texels are used to texture the polygons, causing the object to have miscolored regions. Generally the incorrectly sampled polygons are small, causing the artifacts to look like "dirt". Because these grazing polygons are small in screen space, the number of affected pixels is usually small. Still the effectively random sparkling can be objectionable, particularly in animated scenes. Figure 5.7 shows a scene with sparkle artifacts, a zoomed in section of the scene sparkles at the silhouette edge of the sphere-mapped object.

This problem can be solved by careful splitting of silhouette polygons, forcing the correct texels to be sampled in the resulting polygons. The polygons should be split along the boundary of the polygon where the interpolated reflection vector is parallel to the direction of view (and maps to the the sphere map edge). This can be an expensive operation, however. It may be better to use a more robust technique such as cube mapping.

The final major limitation of sphere maps is that their construction assumes that the center of the sphere map reflects directly back at the viewer. When constructing sphere maps, the construction is based on a particular view orientation. The sphere map image is *view-dependent*. This means unless the sphere map is regenerated for different views, the sphere map will be incorrect as the viewer's relationship to the textured object changes.

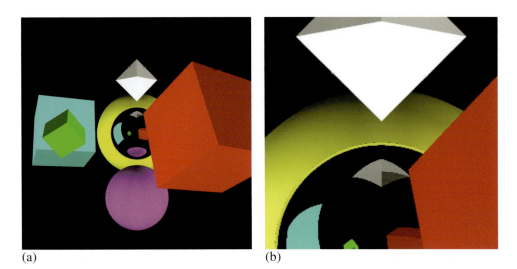

(a)   (b)

Figure 5.7 Example showing sparkle artifacts.

To avoid artifacts, new sphere map texture images must be created and loaded as the viewer/object relationship changes. If the environment mapped object is reflecting a dynamic environment, this continuous updating may be required anyway. This requirement is a major limitation for using sphere maps in dynamic scenes with a moving viewer.

5.5 3D Texture

An important point to note about 3D textures in OpenGL is how similar they are to their 1D and 2D relatives. From the beginning, OpenGL texturing was designed to be extensible. As a result, 3D textures are implemented as a straightforward extension of 2D and 1D textures. Texture command parameters are similar; a GL_TEXTURE_3D target is used in place of GL_TEXTURE_2D or GL_TEXTURE_1D.[6] The texture environment remains unchanged. 3D texture internal and external formats and types are the same, although a particular OpenGL implementation may limit the availability of 3D texture formats.

A 3D texture is indexed with s, t, and r texture coordinates instead of just s and t. The additional texture coordinate complexity, combined with the common uses for 3D textures, means texture coordinate generation is used more commonly for 3D textures

---

6. 3D textures were added to OpenGL 1.2; prior to 1.2 they are available as an extension.

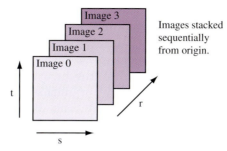

Image 3
Image 2
Image 1
Image 0

Images stacked
sequentially
from origin.

t

r

s

Figure 5.8 3D Texture Maps.

than for 1D and 2D. Figure 5.8 shows a 3D texture, its 2D image components, and how it is indexed with s, t, and r.

3D texture maps take up a large amount of texture memory, and are expensive to change dynamically. This can affect the performance of multipass algorithms that require multiple passes with different textures.

The texture matrix operates on 3D texture coordinates in the same way that it does for 1D and 2D textures. A 3D texture volume can be translated, rotated, scaled, or have any other combination of affine and perspective transforms applied to it. Applying a transformation to the texture matrix is a convenient and high-performance way to manipulate a 3D texture, especially when it is too expensive to alter the texel values directly.

A clear distinction should be made between 3D textures and mipmapped 2D textures. 3D textures can be thought of as a solid block of texture, requiring a third texture coordinate r, to access any given texel. A 2D mipmap is a series of 2D texture maps, each filtered to a different resolution. Texels from the appropriate level(s) are chosen and filtered, based on the relationship between texel and pixel size on the primitive being textured.

Like 2D textures, 3D texture maps may be mipmapped. Instead of resampling a 2D image, at each level the entire texture volume is resampled down to an eighth of its volume. This is done by averaging a group of eight adjacent texels on one level down to a single texel on the next. Mipmapping serves the same purpose in both 2D and 3D texture maps; it provides a means of accurately filtering when the projected texel size is small relative to the pixels being rendered.

5.5.1 Using 3D Textures to Render Solid Materials

A straightforward 3D texture application renders solid objects composed of heterogeneous material. A good example would be rendering an object made of solid marble or wood. The object itself is composed of polygons or non-uniform rational B-splines (NURBS) surfaces bounding the solid. Combined with proper texgen values, rendering the surface using a 3D texture of the material makes the object appear cut out of the material. In contrast, with 2D textures, objects often appear to have the material laminated on the surface. The difference can be striking when there are obvious 3D coherencies in the material texture, especially if the object has sharp angles between its surfaces.

Creating a solid 3D texture starts with material data. The material color data is organized as a three dimensional array. If mipmap filtering is desired, use `glBuild3DMipmaps` to create the mipmap levels. Since 3D textures can use up a lot of texture memory, many implementations limit their maximum allowed size. Verify that the size of the texture to be created is supported by the system and there is sufficient texture memory available for it by calling `glTexImage3D` with `GL_PROXY_TEXTURE_3D` to find a supported size. Alternatively, `glGet` with `GL_MAX_3D_TEXTURE_SIZE` retrieves the maximum allowed size of any dimension in a 3D texture for the OpenGL implementation, though the result may be more conservative than the result of a proxy query, and doesn't take into account the amount of available texture memory.

The key to applying a solid texture accurately on the surface is using the right texture coordinates at the vertices. For a solid surface, using `glTexGen` to create the texture coordinates is the easiest approach. Define planes for s, t, and r in object space to orient the solid material to the object. Adjusting the scale has more effect on texture quality than the position and orientation of the planes, since scaling affects the spacing of the texture samples.

Texturing itself is straightforward. Using `glEnable(GL_TEXTURE_3D)` to enable 3D texture mapping and setting the texture parameters and texture environment appropriately is all that is required. Once properly configured, rendering with a 3D texture is no different than other types of texturing. See Section 14.1 for more information on using 3D textures.

5.6 Filtering

While texture image is a discrete array of texels, texture coordinates vary continuously (at least conceptually) as they are interpolated across textured primitives during rendering. This creates a sampling problem. When rendering textured geometry, the difference between texture and geometric coordinates causes a pixel fragment to cover an arbitrary region of the texture image (called the pixel footprint). Ideally, texture filtering integrates weighted contributions from all the texels covered by the pixel footprint. The discussions in Section 4.1 regarding digital image representation and sampling are equally valid when applied to texture mapping. Texture mapping operations can introduce aliasing artifacts if inadequate sampling is performed. In practice, texture mapping doesn't approach ideal sampling because of the large performance penalty incurred by accessing and integrating all contributing sample values. In some circumstances, filtering results can be improved using special techniques inside the application. For example, Section 14.7 describes techniques for dealing with anisotropic footprints.

OpenGL provides a set of filtering methods for sampling and integrating texel values. The available filtering choices depend on whether the texels are being magnified (when the pixel footprint is smaller than a single texel) or minified (the pixel footprint is larger than a single texel).

The simplest filter method is point sampling: only a single texel value, from the texel nearest the texture coordinate's sample point, is selected. This type of sampling, called GL_NEAREST in OpenGL, is useful when an application requires access to unmodified texel values (e.g., when a texture map is being used as a lookup table). Point sampling seldom gives satisfactory results when used to add surface detail, often creating distracting aliasing artifacts. Instead, most applications use an interpolating filter.

Bilinear texturing is the next step up for filtering texture images. It performs a linear interpolation of the four texels closest to the sample point. In image processing parlance, this is a tent or triangle filter using a 2×2 filter kernel. In OpenGL this type of filtering is referred to as GL_LINEAR. For magnified textures, OpenGL supports GL_LINEAR and GL_NEAREST filtering. For minification, OpenGL supports GL_NEAREST and GL_LINEAR, as well as a number of different mipmapping (Williams, 1983) approaches. The highest quality (and most computationally expensive) mipmap method core OpenGL supports is tri-linear mipmapping. This mipmapping method, called GL_LINEAR_MIPMAP_LINEAR, performs bilinear filtering on the two closest mipmap levels, then interpolates the resulting values based on the sample point's level of detail.

Some OpenGL implementations support an extension called SGIS_texture_filter4. This is a texture filtering method that provides a larger filter kernel. It computes the weighted sum of the 4×4 texel array closest to the sample point. Anisotropic texturing, which handles textures with a higher minification value in a certain direction (this is common in textures applied to geometry that is viewed nearly edge on), is also supported by some OpenGL implementations with the EXT_texture_filter_anisotropic extension. Anisotropic texturing samples a texture along the line of maximum minification. The number of samples depends on the ratio between the maximum and minimum minification at that location.

5.7 Additional Control of Texture Level of Detail

In OpenGL 1.0 and 1.1, all of the mipmap levels of a texture must be specified and consistent. To be consistent, every mipmap level of a texture must have half the dimensions of the previous mipmap level of detail (LOD) until reaching a level having one or both dimensions of length one, excluding border texels. In addition, all of a mipmap's levels must use the same internal format and border configuration (Figure 5.9).

If mipmap filtering is requested for a texture, but all the mipmap levels of a texture are not present or are not consistent, OpenGL silently disables texturing. A common pitfall for OpenGL programmers is to accidently supply an inconsistent or incomplete set

Original texture

Magnified view of textures:
note how texels blur together
at coarser mip levels

Pre-filtered mipmap textures

1/4

1/16

1/64

1/256

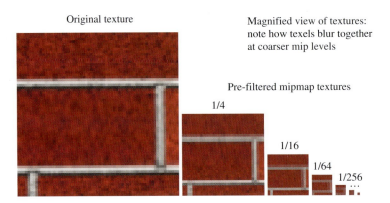

Figure 5.9 Multiple levels of texture detail using mipmaps.

of mipmap levels, resulting in polygons being rendered without texturing. For a common example of this problem, consider an application that specifies a single texture level without setting the minification filter setting. The default minification filter in OpenGL, GL_LINEAR_MIPMAP_LINEAR, requires a consistent mipmap. As a result, the texture is inconsistent with the minification filter being used, and texturing is disabled.

OpenGL 1.2 relaxes the texture consistency requirement by allowing the application to specify a contiguous subset of mipmap levels to use. Only the levels specified must exist and be consistent. For example, this feature permits an application to specify only the 1×1 through 256×256 mipmap levels of a texture with a 1024×1024 level 0 texture, and still mipmap with these levels, even if the 512×512 and 1024×1024 levels are not loaded. The application can do this by setting the texture's GL_TEXTURE_BASE_LEVEL and GL_TEXTURE_MAX_LEVEL parameters appropriately. An OpenGL application will not use texture levels outside the range specified by these values, even if the level of detail parameter indicates that they are the most appropriate ones to use.

The level of detail parameter, λ, is used in the OpenGL specification to describe the size relationship between a pixel in window space, and the corresponding texel(s) that covers it. If the texture coordinates of a textured primitive were overlayed onto the primitive in screen space, and the texture coordinates were scaled by the texture dimensions, the ratio of these coordinates shows how the texels in the texture map correspond to the pixels in the primitive. A ratio can be computed for each texture coordinate relative to the x and y coordinates in window space. Taking log_2 of the largest scale factor produces λ. This parameter is measured to choose between minification and magnification filters, and to select mipmap levels when mipmap minification is enabled.

Limiting OpenGL to a limited range of texture levels is useful if an application must guarantee a constant update rate. From the previous example, if texture load bandwidth is a bottleneck, the application might constrain the base and maximum LODs when it doesn't have enough time to load the 512×512 and 1024×1024 mipmap levels from disk. In this case, the application chooses to settle for lower resolution LODs, possibly resulting

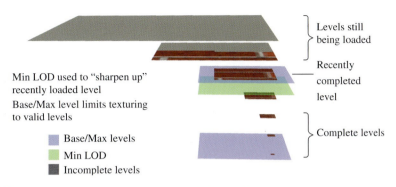

Levels still being loaded

Recently completed level

Complete levels

Min LOD used to "sharpen up" recently loaded level

Base/Max level limits texturing to valid levels

Base/Max levels
Min LOD
Incomplete levels

Figure 5.10 Loading a mipmap over multiple frames using LOD control.

in blurry textured surfaces, rather than not updating the image in time for the next frame. On subsequent frames, when the application gets enough additional time to load the full set of mipmap levels for the texture, it can load the finer levels, change the LOD limits, and render with full texture quality. The OpenGL implementation can be configured to use only the available levels by clamping the λ LOD value to the range of available ones.

OpenGL provides finer control over LOD than specifying a range of texture levels. The minimum and maximum allowable LOD values themselves can be specified. The OpenGL 1.2 GL_TEXTURE_MIN_LOD and GL_TEXTURE_MAX_LOD texture parameters provide a further means to clamp the λ LOD value. The min and max values can be fractional, allowing the application to control the blending of two mipmap levels.[7] An application can use the min and max values to gradually "sharpen up" to a finer mipmap level over a number of frames, or gradually "blur down" to a coarser level.

This functionality can be used to make the use of finer texture levels as they become available less abrupt and noticeable to the user. Section 14.6 applies this feature to the task of texture paging. Figure 5.10 shows how texture level and LOD ranges can work together to allow the application fine control over loading and using a mipmap. In this example, a mipmap's levels are being loaded over a number of frames. LOD control is used to ensure that the mipmap can be put to use while the loading occurs, with minimal visual artifacts.

5.8 Texture Objects

Most texture mapping applications switch among many different textures during the course of rendering a scene. To facilitate efficient switching among multiple textures

---

7. This same functionality for controlling texture level of detail is also available through the SGIS_texture_lod extension.

and to facilitate texture management, OpenGL uses *texture objects* to maintain texture state.[8]

The state of a texture object contains all of the texture images in the texture (including all mipmap levels) and the values of the texturing parameters that control how texels are accessed and filtered. Other OpenGL texture-related states, such as the texture environment or texture coordinate generation modes, are *not* part of a texture object's state.

As with display lists, each texture object is identified by a 32-bit unsigned integer which serves as the texture's name. Like display list names, the application is free to assign arbitrary unused names to new texture objects. The command glGenTextures assists in the assignment of texture object names by returning a set of names guaranteed to be unused. A texture object is bound, prioritized, checked for residency, and deleted by its name. Each texture object has its own texture target type. The four supported texture targets are:

- GL_TEXTURE_1D
- GL_TEXTURE_2D
- GL_TEXTURE_3D
- GL_TEXTURE_CUBE_MAP

The value zero is reserved to name the default texture of each texture target type. Calling glBindTexture binds the named texture object, making it the current texture for the specified texture target. Instead of always creating a new texture object, glBindTexture creates a texture object only when a texture image or parameter is set to an unused texture object name. Once created, a texture object's target (1D, 2D, or 3D) can't be changed. Instead, the old object must be destroyed and a new one created.

The glTexImage, glTexParameter, glGetTexParameter, glGetTexLevel-Parameter, and glGetTexImage commands update or query the state of the currently bound texture of the specified target type. Note that there are really four current textures, one for each texture target type: 1D, 2D, 3D, and cube map. When texturing is enabled, the current texture object (i.e., current for the highest priority enabled texture target) is used for texturing. When rendering geometric objects using more than one texture, glBindTexture can be used to switch among them.

Switching textures is a fairly expensive operation; if a texture is not already resident in the accelerator texture memory, switching to a non-resident texture requires that the texture be loaded into the hardware before use. Even if the texture is already loaded, caches that maximize texture performance may be invalidated when switching textures. The details of switching a texture vary with different OpenGL implementations, but

---

8. Texture objects were added in OpenGL 1.1.

it's safe to assume that an OpenGL implementation is optimized to maximize texturing performance for the currently bound texture, and that switching textures should be minimized.

Applications often derive significant performance gains sorting the objects they are about to render by texture. The goal is to minimize the number of `glBindTexture` commands required to draw the scene. Take a simple example: if a scene uses three different tree textures to draw several dozen trees within a scene, it is a good idea to group the trees by the texture they use. Then each group can be rendered in turn, binding the group's texture, then rendering all the group's members.

5.9 Multitexture

OpenGL 1.3 extends core texture mapping capability by providing a framework to support multiple texture units. This allows two or more distinct textures to be applied to a fragment in one texturing pass.[9] This capability is generally referred to by the name *multitexture*. Each *texture unit* has the ability to access, filter, and supply its own texture color to each rasterized fragment. Before multitexture, OpenGL only supported a single texture unit. OpenGL's multitexture support requires that every texture unit be fully functional and maintain state that is independent of all other texture units. Each texture unit has its own texture coordinate generation state, texture matrix state, texture enable state, and texture environment state. However, each texture unit within an OpenGL context shares the same set of texture objects.

Rendering algorithms that require multiple rendering passes can often be reimplemented to use multitexture and operate with fewer passes. Some effects, due to the number of passes required or the need for high color precision, are only viable using multitexture.

Many games, such as Quake (id Software, 1999) and Unreal (Epic Games, 1999), use light maps to improve the lighting quality within their scenes. Without multitexture, light map textures must be modulated into the scene using a second blended rendering pass, after the first pass renders the surface texture. With multitexture, the light maps and surface texture can be rendered in a single rendering pass. This reduces the transformation overhead almost in half: rendering light maps as part of a single multitextured rendering pass means the polygons are only transformed once. Framebuffer update overhead is also lower when using multitexture to render light maps: when multitexture is used, the overhead of blending in the second rendering pass is eliminated. The computation moves from the framebuffer blending part of the pipeline to the second texture unit's environment stage. This means the light maps only affect the processing of multitextured geometry, rather than the entire scene. Light maps are described in more detail in Section 15.5.

---

9. This functionality was also available earlier as the `ARB_multitexture` extension.

5.9.1 Multitexture Model

The multitexture API adds commands that control the state of one or more texture units. The glActiveTexture command determines which texture unit will be affected by the OpenGL texture commands that follow. For example, to enable 2D texturing on texture unit 0 and 1D texturing on texture unit 1, issue the following OpenGL commands:

```
glActiveTexture(GL_TEXTURE0);
glEnable(GL_TEXTURE_2D);
glActiveTexture(GL_TEXTURE1);
glEnable(GL_TEXTURE_1D);
```

Note that the state of each texture unit is completely independent. When multitexture is supported, other texture commands such as glTexGen, glTexImage2D, and glTexParameter affect the current active texture unit (as set by glActiveTexture). Other commands, such as glDisable, glGetIntegerv, glMatrixMode, glPushMatrix, and glPopMatrix, also operate on the current active texture unit when updating or querying texture state.

The number of texture units available in a given OpenGL implementation can be found by querying the implementation-dependent constant GL_MAX_TEXTURE_UNITS. using glGetIntegerv. To be conformant with the OpenGL specification, implementations should support at least two units, but this may not always be the case. To be safe, the application should query the number available before multitexturing.

OpenGL originally supported a single set of texture coordinates. With the addition of multitexture, vertex attributes have been extended to include a number of texture coordinate *sets* equal to the maximum number of texture units supported by the implementation. Rather than modifying the behavior of the existing glTexCoord command, multitexture provides glMultiTexCoord commands for setting texture coordinates for each texture unit. For example:

```
glMultiTexCoord2f(GL_TEXTURE0, s0, t0);
glMultiTexCoord4f(GL_TEXTURE1, s1, t1, r1, q1);
glMultiTexCoord1i(GL_TEXTURE2, s2);
glVertex3f(x, y, z);
```

The behavior of the glTexCoord family of routines is specified to update just texture unit zero.

Multitexture also supports vertex arrays for multiple texture coordinate sets. In this case, an *active texture* paradigm is used. Because vertex arrays are considered client state, the glClientActiveTexture command is added to control which vertex array texture coordinate set the glTexCoordPointer, glEnableClientState, glDisableClientState, and glGetPointerv commands effect or query. To illustrate, this example code fragment provides no texture coordinates for texture unit zero, but provides an array pointing to the data in `tex_array_ptr` for texture unit one:

```
glClientActiveTexture(GL_TEXTURE0);
glDisableClientState(GL_TEXTURE_COORD_ARRAY);
glClientActiveTexture(GL_TEXTURE1);
glTexCoordPointer(2, GL_FLOAT, 0, tex_array_ptr);
glEnableClientState(GL_TEXTURE_COORD_ARRAY);
```

Multitexturing also extends the current raster position to contain a distinct texture coordinate set for each supported texture unit. Multitexture support was not provided uniformly throughout OpenGL; evaluator and feedback functionality are not extended to support multiple texture coordinate sets. Evaluators and feedback utilize only texture coordinate set zero.

The `glPushAttrib`, `glPopAttrib`, `glPushClientAttrib`, and `glPopClientAttrib` push and pop respectively all the respective server or client texture state of all texture units when texture-related state is pushed or popped.

5.9.2 Multitexture Texture Environments

Much of the multitexture functionality, such as texture coordinate generation, texel lookup, and texture filtering, can be thought of as operating independently in each texture unit. But they must interact during the texture environment stage to provide a single fragment color. The multitexture pipeline uses a cascade model to combine the incoming fragment color with the fragment's texture contribution from each texture unit. The first enabled texture unit uses its state to control how to combine the incoming fragment color with its corresponding texture color.

The resulting color is passed to the next enabled texture unit, where the process is repeated. The texture unit uses its environment state to control how the incoming color (which came from the previous active texture unit), is combined with the corresponding texture color, then passes the resulting color to the next active unit.

This process continues until all the enabled texture units have modified the fragment color. The texture units are accessed by increasing numerical order; texture unit 0 (if active), then texture unit 1 (if active), and so on. Figure 5.11 illustrates the multitexture dataflow.

Multitexture with basic texture environment functionality is extremely useful for streamlining multitexture algorithms such as light maps or environment mapping. But modern multitexture hardware has evolved to support a substantially more flexible facility for combining multiple textures. This evolution is reflected in a number of additions to the texture environment functionality. Multitexturing techniques reach their fullest potential when used with this more advanced version of texture environment. It is implemented in OpenGL through the `ARB_texture_env_combine`, `ARB_texture_env_dot3`, and `ARB_texture_env_crossbar` extensions. The first two extensions was added to

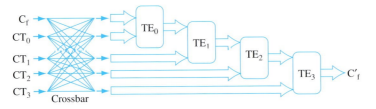

Figure 5.11 Multitexture texture environments. Four texture units are shown; however, the number of units available depends on the implementation. The input fragment color is successively combined with each texture according to the state of the corresponding texture environment, and the resulting fragment color passed as input to the next texture unit in the pipeline.

core OpenGL 1.3, while the last is in OpenGL 1.4. The following section describes this functionality in more detail.

5.10 Texture Environment

The texturing stage that computes the final fragment color value is called the texture environment function (glTexEnv). This stage takes the filtered texel color (the *texture color*) and the untextured color that comes from rasterizing the untextured polygon, called the *fragment color*. In addition to these two input values, the application can also supply an additional color value, called the *environment color*. The application chooses a method to combine these colors to produce a final color. OpenGL provides a fixed set of methods for the application to choose from.

Each of the methods provided by OpenGL produce a particular effect. One of the most commonly used is the GL_MODULATE environment function. The modulate function multiplies or *modulates* the polygon's fragment color with the texel color. Typically, applications generate polygons with per-vertex lighting enabled and then modulate the texture image with the fragment's interpolated lighted color value to produce a lighted, textured surface.

The GL_REPLACE texture environment[10] function is much simpler. It just replaces the fragment color with the texture color. The replace function can be emulated in OpenGL 1.0 by using the modulate environment with a constant white polygon color, though the replace function has a lower computational cost.

The GL_DECAL environment function alpha-blends between the fragment color and an RGBA texture's texture color, using the texture's alpha component to control the interpolation; for RGB textures it simply replaces the fragment color. Decal mode is undefined for other texture formats (luminance, alpha, intensity). The GL_BLEND environment

---

10. Introduced by OpenGL 1.1.

function is a little different. It uses the texture value to control the mixing of the fragment color and the application-supplied texture environment color.

5.10.1 Advanced Texture Environment Functionality

Modern graphics hardware has undergone a substantial increase in power and flexibility, adding multiple texture units and new ways to combine the results of the lookup operations. OpenGL has evolved to better use this functionality by adding multitexturing functionality and by providing more flexible and powerful fixed-function texture environment processing. This evolution has culminated in transition from a fixed-function model to a programmable model, adding an interface for programming texturing hardware directly with a special *shading language*.

As of OpenGL 1.3, three more environment function extensions were added to the core specification. The ARB_texture_env_add extension adds the GL_ADD texture environment function in which the final color is produced by adding the fragment and texture color. This functionality is useful to support additive detail, such as specular highlights, and additive lightmaps.

The ARB_texture_env_combine extension provides a fine-grain orthogonal set of fixed-function texture environment settings. This reorganization of texture environment functionality can take better advantage of programmable texturing hardware. When GL_COMBINE is specified, two different texture environment functions can be specified; one for the RGB components and one for the alpha components of the incoming colors. Each environment function is chosen from a corresponding set of RGB and alpha functions.

Unlike previous texture environment functions, the combine functions are generic; they operate on three arguments, named *Arg0*, *Arg1*, and *Arg2*. These arguments are specified with source and operand enumerants for each argument. Like the environment functions themselves, there are distinct sets of source and operand enumerants for RGB and alpha color components. An argument source can be configured to be the filtered texture color GL_TEXTURE, the application-specified texture environment color GL_CONSTANT, the untextured fragment color from the primitive GL_PRIMARY_COLOR, or the color from the previous texture stage GL_PREVIOUS. The components of the argument's specified color are modified by the operand argument. An operand can choose the RGB or alpha components of the source color, use them unchanged, or invert them (apply a $1 - color$ operation to each component). Figure 5.12 illustrates the relationships between the components that make up the combine function.

Configuring this new functionality may become clearer with an example. It uses the GL_COMBINE functionality to mimic the GL_MODULATE function. The following command sequence will produce the same effect as GL_MODULATE on an RGB texture:

```
glTexEnvi(GL_TEXTURE_ENV, GL_TEXTURE_ENV_MODE, GL_COMBINE);
glTexEnvi(GL_TEXTURE_ENV, GL_COMBINE_RGB, GL_MODULATE);
glTexEnvi(GL_TEXTURE_ENV, GL_SOURCE0_RGB, GL_PRIMARY_COLOR);
```

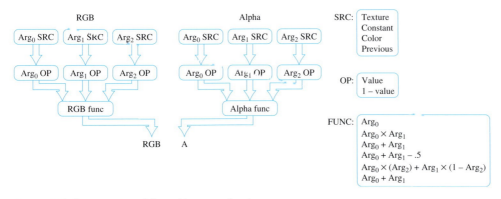

Figure 5.12 The components of the combine texture function.

```
glTexEnvi(GL_TEXTURE_ENV, GL_SOURCE1_RGB, GL_TEXTURE);
glTexEnvi(GL_TEXTURE_ENV, GL_OPERAND0_RGB, GL_SRC_COLOR);
glTexEnvi(GL_TEXTURE_ENV, GL_OPERAND1_RGB, GL_SRC_COLOR);

glTexEnvi(GL_TEXTURE_ENV, GL_COMBINE_ALPHA, GL_REPLACE);
glTexEnvi(GL_TEXTURE_ENV, GL_SOURCE0_ALPHA, GL_PRIMARY_COLOR);
glTexEnvi(GL_TEXTURE_ENV, GL_OPERAND0_ALPHA, GL_SRC_COLOR);
```

The `ARB_texture_env_dot3` extension augments the combine functionality, providing RGB and RGBA dot product RGB functions. Per-pixel dot product functions are useful for a number of techniques, such as implementing a common bump mapping technique.

With OpenGL 1.4 another extension was added to the core; `ARB_texture_env_crossbar`. This extension also augments the *combine* interface. Instead of restricting the source of a previously textured color value to the previous texture unit, the crossbar functionality makes it possible to use the output from any previous active texture unit in the texturing chain. This makes texture environment sequences more flexible; for example, a particular texture unit's output can be used as input by multiple texturing units. This functionality allows the fixed function *combine* interface to more closely approximate a fully programmable one.

5.10.2 Fragment Programs

The evolution of texture environment functionality has progressed to the point where OpenGL can support fully programmable texture (shading) hardware. The `ARB_fragment_program` extension defines a programming language that can be loaded in the pipeline through a set of new commands. Programs can be loaded, made current, and have parameter values assigned.

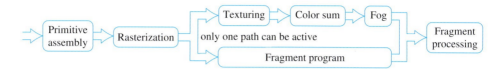

Figure 5.13 Fragment program functionality.

The programming language not only provides a fully programmable replacement for texture environment operations (including support for depth textures), but also supplants the color summation stage (for separate specular color) and fog computations, as shown in Figure 5.13.

Besides a programming language, the fragment program extension provides additional commands for loading, selecting, and modifying fragment programs (which are called *program objects*). The functionality provided is very similar to that used for texture objects. The glProgramStringARB command loads a new fragment program; it can be made current with glBindProgramARB; and deleted with glDeleteProgramsARB. There are also queries and tests that can be used to retrieve a loaded program, or to check for its existence.

Fragment programs can use environment and local variables, called *parameters*. A local parameter can be thought of as a static variable, global to the program. Environment parameters are variable values global to all programs in the implementation. All parameters are an array of four floating-point values (eliminating a multitude of dynamic range and precision problems in the fixed-function pipeline). These values can be changed in a loaded program using various forms of glProgramEnvParameter and glProgramLocalParameter. Since these parameters can be modified in a program even after it is loaded, it makes it possible to use a parameterized program multiple ways, without having to reload it.

Going into the details of the fragment programming language is beyond the scope of this book, but some general comments can give some idea of its capabilities. The currently active fragment program operates on fragments generated during rasterization. Fragment programs appear like assembly language, having simple instructions and operands. The instructions have a digital signal processor (DSP) flavor, supporting trigonometric operations such as sine and cosine, dot and cross products, exponentiation, and multiply-add. Special instructions provide texture lookup capability. Instructions operate on vector and scalar floating-point values, they can come from attributes of the rasterized fragment, temporary variables in the program, or parameters that can be modified by the application. There is built-in support for *swizzling* vector arguments as well as negation.

As mentioned previously, the base extension provides no flow control or looping constructs, but there are conditional set instructions, and instructions that can be used to "kill" (discard) individual fragments. These instructions, in concert with local and environment parameters that can be changed after a program is loaded, make it possible to control (i.e., parameterize) the behavior of a fragment program. The final result of the program execution is a color and depth value that is passed down to the remainder of the fragment pipeline (scissor test, alpha test, etc.).

When available, this extension can replace a significant number of multipass operations with programmable micropass ones. See Section 9.5 for details on the difference between multipass and micropass approaches to complex rendering.

Fragment program functionality is still evolving. There are extensions to this functionality, such as providing conditionals and looping constructs in the language, as well as a set of higher level languages that are "compiled" into fragment programs, such as Cg (NVIDIA, 2004) and GLSL (Kessenich, 2003). Other possible extensions might increase fragment program scope to control more of the fragment processing pipeline, for example, manipulating stencil values. At this time neither fragment or vertex program functionality is part of core OpenGL, but both are expected to be part of OpenGL 2.0. For this reason, and because there are other texts covering fragment and vertex programming, we limit our discussion of them in this book. For detailed information on this extension, look at the documentation on the `ARB_fragment_program` extension and the OpenGL Shading Language at the opengl.org website.

5.11 Summary

Texture mapping is arguably the most important functionality in OpenGL, and is still undergoing significant evolution. Texture mapping functionality, while complex, is well worth the time to study thoroughly. This chapter describes the basic texture mapping machinery, Chapter 14 describes several "building block" techniques, and many of the other chapters make extensive use of texture mapping algorithms as key parts of the overall technique.

Rasterization and Fragment Processing

OpenGL specifies a precise sequence of steps for converting primitives into patterns of pixel values in the framebuffer. An in-depth understanding of this sequence is very useful; proper manipulation of this part of the pipeline is essential to many of the techniques described in this book. This chapter reviews the rasterization and fragment processing parts of the OpenGL pipeline, emphasizing details and potential problems that affect multipass rendering techniques.

OpenGL's rasterization phase is divided into several stages, as shown in Figure 6.1. This part of the pipeline can be broken into two major groups; rasterization and fragment processing. Rasterization comes first: a primitive, described as a set of vertex coordinates, associated colors and texture coordinates, is converted into a series of fragments. Here the pixel locations covered by the primitive are determined, and the associated color and depth values at these locations are computed. The current texturing and fog state are used by the rasterizer to modify the fragments appropriately.

The result of the rasterization step is a set of fragments. A fragment is the part of a primitive contained in (i.e. overlapping) a particular pixel; it includes color, window coordinates, and depth information. After rasterization, the fragments undergo a series of processing steps, called *fragment operations*. These steps include scissoring, alpha test, depth, and stencil test and blending. At the end of fragment operations, the primitive's fragments have been used to update the framebuffer. If multisample antialiasing is enabled, more complex fragments containing multiple color, texture coordinate, depth, and stencil values are generated and processed for each pixel location the primitive covers.

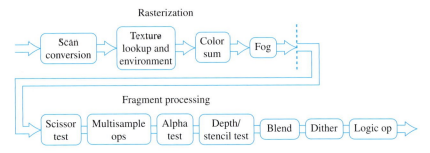

Figure 6.1 Rasterization pipeline.

6.1 Rasterization

OpenGL specifies a specific set of rules to determine which pixels a given primitive covers. Conceptually, the primitive is overlaid on the window space pixel grid. The pixel coverage rules are detailed and vary per primitive, but all pixel coverage is determined by comparing the primitive's extent against one or more *sample points* in each pixel. This *point sampling* method does not compute a primitive's coverage area; it only computes whether the primitive does or doesn't cover each of the pixel's sample points. This means that a primitive can cover a significant portion of a pixel, yet still not affect its color, if none of the pixel's sample points are covered.

If multisampling is not being used, there is one sample point for each pixel, it is located at the pixel center; in window coordinates this means a pixel at framebuffer location (m, n) is sampled at $(m + \frac{1}{2}, n + \frac{1}{2})$. When multisampling is enabled, the number and location of sample points in each pixel is implementation-dependent. In addition to some number of samples per-pixel, there is a single per-pixel coverage value with as many bits as there are pixel samples. The specification allows the color and texture values to be the same for all samples within a pixel; only the depth and stencil information must represent the values at the sample point. When rasterizing, all sample information for a pixel is bundled together into a single fragment. There is always exactly one fragment per-pixel. When multisampling is disabled, two adjacent primitives sharing a common edge also generate one fragment per-pixel. With multisampling enabled, two fragments (one from each primitive) may be generated at pixels along the shared edge, since each primitive may cover a subset of the sample locations within a pixel.

Irrespective of the multisample state, each sample holds color, depth, stencil, and texture coordinate information from the primitive at the sample location. If multitexturing is supported, the sample contains texture coordinates for each texture unit supported by the implementation.

Often implementations will use the same color and texture coordinate values for each sample position within a fragment. This provides a significant performance advantage since it reduces the number of distinct sample values that need to be computed and transmitted through the remainder of the fragment processing path. This form of multisample antialiasing is often referred to as *edge antialiasing*, since the edges of geometric primitives are effectively supersampled but interior colors and texture coordinates are not. When fragments are evaluated at a single sample position, care must be taken in choosing it. In non-multisampled rasterization, the color and texture coordinate values are computed at the pixel center. In the case of multisampling, the color value must be computed at a sample location that is *within the primitive* or the computed color value may be out of range. However, texture coordinate values are sampled at the pixel center since the wrapping behavior defined for texture coordinates will ensure that an in-range value is computed. Two reasonable choices an implementation may use for the color sample location are the sample nearest the center of the pixel or the sample location closest to the *centroid* of the sample locations (the average) within the primitive.

6.1.1 Rasterization Consistency

The OpenGL specification does not dictate a specific algorithm for rasterizing a geometric primitive. This lack of precision is deliberate; it allows implementors freedom to choose the best algorithm for their graphics hardware and software. While good for the implementor, this lack of precision imposes restrictions on the design of OpenGL applications. The application cannot make assumptions about exactly how a primitive is rasterized. One practical implication: an application shouldn't be designed to assume that a primitive whose vertex coordinates don't exactly match another primitive's will still have the same depth or color values. This can be restrictive on algorithms that require coplanar polygons.

This lack of consistency also affects primitives that have matching vertices, but are rendered with different rasterization modes. The same triangle drawn with GL_FILL and GL_LINE rendering modes may not generate matching depth or color values, or even cover the same pixels along its outer boundary.

OpenGL consistency guidelines do require that certain changes, such as changes in vertex color, texture coordinate position, current texture, and a host of other state changes, will not affect the depth or pixel coverage of a polygon. If these consistency rules were not required, it would be very difficult or impossible to perform many of the techniques described in this book. This is because many of the book's techniques draw an object multiple times, each time with different parameter settings. These *multipass* algorithms combine the results of rendering objects multiple times in order to create a desired effect (Figure 6.2).

6.1.2 Z-Fighting

One consequence of inconsistent rendering is depth artifacts. If the depth information of multiple objects (or the same object rendered multiple times) does not match fragment for fragment, the results of depth testing can create artifacts in the color buffer. This problem, commonly known as *z-fighting*, creates unwanted artifacts that have a "stitched"

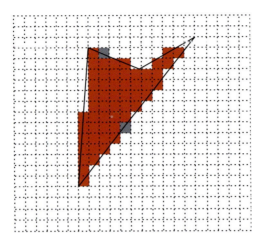

Polygon rasterized with different modes in red
and blue: blue version rasterizes extra pixels.

Figure 6.2 Rasterization consistency.

Blue pixels from bottom triangle
bleed through coplanar red triangle.

Figure 6.3 Coplanar z-fighting.

appearance. They appear where two objects are rasterized into fragments with depth values that differ a very small amount, and were rendered using different algorithms.

Z-fighting can happen when attempting to position and draw two different objects in the same plane. Because of differences in rasterization, the two coplanar objects may not rasterize to the same depth values at all fragments. Figure 6.3 shows two triangles drawn in the same plane. Some of the fragments from the *farther* triangle have replaced fragments from the *closer* triangle. At these fragment locations, rasterization of the farther triangle has generated a depth value that is smaller than the one generated by the closer one. The depth test discards the fragments from the closer triangle, since it is configured to keep fragments with smaller depth values. The problem is exacerbated when the scene is animated, since different pixels may bleed through as the primitives change orientation. These problems result from numerical rounding errors; they become significant because the depth values for the fragments are so close together numerically.

There are a number of ways to avoid z-fighting. If two coplanar polygons are required, the application can take care to use the same vertices for both of them, and set their states to ensure that the same rasterization method is used on both of them. If this isn't possible, the application can choose to disable depth testing altogether, and use the stencil buffer for any masking that is required (Section 16.8). Another approach is to displace one of the two polygons toward the viewer, so the polygons are separated enough in depth that rasterization differences won't cause one polygon to "bleed through" another. Care should be taken with this last approach, since the choice of polygon that should be displaced toward the viewer may be orientation-dependent. This is particularly true if back-facing polygons are used by the application.

OpenGL does provide a mechanism to make the displacement method more convenient, called *polygon offset*. Using the `glPolygonOffset` command allows the programmer to set a displacement for polygons based on their slope and a bias value. The current polygon offset can be enabled separately for points, lines and polygons, and the bias and slope values are signed, so that a primitive can be biased toward or away from the viewer. This relieves the application from the burden of having to apply the appropriate offset to primitive vertices in object space, or adjusting the modelview matrix. Some techniques using polygon offset are described in Section 16.7.2.

6.1.3 Bitmaps and Pixel Rectangles

Points, lines, and polygons are not the only primitives that are rasterized by OpenGL. Bitmaps and pixel rectangles are also available. Since rasterized fragments require window coordinates and texture coordinates as well as color values, OpenGL must generate the x, y, and z values, as well as a set of texture coordinates for each pixel and bitmap fragment. OpenGL uses the notion of a *raster position* to augment the pixel rectangles and bitmaps with additional position information. A raster position corresponds to the lower left corner of the rectangular pixel object. The `glRasterPos` command provides the position of the lower left corner of the pixel rectangle; it is similar to the `glVertex` call in that there are 2-, 3-, and 4-component versions, and because it binds the current texture coordinate set and color to the pixel primitive.

The coordinates of a raster position can be transformed like any vertex, but only the raster position itself is transformed; the pixel rectangle is always perpendicular to the viewer. Its lower left corner is attached to the raster position, and all of its depth values match the raster position's z coordinate. Similarly, the set texture coordinates and color associated with the raster position are used as the texture coordinates for all the fragments in the pixel primitive.

6.1.4 Texture, Color, and Depth Interpolation

Although it doesn't define a specific algorithm, the OpenGL specification provides specific guidelines on how texture coordinates, color values, and depth values are calculated for each fragment of a primitive during rasterization. For example, rasterization of a polygon involves choosing a set of fragments corresponding to pixels "owned" by the polygon, interpolating the polygon's vertex parameters to find their values at each fragment, then sending these fragments down the rest of the pipeline. OpenGL requires that the algorithm used to interpolate the vertex values must behave as if the parameters are calculated using barycentric coordinates. It also stipulates that the x and y values used for the interpolation of each fragment must be computed at the pixel center for that fragment.

Primitive interpolation generates a color, texture coordinates, and a depth value for each fragment as a function of the x and y window coordinates for the fragment (multiple depth values per-pixel may be generated if multisampling is active and multiple texture coordinates may be compared when multitexture is in use). Conceptually, this interpolation is applied to primitives after they have been transformed into window coordinates. This is done so pixel positions can be interpolated relative to the primitive's vertices. While a simple linear interpolation from vertices to pixel locations produces correct depth values for each pixel, applying the same interpolation method to color values is problematic, and texture coordinates interpolated in this manner can cause visual artifacts. A texture coordinate interpolated in window space may simply not produce the same result as would interpolating to the equivalent location on the primitive in clip space.

These problems occur if the transformation applied to the primitive to go from clip space into window space contains a perspective projection. This is a non-linear transform, so a linear interpolation in one space won't produce the same results in the other. To get the same results in both spaces, even if a perspective transform separates them, requires using an interpolation method that is perspective invariant.

A perspective-correct method interpolates the ratio of the interpolants and a w term to each pixel location, then divides out the w term to get the interpolated value. Values at each vertex are transformed by dividing them by the w value at the vertex. Assume a clip-space vertex a with associated texture coordinates s_a and t_a, and a w value of w_a. In order to interpolate these values, create new values at the vertex, $\frac{s_a}{w_a}$, $\frac{t_a}{w_a}$, and $\frac{1}{w_a}$. Do this for the values at each vertex in the primitive, then interpolate all the terms (including the $\frac{1}{w}$ values) to the desired pixel location. The interpolated texture coordinates ratios are obtained by dividing the interpolated $\frac{s}{w}$ and $\frac{t}{w}$ values by the interpolated $\frac{1}{w}$: $\frac{\frac{s}{w}}{\frac{1}{w}}$ and $\frac{\frac{t}{w}}{\frac{1}{w}}$, which results in a perspective-correct s and t.

Here is another example, which shows a simple interpolation using this method in greater detail. A simple linear interpolation of a parameter f, between points a and b uses the standard linear interpolation formula:

$$f = (1 - \alpha)f_a + \alpha f_b.$$

Interpolating in a perspective-correct manner changes the formula to :

$$f = \frac{(1-\alpha)\frac{f_a}{w_a} + \alpha\frac{f_b}{w_b}}{(1-\alpha)\frac{1}{w_a} + \alpha\frac{1}{w_b}} \tag{6.1}$$

The OpenGL specification strongly recommends that texture coordinates be calculated in a "perspective correct" fashion, while depth values should not be (depth values will maintain their correct depth ordering even across a perspective transform). Whether to use a perspective correct interpolation of per-fragment color values is left up to the implementation. Recent improvements in graphics hardware make it possible for some OpenGL implementations to efficiently perform the interpolation operations in clip space rather than window space.

Finally, note that the texture coordinates are subjected to their own perspective division by q. This is included, as part of the texture coordinate interpolation, changing Equation 6.1 to:

$$f = \frac{(1-\alpha)\frac{f_a}{w_a} + \alpha\frac{f_b}{w_b}}{(1-\alpha)\frac{q_a}{w_a} + \alpha\frac{q_b}{w_b}}$$

6.1.5 *w* Buffering

Although the OpenGL specification specifies the use of the z_w fragment component for depth testing, some implementations use a per-fragment w component instead. This may be done to eliminate the overhead of interpolating a depth value; a per-pixel $\frac{1}{w}$ value must be computed for perspective correct texturing, so per-pixel computation and bandwidth can be reduced by eliminating z and using w instead. The w component also has some advantages when used for depth testing. For a typical perspective transform (such as the one generated by using glFrustum), the transformed w component is linearly related to the pre-transformed z component. On the other hand, the post-transformed z is related to the pre-transformed $\frac{1}{z}$ (see Section 2.8 for more details on how z coordinates are modified by a perspective projection).

Using w instead of z results in a depth buffer with a linear range. This has the advantage that precision is distributed evenly across the range of depth values. However, this isn't always an advantage since some applications exploit the improved effective resolution present in the near range of traditional depth buffering in w Pleasure, w Fun (1998), Jim Blinn analyzes the characteristics in detail). Furthermore, depth buffer reads on an implementation using w buffering produces very implementation-specific values, returning w values or possibly $\frac{1}{w}$ values (which are more "z-like"). Care should be taken using an algorithm that depends on retrieving z values when the implementation uses w buffering.

6.2 Fragment Operations

A number of fragment operations are applied to rasterization fragments before they are allowed to update pixels in the framebuffer. Fragment operations can be separated into two categories, operations that test fragments, and operations that modify them. To maximize efficiency, the fragment operations are ordered so that the fragment tests are applied first. The most interesting tests for advanced rendering are: alpha test, stencil test, and depth buffer test. These tests can either pass, allowing the fragment to continue, or fail, discarding the fragment so it can't pass on to later fragment operations or update the framebuffer. The stencil test is a special case, since it can produce useful side effects even when fragments fail the comparison.

All of the fragment tests use the same set of comparison operators: Never, Always, Less, Less than or Equal, Equal, Greater than or Equal, Greater, and Not Equal. In each test, a fragment value is compared against a reference value saved in the current OpenGL state (including the depth and stencil buffers), and if the comparison succeeds, the test passes. The details of the fragment tests are listed in Table 6.1.

The list of comparison operators is very complete. In fact, it may seem that some of the comparison operations, such as GL_NEVER and GL_ALWAYS are redundant, since their functionality can be duplicated by enabling or disabling a given fragment test. There is a use for them, however. The OpenGL invariance rules require that invariance is maintained if a comparison is changed, but not if a test is enabled or disabled. So if invariance must be maintained (because the test is used in a multipass algorithm, for example), the application should enable and disable tests using the comparison operators, rather than enabling or disabling the tests themselves.

Table 6.1 Fragment Test

Constant	Comparison
GL_ALWAYS	always pass
GL_NEVER	never pass
GL_LESS	pass if *incoming* $<$ *ref*
GL_LEQUAL	pass if *incoming* $\leq$ *ref*
GL_GEQUAL	pass if *incoming* $\geq$ *ref*
GL_GREATER	pass if *incoming* $>$ *ref*
GL_EQUAL	pass if *incoming* $=$ *ref*
GL_NOTEQUAL	pass if *incoming* $\neq$ *ref*

6.2.1 Multisample Operations

Multisample operations provide limited ways to affect the fragment coverage and alpha values. In particular, an application can reduce the coverage of a fragment, or convert the fragment's alpha value to another coverage value that is combined with the fragment's value to further reduce it. These operations are sometimes useful as an alternative to alpha blending, since they can be more efficient.

6.2.2 Alpha Test

The alpha test reads the alpha component value of each fragment's color, and compares it against the current alpha test value. The test value is set by the application, and can range from zero to one. The comparison operators are the standard set listed in Table 6.1. The alpha test can be used to remove parts of a primitive on a pixel by pixel basis. A common technique is to apply a texture containing alpha values to a polygon. The alpha test is used to trim a simple polygon to a complex outline stored in the alpha values of the surface texture. A detailed description of this technique is available in Section 14.5.

6.2.3 Stencil Test

The stencil test performs two tasks. The first task is to conditionally eliminate incoming fragments based on a comparison between a reference value and stencil value from the stencil buffer at the fragment's destination. The second purpose of the stencil test is to update the stencil values in the framebuffer. How the stencil buffer is modified depends on the outcome of the stencil and depth buffer tests. There are three possible outcomes of the two tests: the stencil buffer test fails, the stencil buffer test passes but the depth buffer fails, or both tests fail. OpenGL makes it possible to specify how the stencil buffer is updated for each of these possible outcomes.

The conditional elimination task is controlled with `glStencilFunc`. It sets the stencil test comparison operator. The comparison operator can be selected from the list of operators in Table 6.1.

Setting the stencil update requires setting three parameters, each one corresponding to one of the stencil/depth buffer test outcomes. The `glStencilOp` command takes three operands, one for each of the comparison outcomes (see Figure 6.4). Each operand value specifies how the stencil pixel corresponding to the fragment being tested should be modified. Table 6.2 shows the possible values and how they change the stencil pixels.

The stencil buffer is often used to create and use per-pixel masks. The desired stencil mask is created by drawing geometry (often textured with an alpha pattern to produce a complex shape). Before rendering this template geometry, the stencil test is configured to update the stencil buffer as the mask is rendered. Often the pipeline is configured so that the color and depth buffers are not actually updated when this geometry is rendered; this can be done with the `glColorMask` and `glDepthMask` commands, or by setting the depth test to always fail.

Table 6.2 Stencil Update Values

Constant	Description
GL_KEEP	*stencil pixel* ← *old value*
GL_ZERO	*stencil pixel* ← 0
GL_REPLACE	*stencil pixel* ← *reference value*
GL_INCR	*stencil pixel* ← *old value* + 1
GL_DECR	*stencil pixel* ← *old value* − 1
GL_INVERT	*stencil pixel* ← *old value*

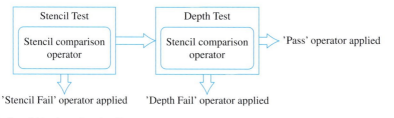

Figure 6.4 Stencil/depth test functionality.

Once the stencil mask is in place, the geometry to be masked is rendered. This time, the stencil test is pre-configured to draw or discard fragments based on the current value of the stencil mask. More elaborate techniques may create the mask using a combination of template geometry and carefully chosen depth and stencil comparisons to create a mask whose shape is influenced by the geometry that was previously rendered. There are are also some extensions for enhancing stencil functionality. One allows separate stencil operations, reference value, compare mask, and write mask to be selected depending on whether the polygon is front- or back-facing.[1] A second allows the stencil arithmetic operations to wrap rather than clamp, allowing a stencil value to temporarily go out of range, while still producing the correct answer if the final answer lies within the representable range.[2]

6.2.4 Blending

One of the most useful fragment modifier operations supported by OpenGL is blending, also called *alpha blending*. Without blending, a fragment that passes all the filtering

---

1. EXT_stencil_two_side
2. EXT_stencil_wrap

Table 6.3 Blend Factors

Constant	Used In	Action
GL_ZERO	src, dst	scale each color element by zero
GL_ONE	src, dst	scale each element by one
GL_SRC_COLOR	dst	scale color with source color
GL_DST_COLOR	src	scale color with destination color
GL_ONE_MINUS_SRC_COLOR	dst	scale color with one minus source color
GL_ONE_MINUS_DST_COLOR	dst	scale color with one minus destination color
GL_SRC_ALPHA	src, dst	scale color with source alpha
GL_ONE_MINUS_SRC_ALPHA	src, dst	scale color with source alpha
GL_DST_ALPHA	src, dst	scale color with destination alpha
GL_ONE_MINUS_DST_ALPHA	src, dst	scale color with one minus destination alpha
GL_SRC_ALPHA_SATURATE	src	scale color by minimum of source alpha and destination alpha
GL_CONSTANT_COLOR	src, dst	scale color with application-specified color
GL_ONE_MINUS_CONSTANT_COLOR	src, dst	scale color with one minus application-specified color
GL_CONSTANT_ALPHA	src, dst	scale color with alpha of application-specified color
GL_ONE_MINUS_CONSTANT_ALPHA	src, dst	scale color with one minus alpha of application-specified color

and modification steps simply replaces the appropriate color pixel in the framebuffer. If blending is enabled, the incoming fragment, the corresponding target pixel, or an application-defined constant color[3] are combined using a linear equation instead. The color components (including alpha) of both the fragment and the pixel are first scaled by a specified *blend factor*, then either added or subtracted.[4] The resulting value is used to update the framebuffer.

There are two fixed sets of blend factors (also called *weighting factors*) for the blend operation; one set is for the source argument, one for the destination. The entire set is listed in Table 6.3; the second column indicates whether the factor can be used

---

3. In implementations supporting OpenGL 1.2 or newer.

4. In OpenGL 1.4 subtraction and min and max blend equations were moved from the ARB_imaging extension to the core.

Table 6.4 Blend Equations

Operand	Result
GL_ADD	soruce + destination
GL_SUBTRACT	source − destination
GL_REVERSE_SUBTRACT	destination − source
GL_MIN	min(source, dest)
GL_MAX	max(source, dest)

with a source, a destination, or both. These factors take a color from one of the three inputs, the incoming fragment, the framebuffer pixel, or the application-specified color, modify it, and insert it into the blending equation. The source and destination arguments are used by the blend equation, one of GL_FUNC_ADD, GL_FUNC_SUBTRACT, GL_FUNC_REVERSE_SUBTRACT, GL_MIN, or GL_MAX. Table 6.4 lists the operations. Note that the result of the subtract equation depends on the order of the arguments, so both subtract and reverse subtract are provided. In either case, negative results are clamped to zero.

Some blend factors are used more frequently than others: GL_ONE is commonly used when an unmodified source or destination color is needed in the equation. Using GL_ONE for both factors, for example, simply adds (or subtracts) the source pixel and destination pixel value. The GL_ZERO factor is used to eliminate one of the two colors. The GL_SRC_ALPHA/GL_ONE_MINUS_ALPHA combination is used for a common transparency technique, where the alpha value of the fragment determines the opacity of the fragment. Another transparency technique uses GL_SRC_ALPHA_SATURATE instead; it is particularly useful for wireframe line drawings, since it minimizes line brightening where multiple transparent lines overlap.

6.2.5 Logic Op

As of OpenGL 1.1, a new fragment processing stage, *logical operation,*[5] can be used instead of blending (if both stages are enabled by the application, logic op takes precedence, and blending is implicitly disabled). Logical operations are defined for both index and RGBA colors; only the latter is discussed here. As with blending, logic op takes the incoming fragment and corresponding pixel color, and performs an operation on it. This *bitwise* operation is chosen from a fixed set by the application using the glLogicOp command. The possible logic operations are shown in Table 6.5 (C-style logical operands are used for clarity).

---

5. In OpenGL 1.0, the logic op stage operated in color index mode only.

Table 6.5 Logic Op Operations

Operand	Result
GL_CLEAR	0
GL_AND	source & destination
GL_AND_REVERSE	source & ~destination
GL_COPY	source
GL_AND_INVERTED	~(source & destination)
GL_NOOP	destination
GL_XOR	source ^ destination
GL_OR	source | destination
GL_NOR	~(source | destination)
GL_EQUIV	~(source ^ destination)
GL_INVERT	~destination
GL_OR_REVERSE	source | ~destination
GL_COPY_INVERTED	~source
GL_OR_INVERTED	~source | destination
GL_NAND	~(source & destination)
GL_SET	1 (all bits)

Logic ops are applied separately for each color component. Color component updates can be controlled per channel by using the glColorMask command. The default command is GL_COPY, which is equivalent to disabling logic op. Most commands are self-explanatory, although the GL_EQUIV operation may lead to confusion. It can be thought of as an equivalency test; a bit is set where the source and destination bits match.

6.3 Framebuffer Operations

There are a set of OpenGL operations that are applied to the entire framebuffer at once. The accumulation buffer is used in many OpenGL techniques and is described below.

6.3.1 Accumulation Buffer

The accumulation buffer provides accelerated support for combining multiple rendered images together. It is an off-screen framebuffer whose pixels have very high color resolution. The rendered frame and the accumulation buffer are combined by adding the pixel values together, and updating the accumulation buffer with the results. The accumulation buffer has a scale value that can be used to scale the pixels in the rendered frame before its contents are merged with the contents of the accumulation buffer.

Accumulation operations allow the application to combine frames to generate high-quality images or produce special effects. For example, rendering and combining multiple images modified with a subpixel jitter can be used to generate antialiased images.

It's important to understand that the accumulation buffer operations only take input from the color buffer; the OpenGL specification provides no way to render directly to the accumulation buffer. There are a number of consequences to this limitation; it is impossible, for example, to replace part of the image, since there is no depth or stencil buffer available to mask part of the image. The accumulation buffer is best thought of as a place to do high-precision scaling, blending, and clamping of color images. Figure 6.5 shows how multiple images rendered to the color buffer are transferred to the accumulation buffer to be combined together.

Besides having limited access from the rendering pipeline, the accumulation buffer differs from a generic off-screen framebuffer in a number of ways. First, the color representation is different. The accumulation buffer represents color values with component ranges from $[-1, 1]$, not just $[0, 1]$ as in a normal OpenGL framebuffer. As mentioned

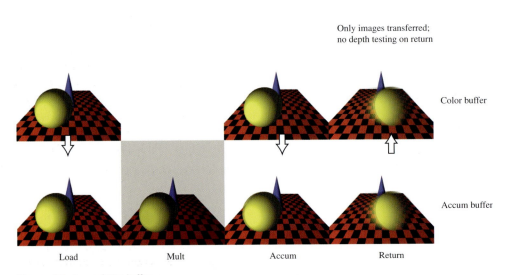

Figure 6.5 Accumulation buffer.

Table 6.6 Accumulation Buffer Operations

Constant	Description
GL_ACCUM	scale the incoming image, add it to the accumulation buffer
GL_LOAD	replace the accumulation buffer with the incoming scaled image
GL_ADD	bias the accumulation buffer image
GL_MULT	scale the accumulation buffer image
GL_RETURN	copy the scaled and clamped accumulation buffer into the color buffer

previously, the color precision of the accumulation buffer is higher than a normal color buffer, often increasing the number of bits representing each color component by a factor of two or more (depending on the implementation). This enhanced resolution increases the number of ways the images can be combined and the number of accumulations that can be performed without degrading image quality.

The accumulation buffer also provides additional ways to combine and modify images. Incoming and accumulation buffer images can be added together, and the accumulation buffer image can be scaled and biased. The return operation, which copies the accumulation buffer back into the framebuffer, also provides implicit image processing functionality: the returned image can be scaled into a range containing negative values, which will be clamped back to the [0, 1] range as it's returned. Images that are loaded or accumulated into the accumulation buffer can also be scaled as they are copied in. The operations are summarized in Table 6.6.

Note that the accumulation buffer is often not well accelerated on commodity graphics hardware, so care must be taken when using it in a performance-critical application. There are techniques mentioned later in the book that maximize accumulation buffer performance, and even a slow accumulation buffer implementation can be useful for generating images "off line". For example, the accumulation buffer can be used to generate high-quality textures and bitmaps to be stored as part of the application, and thus used with no performance penalty.

6.4 Summary

The details of this section of the OpenGL pipeline have a large influence on the design of a multipass algorithm. The rasterization and fragment processing operations provide many mechanisms for modifying a fragment value or discarding it outright.

Over the last several chapters we have covered the rendering pipeline from front to back. In the remainder of this part of the book we will round out our understanding of the pipeline by describing how the rendering pipeline is integrated into the native platform window system, examining some of the evolution of the OpenGL pipeline, and exploring some of the techniques used in implementing hardware and software versions of the pipeline.

Window System and Platform Integration

The OpenGL API is primarily concerned with accepting procedural scene descriptions and generating pixels corresponding to those descriptions. The OpenGL specification *per se* doesn't say where the generated pixels will end up. The final step of sending pixels to their target, such as a window on the screen, is left up to the *embedding* or *platform layer*. This layer defines how the OpenGL renderer attaches or *binds* onto the output device or devices. There can be many possible window system targets; defining this interface is the task of the window system, not the OpenGL rendering pipeline. Most window systems have a specification that defines the OpenGL interaction. Some of these specifications, like the OpenGL specification itself, include an extension mechanism; the specification can evolve over time to reflect the evolution of the underlying window system. Here are embeddings of three of the most popular windows systems: the X Window System embedding (Scheifler and Gettys, 1986), called GLX (Womaeck and Leech, 1998); the embedding into the Win32 API (Microsoft, Inc., 2001b) used by Microsoft's Windows family of operating systems, called WGL (Microsoft, Inc., 2001a) (pronounced wiggle); and the embedding connecting Apple's Macintosh operating system (MacOS) called AGL (Apple Computer, Inc., 2001). The OpenGL ES project (see Section 8.3) also includes a more portable window system embedding layer called EGL (Leech, 2003).

Of course, OpenGL isn't limited to, or required to work with a window system. It can just as readily render to a printer, a full screen video game console, or a linear array of memory in an application's address space. Despite this flexibility, most of our discussions will assume the presence of the most common target, a window system. In particular, terms such as *window space* (described in Section 2.2.5), imply a window system environment.

This chapter limits itself to describing aspects of window system embedding as useful background for later chapters of the book. For more detailed information regarding using GLX on UNIX systems and WGL on Windows systems, see the texts by Kilgard (1996) and Fosner (1996).

7.1 Renderer and Window State

Since OpenGL is concerned with rendering and not display, we should clarify the roles of the renderer and the window system. An application using OpenGL needs to maintain a bundle of OpenGL state, including the current color, normal, texture coordinate, modelview matrix stack, projection matrix stack, and so forth. This collection of state describes everything needed by an OpenGL renderer to convert a set of input primitives into a set of output pixels. This collection of state is termed *renderer state*. The precise definition and scope of OpenGL renderer state is described in the OpenGL specification. The contents of the framebuffer (color, depth, stencil, and accumulation buffers), however, are not part of the renderer state. They are part of the *window state*. While renderer state is governed by the OpenGL renderer, window state is controlled by the window system. Ultimately, window state includes the position and size of the buffers on the display, mapping which bits correspond to the OpenGL front and back buffer, color maps for pseudo-color (color index) windows, gamma lookup tables that correct intensity levels driving output displays, and so on.

The OpenGL renderer state is encapsulated by a *context*. The data types and methods for creating a context are specific to a particular window system embedding, for example, `glxCreateContext` for GLX or `wglCreateContext` for WGL. To render to a window, the context must be bound to that window using a method specific to the window system binding API. This binding notion is not limited to attaching the OpenGL context to a window; it also attaches the context to an application process or thread (Figure 7.1). The exact details of a process or thread are specific to the platform (for example, Windows or Unix). Application calls to OpenGL API methods modify the contents of the current bound context and ultimately the current bound window.

This notion of binding a context to a thread is arguably a little unusual from an API standpoint. One alternative is to pass a *handle* to the context to be updated as a parameter to the API method. A C++ or Java API might define OpenGL operations as methods of an OpenGL context object, making the context parameter implicit. The downside of this approach is the extra overhead needed to call indirectly through a handle to update the specified context. In the more stateful binding model, resolving information about the target context is done once when the context is bound. There is less overhead

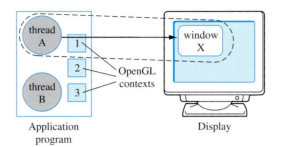

Figure 7.1 Thread A drawing through context 1 to window X.

involved at the cost of some additional complexity. The OpenGL designers considered the performance savings to be worth the complexity trade-off.

Most applications need only a single OpenGL context to do all of their rendering. The requirements for multiple contexts depend on the window system embedding. As a general rule, a window needs a separate context if it is in a different stacking layer or using a pixel format sufficiently different from the other OpenGL windows. This requirement reduces the complexity of an OpenGL implementation and ensures sensible behavior for the renderer state when it is moved from one window to another. Allowing a context to be moved from an RGB window to a color index window presents numerous problems, since the state representations for each of the context types is quite different. It makes more sense to require each window to have a separate context.

7.2 Address Space and Threads

The embedding layer is platform-specific beyond the details of the window system. Data transfers to and from the OpenGL pipeline rely on the (conventional) notion of a process and an address space. When memory addresses are used in OpenGL commands they refer to the address space of the application process. Most OpenGL platform embeddings also support the concept of a thread. A thread is an execution context (a thread of execution) and a process may have multiple threads executing within it. The threads share the process's address space. The OpenGL embedding layer supports the notion of multiple thread-context-window triplets being current (active) simultaneously. However, a context cannot be used with (current to) multiple threads concurrently. Conversely in the GLX embedding, a window can be current to multiple thread-context pairs concurrently, though this seldom provides real utility unless there are multiple accelerators present in the system. In practice, the most useful multi-thread and multi-context scenarios involve using a single thread for rendering and other threads for non-rendering tasks. Usually, it only makes sense to use multiple rendering threads to render to *different* accelerators in parallel.

7.3 Anatomy of a Window

In its simplest form a window is a rectangular region on a display,[1] described by an origin and a size. From the rendering perspective, the window has additional attributes that describe its framebuffer, color index vs. RGB, number of bits per-pixel, depth buffer size, accumulation buffer size, number of color buffers (single buffered or double buffered), and so forth. When the OpenGL context is bound to the window, these attributes are used by the OpenGL renderer to determine how to render to it correctly.

7.3.1 Overlay and Underlay Windows

Some window systems include the concept of an *overlay window*. An overlay window always lies on top of non-overlay windows, giving the contents of the overlay window visual priority over the others. In some window systems, notably the X Window System, the overlay window may be opaque or transparent. If the overlay window is opaque, then all pixels in the overlay window have priority over pixels in windows logically underneath the overlay window (below it in the *window stacking order*). Transparent overlay windows have the property of controlling the visual priority of a pixel using the overlay pixel's color value. Therefore, pixels assigned a special transparent color have lower priority, so the pixel of the window logically underneath this window can be visible.

Overlay windows are useful for implementing popup menus and other graphical user interface components. They can also be useful for overlaying other types of annotations onto a rendered scene. The principal advantage of using an overlay window rather than drawing directly into the main window is that the two windows can be updated independently — to change window annotations requires redrawing only the overlay window. This assumes that overlay window independence is really implemented by the window system and display hardware, and not simulated.[2] Overlays become particularly useful if the contents of the main window are expensive to regenerate. Overlay windows are often used to display data decoded from a multimedia video source on top of other windows with the hardware accelerator decoding the stream directly to a separate overlay framebuffer.

Similar to the concept of overlays, there is the analogous concept of an underlay window with the lowest visual priority. Such a window is only useful when the windows logically above it contain transparent pixels. In general, the need for underlay windows has been minimal; there are few OpenGL implementations that support them.

---

1. Some window systems support non-rectangular windows as well, but for our purposes we can use the bounding rectangle.

2. Sometimes to indicate more clearly that this independence is reflected in the hardware implementation, this support is referred to as *hardware overlays*.

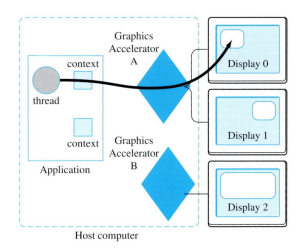

Figure 7.2 Three-display system using two accelerators.

7.3.2 Multiple Displays

Some operating system/window system combinations can support multiple displays. Some configure multiple displays to share the same accelerator or, in the more general case, multiple accelerators each drive multiple displays. In both cases the details of attaching and using a context with windows on different displays becomes more complicated, and depends on window system embedding details.

Figure 7.2 shows an example of a three-display system in which two of the displays are driven from one graphics accelerator, while a third display is driven from a second accelerator. To use all of the available displays typically involves the use of multiple OpenGL contexts. Since an OpenGL context encapsulates the renderer state, and this state may be contained inside hardware, it follows that each hardware accelerator needs an independent context. If the two accelerators were built by different vendors, they would likely use two different OpenGL implementations. A well-designed operating system/window system embedding layer can allow both accelerators to be used from a single application by creating a context corresponding to each accelerator/display combination. For example, in a GLX-based system, the accelerator is identified by its `DISPLAY` name; an application can create GLX contexts corresponding to the individual `DISPLAY` names.

Multiple display systems go by many different names (multimon, dual-head, Twin-View are examples) but all are trying to achieve the same end. They all drive multiple displays, monitors, or video channels from the same accelerator card. The simplest configuration provides a large logical framebuffer from which individual rectangular video or display channels are carved out (as shown in Figure 7.3). This is similar to the way windows are allocated from a framebuffer on a single display. The amount of framebuffer memory used by each channel depends on the resolution of the channel and the pixel formats supported in each channel.

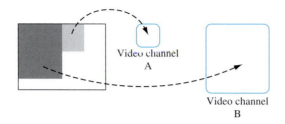

Figure 7.3 Two video channels allocated from one framebuffer.

7.4 Off-Screen Rendering

As mentioned previously, an OpenGL renderer isn't limited to rendering to a window or a video output display device; it can render to any device that implements some sort of framebuffer storage. One technique that has gained popularity is rendering to accelerated framebuffer memory that isn't visible as part of the display. For example, in Figure 7.3 a third of the framebuffer memory isn't allocated as part of a visible video channel, but could be useful for generating intermediate images used to construct a more complicated final image. The back buffer in a double-buffered window can also be used for intermediate storage, but the application is limited to a single back buffer, and the buffer contents cannot persist across multiple frames. The OpenGL specification includes the notion of *auxiliary buffers* (or auxbufs) that serve as additional persistent color buffers, but they suffer from a number of limitations. Auxilliary buffers are the same dimensions as the main color buffer, and they don't provide a way to save the depth buffer. The concept of more general off-screen windows overcomes many of these limitations.

Off-screen windows introduce their own problems, however. The first is how to move data from an off-screen window to some place useful. Assuming that the off-screen image is intended for use as a rendering step in an on-screen window, a mechanism is needed to allow an OpenGL context to use the off-screen window in conjunction with an on-screen window. The mechanism chosen to do this is to separate a window into two components: a read window and a write window. In most situations the read and write window are one and the same, but when it's necessary to retrieve data from another window, the source window is bound to the OpenGL context as a read window — all OpenGL read-related operations (`glReadPixels`, `glCopyPixels`, and `glCopyTexture`) use the read window as the read *source*. Note that the read window does not change the window used for pixel-level framebuffer read operations, such as blending, depth test, stencil, or accumulation buffer returns. Figure 7.4 illustrates a thread-context pair with a separate off-screen read source and a visible write window. The accelerator memory is divided between framebuffers for two displays and a third partition for off-screen surfaces.

To use an off-screen window as part of a complex rendering algorithm, the application renders the relevant parts of the scene to the off-screen window, then binds the context to both the visible window and the off-screen window. The off-screen window

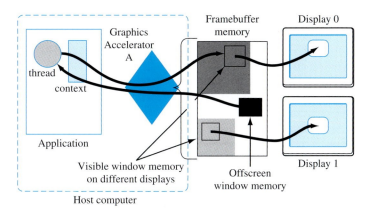

Figure 7.4 Thread with on-screen *write* window and off-screen *read* window.

is bound as a read source, while the visible window is bound as a write source. Then the application performs a pixel copy operation to merge the off-screen buffer contents with the on-screen contents.

The second problem with using off-screen memory is managing the memory itself. In the case of visible windows, the windows are allowed to overlap. The end user can see where windows are being allocated and directly manage the "screen real-estate." For off-screen memory, the end user has no idea how much memory is available, the "shape" of the memory, and whether there are implementation-specific constraints on how the memory can be allocated. If the framebuffer memory can't be treated as a one dimensional array of bytes—this restriction is often true with sophisticated hardware accelerators—the memory allocation and management problem becomes substantially more complicated. In Figure 7.3 the off-screen part of framebuffer memory has an irregular shape that may affect the maximum allowed dimensions of an off-screen window. If multiple off-screen memory allocation requests are made, the outcome of the requests may depend on their order. The window system embedding layer attempts to provide a 90% solution to this problem as simply as possible, but doesn't provide guarantees.

7.4.1 GLX Pbuffers

GLX provides support for rendering to off-screen memory as X Window System *pixmaps*. However, X pixmaps are a little too general and don't provide all of the necessary functionality needed for efficient rendering. In fact, no known GLX+OpenGL implementation supports accelerated rendering to pixmaps. To address the need for efficient off-screen rendering, a form of off-screen *drawable* specifically for OpenGL rendering was added to GLX 1.3. GLX calls these off-screen drawables *pbuffers*—short for pixel buffers.

To support the addition of pbuffers, substantial additions were made to the GLX 1.3 API. These changes separate the description of the framebuffer (bits per color component, depth buffer size, etc.) from the X Window System's visual concept; instead, identifying a framebuffer configuration description as an *FBConfig* rather than a visual. The end result is that the original API using visuals can be layered on the new API using FBConfigs by internally associating an FBConfig with each visual. This new API operates on the three types of drawables: windows, pixmaps, and pbuffers. Windows and pixmaps are created using X Window System commands, while pbuffers are created with a GLX-specific API.

The pbuffer creation command, `glxCreatePbuffer`, includes some additional attributes that help with off-screen memory management. In addition to requesting a pbuffer of specific dimension be created, the application can also specify that if that request fails, a pbuffer of the largest available size should be allocated. This provides a means of *discovering* the largest available pbuffer. The discovery routine also allocates the pbuffer to avoid race conditions with other applications. The created pbuffer also includes an attribute specifying whether the pbuffer is *volatile*; that is, whether the pbuffer contents should be preserved. If the contents need not be preserved, then they may be damaged by rendering operations on other drawables, in much the same way that the contents of one window may be damaged by rendering to another overlapping window. When this happens, the application can be notified by registering for GLX-specific buffer *clobber* events. The idea is to provide a choice to application writers; if the contents of a pbuffer can be regenerated easily or are transient, then volatile pbuffers are the best solution. If the pbuffer contents cannot be easily regenerated, then the application can use a non-volatile pbuffer and the system will save and restore the pbuffer contents when the resources are needed by another drawable. Of course, the save and restore operations may slow the application, so non-volatile pbuffers should only be used when absolutely necessary.

7.4.2 WGL Pbuffers

Pbuffers are also available on the Windows platform through the `WGL_ARB_pbuffer`, `WGL_ARB_pixel_format`, and `WGL_ARB_make_current_read` extensions.

7.5 Rendering to Texture Maps

In many OpenGL implementations the storage for texture maps and the framebuffer comes from the same physical pool of memory. Since they are in the same memory, it suggests the opportunity to improve the efficiency of using the framebuffer contents as a texture map (see Section 5.3) without copying the data from the framebuffer to the texture map. The `ARB_render_texture` WGL extension provides a means to do this using pbuffers.

An application using the extension creates a pbuffer, binds it to the context using `wglMakeCurrent`, renders to it, then unbinds from it. Next, the application binds to a new drawable and uses the extension command `wglBindTexImageARB` to bind the pbuffer to the current texture. In an optimized implementation, subsequent texture-mapped geometry will retrieve texel data directly from the pbuffer. The extension can still be implemented on pipeline implementations that don't share texture and framebuffer storage by simply copying the data from the pbuffer to the texture map. The latter implementation is no worse than the application calling `glCopyTexture` directly, and on implementations that share storage it is considerably more efficient. After using the pbuffer as a texture, it is unbound from the texture (using `wglReleaseTexImageARB`) and can again be used for rendering. The extension does not allow a pbuffer to be used simultaneously for rendering and texturing since this can have unpredictable implementation-specific behavior.

7.6 Direct and Indirect Rendering

Another factor that arises in a discussion of both the window system embedding and the host operating system is the notion of direct and indirect rendering. For X Window System embedding, these notions have a very precise meaning. Indirect rendering means that each OpenGL command issued by a *client* application is encoded in the X11 protocol, as defined by the GLX extension. The encoded stream is then decoded by the *server* and sent to an OpenGL renderer. The advantage of indirect rendering is that it allows OpenGL rendering to be used by any client that implements the client side of the GLX protocol encoder. It can send rendering commands over a network to a remote server and execute the rendering operations and display the results on the remote server. The disadvantage is that the protocol encoding and decoding consumes extra processing and memory resources that can limit the achievable performance. If both the client and server are both on the same computer, then a more efficient mechanism to issue commands to the hardware can be used — *direct rendering*.

GLX doesn't specify a protocol for direct rendering; instead, it specifies a set of ground rules that allow vendors some flexibility in doing their implementations, while retaining indirect rendering compatibility. In a high-performance direct rendering implementation, once a context/window pair has been made current, the application issues commands directly to the hardware mapped into the address space of the application. There is no need to buffer commands or interact with device drivers or the operating system kernel layer. The details for one such implementation are available in *Graphics Interface '95* by Kilgard et al. (1995).

In other embeddings the notion of direct and indirect rendering is more vague. The Windows platform does not provide native support for remote rendering, so it can be said to only support direct rendering. However, mechanisms used to achieve direct rendering may be radically different from those used on UNIX platforms.

OpenGL Implementations

The OpenGL specification offers considerable flexibility to implementors. The OpenGL rendering pipeline is also an evolving design; as implementation technologies advance and new ideas surface and are proven through trial and iteration, they become part of the specification. This has both advantages and disadvantages. It ensures that the standard remains relevant for new applications by embracing new functionality required by those applications. At the same time it creates some fragmentation since different vendors may ship OpenGL implementations that correspond to different versions of the specification. This puts a greater burden on the application developer to understand the differences in functionality between the different versions and also to understand how to take advantage of the new functionality when it is available and how to do without in its absence.

In this chapter we will describe some ways in which OpenGL has evolved and is currently evolving and also discuss some interesting aspects of implementing hardware acceleration of the OpenGL pipeline.

8.1 OpenGL Versions

At the time of writing there are have been five revisions to the OpenGL specification (1.1 through 1.5). The version number is divided into a major and minor number. The change in minor number indicates that these versions are backward-compatible; no pre-existing functionality has been modified or removed. This means that applications written using an older revision of OpenGL will continue to work correctly with a newer version.

When a new version of the specification is released, it includes enhancements that either incorporate new ideas or that generalize some existing part of the pipeline. These enhancements are added as it becomes practical to implement them on existing platforms or platforms that will be available in the near future. Some examples of new functionality are the addition of vertex arrays and texture objects in OpenGL 1.1 or the addition of multitexture and multisample in OpenGL 1.3. In the case of vertex arrays and texture objects they were additions that did not really reflect new technologies. They were for the most part additions that helped improve the performance an application could achieve. Multitexture is a generalization of the texturing operation that allows multiple texture maps to be applied to a single primitive. Multisample is a new feature that introduces a new technology (multiple samples per-pixel) to achieve full-scene antialiasing.

This short list of features helps illustrate a point. Features that require new technologies or modifications to existing technologies are unlikely to be well supported on platforms that were created before the specification was defined. Therefore older platforms, i.e., older accelerators are unlikely to be refitted with new versions of OpenGL or when they do, they typically implement the new features using the host processor and are effectively unaccelerated. This means that application writers may need to be cautious when attempting to use the features from a new version of OpenGL on an older (previous generation) platform. Rather than repeat *caveat emptor* and *your mileage may vary* each time we describe an algorithm that uses a feature from a later version of OpenGL to avoid clutter we'll only state it once here.

A fairly complete list of features added in different versions of the OpenGL specification is as follows:

OpenGL 1.1 Vertex array, polygon offset, RGB logic operation, texture image formats, texture replace environment function, texture proxies, copy texture, texture subimage, texture objects.

OpenGL 1.2 3D textures, BGRA pixel formats, packed pixel formats, normal rescaling, separate specular color, texture coordinate edge clamping, texture LOD control, vertex array draw element range, imaging subset.

OpenGL 1.3 Compressed textures, cube map textures, multisample, multitexture, texture add environment function, texture combine environment function, texture dot3 combine environment operation, texture coordinate border clamp, transpose matrix.

OpenGL 1.4 Automatic mipmap generation, squaring blend function, constant blend color (promoted from the imaging subset), depth textures, fog coordinate, multiple draw arrays, point parameters, secondary color, stencil wrap, texture crossbar environment mode, texture LOD bias, texture coordinate mirror repeat wrap mode, window raster position.

OpenGL 1.5 Buffer objects, occlusion queries, and shadow functions.

8.2 OpenGL Extensions

To accommodate the rapid innovation in the field of computer graphics the OpenGL design also allows an implementation to support additional features. Each feature is packaged as a mini-specification that adds new commands, tokens, and state to the pipeline. These extensions serve two purposes: they allow new features to be "field tested," and if they prove successful they are incorporated into a later version of the specification. This also allows vendors to use their innovations as product differentiators: it provides a mechanism for OpenGL implementation vendors to release new features as part of their OpenGL implementation without having to wait for the feature to become mainstream and go through a standardization process.

Over time it became useful to create standardized versions of some vendor-specific extension specifications. The original idea was to promote an existing vendor-specific extension to "EXT" status when multiple vendors (two or more) supported the extension in their implementation and agreed on the specification. It turned out that this process wasn't quite rigorous enough, so it evolved into a new process where the Architecture Review Board creates a version of specific extensions with their own seal of approval. These "ARB" extensions often serve as previews of new features that will be added in a subsequent version of the standard. For example, multitexture was an ARB extension at the time of OpenGL 1.2 and was added to the base standard as part of OpenGL 1.3. An important purpose of an ARB extension is that it acts as a mini-standard that OpenGL implementation vendors can include in their products when they can support it well. This reduces the pressure to add new features to the base standard before they can be well supported by a broad set of implementation vendors, yet at the same time gives application writers a strong specification and an evolutionary direction.

Sometimes an ARB extension reflects a set of capabilities that are more market-specific. The `ARB_imaging_subset` is an example of such an extension. For this class of extensions the demand is strong enough to create a rigorously defined specification that multiple vendors can consistently implement, but the demand is not broad enough and the features are costly enough to implement so as not to incorporate it into the base standard.

As we stated in the book preface, our intent is to make full use of features available in OpenGL versions 1.0 through 1.5 as well as ARB extensions. Occasionally we will also describe a vendor-specific extension when it is helpful to a particular algorithm. More information about using extensions is included in Appendix A.

8.3 OpenGL ES for Embedded Systems

As applications for 3D graphics have arisen in areas beyond the more traditional personal computers and workstations, the success of the OpenGL standard has made it attractive for use in other areas.

One rapidly growing area is 3D graphics for embedded systems. Embedded systems range from mobile devices such as watches, personal digital assistants, and cellular handsets; consumer appliances such as game consoles, settop boxes, and printers; to more industrial aerospace, automotive, and medical imaging applications. The demands of these systems also encompass substantial diversity in terms of processing power, memory, cost, battery power, and robustness requirements. The most significant problem with the range of potential 3D clients is that many of them can't support a full "desktop" OpenGL implementation. To solve this problem and address the needs of the embedded devices, in 2002 the Khronos Group created a group to work with Silicon Graphics (the owner of the OpenGL trademark) and the OpenGL ARB (the overseer of the OpenGL specification) to create a parallel specification for embedded devices called OpenGL ES. The operating principles of the group are to oversee a standard for embedded devices based on a subset of the existing desktop OpenGL standard. To handle the diverse requirements of all of the different types of embedded devices the Khronos Group decided to create individualized subsets that are tailored to the characteristics of a particular embedded market (Khronos Group, 2002). These subsets are termed *profiles*.

8.3.1 Embedded Profiles

To date, the Khronos Group has completed version 1.0 and 1.1 of the specifications for two profiles (Blythe, 2003) and is in the process of creating the specification for a third. Profile specifications are created by working groups, comprised of Khronos members experienced in creating OpenGL implementations and familiar with the profile's target market. Since a profile is intended to address a specific market, the definition of a profile begins with a characterization of the market being addressed, analyzing the demands and constraints of that market. The characterization is followed by draft proposals of features from the desktop OpenGL specification that match the market characterization document. From the feature proposals a more detailed specification document is created. It defines the exact subset of the OpenGL pipeline included in the profile, detailing the commands, enumerants, and pipeline behavior. Similar to OpenGL ARB extensions, an OpenGL ES profile specification may include new OES extensions that are standardized versions of extensions useful to the particular embedded market. Like desktop OpenGL implementations, implementations of OpenGL ES profiles may also include vendor-specific extensions. The set of extensions include those already defined for desktop OpenGL, as well as new extensions created specifically to address additional market-specific needs of the profile's target market.

A profile includes a strict subset of the desktop OpenGL specification as its base and then adds additional extensions as either *required* or *optional* extensions. Required extensions must be supported by an implementation and optional extensions are at the discretion of the implementation vendor. Similar to desktop OpenGL, OpenGL ES profiles must pass a profile-specific conformance test to be described as an OpenGL ES implementation. The conformance test is also defined and overseen by the Khronos Group.

The two defined profiles are the Common and Common-Lite profiles. The third profile design in progress is the Safety Critical profile.

8.3.2 Common and Common-Lite Profiles

The goal of the Common and Common-Lite profiles is to address a wide range of consumer-related devices ranging from battery-powered hand-held devices such as mobile phones and PDAs to line-powered devices such as kiosks and settop boxes. The requirements of these devices are small memory footprint, modest to medium processing power, and a need for a wide range of 3D rendering features including lighted, texture mapped, alpha blended, depth-buffered triangles, lines, and points.

To span this broad range of devices, there are two versions of the profile. The Common profile effectively defines the feature subset of desktop OpenGL in the two profiles. The Common-Lite profile further reduces the memory footprint and processing requirements by eliminating the floating-point data type from the profile.

The version 1.0 Common profile subset is as follows: Only RGBA rendering is supported, color index mode is eliminated. The double-precision data type is dropped and a new fixed-point data type called *fixed* (suffixed with 'x') is added. Desktop OpenGL commands that only have a double-precision form, such as glDepthRange are replaced with single-precision floating-point and fixed-point versions.

Only triangle, line, and point-based primitives are supported (not pixel images or bitmaps). Geometry is drawn exclusively using vertex arrays (no support for glBegin/glEnd). Vertex arrays are extended to include the byte data type.

The full transformation stack is retained, but the modelview stack minimum is reduced to 16 elements, and the transpose forms of the load and multiply commands are removed. Application-specified clipping planes and texture coordinate generation are also eliminated. Vertex lighting is retained with the exception of secondary color, local viewer mode, and distinct front and back materials (only the combined GL_FRONT_AND_BACK material can be specified). The only glColorMaterial mode supported is the default GL_AMBIENT_AND_DIFFUSE.

Rasterization of triangles, lines, and points are retained including flat and smooth shading and face culling. However, polygon stipple, line stipple, and polygon mode (point and line drawing styles) are not included. Antialiased line and point drawing is included using glLineSmooth and glPointSmooth, but not glPolygonSmooth. Full scene antialiasing is supported through multisampling, though it is an optional feature.

The most commonly used features of texture mapping are included. Only 2D texture maps without borders using either repeat or edge clamp wrap modes are supported. Images are loaded using glTexImage2D or glCopyTexture2D but the number of external image type and format combinations is greatly reduced. Table 8.1 lists the supported combinations of formats and types. The infrastructure for compressed texture images is also supported. The Common and Common-Lite profiles also introduce a simple paletted form of compression. The extension is defined so that images can either be

Table 8.1 OpenGL ES Texture Image Formats and Types

Internal Format	External Format	Type
GL_RGBA	GL_RGBA	GL_UNSIGNED_BYTE
GL_RGB	GL_RGB	GL_UNSIGNED_BYTE
GL_RGBA	GL_RGBA	GL_UNSIGNED_SHORT_4_4_4_4
GL_RGBA	GL_RGBA	GL_UNSIGNED_SHORT_5_5_5_1
GL_RGB	GL_RGB	GL_UNSIGNED_SHORT_5_6_5
GL_LUMINANCE_ALPHA	GL_LUMINANCE_ALPHA	GL_UNSIGNED_BYTE
GL_LUMINANCE	GL_LUMINANCE	GL_UNSIGNED_BYTE
GL_ALPHA	GL_ALPHA	GL_UNSIGNED_BYTE

accelerated in their indexed form or expanded to their non-paletted form at load time operating on them as regular images thereafter.

Multitexturing is supported, but only a single texture unit is required. Texture objects are supported, but the set of texture parameters is reduced, leaving out support for texture priorities and level clamping. A subset of texture environments from the OpenGL 1.3 version are supported: GL_MODULATE, GL_BLEND, GL_REPLACE, GL_DECAL, and GL_ADD. The remainder of the pipeline: fog, scissor test, alpha test, stencil/depth test, blend, dither, and logic op are supported in their entirety. The accumulation buffer is not supported.

Support for operating on images directly is limited. Images can be loaded into texture maps, and images can be retrieved to the host from the framebuffer or copied into a texture map. The glDrawPixels, glCopyPixels, and glBitmap commands are not supported.

More specialized functionality including evaluators, feedback, and selection are not included. Display lists are also omitted because of their sizable implementation burden. State queries are also substantially limited; only *static* state can be queried. Static state is defined as implementation-specific constants such as the depth of a matrix stack, or depth of color buffer components, but does not include state that can be directly or indirectly set by the application. Examples of non-static state include the current blend function, and the current value of the modelview matrix.

Fixed-Point Arithmetic

One of the more significant departures from desktop OpenGL in the Common profile is the introduction of a fixed-point data type. The definition of this type is a 32-bit representation with a 16-bit signed integer part and a 16-bit fraction part. Conversions between a fixed-point representation, x, and a traditional integer or floating-point representation, t, are accomplished with the formulas:

$$x = t * 65536$$

$$t = x/65536,$$

which, of course, may use integer shift instructions in some cases to improve the efficiency of the computation. The arithmetic rules for fixed-point numbers are:

$$add(a, b) = a + b$$

$$sub(a, b) = a - b$$

$$mul(a, b) = (a * b)/65536$$

$$div(a, b) = (a * 65536)/b$$

Note that the simple implementation of multiplication and division need to compute a 48-bit intermediate result to avoid losing information.

The motivation for adding the fixed-point data type is to support a variety of devices that do not include native hardware support for floating-point arithmetic. Given this limitation in the devices, the standard could either:

1. Continue to support single-precision floating-point only, assuming that software emulation will be used for all floating-point operations (in the application and in the profile implementation).

2. Require a floating-point interface but allow the profile implementation to use fixed-point internally by relaxing some of the precision and dynamic range requirements. This assumes that an application will use software floating-point, or will use its own form of fixed-point within the application, and convert to floating-point representation when using profile commands.

3. Support a fixed-point interface and internal implementation including relaxing the precision and dynamic range requirements.

Each of the choices has advantages and disadvantages, but the path chosen was to include a fixed-point interface in both the Common and Common-Lite profiles, while requiring the Common profile to continue to support a dynamic range consistent with IEEE single-precision floating-point. This allows an application to make effective use of either the floating-point data types and command interface while retaining compatibility with Common-Lite profile applications. The Common-Lite profile only supports fixed-point and integer data types and at minimum must support a dynamic range consistent with a straightforward fixed-point implementation with 16 bits each of integer and fraction parts. However, a Common-Lite profile implementation may support larger dynamic range, for example, using floating-point representations and operations internally.

This design decision places more burden on applications written using the fixed-point interface to constrain the ranges of values used within the application, but provides opportunities for efficient implementations across a much wider range of device capabilities.

The principal application concern is avoiding overflow during intermediate calculations. This means that the combined magnitudes of values used to represent vertices and modeling transformations must not exceed $2^{15} - 1$. Conversely, given the nature of fixed-point arithmetic, values less than 1.0 will lose precision rapidly. Some useful rules for avoiding overflow are:

Given a representation that supports numbers in the range $[-X, X]$,

1. Data should start out within this range.

2. Differences between vertex components within a primitive (triangle or line) should be within $[-X, X]$.

3. For any pair of vertices q and p, $|q_i - p_i| + |q_3 - p_3| < X$, for $i = 0 \ldots 2$ (the subscript indices indicate the x, y, z, and w components).

These constraints need to be true for coordinates all the way through the transformation pipeline up to clipping. To check that this constraint is met for each object, examine the composite transformation matrix (projection*modelview) and the components of the object vertices. Take the absolute values of the largest scaling component from the upper 3×3 (s), the largest translational component from the 4th column (t), and the largest component from the object vertices (c), and test that $c * s + t < X/2$.

8.3.3 Safety Critical Profile

The Safety Critical profile addresses the market for highly robust or *mission critical* 3D graphics implementations. Typical applications for this market include avionics and automotive displays. The principal driving factor behind the Safety Critical profile is providing the minimum required 3D rendering functionality and nothing more. Unlike the Common profile, processing power, battery power, and memory footprint are not constraints. Instead, minimizing the number of code paths that need to be tested is much more important. For these reasons, the Safety Critical profile greatly reduces the number of supported input data types, and will make more drastic cuts to existing desktop features to simplify the testing burden.

8.3.4 OpenGL ES Revisions

The OpenGL ES embedded profiles promise to extend the presence of the OpenGL pipeline and OpenGL applications from tens of millions of desktop computers to hundreds of millions of special purpose devices. Similar to the OpenGL specification, the ES profile specifications are also revised at regular intervals, nominally yearly, so that important new features can be incorporated into the standard in a timely fashion.

8.4 OpenGL Pipeline Evolution

Looking at features added to new versions, the most significant changes in OpenGL have occurred in the way data is managed and moved in and out of the pipeline (texture objects, vertex arrays, vertex buffer objects, render-to-texture, pbuffers, packed pixels, internal formats, subimages, etc.) and in the explosive improvement in the capabilities of the texture mapping subsystem (cube maps, LOD control, multitexture, depth textures, combine texture environment, crossbar environment, etc.). The first class of changes reflect a better understanding of how applications manage data and an evolving strategy to tune the data transfer model to the underlying hardware technologies. The second class of changes reflect the desire for more advanced fragment shading capabilities.

However, these changes between versions only tell part of the story. The OpenGL extensions serve as a harbinger of things to come. The most significant feature is the evolution from a *fixed-function* pipeline to a *programmable* pipeline. This evolution manifests itself in two ways: vertex programs and fragment programs. Vertex programs allow an application to tailor its own transform and lighting pipeline, enabling more sophisticated modeling and lighting operations including morphing and skinning, alternate per-vertex lighting models, and so on. Fragment programs bypass the increasingly complex multi-texture pipeline API (combine and crossbar environments), replacing it with a complex but much more expressive programming model allowing nearly arbitrary computation and texture lookup to be performed at each fragment.

The two programmable stages of the pipeline continue to grow in sophistication, supporting more input and computational resources. However, there is another evolutionary stage just now appearing. The programmable parts of the pipeline are following the evolution of traditional computing (to some extent), beginning with programs expressed in a low-level assembly language and progressing through languages with increased expressiveness at a much higher level. These improvements are achieved through the greater use of abstraction in the language. The programmable pipeline is currently making the first transition from assembly language to a higher-level (C-like) language. This step is embodied in the `ARB_shading_language_100` extension, also called the *OpenGL Shading Language* (Kessenich et al., 2003).

The transition to a higher-level shading language is unlikely to be the end of the evolution, but it may signal a marked slow down in the evolution of the structure of the pipeline and greater focus on supporting higher-level programming constructs. Regardless, the transition for devices to the programmable model will take some time, and in the near term there will be devices that, for cost or other reasons, will be limited to earlier versions of the OpenGL standard well after the programmable pipeline becomes part of core OpenGL.[1]

The remainder of this chapter describes some of the details and technologies involved in implementing hardware accelerators. Many of the techniques serve as a basis for

---

1. OpenGL 2.0

hardware-accelerated OpenGL implementations independent of the target cost of the accelerator. Many of the techniques can be scaled down for low-cost or scaled up for very high-performance implementations and the techniques are applicable to both the fixed-function and programmable parts of the pipeline.

8.5 Hardware Implementations of the Pipeline

The speed of modern processors makes it possible to implement the entire OpenGL pipeline in software on the host processor and achieve the performance required to process millions of vertices per second and hundreds of millions of pixels per second. However, the trend to increase realism by increasing the complexity of rendered scenes calls for the use of hardware acceleration on at least some parts of the OpenGL pipeline to achieve interactive performance.

At the time of this writing, hardware acceleration can enable performance levels in the range of 100 to 300 million vertices per second for geometry processing and 100 million to 5 billion pixels per second for rasterization. The raw performance is typically proportional to the amount of hardware acceleration present and this is in turn reflected in the cost and feature set of the accelerator. OpenGL pipelines are being implemented across a tremendous range of hardware and software. This range makes it difficult to describe implementation techniques that are applicable across devices with differing price and performance targets. Instead, the following sections provide an overview of some acceleration techniques in order to provide additional insight into how the pipeline works and how applications can use it more efficiently.

The OpenGL pipeline can be roughly broken into three stages: transform and lighting, primitive setup, and rasterization and fragment processing. Accelerators are usually designed to accelerate one or more of these parts of the pipeline. Usually there is more benefit in accelerating the later stages of the pipeline since there is more data to process.

8.5.1 Rasterization Acceleration

Rasterization accelerators take transformed and lighted primitives and convert them to pixels writing them to the framebuffer. The rasterization pipeline can be broken down into several operations which are described in the following paragraphs.

Scan Conversion

Scan conversion generates the set of fragments corresponding to each primitive. Each fragment contains window coordinates x, y, and z, a color value, and texture coordinates. The fragment values are generated by interpolating the attributes provided at each vertex in the primitive. Scan conversion is computationally intensive since multiple attribute values must be computed for each fragment. Scan conversion computations can be performed using fixed-point arithmetic, but several of the computations must be performed at high precision to avoid producing artifacts. For example, color computations may use 4- or 8-bit (or more) computations and produce satisfactory results, whereas window coordinates and texture coordinates need substantially higher precision. During scan conversion the generated fragments are also tested against the scissor rectangle, and fragments outside the rectangle are discarded.

Texture

Texture mapping uses texture coordinates to look up one or more texel values in a texture map. The texel values are combined together to produce a single color, which is used to update the fragment color. The update method is determined by the current texture environment mode. The texturing operation can be both computationally expensive and memory intensive, depending on the filtering mode. For example, an RGBA texture map using a GL_LINEAR_MIPMAP_LINEAR minification filter retrieves 8 texel values split between 2 texture images. These 8 texel values are combined together using roughly 10 multiplications and 4 additions per color component. The amount of memory bandwidth required is dependent on the component number and depth of the texture map as well as the type of filtering used. It is common for hardware accelerators to design around compact texel representations, for example, 16-bit texels (textures with component sizes summing to 16-bits or less such as GL_RGBA4, GL_RGB5_A1) or a compressed texture representation.

Multitexture increases the bandwidth requirement in a linear way, in that each active texture stage requires a similar set of operations to produce the filtered result and then the result must be combined with those from other texture stages.

Fog and Alpha

This stage calculates an attenuation value, used to blend the fragment color with a fog color. The attenuation computation is dependent on the distance between the eye and the fragment and the current fog mode. Many hardware accelerators use the window z coordinate as an approximation to the distance, evaluating the fog function using a table lookup scheme rather than providing circuitry to evaluate the fog function directly.

The alpha function compares the fragment alpha against a reference value and performs an interpolation between the alpha and selected color components of the fragment. The color components selected depend on the current alpha function.

Depth and Stencil

The depth and stencil tests are memory intensive, since the depth and stencil values must be retrieved from the framebuffer before the tests can be performed. The amount of memory bandwidth required depends on the size of the depth and stencil buffers. Accelerator implementations will often pack the depth and stencil storage together for simultaneous access. For example, a 23-bit depth value and 1-bit stencil value are packed into 3 bytes, or a 24-bit depth value and an 8-bit stencil value are packed into 4 bytes. In the first example, the stencil operation may be no more expensive than the depth test operation if memory is accessed in byte-units; but in the latter case the stencil operation may cost an extra memory access, depending on the structure of the memory interface.

Blending

Framebuffer blending is also memory intensive since the contents of the color buffer must be retrieved as part of the computation. If the blend function uses destination alpha, additional memory bandwidth is required to retrieve the destination alpha value. Depending on the blend function, a moderate number of multiplication and addition operations may also be required. For example, for rendering of transparent surfaces, 6 multiplies and 3 adds are required for each fragment:

$$R_{dst} \leftarrow R_{src}\alpha + (1 - \alpha)R_{dst}$$
$$G_{dst} \leftarrow G_{src}\alpha + (1 - \alpha)G_{dst}$$
$$B_{dst} \leftarrow B_{src}\alpha + (1 - \alpha)B_{dst}$$

Framebuffer Operations

Rasterization accelerators typically accelerate some additional framebuffer operations such as buffer clears and dithering. The clear operations are very memory intensive, since every pixel within the window needs to be written. For example, a 1024×1024 window requires 1 million memory operations to write each pixel in the window. If an application is running at 85 frames per second, 85 million pixel writes per second are required just to clear the window.

Accumulation buffer operations are also computation and memory intensive, but frequently are not implemented directly in lower cost accelerators. The main reason for this is that the accumulation buffer operations require larger multipliers and adders to implement the higher precision arithmetic, but the cost is prohibitive for lower cost accelerators.

The total number of rasterization computations performed for each pixel can exceed 100 operations. To support rasterization rates in excess of 100 million pixels per second the rasterization pipeline must support as many as 1 billion operations per second or more. This is why rasterization acceleration is found in all but the lowest-cost devices that support 3D rendering.

OpenGL implementations that do not use an external accelerator may still take advantage of special CPU instructions to assist with rasterization. For example, Intel's MMX (multimedia extensions) (Peleg et al., 1997) instructions allow the same operation to be simultaneously applied to multiple data elements packed into a wide register. Such instructions are particularly useful for computing all of the components of an RGBA color value at once.

8.5.2 Primitive Setup Acceleration

Primitive setup refers to the set of computations that are required to generate input fragments for the rasterization pipeline. In lowest cost accelerators, these computations are performed on the host computer for each primitive and sent to the rasterizer. These computations can easily become the bottleneck in the system, however, when a large number of primitives are drawn. The computations require computing the edge equations for each active parameter in a triangle's vertices (color, depth, texture coordinates), performed at high precision to avoid artifacts. There is a large amplification of the amount of data in the pipeline, as each triangle generates a large number of fragments from three vertices.

8.5.3 Transform and Lighting Acceleration

Mid-range and high-end accelerators often provide hardware acceleration for the OpenGL transform and lighting (also called geometry) operations. These operations include the transformation of vertex coordinates to eye space, lighting computations, projection to window coordinates, clipping, texture coordinate generation, and transform. These operations typically use IEEE-754 single-precision floating-point computations[2] and require in excess of 90 operations per-vertex when lighting or texturing is enabled. To achieve rates of 10 million triangles per second, more than 100 million floating-point operations per second are necessary in addition to data movement and other operations. High vertex rates preclude using the host CPU except in cost-sensitive applications.

Even with accelerator support, some operations need to be implemented carefully to achieve good performance. For many computations, it is not necessary to evaluate the result to full single-precision accuracy. For example, color computations may only need 8- or 12-bits of precision, and specular power and spotlight power functions are often implemented using table lookup rather than direct function evaluation. The OpenGL glRotate command may use limited precision polynomial approximations to evaluate trigonometric functions. Division may be implemented using fast reciprocal approximations (Soderquist and Leeser, 1996) rather than a much more expensive divide operation. The accelerator architecture may be tuned to compute inner product operations since much of the transformation and lighting computations are composed of inner product computations.

Implementations that support programmable vertex operations (vertex programs), map or translate the application-specified vertex programs onto an internal instruction set. This internal instruction set shares much in common with the operations required to implement the fixed vertex pipeline: vector add, multiply, reciprocal, inner product, matrix operations, limited conditional branching and looping, and miscellaneous operations to assist in computing some parts of the vertex lighting equation (e.g., attenuation or specular power). Programmable fragment processing requires similar types of instructions

---

2. In practice, a subset of IEEE floating-point is used since some of the more expensive capabilities (e.g., support for different rounding modes), are unnecessary.

as well, particularly to support per-fragment lighting computations, only in the near-term with lower precision and range requirements than those needed for vertex processing.

Over the past five years, it has become cost-effective to fit rasterization, setup, and transform and lighting acceleration into a single chip, paving the way for low-cost implementations to hardware accelerate the majority of the OpenGL pipeline. These implementations range from desktop to handheld devices. High-end desktop versions are capable of rendering hundreds of millions of triangles per second and billions of pixels per second, while low-power consumption, low-cost implementations for hand-held devices are capable of hundreds of thousands of triangles and tens of millions of pixels per second.[3]

8.5.4 Pipeline Balance

The data explosion that occurs as vertices are processed and converted to pixels leads to the notion of balancing the stages of the pipeline to match the increases in the amount of data to be processed. An unbalanced pipeline leaves a bottleneck at one of the pipeline stages, leaving earlier and later stages idle, wasting resources. The question arises on how to determine the correct balance between pipeline stages. The difficulty is that the correct answer is application-dependent. An application that generates large numbers of very small triangles may require more power in the earlier transform, lighting, and setup stages of the pipeline, whereas applications that generate smaller numbers of triangles with larger areas may require more rasterization and pixel fill capabilities. Sometimes application classes can be grouped into categories such as *geometry-limited* or *fill-limited*. Generally CAD applications fit in the former category, whereas games and visual simulation applications fit in the latter, so it is not uncommon for accelerator designers to bias their implementations toward their target audience.

One way to describe the balance is in terms of the number of input triangles (or other primitives) and the average area of the primitive. For example, 100 million triangles per second with 10 pixels per triangle requires 1 billion pixels to be processed per second. Similarly, 50 million 10-pixel aliased lines may require 500 million pixels per second, and 50 million antialiased lines where each antialiased pixel has a 3-pixel footprint requires 1.5 billion pixels per second. System designers will then assign properties to the primitives and pixels, (e.g., a single infinite light; normal, color, one texture coordinate per-vertex; average triangle strip length 10; 2 mipmapped textures; depth buffering; 8-bit RGBA framebuffer; 24-bit depth buffer, etc.) and determine the raw processing requirements to meet these objectives.

8.5.5 Parallelism Opportunities

The OpenGL specification allows the use of parallel processing to improve performance, but imposes constraints on its use. The most important constraint requires that images are

---

3. In the year 2004.

rendered as if their primitives were processed in the order they were received, throughout the pipeline. This means that the fragments from one triangle shall not reach the framebuffer before the fragments of a triangle that was sent to the pipeline earlier. This constraint is essential for the correct operation of *order-dependent* algorithms such as transparency. However, the specification does not prohibit primitives from being processed out of order, as long as the end result isn't changed.

Parallelism can be exploited in the transform and lighting stages by processing vertices in parallel, that is, by processing two or more vertices simultaneously. Much of the vertex processing can be performed completely in parallel (transforms, lighting, clip testing) and the results accumulated for primitive assembly and rasterization. A parallel implementation can take several forms. Individual primitives can be sent to independent processors for processing, and the resultant primitives merged back in order before rasterization, as shown in Figure 8.1. In such an implementation, the incoming primitives are passed through a distributor that determines to which geometry processor to send each primitive. The distributor may choose processors in a round-robin fashion or implement a more sophisticated load-balancing scheme to ensure that primitives are sent to idle processors. The output of each geometry processor is sent to a recombiner that merges the processed primitives in the order they were originally sent. This can be accomplished by tagging the primitives in the distributor and then reassembling them in the order specified by the tags.

Using multiple-instruction-multiple-data (MIMD) processors, the processors can run independently of one another. This allows different processors to process differing primitive types or lengths or even execute different processing paths, such as clipping a primitive, in parallel. MIMD-based processing can support workloads with greater variation, but incurs the extra cost of supporting a complete processor with instruction sequencing and data processing. An alternative is to run the processors in lockstep using a single instruction stream.

A single-instruction-multiple-data (SIMD) processor can be used to process the vertices for a single primitive in parallel. For example, a SIMD processor with three

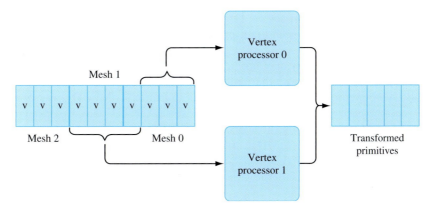

Figure 8.1 MIMD vertex processing.

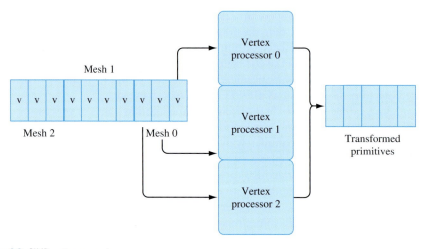

Figure 8.2 SIMD vertex processing.

processors can simultaneously process the three vertices in an independent triangle, or three vertices at a time from a triangle strip, as shown in Figure 8.2. Clipping computations are more difficult to process in parallel on an SIMD processor, so most SIMD implementations use a single processor to clip a primitive.

In both these cases, difficulties arise from state changes, such as changing the modelview matrix or the current color. These changes must be applied to the correct set of primitives. One reason that OpenGL allows so few commands between `glBegin/glEnd` sequences is to facilitate parallel processing without interference from state changes.

When there are no state changes between primitives, all of the vertices for the set of primitives can be processed in the same way. This allows the simple SIMD model to be extended to process vertices from multiple primitives at once, increasing the width of the SIMD array. As the vertices are being processed, the information defining which vertices are contained within each input primitive must be preserved and the primitives re-assembled before clipping.

A single large SIMD array may not be effectively utilized if there are frequent state changes between primitives, since that reduces the number of vertices that are processed identically. One method to maintain efficiency is to utilize an MIMD array of smaller SIMD processors where each MIMD element processes vertices with a particular set of state. Multiple MIMD elements can work independently on different primitives, while within each MIMD element, a SIMD array processes multiple vertices in parallel.

Vertex Efficiency

Most hardware accelerators are tuned to process connected primitives with no interleaved state changes with maximum efficiency. Connected primitives, such as triangle strips, allow the cost of processing a vertex to be amortized over multiple primitives. By avoiding state changes, the geometry accelerator is free to perform long sequences of regular vector and matrix computations and make very efficient use of the arithmetic logic in the accelerator. This an area where the use of vertex arrays can improve performance, since state changes cannot be interspersed in the vertex data and the vertex array semantics leave the current color, normal, and texture coordinate state undefined at the end of the array.

Vertex Caching

Implicitly connected primitives such as strips and fans are not the only mechanism for amortizing vertex computations. Vertex arrays can also be used to draw *triangle lists*, that is, indexed arrays of triangles using the glDrawElements command. At first glance, indexed arrays may seem inefficient since an index must first be fetched before the vertex data can be fetched. However, if the index values are compact (16-bits) and can be fetched efficiently by the accelerator, indexing allows more complex topologies than strips and fans to be specified in a single rendering command. This allows meshes to be specified in which more than two primitives can share each vertex. For example, a regular rectangular grid of triangles will reuse each vertex in four triangles in the interior. This means that the cost of fetching index values can be overcome by the savings from avoiding re-transforming vertices. To realize the savings the accelerator needs to be able to track the post-transform vertex data and re-use it.

With connected primitives the vertex data is re-used immediately as part of the next primitive. However, with mesh data each triangle must be specified completely, so some vertices must be re-specified. Fortunately, vertices are uniquely indexed by their index value, so the index value can also be used to index a *post-transform vertex cache* to retrieve already transformed values. This cache can be implemented as a software-managed cache (for example, in implementations that do software vertex processing), or it can be implemented directly in hardware. A relatively small cache of 8 to 16 entries, combined with careful ordering of the individual primitives in the triangle list, can result in very good vertex re-use, so this technique is commonly employed.

Rasterization

Parallelism can be exploited in the rasterization stage during fragment processing. Once a fragment is generated during scan conversion, it can be processed independently of other fragments as long as order is preserved. One way to accomplish this is to subdivide the screen into regions and assign fragment processors to different regions as shown in Figure 8.3. After scan conversion, each fragment is assigned to a processor according to its window coordinates. A coarse screen subdivision may result in poor processor utilization if the polygons are not evenly distributed among the subdivided regions. To achieve better load balancing, the screen may be more finely subdivided and multiple regions assigned to a single fragment processor. Scan-line interleave is one such form of

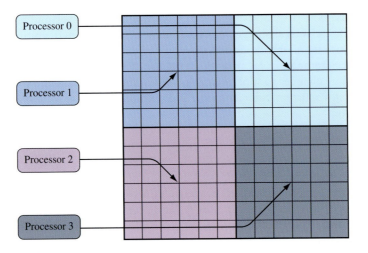

Figure 8.3 Screen tiling.

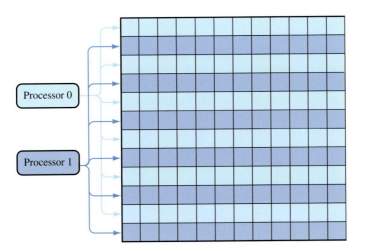

Figure 8.4 Scan line interleave.

fine-grain subdivision: each region is a scan line, and multiple scan lines are assigned to a single processor using an interleaving scheme, as shown in Figure 8.4

Similar SIMD processing techniques can also be used for fragment processing. Since all of the pixels of a primitive are subject to the identical processing, they can be processed in parallel.

One place where parallelism is particularly effective is in improving memory access rates. Two places where external memories are heavily accessed are texture lookup and framebuffer accesses. Rasterization bottlenecks often occur at the memory interfaces. If external memory can't keep up with the rest of the rasterizer, the pixel rate will be limited by the rate at which memory can be accessed; that is, by the *memory bandwidth*. Parallelism increases the effective memory bandwidth, by spreading the burden of memory accesses over multiple memory interfaces. Since pixels can be processed independently, it is straightforward to allocate memory interfaces to different pixel regions using the tiling technique described previously.

For texture memory accesses, there are several ways of achieving some parallelism. For mipmapping operations using `GL_LINEAR_MIPMAP_LINEAR` filtering, eight texel values are retrieved from two mipmap levels. Rather than fetch the texel values serially, waiting for each access to complete before starting the next one, the mipmap levels can be distributed between multiple memories using a tiling pattern. Interleaving data across multiple memory interfaces can benefit any texture filter that uses more than one sample. In addition to interleaving, entire levels can also be replicated in independent memories, trading space for improved time by allowing parallel conflict-free access. Figure 8.5 illustrates an example where texture memory is replicated four ways and even and odd mipmap levels are interleaved.

An alternative to multiple external texture memories is to use a hierarchical memory system. This system has a single external interface, combined with an internal cache memory, which allows either faster or parallel access. Hierarchical memory schemes rely on coherency in the memory access pattern in order to re-use previous memory fetches. Fortunately, mipmapping can exhibit a high level of coherency making caching effective. The coherency can be further improved using texture compression to reduce the effective

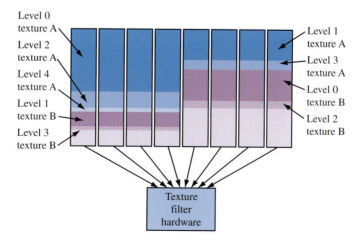

Figure 8.5 Mipmap levels replicated four ways and interleaved.

memory footprint for a texture at the cost of additional hardware to decompress the texture samples during lookup. The organization of memory affects the performance of the texturing subsystem in significant way; in older accelerators it was common for mipmapping to be slower than linear or other filters in the absence of replication and interleaving. In modern low-cost accelerators it is common for applications using mipmap filters to achieve better performance than linear filters since small mipmap levels have better cache coherency than larger linear maps.

A second way to increase parallelism can be exploited for multitexturing operations. If multiple textures are active and the texture coordinates are independent of one another, then the texel values can be retrieved in parallel. Again, rather than multiple external memories, a single external memory can be used with a parallel or high-speed internal cache. Like modern processor memory systems, the caching system used for texturing can have multiple levels creating a hierarchy. This is particularly useful for supporting the multiple texture image references generated by multitexturing and mipmapping.

Latency Hiding

One of the problems with using memory caching is that that the completion times for memory reads become irregular and unpredictable. This makes it much more difficult to interleave memory accesses and computations in such a way as to minimize the time spent idle waiting for memory reads to complete. There can be substantial inefficiency in any processing scheme if the processing element spends a lot of time idle while waiting for memory references to complete. One way to improve efficiency is to use a technique called *hyperthreading*. In hyperthreading, instead of having the processing element sit idle, the processor state is saved and the processor executes another waiting task, called a *thread*. If the second thread isn't referencing memory and executes some amount of computation, it can overlap the waiting time or *latency*, of the memory reference from the first thread. When the memory reference for the first thread completes, that thread is marked as "ready" and executes the next time the processing element stalls waiting for a memory reference. The cost of using the hyperthreading technique is that extra hardware resources are required to store the thread state and some extra work to stop and start a thread.

Hyperthreading works well with highly parallel tasks such as fragment processing. As fragments are generated during rasterization, new threads corresponding to fragments are constructed and are scheduled to run on the processing elements. Hyperthreading can be mixed with SIMD processing, since a group of fragments equal to the SIMD array width can be treated as a single thread. SIMD processing has the nice property that its lockstep execution means that all fragments require memory reads at the same instant. This means that its thread can be suspended once while its read requests for all of the fragments are serviced.

Early-Z Processing

Another method for improving rasterization and fragment processing performance is to try to eliminate fragments that are not visible before they undergo expensive shading operations. One way to accomplish this is to perform the depth test as fragments are generated. If the fragment is already occluded then it is discarded immediately avoiding texture mapping and other operations. To produce correct images, the early test must produce identical results compared to depth testing at the end of the pipeline. This means that when depth testing is disabled, or the depth function is modified, the early depth test must behave correctly.

While early testing against the depth buffer can provide a useful optimization, it still requires comparing each fragment against the corresponding depth buffer location. In implementations with deep buffers of fragments traveling through the fragment processing path on the way to the framebuffer, the test may be using stale depth data. An alternative is to try to reject more fragments from a primitive in a single test, by using a coarser depth buffer consisting of a single value for a tile or *super-pixel*. The coarser buffer need only store information indicating whether the super-pixel is completely occluded and if so, its min and max depth values in the area covered. Correspondingly large areas from an incoming primitive are tested against the depth range stored in the super-pixel. The results of the test: completely behind the super-pixel, completely in front of the super-pixel, or intersects determine if the incoming block of pixels is discarded, or processed as normal (with the depth range in the super-pixel updated as necessary).

Special cases arise when the incoming area intersects the depth range of the super-pixel, or the incoming area is completely in front, but doesn't completely cover the super-pixel. In both cases the fragments in the incoming area proceeds through the rest of the pipeline, but the super-pixel is invalidated since it isn't completely covered by the incoming primitive.

Despite the additional complexity of the coarser area approximation, it has two advantages. First, it can reject larger groups of incoming fragments with few tests. Second, if the areas are large enough (16×16), the buffer storing the depth range and valid flag for the super-pixel becomes small enough to fit on-chip in a hardware accelerator, avoiding additional delays retrieving values from memory. To further improve the efficiency of rejection, the scheme can be extended to a hierarchy of tile sizes (Greene et al., 1993).

8.5.6 Reordering the Pipeline

The early-Z processing mechanism is one of a number of places where processing steps can be reordered to eliminate unnecessary work as a form of performance optimization. The idea is to move work earlier in the pipeline to eliminate other potentially unnecessary processing later in the pipeline. Some examples of this are trivial rejection of primitives and backface culling. The logical order for processing primitives is to transform them to eye-space; light them; project to clip space; clip or discard primitives outside the view volume; perform the perspective division and viewport transformation. However, it can be more efficient to defer the vertex lighting computation until after the trivial rejection test, to avoid lighting vertices that will be discarded. Similarly, polygon face culling logically happens as part of polygon rasterization, but it can be a significant performance improvement to cull polygons first, before lighting them.

In the rasterization and fragment processing stages, it is similarly common to perform the scissor test during rasterization. This ensures that fragments are discarded before texture mapping or expensive shading operations. Early-Z and stencil processing are perhaps the most complex examples, since all application-visible side effects must be maintained. This is the key constraint with reordering the pipeline; it must be done in such a way that the application is unaware of the ordering change; all side effects must be preserved. Side effects might include updates to ancillary buffers, correct output of feedback and selection tokens, and so forth.

The idea of eliminating work as early as possible isn't limited to the internal implementation of the pipeline. It is also beneficial for applications to try to take similar steps, for example, using alpha testing with framebuffer blending to discard "empty" fragments before they reach the more expensive blending stage of the pipeline. Chapter 21 discusses these additional performance optimization techniques.

8.5.7 Mixed Software and Hardware Implementations

As OpenGL continues to evolve, and this single standard is used to satisfy a wide range of applications over an even larger range of performance levels, it is rare for implementations to hardware accelerate all OpenGL primitives for every possible combination of OpenGL states.

Instead, most implementations have a mixture of hardware accelerated and unaccelerated *paths*. The OpenGL specification describes pipelines of steps that primitives must go through to be rendered. These pipelines may be implemented in software or accelerated in hardware. One can think of an implementation containing multiple pipelines, each associated with a set of OpenGL state settings, called a *state vector*. Each one of these pipeline/state combinations is a *path*.

A hardware designer may choose to hardware accelerate only a subset of all possible OpenGL states to reduce hardware costs. If an application sets a combination of state settings that aren't accelerated, primitives processed under that state will be rendered using software on the host processor. This concept gives rise to a number of notions, including *fast paths*, *slow paths*, and *fall back to software*, to indicate whether an implementation is or is not using a high-performance path for a particular combination of modes.

The existence of software and hardware paths has obvious performance implications, but it also introduces some subtler issues. In Section 6.1.1 the importance of invariance in rasterization for multipass algorithms was emphasized. As a practical matter, however, it can be very difficult for an implementation with mixed software and hardware paths to guarantee consistency between them. For example, if a new blending mode is introduced, a software rasterization path may be added to the implementation to support the new mode on legacy hardware. It may be difficult to use this mode in a multipass algorithm since the software rasterizer is unlikely to rasterize triangles in the same way as the hardware.

It may not be an entire path that is implemented in software, but just a single operation. For example, accumulation buffer operations are commonly performed on the host processor, as the extended precision arithmetic is too expensive to implement in commodity hardware. Another example is texture borders. Texture borders, by their nature, tend to complicate hardware texturing implementations and they are not used by many applications;[4] as a result, they are often relegated to software paths, or occasionally not supported at all.

8.6 The Future

It's difficult to predict exactly how the OpenGL pipeline will continue to evolve, but some directions seem promising. In particular, the enhancement of the programmable parts of the pipeline (vertex and fragment programs) will continue, adding storage and computational resources, as well as enhanced arithmetic. Concurrently, new processing structuring paradigms such as stream processing (Owens et al., 2000) may help scale hardware accelerators to the next order of magnitude in performance improvement. At the same time, interest continues in adding new functionality to the pipeline, such as support for subdivision surfaces and displacement mapping (Lee et al., 2000). The demand for efficient implementations of such features may see the evolution of the traditional polygon-based OpenGL rendering pipeline to other formulations such as REYES (render everything you ever saw) (Cook et al., 1987; Owens et al., 2002) allowing hardware accelerators to achieve the next level of interactive realism. In the meantime, the software and hardware implementation techniques described here will enjoy continued use across a variety of devices for the foreseeable future.

---

4. This is a catch-22, since lack of application support is a disincentive to accelerate a feature and vice versa.

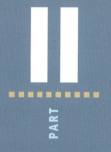

Basic Techniques

Multiple Rendering Passes

One of the most powerful features of the OpenGL pipeline is the ability to render a primitive multiple times using different modes, combining the results together to produce the final image (Figure 9.1). This approach implements the equation $I_{final} = I_1 \text{op}_1 I_2 \text{op}_2 \ldots I_n$, where op_i represents an arbitrary combining operation. In essence, a multipass approach combines the individual functional elements of OpenGL into a programming language, increasing the power and generality of the implementation. An application can do more computations than can be performed in OpenGL during a single pass over each primitive, and can achieve a wide variety of additional effects.

Using multiple rendering passes to draw a single frame can significantly impact rendering performance, which can lead to unacceptable frame rates. As the raw performance of graphics hardware improves, however, applications can budget multiple rendering passes to increase the frame quality, yet still maintain their desired frame rate. Investing computation time on multipass algorithms can often yield more improvement to image quality than applying it to increasing polygon counts. Many of the algorithms described in the remainder of the book use multiple rendering passes to implement algorithms; becoming familiar with these basic multipass principles provides the framework for modifying and extending them.

9.1 Invariance

Section 6.1.1 describes the concept of invariance and how it applies to rasterization operations. The invariance rules are vital to ensure correct multipass rendering; without

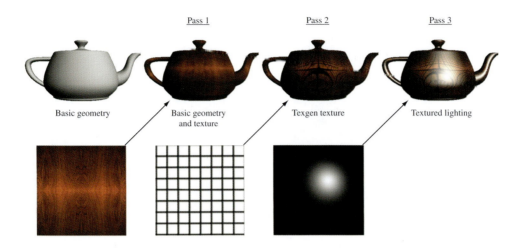

Figure 9.1 Basic multipass concept: combine computations from multiple frames.

invariance there is no guarantee that a given primitive, re-rendered with different attributes by a multipass algorithm, will render predictably and generate the desired result. Application writers should be aware that sometimes the OpenGL invariance rules can be subtle.

For example, a primitive doesn't have to produce the same fragments if blending is enabled and disabled, but it must do so if blending is *effectively disabled* by setting the source and destination blend factors to GL_ONE and GL_ZERO. Since the invariance rules allow for a lot of diversity between implementations, many vendor's implementations may be invariant even when a feature such as blending is explicitly enabled or disabled. While convenient, this additional implementation-dependent invariance can lure application writers into believing that this is the case for all implementations.

Table 9.1 lists methods for effectively disabling a particular feature that still maintains invariance. These methods are guaranteed by the OpenGL specification; they should work on any compliant implementation.

9.2 Multipass Overview

Each stage of a multipass algorithm splits into two steps: how to render one or more primitives, and how the resulting image should be merged with the image from previous steps. Care must be taken at each step, not only to ensure that the desired effect was achieved, but also to ensure that all the buffers affected by this step contain the proper values for the operations that follow.

Table 9.1 Disabling Operations while Maintaining Invariance

State Enable	Function	Disable Arguments
GL_POLYGON_OFFSET_POINT	glPolygonOffset	factor = 0.0
GL_POLYGON_OFFSET_LINE		units = 0.0
GL_POLYGON_OFFSET_FILL		
GL_SCISSOR_TEST	glScissor	x = 0
		y = 0
		width = *window width*
		height = *window height*
GL_ALPHA_TEST	glAlphaFunc	func = GL_ALWAYS
GL_DEPTH_TEST	glDepthFunc	func = GL_ALWAYS
GL_STENCIL_TEST	glStencilOp	zfail = GL_KEEP
		zpass = GL_KEEP
	glStencilFunc	func = GL_ALWAYS
GL_COLOR_LOGIC_OP	glLogicOp	opcode = GL_COPY
GL_INDEX_LOGIC_OP		
GL_BLEND		sfactor = GL_ONE
		dfactor = GL_ZERO

A simple example that illustrates what must be considered when constructing multipass techniques is an implementation of separate specular color functionality. The separate specular color is part of core OpenGL 1.2; it is described in Section 3.3.4.

The multipass implementation of this lighting mode requires two passes. In the first pass, primitives are rendered with vertex lighting enabled, but with the material's specular reflectance set to zero. Zeroing the material specular component ensures that the color from this pass doesn't include a specular contribution. In the second pass, the primitives are re-rendered, this time with the ambient, diffuse, and emissive reflectances set to zero, and the specular reflectance set to the desired value. The result is two separate renderings of the primitive; one with primary (diffuse), one with secondary (specular) colors.

In the specification of separate specular color, OpenGL computes the secondary color separately, then adds it to the the fragment color after texturing. Since the secondary color isn't modified by texturing, our multipass algorithm can duplicate this algorithm by disabling texturing during the second rendering pass. Adding together the primary and secondary light contributions can be done with blending. Blending is enabled during the second pass, with both the source and destination blend factors set to GL_ONE.

This blending equation causes the fragment colors from the two computations to be added together in the framebuffer. When blending two separate renderings of an object, there are several details that must be considered. If depth testing is enabled for both passes, the default depth function, GL_LESS, discards all of the fragments from the second pass before blending. Changing the depth function to GL_EQUAL results in better behavior, since fragments from the second pass with depth values equal to the visible fragments of the first pass now pass the depth test and are blended.

For most situations this method is sufficient. If the rendered geometry is not well behaved, however, multiple fragments might be rasterized to the same depth value as the visible pixel. This effect would be invisible when blending isn't enabled, but in this case the extra fragments will be included in the blending computation, generating undesirable artifacts. One way around this problem is to render each image separately without blending, trim to the geometry of interest (with stencil, for example), then blend the color images in a separate step. In general, the complexity of the merge step can vary, depending on details of the scene, the image quality required, and how the application will use the modified buffers after the algorithm is finished.

To illustrate these trade-offs, consider the separate specular color example in more detail. Care should be taken if the alpha component of the lighted polygon will be used later by the application (for example, if the lighted geometry is being alpha tested or a framebuffer containing alpha components is used to store the alpha components of the pixels for use later on). There are some subtleties here; regular vertex lighting (and therefore OpenGL's separate specular color method) uses the alpha from the diffuse material as the final alpha component of the lighted primitive; the alpha components of the ambient, emissive, and specular reflectance are not used.

If the algorithm must compute the final alpha components correctly, we should consider how these alpha values may be used. The requirement may be that only the final alpha values stored in the framebuffer image must be correct. This could be done by rendering the first, diffuse pass of the algorithm with the diffuse alpha components, and using alpha values of zero for the second, specular pass. However, this approach doesn't work if the application is using alpha testing while the specular primitives are being rendered. The specular components won't have the correct alpha components, and the specular highlights may be masked incorrectly by the alpha test.

To get both the correct final alpha values and the correct alpha test behavior, we need to render both passes using the diffuse alpha components. If this is all we did, we would get incorrect alpha values in the framebuffer; the blend equation we're using would add together the diffuse alpha values from both passes, doubling them. This can be fixed by discarding the alpha component of the second blending pass with the glColorMask(1,1,1,0). The first pass uses the diffuse alphas, producing proper alpha test results, and updating the framebuffer with the proper alpha values. The second pass would also be using the right alpha values, so the alpha test results for the specular part of the image would be correct. The alpha results from this pass would be doubled by the blend, but then discarded by the color mask, leaving the proper alpha components in the framebuffer.

So far, we have focused on creating the proper image in the color buffer. The color buffer is a common target for multipass techniques, but not the only one. In some cases the desired result of a rendering pass is not an updated color buffer, but changes in one or more of the ancillary buffers: depth, stencil, or accumulation. These buffers may be updated directly, or as a side effect of one or more multipass operations. For example, updating the depth or stencil buffer is usually done as a side effect of rendering geometry. Getting the final values of these buffers right (if they will be needed later) is part of the algorithm design process.

9.3 The Multipass Toolbox

As the previous example illustrates, designing a good multipass algorithm requires attention to detail. But there is a more general framework that can be used to guide multipass algorithm design. Here we provide a "toolbox" of building blocks within a programming paradigm that is applicable to a wide range of algorithms.

A rendering algorithm or technique can be thought of as a specialized type of computer algorithm. They can be expressed as a programming language, containing data manipulation operations such as variable assignment, arithmetic and logic operations, and control flow constructs such as loops and conditionals. The operations available in the OpenGL pipeline itself can be mapped into constructs found in programming languages. This language can then be used to express rendering algorithms. From this more general view of OpenGL, it becomes an easier task to map a rendering algorithm into a sequence of OpenGL pipeline operations.

9.3.1 Arithmetic Operations

At every stage of the OpenGL pipeline some form of computation is performed. A few of these stages can be controlled enough by applications so that general arithmetic operations can be performed. In the two-pass specular lighting example, the arithmetic operations available through blending were used. Using OpenGL 1.3 as a reference, the blending functions provide operators for multiplication, addition, subtraction, minimum, and maximum. The constant blending function in the ARB imaging subset provides efficient operators for adding, subtracting, and multiplying by a constant. The logic op function supplies bit-wise logical operations.

There are two difficulties with color buffer blending; the values are restricted to the [0,1] range and the color precision available for each color component may be limited. The use of scaled and biased arithmetic to work around the range limitation is described in Section 3.4.1. The accumulation buffer also allows some arithmetic operations to be performed with increased range and precision. The accumulation buffer doesn't support multiplication of a pixel color by another pixel color, but it does support multiplication by a constant. A disadvantage of the accumulation buffer is that it is not hardware accelerated on some commodity hardware. Ultimately, this problem is solved on new implementations that support floating-point operations and programmable pipeline processing, but for implementations without such support the problem is still cumbersome.

As OpenGL and hardware accelerators have evolved, the texture environment stage has become increasingly sophisticated. With the advent of multitexture's new texture environment functions, many of the operators available for color buffer blending are also available in texture environment functionality. OpenGL 1.3 provides important new texture environment functionality: the texture environment function GL_COMBINE is a generalization of texture environment functions, such as GL_MODULATE or GL_ADD.

The GL_COMBINE function supplies an orthogonal set of operations and sources for texture functions. Sources, operators, and texgen functions can be selected separately to provide a more orthogonal mix of possible texgen operations. RGB and alpha color sources, operations, and texgen functions can be selected separately. Functionality in the texgen stage of the OpenGL pipeline is important because of multitexturing. If the implementation supports multitexturing, chains of arithmetic operations can be performed in a single pass, which can produce higher quality images and significant performance gains. The implications of multitexturing are described in more detail in Section 9.5.1, later in this chapter.

The GL_DOT3_RGB and GL_DOT3_RGBA texture environment functions go beyond blending functionality by introducing dot product operations to the list of combine operations. Two types of dot products can be generated from a pair of color values; one operates on RGB, the other on RGBA. As with the other GL_COMBINE functions, the alpha value can be processed separately. See Section 5.10.1 for more details on texenv functionality.

If the OpenGL implementation supports the ARB imaging subset, some additional powerful operators become available to the application. The color matrix function can be used to perform affine operations on the components of a pixel, including *swizzling* components from one channel to another. For example, the following matrix swaps the R and G channels in an image:

$$\begin{pmatrix} 0 & 1 & 0 & 0 \\ 1 & 0 & 0 & 0 \\ 0 & 0 & 1 & 0 \\ 0 & 0 & 0 & 1 \end{pmatrix} \begin{pmatrix} R \\ G \\ B \\ A \end{pmatrix}$$

Note that this functionality is only available when loading or reading images or texture maps. The highest performance path that provides pixel operations is usually glCopyTexImage2D and glCopyPixels, since they don't read or write pixels to system memory.

9.3.2 Arbitrary Functions

Notably missing from the standard arithmetic operators is division. Division can be emulated to some degree by multiplying by the reciprocal of the divisor. One advantage of using reciprocals is that the reciprocal often fits within the [0,1] range constraint for color and texture components. Going beyond division, it is also often desirable to apply other functions such as sine, cosine, and so on.

One way to efficiently approximate arbitrary functions is to implement them as lookup tables. OpenGL provides several types of lookup tables: pixel maps, color tables, and texture maps. Pixel maps and color tables provide a way to map an input color value to an output color value; in other words, evaluate $y = f(x)$, where the domain and the range of f are constrained to [0,1].

Texture maps can be treated in a similar way, except that 1-, 2-, and 3-input functions can be implemented using 1-, 2-, and 3-D texture maps. The difficulty comes in providing a more flexible way to provide input values: we would like to provide greater control over the texture coordinate values used to index the texture maps. Texture coordinates can be supplied as vertex parameters, generated automatically, and transformed using the texture matrix. This makes it possible to use simple functions of the object or eye space x, y, or z values, but makes it difficult to use the results of arithmetic operations on individual pixels as the input to these functions.

The `SGIS_pixel_texture` extension solves this problem by providing a means to interpret color values in pixel images as texture coordinates. Using `SGIS_pixel_texture`, the first pass of an algorithm can generate an image I, and then the resulting image can be copied over itself using `glCopyPixels` with texturing enabled to compute $f(I)$. The `ARB_fragment_program` extension also provides this functionality, sometimes called *dependent texturing*, as part of a programmable texturing interface. See Section 5.10.2 for more details on programmable texturing.

Using texel values to index into other textures doesn't have to be enormously expensive. If pixel colors are stored in the color buffer using 8-bit components, then the texture memory requirements are modest for 1D and 2D functions, needing only 256×1 and 256×256 texture maps.

9.3.3 Conditionals

The OpenGL pipeline performs conditional or selection operations at a number of stages in the pipeline. One or more of these stages can be used together to implement simple conditional operations in a multipass algorithm. Examples include the depth and alpha tests. Alpha test performs per-fragment comparisons against a reference value and rejects the fragments that fail the test. Even though the test only examines the alpha value, it can be made more general by using other OpenGL operators to map RGBA colors that need testing to specific alpha values. For example, to reject pixels that have 0 for both the R and G components, use the color matrix to put the sum of $R + G$ in the A component and reject pixels with $A = 0$.

Using the stencil and depth buffer together provides powerful conditional logic. Simple arithmetic and logical operations such as counting and exclusive-or, can be performed in the stencil buffer and the result used to selectively update the color buffer.

Additional blending functions such min/max and constant factors are also useful accelerators for conditional logic. Logic operations (expanded to include RGBA support in OpenGL 1.1) provide a large set of bitwise boolean operators, including AND, OR, XOR, COPY, SET, and inverted versions of these operations.

Conditional tests in earlier stages of the pipeline may prove useful as well. Culling and clipping operations use the value of vertices to reject all or part of a primitive. With appropriate transformation matrices, these tests can be used to reject primitives subject to more complex conditions than 'inside' or 'outside' the viewing frustum. For example, the diffuse and specular terms of the lighting equation are clamped to zero if the surface normal points away from the light source. The resulting color can be used as a flag that can be tested in later parts of the pipeline.

These examples may seem odd or even absurd; after all, OpenGL isn't a general purpose programming language. But our intent isn't to promote obfuscated or general purpose programming with OpenGL. Instead the goal is to consider various parts of the pipeline and think of them as building blocks for multipass algorithms. We are using OpenGL functionality in a more general way, being true to the spirit of OpenGL as a graphics assembly language. We don't have to limit the use of a pipeline feature to the specific intent or algorithms the OpenGL designers may have had in mind.

9.3.4 Variables

Early on in the evolution of OpenGL, it became clear that it was useful to have additional color buffers to temporarily hold parts of an image or scene. When constructing multipass algorithms, these temporary buffers play a role analogous to temporary variables in regular programming languages, since they both hold intermediate results. To store a result, the application could copy the contents of the color buffer to system memory until it is needed again. But the performance of an algorithm using this approach would suffer. It is usually much faster if the temporary results are stored in buffers managed by the graphics accelerator. For applications that can tolerate some visual distractions, both the front and back buffers of a double-buffered window can be used. Double-buffered stereo windows (also called quad-buffered) provide 4 buffers, but at the time of this writing, implementations that accelerate double-buffered stereo windows are not common. OpenGL defines additional color buffers called auxiliary or aux buffers, but again very few accelerators support these. One difficulty with quad buffers and aux buffers is that they are constrained to be the same dimensions as the window, whereas the application may need either a smaller or larger buffer.

One straightforward solution to the problem is to use texture memory for temporary buffers. The `glCopyTexImage2D` command added in OpenGL 1.1 provides an efficient mechanism to copy the results of a computation to texture memory. The temporary value can be "read" by drawing a textured quadrilateral with texture coordinates spanning the texture, using the `GL_REPLACE` texture environment.

Though using textures as variable storage is a good general solution, there is another more attractive location — off-screen memory. Even though off-screen memory (we will use the term *drawables*) may share the same location as texture memory in some accelerator implementations, there are still compelling reasons to expose it as a window-like resource: drawables can have ancillary buffers such as depth and stencil, their dimensions are not constrained to be a power of two, and they can be shared between multiple applications more easily than textures.[1] In GLX and WGL OpenGL specifications, these off-screen drawables are called pixel buffers, or *pbuffers* for short. They are similar to aux buffers, in that they are off-screen memory, but unlike aux buffers, their access is accelerated by the graphics hardware. For more information on pbuffers see Section 7.4.1.

9.3.5 Parameters

We can further augment the multipass paradigm by adding the notion of parameters. Just as the parameters of a function call supply input to the body of the function, multipass parameters supply data that a multipass algorithm uses as input. The most obvious source of input data is the geometry's vertex data and texture images supplied to the pixel pipeline. Vertex position, normal direction, and color can all be used to supply data to the pipeline executing a multipass algorithm. A problem may arise however: sometimes an important input parameter, such as the normal vector for surface orientation, is discarded early in the OpenGL pipeline but is needed by the algorithm in a later pipeline stage. The general solution to this problem is simple; an input parameter can always be computed in the application and sent down as a color or texture coordinate in order to reach later pipeline stages.

However, this solution may lead to large amounts of computation being performed on the host, or result in expensive pixel reads and writes to host memory. A better solution is to use OpenGL to map the desired parameters into texture coordinates. OpenGL supports a number of ways to convert vertex positions and normals into texture coordinates. Useful conversions include object or eye-space coordinates mapped to texture coordinates or fragment colors; object- or eye-space normals mapped to texture coordinates; eye reflection vector, light position, or light reflection vector, etc. mapped to texture coordinates. Details on performing these conversions to make parameters available to later pipeline stages are described below.

Vertex Coordinates Object coordinates enter the pipeline optionally with colors, texture coordinates, and normals. Vertex coordinates may be mapped to texture coordinates using texture-coordinate generation. Both object-space and eye-space coordinates are available; it can be useful to use the latter to take advantage of the transforms available with the modelview matrix. To avoid clamping, coordinates need to be scaled and biased into the standard [0,1] texture coordinate range by either folding the scaling operation into the texture-generation equations, or by

---

1. No OpenGL implementation known to the authors allows textures to be shared between independent processes, though GLX and WGL both allow textures to be shared between threads in the same process.

using the texture transform matrix. The texture matrix may also be used to project the generated texture coordinates into two dimensions.

Mapping vertex coordinates to texture coordinates is a good way to generate distance parameters. Such parameters include distance from the viewer, distance from a light source, distances between objects, and so forth.

Vertex Normals Vertex normal vectors are discarded too early in the pipeline to be useful in many algorithms. Normals can be converted into texture coordinates within the application by issuing them directly as texture coordinates or as vertex coordinates transformed by a texgen function. Normals issued as vertex coordinates will be transformed by the modelview matrix directly, rather than the adjoint transpose of the modelview as a normal vector would be (see Section 2.3 for details).

The texture transform matrix can be used to apply a corrective transformation to normal vectors processed as vertex, then texture values. A texture coordinate standing in for a normal will have its components linearly interpolated during rasterization. This isn't the correct way to interpolate normals, but the discrepancy may be acceptable if the surface triangles are small. Another approach is to apply a mapping function using a texture map operation to create a more accurate interpolation.

OpenGL 1.3 includes a more direct solution, the texture coordinate generation function `GL_NORMAL_MAP`. This function uses the eye-coordinate normal vectors as the texture coordinates. Again scaling and biasing using the texture matrix are necessary to compress the range to $[0, 1]$. If the values should be in the range $[-1, 1]$, indexing a cube map with the generated texture coordinates may be a better solution. It will use all three texture coordinates to choose a cube map face and location within that face. It is a good solution if the length of the normal is not important.

Eye Reflection Vector If the eye-space reflection vector is needed, sphere map texture generation can be used to capture it as a set of texture coordinates. The sphere map texture generation computes an eye-space reflection vector and projects it to a set of 2D texture coordinates.

Again, after noting the usefulness of the reflection vector, OpenGL 1.3 also provides a more direct solution via the `GL_REFLECTION_MAP` texture coordinate generation function. As with normals, indexing with a cube map makes it possible to use all three direction components.

Light Position Light position or direction information is frequently used in illumination model computations (see Section 3.3). To perform similar types of computations, using a light position in other parts of the vertex processing or fragment processing pipeline may be necessary. For example, $\mathbf{N} \cdot \mathbf{L}$ may be computed as part of texture-coordinate processing in the geometry pipeline. This can be accomplished by copying the vertex normals into texture coordinates, and storing the light direction in the first row of the texture matrix, such that

$$
\begin{pmatrix} s \\ t \\ r \\ q \end{pmatrix}' = \begin{pmatrix} L_x & L_y & L_z & 0 \\ 0 & 0 & 0 & 0 \\ 0 & 0 & 0 & 0 \\ 0 & 0 & 0 & 0 \end{pmatrix} \begin{pmatrix} s \\ t \\ r \\ q \end{pmatrix}
$$

the resulting transform will compute the dot product of $\mathbf{N}$ and $\mathbf{L}$ and store the result in s'. Similarly, the light vector may be used in color computations. This can be done, for example, using the dot product texture environment function.

9.4 Multipass Limitations

Using multiple passes to implement rendering algorithms provides a very general way to enhance the set of operations in the OpenGL pipeline. This process does incur performance overhead; each pass requires re-issuing and re-rasterizing the object geometry. If interactivity is an objective, then the amount of time available for rendering a frame at the desired refresh rate places an upper bound on the number of passes that can be used.

Beyond the time limitation, there are also precision restrictions. The limited precision present in the color processing path of most hardware accelerators, particularly fixed-function pipeline implementations, doesn't allow a large number of passes without introducing a substantial amount of error in the resulting image. The number of passes that can be practically added to an interactive application typically will be less than ten, limiting the opportunities for the application designer trying to minimize frame rendering time.

Even without time and precision issues, it may be difficult to get exactly the set of input parameters or derived parameters into the pipeline needed for further computation. To work around this, the application may have to do additional processing on the host computer, again limiting the speed of the algorithm. The evolution of the pipeline through vertex and fragment programmability has improved the situation greatly, but OpenGL needs to continue to evolve to make more operations and input parameters available to the application.

9.5 Multipass vs. Micropass

One way to think about the multipass approach is to contrast it with an (perhaps hypothetical) OpenGL implementation that allows the entire algorithm to be expressed in a single pass. Each step must be expressible as a set of operations in the OpenGL pipeline that occur in the correct sequence relative to the other steps. For example, the built-in secondary color support in OpenGL 1.2 makes it possible to add a specular contribution to the texture computation without requiring a separate pass. When multiple computational steps are performed within a single rendering pass, we refer to them as *micropasses*.

As OpenGL evolves, computational steps in popular multipass algorithms will inevitably make their way into the OpenGL pipeline. This is one way to evolve the pipeline in an incremental fashion. For example, rather than add all of the hardware necessary to compute the entire Blinn lighting model per fragment, a more incremental step might be to support part of the computation or to add functional blocks that can be used to achieve the same result. For the case of fragment lighting, the secondary color support is the first step to performing the entire lighting computation at each pixel.

Multitexture can be thought of as a similar incremental step: one texture map may include the diffuse contribution and a second texture map may include the specular contribution. Using texture maps as table lookup functions allows the application to approximate simple illumination computations. Incremental improvements to the texture environments such as texture combine and texture dot product environment modes are examples of small functional blocks that have been added to the fragment processing pipeline and allow some parts of multipass algorithms to be converted to micropasses. As we describe various multipass algorithms in later sections, we will point out steps that can be converted to micropasses.

The clearest direction that OpenGL appears to be evolving is programmability. Both vertex program and fragment program extensions have been accepted by the ARB, and have been implemented in hardware by major graphics hardware vendors. These extensions make parts of the the pipeline controlled by a programming language loaded by the application. Programmability is expected to permeate more stages in the OpenGL pipeline going forward, and these extensions will undoubtedly become an important part of core OpenGL. See Section 2.9 and Section 5.10.2 for more details.

9.5.1 Multitexture

As mentioned previously, multitexture adds a form of programmable micropass support to OpenGL. Multitexture provides the application with the ability to choose a sequence of operations from a set of fixed choices, and chain them together. Texture maps are used to pass in additional input data at each stage. The number of sequences in the chain is limited to the number of texture units supported in the implementation. The simple cascade of multitexture texture environments supports a fixed order of operations starting with the fragment color and modifying it with a texture in each stage, $C_{final} = (((C_f \text{ op}_0 C_{t0}) \text{ op}_1 C_{t1}) \ldots \text{op}_n C_{tn})$. The GL_COMBINE environment function, along with its crossbar extension, provides greater flexibility in controlling the inputs for each texture environment stage and includes most of the arithmetic operations of framebuffer blending, plus several additional capabilities, such as dot product.

Note that a multitexture sequence can be more efficient than the equivalent multipass one. A multitexture sequence only executes the post-texturing part of the OpenGL pipeline once per sequence, reducing overhead. The hardware implementation may further optimize the stages in a multitexture operation. It may parallelize texture operations, for example, or cache the intermediate results between texture stages.

9.6 Deferred Shading

A general technique related to the idea of multipass processing, is *deferred shading*. In its basic form, the idea behind deferred shading is to avoid performing expensive shading computations until the visible pixels have been determined. One way to achieve this is to render all of the geometry and store the attributes required to compute the shading values at each pixel in the framebuffer with the pixel. After all of the geometry is rendered, a second pass is done over the framebuffer pixels, computing the shading for each pixel based on the saved attribute values.

There are several difficulties with this approach. The first is determining where to store the attribute values. A small number of values can be stored in the color buffer and later retrieved using a texture mapping operation. However, even with fragment programs and complex packing of values into the color buffer it is difficult to store many attributes. A second problem is aliasing of attribute values. Techniques such as multisampling and area sampling (see Chapter 10) can be employed to solve some of the aliasing problems during rendering, but these techniques operate on the final color and depth values and are not suitable for merging multiple attribute values together. Super-sampling can be used at some additional cost to store the high-resolution attribute samples.

An alternate two-pass approach is to draw the entire scene twice, relying on early-Z processing (see Section 8.5) to eliminate extra work. In the first pass the geometry is drawn without any shading computations with the objective of resolving the final depth values for the scene. In the second pass the scene is drawn again, using the GL_EQUAL depth comparison function and the shading computations enabled. The second pass relies on early-Z processing to discard non-visible fragments before fragment shading computations are performed. This version can be very effective when complex fragment programs are used in the programmable pipeline. It has the advantage of not requiring extra storage at the cost of extra vertex processing and needing early-Z processing support in the OpenGL implementation. Deferred techniques such as these and the compositing-based techniques described in Chapter 11 are likely to see increased use in the future.

9.7 Summary

This chapter has provided some useful insights in thinking about OpenGL as a programming language for implementing graphics algorithms. We have focused on general approaches; it can be thought of as the theory supporting the practices demonstrated elsewhere in this book.

Antialiasing

Aliasing refers to the jagged edges and other rendering artifacts commonly associated with computer-generated images. They are caused by simplifications incorporated in various algorithms in the rendering pipeline, resulting in inaccuracies in the generated image. Usually these simplifications are necessary to create a pipeline implementation that is low in cost and capable of achieving good interactive frame rates. In this chapter we will review some of the causes of aliasing artifacts and describe some of the techniques that can be used to reduce or eliminate them.

Chapter 4 provides some of the background information regarding how images are represented digitally; the ideas behind sampling and reconstructing the spatial signals comprising an image; and some of the problems that can arise. The *spatial aliasing* problem appears when the sample rate of the digital image is insufficient to represent all of the high-frequency detail in the original image signal. In computer-generated or *synthetic* images the problem is acute because the algebraic representation of primitives can define arbitrarily high frequencies as part of an object description. One place where these occur is at the edges of objects. Here the abrupt change in the signal that occurs when crossing the edge of an object corresponds to infinitely high-frequency components. When a simple point-sampling rasterization process tries to represent these arbitrarily high frequencies, the result is aliasing artifacts.

Object edges aren't the only place spatial aliasing artifacts appear. Aliasing artifacts are also introduced when a texture image is projected to an area that is much smaller than the original texture map. Mipmapping reduces the amount of aliasing by first creating multiple, alias-free texture images of progressively smaller sizes as a pre-processing step. During texture mapping, the projected area is used to determine the two closest texture image sizes that bracket the exact size. A new image is then created by taking a weighted sum of texels from the two images. This minimizes the more visually jarring artifacts that can appear on moving objects that are textured without using mipmapping. This aliasing problem is severe enough that mipmapping support is both defined and well-implemented in most OpenGL implementations. Antialiasing for the edges of lines, points, and polygons is also defined, but is traditionally less well supported by implementations. In particular, polygon edge antialiasing using `GL_POLYGON_SMOOTH` is often poorly implemented.

The simple solution to the aliasing problem is to not introduce frequency aliases during rasterization—or at least minimize them. This requires either increasing the spatial sampling rate to correctly represent the original signals, or removing the frequency components that would otherwise alias before sampling (prefiltering). Increasing the sampling rate, storing the resulting image, and reconstructing that image for display greatly increases the cost of the system. The infinitely high-frequency contributions from edge discontinuities would also imply a need for arbitrarily high sampling rates. Fortunately, the *magnitude* of the contribution typically decreases rapidly with increasing frequency, and these lower-magnitude, high-frequency contributions can be made much less noticeable. As a result, most of the benefit of increasing the sampling rate can be attained by increasing it by a finite amount. Despite this upper limit, it is still not very practical to double or quadruple the size of the framebuffer and enhance the display circuitry to accommodate the higher sampling rate; increasing the sampling rate alone isn't the solution.

A second solution is to eliminate the high-frequency signal contributions before the pixel samples are created. The distortions to the image resulting from eliminating the high-frequency components, *blurring*, are much less objectionable compared to the distortions from aliasing. The process of eliminating the high-frequency components is referred to as *band-limiting*; the resulting image contains a more limited number of frequency bands. The filtering required to accomplish the band-limiting requires more computations to be performed during rasterization; depending on the specifics of the algorithm, it can be a practical addition to the rendering implementation.

10.1 Full-Scene Antialiasing

Ideally, after rendering a scene, the image should be free of aliasing artifacts. As previously described, the best way to achieve this is by eliminating as much of the aliased high-frequency information as possible while generating the pixel samples to be stored in the color buffer. First we will describe some general techniques that work on any type of primitive. Then we will describe methods that take advantage of the characteristics of polygons, lines, and points that allow them to be antialiased more effectively. Primitive-independent methods may be applied to an entire scene. Primitive-dependent methods require grouping the rendering tasks by primitive type, or choosing and configuring the appropriate antialiasing method before each primitive is drawn.

10.2 Supersampling

One popular class of antialiasing techniques samples the image at a much higher sampling rate than the color buffer resolution (for example, by a factor of 4 or 8), then *postfilters* these extra samples to produce the final set of pixel values. Only the postfiltered values are saved in the framebuffer; the high-resolution samples are discarded after they are filtered. This type of antialiasing method is called *supersampling* and the high-resolution pixels are called *supersamples*.[1]

The net effect of supersampling is to eliminate some of the high-frequency detail that would otherwise alias to low-frequency artifacts in the sample values. The process does not eliminate all of the aliasing, since the supersamples themselves contain aliased information from frequencies above the higher resolution sample rate. The aliasing artifacts from these higher frequencies are usually less noticeable, since the magnitude of the high-frequency detail does diminish rapidly as the frequency increases. There is a limit to the amount of useful supersampling. In practice, the most significant improvement comes with 4 to 16 samples; beyond that the improvements diminish rapidly.

When designing a supersampling method, the first decision to make is selecting the number of samples. After that there are two other significant choices to make: the choice of supersample locations, which we will call the *sample pattern*, and the method for filtering the supersamples.

The natural choice for supersample locations is a regular grid of sample points, with a spacing equal to the new sample rate. In practice, this produces poor results, particularly when using a small number of supersamples. The reason for this is that remaining aliasing artifacts from a regularly spaced sample grid tend to occur in regular patterns. These patterns are more noticable to the eye than errors with random spacings.

A remedy for this problem is to choose a more random sample pattern. This changes the high-frequency aliasing to less noticeable uncorrelated noise in the image. Methods for producing random sample patterns as described by Cook (1986) are part of a technique called *stochastic supersampling*. Perhaps the most useful is *jittered* sample patterns. They are constructed by displacing (jittering) the points on a regular super-grid with small, random displacements.

A point sample reflects the value of a single point, rather than being representative of all of the features in the pixel. Consider the case of a narrow, tall, vertical rectangle, $\frac{1}{8}$ of a pixel wide, moving horizontally from left to right across the window in 1/8th pixel steps. Using the top left sample pattern (*a*) shown in Figure 10.1 and the normal point sampling rules, the rectangle will alternately be sampled by the left-most two sample points, by no sample points, and then by the right-most sample points. If the same exercise is repeated using the top right sample pattern (*c*), at least some contribution from the rectangle will be detected more often than with sample pattern (*a*), since the sample points include 4

---

1. The term *subsamples* is also frequently used.

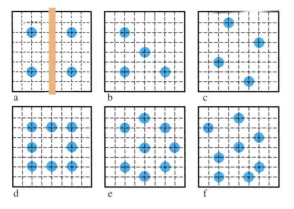

Figure 10.1 Sample patterns for 4 and 8 subsamples.

distinct x positions rather than just 2. Although this example is engineered for a vertical rectangle, it demonstrates some basic ideas for choosing better sample patterns:

- Use a subpixel grid that is at least 4 times the sample rate in each direction.

- Choose sample points that have unique x and y coordinates.

- Include one sample point close to the center of the pixel.

A further consideration that arises when choosing sample locations is whether to use sample points beyond a pixel's extent and into neighboring pixels. The idea of a pixel as rectangle with rigid boundaries is no more than a useful conceptual tool; there is nothing that forbids sampling outside of this region. The answer lies in the sampling and reconstruction process. Since the final pixel value results from reconstructing the signal from its supersamples, the choice of sample locations and reconstruction (postfilter) functions are intertwined. Although the results vary depending on the sample locations and filter function used, the short answer is that using overlapping supersampled regions can result in a better image.

As described in Section 4.2, a number of different low-pass filters are available to choose from to eliminate the high-frequency details. These can range from simple box or triangle filters to more computationally intensive Gaussian or other filters.

10.2.1 Supersampling by Overdrawing

A simple way to implement supersampling is to render a scene in a larger window, then postfilter the result. Although simple to implement, there are a few difficulties with this solution. One issue is that the maximum window size will limit the number of samples per-pixel, especially if the objective is to produce a large final image. The sample locations themselves use the framebuffer pixel locations, which are on a regular grid, resulting in regular patterns of aliasing artifacts.

A second problem is finding an efficient method for implementing the reconstruction filter. A simple solution is to implement the filter within the application code, but it is generally faster to use texture mapping with blending or accumulation buffer hardware as described in Section 6.3.1. Despite these limitations, the algorithm can be used effectively in many applications, particularly those where rendering time is not an issue. Some hardware accelerator vendors include this capability as an antialiasing feature that doesn't require any changes to an existing application. Once the feature is built into the OpenGL implementation, it is often possible to support an irregular sampling pattern, further improving the antialiasing effectiveness.

10.2.2 Supersampling with the Accumulation Buffer

An approach that offers better results than overdrawing uses the accumulation buffer. It can be used very effectively to implement multipass supersampling. In each pass one supersample from the sample pattern is computed for each pixel in the scene, followed by one step of an incremental postfiltering algorithm using the accumulation buffer.

The supersamples are really just the normal pixel point samples taken at specific subpixel sample locations. The subpixel sample is generated by modifying the projection matrix with a translation corresponding to the difference between the original pixel center and the desired subpixel position. Ideally the application modifies the window coordinates by subpixel offsets directly; the most effective way to achieve this is by modifying the projection matrix. Care must be taken to compute translations to shift the scene by the appropriate amount in window coordinate space.

If a translation is multiplied onto the projection matrix stack after the projection matrix has been loaded, then the displacements need to be converted to eye coordinates. To convert a displacement in pixels to eye coordinates, multiply the displacement amount by the dimension of the eye coordinate scene, and divide by the appropriate viewport dimension:

$$dx_{eye} = \frac{right - left}{width} \, dx_{window}$$

$$dy_{eye} = \frac{top - bottom}{height} \, dy_{window}$$

Eye coordinate displacements are incorporated into orthographic projections using glOrtho, and into perspective projections using glFrustum:

```
glOrtho(left - dx, right - dx,
        top - dy, bottom - dy, near, far);
glFrustum(left - dx, right - dx,
        top - dy, bottom - dy, near, far);
```

Example subpixel jitter values, organized by the number of samples needed, are taken from the *OpenGL Programming Guide*, and are shown in Table 10.1. (Note that

Table 10.1 Subpixel Displacement Values

Count	Values
2	{0.25, 0.75}, {0.75, 0.25}
3	{0.5033922635, 0.8317967229}, {0.7806016275, 0.2504380877}, {0.2261828938, 0.4131553612}
4	{0.375, 0.25}, {0.125, 0.75}, {0.875, 0.25}, {0.625, 0.75}
5	{0.5, 0.5}, {0.3, 0.1}, {0.7, 0.9}, {0.9, 0.3}, {0.1, 0.7}
6	{0.4646464646, 0.4646464646}, {0.1313131313, 0.7979797979}, {0.5353535353, 0.8686868686}, {0.8686868686, 0.5353535353}, {0.7979797979, 0.1313131313}, {0.2020202020, 0.2020202020}
8	{0.5625, 0.4375}, {0.0625, 0.9375}, {0.3125, 0.6875}, {0.6875, 0.8125}, {0.8125, 0.1875}, {0.9375, 0.5625}, {0.4375, 0.0625}, {0.1875, 0.3125}
9	{0.5, 0.5}, {0.1666666666, 0.9444444444}, {0.5, 0.1666666666}, {0.5, 0.8333333333}, {0.1666666666, 0.2777777777}, {0.8333333333, 0.3888888888}, {0.1666666666, 0.6111111111}, {0.8333333333, 0.7222222222}, {0.8333333333, 0.0555555555}
12	{0.4166666666, 0.625}, {0.9166666666, 0.875}, {0.25, 0.375}, {0.4166666666, 0.125}, {0.75, 0.125}, {0.0833333333, 0.125}, {0.75, 0.625}, {0.25, 0.875}, {0.5833333333, 0.375}, {0.9166666666, 0.375}, {0.0833333333, 0.625}, {0.583333333, 0.875}
16	{0.375, 0.4375}, {0.625, 0.0625}, {0.875, 0.1875}, {0.125, 0.0625}, {0.375, 0.6875}, {0.875, 0.4375}, {0.625, 0.5625}, {0.375, 0.9375}, {0.625, 0.3125}, {0.125, 0.5625}, {0.125, 0.8125}, {0.375, 0.1875}, {0.875, 0.9375}, {0.875, 0.6875}, {0.125, 0.3125}, {0.625, 0.8125}

some of these patterns are a little more regular horizontally and vertically than is optimal.)

The reconstruction filter is defined by the sample locations and the scale factor used in each accumulation operation. A box filter is implemented by accumulating each image with a scale factor equal to $1/n$, where n is the number of supersample passes. More sophisticated filters are implemented by using different weights for each sample location.

Using the accumulation buffer, it is easy to make trade-offs between quality and speed. For higher quality images, simply increase the number of scenes that are accumulated. Although it is simple to antialias the scene using the accumulation buffer, it is much more computationally intensive and probably slower than the more specific antialiasing algorithms that are described next.

10.2.3 Multisample Antialiasing

Multisampling is a form of single-pass supersampling that is directly supported in OpenGL.[2] When using hardware with this support, multisampling produces high-quality results with less performance overhead, and requires minimal changes to an existing application. It was originally available as an OpenGL extension and later added to the core specification in version 1.3. The multisampling specification largely defines a set of rules for adding supersampling to the rendering pipeline. The number of samples can vary from implementation to implementation, but typically ranges between 2 and 8.

Each pixel fragment is extended to include a fixed number of additional texture coordinates and color, depth, and stencil values. These sample values are stored in an extra buffer called the *multisample buffer*. The regular color buffer continues to exist and contains the *resolved* color — the postfiltered result. There are no equivalent resolved depth and stencil buffers however; all depth and stencil values are part of the multisample buffer. It is less useful to compute postfiltered depth or stencil results since they are typically used for resolving visible surfaces, whereas the resolved color is used for display. Some implementations may defer computation of the resolved color values until the multisample buffer is read for display or the color buffer is used as a source in another OpenGL operation, for example, `glReadPixels`. For the most part, multisampling doesn't change the operation of the rendering pipeline, except that each pipeline step operates on each sample in the fragment individually.

A multisample fragment also differs from a non-multisample fragment because it contains a bitmask value termed *coverage*. Each bit in the mask corresponds to a sample location. The value of the bit indicates whether the primitive fragment intersects (covers) that sample point. One way to think of the coverage value is as a mask indicating which samples in the fragment correspond to part of the primitive and which do not. Those that are not part of the primitive can be ignored in most of the pipeline processing. There are many ways to make a multisample implementation more efficient. For example, the same color value or texture coordinate may be used for all samples within a fragment. The multisample buffer may store its contents with some form of compression to reduce space requirements. For example, the multisample buffer contents may be encoded so as to exploit coherence between samples within a pixel.

---

2. Introduced in OpenGL 1.3.

The OpenGL specification does not define the sample locations and they are not queriable by the application. The sample points may extend outside a pixel and the locations may vary from pixel to pixel. This latter allowance makes it possible to implement some form of stochastic sampling, but it also breaks the invariance rules, since the values computed for a fragment are dependent on the pixel location.

As described in Section 6.1, implementations often use the same color and texture coordinate values at all sample locations. This affords a substantial performance improvement over true supersampling since color and texture coordinate values are evaluated once per-pixel and the amount of data associated with a fragment is greatly reduced. However, distinct depth and stencil values are maintained for each sample location to ensure that the edges of interpenetrating primitives are resolved correctly. A disadvantage of this optimization is that interior portions of primitives may still show aliasing artifacts. This problem becomes more apparent with the use of complex per-fragment shading computations in fragment programs. If the fragment program doesn't filter the results of the shading calculations, then aliasing artifacts may result.

Generally, multisampling provides a good full-scene (edge) antialiasing solution. Most importantly, to use it only requires turning it on; other than that, there are no changes required of the application. Using multisampling can be completely automatic. If the application selects a multisample-capable framebuffer configuration, multisampling is enabled by default. The OpenGL implementation pays the cost of extra storage for the the multisample buffer and additional per-sample processing at each fragment, but this cost will be reduced over time with advances in the state of the art. Some implementations may even combine multisampling with the brute force overdraw supersampling technique to further increase the effective sampling rate. Unfortunately, supersampling with a small number of samples (less than 16) is not an antialiasing panacea. By contrast, film-quality software renderers often use supersampling with considerably larger numbers of samples, relying on adaptive sampling techniques to determine the number of samples required within each pixel to reduce the computational requirements.

While supersampling with a small number of samples may produce good results, the results for point and line primitives using primitive-specific methods may be substantially better. Fortunately, these other techniques can be used in concert with multisampling.

10.2.4 Drawbacks

In some cases, the ability to automatically antialias the images rendered by an application can be a drawback. Taking advantage of the flexibility of the approach, some hardware vendors have provided methods for turning on full scene antialiasing without requiring any support from the application. In some cases, this can cause problems for an application not designed to be used with antialiasing.

For example, an application may use bitmapped fonts to display information to the viewer. Quite often, this text will show artifacts if full scene antialiasing is applied to it, especially if the text is moved across the screen. Sampling errors will make the text appear "blotchy"; if the text is small enough, it can become unreadable. Since most antialiasing implementations filter samples in different ways, it can be difficult for the application developer to correct for this on all hardware. In the end, full scene antialiasing is not always appropriate. Care must be taken to understand an application's display techniques before turning it on.

10.3 Area Sampling

Another class of antialiasing algorithms uses a technique called *area sampling*. The idea behind area sampling is that the value of a pixel sample should be proportional to the area of the pixel intersected by the primitive. This is in contrast to point sampling and supersampling which derive a pixel value from the intensity of the primitive at one or more infinitely small sample points. With area sampling, the contribution from a primitive partially overlapping a pixel is always accounted for. In contrast, a point-sampled primitive makes no contribution to a pixel if it doesn't overlap a sample point.

Mathematically, area sampling is equivalent to sampling at infinitely many points followed by filtering. The choice of point locations and filter types leads to several variations of area sampling. The simplest form, called *unweighted* area sampling, uses a box filter to produce an average of the samples. A disadvantage of unweighted area sampling is that moving objects can still generate pixel flicker, since a pixel sample can change abruptly as a primitive moves in and out of the area associated with the pixel (as illustrated in Figure 10.2). The flicker can be corrected by overlapping sample areas with adjacent pixels. The contributions from the neighboring pixels are given a lower weight than contributions from within the pixel. This type of sampling is called *weighted* area sampling. It is similar to using a supersampling approach that includes some supersamples outside of the pixel followed by a triangle or Gaussian low-pass filter to perform the reconstruction.

One of the main difficulties with area sampling techniques is computing the correct result when multiple primitives overlap the same pixel. If two primitives overlap different

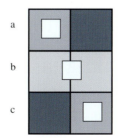

Figure 10.2 Flicker artifacts with unweighted area sampling. A bright fragment 1/4th of a pixel in size moves horizontally across the screen in successive rows.

parts of the pixel, then both should contribute to it. The pixel then becomes the area-weighted sum of the two primitive colors. If part of one primitive is occluded by the other primitive, then the correct approach becomes more complicated. Only the visible parts of two overlapping primitives should contribute. Therein lies the problem — correctly combining visible surface determination with area computations. The supersampling algorithms described previously work correctly and automatically for interpenetrating surfaces since each supersample is correctly depth-buffered before postfiltering. To render an image correctly using area sampling, the visible surface and area sampling processing must be performed together so that the weighted areas for the visible parts of each primitive within each pixel can be computed correctly.

The processing implications of this approach can be severe. It requires that the visible part of each primitive overlapping a pixel must be computed before the area can be determined. There are several algorithms for doing this (Catmill, 1978; Carpenter, 1984); typically one row of pixels (a scan line) or a small rectangular area of pixels, called a *tile*, are processed one at a time. All primitives that intersect a pixel row or tile are processed together. Fragments are computed at each pixel for each primitive, the fragments are depth-sorted, and the visible areas of each fragment are determined. The normalized areas are then used to compute the weighted sum of fragment colors to produce the pixel color. The mathematically correct algorithm clips each fragment against every other fragment in the pixel and sorts the results from front to back. Other algorithms trade off the pixel-level clipping cost for approximations of coverage, using a supersampling-like subpixel grid to track which parts of a pixel a fragment covers while retaining the area-based color value.

In general, adding such an algorithm to the OpenGL pipeline requires considerable effort. To implement the visible surface algorithm, the entire scene must be buffered within the pipeline. Multipass algorithms become more complicated if the combined results need to be antialiased. There is no depth buffer, since a different visible surface algorithm is used. This requires reformulation of techniques that use the stencil and depth buffers.

Nevertheless, the area sampling ideas are quite useful when applied in more specific circumstances. Good candidates for this approach are antialiased lines and points. Their area coverage is easier to compute analytically and the correctness of hidden surface resolution is not as critical as it is for polygons.

10.4 Line and Point Antialiasing

Line and point antialiasing are often considered separately from polygon antialiasing, since there are additional techniques that can be used specifically for these simpler primitives. For certain applications, such as computer-aided design programs, line rendering is pervasive enough that it is worth having special purpose hardware to improve the rendering quality.

Mathematically, a line is infinitely thin. Attempting to compute the percentage of a pixel covered by an infinitely thin object would result in no coverage, so generally one of the following two methods is used:

1. The line is modeled as a long, thin, single-pixel-wide quadrilateral. Area sampling computes the percentage of pixel coverage for each pixel touching the line and this coverage percentage is used as an alpha value for blending.

2. The line is modeled as an infinitely thin transparent glowing object. This method treats a line as if it were drawn on a vector stroke display; these displays draw lines by deflecting the electron beam along the length of the line. This approach requires the implementation to compute the effective shape of a simulated beam that moves across the CRT phosphors.

OpenGL has built-in support for antialiasing lines and points, selected by enabling GL_POINT_SMOOTH or GL_LINE_SMOOTH. Quality hints are provided using glHint. The hint parameter can be GL_FASTEST to indicate that the most efficient option should be chosen, GL_NICEST to indicate the highest quality option should be chosen, or GL_DONT_CARE to indicate no preference.

When antialiasing is enabled, OpenGL computes an alpha value representing either the fraction of each pixel that is covered by the line or point or the beam intensity for the pixel as a function of the distance of the pixel center from the line center. The setting of the GL_LINE_SMOOTH and the GL_POINT_SMOOTH hints determines the accuracy of the calculation used when rendering lines and points, respectively. When the hint is set to GL_NICEST, a larger filter footprint may be applied, causing more fragments to be generated and rendering to run more slowly.

Regardless of which line antialiasing method is used in a particular implementation of OpenGL, it can be approximated by choosing the right blend equation. The critical insight is realizing that antialiased lines and points are a form of *transparent primitive* (see Section 11.8). This requires blending to be enabled so that each incoming pixel fragment will be combined with the value already in the framebuffer, controlled by the alpha value.

The best approximation of a one-pixel-wide quadrilateral is achieved by setting the blending factors to GL_SRC_ALPHA (source) and GL_ONE_MINUS_SRC_ALPHA (destination). To best approximate the lines of a stroke display, use GL_ONE for the destination factor. Note that this second blend equation only works well on a black background and does not produce good results when drawn over bright objects.

As with all transparent primitives, antialiased lines and points should not be drawn until all opaque objects have been drawn first. Depth buffer testing remains enabled, but depth buffer updating is disabled using glDepthMask(GL_FALSE). This allows the antialiased lines and points to be occluded by opaque objects, but not by one another. Antialiased lines drawn with full depth buffering enabled produce incorrect line crossings and can result in significantly worse rendering artifacts than with antialiasing disabled. This is especially true when many lines are drawn close together.

Setting the destination blend mode to GL_ONE_MINUS_SRC_ALPHA may result in order-dependent rendering artifacts if the antialiased primitives are not drawn in back to front order. There are no order-dependent problems when using a setting of GL_ONE, however. Pick the method that best suits the application.

Incorrect monitor gamma settings are much more likely to become apparent with antialiased lines than with shaded polygons. Gamma should typically be set to 2.2, but some workstation manufacturers use values as low as 1.6 to enhance the perceived contrast of rendered images. This results in a noticable intensity nonlinearity in displayed images. Signs of insufficient gamma are "roping" of lines and moire patterns where many lines come together. Too large a gamma value produces a "washed out" appearance. Gamma correction is described in more detail in Section 3.1.2.

Antialiasing in color index mode can be tricky. A correct color map must be loaded to get primitive edges to blend with the background color. When antialiasing is enabled, the last four bits of the color index indicate the coverage value. Thus, 16 contiguous color map locations are needed, containing a color ramp ranging from the background color to the object's color. This technique only works well when drawing wireframe images, where the lines and points typically are blended with a constant background. If the lines and/or points need to be blended with background polygons or images, RGBA rendering should be used.

10.5 Antialiasing with Textures

Points and lines can also be antialiased using the filtering provided by texturing by using texture maps containing only alpha components. The texture is an image of a circle starting with alpha values of one at the center and rolling off to zero from the center to the edge. The alpha texel values are used to blend the point or rectangle fragments with the pixel values already in the framebuffer. For example, to draw an antialiased point, create a texture image containing a filled circle with a smooth (antialiased) boundary. Then draw a textured polygon at the point location making sure that the center of the texture is aligned with the point's coordinates and using the texture environment GL_MODULATE. This method has the advantage that a different point shape may be accommodated by varying the texture image.

A similar technique can be used to draw antialiased line segments of any width. The texture image is a filtered line. Instead of a line segment, a texture-mapped rectangle, whose width is the desired line width, is drawn centered on and aligned with the line segment. If line segments with squared ends are desired, these can be created by using a one dimensional texture map aligned across the width of the rectangle polygon.

This method can work well if there isn't a large disparity between the size of the texture map and the window-space size of the polygon. In essence, the texture image serves as a pre-filtered, supersampled version of the desired point or line image. This means that the roll-off function used to generate the image is a filtering function and the image can be generated by filtering a constant intensity line, circle or rectangle. The texture mapping operation serves as a reconstruction filter and the quality of the reconstruction is determined by the choice of texture filter. This technique is further generalized to the concept of texture brushes in Section 19.9.

10.6 Polygon Antialiasing

Antialiasing the edges of filled polygons using area sampling is similar to antialiasing points and lines. Unlike points and lines, however, antialiasing polygons in color index mode isn't practical. Object intersections are more prevalent, and OpenGL blending is usually necessary to get acceptable results.

As with lines and points, OpenGL has built-in support for polygon antialiasing. It is enabled using glEnable with GL_POLYGON_SMOOTH. This causes pixels on the edges of the polygon to be assigned fractional alpha values based on their pixel coverage. The quality of the coverage values are controlled with GL_POLYGON_SMOOTH_HINT.

As described in Section 10.3, combined area sampling and visibility processing is a difficult problem. In OpenGL an approximation is used. To make it work, the *application* is responsible for part of the visibility algorithm by sorting the polygons from front to back in eye space and submitting them in that order. This antialiasing method does not work without sorting. The remaining part of resolving visible surfaces is accomplished using blending. Before rendering, depth testing is disabled and blending is enabled with the blending factors GL_SRC_ALPHA_SATURATE (source) and GL_ONE (destination). The final color is the sum of the destination color and the scaled source color; the scale factor is the smaller of either the incoming source alpha value or one minus the destination alpha value. This means that for a pixel with a large alpha value, successive incoming pixels have little effect on the final color because one minus the destination alpha is almost zero.

At first glance, the blending function seems a little unusual. Section 11.1.2 describes an algorithm for doing front-to-back compositing which uses a different set of blending factors. The polygon antialiasing algorithm uses the saturate source factor to ensure that surfaces that are stitched together from multiple polygons have the correct appearance. Consider a pixel that lies on the shared edge of two adjacent, opaque, visible polygons sharing the same constant color. If the two polygons together cover the entire pixel, then the pixel color should be the polygon color. Since one of the fragments is drawn first, it will contribute the value $\alpha_1 C$. When the second contributing fragment is drawn, it has alpha value α_2. Regardless of whether α_1 or α_2 is larger, the resulting blended color will be $\alpha_1 C + (1 - \alpha_1)C = C$, since the two fragments together cover the entire pixel $\alpha_2 = 1 - \alpha_1$.

Conversely, if the fragments are blended using a traditional compositing equation, the result is $\alpha_1 C + (1 - \alpha_1)\alpha_2 C + (1 - \alpha_1)(1 - \alpha_2)C_{background}$ and some of the background color "leaks" through the shared edge. The background leaks through because the second fragment is weighted by $(1 - \alpha_1)\alpha_2$. Compare this to the first method that uses either α_2 or $(1 - \alpha_1)$, whichever is smaller (in this case they are equal). This blending equation ensures that shared edges do not have noticable blending artifacts and it still does a reasonable job of weighting each fragment contribution by its coverage, giving priority to the fragments closest to the eye. More details regarding this antialiasing formula versus the other functions that are available are described in Section 11.1.2. It useful to note that A-buffer-related algorithms avoid this problem by tracking which parts of the pixel are covered by each fragment, while compositing does not.

Since the accumulated coverage is stored in the color buffer, the buffer must be able to store an alpha value for every pixel. This capability is called "destination alpha," and is required for this algorithm to work. To get a framebuffer with destination alpha, you must request a visual or pixel format that has it. OpenGL conformance does not require implementations to support a destination alpha buffer so an attempt to select this visual may not succeed.

This antialiasing technique is often poorly supported by OpenGL implementations, since the edge coverage values require extra computations and destination alpha is required. Implementations that support multisample antialiasing can usually translate the coverage mask into an alpha coverage value providing a low-resolution version of the real coverage. The algorithm also doesn't see much adoption since it places the sorting burden on the application. However, it can provide very good antialiasing results; it is often used by quality-driven applications creating "presentation graphics" for slide shows and printing.

A variant polygon antialiasing algorithm that is frequently tried is outlining non-antialiased polygons with antialiased lines. The goal is to soften the edges of the polygons using the antialiased lines. In some applications it can be effective, but the results are often of mixed quality since the polygon edges and lines are not guaranteed to rasterize to the same set of pixel locations.

10.7 Temporal Antialiasing

Thus far, the focus has been on aliasing problems and remedies in the spatial domain. Similar sampling problems also exist in the time domain. When an animation sequence is rendered, each frame in the sequence represents a point in time. The positions of moving objects are point-sampled at each frame; the animation frame rate defines the sampling rate. An aliasing problem analogous to the spatial aliasing occurs when object positions are changing rapidly and the motion sampling rate is too low to correctly capture the changes. This produces the familiar strobe-like temporal aliasing artifacts, such as vehicle wheels appearing to spin more slowly than they should or even spinning backward. Similar to pixel colors and attributes, the motion of each object can be thought of as a signal, but in the time domain instead of the spatial one. These time domain signals also have corresponding frequency domain representations; aliasing artifacts occur when the high-frequency parts of the signal alias to lower frequency signals during signal reconstruction.

The solutions for temporal aliasing are similar to those for spatial aliasing; the sampling rate is increased to represent the highest frequency present, or the high-frequency components are filtered out before sampling. Increasing the sampling rate alone isn't practical, since the reconstruction and display process is typically limited to the video refresh rate, usually ranging between 30Hz and 120Hz. Therefore, some form of filtering during sampling is used. The result of the filtering process is similar to the results achieved in cinematography. When filming, during the time period when the shutter is held open to expose the film, the motion of each object for the entire exposure period is captured. This results in the film integrating an infinite number of time sample points over the exposure time. This is analogous to performing a weighted average of point samples. As with supersampling, there are quality vs. computation trade-offs in the choice of filter function and number of sample points.

10.7.1 Motion Blur

The idea of generating a weighted average of a number of time samples from an animation is called *motion blur*. It gets this name from the blurry image resulting from averaging together several samples of a moving object, just as a camera with too low of a shutter speed captures a blurred image of a moving object.

One simple way to implement motion blur is with the accumulation buffer. If the display rate for an animation sequence is 30 frames per second and we wish to include 10 temporal samples for each frame, then the samples for time t seconds are generated from the sequence of frames computed at $t - 5x, t - 4x, t - 3x, \ldots, t, t + 1x, t + 2x, \ldots t + 4x$, where $x = \frac{1}{300}$. These samples are accumulated with a scale of $\frac{1}{10}$ to apply a box filter. As with spatial filtering, the sample sets for each frame may overlap to create a better low-pass filter, but typically this is not necessary.

For scenes in which the moving objects are in front of the static ones, an optimization can be performed. Only the objects that are moving need to be re-rendered at each sample. All of the static objects are rendered and accumulated with full weight, then the objects that are moving are drawn at each time sample and accumulated. For a single moving object, the steps are:

1. Render the scene without the moving object, using `glAccum(GL_LOAD, 1.0f)`.

2. Accumulate the scene n times, with the moving object drawn against a black background, using `glAccum(GL_ACCUM, 1.0f/n)`.

3. Copy the result back to the color buffer using `glAccum(GL_RETURN, 1.0f)`.

This optimization is only correct if the static parts of the scene are completely unchanging. If depth buffering is used, the visible parts of static objects may change as the amount of occlusion by moving objects changes. A different optimization is to store the contents of the color and depth buffer for the static scene in a pbuffer and then restore the buffers before drawing the moving objects for each sample. Of course, this optimization can only improve performance if the time to restore the buffers is small relative to the amount of time it takes to draw the static parts of the scene.

The filter function can also be altered empirically to affect the perceived motion. For example, objects can be made to appear to accelerate or decelerate by varying the weight for each accumulation. If the weights are sequentially decreased for an object, then the object appears to accelerate. The object appears to travel further in later samples. Similarly, if the weights are increased, the object appears to decelerate.

10.8 Summary

In this chapter we reviewed supersampling and area sampling spatial antialiasing methods and how they are supported in the OpenGL pipeline. We also described temporal antialiasing for animation, and its relationship to spatial antialiasing.

In the next chapter we look at how blending, compositing, and transparency are supported in the pipeline. These ideas and algorithms are interrelated: they overlap with some of the algorithms and ideas described for area sampling-based antialiasing.

Compositing, Blending, and Transparency

Blending and compositing describe the task of merging together disparate collections of pixels that occupy the same locations in the output image. The basic task can be described as combining the pixels from two or more input images to form a single output image. In the general case, compositing results depend on the order in which the images are combined. Compositing is useful in many areas of computer graphics. It makes it possible to create complex scenes by rendering individual components of the scene, then combining them. The combining process itself can also add complexity and interest to images.

Semi-transparent surfaces reflect some light while allowing some light from other surfaces to pass through them. Rendering semi-transparent objects is closely related to the ideas used for compositing multiple images. The details of blending images or image elements is an almost universal building block for the rendering techniques in this book, so it is valuable to explore the operations in detail.

11.1 Combining Two Images

Given two input images A and B, an output image C can be expressed as a linear combination of the two input images:

$$C = w_a A + w_b B \tag{11.1}$$

where w_a and w_b are weighting factors. Constant weighting factors are used to implement simple effects such as cross fades or dissolves. For example, to cross fade from A to B, set w_b in terms of w_a ($w_b = 1 - w_a$) and smoothly vary w_a from 0 to 1.

Blending two source images (also called *elements*) with constant weights isn't selective enough to create certain effects. It's more useful to be able to select an object or subregion from element A and a subregion from element B to produce the output composite. These subregions are arbitrary regions of pixels embedded in rectangular images. Distinguishing an arbitrary shaped subregion in an image can be done by varying the weighting function for each pixel in the image. This per-pixel weighting changes Equation 11.1 to

$$C[i, j] = w_a[i, j]A[i, j] + w_b[i, j]B[i, j] \tag{11.2}$$

For convenience we will drop the indices $[i, j]$ from this point on and assume the weights are distinct for each pixel.

To select a subregion from image A, the pixels in the subregion are given a weight of 1, while the pixels not in the subregion are given a weight of 0. This works well if the edges of the subregion are sharp and end at pixel boundaries. However, antialiased images often contain partially covered pixels at the boundary edges of objects. These boundary pixels may contain color contributions from the background, or other objects in the image in addition to the source object's color (see the discussion of digital image representation in Chapter 4). To correct for this, the per-pixel weighting factor for these pixels is scaled to be proportional to the object's contribution. This ensures that the contribution in the final image is the same as in the input image.

OpenGL provides this weighted per-pixel merge capability through the framebuffer blending operation. In framebuffer blending the weights are stored as part of the images themselves. Both the alpha component and the R, G, and B color components can be used as per-pixel weights or as parameters to a simple weight function, such as $1 - \text{alpha}$. Framebuffer blending is often called *alpha-blending* since the alpha values are most often used as the weights.

11.1.1 Compositing

A common blending operation is to *composite* a background image, perhaps from a film or video, with a computer-generated object. In this context, the word "composite" represents a very specific image-combining operation involving images whose pixels include an α (alpha) value. The alpha value indicates either the transparency or the coverage of the object intersecting the pixel. The most common type of composite is the *over* operator, in which a foreground element is composited over a background element.

In traditional film technology, compositing a foreground and background image is achieved using a *matte*: a piece of film, aligned with the foreground image, in which areas of interest are transparent and the rest is opaque. The matte allows only the areas of interest from the foreground image to pass through. Its complement, the *holdout matte*, is used with digital images. A holdout matte is opaque in the areas of interest and transparent everywhere else. A digital holdout matte is the set of opacity α values for the corresponding image pixels. To combine two pixels together, the source element color is multiplied by the matte's α value, and added to the corresponding color from the background image, scaled by $1 - \alpha$. The resulting equation is $C_{new} = \alpha_f C_f + (1 - \alpha_f)C_b$. The entire contribution of the object in the source element α is transferred to the new pixel while the background image contributes $1 - \alpha$, the remaining unclaimed portion of the new pixel.

OpenGL can be used to composite geometry against a background image by loading it into the framebuffer, then rendering the geometry on top of the background with blending enabled. Set the source and destination blend factors to `GL_SRC_ALPHA` and `GL_ONE_MINUS_SRC_ALPHA`, respectively, and assign α values of 1.0 to the rendered primitives when they are sent to the OpenGL pipeline. If the geometry is opaque and there is no antialiasing algorithm modifying the α values, the rasterized fragments will have α values of 1.0, reducing the compositing operation to a simple selection process. Without antialiasing, the computer-generated object will be composited with sharp silhouette edges, making it look less realistic than the objects in the background image that have softer edges.

The antialiasing algorithms described in Chapter 10 can be used to antialias the geometry and correct this problem. They are often a good solution, even if they are slower to generate, for compositing applications that do not need to be highly interactive during the compositing process.

Transparent objects are also represented with fractional α values. These values may come from the color assigned each vertex, the diffuse material specification, or a texture map. The α value represents the amount of light reflected by the object and $1 - \alpha$ represents the amount of light transmitted through the object. Transparency will be discussed later in this chapter.

11.1.2 Compositing Multiple Images

The preceding algorithm is mathematically correct for compositing an arbitrary foreground image with an opaque background. Problems arise, however, if it is used to combine several elements together. If the background image is not opaque, then the compositing equation should be:

$$C_{new} = \alpha_f C_f + (1 - \alpha_f)\alpha_b C_b$$

so that the background pixel is scaled by its α value to calculate its contribution correctly. This new equation works correctly for compositing any two images together. There is a subtlety when using both this equation and the opaque-background version; while the input images are explicitly scaled by their α values as part of the compositing equation, the resulting pixel value is implicitly scaled by the new composite α value. The equation expects that the C_f and C_b inputs do not include a *premultiplied* alpha, but it creates a

C_{new} that does. The corresponding α value for the composited pixel, α_{new}, is $\alpha_f +$ $(1 - \alpha_f)\alpha_b$. To undo the alpha scaling, C_{new} should be divided by α_{new}.

This side effect of the compositing equation creates some confusion when discussing the compositing of multiple images, especially if the input images and intermediate images don't consistently include a premultiplied alpha. To simplify the discussion, we use the notation $\bar{C}_x$ to indicate a color value with a premultiplied α value ($\bar{C}_x = \alpha_x C_x$). Using this notation, the compositing equation simplifies to:

$$\bar{C}_{new} = \bar{C}_f + (1 - \alpha_f)\bar{C}_b$$

and

$$\alpha_{new} = \alpha_f + (1 - \alpha_f)\alpha_b$$

Now the case of compositing a foreground image with a background image where the background is itself the result of compositing two images C_1 and C_2 becomes:

$$\bar{C}_{new} = \bar{C}_f + (1 - \alpha_f)\left[\bar{C}_1 + (1 - \alpha_1)\bar{C}_2\right]$$

This is the algorithm for doing *back-to-front* compositing, in which the background is built up by combining it with the element that lies closest to it to produce a new background image. It can be generalized to include an arbitrary number of images by expanding the innermost background term:

$$\bar{C} = \bar{C}_n + (1 - \alpha_n)\left[\bar{C}_{n-1} + (1 - \alpha_{n-1})\left[\bar{C}_{n-2} + (1 - \alpha_{n-2})[\ldots]\right]\right] \qquad \textbf{(11.3)}$$

Notice that the OpenGL algorithm described previously for compositing geometry over a pre-existing opaque image works correctly for an arbitrary number of geometry elements rendered sequentially.

The algorithm is extended to work for a non-opaque background image in a number of ways. Either a background image whose color values are pre-multiplied by alpha is loaded, or the premultiplication is performed as part of the image-loading operation. This is done by clearing the color buffer to zero, enabling blending with GL_SRC_ALPHA, GL_ZERO source and destination blend factors, and transferring an image containing both color and α values to the framebuffer. If the OpenGL implementation supports fragment programs, then the fragment program can perform the premultiplication operation explicitly.

A sequence of compositing operations can also be performed *front-to-back*. Each new input image is composited *under* the current accumulated image. Renumbering the indices so that n becomes 0 and *vice versa* and expanding out the products, Equation 11.3

becomes:

$$\bar{C} = \bar{C}_0 + (1 - \alpha_0)\bar{C}_1 + (1 - \alpha_0)(1 - \alpha_1)\bar{C}_2 + \cdots + (1 - \alpha_0)\ldots(1 - \alpha_{n-1})\bar{C}_n$$
$$= \bar{C}_0 + w_0\bar{C}_1 + w_1\bar{C}_2 + \cdots + w_{n-1}\bar{C}_n$$

To composite from front to back, each image must be multiplied by its own alpha value and the product of $(1 - \alpha_k)$ of all preceding images. This means that the calculation used to compute the color values isn't the same as those used to compute the intermediate weights. Considering only premultiplied alpha inputs, the intermediate result image is $\bar{C}_j' = \bar{C}_{j-1}' + w_{j-1}\bar{C}_j$ and the running composite weight is $w_j = (1 - \alpha_j)w_{j-1}$. This set of computations can be computed using OpenGL alpha blending by accumulating the running weight in the destination alpha buffer. However, this also requires separate specification of RGB color and alpha blend functions.[1] If separate functions are supported, then GL_DST_ALPHA and GL_ONE are used for the RGB source and destination factors and GL_ZERO and GL_ONE_MINUS_SRC_ALPHA are used to accumulate the weights. For non-premultiplied alpha images, a fragment program or multipass algorithm is required to produce the correct result, since the incoming fragment must be weighted and multiplied by both the source and destination α values. Additionally, if separate blend functions are not supported, emulating the exact equations becomes more difficult.

The coverage-based polygon antialiasing algorithm described in Section 10.6 also uses a front-to-back algorithm. The application sorts polygons from front to back, blending them in that order. It differs in that the source and destination weights are $\min(\alpha_s, 1 - \alpha_d)$ and 1 rather than α_d and 1. Like the front-to-back compositing algorithm, as soon as the pixel is opaque, no more contributions are made to the pixel. The compositing algorithm achieves this as the running weight w_j stored in destination alpha reaches zero, whereas polygon antialiasing achieves this by accumulating an approximation of the α value for the resulting pixel in destination α converging to 1. These approaches work because OpenGL defines separate blend functions for the GL_SRC_ALPHA_SATURATE source factor. For the RGB components the factor is $\min(\alpha_s, 1 - \alpha_d)$; however, for the α component the blend factor is 1. This means that the value computed in destination α is $\alpha_j = \alpha_s + \alpha_{j-1}$ where α_s is the incoming source α value. So, with the saturate blend function, the destination α value increases while the contribution of each sample decreases.

The principle reason for the different blend functions is that both the back-to-front and front-to-back composition algorithms make a *uniform opacity assumption*. This means the material reflecting or transmitting light in a pixel is uniformly distributed throughout the pixel. In the absence of extra knowledge regarding how the geometry fragments are distributed within the pixel, every sub-area of the pixel is assumed to contain an equal distribution of geometry and empty space.

---

1. Added in OpenGL 1.4.

In the polygon antialiasing algorithm, the uniform opacity assumption is not appropriate for polygons that share a common edge. In those situations, the different parts of the polygon don't overlap, and rendering with the uniform assumption causes the polygons under-contributing to the pixel, resulting in artifacts at the shared edges. The source fragments generated from polygon antialiasing also need to be weighted by the source α value (i.e., premultiplied). The saturate function represents a reasonable compromise between weighting by the source alpha when it is small and weighting by the unclaimed part of the pixel when its value is small. The algorithm effectively implements a complementary opacity assumption where the geometry for two fragments within the same pixel are assumed to not overlap and are simply accumulated. Accumulation is assumed to continue until the pixel is completely covered. This results in correct rendering for shared edges, but algorithms that use the uniform opacity assumption, such as rendering transparent objects, are not blended correctly.

Note that the back-to-front algorithm accumulates the correct composite α value in the color buffer (assuming destination alpha is available), whereas this front-to-back method does not. The correct α term at each step is computed using the same equation as for the RGB components $\alpha'_j = \alpha'_{j-1} + w_{j-1}\alpha_j$. The saturate function used for polygon antialiasing can be used as an approximation of the functions needed for front-to-back compositing, but it will introduce errors since it doesn't imply uniform opacity. However, the value accumulated in destination alpha is the matching α value for the pixel.

11.1.3 Alpha Division

Both the back-to-front and front-to-back compositing algorithms (and the polygon antialiasing algorithm) compute an RGB result that has been premultiplied by the corresponding α value; in other words, $\bar{C}$ is computed rather than C. Sometimes it is necessary to recover the original non-premultiplied color value. To compute this result, each color value must be divided by the corresponding α value. Only the programmable fragment pipeline supports division directly. However, a multipass algorithm can be used to approximate the result in the absence of programmability. As suggested in Section 9.3.2, a division operation can be implemented using pixel textures if they are supported.

11.2 Other Compositing Operators

Porter and Duff (1984) describe a number of operators that are useful for combining multiple images. In addition to *over*, these operators include *in*, *out*, *atop*, *xor*, and *plus*, as shown in Table 11.1. These operators are defined by generalizing the compositing equation for two images, A and B to

$$\bar{C}_{new} = \bar{C}_A F_A + \bar{C}_B F_B$$

and substituting F_A and F_B with the terms from Table 11.1.

Table 11.1 Compositing Operators

operation	F_A	F_B
A over B	1	$1 - \alpha_A$
B over A	$1 - \alpha_A$	1
A in B	α_B	0
B in A	0	α_A
A out B	$1 - \alpha_B$	0
B out A	0	$1 - \alpha_A$
A atop B	α_B	$1 - \alpha_A$
B atop A	$1 - \alpha_B$	α_A
A xor B	$1 - \alpha_B$	$1 - \alpha_A$
A plus B	1	1

This equation assumes that the two images A and B have been pre-multiplied by their α values. Using OpenGL, these operators are implemented using framebuffer blending, modifying the source and destination blend factors to match F_A and F_B. Assuming that the OpenGL implementation supports a destination alpha buffer with double buffering, alpha premultiplication can be incorporated by first loading the front and back buffers with the A and B images using `glBlendFunc(GL_ONE, GL_ZERO)` to do the premultiplication. The blending factors are then changed to match the factors from Table 11.1. `glCopyPixels` is used to copy image A onto image B. This simple and general method can be used to implement all of the operators. Some of them, however, may be implemented more efficiently. If the required factor from Table 11.1 is 0, for example, the image need not be premultiplied by its α value, since only its α value is required. If the factor is 1, the premultiplication by alpha can be folded into the same blend as the operator, since the 1 performs no useful work and can be replaced with a multiplication by α.

In addition to framebuffer blending, the multitexture pipeline can be used to perform similar blending and compositing operations. The combine and crossbar texture environment functions enable a number of useful equations using source operands from texture images and the source fragment. The fundamental difference is that results cannot be directly accumulated into one of the texture images. However, using the render-to-texture techniques described in Sections 5.3 and 7.5, a similar result can be achieved.

11.3 Keying and Matting

The term *chroma keying* has its roots in broadcast television. The principal subject is recorded against a constant color background — traditionally blue. As the video signal is displayed, the parts of the signal corresponding to the constant color are replaced with an alternate image. The resulting effect is that the principal subject appears overlayed on the alternate background image. The chroma portion of the video signal is used for the comparison, hence the name. Over time the term has been generalized. It is now known by a number of other names including color keying, blue and green screening, or just plain keying, but the basic idea remains the same. More recently the same basic idea is used, recording against a constant color background, but the keying operation has been updated to use digital compositing techniques.

Most of the aspects of compositing using blending and the α channel also apply to keying. The principal difference is that the opacity or coverage information is in one of the color channels rather than in the α channel. The first step in performing keying digitally is moving the opacity information into the alpha channel. In essence, a holdout matte is generated from the information in the color channels. Once this is done, then the alpha channel compositing algorithms can be used.

11.4 Blending Artifacts

A number of different types of artifacts may result when blending or compositing multiple images together. In this section we group the sources of errors into common classes and look at each individually.

11.4.1 Arithmetic Errors

The arithmetic operations used to blend pixels together can be a source of error in the final image. Section 3.4 discusses the use of fixed-point representation and arithmetic in the fragment processing pipeline and some of the inherent problems. When compositing a 2- or 3- image sequence, there is seldom any issue with 8-bit framebuffer arithmetic. When building up complex scenes with large numbers of compositing operations, however, poor arithmetic implementations and quantization errors from limited precision can quickly accumulate and result in visible artifacts.

A simple rule of thumb is that each multiply operation introduces at least $\frac{1}{2}$-bit error when a $2 \times n$-bit product is reduced to n-bits. When performing a simple *over* composite the αC term may, conservatively, be in error by as much as 1 bit. With 8-bit components, this translates to roughly 0.4% error per compositing operation. After 10 compositing operations, this will be 4% error and after 100 compositing operations, 40% error. The ideal solution to the problem is to use more precision (deeper color buffer) and better arithmetic implementations. For high-quality blending, 12-bit color components provide enough precision to avoid artifacts. Repeating the 1-bit error example with 12-bit component resolution, the error changes to approximately 0.025% after each compositing operation, 0.25% after 10 operations, and 2.5% after 100 operations.

11.4.2 Blending with the Accumulation Buffer

While the accumulation buffer is designed for combining multiple images with high precision, its ability to reduce compositing errors is limited. While the accumulation buffer does act as an accumulator with higher precision than found in most framebuffers, it only supports scaling by a constant value, not by a per-pixel weight such as α. This means that per-pixel scaling must still be performed using blending; only the result can be accumulated. The accumulation buffer is most effective at improving the precision of multiply-add operations, where the multiplication is by a constant. The real value of the accumulation buffer is that it can accumulate a large number of very small values, whereas the normal color buffer likely does not have enough dynamic range to represent both the end result and a single input term at the same time.

11.4.3 Approximation Errors

Another, more subtle, error can occur with the use of opacity to represent coverage at the edges of objects. The assumption with coverage values is that the background color and object color are uniformly spread across the pixel. This is only partly correct. In reality, the object occupies part of the pixel area and the background (or other objects) covers the remainder. The error in the approximation can be illustrated by compositing a source element containing an opaque object with itself. Since the objects are aligned identically and one is in front of the other, the result should be the source element itself. However, a source element pixel where α is not equal to 1 will contribute $\bar{C}_f + (1 - \alpha_f)\bar{C}_f$ to the new pixel. The overall result is that the edges become brighter in the composite. In practice, the problem isn't as bad as it might seem since the equal-distribution assumption is valid if there isn't a lot of correlation between the edges in the source elements. This is one reason why the polygon antialiasing algorithm described in Section 10.6 does not use the regular compositing equations.

Alpha-compositing does work correctly when α is used to model transparency. If a transparent surface completely overlaps a pixel, then the α value represents the amount of light that is reflected from the surface and $1 - \alpha$ represents the amount of light transmitted through the surface. The assumption that the ratios of reflected and transmitted light are constant across the area of the pixel is reasonably accurate and the correct results are obtained if a source element with a semi-transparent object is composited with itself.

11.4.4 Gamma Correction Errors

Another frequent source of error occurs when blending or compositing images with colors that are not in a linear space. Blending operators are linear and assume that the operands in the equations have a linear relationship. Images that have been gamma-corrected no longer have a linear relationship between color values. To correctly composite two gamma-corrected images, the images should first be converted back to linear space, composited, then have gamma correction re-applied. Often applications skip the linear conversion and re-gamma correction step. The amount of error introduced depends on where the input color values are on the gamma correction curve. In A Ghost in a Snowstorm (1998a), Jim Blinn analyzes the various error cases and determines that the worst errors occur with when mixing colors at opposite ends of the range, compositing white over black or black over white. The resulting worst case error can be greater than 25%.

11.5 Compositing Images with Depth

Section 11.1 discusses algorithms for compositing two images together using alpha values to control how pixels are merged. One drawback of this method is that only simple visibility information can be expressed using mattes or masks. By retaining depth information for each image pixel, the depth information can be used during the compositing operation to provide more visible surface information. With alpha-compositing, elements that occupy the same destination area rely on the alpha information and the back-to-front ordering to provide visibility information. Objects that interpenetrate must be rendered together to the same element using a hidden surface algorithm, since the back-to-front algorithm cannot correctly resolve the visible surfaces.

Depth information can greatly enhance the applicability of compositing as a technique for building up a final image from separate elements (Duff, 1985). OpenGL allows depth and color values to be read from the framebuffer using glReadPixels and saved to secondary storage for later compositing. Similarly, rectangular images of depth or color values can be independently written to the framebuffer using glDrawPixels. However, since glDrawPixels works on depth and color images one at a time, some additional work is required to perform a true 3D composite, in which the depth information is used in the visibility test.

Both color and depth images can be independently saved to memory and later drawn to the screen using glDrawPixels. This is sufficient for 2D style composites, where objects are drawn on top of each other to create the final scene. To do true 3D compositing, it is necessary to use the color and depth values simultaneously, so that depth testing can be used to determine which surfaces are obscured by others.

The stencil buffer can be used to implement true 3D compositing as a two-pass operation. The color buffer is disabled for writing, the stencil buffer is cleared, and the saved depth values are copied into the framebuffer. Depth testing is enabled, ensuring that only depth values that are closer to the original can update the depth buffer. glStencilOp is used to configure the stencil test so that the stencil buffer bit is set if the depth test passes.

The stencil buffer now contains a mask of pixels that were closer to the view than the pixels of the original image. The stencil function is changed to accomplish this masking operation, the color buffer is enabled for writing, and the color values of the saved image are drawn to the framebuffer.

This technique works because the fragment operations, in particular the depth test and the stencil test, are part of both the geometry and imaging pipelines in OpenGL. The technique is described here in more detail. It assumes that both the depth and color values of an image have been saved to system memory, and are to be composited using depth testing to an image in the framebuffer:

1. Clear the stencil buffer using `glClear` with `GL_STENCIL_BUFFER_BIT` set in the bitmask.

2. Disable the color buffer for writing with `glColorMask`.

3. Set stencil values to 1 when the depth test passes by calling `glStencilFunc(GL_ALWAYS, 1, 1)`, and `glStencilOp(GL_KEEP, GL_KEEP, GL_REPLACE)`.

4. Ensure depth testing is set; `glEnable(GL_DEPTH_TEST)`, `glDepthFunc(GL_LESS)`.

5. Draw the depth values to the framebuffer with `glDrawPixels`, using `GL_DEPTH_COMPONENT` for the format parameter.

6. Set the stencil buffer to test for stencil values of 1 with `glStencilFunc(GL_EQUAL, 1, 1)` and `glStencilOp(GL_KEEP, GL_KEEP, GL_KEEP)`.

7. Disable the depth testing with `glDisable(GL_DEPTH_TEST)`.

8. Draw the color values to the framebuffer with `glDrawPixels`, using `GL_RGBA` as the format parameter.

At this point, both the depth and color values will have been merged, using the depth test to control which pixels from the saved image update the framebuffer. Compositing can still be problematic when merging images with coplanar polygons.

This process can be repeated to merge multiple images. The depth values of the saved image can be manipulated by changing the values of `GL_DEPTH_SCALE` and `GL_DEPTH_BIAS` with `glPixelTransfer`. This technique makes it possible to squeeze the incoming image into a limited range of depth values within the scene.

11.6 Other Blending Operations

So far we have described methods that use the alpha component for weighting pixel values. OpenGL blending supports additional source and destination blend factors which can be used to implement other algorithms. A short summary of the more common operations follows.

Summing Two Images Using GL_ONE as the source and destination blend factors, the source image is added to the destination image. This operation is useful in multipass sequences to combine the results of two rendering passes.

Modulating an Image In the alpha-blending discussion, each of the color components have been weighted equally by a value in the alpha channel. Some applications require scaling the color components by different amounts depending on their relative contributions. For example, in the OpenGL lighting equation the lighting computations may produce a different result for each color channel. To reproduce the result of scaling an image by different light colors, each color component of the image must be scaled separately. This can be done using either the GL_SRC_COLOR destination or GL_DST_COLOR source factor to scale the current framebuffer contents. For example, drawing a constant-colored window-sized rectangle with GL_DST_COLOR and GL_ZERO as the source and destination factors scales the color buffer contents by the color of the rectangle.

Constant Colors The ARB imaging subset and OpenGL 1.4 support constant blending factors. These are useful to perform constant scaling operations, for example simple cross fades.

Subtraction The ARB imaging subset also supports a subtraction equation (actually both subtract and reverse subtract) in addition to the original addition operation. These allow more general purpose arithmetic to be performed in the framebuffer, most usefully as part of a multipass toolbox as described in Section 9.3.

Min/Max Arguably stretching the idea of blending a bit, the min and max functions allow per-pixel computation of the minimum and maximum values for each component for each pixel. These functions can be useful for a number of imaging operations, as described in Chapter 12.

11.7 Dissolves

A common film technique is the "dissolve", where one image or animated sequence is replaced with another, in a smooth transition. One simple version alpha blends the two images together, fading out the first image with α and fading in the second with $1 - \alpha$. One way to think about the dissolve sequence is as a dynamic mask that changes each frame and is applied to the two target images. As discussed at the beginning of the chapter, the masks may be simple selection operations in which the pixel is selected from either the first or second image. A more general form is to take a weighted sum of the two pixels. For a simple selection operation, there are additional methods for performing it. The alpha-test fragment operation can be used to discard fragments based on their alpha value. Often dissolves are used to describe transitions between two static images, or sequences of pre-generated images. The concept can be equally well applied to sequences of images that are generated dynamically. For example, the approach can be used to dissolve between two dynamically rendered 3D scenes.

Alpha testing can be used to implement very efficient selection operations, since it discards pixels before depth and stencil testing and blending operations. One issue with using alpha testing is generating the alpha values themselves. For a dissolve the mask is usually independent and unrelated to the source image. One way to "tack on" a set of alpha values during rasterization is to use an alpha texture. A linear texture coordinate generation function is used to produce texture coordinates, indexing the texture map as a screen-space matte. To achieve the dynamic dissolve, the texture is updated each frame, either by binding different texture objects or by replacing the contents of the texture map. An alpha-texture-based technique works well when multitexture is supported since an unused texture unit may be available for the operation. The alpha-texture-based technique works with both alpha-testing or alpha-blending style algorithms.

Another option for performing masking operations is the stencil buffer. The stencil buffer can be used to implement arbitrary dissolve patterns. The alpha planes of the color buffer and the alpha function can also be used to implement this kind of dissolve, but using the stencil buffer frees up the alpha planes for motion blur, transparency, smoothing, and other effects.

The basic approach to a stencil buffer dissolve is to render two different images, using the stencil buffer to control where each image can draw to the framebuffer. This can be done very simply by defining a stencil test and associating a different reference value with each image. The stencil buffer is initialized to a value such that the stencil test will pass with one of the images' reference values, and fail with the other. An example of a dissolve part way between two images is shown in Figure 11.1.

At the start of the dissolve (the first frame of the sequence), the stencil buffer is all cleared to one value, allowing only one of the images to be drawn to the framebuffer. Frame by frame, the stencil buffer is progressively changed (in an application-defined

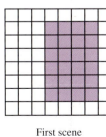
First scene

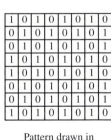
Pattern drawn in
stencil buffer

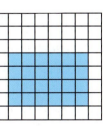
Second scene drawn with
glStencilFunc(GL_EQUAL, 1, 1)

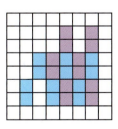
Resulting image

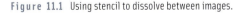

Figure 11.1 Using stencil to dissolve between images.

pattern) to a different value, one that passes only when compared against the second image's reference value. As a result, more and more of the first image is replaced by the second.

Over a series of frames, the first image "dissolves" into the second under control of the evolving pattern in the stencil buffer.

Here is a step-by-step description of a dissolve.

1. Clear the stencil buffer with `glClear(GL_STENCIL_BUFFER_BIT)`.

2. Disable writing to the color buffer, using `glColorMask(GL_FALSE, GL_FALSE, GL_FALSE, GL_FALSE)`.

3. If the values in the depth buffer should not change, use `glDepthMask(GL_FALSE)`.

For this example, the stencil test will always fail, setting the stencil operation to write the reference value to the stencil buffer. The application should enable stenciling before beginning to draw the dissolve pattern.

1. Turn on stenciling: `glEnable(GL_STENCIL_TEST)`.

2. Set stencil function to always fail: `glStencilFunc(GL_NEVER, 1, 1)`.

3. Set stencil op to write 1 on stencil test failure: `glStencilOp(GL_REPLACE, GL_KEEP, GL_KEEP)`.

4. Write the dissolve pattern to the stencil buffer by drawing geometry or using `glDrawPixels`.

5. Disable writing to the stencil buffer with `glStencilMask(GL_FALSE)`.

6. Set stencil function to pass on 0: `glStencilFunc(GL_EQUAL, 0, 1)`.

7. Enable color buffer for writing with `glColorMask(GL_TRUE, GL_TRUE, GL_TRUE, GL_TRUE)`.

8. If you're depth testing, turn depth buffer writes back on with `glDepthMask`.

9. Draw the first image. It will only be written where the stencil buffer values are 0.

10. Change the stencil test so only values that equal 1 pass: `glStencilFunc(GL_EQUAL, 1, 1)`.

11. Draw the second image. Only pixels with a stencil value of 1 will change.

12. Repeat the process, updating the stencil buffer so that more and more stencil values are 1. Use the dissolve pattern and redraw image 1 and 2 until the entire stencil buffer has 1's in it and only image 2 is visible.

If each new frame's dissolve pattern is a superset of the previous frame's pattern, image 1 doesn't have to be re-rendered. This is because once a pixel of image 1 is replaced with image 2, image 1 will never be redrawn there. Designing the dissolve pattern with this restriction can improve the performance of this technique.

11.8 Transparency

Accurate rendering of transparent objects is an important element of creating realistic scenes. Many objects, both natural and artificial, have some degree of transparency. Transparency is also a useful feature when visualizing the positional relationships of multiple objects. Pure transparency, unless refraction is taken into account, is straight-forward. In most cases, when a transparent object is desired, what is really wanted is a partially transparent object. By definition, a partially transparent object has some degree of opacity: it is measured by the percentage of light that won't pass through an object. Partially transparent objects don't just block light; they also add their own color, which modifies the color of the light passing through them.

Simulating transparency is not just a useful technique in and of itself. The blending techniques used to create the most common form of transparency are also the basis of many other useful graphics algorithms. Examples include material mapping, line antialias-ing, billboarding, compositing, and volume rendering. This section focuses on basic transparency techniques, with an emphasis on the effective use of blending techniques.

In computer graphics, transparent objects are modeled by creating an opaque ver-sion of a transparent object, then modifying its transparency. The opacity of an object is defined independently of its color and is expressed as a fraction between 0 and 1, where 1 means fully opaque. Sometimes the terms *opacity* and *transparency* are used inter-changably; strictly speaking, transparency is defined as $1 - opacity$; a fully transparent object has an opacity of 0.

An object is made to appear transparent by rendering a weighted sum of the color of the transparent object and the color of the scene obscured by the transparent object. A fully opaque object supplies all of its color, and none from the background; a fully transparent object does the opposite. The equation for computing the output color of a transparent object, A, with opacity, o_A, at a single point is:

$$C_{outA} = o_A C_A + (1 - o_A) C_{background} \tag{11.4}$$

Applying this equation properly implies that everything behind the transparent object is rendered already as $C_{background}$ so that it is available for blending. If multiple transparent objects obscure each other, the equation is applied repeatedly. For two objects A and B (with A in front of B), the resulting color depends on the order of the transparent objects relative to the viewer. The equation becomes:

$$C_{outA} = o_A C_A + (1 - o_A) C_{outB}$$
$$C_{outB} = o_B C_B + (1 - o_B) C_{background}$$
$$C_{outAB} = o_A C_A + (1 - o_A)(o_B C_B + (1 - o_B) C_{background}) \tag{11.5}$$

The technique for combining transparent surfaces is identical to the back-to-front compositing process described in Section 11.1. The simplest transparency model assumes that a pixel displaying the transparent object is completely covered by a transparent surface. The transparent surface transmits $1 - o$ of the light reflected from the objects behind it and reflects o of its own incident light. For the case in which boundary pixels are only partially covered by the transparent surface, the uniform distribution (uniform opacity) assumption described in Section 11.1.2 is combined with the transparency model.

The compositing model assumes that when a pixel is partially covered by a surface, pieces of the overlapping surface are randomly distributed across the pixel such that any subarea of the pixel contains α of the surface. The two models can be combined such that a pixel partially covered by a transparent surface can have its α and o values combined to produce a single weight, αo. Like the compositing algorithm, the combined transparency compositing process can be applied back-to-front or front-to-back with the appropriate change to the equations.

11.9 Alpha-Blended Transparency

The most common technique used to draw transparent geometry is alpha blending. This technique uses the alpha value of each fragment to represent the opacity of the object. As an object is drawn, each fragment is combined with the values in the framebuffer pixel (which is assumed to represent the background scene) using the alpha value of the fragment to represent opacity:

$$C_{final} = \alpha_{src} C_{src} + (1 - \alpha_{src}) C_{dst}$$

The resulting output color, C_{final}, is written to the frame buffer. C_{src} and α_{src} are the fragment source color and alpha components. C_{dst} is the destination color, which is already in the framebuffer. This blending equation is specified using glBlendFunc with GL_SRC_ALPHA and GL_ONE_MINUS_SRC_ALPHA as the source and destination blend factors. The alpha blending algorithm implements the general transparency formula (Equation 11.5) and is order-dependent.

An illustration of this effect is shown in Figure 11.2, where two pairs of triangles, one pair on the left and one pair on the right, are drawn partially overlapped. Both pairs of triangles have the same colors, and both have opacities of 15. In each pair, the triangle on the left is drawn first. Note that the overlapped regions have different colors; they differ because the yellow triangle of the left pair is drawn first, while the cyan triangle is the first one drawn in the right pair.

As mentioned previously, the transparency blending equation is order-dependent, so transparent primitives drawn using alpha blending should *always* be drawn after all opaque primitives are drawn. If this is not done, the transparent objects won't show the color contributions of the opaque objects behind them. Where possible, the opaque objects should be drawn with depth testing on, so that their depth relationships are correct, and so the depth buffer will contain information on the opaque objects.

Figure 11.2 Alpha transparency ordering.

When drawing transparent objects in a scene that has opaque ones, turning on depth buffer testing will prevent transparent objects from being incorrectly drawn over the opaque ones that are in front of them.

Overlapping transparent objects in the scene should be sorted by depth and drawn in back-to-front order: the objects furthest from the eye are drawn first, those closest to the eye are drawn last. This forces the sequence of blending operations to be performed in the correct order.

Normal depth buffering allows a fragment to update a pixel only if the fragment is closer to the viewer than any fragment before it (assuming the depth compare function is GL_LESS). Fragments that are farther away won't update the framebuffer. When the pixel color is entirely replaced by the fragment's color, there is no problem with this scheme. But with blending enabled, every pixel from a transparent object affects the final color.

If transparent objects intersect, or are not drawn in back to front order, depth buffer updates will prevent some parts of the transparent objects from being drawn, producing incorrect results. To prevent this, depth buffer updates can be disabled using glDepthMask(GL_FALSE) after all the opaque objects are drawn. Note that depth testing is still active, just the depth buffer updates are disabled. As a result, the depth buffer maintains the relationship between opaque and transparent objects, but does not prevent the transparent objects from occluding each other.

In some cases, sorting transparent objects isn't enough. There are objects, such as transparent objects that are lit, that require more processing. If the back and front faces of the object aren't drawn in back-to-front order, the object can have an "inside out" appearance. Primitive ordering within an object is required. This can be difficult, especially if the object's geometry wasn't modeled with transparency in mind. Sorting of transparent objects is covered in more depth in Section 11.9.3.

If sorting transparent objects or object primitives into back-to-front order isn't feasible, a less accurate, but order-independent blending method can be used instead. Blending is configured to use GL_ONE for the destination factor rather than GL_ONE_MINUS_SRC_ALPHA. The blending equation becomes:

$$C_{final} = \alpha_{src} C_{src} + C_{dst} \tag{11.6}$$

This blending equation weights transparent surfaces by their opacity, but the accumulated background color is not changed. Because of this, the final result is independent of the surface drawing order. The multi-object blending equation becomes:

$$\alpha_A C_A + \alpha_B C_B + \alpha_C C_C + \cdots + C_{background}.$$

There is a cost in terms of accuracy with this approach; since the background color attenuation from Equation 11.5 has been eliminated, the resulting colors are too bright and have too much contribution from the background objects. It is particularly noticeable if transparent objects are drawn over a light-colored background or bright background objects.

Alpha-blended transparency sometimes suffers from the misconception that the technique requires a framebuffer with alpha channel storage. For back-to-front algorithms, the alpha value used for blended transparency comes from the fragments generated in the graphics pipeline; alpha values in the framebuffer (GL_DST_ALPHA) are not used in the blending equation, so no alpha buffer is required to store them.

11.9.1 Dynamic Object Transparency

It is common for an object's opacity values to be configured while modeling its geometry. Such static opacity can be stored in the alpha component of the vertex colors or in per-vertex diffuse material parameters. Sometimes, though, it is useful to have dynamic control over the opacity of an object. This might be as simple as a single value that dynamically controls the transparency of the entire object. This setting is useful for fading an object in or out of a scene (see Section 16.4 for one use of this capability). If the object being controlled is simple, using a single color or set of material parameters over its entire surface, the alpha value of the diffuse material parameter or object color can be changed and sent to OpenGL before rendering the object each frame.

For complex models that use per-vertex reflectances or surface textures, a similar global control can be implemented using constant color blending instead. The ARB imaging subset provides an application-defined constant blend color that can be used as the source or destination blend factor.[2] This color can be updated each frame, and used to modify the object's alpha value with the blend value GL_CONSTANT_ALPHA for the source and GL_ONE_MINUS_CONSTANT_ALPHA for the destination blend factor.

If the imaging subset is not supported, then a similar effect can be achieved using multitexture. An additional texture unit is configured with a 1D texture containing a single component alpha ramp. The unit's texture environment is configured to modulate the fragment color, and the unit is chained to act on the primitive after the surface texturing has been done. With this approach, the s coordinate for the additional texture unit is

---

2. Constant color blending is also present in OpenGL 1.4.

set to index the appropriate alpha value each time the object is drawn. This idea can be extended to provide even finer control over the transparency of an object. One such algorithm is described in Section 19.4.

11.9.2 Transparency Mapping

Because the key to alpha transparency is control of each fragment's alpha component, OpenGL's texture machinery is a valuable resource as it provides fine control of alpha. If texturing is enabled, the source of the alpha component is controlled by the texture's internal format, the current texture environment function, and the texture environment's constant color. Many intricate effects can be implemented using alpha values from textures.

A common example of texture-controlled alpha is using a texture with alpha to control the outline of a textured object. A texture map containing alpha can define an image of an object with a complex outline. Beyond the boundaries of the outline, the texel's alpha components can be zero. The transparency of the object can be controlled on a per-texel basis by controlling the alpha components of the textures mapped on its surface.

For example, if the texture environment mode is set to GL_REPLACE (or GL_MODULATE, which is a better choice for lighted objects), textured geometry is "clipped" by the texture's alpha components. The geometry will have "invisible" regions where the texel's alpha components go to zero, and be partially transparent where they vary between zero and one. These regions colored with alpha values below some threshold can be removed with either alpha testing or alpha blending. Note that texturing using GL_MODULATE will only work if the alpha component of the geometry's color is one; any other value will scale the transparency of the results. Both methods also require that blending (or alpha test) is enabled and set properly.

This technique is frequently used to draw complicated geometry using texture-mapped polygons. A tree, for example, can be rendered using an image of a tree texture mapped onto a single rectangle. The parts of the texture image representing the tree itself have an alpha value of 1; the parts of the texture outside of the tree have an alpha value of 0. This technique is often combined with billboarding (see Section 13.5), a technique in which a rectangle is turned to perpetually face the eye point.

Alpha testing (see Section 6.2.2) can be used to efficiently discard fragments with an alpha value of zero and avoid using blending, or it can be used with blending to avoid blending fragments that make no contribution. The threshold value may be set higher to retain partially transparent fragments. For example the alpha threshold can be set to 0.5 to capture half of the semi-transparent fragments, avoiding the overhead of blending while still getting acceptable results. An alternative is to use two passes with different alpha tests. In the first pass, draw the opaque fragments with depth updates enabled and transparent fragments discarded; in the second pass, draw the non-opaque parts with blending enabled and depth updates disabled. This has the advantage of avoiding blending operations for large opaque regions, at the cost of two passes.

11.9.3 Transparency Sorting

The sorting required for proper alpha transparency can be complex. Sorting is done using eye coordinates, since the back-to-front ordering of transparent objects must be done relative to the viewer. This requires the application transform geometry to eye space for sorting, then send the transparent objects in sorted order through the OpenGL pipeline.

If transparent objects interpenetrate, the individual triangles comprising each object should be sorted and drawn from back to front to avoid rendering the individual triangles out of order. This may also require splitting interpenetrating polygons along their intersections, sorting them, then drawing each one independently. This work may not be necessary if the interpenetrating objects have similar colors and opacity, or if the results don't have to be extremely realistic. Crude sorting, or even no sorting at all, can give acceptable results, depending on the requirements of the application.

Transparent objects can produce artifacts even if they don't interpenetrate other complex objects. If the object is composed of multiple polygons that can overlap, the order in which the polygons are drawn may not end up being back to front. This case is extremely common; one example is a closed surface representation of an object. A simple example of this problem is a vertically oriented cylinder composed of a single tri-strip. Only a limited range of orientations of the cylinder will result in all of the more distant triangles being drawn before all of the nearer ones. If lighting, texturing, or the cylinder's vertex colors resulted in the triangles of the cylinder having significantly different colors, visual artifacts will result that change with the cylinder's orientation.

This orientation dependency is shown in Figure 11.3. A four-sided cylinder is rendered with differing orientations in three rows. The top row shows the cylinder opaque. The middle row shows a properly transparent cylinder (done with the front-and-back-facing technique described in this chapter). The bottom row shows the cylinder made transparent with no special sorting. The cylinder walls are rendered in the order magenta,

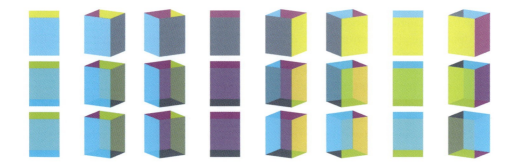

Figure 11.3 Orientation sensitivity in transparency objects.

yellow, gray, and cyan. As long as the walls rendered earlier are obscured by walls rendered later, the transparent cylinder is properly rendered, and the middle and bottom rows match. When the cylinder rotates to the point were the render ordering doesn't match the depth ordering, the bottom row is incorrectly rendered. This begins happening on the fifth column, counting from left to right. Since this cylinder has only four walls, it has a range of rotations that are correct. A rounder cylinder with many facets of varying colors would be much more sensitive to orientation.

If the scene contains a single transparent object, or multiple transparent objects which do not overlap in screen space (i.e., each screen pixel is touched by at most one of the transparent objects), a shortcut may be taken under certain conditions. If the transparent objects are closed, convex, and can't be viewed from the inside, backface culling can be used. The culling can be used to draw the back-facing polygons prior to the front-facing polygons. The constraints given previously ensure that back-facing polygons are farther from the viewer than front-facing ones.

For this, or any other face-culling technique to work, the object must be modeled such that all polygons have consistent orientation (see Section 1.3.1). Each polygon in the object should have its vertices arranged in a counter-clockwise direction when viewed from outside the object. With this orientation, the back-facing polygons are always farther from the viewer. The `glFrontFace` command can be used to invert the sense of front-facing for models generated with clockwise-oriented front-facing polygons.

11.9.4 Depth Peeling

An alternative to sorting is to use a multipass technique to extract the surfaces of interest. These *depth-peeling* techniques dissect a scene into layers with narrow depth ranges, then composite the results together. In effect, multiple passes are used to crudely sort the fragments into image layers that are subsequently composited in back-to-front order. Some of the original work on depth peeling suggested multiple depth buffers (Mammen, 1989; Diefenbach, 1996); however, in an NVIDIA technical report, Cass Everitt suggests reusing fragment programs and texture depth-testing hardware, normally used to support shadow maps, to create a mechanism for multiple depth tests, that in turn can be used to do depth peeling.

11.10 Screen-Door Transparency

Another simple transparency technique is *screen-door transparency*. A transparent object is created by rendering only a percentage of the object's pixels. A bitmask is used to control which pixels in the object are rasterized. A 1 bit in the bitmask indicates that the transparent object should be rendered at that pixel; a 0 bit indicates the transparent object shouldn't be rendered there, allowing the background pixel to show through.

The percentage of bits in the bitmask which are set to 0 is equivalent to the transparency of the object (Foley et al., 1990).

This method works because the areas patterned by the screen-door algorithm are spatially integrated by the eye, making it appear as if the weighted sums of colors in Equation 11.4 are being computed, but no read-modify-write blending cycles need to occur in the framebuffer. If the viewer gets too close to the display, then the individual pixels in the pattern become visible and the effect is lost.

In OpenGL, screen-door transparency can be implemented in a number of ways; one of the simplest uses *polygon stippling*. The command glPolygonStipple defines a 32×32 bit stipple pattern. When stippling is enabled (using glEnable with a GL_POLYGON_STIPPLE parameter), it uses the low-order x and y bits of the screen coordinate to index into the stipple pattern for each fragment. If the corresponding bit of the stipple pattern is 0, the fragment is rejected. If the bit is 1, rasterization of the fragment continues.

Since the stipple pattern lookup takes place in screen space, the stipple patterns for overlapping objects should differ, even if the objects have the same transparency. If the same stipple pattern is used, the same pixels in the framebuffer are drawn for each object. Because of this, only the last (or the closest, if depth buffering is enabled) overlapping object will be visible. The stipple pattern should also display as fine a pattern as possible, since coarse features in the stipple pattern will become distracting artifacts.

One big advantage of screen-door transparency is that the objects do not need to be sorted. Rasterization may be faster on some systems using the screen-door technique than by using other techniques such as alpha blending. Since the screen-door technique operates on a per-fragment basis, the results will not look as smooth as alpha transparency. However, patterns that repeat on a 2×2 grid are the smoothest, and a 50% transparent "checkerboard" pattern looks quite smooth on most systems.

Screen-door transparency does have important limitations. The largest is the fact that the stipple pattern is indexed in screen space. This fixes the pattern to the screen; a moving object makes the stipple pattern appear to move across its surface, creating a "crawling" effect. Large stipple patterns will show motion artifacts. The stipple pattern also risks obscuring fine shading details on a lighted object; this can be particularly noticeable if the stippled object is rotating. If the stipple pattern is attached to the object (by using texturing and GL_REPLACE, for example), the motion artifacts are eliminated, but strobing artifacts might become noticeable as multiple transparent objects overlap.

Choosing stipple patterns for multiple transparent objects can be difficult. Not only must the stipple pattern accurately represent the transparency of the object, but it must produce the proper transparency with other stipple patterns when transparent objects overlap. Consider two 50% transparent objects that completely overlap. If the same stipple pattern is used for both objects, then the last object drawn will capture all of the pixels and the first object will disappear. The constraints in choosing patterns quickly becomes intractable as more transparent objects are added to the scene.

The coarse pixel-level granularity of the stipple patterns severely limits the effectiveness of this algorithm. It relies heavily on properties of the human eye to average out the individual pixel values. This works quite well for high-resolution output devices such as color printers (> 1000 dot-per-inch), but clearly fails on typical 100 dpi computer graphics displays. The end result is that the patterns can't accurately reproduce the transparency levels that should appear when objects overlap and the wrong proportions of the surface colors are mixed together.

11.10.1 Multisample Transparency

OpenGL implementations supporting multisampling (OpenGL 1.3 or later, or implementations supporting ARB_multisample) can use the per-fragment sample coverage, normally used for antialiasing (see Section 10.2.3), to control object transparency as well. This method is similar to screen-door transparency described earlier, but the masking is done at each sample point within an individual fragment.

Multisample transparency has trade-offs similar to screen-door transparency. Sorting transparent objects is not required and the technique may be faster than using alpha-blended transparency. For scenes already using multisample antialiasing, a performance improvement is more likely to be significant: multisample framebuffer blending operations use all of the color samples at each pixel rather than a single pixel color, and may take longer on some implementations. Eliminating a blending step may be a significant performance gain in this case.

To implement screen-door multisample transparency, the multisample coverage mask at the start of the fragment processing pipeline must be modified (see Section 6.2) There are two ways to do this. One method uses GL_SAMPLE_ALPHA_TO_COVERAGE. When enabled, this function maps the alpha value of each fragment into a sample mask. This mask is bitwise AND'ed with the fragment's mask. Since the mask value controls how many sample colors are combined into the final pixel color, this provides an automatic way of using alpha values to control the degree of transparency. This method is useful with objects that do not have a constant transparency value. If the transparency value is different at each vertex, for example, or the object uses a surface texture containing a transparency map, the per-fragment differences in alpha value will be transferred to the fragment's coverage mask.

The second transparency method provides more direct control of the sample coverage mask. The glSampleCoverage command updates the GL_SAMPLE_COVERAGE_VALUE bitmask based on the floating-point *coverage* value passed to the command. This value is constrained to range between 0 and 1. The coverage value bitmask is bitwise AND'ed with each fragment's coverage mask. The glSampleCoverage command provides an *invert* parameter which inverts the computed value of GL_SAMPLE_COVERAGE_VALUE. Using the same *coverage* value, and changing the *invert* flag makes it possible to create two transparency masks that don't overlap. This method is most useful when the transparency is constant for a given object; the coverage value can be set once before each object is rendered. The invert option is also useful for gradually fading between two objects; it is used by some geometry level-of-detail management techniques (see Section 16.4 for details).

Multisample screen-door techniques have the advantage over per-pixel screen-door algorithms; that subpixel transparency masks generate fewer visible pixel artifacts. Since each transparency mask pattern is contained within a single pixel, there is no pixel-level pattern imposed on polygon surfaces. A lack of a visible pattern also means that moving objects won't show a pattern crawl on their surfaces. Note that it is still possible to get *subpixel* masking artifacts, but they will be more subtle; they are limited to pixels that are partially covered by a transparent primitive. The behavior of these artifacts are highly implementation-dependent; the OpenGL specification imposes few restrictions on the layout of samples within a fragment.

The multisample screen-door technique is constrained by two limitations. First, it is not possible to set an exact bit pattern in the coverage mask: this prevents the application from applying precise control over the screen-door transparency patterns. While this restriction was deliberately placed in the OpenGL design to allow greater flexibility in implementing multisample, it does remove some control from the application writer. Second, the transparency resolution is limited by the number of samples available per fragment. If the implementation supports only four multisamples, for example, each fragment can represent at most five transparency levels $(n+1)$, including fully transparent and fully opaque. Some OpenGL implementations may try to overcome this restriction by spatially dithering the subpixel masks to create additional levels. This effectively creates a hybrid between subpixel-level and pixel-level screen-door techniques. The limited number of per-fragment samples creates a limitation which is also found in the the per-pixel screen-door technique: multisample transparency does not work well when many transparent surfaces are stacked on top of one another.

Overall, the multisample screen-door technique is a significant improvement over the pixel-level screen door, but it still suffers from problems with sample resolution. Using sorting with alpha blending can generate better results; the alpha channel can usually represent more opacity levels than sample coverage and the blending arithmetic computes an exact answer at each pixel. However, for performance-critical applications, especially when the transparent objects are difficult to sort, the multisample technique can be a good choice. Best results are obtained if there is little overlap between transparent objects and the number of different transparency levels represented is small.

Since there is a strong similarity between the principles used for modeling surface opacity and compositing, the subpixel mask operations can also be used to perform some of the compositing algorithms without using framebuffer blending. However, the limitations with respect to resolution of mask values preclude using these modified techniques for high-quality results.

11.11 Summary

In this chapter we described some of the underlying theory for image compositing and transparency modeling. We also covered some common algorithms using the OpenGL pipeline and the various advantages and limitations of these algorithms. Efficient rendering of semi-transparent objects without extra burdens on the application, such as sorting, continues to be a difficult problem and will no doubt be a continuing area of investigation. In the next chapter we examine using other parts of the pipeline for operating on images directly.

Image Processing Techniques

A comprehensive treatment of image processing techniques is beyond the scope of this book. However, since image processing is such a powerful tool, even a subset of image processing techniques can be useful, and is a powerful adjunct to computer graphics approaches. Some of the more fundamental processing algorithms are described here, along with methods for accelerating them using the OpenGL pipeline.

12.1 OpenGL Imaging Support

Image processing is an important component of applications used in the publishing, satellite imagery analysis, medical, and seismic imaging fields. Given its importance, image processing functionality has been added to OpenGL in a number of ways. A bundle of extensions targeted toward accelerating common image processing operations, referred to as the *ARB imaging subset*, is defined as part of the OpenGL 1.2 and later specifications. This set of extensions includes the color matrix transform, additional color lookup tables, 2D convolution operations, histogram, min/max color value tracking, and additional color buffer blending functionality. These extensions are described in Section 4.8. While these extensions are not essential for all of the image processing techniques described in this chapter, they can provide important performance advantages.

Since the imaging subset is optional, not all implementations of OpenGL support them. If it is advertised as part of the implementation, the entire subset must be implemented. Some implementations provide only part of this functionality by implementing a subset of the imaging extensions, using the EXT versions. Important functionality, such as the color lookup table (EXT_color_table) and convolution (EXT_convolution) can be provided this way.

With the evolution of the fragment processing pipeline to support programmability, many of the functions provided by the imaging subset can be implemented using fragment programs. For example, color matrix arithmetic becomes simple vector operations on color components, color lookup tables become dependent texture reads with multitexture, convolution becomes multiple explicit texture lookup operations with a weighted sum. Other useful extensions, such as pixel textures, are implemented using simple fragment program instructions. However, other image subset operations such as histogram and minmax don't have direct fragment program equivalents; perhaps over time sufficient constructs will evolve to efficiently support these operations.

Even without this extended functionality, the basic imaging support in OpenGL, described in Chapter 4, provides a firm foundation for creating image processing techniques.

12.2 Image Storage

The multipass concept described in Chapter 9 also applies to image processing. To combine image processing elements into powerful algorithms, the image processing operations must be coupled with some notion of temporary storage, or image variables, for intermediate results. There are three main locations for storing images: in application memory on the host, in a color buffer (back, front, aux buffers, and stereo buffers), or in a texture. A fourth storage location, off-screen memory in pbuffers, is available if the implementation supports them. Each of these storage areas can participate in image operations in one form or another. The biggest difference occurs between images stored as textures and those stored in the other buffers types. Texture images are manipulated by drawing polygonal geometry and operating on the fragment values during rasterization and fragment processing.

Images stored in host memory, color buffers, or pbuffers can be processed by the pixel pipeline, as well as the rasterization and fragment processing pipeline. Images can be easily transferred between the storage locations using glDrawPixels and glReadPixels to transfer images between application memory and color buffers, glCopyTexImage2D to copy images from color buffers to texture memory, and by drawing scaled textured quadrilaterals to copy texture images to a color buffer. To a large extent the techniques discussed in this chapter can be applied regardless of where the image is stored, but some techniques may be more efficient if the image is stored in one particular storage area over another.

If an image is to be used repeatedly as a source operand in an algorithm or by applying the algorithm repeatedly using the same source, it's useful to optimize the location of the image for the most efficient processing. This will invariably require moving the image from host memory to either texture memory or a color buffer.

12.3 Point Operations

Image processing operations are often divided into two broad classes: *point-based* and *region-based* operations. Point operations generate each output pixel as a function of a single corresponding input pixel. Point operations include functions such as thresholding and color-space conversion. Region-based operations calculate a new pixel value using the values in a (usually small) local neighborhood. Examples of region-based operations include convolution and morphology operations.

In a point operation, each component in the output pixel may be a simple function of the corresponding component in the input pixel, or a more general function using additional, non-pixel input parameters. The multipass toolbox methodology outlined in Section 9.3, i.e., building powerful algorithms from a "programming language" of OpenGL operations and storage, is applied here to implement the algorithms outlined here.

12.3.1 Color Adjustment

A simple but important local operation is adjusting a pixel's color. Although simple to do in OpenGL, this operation is surprisingly useful. It can be used for a number of purposes, from modifying the brightness, hue or saturation of the image, to transforming an image from one color space to another.

12.3.2 Interpolation and Extrapolation

Haeberli and Voorhies (1994) have described several interesting image processing techniques using linear interpolation and extrapolation between two images. Each technique can be described in terms of the formula:

$$O = (1 - x)I_0 + xI_1 \qquad \textbf{(12.1)}$$

The equation is evaluated on a per-pixel basis. I_0 and I_1 are the input images, O is the output image, and x is the blending factor. If x is between 0 and 1, the equations describe a linear interpolation. If x is allowed to range outside $[0, 1]$, the result is extrapolation.

In the limited case where $0 \leq x \leq 1$, these equations may be implemented using constant color blending or the accumulation buffer. The accumulation buffer version uses the following steps:

1. Draw I_0 into the color buffer.

2. Load I_0, scaling by $(1 - x)$: `glAccum(GL_LOAD, (1-x))`.

3. Draw I_1 into the color buffer.

4. Accumulate I_1, scaling by x: `glAccum(GL_ACCUM,x)`.

5. Return the results: `glAccum(GL_RETURN, 1)`.

It is assumed that component values in I_0 and I_1 are between 0 and 1. Since the accumulation buffer can only store values in the range $[-1, 1]$, for the case $x < 0$ or $x > 1$, the equation must be implemented in a such a way that the accumulation operations stay within the $[-1, 1]$ constraint. Given a value x, equation Equation 12.1 is modified to prescale with a factor such that the accumulation buffer does not overflow. To define a scale factor s such that:

$$s = \max(x, 1 - x)$$

Equation 12.1 becomes:

$$O = s \left(\frac{(1 - x)}{s} I_0 + \frac{x}{s} I_1 \right)$$

and the list of steps becomes:

1. Compute s.

2. Draw I_0 into the color buffer.

3. Load I_0, scaling by $\frac{(1-x)}{s}$: `glAccum(GL_LOAD, (1-x)/s)`.

4. Draw I_1 into the color buffer.

5. Accumulate I_1, scaling by $\frac{x}{s}$: `glAccum(GL_ACCUM, x/s)`.

6. Return the results, scaling by s: `glAccum(GL_RETURN, s)`.

The techniques suggested by Haeberli and Voorhies use a degenerate image as I_0 and an appropriate value of x to move toward or away from that image. To increase brightness, I_0 is set to a black image and $x > 1$. Saturation may be varied using a luminance version of I_1 as I_0. (For information on converting RGB images to luminance, see Section 12.3.5.) To change contrast, I_0 is set to a gray image of the average luminance value of I_1. Decreasing x (toward the gray image) decreases contrast; increasing x increases contrast. Sharpening (*unsharp masking*) may be accomplished by setting I_0 to a blurred version of I_1. These latter two examples require the application of a region-based operation to compute I_0, but once I_0 is computed, only point operations are required.

12.3.3 Scale and Bias

Scale and bias operations apply the affine transformation $C_{out} = sC_{in} + b$ to each pixel. A frequent use for scale and bias is to compress the range of the pixel values to compensate for limited computation range in another part of the pipeline or to undo this effect by expanding the range. For example, color components ranging from [0, 1] are scaled to half this range by scaling by 0.5; color values are adjusted to an alternate signed representation by scaling by 0.5 and biasing by 0.5. Scale and bias operations may also be used to trivially null or saturate a color component by setting the scale to 0 and the bias to 0 or 1.

Scale and bias can be achieved in a multitude of ways, from using explicit pixel transfer scale and bias operations, to color matrix, fragment programs, blend operations or the accumulation buffer. Scale and bias operations are frequently chained together in image operations, so having multiple points in the pipeline where they can be performed can improve efficiency significantly.

12.3.4 Thresholding

Thresholding operations select pixels whose component values lie within a specified range. The operation may change the values of either the selected or the unselected pixels. A pixel pattern can be highlighted, for example, by setting all the pixels in the pattern to 0. Pixel maps and lookup tables provide a simple mechanism for thresholding using individual component values. However, pixel maps and lookup tables only allow replacement of one component individually, so lookup table thresholding is trivial only for single component images.

To manipulate all of the components in an RGB pixel, a more general lookup table operation is needed, such as pixel textures, or better still, fragment programs. The operation can also be converted to a multipass sequence in which individual component selection operations are performed, then the results combined together to produce the thresholded image. For example, to determine the region of pixels where the R, G, and B components are all within the range [25, 75], the task can be divided into four separate passes. The results of each component threshold operation are directed to the alpha channel; blending is then used to perform simple logic operations to combine the results:

1. Load the `GL_PIXEL_MAP_A_TO_A` with a values that map components in the range [0.25, 0.75] to 1 and everything else to 0. Load the other color pixel maps with a single entry that maps all components to 1 and enable the color pixel map.

2. Clear the color buffer to (1, 1, 1, 0) and enable blending with source and destination blend factors `GL_SRC_ALPHA`, `GL_SRC_ALPHA`.

3. Use `glDrawPixels` to draw the image with the R channel in the A position.

4. Repeat the previous step for the G and B channels.

5. At this point the color buffer has 1 for every pixel meeting the condition $0.25 \leq x \leq 0.75$ for the three color components. The image is drawn one more

time with the blend function set to `glBlendFunc(GL_DST_COLOR, GL_ZERO)` to modulate the image.

One way to draw the image with the R, G, or B channels in the A position is to use a color matrix *swizzle* as described in Section 9.3.1. Another approach is to pad the beginning of an RGBA image with several extra component instances, then adjust the input image pointer to `glDrawPixels` by a negative offset. This will ensure that the desired component starts in the A position. Note that this approach works only for 4-component images in which all of the components are equal size.

12.3.5 Conversion to Luminance

A color image is converted to a luminance image (Figure 12.1) by scaling each component by its weight in the luminance equation.

$$
\begin{pmatrix} L \\ L \\ L \\ 0 \end{pmatrix} = \begin{pmatrix} R_w & G_w & B_w & 0 \\ R_w & G_w & B_w & 0 \\ R_w & G_w & B_w & 0 \\ 0 & 0 & 0 & 0 \end{pmatrix} \begin{pmatrix} R \\ G \\ B \\ A \end{pmatrix}
$$

The recommended weight values for R_w, G_w, and B_w are 0.2126, 0.7152, and 0.0722, respectively, from the ITU-R BT.709-5 standard for HDTV. These values are identical to the luminance component from the CIE XYZ conversions described in Section 12.3.8. Some authors have used the values from the NTSC YIQ color conversion equation (0.299, 0.587, and 0.114), but these values are inappropriate for a linear RGB color space (Haeberli, 1993). This operation is most easily achieved using the color matrix, since the computation involves a weighted sum across the R, G, and B color components.

In the absence of color matrix or programmable pipeline support, the equivalent result can be achieved, albeit less efficiently, by splitting the operation into three passes. With each pass, a single component is transferred from the host. The appropriate scale factor is set, using the scale parameter in a scale and bias element. The results are summed together in the color buffer using the source and destination blend factors `GL_ONE`, `GL_ONE`.

12.3.6 Manipulating Saturation

The *saturation* of a color is the distance of that color from a gray of equal intensity (Foley et al., 1990). Haeberli modifies saturation using the equation:

$$
\begin{pmatrix} R' \\ G' \\ B' \\ A \end{pmatrix} = \begin{pmatrix} a & d & g & 0 \\ b & e & h & 0 \\ c & f & i & 0 \\ 0 & 0 & 0 & 1 \end{pmatrix} \begin{pmatrix} R \\ G \\ B \\ A \end{pmatrix}
$$

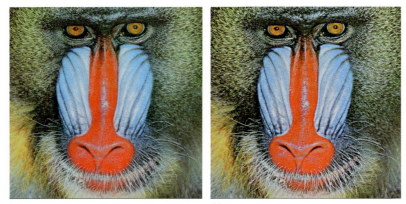

(a) (b)

(c)

Figure 12.1 Image operations: original, sharpened, luminance.

where:

$$a = (1 - s) * R_w + s$$
$$b = (1 - s) * R_w$$
$$c = (1 - s) * R_w$$
$$d = (1 - s) * G_w$$
$$e = (1 - s) * G_w + s$$
$$f = (1 - s) * G_w$$
$$g = (1 - s) * B_w$$
$$h = (1 - s) * B_w$$
$$i = (1 - s) * B_w + s$$

with R_w, G_w, and B_w as described in the previous section. Since the saturation of a color is the difference between the color and a gray value of equal intensity, it is comforting to note that setting s to 0 gives the luminance equation. Setting s to 1 leaves the saturation unchanged; setting it to -1 takes the complement of the colors (Haeberli, 1993).

12.3.7 Rotating Hue

Changing the hue of a color can be accomplished by a color rotation about the gray vector $(1, 1, 1)^t$ in the color matrix. This operation can be performed in one step using the glRotate command. The matrix may also be constructed by rotating the gray vector into the z-axis, then rotating around that. Although more complicated, this approach is the basis of a more accurate hue rotation, and is shown later. The multistage rotation is shown here (Haeberli, 1993):

1. Load the identity matrix: glLoadIdentity.

2. Rotate such that the gray vector maps onto the z-axis using the glRotate command.

3. Rotate about the z-axis to adjust the hue: glRotate(<degrees>, 0, 0, 1).

4. Rotate the gray vector back into position.

Unfortunately, this naive application of glRotate will not preserve the luminance of an image. To avoid this problem, the color rotation about z can be augmented. The color space can be transformed so that areas of constant luminance map to planes perpendicular to the z-axis. Then a hue rotation about that axis will preserve luminance. Since the luminance of a vector (R, G, B) is equal to:

$$(R, G, B) \cdot (R_w, G_w, B_w)^T$$

the plane of constant luminance k is defined by:

$$(R, G, B) \cdot (R_w, G_w, B_w)^T = k$$

Therefore, the vector (R_w, G_w, B_w) is perpendicular to planes of constant luminance. The algorithm for matrix construction becomes the following (Haeberli, 1993):

1. Load the identity matrix.

2. Apply a rotation matrix M such that the gray vector $(1, 1, 1)^t$ maps onto the positive z-axis.

3. Compute $(R_w', G_w', B_w')^t = M(R_w, G_w, B_w)^t$. Apply a skew transform which maps $(R_w', G_w', B_w')^t$ to $(0, 0, B_w')^t$. This matrix is:

$$\begin{pmatrix} 1 & 0 & \dfrac{-R_w'}{B_w'} & 0 \\ 0 & 1 & \dfrac{-G_w'}{B_w'} & 0 \\ 0 & 0 & 1 & 0 \\ 0 & 0 & 0 & 1 \end{pmatrix}$$

4. Rotate about the z-axis to adjust the hue.

5. Apply the inverse of the shear matrix.

6. Apply the inverse of the rotation matrix.

It is possible to create a single matrix which is defined as a function of R_w, G_w, B_w, and the amount of hue rotation required.

12.3.8 Color Space Conversion

CIE XYZ Conversion The CIE (Commission Internationale de L'Éclairage) color space is the internationally agreed on representation of color. It consists of three spectral weighting curves $\bar{x}, \bar{y}, \bar{z}$ called *color matching functions* for the CIE Standard Observer. A tristimulus color is represented as an XYZ triple, where Y corresponds to luminance and X and Z to the response values from the two remaining color matching functions. The CIE also defines a representation for "pure" color, termed *chromaticity* consisting of the two values

$$x = \frac{X}{X + Y + Z} \qquad y = \frac{Y}{X + Y + Z}$$

A chromaticity diagram plots the chromaticities of wavelengths from 400 nm to 700 nm resulting in the inverted "U" shape shown in Figure 12.2. The shape

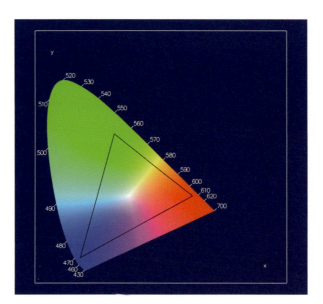

Figure 12.2 The CIE (1931) (x,y) chromaticity diagram.

defines the gamut of visible colors. The CIE color space can also be plotted as a 3D volume, but the 2D chromaticity projection provides some useful information. RGB color spaces project to a triangle on the chromaticity diagram, and the triangle defines the gamut of the RGB color space. Each of the R, G, and B primaries form a vertex of the triangle. Different RGB color spaces map to different triangles in the chromaticity diagram. There are many standardized RGB color space definitions, each with a different purpose. Perhaps the most important is the ITU-R BT.709-5 definition. This RGB color space defines the RGB gamut for digital video signals and roughly matches the range of color that can be reproduced on CRT-like display devices. Other RGB color spaces represent gamuts of different sizes. For example, the Adobe RGB (1998) color space projects to a larger triangle and can represent a large range of colors. This can be useful for transfer to output devices that are capable of reproducing a larger gamut. Note that with a finite width color representation, such as 8-bit RGB color components, there is a trade-off between the representable range of colors and the ability to differentiate between distinct colors. That is, there is a trade-off between dynamic range and precision.

To transform from BT.709 RGB to the CIE XYZ color space, use the following matrix:

$$\begin{pmatrix} X \\ Y \\ Z \\ A \end{pmatrix} = \begin{pmatrix} 0.412391 & 0.357584 & 0.180481 & 0 \\ 0.212639 & 0.715169 & 0.072192 & 0 \\ 0.019331 & 0.119193 & 0.950532 & 0 \\ 0.000000 & 0.000000 & 0.000000 & 1 \end{pmatrix} \begin{pmatrix} R \\ G \\ B \\ A \end{pmatrix}$$

The XYZ values of each of the R, G, and B primaries are the columns of the matrix. The inverse matrix is used to map XYZ to RGBA (Foley et al., 1990). Note that the CIE XYZ space can represent colors outside the RGB gamut. Care should be taken to ensure the XYZ colors are "clipped" as necessary to produce representable RGB colors (all components lie within the 0 to 1 range).

$$\begin{pmatrix} R \\ G \\ B \\ A \end{pmatrix} = \begin{pmatrix} 3.240970 & -1.537383 & -0.498611 & 0 \\ -0.969244 & 1.875968 & 0.041555 & 0 \\ 0.055630 & -0.203977 & 1.056972 & 0 \\ 0.000000 & 0.000000 & 0.000000 & 1 \end{pmatrix} \begin{pmatrix} X \\ Y \\ Z \\ A \end{pmatrix}$$

Conversion between different RGB spaces is achieved by using the CIE XYZ space as a common intermediate space. An RGB space definition should include CIE XYZ values for the RGB primaries. Color management systems use this as one of the principles for converting images from one color space to another.

CMY Conversion The CMY color space describes colors in terms of the subtractive primaries: cyan, magenta, and yellow. CMY is used for hardcopy devices such as color printers, so it is useful to be able to convert to CMY from RGB color space. The conversion from RGB to CMY follows the equation (Foley, et al., 1990):

$$\begin{pmatrix} C \\ M \\ Y \end{pmatrix} = \begin{pmatrix} 1 \\ 1 \\ 1 \end{pmatrix} - \begin{pmatrix} R \\ G \\ B \end{pmatrix}$$

CMY conversion may be performed using the color matrix or as a scale and bias operation. The conversion is equivalent to a scale by -1 and a bias by $+1$. Using the 4×4 color matrix, the equation can be restated as:

$$\begin{pmatrix} C \\ M \\ Y \\ 1 \end{pmatrix} = \begin{pmatrix} -1 & 0 & 0 & 1 \\ 0 & -1 & 0 & 1 \\ 0 & 0 & -1 & 1 \\ 0 & 0 & 0 & 1 \end{pmatrix} \begin{pmatrix} R \\ G \\ B \\ 1 \end{pmatrix}$$

To produce the correct bias from the matrix multiply, the alpha component of the incoming color must be equal to 1. If the source image is RGB, the 1 will be added automatically during the format conversion stage of the pipeline.

A related color space, CMYK, uses a fourth channel (K) to represent black. Since conversion to CMYK requires a *min()* operation, it cannot be done using the color matrix.

The OpenGL extension EXT_CMYKA adds support for CMYK and CMYKA (CMYK with alpha). It provides methods to read and write CMYK and CMYKA values stored in system memory (which also implies conversion to RGB and RGBA, respectively).

YIQ Conversion The YIQ color space was explicitly designed to support color television, while allowing backwards compatibility with black and white TVs. It is still used today in non-HDTV color television broadcasting in the United States. Conversion from RGBA to YIQA can be done using the color matrix:

$$\begin{pmatrix} Y \\ I \\ Q \\ A \end{pmatrix} = \begin{pmatrix} 0.299 & 0.587 & 0.114 & 0 \\ 0.596 & -0.275 & -0.321 & 0 \\ 0.212 & -0.523 & 0.311 & 0 \\ 0.000 & 0.000 & 0.000 & 1 \end{pmatrix} \begin{pmatrix} R \\ G \\ B \\ A \end{pmatrix}$$

(Generally, YIQ is not used with an alpha channel so the fourth component is eliminated.) The inverse matrix is used to map YIQ to RGBA (Foley et al., 1990):

$$\begin{pmatrix} R \\ G \\ B \\ A \end{pmatrix} = \begin{pmatrix} 1.0 & 0.956 & 0.621 & 0 \\ 1.0 & -0.272 & -0.647 & 0 \\ 1.0 & -1.105 & 1.702 & 0 \\ 0.0 & 0.000 & 0.000 & 1 \end{pmatrix} \begin{pmatrix} Y \\ I \\ Q \\ A \end{pmatrix}$$

HSV Conversion The hue saturation value (HSV) model is based on intuitive color characteristics. Saturation characterizes the purity of the color or how much white is mixed in, with zero white being the purest. Value characterizes the brightness of the color. The space is defined by a hexicone in cylindrical coordinates, with hue ranging from 0 to 360 degrees (often normalized to the [0, 1] range), saturation from 0 to 1 (purest), and value from 0 to 1 (brightest). Unlike the other color space conversions, converting to HSV can't be expressed as a simple matrix transform. It can be emulated using lookup tables or by directly implementing the formula:

$$V = \max(R, G, B)$$

$$\Delta = V - \min(R, G, B)$$

$$S = \begin{cases} \Delta/V & \text{if } V \neq 0 \\ 0 & \text{if } V = 0 \end{cases}$$

$$h = \begin{cases} 0 + 60(G - B)/\Delta & \text{if } R = V \\ 120 + 60(B - R)/\Delta & \text{if } G = V \\ 240 + 60(R - G)/\Delta & \text{if } B = V \end{cases}$$

$$H = \begin{cases} 0 & \text{if } S = 0 \\ h & \text{if } h \geq 0 \\ h + 360 & \text{if } h < 0 \end{cases}$$

The conversion from HSV to RGB requires a similar strategy to implement the formula:

$$sector = \text{floor}(H/60)$$

$$frac = (H/60) - sector$$

$$o = V(1 - S)$$

$$p = V(1 - S\,frac)$$

$$q = V(1 - S(1 - frac))$$

$$(R \quad G \quad B) = \begin{cases} (V \quad V \quad V) & \text{if } S = 0 \\ (V \quad q \quad o) & \text{if } sector = 0 \\ (p \quad V \quad o) & \text{if } sector = 1 \\ (o \quad V \quad q) & \text{if } sector = 2 \\ (o \quad p \quad V) & \text{if } sector = 3 \\ (q \quad o \quad V) & \text{if } sector = 4 \\ (V \quad o \quad p) & \text{if } sector = 5 \end{cases}$$

12.4 Region-based Operations

A region-based operation generates an output pixel value from multiple input pixel values. Frequently the input value's spatial coordinates are near the coordinates of the output pixel, but in general an output pixel value can be a function of any or all of the pixels in the input image. An example of such a function is the minmax operation, which computes the minimum and maximum component values across an entire pixel image. This class of image processing operations is very powerful, and is the basis of many important operations, such as edge detection, image sharpening, and image analysis.

OpenGL can be used to create several toolbox functions to make it easier to perform non-local operations. For example, once an image is transferred to texture memory, texture mapped drawing operations can be used to shift the texel values to arbitrary window coordinates. This can be done by manipulating the window or texture coordinates of the accompanying geometry. If fragment programs are supported, they can be used to sample from arbitrary locations within a texture and combine the results (albeit with limits on the number of instructions or samples). Histogram and minmax operations can be used to compute statistics across an image; the resulting values can later be used as weighting factors.

12.4.1 Contrast Stretching

Contrast stretching is a simple method for improving the contrast of an image by linearly scaling (*stretching*) the intensity of each pixel by a fixed amount. Images in which the intensity values are confined to a narrow range work well with this algorithm. The linear scaling equation is:

$$I_{out} = \left(\frac{I_{in} - \min(I_{in})}{\max(I_{in}) - \min(I_{in})} \right)$$

where $\min(I_{in})$ and $\max(I_{in})$ are the minimum and maximum intensity values in the input image. If the intensity extrema are already known, the stretching operation is really a point operation using a simple scale and bias. However, the search operation required to find the extrema is a non-local operation. If the imaging subset is available, the minmax operation can be used to find them.

12.4.2 Histogram Equalization

Histogram equalization is a more sophisticated technique, modifying the dynamic range of an image by altering the pixel values, guided by the intensity histogram of that image. Recall that the intensity histogram of an image is a table of counts, each representing a range of intensity values. The counts record the number of times each intensity value range occurs in the image. For an RGB image, there is a separate table entry for each of the R, G, and B components. Histogram equalization creates a non-linear mapping, which reassigns the intensity values in the input image such that the resultant images contain a uniform distribution of intensities, resulting in a flat (or nearly flat) histogram. This mapping operation is performed using a lookup table. The resulting image typically brings more image details to light, since it makes better use of the available dynamic range.

The steps in the histogram equalization process are:

1. Compute the histogram of the input image.

2. Normalize the resulting histogram to the range [0, 1].

3. Transfer the normalized histogram to a color table.

4. Transfer the input image through the lookup table.

12.5 Reduction Operations

The minmax and histogram computations are representative of a class of *reduction operations* in which an entire image is scanned to produce a small number of values. For minmax, two color values are computed and for luminance histograms, an array of counts is computed corresponding to the luminance bins. Other examples include computing the average pixel value, the sum of all the pixel values, the count of pixel values of a particular color, etc. These types of operations are difficult for two reasons. First, the range of intermediate or final values may be large and not easily representable using a finite width color value. For example, an 8-bit color component can only represent 256 values. However, with increasing support for floating-point fragment computations and floating-point colors, this limitation disappears.

The second problem is more architectural. The reduction algorithms can be thought of as taking many inputs and producing a single (or small number of) outputs. The vertex and fragment processing pipelines excel at processing large numbers of inputs (vertices or fragments) and producing a large number of outputs. Parallel processing is heavily exploited in hardware accelerator architectures to achieve significant processing speed increases. Ideally a reduction algorithm should try to exploit this parallel processing capability. One way to accomplish this is by using *recursive folding* operations to successively reduce the size of the input data. For example, an $n \times n$ image is reduced to an $n/2 \times n/2$ image of min or max values of neighbor pixels (texels) using texture mapping and a fragment program to compute the minmax of neighboring values. This processing continues by copying the previous result to a texture map and repeating the steps. This reduces the generated image size by 2 along each dimension in each pass until a 1×1 image is left. For an $n \times n$ image it takes $1 + \lceil \log_2 n \rceil$ passes to compute the final result, or for an $n \times m$ image it takes $1 + \lceil \log_2(\max\{n, m\}) \rceil$ passes (Figure 12.3).

As the intermediate result reduces in size, the degree of available parallelism decreases, but large gains can still be achieved for the early passes, typically until $n = 4$. When n is sufficiently small, it may be more efficient to transfer the data

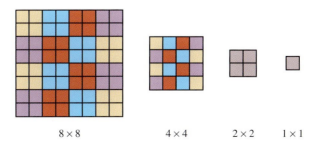

8×8 4×4 2×2 1×1

Figure 12.3 Recursive 2-way folding.

to the host and complete the computation there if that is the final destination for the result. However, if the result will be used as the input for another OpenGL operation, then it is likely more efficient to complete the computation within the pipeline.

If more samples can be computed in the fragment program, say $k \times k$, then the image size is reduced by k in each dimension at each pass and the number of passes is $1 + [\log_k (\max\{n, m\})]$. The logical extreme occurs when the fragment program is capable of indexing through the entire image in a single fragment program instance, using conditional looping. Conditional looping support is on the horizon for the programmable pipeline, so in the near future the single pass scenario becomes viable. While this may seem attractive, it is important to note that executing the entire algorithm in a single fragment program eliminates all of the inherent per-pixel parallelism. It is likely that maintaining some degree of parallelism throughout the algorithm makes more effective use of the hardware resources and is therefore faster.

Other reduction operations can be computed using a similar folding scheme. For example, the box-filtered mipmap generation algorithm described later in Section 14.15 is the averaging reduction algorithm in disguise. Futhermore, it doesn't require a fragment program to perform the folding computations. Other reduction operations may also be done using the fixed-function pipeline if they are simple sums or counts.

The histogram operation is another interesting reduction operation. Assuming that a luminance histogram with 256 bins is desired, the computation can be performed by using a fragment program to target one bin at a time. A single texel is sampled at a time, generating 0 or 1 for the texel sample depending on whether it is outside or inside the bin range. Framebuffer blending with GL_ONE, GL_ONE factors is used to sum the results. This requires $n \times n \times 256$ passes to process the entire image. To improve upon the parallelism, a 256×1 quad can be drawn to sample one texel and compare it against all 256 bins at a time. The window x coordinate is used to determine which bin to compare the texel value against. This reduces the number of passes to $n \times n$. To further reduce the number of passes, the fragment program can be modified to sample some small number of texels at a time, for example 4 to 16. This reduces the number of passes to $(n \times n)/k$.

Ideally we would like to achieve the same logarithmic reduction in passes as with the folding scheme. A final improvement to the strategy is to process all rows of the image in parallel, drawing a $256 \times n$ quad to index all of the image rows. Multiple rows of output bins are aligned vertically and the y window coordinate chooses the correct row of bins. This leaves a result that is distributed across the multiple rows of bins, so another set of passes is required to reduce the n rows to a single row. This uses the same folding scheme to pairwise sum two rows, one pair of bins, per fragment program. This reduces the number of rows by two in each pass. The end result is an algorithm requiring $(1 + [\log_2 n])n/k$ passes. Figure 12.4 illustrates the algorithm for a 4-bin histogram on an 8×8 image. Eight rows of bins are simultaneously computed across the columns of the image, producing the final 8 rows of bins. Three sets of folded sums are computed reducing the number of rows of bins by 2 at each step, culminating in the single row of bins on the right.

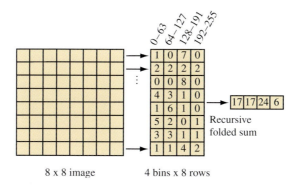

8 x 8 image   4 bins x 8 rows

Figure 12.4 Multi-row histogram and folded sum.

12.6 Convolution

Convolution is used to perform many common image processing operations. These operations include sharpening, blurring, noise reduction, embossing, and edge enhancement. The mathematics of the convolution operation are described in Section 4.3. This section describes two ways to perform convolutions using OpenGL: with the accumulation buffer and using the convolution operation in the imaging subset.

12.6.1 Separable Filters

Section 4.3 briefly describes the signal processing motivation and the equations behind the general 2D convolution. Each output pixel is the result of the weighted sum of its neighboring pixels. The set of weights is called the filter *kernel*; the width and height of the kernel determines the number of neighbor pixels ($width \times height$) included in the sum.

In the general case, a 2D convolution operation requires ($width \times height$) multiplications for each output pixel. Separable filters are a special case of general convolution in which the horizontal and vertical filtering components are orthogonal. Mathematically, the filter

$$G[0..(width - 1)][0..(height - 1)]$$

can be expressed in terms of two vectors

$$G_{row}[0..(width - 1)]G_{col}[0..(height - 1)]$$

such that for each $(i, j) \epsilon ([0..(width - 1)], [0..(height - 1)])$

$$G[i][j] = G_{row}[i] * G_{col}[j]$$

This case is important; if the filter is separable, the convolution operation may be performed using only ($width + height$) multiplications for each output pixel. Applying the separable filter to Equation 4.3 becomes:

$$H[x][y] = \sum_{j=0}^{height-1} \sum_{i=0}^{width-1} F[x+i][y+j]G_{row}[i]G_{col}[j]$$

Which simplifies to:

$$H[x][y] = \sum_{j=0}^{height-1} G_{col}[j] \sum_{i=0}^{width-1} F[x+i][y+j]G_{row}[i]$$

To apply the separable convolution to an image, first apply G_{row} as though it were a $width \times 1$ filter. Then apply G_{col} as though it were a $1 \times height$ filter.

12.6.2 Convolutions Using the Accumulation Buffer

Instead of using the ARB imaging subset, the convolution operation can be implemented by building the output image in the accumulation buffer. This allows the application to use the important convolution functionality even with OpenGL implementations that don't support the subset. For each kernel entry $G[i][j]$, translate the input image by $(-i, -j)$ from its original position, then accumulate the translated image using the command glAccum(GL_ACCUM, G[i][j]). This translation can be performed by glCopyPixels but an application may be able to redraw the image shifted using glViewport more efficiently. *Width* $\times$ *height* translations and accumulations (or *width* + *height* if the filter is separable) must be performed.

An example that uses the accumulation buffer to convolve with a Sobel filter, commonly used to do edge detection is shown here. This filter is used to find horizontal edges:

$$\begin{pmatrix} -1 & -2 & -1 \\ 0 & 0 & 0 \\ 1 & 2 & 1 \end{pmatrix}$$

Since the accumulation buffer can only store values in the range $[-1, 1]$, first modify the kernel such that at any point in the computation the values do not exceed this range (assuming the input pixel values are in the range $[0, 1]$):

$$\begin{pmatrix} -1 & -2 & -1 \\ 0 & 0 & 0 \\ 1 & 2 & 1 \end{pmatrix} = 4 \begin{pmatrix} -\frac{1}{4} & -\frac{2}{4} & -\frac{1}{4} \\ 0 & 0 & 0 \\ \frac{1}{4} & \frac{2}{4} & \frac{1}{4} \end{pmatrix}$$

To apply the filter:

1. Draw the input image.

2. `glAccum(GL_LOAD, 1/4)`

3. Translate the input image left by one pixel.

4. `glAccum(GL_ACCUM, 2/4)`

5. Translate the input image left by one pixel.

6. `glAccum(GL_ACCUM, 1/4)`

7. Translate the input image right by two pixels and down by two pixels.

8. `glAccum(GL_ACCUM, -1/4)`

9. Translate the input image left by one pixel.

10. `glAccum(GL_ACCUM, -2/4)`

11. Translate the input image left by one pixel.

12. `glAccum(GL_ACCUM, -1/4)`

13. Return the results to the framebuffer: `glAccum(GL_RETURN, 4)`.

In this example, each pixel in the output image is the combination of pixels in the 3×3 pixel square whose lower left corner is at the output pixel. At each step, the image is shifted so that the pixel that would have been under a given kernel element is under the lower left corner. An accumulation is then performed, using a scale value that matches the kernel element. As an optimization, locations where the kernel value is equal to zero are skipped.

The scale value 4 was chosen to ensure that intermediate results cannot go outside the range $[-1, 1]$. For a general kernel, an upper estimate of the scale value is computed by summing all of the positive elements of kernel to find the maximum and all of the negative elements to find the minimum. The scale value is the maximum of the absolute value of each sum. This computation assumes that the input image pixels are in the range $[0, 1]$ and the maximum and minimum are simply partial sums from the result of multiplying an image of 1's with the kernel.

Since the accumulation buffer has limited precision, more accurate results can be obtained by changing the order of the computation, then recomputing scale factor. Ideally, weights with small absolute values should be processed first, progressing to larger weights. Each time the scale factor is changed the `GL_MULT` operation is used to scale the current partial sum. Additionally, if values in the input image are constrained to a range smaller than $[0, 1]$, the scale factor can be proportionately increased to improve the precision.

For separable kernels, convolution can be implemented using *width + height* image translations and accumulations. As was done with the general 2D filter, scale factors for the row and column filters are determined, but separately for each filter. The scale values should be calculated such that the accumulation buffer values will never go out of the accumulation buffer range.

12.6.3 Convolution Using Extensions

If the imaging subset is available, convolutions can be computed directly using the convolution operation. Since the pixel transfer pipeline is calculated with extended range and precision, the issues that occur when scaling the kernels and reordering the sums are not applicable. Separable filters are supported as part of the convolution operation as well; they result in a substantial performance improvement.

One noteworthy feature of pipeline convolution is that the filter kernel is stored in the pipeline and it can be updated directly from the framebuffer using `glCopyConvolutionFilter2D`. This allows an application to compute the convolution filter in the framebuffer and move it directly into the pipeline without going through application memory.

If fragment programs are supported, then the weighted samples can be computed directly in a fragment program by reading multiple point samples from the same texture at different texel offsets. Fragment programs typically have a limit on the number of instructions or samples that can be executed, which will in turn limit the size of a filter that can be supported. Separable filters remain important for reducing the total number of samples that are required. To implement separable filters, separate passes are required for the horizontal and vertical filters and the results are summed using alpha blending or the accumulation buffer. In some cases linear texture filtering can be used to perform piecewise linear approximation of a particular filter, rather than point sampling the function. To implement this, linear filtering is enabled and the sample positions are carefully controlled to force the correct sample weighting. For example, the linear 1D filter computes $\alpha T_0 + (1 - \alpha)T_1$, where α is determined by the position of the s texture coordinate relative to texels T_0 and T_1. Placing the s coordinate midway between T_0 and T_1 equally weights both samples, positioning s 3/4 of the way between T_0 and T_1 weights the texels by 1/4 and 3/4. The sampling algorithm becomes one of extracting the slopes of the lines connecting adjacent sample points in the filter profile and converting those slopes to texture coordinate offsets.

12.6.4 Useful Convolution Filters

This section briefly describes several useful convolution filters. The filters may be applied to an image using either the convolution extension or the accumulation buffer technique. Unless otherwise noted, the kernels presented are normalized (that is, the kernel weights sum to zero).

Keep in mind that this section is intended only as a very basic reference. Numerous texts on image processing provide more details and other filters, including Myler and Weeks (1993).

Line detection Detection of lines one pixel wide can be accomplished with the following filters:

Horizontal Edges

$$\begin{pmatrix} -1 & -1 & -1 \\ 2 & 2 & 2 \\ -1 & -1 & -1 \end{pmatrix}$$

Vertical Edges

$$\begin{pmatrix} -1 & 2 & -1 \\ -1 & 2 & -1 \\ -1 & 2 & -1 \end{pmatrix}$$

Left Diagonal Edges

$$\begin{pmatrix} 2 & -1 & -1 \\ -1 & 2 & -1 \\ -1 & -1 & 2 \end{pmatrix}$$

Right Diagonal Edges

$$\begin{pmatrix} -1 & -1 & 2 \\ -1 & 2 & -1 \\ 2 & -1 & -1 \end{pmatrix}$$

Gradient Detection (Embossing) Changes in value over 3 pixels can be detected using kernels called *gradient masks* or *Prewitt masks*. The filter detects changes in gradient along limited directions, named after the points of the compass (with north equal to the up direction on the screen). The 3×3 kernels are shown here:

North

$$\begin{pmatrix} -1 & -2 & -1 \\ 0 & 0 & 0 \\ 1 & 2 & 1 \end{pmatrix}$$

West

$$\begin{pmatrix} -1 & 0 & 1 \\ -2 & 0 & 2 \\ -1 & 0 & 1 \end{pmatrix}$$

East

$$\begin{pmatrix} 1 & 0 & -1 \\ 2 & 0 & -2 \\ 1 & 0 & -1 \end{pmatrix}$$

South

$$\begin{pmatrix} 1 & 2 & 1 \\ 0 & 0 & 0 \\ -1 & -2 & -1 \end{pmatrix}$$

Northeast

$$\begin{pmatrix} 0 & -1 & -2 \\ 1 & 0 & -1 \\ 2 & 1 & 0 \end{pmatrix}$$

Southwest

$$\begin{pmatrix} 0 & 1 & 2 \\ -1 & 0 & 1 \\ -2 & -1 & 0 \end{pmatrix}$$

Smoothing and Blurring Smoothing and blurring operations are low-pass spatial filters. They reduce or eliminate high-frequency intensity or color changes in an image.

Arithmetic Mean The arithmetic mean simply takes an average of the pixels in the kernel. Each element in the filter is equal to 1 divided by the total number of elements in the filter. Thus, the 3×3 arithmetic mean filter is:

$$\begin{pmatrix} \dfrac{1}{9} & \dfrac{1}{9} & \dfrac{1}{9} \\ \dfrac{1}{9} & \dfrac{1}{9} & \dfrac{1}{9} \\ \dfrac{1}{9} & \dfrac{1}{9} & \dfrac{1}{9} \end{pmatrix}$$

Basic Smooth These filters approximate a Gaussian shape.

3×3 (not normalized) 5×5 (not normalized)

$$\begin{pmatrix} 1 & 2 & 1 \\ 2 & 4 & 2 \\ 1 & 2 & 1 \end{pmatrix} \qquad \begin{pmatrix} 1 & 1 & 1 & 1 & 1 \\ 1 & 4 & 4 & 4 & 1 \\ 1 & 4 & 12 & 4 & 1 \\ 1 & 4 & 4 & 4 & 1 \\ 1 & 1 & 1 & 1 & 1 \end{pmatrix}$$

High-pass Filters A high-pass filter enhances the high-frequency parts of an image by reducing the low-frequency components. This type of filter can be used to sharpen images.

Basic High-Pass Filter: 3×3 Basic High-Pass Filter: 5×5

$$\begin{pmatrix} -1 & -1 & -1 \\ -1 & 9 & -1 \\ -1 & -1 & -1 \end{pmatrix} \qquad \begin{pmatrix} 0 & -1 & -1 & -1 & 0 \\ -1 & 2 & -4 & 2 & -1 \\ -1 & -4 & 13 & -4 & -1 \\ -1 & 2 & -4 & 2 & -1 \\ 0 & -1 & -1 & -1 & 0 \end{pmatrix}$$

Laplacian Filter The *Laplacian* filter enhances discontinuities. It outputs brighter pixel values as it passes over parts of the image that have abrupt changes in intensity, and outputs darker values where the image is not changing rapidly.

3×3 5×5

$$\begin{pmatrix} 0 & -1 & 0 \\ -1 & 4 & -1 \\ 0 & -1 & 0 \end{pmatrix} \qquad \begin{pmatrix} -1 & -1 & -1 & -1 & -1 \\ -1 & -1 & -1 & -1 & -1 \\ -1 & -1 & 24 & -1 & -1 \\ -1 & -1 & -1 & -1 & -1 \\ -1 & -1 & -1 & -1 & -1 \end{pmatrix}$$

Sobel Filter The *Sobel* filter consists of two kernels which detect horizontal and vertical changes in an image. If both are applied to an image, the results can be used to compute the magnitude and direction of edges in the image. Applying the Sobel kernels results in two images which are stored in the arrays `Gh[0..(height-1)][0..(width-1)]` and `Gv[0..(height-1)][0..(width-1)]`. The magnitude of the edge passing through the pixel `x`, `y` is given by:

$$M_{sobel}[x][y] = \sqrt{Gh[x][y]^2 + Gv[x][y]^2} \approx \left| Gh[x][y] \right| + \left| Gv[x][y] \right|$$

(Using the magnitude representation is justified, since the values represent the magnitude of orthogonal vectors.) The direction can also be derived from `Gh` and `Gv`:

$$\phi_{sobel}[x][y] = \tan^{-1}\left(\frac{Gv[x][y]}{Gh[x][y]} \right)$$

The 3×3 Sobel kernels are:

Horizontal

$$\begin{pmatrix} -1 & -2 & -1 \\ 0 & 0 & 0 \\ 1 & 2 & 1 \end{pmatrix}$$

Vertical

$$\begin{pmatrix} -1 & 0 & 1 \\ -2 & 0 & 2 \\ -1 & 0 & 1 \end{pmatrix}$$

12.6.5 Correlation and Feature Detection

Correlation is useful for feature detection; applying correlation to an image that possibly contains a target feature and an image of that feature forms local maxima or pixel value "spikes" in candidate positions. This is useful in detecting letters on a page or the position of armaments on a battlefield. Correlation can also be used to detect motion, such as the velocity of hurricanes in a satellite image or the jittering of an unsteady camera.

The *correlation* operation is defined mathematically as:

$$h(x) = f(x) \circ g(x) = \int_{-\infty}^{+\infty} f^*(\tau) g(x + \tau) d\tau \qquad (12.2)$$

The $f^*(\tau)$ is the complex conjugate of $f(\tau)$, but since this section will limit discussion to correlation for signals which only contain real values, $f(\tau)$ can be substituted instead.

For 2D discrete images, Equation 4.3, the convolution equation, may be used to evaluate correlation. In essence, the target feature is stored in the convolution kernel. Wherever the same feature occurs in the image, convolving it against the same image in the kernel will produce a bright spot, or spike.

Convolution functionality from the imaging subset or a fragment program may be used to apply correlation to an image, but only for features no larger than the maximum

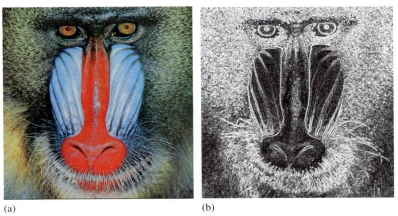

(a)

(b)

(c)

Figure 12.5 Convolution operations: original, edge detect, emboss.

available convolution kernel size (Figure 12.5). For larger images or for implementation without convolution functionality, convolve with the accumulation buffer technique. It may also be worth the effort to consider an alternative method, such as applying a multiplication in the frequency domain (Gonzalez and Wintz, 1987) to improve performance, if the feature and candidate images are very large.

After applying convolution, the application will need to find the "spikes" to determine where features have been detected. To aid this process, it may be useful to apply thresholding with a color table to convert candidate pixels to one value and non-candidate pixels to another, as described in Section 12.3.4.

Features can be found in an image using the method described below:

1. Draw a small image containing just the feature to be detected.

2. Create a convolution filter containing that image.

3. Transfer the image to the convolution filter using `glCopyConvolutionFilter2D`.

4. Draw the candidate image into the color buffers.

5. Optionally configure a threshold for candidate pixels:

   • Create a color table using `glColorTable`.

   • `glEnable(GL_POST_CONVOLUTION_COLOR_TABLE)`.

6. `glEnable(GL_CONVOLUTION_2D)`.

7. Apply pixel transfer to the candidate image using `glCopyPixels`.

8. Read back the framebuffer using `glReadPixels`.

9. Measure candidate pixel locations.

If features in the candidate image are not pixel-exact, for example if they are rotated slightly or blurred, it may be necessary to create a blurry feature image using jittering and blending. Since the correlation spike will be lower when this image matches, it is necessary to lower the acceptance threshold in the color table.

12.7 Geometric Operations

12.7.1 Pixel Zoom

An application may need to magnify an image by a constant factor. OpenGL provides a mechanism to perform simple scaling by replicating or discarding fragments from pixel rectangles with the pixel zoom operation. Zoom factors are specified using `glPixelZoom` and they may be non-integer, even negative. Negative zoom factors reflect the image about the window coordinate x- and y-axis. Because of its simple operation, an advantage in using pixel zoom is that it is easily accelerated by most implementations. Pixel zoom operations do not perform filtering on the result image, however. In Section 4.1 we described some of the issues with digital image representation and with performing sampling and reconstruction operations on images. Pixel zoom is a form of sampling and reconstruction operation that reconstructs the incoming image by replicating pixels, then samples these values to produce the zoomed image. Using this method to increase or reduce the size of an image introduces aliasing artifacts, therefore it may not provide satisfactory results. One way to minimize the introduction of artifacts is to use the filtering available with texture mapping.

12.7.2 Scaling Using Texture Mapping

Another way to scale an image is to create a texture map from the image and then apply it to a quadrilateral drawn perpendicular to the viewing direction. The interpolated texture coordinates form a regular grid of sample points. With nearest filtering, the resulting image is similar to that produced with pixel zoom. With linear filtering, a weighted average of the four nearest texels (original image pixels) is used to compute each new sample. This triangle filter results in significantly better images when the scale factors are close to unity (0.5 to 2.0) and the performance should be good since texture mapping is typically well optimized. If the scale factor is exactly 1, and the texture coordinates are aligned with texel centers, the filter leaves the image undisturbed. As the scale factors progress further from unity the results become worse and more aliasing artifacts are introduced. Even with its limitations, overall it is a good general technique. An additional benefit: once a texture map has been constructed from the image, texture mapping can be used to implement other geometric operations, such as rotation.

Using the convolution techniques, other filters can be used for scaling operations. Figure 12.6 illustrates 1D examples of triangle, box, and a 3-point Gaussian filter approximation. The triangle filter illustrates the footprint of the OpenGL linear filter. Filters with greater width will yield better results for larger scale factors. For magnification operations, a bicubic (4 × 4 width) filter provides a good trade-off between quality and performance. As support for the programmable fragment pipeline increases, implementing a bicubic filter as a fragment program will become both straightforward and achieve good performance.

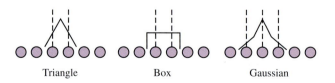

Triangle   Box   Gaussian

Figure 12.6 Triangle, box, and 3-point Gaussian filters.

12.7.3 Rotation Using Texture Mapping

There are many algorithms for performing 2D rotations on an image. Conceptually, an algebraic transform is used to map the coordinates of the center of each pixel in the rotated image to its location in the unrotated image. The new pixel value is computed from a weighted sum of samples from the original pixel location. The most efficient algorithms factor the task into multiple shearing transformations (Foley et al., 1990) and filter the result to minimize aliasing artifacts. Image rotation can be performed efficiently in OpenGL by using texture mapping to implement the simple conceptual algorithm. The image is simply texture mapped onto geometry rotated about its center. The texture coordinates follow the rotated vertex coordinates and supply that mapping from rotated pixel position to the original pixel position. Using linear filtering minimizes the introduction of artifacts.

In general, once a texture map is created from an image, any number of geometric transformations can be performed by either modifying the texture or the vertex coordinates. Section 14.11 describes methods for implementing more general image warps using texture mapping.

12.7.4 Distortion Correction

Distortion correction is a commonly used geometric operation. It is used to correct distortions resulting from projections through a lens, or other optically active medium. Two types of distortion commonly occur in camera lenses: *pincushion* and *barrel* distortion. Pincushion distortion causes horizontal and vertical lines to bend in toward the center of the image and commonly occurs with zoom or telephoto lenses. Barrel distortion cause vertical and horizontal lines to bend outwards from the center of the image and occurs with wide angle lenses (Figure 12.7).

Distortion is measured as the relative difference of the distance from image center to the distorted position and to the correct position, $D = (h' - h)/h$. The relationship is usually of the form $D = ah^2 + bh^4 + ch^6 + \dots$. The coefficient a is positive for pincushion and negative for barrel distortion. Usually the quadratic term dominates the

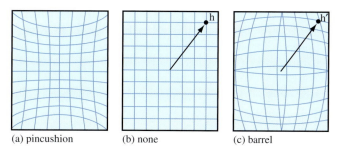

(a) pincushion   (b) none   (c) barrel

Figure 12.7 Pincushion and barrel distortion.

other terms, so approximating with the quadratic term alone often provides good results. The algorithm to correct a pincushion or barrel distortion is as follows:

1. Construct a high-resolution rectangular 2D mesh that projects to a screen-space area the size of the input image. The mesh should be high-enough resolution so that the pixel spacing between mesh points is small (2–3 pixels).

2. Each point in the mesh corresponds to a corrected position in virtual image coordinates ranging from $[-1, 1]$ in each direction. For each correct position, (x, y), compute the corresponding uncorrected position, $h'(x, y)$, where $h' = a(\sqrt{x^2 + y^2})^2$.

3. Assign the uncorrected coordinates as s and t texture coordinates, scaling and biasing to map the virtual coordinate range $[-1, 1]$ to $[0, 1]$.

4. Load the uncorrected image as a 2D texture image and map it to the mesh using linear filtering. When available, a higher order texture filter, such as a bicubic (implemented in a fragment program), can be used to produce a high-quality result.

A value for the coefficient a can be determined by trial and error; using a calibration image such as a checkerboard or regular grid can simplify this process. Once the coefficient has been determined, the same value can be used for all images acquired with that lens. In practice, a lens may exhibit a combination of pincushion and barrel distortion or the higher order terms may become more important. For these cases, a more complex equation can be determined by using an optimization technique, such as least squares, to fit a set of coefficients to calibration data. Large images may exceed the maximum texture size of the OpenGL implementation. The tiling algorithm described in Section 14.5 can be used to overcome this limitation. This technique can be generalized for arbitrary image warping and is described in more detail in Section 14.11.

12.8 Image-Based Depth of Field

Section 13.3 describes a geometric technique for modeling the effects of depth of field, that is, a method for simulating a camera with a fixed focal length. The result is that there is a single distance from the eye where objects are in perfect focus and as objects approach the viewer or receed into the distance they appear increasingly blurry.

The image-based methods achieve this effect by creating multiple versions of the image of varying degrees of blurriness, then selecting pixels from the image based on the distance from the viewer of the object corresponding to the pixel. A simple, but manual, method for achieving this behavior is to use the texture LOD biasing[1] to select lower resolution texture mipmap levels for objects that are further away. This method is limited to a constant bias for each object, whereas a bias varying as a function of focal plane to object distance is more desirable.

---

1. A core feature in OpenGL 1.4 or as the EXT_texture_lod_bias extension.

A generalization of this technique, using the programmable pipeline, renders the scene using a texture coordinate to interpolate the distance to the viewer (or focal plane) at each pixel and uses this value to look up a blurriness interpolation coefficient. This coefficient is stored in destination alpha with the rest of the scene. In subsequent passes the blurred versions of the image are created, using the techniques described previously and in Section 14.15. In the final pass a single quadrilateral the size of the window is drawn, with the orginal and blurred images bound as textures. As the quad is drawn, samples are selected from each of the bound textures and merged using the interpolation coefficient. Since the interpolation coeffecient was originally rendered to the alpha channel of the scene, it is in the alpha channel of the unblurred texture. A blurred version of the coefficient is also computed along with the RGB colors of the scene in each of the blurred texture maps. The actual blur coefficient used for interpolation is computed by averaging the unblurred and most-blurred versions of the coefficient.

If a single blurry texture is used, then a simple interpolation is done between the unblurred and blurry texture. If multiple blurrier textures are used, then the magnitude of the interpolation coefficient is used to select between two of the textures (much like LOD in mipmapping) and the samples from the two textures are interpolated.

So far, we have described how to compute the resulting image based on an interpolated bluriness coefficient, but haven't shown how to derive the coefficient. The lens and aperture camera model described by Potmesil and Chakravarty (1981) develops a model for focus that takes into account the focal length and aperture of the lens. An in-focus point in 3D projects to a point on the image plane. A point that is out of focus maps to a circle, termed the *circle of confusion*, where the diameter is proportional to the distance from the plane of focus. The equation for the diameter depends on the distance from the camera to the point z, the lens focal length F, the lens aperature number n, and the focal distance (distance at which the image is in perfect focus), z_f:

$$c(z) = \alpha \frac{|z - z_f|}{z} \qquad \text{where } \alpha = \frac{F^2}{n(z_f - F)}$$

Circles of diameter less than some threshold d_{min} are considered in focus. Circles greater than a second threshold d_{max} are considered out of focus and correspond to the blurriest texture. By assigning a texture coordinate with the distance from the viewer, the interpolated coordinate can be used to index an alpha texture storing the function:

$$\frac{c(z) - d_{min}}{d_{max} - d_{min}}$$

This function defines the $[0, 1]$ bluriness coefficient and is used to interpolate between the RGB values in the textures storing the original version of the scene and one or more blurred versions of the scene as previously described (Figure 12.8).

The main advantage of this scheme over a geometric scheme is that the orignal scene only needs to be rendered once. However, there are also some shortcommings. It requires

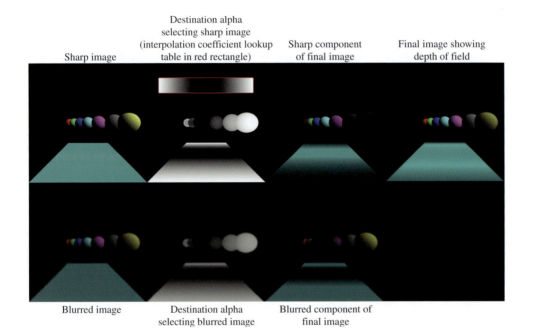

Figure 12.8 Depth of field effect.

fragment program support to implement the multiway interpolation, the resolution of the interpolation coefficient is limited by the bit-depth of the alpha buffer, and the fidelity is limited by the number of blurry textures used (typically 2 or 3). Some simple variations on the idea include using a fragment-program-controlled LOD bias value to alter which texture level is selected on a per-fragment basis. The $c(z)$ value can be computed in a similar fashion and be used to control the LOD bias.

12.9 High-Dynamic Range Imaging

Conventional 8-bit per component RGB color representations can only represent two orders of magnitude in luminance range. The human eye is capable of resolving image detail spanning 4 to 5 orders of magnitude using local adaptation. The human eye, given several minutes to adjust (for example, entering a dark room and waiting), can span 9 orders of magnitude (Ward, 2001). To generate images reproducing that range requires solving two problems: enabling computations that can capture this much larger dynamic range, and mapping a high-dynamic range image to a display device with a more limited gamut.

12.9.1 Dynamic Range

One way to solve the dynamic range computation problem is to use single-precision floating-point representations for RGB color components. This can solve the problem at the cost of increased computational, storage, and bandwidth requirements. In the programmable pipeline, vertex and fragment programs support floating-point processing for all computations, although not necessarily with full IEEE-754 32-bit precision.[2] While supporting single-precision floating-point computation in the pipeline is unlikely to be an issue for long, the associated storage and bandwidth requirements for 96-bit floating-point RGB colors as textures and color buffers can be more of an issue. There are several, more compact representations that can be used, trading off dynamic range and precision for compactness. The two most popular representations are the "half-float" and "shared-exponent" representations.

Half Float

The half-float representation uses a 16-bit floating representation with 5 bits of exponent, 10 bits of significand (mantissa), and a sign bit. Like the IEEE-754 floating-point formats, normalized numbers have an implied or hidden most significant mantissa bit of 1, so the mantissa is effectively 11 bits throughout most of the range. The range of numbers that can be represented is roughly $[2^{-16}, 2^{16}]$ or about 10 orders of magnitude with 11 bits of precision. This representation captures the necessary dynamic range while maintaining

---

2. Hardware implementations make various cost vs. accuracy vs. performance trade-offs and fragment processing representations may be limited to 24-bit or even 16-bit floating point precision.

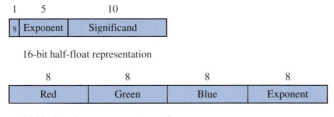

Figure 12.9 Half-float and RGBE HDR representations.

good accuracy, at a cost of twice the storage and bandwidth of an 8-bit per-component representation. This format is seeing moderate adoption as an external image representation and rapid adoption in graphics accelerators as a texture and color buffer format.

Shared Exponent

Shared exponent representations reduce the number of bits by sharing a single exponent between all three of the RGB color components. The name RGBE is often used to describe the format. A typical representation uses a shared 8-bit exponent with three 8-bit significands for a total of 32 bits. Since the exponent is shared, the exponent from the component with largest magnitude is chosen and the mantissas of the remaining two components are scaled to match the exponent. This results in some loss of accuracy for the remaining two components if they do not have similar magnitudes to the largest component.

The RGBE representation, using 8-bit for significands and exponent, is convenient to process in an application since each element fits in a byte, but it is not an optimal distribution of the available bits for color representation. The large exponent supports a dynamic range of 76 orders of magnitude, which is much larger than necessary for color representation; the 8-bit mantissa could use more bits to retain accuracy, particularly since the least significant bits are truncated to force two of the components to match the exponent. An example of an alternative distribution of bits might include a 5-bit exponent, like the half-float representation, and a 9-bit significand (Figure 12.9).

The shared-exponent format does a good job of reducing the overall storage and bandwidth requirements. However, the extra complexity in examining a set of 3 color components, determining the exponent and adjusting the components makes the representation more expensive to generate. Furthermore, to minimize visual artifacts from truncating components the neighboring pixel values should also be examined. This extra cost results in a trend to use the representation in hardware accelerators as a read-only source format, for example, in texture maps, rather than a more general writable color buffer format.

12.9.2 Tone Mapping

Once we can represent high-dynamic range (HDR) images, we are still left with the problem of displaying them on low-dynamic range devices such as CRTs and LCD panels.

One way to accomplish this is to mimic the human eye. The eye uses an adaptation process to control the range of values that can be resolved at any given time. This amounts to controlling the exposure to light, based on the incoming light intensity. This adaptation process is analogous to the exposure controls on a camera in which the size of the lens aperture and exposure times are modified to control the amount of light that passes to the film or electronic sensor.

Note that low-dynamic range displays only support two orders of magnitude of range, whereas the eye accommodates four to five orders *before* using adaptation. This means that great care must be used in mapping the high-dynamic range values. The default choice is to clamp the gamut range, for example, to the standard OpenGL [0, 1] range, losing all of the high-intensity and low-intensity detail. The class of techniques for mapping high-dynamic range to low-dynamic range is termed *tone mapping*; a specific technique is often called a *tone mapping operator*. Other classes of algorithms include:

1. Uniformly scaling the image gamut to fit within the display gamut, for example, by scaling about the average luminance of the image.

2. Scaling colors on a curve determined by image content, for example, using a global histogram (Ward Larson et al., 1997).

3. Scaling colors locally based on nearby spatial content. In a photographic context, this corresponds to dodging and burning to control the exposure of parts of a negative during printing (Chui et al., 1993).

Luminance Scaling

The first mapping method involves scaling about some approximation of the neutral scene luminance or *key* of the scene. The log-average luminance is a good approximation of this and is defined as:

$$L_{avg} = exp\left(\frac{1}{N}\sum_{x,y}\log(\delta + L(x,y))\right)$$

The δ value is a small bias included to allow log computations of pixels with zero luminance. The log-average luminance is computed by summing the log-luminance of the pixel values of the image. This task can be approximated by sparsely sampling the image, or operating on an appropriately resampled smaller version of the image. The latter can be accomplished using texture mapping operations to reduce the image size to 64×64 before computing the sum of logs. If fragment programs are supported, the 64×64 image can be converted to log-luminance directly, otherwise color lookup tables can be used on the color values. The average of the 64×64 log-luminance values is also computed using successive texture mapping operations to produce 16×16, 4×4, and 1×1 images, finally computing the antilog of the 1×1 image.

The log-average luminance is used to compute a per-pixel scale factor

$$L_{scale}(x,y) = \frac{a}{L_{avg}} L(x,y)$$

where a is a value between $[0, 1]$ and represents the *key* of the scene, typically about 0.18. By adjusting the value of a, the linear scaling controls how the parts of the high-dynamic range image are mapped to the display. The value of a roughly models the exposure setting on a camera.

Curve Scaling

The uniform scaling operator can be converted to the non-linear operator (Reinhard, 2002)

$$L_d(x,y) = \frac{L_{scale}(x,y)}{1 + L_{scale}(x,y)}$$

which compresses high-luminace regions by $\frac{1}{L}$ while leaving low-luminace regions untouched. It is applied as a scale factor to the color components of each image pixel.

It can be modified to allow high luminances to burn out:

$$L_d(x,y) = \frac{L_{scale}(x,y) \left(1 + \frac{L_{scale}(x,y)}{L_{white}^2} \right)}{1 + L_{scale}(x,y)}$$

where L_{white} is the smallest luminance value to be mapped to white. These methods preserve some detail in low-contrast areas while compressing the high luminances into a displayable range. For very high-dynamic range scenes detail is lost, leading to a need for a local tone reproduction operator that considers the range of luminance values in a local neighborhood.

Local Scaling

Local scaling emulates the photographic techniques of dodging and burning with a spatially varying operator of the form

$$L_d(x,y) = \frac{L_{scale}(x,y)}{1 + V(x,y,s(x,y))}$$

where V is the spatially varying function evaluated over the region s. Contrast is measured at multiple scales to determine the size of the region. An example is taking the difference between two images blurred with Gaussian filters. Additional details on spatially varying operators can be found in Reinhard et al. (2002).

12.9.3 Modeling Adaptation

The adaption process of the human visual system can be simulated by varying the tone operator over time. For example, as the scene changes in response to changes to the viewer position one would normally compute a new average scene luminance value for the new scene. To model the human adaptation process, a transition is made from the current adaption level to the new scene average luminance. After a length of time in the same position the current adaption level converges to the scene average luminance value. A good choice for weighting functions is an exponential function.

12.10 Summary

This chapter describes a sampling of important image processing techniques that can be implemented using OpenGL. The techniques include a range of point-based, region-based, and geometric operations. Although it is a useful addition, the ARB imaging subset is not required for most of the techniques described here. We also examine the use of the programmable pipeline for image processing techniques and discuss some of the strengths and weaknesses of this approach. Several of the algorithms described here are used within other techniques described in later chapters. We expect that an increasing number of image processing algorithms will become important components of other rendering algorithms.

Basic Transform Techniques

OpenGL's transformation pipeline is a powerful component for building rendering algorithms; it provides a full 4×4 transformation and perspective division that can be applied to both geometry and texture coordinates. This general transformation ability is very powerful, but OpenGL also provides complete orthogonality between transform and rasterization state. Being able to pick and choose the values of both states makes it possible to freely combine transformation and rasterization techniques.

This chapter describes a toolbox of basic techniques that use OpenGL's transformation pipeline. Some of these techniques are used in many applications, others show transform techniques that are important building blocks for advanced transformation algorithms. This chapter also focuses on transform creation, providing methods for efficiently building special transforms needed by many of the techniques described later. These techniques are applicable for both the fixed-function pipeline and for vertex programs. With vertex programs it may be possible to further optimize some of the computations to match the characteristics of the algorithm, for example, using a subset of a matrix.

13.1 Computing Inverse Transforms Efficiently

In general, when geometry is transformed by a 4×4 matrix, normals or other vectors associated with that geometry have to be transformed by the inverse transpose of that matrix. This is done to preserve angles between vectors and geometry (see Section 2.3 for details). Finding the inverse transpose of a general 4×4 matrix can be an expensive computation, since it requires inverting a full 4×4 matrix. The general procedure is shown below; a matrix M is inverted to M', then transposed.

$$\begin{pmatrix} m_{11} & m_{12} & m_{13} & m_{14} \\ m_{21} & m_{22} & m_{23} & m_{24} \\ m_{31} & m_{32} & m_{33} & m_{34} \\ m_{41} & m_{42} & m_{43} & m_{44} \end{pmatrix} \Rightarrow \begin{pmatrix} m'_{11} & m'_{12} & m'_{13} & m'_{14} \\ m'_{21} & m'_{22} & m'_{23} & m'_{24} \\ m'_{31} & m'_{32} & m'_{33} & m'_{34} \\ m'_{41} & m'_{42} & m'_{43} & m'_{44} \end{pmatrix} \Rightarrow \begin{pmatrix} m'_{11} & m'_{21} & m'_{31} & m'_{41} \\ m'_{12} & m'_{22} & m'_{32} & m'_{42} \\ m'_{13} & m'_{23} & m'_{33} & m'_{43} \\ m'_{14} & m'_{24} & m'_{34} & m'_{44} \end{pmatrix}$$

OpenGL performs this computation for the application as part of the transform pipeline, which provides the functionality needed for basic lighting, texture coordinate generation, and environment operations. There are times when an application may need to construct more complex transforms not provided in the pipeline. Some techniques require a special per-vertex vector, such as the bi-normal vector used in bump mapping (Section 15.10) and anisotropic lighting (Section 15.9.3). Other algorithms, such as those modeling curved reflectors (Section 17.1.3) subdivide surfaces based on the values of adjacent normal or reflection vectors. In these, and many other algorithms, an efficient way to compute vector transform matrices is needed.

Although finding the inverse of a general 4×4 matrix is expensive, many graphics applications use only a small set of matrix types in the modelview matrix, most of which are relatively easy to invert. A common approach, used in some OpenGL implementations, is to recognize the matrix type used in the modelview matrix (or tailor the application to limit the modelview matrix to a given type), and apply an appropriate shortcut. Matrix types can be identified by tracking the OpenGL commands used to create them. This can be simple if `glTranslate`, `glScale`, and `glRotate` commands are used. If `glLoadMatrix` or `glMultMatrix` are used, it's still possible to rapidly check the loaded matrix to see if it matches one of the common types. Once the type is found, the corresponding inverse can be applied. Some of the more common matrix types and inverse transpose shortcuts are described below.

An easy (and common) case arises when the transform matrix is composed of only translates and rotates. A vector transformed by the inverse transpose of this type of matrix is the same as the vector transformed by the original matrix, so no inverse transpose operation is needed.

If uniform scale operations (a matrix M with elements $m_{11} = m_{22} = m_{33} = s$) are also used in the transform, the length of the transformed vector changes. If the vector length doesn't matter, no inverse is needed. Otherwise, renormalization or rescaling is required. Renormalization scales each vector to unit length. While renormalization is computationally expensive, it may be required as part of the algorithm anyway (for example, if unit normals are required and the input normals are not guaranteed to be unit length). Rescaling applies an inverse scaling operation after the transform to undo its scaling effect. Although it is less expensive than renormalization, it won't produce unit vectors unless the untransformed vectors were already unit length. Rescaling uses the

Table 13.1 Inverse Transpose of Upper 3×3 of Simple Transforms

	Transform	Inverse-Transpose
translate	$(T^{-1})^T$	T (discard elements)
rotate	$(R(\theta)^{-1})^T$	$R(\theta)$
uniform scale	$(S^{-1})^T$	$\frac{1}{s}I$
composite	$((ABC)^{-1})^T$	$(A^{-1})^T(B^{-1})^T(C^{-1})^T$

inverse of the transform's scaling factor, creating a new matrix $S^{-1} = \frac{1}{s}I$; the diagonal element's scale factor is inverted and used to scale the matrix.

Table 13.1 summarizes common shortcuts. However, it's not always practical to characterize the matrix and look up its corresponding inverse shortcut. If the modelview transform is constructed of more than translates, rotates, and uniform scales, computing the inverse transpose is necessary to obtain correct results. But it's not always necessary to find the full inverse transpose of the composited transform.

An inverse transpose of a composite matrix can be built incrementally. The elements of the original transform are inverted and transposed individually. The resulting matrices can then be composed, in their original order, to construct the inverse transpose of the original sequence. In other words, given a composite matrix built from matrices A, B, and C, $((ABC)^{-1})^T$ is equal to $(A^{-1})^T(B^{-1})^T(C^{-1})^T$. Since these matrices are transposed, the order of operations doesn't change. Many basic transforms, such as pure translates, rotates, and scales, have trivial special case inversions, as shown previously. The effort of taking the inverse transpose individually, then multiplying, can be much less in these cases.

If the transform is built from more complex pieces, such as arbitrary 4×4 matrices, then using an efficient matrix inversion algorithm may become necessary. Even in this case, trimming down the matrix to 3×3 (all that is needed for transforming vectors) will help.

13.2 Stereo Viewing

Stereo viewing is used to enhance user immersion in a 3D scene. Two views of the scene are created, one for the left eye, one for the right. To display stereo images, a special display configuration is used, so the viewer's eyes see different images. Objects in the scene appear to be at a specific distance from the viewer based on differences in their positions in the left and right eye views. When done properly, the positions of objects in the scene appear more realistic, and the image takes on a solid feeling of "space".

OpenGL natively supports stereo viewing by providing left and right versions of the front and back buffers. In normal, non-stereo viewing, the default buffer is the left one for both front and back. When animating stereo, both the left and right back buffers are used,

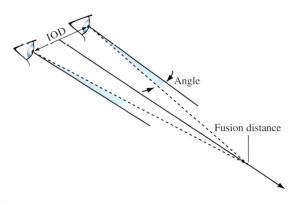

Figure 13.1 Stereo viewing geometry.

and both must be updated each frame. Since OpenGL is window system independent, there are no interfaces in OpenGL for stereo glasses or other stereo viewing devices. This functionality is part of the OpenGL/Window system interface library; the extent and details of this support are implementation-dependent and varies widely.

A stereo view requires a detailed understanding of viewer/scene relationship (Figure 13.1). In the real world, a viewer sees two separate views of the scene, one for each eye. The computer graphics approach is to create a transform to represent each eye's view, and change other parameters for each view as needed by the stereo display hardware. Since a real viewer will shift view direction to focus on an object of interest, an OpenGL application does the same. Ideally, the eye transforms are updated based on the object the user of the stereo application is looking at, but this requires some method of tracking the viewer's focus of attention.

A less ambitious technique uses the viewing direction instead, and stereo parameters that describe the position of the left and right eyes. The model requires that both eye views are aimed at a single point along the line of sight; another stereo parameter is added to represent the distance to that point from the eye point. This parameter is called the *fusion distance* (FD). When the two scenes are rendered together to form a stereo image, objects at this distance will appear to be embedded in the front surface of the display ("in the glass"). Objects farther than the fusion distance from the viewer will appear to be "behind the glass" while objects in front will appear to float in front of the display. The latter effect can be hard to maintain, since objects visible to the viewer beyond the edge of the display tend to destroy the illusion.

To compute the left and right eye views, the scene is rendered twice, each with the proper eye transform. These transforms are calculated so that the camera position, view, direction and up direction correspond to the view from each of the viewer's two eyes. The normal viewer parameters are augmented by additional information describing the position of the viewer's eyes, usually relative to the traditional OpenGL eye point. The distance separating the two eyes is called the *interocular distance* or IOD. The IOD is chosen to give the proper spacing of the viewer's eyes relative to the scene being viewed.

The IOD value establishes the size of the imaginary viewer relative to the objects in the scene. This distance should be correlated with the degree of perspective distortion present in the scene in order to produce a realistic effect.

To formalize the position and direction of views, consider the relationship between the view direction, the view up vector, and the vector separating the two eye views. Assume that the view direction vector, the eye position vector (a line connecting both eye positions), and the up vectors are all perpendicular to each other. The fusion distance is measured along the view direction. The position of the viewer can be defined to be at one of the eye points, or halfway between them. The latter is used in this description. In either case, the left and right eye locations can be defined relative to it.

Using the canonical OpenGL view position, the viewer position is at the origin in eye space. The fusion distance is measured along the negative z-axis (as are the near and far clipping planes). Assuming the viewer position is halfway between the eye positions, and the up vector is parallel to the positive y-axis, the two viewpoints are on either side of the origin along the x-axis at $(-IOD/2, 0, 0)$ and $(IOD/2, 0, 0)$.

Given the spatial relationships defined here, the transformations needed for correct stereo viewing involve simple translations and off-axis projections (Deering, 1992). The stereo viewing transforms are the last ones applied to the normal viewing transforms. The goal is to alter the transforms so as to shift the viewpoint from the normal viewer position to each eye. A simple translation isn't adequate, however. The transform must also aim each to point at the spot defined by view vector and the fusion distance.

The stereo eye transformations can be created using the `gluLookAt` command for each eye view. The `gluLookAt` command takes three sets of three-component parameters; an eye position, a center of attention, and an up vector. For each eye view, the `gluLookAt` function receives the eye position for the current eye $(\pm IOD/2, 0, 0)$, an up vector (typically $0, 1, 0$), and the center of attention position $(0, 0, FD)$. The center of attention position should be the same for both eye views. `gluLookAt` creates a composite transform that rotates the scene to orient the vector between the eye position and center of view parallel to the z-axis, then translates the eye position to the origin.

This method is slightly inaccurate, since the rotation/translation combination moves the fusion distance away from the viewer slightly. A shear/translation combination is more correct, since it takes into account differences between a physical stereo view and the properties of a perspective transform. The shear orients the vector between the eye and the center of attention to be parallel to the z-axis. The shear should subtract from x values when the x coordinate of the eye is negative, and add to the x values when the x component of the eye is positive. More precisely, it needs to shear $x \pm \frac{IOD}{2}$ when z equals the $-FD$. The equation is $x \pm \left(\frac{IOD}{2}\right)\left(\frac{z}{FD}\right)$. Converting this into a 4×4 matrix becomes:

$$\begin{pmatrix} 1 & 0 & \dfrac{IOD}{2FD} & 0 \\ 0 & 1 & 0 & 0 \\ 0 & 0 & 1 & 0 \\ 0 & 0 & 0 & 1 \end{pmatrix}$$

Compositing a transform to move the eye to the origin completes the transform. Note that this is only one way to compute stereo transforms; there are other popular approaches in the literature.

13.3 Depth of Field

The optical equivalent to the standard viewing transforms is a perfect pinhole camera: everything visible is in focus, regardless of how close or how far the objects are from the viewer. To increase realism, a scene can be rendered to vary focus as a function of viewer distance, more accurately simulating a camera with a fixed focal length. There is a single distance from the eye where objects are in perfect focus. Objects farther and nearer to the viewer become increasingly fuzzy.

The depth-of-field problem can be seen as an extension of stereo viewing. In both cases, there are multiple viewpoints, with all views converging at a fixed distance from the viewer on the direction of view vector. Instead of two eye views, the depth of field technique creates a large number of viewpoints that are scattered in a plane perpendicular to the view direction. The images generated from each view rendered are then blended together.

Rendering from these viewpoints generates images which show objects in front of and behind the fusion distance shifted from their normal positions. These shifts vary depending on how far the viewpoint is shifted from the eye position. Like the eye views in stereo viewing, all viewpoints are oriented so their view directions are aimed at a single point located on the original direction of view. As a result, the farther an object is from this aim point, the more the object is shifted from its original position.

Blending these images together combines each set of shifted objects, creating a single blurry one. The closer an object is to the aim point (focal) distance, the less it shifts, and the sharper it appears. The field of view can be expanded by reducing the average amount of viewpoint shift for a given fusion distance. If viewpoints are closer to the original eye point, objects have to be farther from the fusion distance in order to be shifted significantly.

Choosing a set of viewpoints and blending them together can be seen as modeling a physical lens—blending together pinhole views sampled over the lens' area. Real lenses have a non-zero area, which causes only objects within a limited range of distances to be in perfect focus. Objects closer or farther from the camera focal length are progressively more blurred.

To create depth of field blurring, both the perspective and modelview transforms are changed together to create an offset eye point. A shearing transform applied along the direction of view (-z-axis) is combined into the perspective transform, while a translate is added to the modelview. A shear is chosen so that the changes to the transformed objects are strictly a function of distance from the viewer (the blurriness shouldn't change based on the perpendicular distance from the view direction), and to ensure that distance of the objects from the viewer doesn't change.

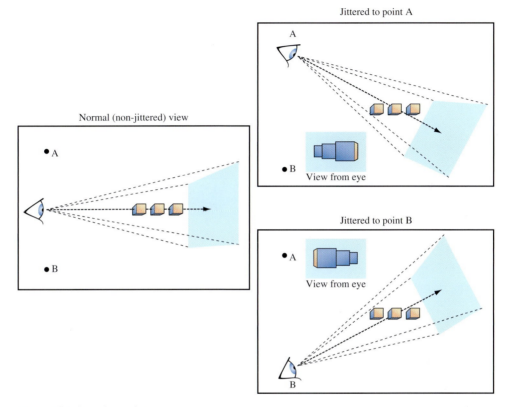

Figure 13.2 Jittered eye points.

These transform changes can be implemented easily using glFrustum to change the perspective transform, and glTranslate to change the modelview matrix. Given jitter variables *xoff* and *yoff*, and a focal length *focus*, the parameters for the commands are given in Table 13.2.

The jitter translation should be the last transform applied in the current modelview sequence, so glTranslate should be called first in the modelview transform code. The final issue to consider is the the number of jitter positions to use, and how to choose those positions. These choices are similar to many other jittering problems. A pattern of irregular positions causes sampling artifacts to show up as noise, rather than more noticeable image patterns. The jitter values shown in Section 10.1 provide good results.

The number of jittered images will be limited to the color resolution available for blending. See Section 11.4.1 for a discussion of blending artifacts and how to calculate blend error. A deep color buffer or accumulation buffer allows more images to be blended together while minimizing blending errors. If the color resolution allows it, and there is time available in the frame to render more images, more samples results in smoother

Table 13.2 Jittering Eye Position to Produce Depth of Field

Command	Parameter	Value
glFrustum	left	$left - \frac{(xoff)(near)}{focus}$
	right	$right - \frac{(xoff)(near)}{focus}$
	top	$top - \frac{(yoff)(near)}{focus}$
	bottom	$bottom - \frac{(yoff)(near)}{focus}$
	near	$near$
	far	far
glTranslate	x	$-xoff$
	y	$-yoff$

blurring of out of focus objects. Extra samples may be necessary if there are objects close to the viewer and far from the fusion point. Very blurry large objects require more samples in order to hide the fact that they are made of multiple objects.

13.4 Image Tiling

When rendering a scene in OpenGL, the maximum resolution of the image is normally limited to the workstation screen size. For interactive applications screen resolution is usually sufficient, but there may be times when a higher resolution image is needed. Examples include color printing applications and computer graphics images being recorded to film. In these cases, higher resolution images can be divided into tiles that fit within the framebuffer. The image is rendered tile by tile, with the results saved into off-screen memory or written to a file. The image can then be sent to a printer or film recorder, or undergo further processing, such as using down-sampling to produce an antialiased image.

Rendering a large image tile by tile requires repositioning the image to make different tiles visible in the framebuffer. A straightforward way to do this is to manipulate the parameters to glFrustum. The scene can be rendered repeatedly, one tile at a time, by changing the *left*, *right*, *bottom*, and *top* parameters of glFrustum for each tile.

Computing the argument values is straightforward. Divide the original width and height range by the number of tiles horizontally and vertically, and use those values to parametrically find the left, right, top, and bottom values for each tile.

$$tile(i, j); \; i : 0 \rightarrow nTiles_{horiz}, \; j : 0 \rightarrow nTiles_{vert}$$

$$right_{tiled}(i) = left_{orig} + \frac{right_{orig} - left_{orig}}{nTiles_{horiz}} * (i + 1)$$

$$left_{tiled}(i) = left_{orig} + \frac{right_{orig} - left_{orig}}{nTiles_{horiz}} * i$$

$$top_{tiled}(j) = bottom_{orig} + \frac{top_{orig} - bottom_{orig}}{nTiles_{vert}} * (j + 1)$$

$$bottom_{tiled}(j) = bottom_{orig} + \frac{top_{orig} - bottom_{orig}}{nTiles_{vert}} * j$$

In these equations each value of i and j corresponds to a tile in the scene. If the original scene is divided into $nTiles_{horiz}$ by $nTiles_{vert}$ tiles, then iterating through the combinations of i and j generate the left, right, top, and bottom values for glFrustum to create the tile. Since glFrustum has a shearing component in the matrix, the tiles stitch together seamlessly to form the scene, avoiding artifacts that result from changing the viewpoint. This technique must be modified if gluPerspective or glOrtho is used instead of glFrustum.

There is a better approach than changing the perspective transform, however. Instead of modifying the transform command directly, apply tiling transforms *after* the perspective one. A subregion of normalized device coordinate (NDC) space corresponding to the tile of interest can be translated and scaled to fill the entire NDC cube. Working in NDC space instead of eye space makes finding the tiling transforms easier, and is independent of the type of projection transform. Figure 13.3 summarizes the two approaches.

For the transform operations to take place after the projection transform, the OpenGL commands must happen before it. A typical sequence of operations is:

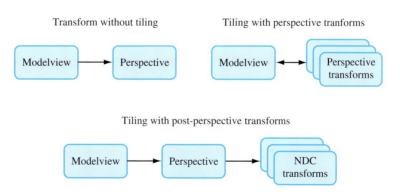

Transform without tiling   Tiling with perspective tranforms

Modelview → Perspective   Modelview ↔ Perspective transforms

Tiling with post-perspective transforms

Modelview → Perspective → NDC transforms

Figure 13.3 Image tiling transforms.

```
glMatrixMode(GL_PROJECTION);
glLoadIdentity();
/* scale is applied last */
glScalef(xScale, yScale);
glTranslatef(xOffset, yOffset, 0.f);
/* projection occurs before translate and scale */
setProjectionTransform();
```

The scale factors *xScale* and *yScale* scale the tile of interest to fill the the entire scene:

$$xScale = \frac{sceneWidth}{tileWidth} \qquad yScale = \frac{sceneHeight}{tileHeight}$$

The offsets *xOffset* and *yOffset* are used to offset the tile so it is centered about the *z*-axis. In this example, the tiles are specified by their lower left corner relative to their position in the scene, but the translation needs to move the center of the tile into the origin of the *x-y* plane in NDC space:

$$xOffset = \frac{-2*left}{sceneWidth} + \left(1 - \frac{1}{nTiles_{horiz}}\right) \qquad yOffset = \frac{-2*bottom}{sceneHeight} + \left(1 - \frac{1}{nTiles_{vert}}\right)$$

Like the previous example, $nTiles_{horiz}$ is the number of tiles that span the scene horizontally, while $nTiles_{vert}$ is the number of tiles that span the scene vertically. Some care should be taken when computing *left*, *bottom*, *tileWidth*, and *tileHeight* values. It is important that each tile is abutted properly with its neighbors. This can be ensured by guarding against round-off errors. The following code shows an example of this approach. Note that parameter values are computed so that *left* + *tileWidth* is guaranteed to be equal to *right* and equal to *left* of the next tile over, even if *tileWidth* has a fractional component. If the frustum technique is used, similar precautions should be taken with the *left*, *right*, *bottom*, and *top* parameters to glFrustum.

```
/* tileWidth and tileHeight are GLfloats */
GLint bottom, top;
GLint left, right;
GLint width, height;
for(j = 0; j < num_vertical_tiles; j++) {
    for(i = 0; i < num_horizontal_tiles; i++) {
        left = i * tileWidth;
        right = (i + 1) * tileWidth;
        bottom = j * tileHeight;
        top = (j + 1) * tileHeight;
        width = right - left;
        height = top - bottom;
        /* compute xScale, yScale, xOffset, yOffset */
    }
}
```

It is worth noting that primitives with sizes that are specified in object space dimensions automatically scale in size. If the scene contains primitives with sizes that are implicitly defined in window space dimensions, such as point sizes, line widths, bitmap sizes and pixel-rectangle, dimensions remain the same in the tiled image. An application must do extra work to scale the window space dimensions for these primitives when tiling.

13.5 Billboarding Geometry

A common shortcut used to reduce the amount of geometry needed to render a scene is to billboard the objects in the scene that have one or more axes of symmetry. Billboarding is the technique of orienting a representation of a symmetrical object toward the viewer. The geometry can be simplified to approximate a single view of an object, with that view always facing the viewer.

This technique works if the object being billboarded has an appearance that doesn't change significantly around its axis of symmetry. It is also helpful if the objects being billboarded are not a central item in the scene. The principle underlying billboarding is that complexity of an object representation is reduced in a way that is not noticeable. If successful, this approach can reduce the rendering time while maintaining image quality. Good examples of billboarded objects are trees, which have cylindrical symmetry, and clouds which have spherical symmetry. Billboarding can also be a useful technique on its own. For example, text used to annotate objects in a 3D scene can be billboarded to ensure that the text always faces the viewer and is legible.

While simplifying the geometry of an object being billboarded, it is desirable to retain its (possibly complex) outline in order to maintain a realistic result. One way to do this is to start with simple geometry such as a quadrilateral, then apply a texture containing colors that capture the surface detail and alpha components that match the object's outline. If the texture is rendered with alpha testing or alpha blending enabled, the pattern of alpha values in the texture can control which parts of the underlying geometry are rendered. The alpha texture acts as a per-pixel template, making it possible to cut out complex outlines from simple geometry. For additional details regarding using alpha to trim outlines see Section 11.9.2.

The billboarding technique is not limited to simple texture-mapped geometry though. Billboarding can also be used to draw a tessellated hemisphere, giving the illusion that a full sphere is being drawn. A similar result can be accomplished using backface culling to eliminate rasterization of the back of the sphere, but the vertices for the entire sphere are processed first. Using billboarding, only half of the sphere is transformed and rendered; however, the correct orienting transform must be computed for each hemisphere.

The billboard algorithm uses the object's modeling transform (modelview transform) to position the geometry, but uses a second transform to hold the object's orientation fixed with respect to the viewer. The geometry is always face-on to the viewer, presenting a complex image and outline with its surface texture. Typically, the billboard transform consists of a rotation concatenated to the object's modelview transform, reorienting it. Using a tree billboard as an example, an object with roughly cylindrical symmetry, an axial rotation is used to rotate the simple geometry supporting the tree texture, usually a quadrilateral, about the vertical axis running parallel to the tree trunk.

Assume that the billboard geometry is modeled so that it is already oriented properly with respect to the view direction. The goal is to find a matrix R that will rotate the geometry back into its original orientation after it is placed in the scene by the modelview transform M. This can be done in two steps. Start with the eye vector, representing the direction of view, and apply the inverse of M to it. This will transform the viewing direction vector into object space. Next, find the angle the transformed vector makes relative to canonical view direction in eye space (usually the negative z-axis) and construct a transform that will rotate the angle back to zero, putting the transformed vector into alignment with the view vector.

If the viewer is looking down the negative z-axis with an up vector aligned with the positive y-axis, the view vector is the negative z-axis. The angle of rotation can be determined by computing the vector after being transformed by the modelview matrix M

$$\mathbf{V}_{eye} = M^{-1} \begin{pmatrix} 0 \\ 0 \\ -1 \\ 0 \end{pmatrix}$$

Applying the correction rotation means finding the angle θ needed to rotate the transformed vector (and the corresponding geometry) into alignment with the direction of view. This can be done by finding the dot product between the transformed vector and the two major axes perpendicular to the axis of rotation; in this case the x and z axes.

$$\cos\theta = \mathbf{V}_{eye} \cdot \mathbf{V}_{front}$$

$$\sin\theta = \mathbf{V}_{eye} \cdot \mathbf{V}_{right}$$

where

$$\mathbf{V}_{front} = (0, 0, 1)$$

$$\mathbf{V}_{right} = (1, 0, 0)$$

The sine and cosine values are used to construct a rotation matrix R representing this rotation about the y-axis ($\mathbf{V}_{up}$). Concatenate this rotation matrix with the modelview matrix to make a combined matrix *MR*. This combined matrix is the transform applied to the billboard geometry.

To handle the more general case of an arbitrary billboard rotation axis, compute an intermediate alignment rotation *A* to rotate the billboard axis into the $\mathbf{V}_{up}$ vector. This algorithm uses the OpenGL `glRotate` command to apply a rotation about an arbitrary axis as well as an angle. This transform rotates the billboard axis into the vertical axis in eye space. The rotated geometry can then be rotated again about the vertical axis to face the viewer. With this additional rotation,

$$\mathbf{axis} = \mathbf{V}_{up} \times \mathbf{V}_{billboard}$$

$$\cos\theta = \mathbf{V}_{up} \cdot \mathbf{V}_{billboard}$$

$$\sin\theta = \|\mathbf{axis}\|$$

the complete matrix transformation is *MAR*. Note that these calculations assume that the projection matrix contains no rotational component.

Billboarding is not limited to objects that are cylindrically symmetric. It is also useful to billboard spherically symmetric objects such as smoke, clouds, and bushes. Spherical symmetry requires a billboard to rotate around two axes (up/down and left/right), whereas cylindrical behavior only requires rotation around a single axis (usually up/down) (Figure 13.4). Although it is more general, spherically symmetric billboarding is not suited for all objects; trees, for example, should not bend backward to face a viewer whose altitude increases.

Spherically symmetric objects are rotated about a point to face the viewer. This adds another degree of freedom to the rotation computation. Adding an additional alignment constraint can resolve this degree of freedom, such as one that keeps the object oriented consistently (e.g., constraining the object to remain upright).

This type of constraint helps maintain scene realism. Constraining the billboard to maintain its orientation in object space ensures that the orientation of a plume of smoke doesn't change relative to the other objects in a scene from frame to frame. A constraint can also be enforced in eye coordinates. An eye coordinate constraint can maintain alignment of an object relative to the screen (e.g., keeping text annotations aligned horizontally).

The computations for a spherically symmetric billboard are a minor extension of those used for the arbitrarily aligned cylindrical one (Figure 13.5). There is still a billboard axis, as there was in the cylindrical case, but now that axis is rotated to vertical alignment before it is used as an axis for the second rotation. An alignment transformation, *A*, rotates about a vector perpendicular to the billboard's transformed alignment axis and the up direction. The up direction is either transformed by the modelview matrix, or left untransformed, depending on whether eye-space or object-space alignment is required.

Usually the billboard axis is modeled to be parallel with a major axis in the untransformed geometry. If this is the case, *A*'s axis of rotation is computed by taking the cross product of the billboard axis and the up vector. In the more general case, if the billboard

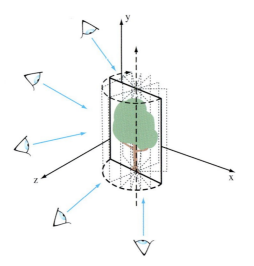

Figure 13.4 Billboard with cylindrical symmetry.

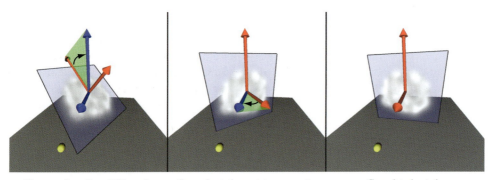

First rotation aligns billboard with eye space vertical; in general not aligned with rotation axis

Second rotation rotates geometry around vertical to face viewer

Completed rotation

Figure 13.5 Transforming a billboard with spherical symmetry.

axis is arbitrary, the transformed billboard axis must be processed before use in the cross product. Project the billboard axis to remove any component parallel to the transformed eye vector, as shown in the following equation.

The sine and cosine of the angle of rotation are computed like they were in the cylindrical case. Cosine is derived from the dot product; sine from the length of the cross product.

A is computed as:

$$\mathbf{axis} = \mathbf{V}_{up} \times \mathbf{V}_{alignment}$$

$$\cos\theta = \mathbf{V}_{up} \cdot \mathbf{V}_{alignment}$$

$$\sin\theta = \|\mathbf{axis}\|$$

where $\mathbf{V}_{alignment}$ is the billboard alignment axis with the component in the direction of the eye direction vector removed:

$$\mathbf{V}_{alignment} = \mathbf{V}_{billboard} - (\mathbf{V}_{eye} \cdot \mathbf{V}_{billboard})\mathbf{V}_{eye}$$

Rotation by the A matrix doesn't change the calculations needed to rotate about the now vertical axis. This means the left/right rotation about the up vector can still be computed from the original modelview transform in exactly the same way as a basic cylindrical billboard.

To compute the A and R matrices, it is necessary to use elements of the geometry's modelview transform. Retrieving transformation matrices using `glGet` introduces a large performance penalty on most OpenGL implementations and should be avoided. The application should either read the transformation once per frame, or shadow the current modelview transform to avoid reading it back from OpenGL altogether. Fortunately, it is fairly simple to duplicate the standard OpenGL transform commands in software and provide some simple vector and matrix operations. Matrix equivalents for `glTranslate`, `glRotate`, and `glScale` operations are described in Appendix B. Computing the inverse for each of these three operations is trivial; see Section 13.1 for details.

13.6 Texture Coordinate vs. Geometric Transformations

The texture coordinate pipeline has a significant amount of transformation power. There is a single transformation matrix (called the texture transformation matrix), but it is a full 4×4 matrix with perspective divide functionality. Even if the target is a 2D texture, the perspective divide capability makes the fourth texture coordinate, q, a useful tool, while a 3D texture target can make use of all four coordinates. The texture transform pipeline has nearly the same transformation capabilities as the geometry pipeline, only lacking the convenience of two independent transform matrices and an independent viewport transform.

The texture coordinate path has an additional benefit, automatic texture coordinate generation, which allows an application to establish a linear mapping between vertex coordinates in object or eye space and texture coordinates. The environment mapping functionality is even more powerful, allowing mappings between vertex normals or reflection vectors and texture coordinates.

Geometric transforms are applied in a straightforward way to texture coordinates; a texture coordinate transform can be assembled and computed in the same way it is done in the geometry pipeline. Convenience functions such as `glFrustum`, `glOrtho`, and `gluLookAt`, are available, as well as the basic matrix commands such as `glLoadMatrix`. Since there is only one matrix to work with, some understanding of matrix composition is necessary to produce the same effects the modelview and projection matrices do in the geometry pipeline. It's also important to remember that NDC space, the result of these two transformations, ranges from −1 to 1 in three dimensions, while texture coordinates range from 0 to 1. This usually implies that a scale and bias term must be added to texture transforms to ensure the resulting texture coordinates map to the texture map.

To apply a geometric transform into texture coordinates, the transformations for texture coordinates are applied in the same order as they are in the vertex coordinate pipeline: modelview, projection, and scale and bias (to convert NDC to texture space). A summary of the steps to build a typical texture transformation using geometry pipeline transforms is as follows:

1. Select the texture matrix: `glMatrixMode(GL_TEXTURE)`.

2. Load the identity matrix: `glLoadIdentity()`.

3. Load the bias: `glTranslatef(.5f, .5f, 0.f)`.

4. Load the scale: `glScalef(.5f, .5f, 1.f)`.

5. Set the perspective transform: `glFrustum(...)`.

6. Set the modelview transform: `gluLookAt(...)`.

With the texture transform matrix set, the last step is to choose the values for the input texture coordinates. As mentioned previously, it's possible to map certain vertex attributes into texture coordinates. The vertex position, normal, or reflection vector (see Section 5.4), is transformed, then used as the vertex's texture coordinate. This functionality, called *texture generation* (or texgen), is a branch point for creating texture coordinates. Texture coordinate generation can take place in object or eye space. After branching, the texture coordinates and the vertex attributes that spawned them are processed by the remainder of the vertex pipeline.

The following sections illustrate some texgen/texture coordinate transform techniques. These are useful building block techniques as well as useful solutions to some common texture coordinate problems.

13.6.1 Direct Vertex to Texture Coordinate Mapping

If the projection and modelview parts of the matrix are defined in terms of eye space (where the entire scene is assembled), a basic texture coordinate generation method is to create a one-to-one mapping between eye-space and texture space. The s, t, and r values at a vertex must be the same as the x, y, and z values of the vertex in eye space. This is done by enabling eye-linear texture generation and setting the eye planes to a one-to-one mapping:

$$S_{eye} = (1, 0, 0, 0)$$

$$T_{eye} = (0, 1, 0, 0)$$

$$R_{eye} = (0, 0, 1, 0)$$

$$Q_{eye} = (0, 0, 0, 1)$$

Instead of mapping to eye space, an object-space mapping can be used. This is useful if the texture coordinates must be created before any geometric transformations have been applied.

When everything is configured properly, texture coordinates matching the x, y, and z values transformed by the modelview matrix are generated, then transformed by the texture matrix. This method is a good starting point for techniques such as projective textures; see Section 14.9 for details.

13.6.2 Overlaying an Entire Scene with a Texture

A useful technique is overlaying a texture map directly onto a scene rendered with a perspective transform. This mapping establishes a fixed relationship between texels in the texture map and every pixel on the viewport; the lower left corner in the scene corresponds to the lower left corner of the texture map; the same holds true for the upper right corner. The relative size of the pixels and texels depends on the relative resolutions of the window and the texture map. If the texture map has the same resolution as the window, the texel to pixel relationship is one to one.

When drawing a perspective view, the near clipping plane maps to the viewport in the framebuffer. To overlay a texture, a texture transformation must be configured so that the near clipping plane maps directly to the [0, 1] texture map range. That is, find a transform that maps the x, y, and z values to the appropriate s and t values. As mentioned previously, it is straightforward to map NDC space to texture space. All coordinates in

NDC space range from $[-1, 1]$ and texture coordinates range from $[0, 1]$. Given a texgen function that maps x, y NDC values into s, t texture coordinate values, all that is required is to add a scale and translate into the texture matrix. The NDC-space z values are unused since they do not affect the x, y position on the screen.

1. Use texgen to map from NDC space to texture coordinates.

2. Set up translate and scale transforms in the texture matrix to map from -1 to 1 to 0 to 1.

Unfortunately, OpenGL doesn't provide texgen function to map vertex coordinates to NDC space. The closest available is eye-space texgen. Translating from eye space to NDC space can be done using an additional transform in the texture transformation pipeline, emulating the remainder of the vertex transformation pipeline. This is done by concatenating the projection transform, which maps from eye space to NDC space in the geometry transform pipeline. This transform is then composited with the translate and scale transforms needed to convert from NDC to texture coordinates, ordering the transforms such that the projection matrix transform is applied to the texture coordinates first. Summing up the steps in order results in the following:

1. Configure texgen to generate texture coordinates from eye-space geometry.

2. Set the texture transform matrix to translate and scale the range -1 to 1 to 0 to 1.

3. Concatenate the contents of the projection matrix onto the texture transform matrix.

13.6.3 Overlaying a Scene with an Independent Texture Projection

The previous technique can be seen as a simplified version of the more general problem; how to map objects as seen from one viewpoint to a full scene texture but using a different viewpoint to render the objects. To accomplish this, texture coordinates need to be generated from vertices earlier in the geometry pipeline: texgen is applied in untransformed object space. The x, y, z positions are converted into s, t, r values before any transforms are applied; the texture coordinates can then be transformed completely separately from the geometric coordinates. Since texgen is happening earlier, mapping the texture coordinates to the near clip plane, as described previously, requires transforming the texture coordinates with a modelview and projection transform (including a perspective divide) to go from object space all the way to NDC space, followed by the scale and bias necessary to get to texture space.

Doing the extra transform work in the texture matrix provides extra flexibility: the texture coordinates generated from the vertices can be transformed with one set of modelview (and perspective) transforms to create one view, while the original geometry can be transformed using a completely separate view.

To create the proper texture transformation matrix, both the modelview and projection matrices are concatenated with the scale and bias transforms. Since the modelview matrix should be applied first, it should be multiplied into the transform last.

1. Configure texgen to map to texture coordinates from eye-space geometry.

2. Set the texture transform matrix to translate and scale the range −1 to 1 to 0 to 1.

3. Concatenate the contents of the projection matrix with the texture transform matrix.

4. Concatenate a (possibly separate) modelview matrix with the texture transform matrix.

When using the geometry pipeline's transform sequence from a modelview or perspective transform to build a transform matrix, be sure to strip any `glLoadIdentity` commands from projection and modelview commands. This is required since all the transforms are being combined into a single matrix. This transform technique is a key component to techniques such as shadow mapping, a texture-based method of creating inter-object shadows. This technique is covered in Section 17.4.3.

13.7 Interpolating Vertex Components through a Perspective Transformation

The rasterization process interpolates vertex attributes in window space and sometimes it's useful to perform similar computations within the application. Being able to do so makes it possible to efficiently calculate vertex attributes as a function of pixel position. For example, these values can be used to tessellate geometry as a function of screen coverage. Differences in texture coordinates between adjacent pixels can be used to compute LOD and texture coordinate derivatives $\left(\frac{\partial u}{\partial x}, \frac{\partial u}{\partial y}, \frac{\partial v}{\partial x}, \frac{\partial v}{\partial y}\right)$ as a function of screen position. Techniques that require this functionality include detail textures (Section 14.13.2), texture sharpening (Section 14.14), and using prefiltered textures to do anisotropic texturing (Section 14.7).

Interpolating a vertex attribute to an arbitrary location in window space is a two-step process. First the vertex coordinates to be interpolated are transformed to window coordinates. Then the attributes of interest are interpolated to the desired pixel location. Since the transform involves a perspective divide, the relationship between object and window coordinates isn't linear.

13.7.1 Transforming Vertices in the Application

Finding the transformed values of the vertex coordinates can be done using feedback mode, but this path is slow on most OpenGL implementations. Feedback also doesn't provide all the information that will be needed to compute vertex attributes, such as texture coordinate values, efficiently. Instead an application can transform and (optionally) clip vertices using the proper values of the modelview, projection, and viewport transforms.

The current modelview and perspective transforms can be shadowed in the application, so they don't have to be queried from OpenGL (which can be slow). The viewport transformation can be computed from the current values of the glViewport command's parameters x_o, y_o, *width*, and *height*. The transformation equations for converting x_{ndc} and y_{ndc} from NDC space into window space is:

$$x_{win} = \left(\frac{width}{2}\right) x_{ndc} + x_o$$

$$y_{win} = \left(\frac{height}{2}\right) y_{ndc} + y_o$$

$$z_{win} = \left(\frac{f - n}{2}\right) z_{ndc} + \left(\frac{n + f}{2}\right)$$

where n and f are near and far depth range values; the default values are 0 and 1, respectively. If only texture values are being computed, the equation for computing z_{win} is not needed. The equations can be further simplified for texture coordinates since the viewport origin doesn't affect these values either; all that matters is the size ratio between texels and pixels:

$$x_{win} = \left(\frac{width}{2}\right) x_{ndc}$$

$$y_{win} = \left(\frac{height}{2}\right) y_{ndc}$$

(13.1)

13.7.2 Interpolating Vertex Components

Finding vertex locations in screen space solves only half of the problem. Since the vertex coordinates undergo a perspective divide as they are transformed to window space, the relationship between object or eye space and window space is non-linear. Finding the values of a vertex attribute, such as a texture coordinate, at a given pixel takes a special approach. It is not accurate to simply transform the vertex coordinates to window space, then use their locations on the screen to linearly interpolate attributes of interest to a given pixel.

In order to interpolate attributes on the far side of the perspective divide accurately, the interpolation must be done *hyperbolically*, taking interpolated w values into account. Blinn (1992) describes an efficient interpolation and transformation method. We'll present the results here within the context of OpenGL.

To interpolate a vertex attribute hyperbolically, every attribute of interest must be scaled before interpolation. The attributes must be divided by the transformed w attribute of the vertex. This w value, which we'll call w', has had all of its geometry transforms applied, but hasn't been modified by a perspective divide yet. Each attribute in the vertex to be interpolated is divided by w'. The value of $1/w'$ is also computed and stored for each vertex. To interpolate attributes, the vertex's scaled attributes and its $1/w'$ are all interpolated independently.

If the interpolation needs to be done to a particular location in window space, each vertex's x and y values are transformed and perspective divided to transform into window space first. The relationship between the desired pixel position and the vertex's x_{win} and y_{win} values are used to compute the correct interpolation parameters.

Once the vertex attributes are interpolated, they are divided by the interpolated value of $1/w'$, yielding the correct attribute values at that window space location.

13.7.3 Computing LOD

As an example, consider finding an LOD value for a particular location on a triangle in object space. An LOD value measures the size ratio between texel and pixel at a given location. First, each vertex's transformed texture coordinates (s and t) are divided by the vertex coordinates' post-transform w' value. The s/w', t/w', and the $1/w'$ values are computed at the triangle vertices. All three attributes are interpolated to the location of interest. The interpolated s/w' and t/w' values ($\tilde{s}, \tilde{t}$) are divided by the interpolated $1/w'$ value ($\tilde{1}$), which produces the proper s and t values.

To find the LOD at window-space location, the texture coordinate derivatives must be computed. This means finding $\partial s/\partial x$, $\partial t/\partial x$, $\partial s/\partial y$, and $\partial t/\partial y$ in window space. These derivatives can be approximated using divided differences. One method of doing this is to find the s and t values one pixel step away in the x and y directions in window space, then compute the differences. Finding these values requires computing new interpolation parameters for window space positions. This is done by computing the x_{win} and y_{win} values for the vertices of the triangle, then using the x_{win} and y_{win} at the locations of interest to compute barycentric interpolation parameters. These new interpolation parameters are used to hyperbolically interpolate s and t coordinates for each point and then to compute the differences.

Using s and t values directly won't produce usable texture derivatives. To compute them, texture coordinates s and t must be converted to *texel coordinates* u and v. This is done by scaling s and t by the width and height of the texture map. With these values in place, the differences in u and v relative to x_{win} and y_{win} will reflect the size relationship between pixels and texels. To compute the LOD, the differences must be combined to provide a single result. An accurate way to do this is by applying the formula:

$$\rho = \max\left\{ \sqrt{\left(\frac{\partial u}{\partial x}\right)^2 + \left(\frac{\partial v}{\partial x}\right)^2}, \sqrt{\left(\frac{\partial u}{\partial y}\right)^2 + \left(\frac{\partial v}{\partial y}\right)^2} \right\} \qquad \textbf{(13.2)}$$

Other methods that are less accurate but don't require as much computation can also be used (and may be used in the OpenGL implementation). These methods include choosing the largest absolute value from the four approximated derivative values computed in Equation 13.2.

Once a single value is determined, the LOD is computed as log_2 of that value. A negative LOD value indicates texture magnification; a positive one, minification.

Combining Transforms

The transforms applied to the vertex values can be concatenated together for efficiency. Some changes are necessary: the perspective divide shouldn't change the w value of the vertex, since the transformed w will be needed to interpolate the texture coordinates properly. Since the post-divide w won't be 1, the viewport transform should be based on Equation 13.1 so it is independent of w values. If the exact window positions are necessary, the results can be biased by the location of the window center.

Window Space Clipping Shortcuts

In some cases, the clipping functionality in the transformation pipeline must also be duplicated by the application. Generalized primitive clipping can be non-trivial, but there are a number of shortcuts that can be used in some cases. One is to simply not clip the primitive. This will work as long as the primitive doesn't go through the eye point, resulting in w' values of zero. If it does, clipping against the near clip plane is required. If the primitive doesn't go through the viewpoint and simplified clipping is needed for efficiency, the clipping can be applied in window space against the viewport rectangle. If this is done, care should be taken to ensure that the perspective divide doesn't destroy the value of w'. The vertex attributes should be hyperbolically interpolated to compute their values on new vertices created by clipping.

13.8 Summary

This chapter describes a number of viewing, projection, and texture transformations frequently employed in other techniques. The algorithms described are representative of a broad range of techniques that can be implemented within the OpenGL pipeline. The addition of the programmable vertex pipeline greatly increases the flexibility of the transformation pipeline but these basic transformation algorithms remain important as building blocks for other techniques. The remaining chapters incorporate and extend several of these basic ideas as important constituents of more complex techniques.

Texture Mapping Techniques

Texture mapping is a powerful building block of graphics techniques. It is used in a wide range of applications, and is central to many of the techniques used in this book. The basics of texture mapping have already been covered in Chapter 5 and serves as a background reference for texture-related techniques.

The traditional use of texture mapping applies images to geometric surfaces. In this chapter we'll go further, exploring the use of texture mapping as an elemental tool and building block for graphics effects. The techniques shown here improve on basic texture mapping in two ways. First, we show how to get the most out of OpenGL's native texturing support, presenting techniques that allow the application to maximize basic texture mapping functionality. Examples of this include rendering very large textures using texture paging, prefiltering textures to improve quality, and using image mosaics (or atlases) to improve texture performance.

We also re-examine the uses of texture mapping, looking at texture coordinate generation, sampling, and filtering as building blocks of functionality, rather than just a way of painting color bitmaps onto polygons. Examples of these techniques include texture animation, billboards, texture color coding, and image warping. We limit our scope to the more fundamental techniques, focusing on the ones that have potential to be used to build complex approaches. More specialized texturing techniques are covered in the chapters where they are used. For example, texture mapping used in lighting is covered in Chapter 15. Volumetric texturing, a technique for visualizing 3D datasets, is presented in Section 20.5.8.

14.1 Loading Texture Images into a Framebuffer

Although there is no direct OpenGL support for it, it is easy to copy an image from a texture map into the framebuffer. It can be done by drawing a rectangle of the desired size into the framebuffer, applying a texture containing the desired texture image. The rectangle's texture coordinates are chosen to provide a one-to-one mapping between texels and pixels. One side effect of this method is that the depth values of the textured image will be changed to the depth values of the textured polygon. If this is undesirable, the textured image can be written back into the framebuffer without disturbing existing depth buffer values by disabling depth buffer updates when rendering the textured rectangle. Leaving the depth buffer intact is very useful if more objects need to be rendered into the scene with depth testing after the texture image has been copied into the color buffer.

The concept of transferring images back and forth between a framebuffer and texture map is a useful building block. Writing an image from texture memory to the framebuffer is often faster than transferring it from system memory using `glDrawPixels`. If an image must be transferred to the framebuffer more than once, using a texture can be the high-performance path. The texture technique is also very general, and can be easily extended. For example, when writing an image back into the framebuffer with a textured polygon, the texture coordinates can be set to arbitrarily distort the resulting image. The distorted image could be the final desired result, or it could be transferred back into the texture, providing a method for creating textures with arbitrarily warped images.

14.2 Optimizing Texture Coordinate Assignment

Rather than using it to create special effects, in some cases distorting a texture image can be used to improve quality. Sloan et al. (1997) have explored optimizing the assignment of texture coordinates based on an "importance map" that can encode both intrinsic texture properties as well as user-guided highlights. This approach highlights the fact that texture images can have separate "interesting" regions in them. These can be areas of high contrast, fine detail, or otherwise draw the viewer's attention based on its content. A simple example is a light map containing a region of high contrast and detail near the light source with the rest of the texture containing a slowly changing, low-contrast image.

A common object modeling approach is to choose and position vertices to represent an object accurately, while maintaining a "vertex budget" constraint to manage geometry size and load bandwidth. As a separate step, the surface is parameterized with texture coordinates so surface textures can be applied. Adding the notion of textures with regions of varying importance can lead to changes in this approach.

The first step is to distort a high-resolution version of the texture image so the regions of interest remain large but the remainder shrinks. The resulting texture image is smaller than the original, which had high-image resolution everywhere, even where it wasn't needed. The technique described in Section 5.3 can be used to generate the new image. The parameterization of the geometry is also altered, mapping the texture onto the surface so that the high and low importance regions aren't distorted, but instead vary in texel resolution. This concept is shown in Figure 14.1.

To do this properly both the texture, with its regions of high and low interest, and the geometry it is applied to must be considered. The tessellation of the model may have to be changed to ensure a smooth transition between high- and low-resolution regions of the texture. At least two rows of vertices are needed to transition between a high-resolution scaling to a low-resolution one; more are needed if the transition region requires fine control.

The idea of warping the texture image and altering the texture coordinate assignment can be thought of as a general approach for improving texture appearance without increasing texture size. If the OpenGL implementation supports multitexturing, a single texture can be segmented into multiple textures with distinct low and high interest regions.

14.3 3D Textures

The classic application of 3D texture maps is to to use them to represent the visual appearance of a solid material. One example would be to procedurally generate a solid representation of marble, then apply it to an object, so that the object appears to be carved out of the stone. Although this 3D extension of the surface mapping application is certainly valuable, 3D texture maps can do more. Put in a more general context, 3D textures can be thought of as a 2D texture map that varies as a function of its r coordinate value. Since the 3D texture filters in three dimensions, changing the r value smoothly will linearly blend from one 2D texture image slice to the next (Figure 14.2). This technique can be used to create animated 2D textures and is described in more detail in Section 14.12.

Two caveats should be considered when filtering a 3D texture. First, OpenGL doesn't make any distinction between dimensions when filtering; if GL_LINEAR filtering is chosen, both the texels in the r direction, and the ones in the s and t directions, will be linearly filtered. For example, if the application uses nearest filtering to choose a specific slice, the resulting image can't be linearly filtered. This lack of distinction between dimensions also leads to the second caveat. When filtering, OpenGL will choose to minify or magnify isotropically based on the size ratio between texel and pixel in all dimensions. It's not possible to stretch an image slice and expect minification filtering to be used for sampling in the r direction.

| High resolution texture with region of interest | Distortion function applies to image; area surrounding region of interest shrunk and distorted | Inverse of distortion function (applied to texture coordinates) |

Texture coordinates invert distortion function applied to image; areas surrounding region of interest are low resolution

Figure 14.1 Segmenting a texture into resolution regions.

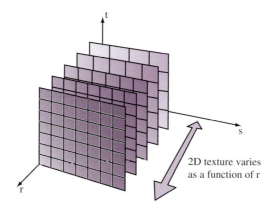

Figure 14.2 3D textures as 2D textures varying with R.

The safest course of action is to set GL_TEXTURE_MIN_FILTER and GL_TEXTURE_MAG_FILTER to the same values. It is also prudent to use GL_LINEAR instead of GL_NEAREST. If a single texture slice should be used, compute r to index exactly to it: the OpenGL specification is specific enough that the proper r value is computable, given the texture dimensions. Finally, note that using r for the temporal direction in a 3D texture is arbitrary; OpenGL makes no distinction, the results depend solely on the configuration set by the application.

3D textures can also be parameterized to create a more elaborate type of billboard. A common billboard technique uses a 2D texture applied to a polygon that is oriented to always face the viewer. Billboards of objects such as trees behave poorly when the object is viewed from above. A 3D texture billboard can change the textured image as a function of viewer elevation angle, blending a sequence of images between side view and top view, depending on the viewer's position.

If the object isn't seen from above, but the view around the object must be made more realistic, a 3D texture can be composed of 2D images taken around the object. An object, real or synthetic, can be imaged from viewpoints taken at evenly spaced locations along a circle surrounding it. The billboard can be textured with the 3D texture, and the r coordinate can be selected as a function of viewer position. This sort of "azimuth billboard" will show parallax motion cues as the view moves around the billboard, making it appear that the billboard object has different sides that come into view. This technique also allows a billboard to represent an object that isn't as cylindrically symmetric about its vertical access.

This technique has limits, as changes in perspective are created by fading between still images taken at different angles. The number of views must be chosen to minimize the differences between adjacent images, or the object itself may need to be simplified. Using a billboard of any variety works best if the object being billboarded isn't the focus of the viewer's attention. The shortcuts taken to make a billboard aren't as noticeable if billboards are only used for background objects.

The most general use of 3D textures is to represent a 3D function. Like the 2D version, each texel stores the result of evaluating a function with a particular set of parameter values. It can be useful to process the s, t, and r values before they index the texture, to better represent the function. This processing can be done with texgen or a texture transform matrix functionality. As with the previous two methods, using GL_LINEAR makes it possible to interpolate between arbitrary sample points. A non-linear function is often approximately linear between two values, if the function values are sampled at close enough intervals.

14.4 Texture Mosaics

Many complex scenes have a large number of "odds and ends" textures. These low-resolution textures are used to add diversity and realism to the scene's appearance. Additionally, many small textures are often needed for multipass and multitexture surfaces, to create light maps, reflectance maps, and so forth. These "surface realism" textures are often low resolution; their pattern may be replicated over the surface to add small details, or stretched across a large area to create a slowly changing surface variation.

Supporting such complex scenes can be expensive, since rendering many small, irregularly sized textures requires many texture binds per scene. In many OpenGL implementations the cost of binding a texture object (making it the currently active texture) is relatively high, limiting rendering performance when a large number of textures are being used in each rendered frame. If the implementation supports multitexturing, the binding and unbinding of each texture unit can also incur a high overhead.

Beyond binding performance, there are also space issues to consider. Most implementations restrict texture map sizes to be powers of two to support efficient addressing of texels in pipeline implementations. There are extensions that generalize the addressing allowing non-power-of-two sizes, such as ARB_texture_non_power_of_two and EXT_texture_rectangle. Nevertheless, to meet a power-of-two restriction, small texture images may have to be embedded in a larger texture map, surrounded by a large boundary. This is wasteful of texture memory, a limited resource in most implementations. It also makes it more likely that fewer textures in the scene fit into texture memory simultaneously, forcing the implementation to swap textures in and out of the graphics hardware's texture memory, further reducing performance.

Each image in
separate texture

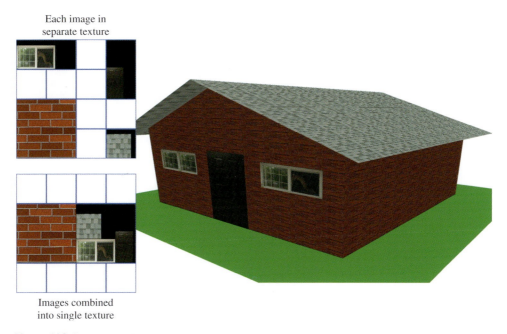

Images combined
into single texture

Figure 14.3 Texture mosaicing.

Both the texture binding and space overhead of many small textured images can be reduced by using a technique called *texture mosaicing* (or sometimes *texture atlasing*) (Figure 14.3). In this technique, many small texture images are packed together into a single texture map. Binding this texture map makes all of its texture images available for rendering, reducing the number of texture binds needed. In addition, less texture memory is wasted, since many small textures can be packed together to form an image close to power-of-two dimensions.

Texture mosaicing can also be used to reduce the overhead of texture environment changes. Since each texture often has a specific texture environment associated with it, a mosaic can combine images that use the same texture environment. When the texture is made current, the texture environment can be held constant while multiple images within the texture map are used sequentially. This combining of similar texture images into a single texture map can also be used to group textures that will be used together on an object, helping to reduce texture binding overhead.

The individual images in the mosaic must be separated enough so that they do not interfere with each other during filtering. If two images are textured using nearest filtering, then they can be adjacent, but linear filtering requires a one-pixel border around each texture, so the adjacent texture images do not overlap when sampled near their shared boundaries.

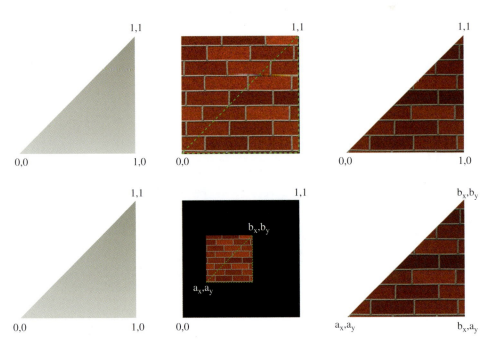

Figure 14.4 Texture mosaicing.

Mosaicing mipmapped textures requires greater separation between images. If a series of mipmap layers contain multiple images, then each image must be enclosed in a power-of-two region, even if the image doesn't have a power-of-two resolution. This avoids sampling of adjacent images when coarse mipmap levels are used. This space-wasting problem can be mitigated somewhat if only a subset of the mipmap levels (LODs) are needed. OpenGL 1.2 supports texture LOD clamping which constrains which LODs are used and therefore which levels need to be present. Blending of coarse images also may not be a problem if the adjacent textures are chosen so that their coarser layers are very similar in appearance. In that case, the blending of adjacent images may not be objectionable.

A primitive textured using mosaiced textures must have its texture coordinates modified to access the proper region of the mosaic texture map. Texture coordinates for an unmosaiced texture image will expect the texture image to range from 0 to 1. These values need to be scaled and biased to match the location of desired image in the mosaic map (Figure 14.4). The scaled and biased texture coordinates can be computed once, when the objects in the scene are modeled and the mosaiced textures created, or dynamically, by using OpenGL's texgen or texture matrix functions to transform the texture coordinates as the primitives are rendered. It is usually better to set the coordinates at modeling time, freeing texgen for use in other dynamic effects.

14.5 Texture Tiling

There is an upper limit to the size of a texture map that an implementation can support. This can make it difficult to define and use a very large texture as part of rendering a high-resolution image. Such images may be needed on very high-resolution displays or for generating an image for printing. Texture tiling provides a way of working around this limitation. An arbitrarily large texture image can be broken up into a rectangular grid of tiles. A tile size is chosen that is supported by the OpenGL implementation. This texture tiling method is related to texture paging, described in Section 14.6.

OpenGL supports texture tiling with a number of features. One is the strict specification of the texture minification filters. On conformant implementations, this filtering is predictable, and can be used to seamlessly texture primitives applied one at a time to adjacent regions of the textured surface.

To apply a texture to these regions, a very large texture is divided into multiple tiles. The texture tiles are then loaded and used to texture in several passes. For example, if a 1024×1024 texture is broken up into four 512×512 images, the four images correspond to the texture coordinate ranges $(0 \to \frac{1}{2}, 0 \to \frac{1}{2})$, $(\frac{1}{2} \to 1, 0 \to \frac{1}{2})$, $(0 \to \frac{1}{2}, \frac{1}{2} \to 0)$, and $(\frac{1}{2} \to 1, \frac{1}{2} \to 1)$.

As each tile is loaded, only the portions of the geometry that correspond to the appropriate texture coordinate ranges for a given tile should be drawn. To render a single triangle whose texture coordinates are (0.1, 0.1), (0.1, 0.7), and (0.8, 0.8), the triangle must be clipped against each of the four tile regions in turn. Only the clipped portion of the triangle—the part that intersects a given texture tile—is rendered, as shown in Figure 14.5. As each piece is rendered, the original texture coordinates must be adjusted to match the scaled and translated texture space represented by the tile. This transformation is performed by loading the appropriate scale and translation onto the texture matrix.

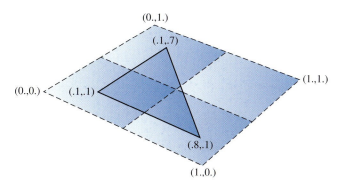

Figure 14.5 Texture tiling.

Normally clipping the geometry to the texture tiles is performed as part of the modeling step. This can be done when the relationship between the texture and geometry is known in advance. However, sometimes this relationship isn't known, such as when a tiled texture is applied to arbitrary geometry. OpenGL does not provide direct support for clipping the geometry to the tile. The clipping problem can be simplified, however, if the geometry is modeled with tiling in mind. For a trivial example, consider a textured primitive made up of quads, each covered with an aligned texture tile. In this case, the clipping operation is easy. In the general case, of course, clipping arbitrary geometry to the texture tile boundaries can involve substantially more work.

One approach that can simplify the clipping stage of texture tiling is to use stenciling (Section 6.2.3) and transparency mapping (Section 11.9.2) to trim geometry to a texture tile boundary. Geometry clipping becomes unnecessary, or can be limited to culling geometry that doesn't intersect a given texture tile to improve performance. The central idea is to create a stencil mask that segments the polygons that is covered by a given texture tile from the polygons that aren't. The geometry can be rendered with the proper tile texture applied, and the stencil buffer can be set as a side effect of rendering it. The resulting stencil values can be used in a second pass to only render the geometry where it is textured with the tile (Figure 14.6).

Creating the stencil mask itself can be done by using a "masking" texture. This texture sets an alpha value only where it's applied to the primitive. Alpha test can then be used to discard anything not drawn with that alpha value (see Section 6.2.2). The undiscarded fragments can then be used with the proper settings of stencil test and stencil operation to create a stencil mask of the region being textured. Disabling color and depth buffer updates, or setting the depth test to always fail will ensure that only the stencil buffer is updated.

One area that requires care is clamping. Since the tiling scenario requires applying a masking texture that only covers part of the primitive, what happens outside the texture

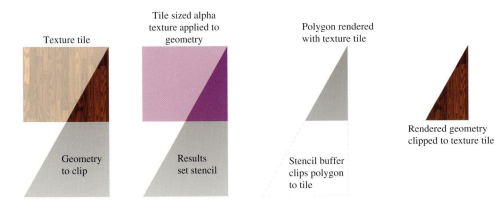

Figure 14.6 Clipping geometry to tile with alpha texture and stencil.

coordinate range of [0, 1] must be considered. One approach is to configure the masking texture to use the GL_CLAMP_TO_BORDER wrap mode, so all of the geometry beyond the applied texture will be set to the border color. Using a border color with zero components (the default) will ensure that the geometry not covered by the texture will have a different alpha value.

Here is a procedure that puts all of these ideas together:

1. Create a texture of internal type GL_ALPHA. It can have a single texel if desired.

2. Set the parameters so that GL_NEAREST filtering is used, and set the wrap mode appropriately.

3. Set the texture environment to GL_REPLACE.

4. Apply the texture using the same coordinate, texgen, and texture transform matrix settings that will be used in the actual texture tile.

5. Enable and set alpha testing to discard all pixels that don't have an alpha value matching the masking texture.

6. Set up the stencil test to set stencil when the alpha value is correct.

7. Render the primitive with the masking texture applied. Disable writes to the color and depth buffer if they should remain unchanged.

8. Re-render the geometry with the actual tiled texture, using the new stencil mask to prevent any geometry other than the tiled part from being rendered.

If the tiled textures are applied using nearest filtering, the procedure is complete. In the more common case of linear or mipmap filtered textures, there is additional work to do. Linear filtering can generate artifacts where the texture tiles meet. This occurs because a texture coordinate can sample beyond the edge of the texture. The simple solution to this problem is to configure a one-texel border on each texture tile. The border texels should be copied from the adjacent edges of the neighboring tiles.

A texture border ensures that a texture tile which samples beyond its edges will sample from its neighbors texels, creating seamless boundaries between tiles. Note that borders are only needed for linear or mipmap filtering. Clamp-to-edge filtering can also be used instead of texture borders, but will produce lower quality results. See Section 5.1.1 for more information on texture borders.

14.6 Texture Paging

As applications simulate higher levels of realism, the amount of texture memory they require can increase dramatically. Texture memory is a limited, expensive resource, so directly loading a high-resolution texture is not always feasible. Applications are often forced to resample their images at a lower resolution to make them fit in texture memory, with a corresponding loss of realism and image quality. If an application must view the entire textured image at high resolution, this, or a texture tiling approach (as described in Section 14.5) may be the only option.

But many applications have texture requirements that can be structured so that only a small area of large texture has to be shown at full resolution. Consider a flight simulation example. The terrain may be modeled as a single large triangle mesh, with texture coordinates to map it to a single, very large texture map, possibly a mipmap. Although the geometry and the texture are large, only terrain close to the viewer is visible in high detail. Terrain far from the viewer must be textured using low-resolution texture levels to avoid aliasing, since a pixel corresponding to these areas covers many texels at once. For similar reasons, many applications that use large texture maps find that the maximum amount of texture memory in use for any given viewpoint is bounded.

Applications can take advantage of these constraints through a technique called *texture paging*. Rather than loading complete levels of a large image, only the portion of the image closest to the viewer is kept in texture memory. The rest of the image is stored in system memory or on disk. As the viewer moves, the contents of texture memory are updated to keep the closest portion of the image loaded.

Two different approaches can be used to implement this technique. The first is to use a form of texture tiling. The texture is subdivided into fixed sized tiles. Textured geometry is matched up with the tiles that cover it, and segmented to match the tile boundaries. This segmentation can happen when the geometry is modeled, by re-tessellating it into tile-sized pieces (with its texture coordinates changed to map the tile properly) or it can be done at runtime through clipping combined with texgen or the texture transform matrix.

When tiled geometry is rendered, it is rendered one tile at a time, with texture coordinates set appropriately to apply the tile to the surface. Texture memory is reloaded when a new tile is needed. For geometry that is farther from the viewer, tiles containing lower resolution texture levels are used to avoid aliasing artifacts. Figure 14.7 shows a

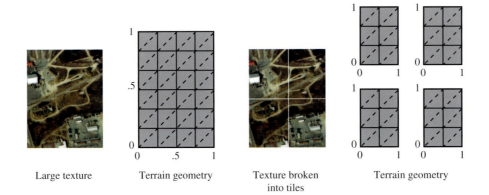

| Large texture | Terrain geometry | Texture broken into tiles | Terrain geometry |

Figure 14.7 Modeling a large texture as a grid of tiles.

texture broken up into tiles, and its geometry tessellated and texture coordinates changed to match.

The tiling technique is conceptually straightforward, and is used in some form by nearly all applications that need to apply a large texture to geometry (see Section 14.5). There are some drawbacks to using a pure tiling approach, however. The part of the technique that requires segmenting geometry to texture tiles is the most problematic. Segmenting geometry requires re-tessellating it to match tile boundaries, or using techniques to clip it against the current tile. In addition, the geometry's texture coordinates must be adjusted to properly map the texture tile to the geometry segment.

For linear filtering, tile boundaries can be made invisible by carefully clipping or tessellating the geometry so that the texture coordinates are kept within the tile's [0.0, 1.0] range, and using texture borders containing a strip of texels from each adjacent tile (see Section 5.1.1 for more details on texture borders). This ensures that the geometry is textured properly across the edge of each tile, making the transition seamless. A clean solution is more elusive when dealing with the boundary between tiles of different texture resolution, however. One approach is to blend the two resolutions at boundary tiles, using OpenGL's blend functionality or multitexturing. Figure 14.8 shows how tiles of different resolution are used to approximate mipmapping, and how tiles on each LOD boundary can be blended. Alternatively, linear filtering with mipmapping handles the border edges, at the expense of loading a full mipmap pyramid rather than a single level.

The process of clipping or re-tessellating dynamic geometry to match each image tile itself is not always easy. An example of dynamic geometry common to visual simulation applications is dynamic terrain tessellation. Terrain close to the viewer is replaced with more highly tessellated geometry to increase detail, while geometry far from the viewer is tessellated more coarsely to improve rendering performance. In general, forcing a

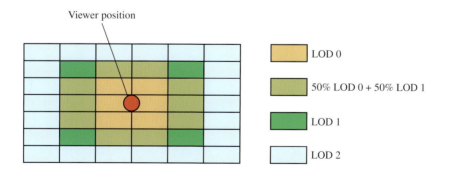

Texture paging approximates mipmapping: coarser resolution tiles as distance from the viewer increases. Tiles can blend LOD levels.

Figure 14.8 Tiling a large texture with different LOD levels.

correspondence between texture and geometry beyond what is established by texture coordinates should be avoided, since it increases complication and adds new visual quality issues that the application has to cope with.

Given sufficient texture memory, geometry segmentation can be avoided by combining texture tiles into a larger texture region, and applying it to the currently visible geometry. Although it uses more texture memory, the entire texture doesn't need to be loaded, only the region affecting visible geometry. Clipping and tessellation is avoided because the view frustum itself does the clipping. To avoid explicitly changing the geometry's texture coordinates, the texture transform matrix can be used to map the texture coordinates to the current texture region.

To allow the viewer to move relative to the textured geometry, the texture memory region must be updated. As the viewer moves, both the geometry and the texture can be thought of as scrolling to display the region closest to the viewer. In order to make the updates happen quickly, the entire texture can be stored in system memory, then used to update the texture memory when the viewer moves.

Consider a single level texture. Define a viewing frustum that limits the amount of visible geometry to a small area, — small enough that the visible geometry can be easily textured. Now imagine that the entire texture image is stored in system memory. As the viewer moves, the image in texture memory can be updated so that it exactly corresponds to the geometry visible in the viewing frustum:

1. Given the current view frustum, compute the visible geometry.

2. Set the texture transform matrix to map the visible texture coordinates into 0 to 1 in s and t.

3. Use `glTexImage2D` to load texture memory with the appropriate texel data, using `GL_SKIP_PIXELS` and `GL_SKIP_ROWS` to index to the proper subregion.

This technique remaps the texture coordinates of the visible geometry to match texture memory, then loads the matching system memory image into texture memory using `glTexImage2D`.

14.6.1 Texture Subimage Loading

While the technique described previously works, it is a very inefficient use of texture load bandwidth. Even if the viewer moves a small amount, the entire texture level must be reloaded to account for the shift in texture. Performance can be improved by loading only the part of the texture that's newly visible, and somehow shifting the rest.

Shifting the texture can be accomplished by taking advantage of texture coordinate wrapping (also called *torroidal mapping*). Instead of completely reloading the contents of texture memory, the section that has gone out of view from the last frame is loaded with the portion of the image that has just come into view with this frame. This technique works because texture coordinate wrapping makes it possible to create a single, seamless texture, connected at opposite sides. When `GL_TEXTURE_WRAP_S` and `GL_TEXTURE_WRAP_T` are set to GL_REPEAT (the default), the integer part of texture coordinates are discarded when mapping into texture memory. In effect, texture coordinates that go off the edge of texture memory on one side, and "wrap around" to the opposite side. The term "torrodial" comes from the fact that the wrapping happens across both pairs of edges. Using subimage loading, the updating technique looks like this:

1. Given the current and previous view frustum, compute how the range of texture coordinates have changed.

2. Transform the change of texture coordinates into one or more regions of texture memory that need to be updated.

3. Use glTexSubImage to update the appropriate regions of texture memory, use GL_SKIP_PIXELS and GL_SKIP_ROWS to index into the system memory image.

When using texture coordinate wrapping, the texture transform matrix can be used to remap texture coordinates on the geometry. Instead of having the coordinates range from zero to one over the entire texture, they can increase by one unit when moving across a single tile along each major axis. Texture matrix operations are not needed if the geometry is modeled with these coordinate ranges. Instead, the updated relationship between texture and geometry is maintained by subimage loading the right amount of new texture data as the viewer moves. Depending on the direction of viewer movement, updating texture memory can take from one to four subimage loads. Figure 14.9 shows how the geometry is remodeled to wrap on tile boundaries.

On most systems, texture subimage loads can be very inefficient when narrow regions are being loaded. The subimage loading method can be modified to ensure that only subimage loads above a minimum size are allowed, at the cost of some additional texture memory. The change is simple. Instead of updating every time the view position changes, ignore position changes until the accumulated change requires a subimage load above the minimum size. Normally this will result in some out of date texture data being visible

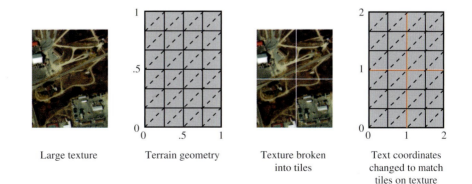

| Large texture | Terrain geometry | Texture broken into tiles | Text coordinates changed to match tiles on texture |

Figure 14.9 Modeling geometry to use texture wrapping.

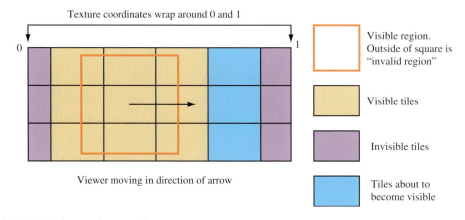

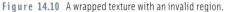

Figure 14.10 A wrapped texture with an invalid region.

around the edges of the textured geometry. To avoid this, an *invalid region* is specified around the periphery of the texture level, and the view frustum is adjusted so the that geometry textured from the texels from the invalid region are never visible. This technique allows updates to be cached, improving performance. A wrapped texture with its invalid region is shown in Figure 14.10.

The wrapping technique, as described so far, depends on only a limited region of the textured geometry being visible. In this example we are depending on the limits of the view frustum to only show properly textured geometry. If the view frustum was expanded, we would see the texture image wrapping over the surrounding geometry. Even with these limitations, this technique can be expanded to include mipmapped textures.

Since OpenGL implementations (today) typically do not transparently page mipmaps, the application cannot simply define a very large mipmap and not expect the OpenGL implementation to try to allocate the texture memory needed for all the mipmap levels. Instead the application can use the texture LOD control functionality in OpenGL 1.2 (or the EXT_texture_lod extension) to define a small number of active levels, using the GL_TEXTURE_BASE_LEVEL, GL_TEXTURE_MAX_LEVEL, GL_TEXTURE_MIN_LOD, and GL_TEXTURE_MAX_LOD with the glTexParameter command. An invalid region must be established and a minimum size update must be set so that all levels can be kept in sync with each other when updated. For example, a subimage 32 texels wide at the top level must be accompanied by a subimage 16 texels wide at the next coarser level to maintain correct mipmap filtering. Multiple images at different resolutions will have to be kept in system memory as source images to load texture memory.

If the viewer zooms in or zooms out of the geometry, the texturing system may require levels that are not available in the paged mipmap. The application can avoid this problem by computing the mipmap levels that are needed for any given viewer position, and keeping a set of paged mipmaps available, each representing a different set of LOD levels. The coarsest set could be a normal mipmap for use when the viewer is very far away from that region of textured geometry.

14.6.2 Paging Images in System Memory

Up to this point, we've assumed that the texel data is available as a large contiguous image in system memory. Just as texture memory is a limited resource that must be rationed, it also makes sense to conserve system memory. For very large texture images, the image data can be divided into tiles, and paged into system memory from disk. This paging can be kept separate from the paging going on from system memory to texture memory. The only difference will be in the offsets required to index the proper region in system memory to load, and an increase in the number of subimage loads required to update texture memory. A sophisticated system can wrap texture image data in system memory, using modulo arithmetic, just as texture coordinates are wrapped in texture memory.

Consider the case of a 2D image roam, illustrated in Figure 14.11, in which the view is moving to the right. As the view pans to the right, new texture tiles must be added to the right edge of the current portion of the texture and old tiles are discarded from the left edge. Since texture wrapping connects these two edges together, the discarding and replacing steps can be combined into a single update step on the tiles that are no longer visible on the left edge, which are about to wrap around and become visible on the right.

The ability to load subregions within a texture has other uses besides these paging applications. Without this capability textures must be loaded in their entirety and their widths and heights must be powers of two. In the case of video data, the images are typically not powers of two, so a texture of the nearest larger power-of-two can be created and only the relevant subregion needs to be loaded. When drawing geometry, the texture coordinates are simply constrained to the fraction of the texture which is occupied with valid data. Mipmapping cannot easily be used with non-power-of-two image data, since the coarser levels will contain image data from the invalid region of the texture. If it's required, mipmapping can be implemented by padding the non-power-of-two images up to the

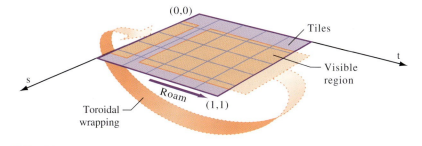

Figure 14.11 2D image roam.

next power-of-two size, or by using one of the non-power-of-two OpenGL extensions, such as `ARB_texture_non_power_of_two`, if it is supported by the implementation. Note that not all non-power-of-two extensions support mipmappped non-power-of-two textures.

14.6.3 Hardware Support for Texture Paging

Instead of having to piece together the components of a mipmapped texture paging solution using torroidal mapping, some OpenGL implementations help by providing this functionality in hardware.

Tanner et al. (1998) describe a hardware solution called *clip mapping* for supporting extremely large textures. The approach is implemented in SGI's InfiniteReality graphics subsystem. The basic clip mapping functionality is accessed using the `SGIX_clipmap` extension. In addition to requiring hardware support, the system also requires significant software management of the texture data as well. In part, this is simply due to the massive texture sizes that can be supported. While the clip map approach has no inherent limit to its maximum resolution, the InfiniteReality hardware implementation supports clip map textures to sizes up to $32,768 \times 32,768$ (Montrym et al., 1997).

The clip map itself is essentially a dynamically updatable partial mipmap. Highest resolution texture data is available only around a particular point in the texture called the *clip center*. To ensure that clip-mapped surfaces are shown at the highest possible texture resolution, software is required to dynamically reposition the clip center as necessary. Repositioning the clip center requires partial dynamic updates of the clip map texture data. With software support for repositioning the clip center and managing the off-disk texture loading and caching required, clip mapping offers the opportunity to dynamically roam over and zoom in and out of huge textured regions. The technique has obvious applications for applications that use very large, detailed textures, such as unconstrained viewing of high-resolution satellite imagery at real-time rates.

Hüttner (1998) describes another approach using only OpenGL's base mipmap functionality to support very high-resolution textures, similar to the one described previously. Hüttner proposes a data structure called a *MIPmap pyramid grid* or MP-grid. The MP-grid is essentially a set of mipmap textures arranged in a grid to represent an aggregate high-resolution texture that is larger than the OpenGL implementation's largest supported texture. For example, a 4×4 grid of 1024×1024 mipmapped textures could be used to represent a 4096×4096 aggregate texture. Typically, the aggregate texture is terrain data intended to be draped over a polygonal mesh representing the terrain's geometry. Before rendering, the MP-grid algorithm first classifies each terrain polygon based on which grid cells within the MP-grid the polygon covers. During rendering, each grid cell is considered in sequence. Assuming the grid cell is covered by polygons in the scene, the mipmap texture for the grid cell is bound. Then, all the polygons covering the grid cell are rendered with texturing enabled. Because a polygon may not exist completely within a single grid cell, care must be taken to intersect such polygons with the boundary of all the grid cells that the polygon partially covers.

Hüttner compares the MP-grid scheme to the clip map scheme and notes that the MP-grid approach does not require special hardware and does not depend on determining a single viewer-dependent clip center, as needed in the clip map approach. However, the MP-grid approach requires special clipping of the surface terrain mesh to the MP-grid. No such clipping is required when clip mapping. Due to its special hardware support, the clip mapping approach is most likely better suited for the support of the very largest high-resolution textures.

Although not commonly supported at the time of this writing, clip mapping may be an interesting prelude to OpenGL support for dynamically updatable cached textures in future implementations.

14.7 Prefiltered Textures

Currently, some OpenGL implementations still provide limited or no support beyond 4-texel linear isotropic filtering.[1] Even when mipmapping, the filtering of each mipmap level is limited to point-sampled (GL_NEAREST) or linear (GL_LINEAR) filtering. While adequate for many uses, there are applications that can greatly benefit from a better filter kernel. One example is anisotropic filtering. Textured geometry can be rendered so that the ideal minification is greater in one direction than another. An example of this is textured geometry that is viewed nearly edge-on. Normal isotropic filtering will apply the maximum required minification uniformly, resulting in excessive blurring of the texture.

If anisotropic texturing is not supported by the implementation,[2] the application writer can approach anisotropic sampling by generating and selecting from a series of prefiltered textures. The task of generating and using prefiltered textures is greatly simplified if the application writer can restrict how the texture will be viewed. Prefiltered textures can also be useful for other applications, where the texel footprint isn't square. If textures are used in such a way that the texel footprints are always the same shape, the number of prefiltered textures needed is reduced, and the approach becomes more attractive.

The technique can be illustrated using anisotropic texturing as an example. Suppose a textured square is rendered as shown in the left of Figure 14.12. The primitive and a selected fragment are shown on the left. The fragment is mapped to a normal mipmapped texture on the upper right, and a prefiltered one on the lower right. In both cases, the ideal texture footprint of the fragment is shown with a dark inner region.

In the upper right texture, the isotropic minification filter forces the actual texture footprint to encompass the square enclosing the dark region. A mipmap level is chosen in which this square footprint is properly filtered for the fragment. In other words, a mipmap

---

1. The vendor specific extension, SGIS_texture_filter4, allows an application-defined 4 × 4 sample filter, but it has very limited availability.

2. There is an EXT_texture_filter_anisotropic extension.

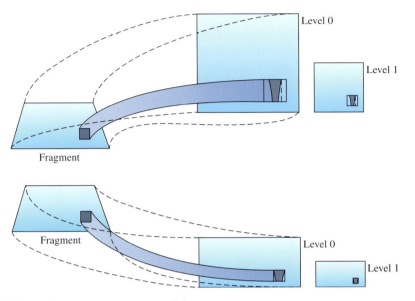

Figure 14.12 Pixel footprint on anisotropically scaled texture.

level is selected in which the size of this square is closest to the size of the fragment. The resulting mipmap is not level 0 but level 1 or higher. Hence, at that fragment more filtering is needed along t than along s, but the same amount of filtering is done in both. The resulting texture will be more blurred than the ideal.

To avoid this problem, the texture can be *prefiltered*. In the lower right texture of Figure 14.12, extra filtering is applied in the t direction when the texture is created. The aspect ratio of the texture image is also changed, giving the prefiltered texture the same width but only half the height of the original. The footprint now has a squarer aspect ratio; the enclosing square no longer has to be much larger, and is closer to the size to the fragment. Mipmap level 0 can now be used instead of a higher level. Another way to think about this concept: using a texture that is shorter along t reduces the amount of minification required in the t direction.

The closer the filtered mipmap's aspect ratio matches the projected aspect ratio of the geometry, the more accurate the sampling will be. The application can minimize excessive blurring at the expense of texture memory by creating a set of resampled mipmaps with different aspect ratios (Figure 14.13).

14.7.1 Computing Texel Aspect Ratios

Once the application has created a set of prefiltered textures, it can find the one that most closely corresponds to the current texture scaling aspect ratio, and use that texture map to texture the geometry (Figure 14.14). This ratio can be quickly estimated by computing

Figure 14.13 Creating a set of anisotropically filtered images.

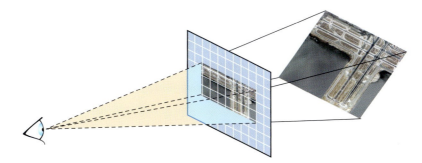

Figure 14.14 Geometry orientation and texture aspect ratio.

the angle between the viewer's line of sight and a plane representing the orientation of the textured geometry. Using texture objects, the application can switch to the mipmap that will provide the best results. Depending on performance requirements, the texture selection process can be applied per triangle or applied to a plane representing the average of a group of polygons can be used.

In some cases, a simple line of sight computation isn't accurate enough for the application. If the textured surface has a complex shape, or if the texture transform matrix is needed to transform texture coordinates, a more accurate computation of the texture coordinate derivatives may be needed. Section 13.7.2 describes the process of computing texture coordinate derivatives within the application. In the near future the programmable pipeline will be capable of performing the same computations efficiently in the pipeline and be able to select from one of multiple-bound texture maps.

Since most OpenGL implementations restrict texture levels to have power-of-two dimensions, it would appear that the only aspect ratios that can be anisotropically prefiltered are 1:4, 1:2, 1:1, 2:1, 4:1, etc. Smaller aspect ratio step sizes are possible, however, by generating incomplete texture images, then using the texture transform matrix to scale the texture coordinates to fit. For a ratio of 3:4, for example, fill a 1:1 ratio mipmap with prefiltered 3:4 texture images partially covering each level (the rest of the texture image is set to black). The unused part of the texture (black) should be along the top (maximum t coordinates) and right (maximum s coordinates) of the texture image. The prefiltered image can be any size, as long as it fits within the texture level. Other than prefiltering the images, the mipmap is created in the normal way.

Using this mipmap for textured geometry with a 3:4 ratio results in an incorrect textured image. To correct it, the texture transform matrix is used to rescale the narrower side of the texture (in our example in the t direction) by 3/4 (Figure 14.15). This will change the apparent size ratio between the pixels and textures in the texture filtering system, making them match, and producing the proper results. This technique would not work well with a repeated texture; in our example, there will be a discontinuity in the image if filtered outside the range of 0 to 1 in t. However, the direction that isn't scaled can be wrapped; in our example, wrapping in s would work fine.

Generalizing from the previous example, the prefiltering procedure can be broken down as follows:

1. Look for textures that have elongated or distorted pixel footprints.

2. Determine the range of pixel footprint shapes on the texture of interest to determine the number of prefiltered images needed.

3. Using convolution or some other image processing technique (see Chapter 12), prefilter the image using the footprint shape as a filter kernel. The prefiltered images should be filtered from higher resolution images to preserve image quality.

4. Generate a range of prefiltered textures matching the range of footprint shapes.

5. Design an algorithm to choose the most appropriate prefiltered image for the texture's viewing conditions.

6. The texture transform matrix can be used to change the relationship between texture and geometric coordinates to support a wider range of prefiltered images.

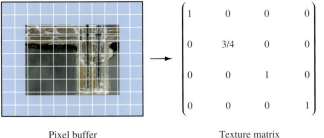

$$\begin{pmatrix} 1 & 0 & 0 & 0 \\ 0 & 3/4 & 0 & 0 \\ 0 & 0 & 1 & 0 \\ 0 & 0 & 0 & 1 \end{pmatrix}$$

Pixel buffer   Texture matrix   Texture map

Figure 14.15 Non-power-of-two aspect ratio using texture matrix.

Prefiltered textures are a useful tool but have limitations compared to true anisotropic texturing. Storing multiple prefiltered images consumes a lot of texture memory; the algorithm is most useful in applications that only need a small set of prefiltered images to choose from. The algorithm for choosing a prefiltered texture should be simple to compute; it can be a performance burden otherwise, since it may have to be run each time a particular texture is used in the scene. Prefiltered images are inadequate if the pixel footprint changes significantly while rendering a single texture; segmenting the textured primitive into regions of homogeneous anisotropy is one possible solution, although this can add still more overhead. Dynamically created textures are a difficult obstacle. Unless they can be cached and reused, the application may not tolerate the overhead required to prefilter them on the fly.

On the other hand, the prefiltered texture solution can be a good fit for some applications. In visual simulation applications, containing fly over or drive-through viewpoints, prefiltering the terrain can lead to significant improvements in quality without high overhead. The terrain can be stored prefiltered for a number of orientations, and the algorithm for choosing the anisotropy is a straightforward analysis of the viewer/terrain orientation. The situation is further simplified if the viewer has motion constraints (for example, a train simulation), which reduce the number of prefiltered textures needed.

Hardware anisotropic filtering support is a trade-off between filtering quality and performance. Very high-quality prefiltered images can be produced if the pixel footprint is precisely known. A higher-quality image than what is achievable in hardware can also be created, making it possible to produce a software method for high-quality texturing that discards all the speed advantages of hardware rendering. This approach might be useful for non-real-time, high-quality image generation.

14.8 Dual-Paraboloid Environment Mapping

An environment map parameterization different from the ones directly supported by OpenGL (see Section 5.4) was proposed by Heidrich and Seidel (1998b). It avoids many of the disadvantages of sphere mapping. The dual-paraboloid environment mapping approach is view-independent, has better sampling characteristics, and, because the singularity at the edge of the sphere map is eliminated, there are no sparkling artifacts at glancing angles. The view-independent advantage is important because it allows the viewer, environment-mapped object, and the environment to move with respect to each other without having to regenerate the environment map.

14.8.1 The Mathematics of Dual-Paraboloid Maps

The principle that underlies paraboloid maps is the same one that underlies a parabolic lens or satellite dish. The geometry of a paraboloid can focus parallel rays to a point.

Figure 14.16 Two paraboloids.

The paraboloid used for dual-paraboloid mapping is:

$$f(x, y) = \frac{1}{2} - \frac{1}{2}(x^2 + y^2), \qquad x^2 + y^2 \leq 1$$

Figure 14.16 shows how two paraboloids can focus the entire environment surrounding a point into two images.

Unlike the sphere-mapping approach, which encodes the entire surrounding environment into a single texture, the dual-paraboloid mapping scheme requires two textures to store the environment, one texture for the "front" environment and another texture for the "back". Note that the sense of "front" and "back" is completely independent of the viewer orientation. Figure 14.17 shows an example of two paraboloid maps. Because two textures are required, the technique must be performed in two rendering passes.

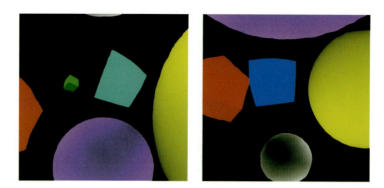

Figure 14.17 Example of dual-paraboloid texture map images.

If multitexturing is supported by the implementation, the passes can be combined into a single rendering pass using two texture units.

Because the math for the paraboloid is all linear (unlike the spherical basis of the sphere map), Heidrich and Seidel observe that an application can use the OpenGL texture matrix to map an eye-coordinate reflection vector **R** into a 2D texture coordinate (s, t) within a dual-paraboloid map. The necessary texture matrix can be constructed as follows:

$$\begin{pmatrix} s \\ t \\ 1 \\ 1 \end{pmatrix} = A \cdot P \cdot S \cdot (M_l)^{-1} \cdot \begin{pmatrix} R_x \\ R_y \\ R_z \\ 1 \end{pmatrix}$$

where

$$A = \begin{pmatrix} \frac{1}{2} & 0 & 0 & \frac{1}{2} \\ 0 & \frac{1}{2} & 0 & \frac{1}{2} \\ 0 & 0 & 1 & 0 \\ 0 & 0 & 0 & 1 \end{pmatrix}$$

is a matrix that scales and biases a 2D coordinate in the range $[-1, 1]$ to the texture image range $[0, 1]$. This matrix

$$P = \begin{pmatrix} 1 & 0 & 0 & 0 \\ 0 & 1 & 0 & 0 \\ 0 & 0 & 1 & 0 \\ 0 & 0 & 1 & 0 \end{pmatrix}$$

is a projective transform that divides by the z coordinate. It serves to flatten a 3D vector into 2D. This matrix

$$S = \begin{pmatrix} -1 & 0 & 0 & D_x \\ 0 & -1 & 0 & D_y \\ 0 & 0 & 1 & D_z \\ 0 & 0 & 0 & 1 \end{pmatrix}$$

subtracts the supplied 3D vector from an orientation vector $\mathbf{D}$ that specifies a view direction. The vector is set to $\mathbf{D}$ either $(0, 0, -1)^T$ or $(0, 0, 1)^T$ depending on whether the front or back paraboloid map is in use, respectively. Finally, the matrix $(M_l)^{-1}$ is the inverse of the linear part (the upper 3×3) of the current (affine) modelview matrix. The matrix $(M_l)^{-1}$ transforms a 3D eye-space reflection vector into an object-space version of the vector.

14.8.2 Using Dual-Paraboloid Maps

For the rationale for these transformations, consult Heidrich and Siedel (1998b). Since all the necessary component transformations can be represented as 4×4 matrices, the entire transformation sequence can be concatenated into a single 4×4 projective matrix and then loaded into OpenGL's texture matrix. The per-vertex eye-space reflection normal can be supplied as a vertex texture coordinate via `glTexCoord3f` or computed from the normal vector using the `GL_REFLECTION_MAP` texture coordinate generation mode.[3] When properly configured this 3D vector will be transformed into a 2D texture coordinate in a front or back paraboloid map, depending on how $\mathbf{D}$ is oriented.

The matrix M_l^{-1} is computed by retrieving the current modelview matrix, replacing the outer row and column with the vector $(0, 0, 0, 1)$, and inverting the result. Section 13.1 discusses methods for computing the inverse of the modelview matrix.

Each dual-paraboloid texture contains an incomplete version of the environment. The two texture maps overlap as shown in Figure 14.17 at the corner of each image. The corner regions in one map are distorted so that the other map has better sampling of the same information. There is also some information in each map that is simply not in the other; for example, the information in the center of each map is not shared. Figure 14.18 shows that each map has a centered circular region containing texels with better sampling than the corresponding texels in the other map. This centered region of each dual-paraboloid map is called the *sweet circle*.

The last step is to segregate transformed texture coordinates, applying them to one of the two paraboloid maps. The decision criteria are simple; given the projective transformation discussed earlier, if a reflection vector falls within the sweet circle

---

3. In OpenGL 1.3.

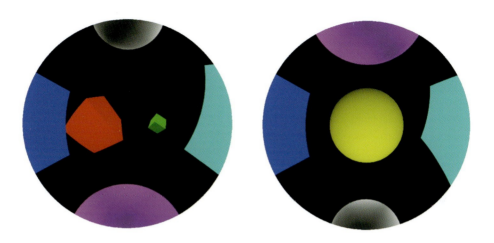

Figure 14.18 The sweet circles of a dual-paraboloid map.

of one dual-paraboloid map, it will be guaranteed to fall outside the sweet circle of the opposite map.

Using OpenGL's alpha testing capability, we can discard texels outside the sweet circle of each texture. The idea is to encode in the alpha channel of each dual-paraboloid texture an alpha value of 1.0 if the texel is within the sweet circle and 0.0 if the texel is outside the sweet circle. To avoid artifacts for texels that land on the circle edges, the circle ownership test should be made conservative.

In the absence of multitexture support, a textured object is rendered in two passes. First, the front dual-paraboloid texture is bound and the $\mathbf{D}$ value is set to $(0, 0, -1)^T$ when constructing the texture matrix. During the second pass, the back texture is bound and a $\mathbf{D}$ value of $(0, 0, 1)^T$ is used. During both passes, alpha testing is used to eliminate fragments with an alpha value less than 1.0. The texture environment should be configured to replace the fragment's alpha value with the texture's alpha value. The result is a complete dual-paraboloid mapped object.

When multiple texture units are available, the two passes can be collapsed into a single multitextured rendering pass. Since each texture unit has an independent texture matrix, the first texture unit uses the front texture matrix, while the second texture unit uses the back one. The first texture unit uses a GL_REPLACE texture environment while the second texture unit should use GL_BLEND. Together, the two texture units blend the two textures based on the alpha component of the second texture. A side benefit of the multitextured approach is that the transition between the two dual-paraboloid map textures is less noticeable. Even with simple alpha testing, the seam is quite difficult to notice.

If a programmable vertex pipeline is supported, the projection operation can be further optimized by implementing it directly in a vertex program.

14.8.3 OpenGL Dual-Paraboloid Support

Although OpenGL doesn't include direct support for dual-paraboloid maps, OpenGL 1.3 support for reflection mapping and multitexture allows efficient implementation by an application. The view independence, good sampling characteristics, and ease of generation of maps makes dual-paraboloid maps attractive for many environment mapping applications.

Besides serving as an interesting example of how OpenGL functionality can be used to build up an entirely new texturing technique, dual-paraboloid mapping is also a useful approach to consider when the OpenGL implementation doesn't support cube mapping. This technique provides some clear advantages over sphere mapping; when the latter isn't adequate, and the rendering resources are available, dual-paraboloid mapping can be a good high-performance solution.

14.9 Texture Projection

Projected textures (Segal et al., 1992) are texture maps indexed by texture coordinates that have undergone a projective transform. The projection is applied using the texture transform matrix, making it possible to apply a projection to texture coordinates that is independent of the geometry's viewing projection. This technique can be used to simulate slide projector or spotlight illumination effects, to apply shadow textures (Section 17.4.3), create lighting effects (Section 15.3), and to re-project an image onto an object's geometry (Section 17.4.1).

Projecting a texture image onto geometry uses nearly the same steps needed to project the rendered scene onto the display. Vertex coordinates have three transformation stages available for the task, while texture coordinates have only a single 4×4 transformation matrix followed by a perspective divide operation. To project a texture, the texture transform matrix contains the concatenation of three transformations:

1. A modelview transform to orient the projection in the scene.

2. A projective transform (e.g., perspective or parallel).

3. A scale and bias to map the near clipping plane to texture coordinates, or put another way, to map the $[-1, 1]$ normalized device coordinate range to $[0, 1]$.

When choosing the transforms for the texture matrix, use the same transforms used to render the scene's geometry, but anchored to the view of a "texture light", the point that appears to project the texture onto an object, just as a light would project a slide onto a surface. A texgen function must also be set up. It creates texture coordinates from the vertices of the target geometry. Section 13.6 provides more detail and insight in setting up the proper texture transform matrix and texgen for a given object/texture configuration.

Configuring the texture transformation matrix and texgen function is not enough. The texture will be projected onto all objects rendered with this configuration; in order to produce an "optical" projection, the projected texture must be "clipped" to a single area.

There are a number of ways to do this. The simplest is to only render polygons that should have the texture projected on them. This method is fast, but limited; it only clips the projected texture to the boundaries defined by individual polygons. It may be necessary to limit the projected image within a polygon. Finer control can be achieved by using the stencil buffer to control which parts of the scene are updated by a projected texture. See Section 14.6 for details.

If the texture is non-repeating and is projected onto an untextured surface, clipping can be done by using the GL_MODULATE environment function with a GL_CLAMP texture wrap mode and a white texture border color. As the texture is projected, the surfaces beyond the projected [0, 1] extent are clamped and use the texture border color. They end up being modulated with white, leaving the areas textured with the border color unchanged. One possible problem with this technique is poor support of texture borders on some OpenGL implementations. This should be less of a problem since the borders are a constant color. There are other wrap modes, such as GL_CLAMP_TO_BORDER, which can be used to limit edge sampling to the border color.

The parameters that control filtering for projective textures are the same ones controlling normal texturing; the size of the projected texels relative to screen pixels determines minification or magnification. If the projected image is relatively small, mipmapping may be required to get good quality results. Using good filtering is especially important if the projected texture is being applied to animated geometry, because poor sampling can lead to scintillation of the texture as the geometry moves.

Projecting a texture raises the issue of perspective correct projection. When texture coordinates are interpolated across geometry, use of the transformed w coordinate is needed to avoid artifacts as the texture coordinates are interpolated across the primitive, especially when the primitive vertices are projected in extreme perspective. When the texture coordinates themselves are projected, the same "perspective correct" issue (see Section 6.1.4) must be dealt with (Figure 14.19).

The problem is avoided by interpolating the transformed q coordinate, along with the other texture coordinates. This assures that the texture coordinates are interpolated correctly, even if the texture image itself is projected in extreme perspective. For more details on texture coordinate interpolation see Section 5.2. Although the specification requires it, there may be OpenGL implementations that do not correctly support this interpolation. If an implementation doesn't interpolate correctly, the geometry can be more finely tessellated to minimize the difference in projected q values between vertices.

Like viewing projections, a texture projection only approximates an optical projection. The geometry affected by a projected texture won't be limited to a region of space. Since there is no implicit texture-space volume clipping (as there is in the OpenGL viewing pipeline), the application needs to explicitly choose which primitives to render when a projected texture is enabled. User-defined clipping planes, or stencil masking may be required if the finer control over the textured region is needed.

Geometry is face on to the viewer, no perspective distortion.

Texture is highly distorted by projection of texture coordinates and may show perspective artifacts if geometry is not tessellated and texture coordinates are not interpolated using q/w.

Figure 14.19 Texture projected with perspective.

14.10 Texture Color Coding and Contouring

Texture coordinate generation allows an application to map a vertex position or vector to a texture coordinate. For *linear transforms*, the transformation is *texcoord* $= f(x, y, z, w)$, where *texcoord* can be any one of s, t, r, or q, and $f(x, y, z, w) = Ax + By + Cz + Dw$, where the coefficients are set by the application. The generation can be set to happen before or after the modelview transform has been applied to the vertex coordinates. See Section 5.2.1 for more details on texture coordinate generation.

One interesting texgen application is to use generated texture coordinates as measurement units. A texture with a pattern or color coding can be used to delimit changes in texture coordinate values. A special texture can be applied to target geometry, marking the texture coordinate changes across its surface visible. This approach makes it possible to annotate target geometry with measurement information. If relationships between objects or characteristics of the entire scene need to be measured, the application can create and texture special geometry, either solid or semitransparent, to make these values visible.

One or more texture coordinates can be used simultaneously for measurement. For example, a terrain model can be colored by altitude using a 1D texture map to hold the coloring scheme. The texture can map s as the distance from the plane $y = 0$, for example. Generated s and t coordinates can be mapped to the $x = 0$ and $z = 0$ planes, and applied to a 2D texture containing tick marks, measuring across a 2D surface.

Much of the flexibility of this technique comes from choosing the appropriate measuring texture. In the elevation example, a 1D texture can be specified to provide different colors for different elevations, such as that used in a topographic map. For example, if vertex coordinates are specified in meters, distances less than 50 meters can be colored blue, from 50 to 800 meters in green, and 800 to 1000 meters in white. To produce this effect, a 1D texture map with the first 5% blue, the next 75% green, and the remaining 20% of texels colored white is needed. A 64- or 128-element texture map provides enough resolution to distinguish between levels. Specifying GL_OBJECT_LINEAR for the texture generation mode and an GL_OBJECT_PLANE equation of (0, 1/1000, 0, 0) for the s coordinate will set s to the y value of the vertex scaled by 1/1000 (i.e., $s = (0, 1/1000, 0, 0) \cdot (x, y, z, w)$).

Different measuring textures provide different effects. Elevation can be shown as contour lines instead of color coding, using a 1D texture map containing a background color, marked with regularly spaced tick marks. Using a GL_REPEAT wrap mode creates regularly repeating lines across the object being contoured. Choosing whether texture coordinate generation occurs before or after the modelview transform affects how the measuring textures appear to be anchored. In the contour line example, a GL_OBJECT_LINEAR generation function anchors the contours to the model (Figure 14.20). A GL_EYE_LINEAR setting generates the coordinates in eye space, fixing the contours in space relative to the viewer.

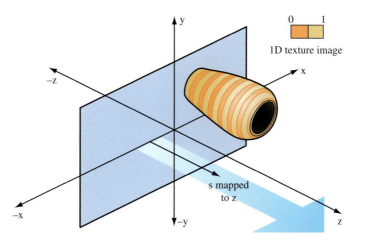

Figure 14.20 Contour generation using glTexGen.

Textures can do more than measure the relative positions of points in 3D space; they can also measure orientation. A sphere or cube map generation function with an appropriately colored texture map can display the orientation of surface normals over a surface. This functionality displays the geometry's surface orientation as color values on a per-pixel basis. Texture sampling issues must be considered, as they are for any texturing application. In this example, the geometry should be tessellated finely enough that the change in normal direction between adjacent vertices are limited enough to produce accurate results; the texture itself can only linearly interpolate between vertices.

14.11 2D Image Warping

OpenGL can warp an image by applying it to a surface with texturing. The image is texture mapped onto planar geometry, using non-uniform texture coordinates to distort it. Image warping takes advantage of OpenGL's ability to establish an arbitrary relationship between texture coordinates and vertex coordinates. Although any geometry can be used, a common technique is to texture onto a uniform polygonal mesh, adjusting the texture coordinates at each vertex on the mesh. This method is popular because the mesh becomes a regular sampling grid, and the changes in texture coordinates can be represented as a function of the texture coordinate values. The interpolation of texture coordinates between vertices gives the warp a smooth appearance, making it possible to approximate a continuous warping function.

Warping may be used to change the framebuffer image (for example, to create a fish-eye lens effect), or as part of preprocessing of images used in texture maps or bitmaps. Repeated warping and blending steps can be concatenated to create special effects, such as streamline images used in scientific visualization (see Section 20.6.3). Warping can also be used to *remove* distortion from an image, undoing a preexisting distortion, such as that created by a camera lens (see Section 12.7.4).

A uniform mesh can be created by tessellating a 2D rectangle into a grid of vertices. In the unwarped form, texture coordinates ranging from zero to one are distributed evenly across the mesh. The number of vertices spanning the mesh determines the sampling rate across the surface. Warped texture coordinates are created by applying the 2D warping function $warp(s, t) = (s + \Delta s, t + \Delta t)$ to the unwarped texture coordinates at each vertex in the mesh. The density of vertices on the mesh can be adjusted to match the amount of distortion applied by the warping function; ideally, the mesh should be fine enough that the change in the warped coordinate is nearly linear from point to point (Figure 14.21). A sophisticated scheme might use non-linear tessellation of the surface to ensure good sampling. This is useful if the warping function produces a mixture of rapidly changing and slowly changing warp areas.

The warped texture coordinates may be computed by the application when the mesh is created. However, if the warp can be expressed as an affine or projective transform, a faster method is to modify the texture coordinates with the texture transform matrix.

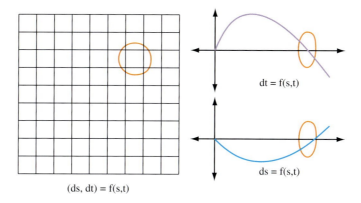

$$(ds, dt) = f(s,t)$$

Warp function sampled at grid points; offsets texture coordinates

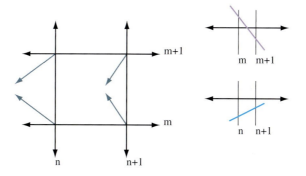

Warp function offsetting texture coordinates at a grid square

Figure 14.21 Distortion function.

This takes advantage of the OpenGL implementation's acceleration of texture coordinate transforms. An additional shortcut is possible; texgen can be configured to generate the unwarped texture coordinate values. How the image is used depends on the intended application.

By rendering images as textured geometry, warped images are created in the framebuffer (usually the back buffer). The resultant image can be used as-is in a scene, copied into a texture using `glCopyTexImage2D`, or captured as an application memory image using `glReadPixels`.

The accuracy of the warp is a function of the texture resolution, the resolution of the mesh (ratio of the number of vertices to the projected screen area), and the filtering function used with the texture. The filtering is generally `GL_LINEAR`, since it is a commonly accelerated texture filtering mode, although mipmapping can be used if the distortion creates regions where many texels are to be averaged into a single pixel color.

The size of the rendered image is application-dependent; if the results are to be used as a texture or bitmap, then creating an image larger than the target size is wasteful; conversely, too small an image leads to coarse sampling and pixel artifacts.

14.12 Texture Animation

Although movement and change in computer graphics is commonly done by modifying geometry, animated surface textures are also a useful tool for creating dynamic scenes. Animated textures make it possible to add dynamic complexity without additional geometry. They also provide a flexible method for integrating video and other dynamic image-based effects into a scene. Combining animated images and geometry can produce extremely realistic effects with only moderate performance requirements. Given a system with sufficient texture load and display performance, animating texture maps is a straightforward process.

Texture animation involves continuously updating the image used to texture a surface. If the updates occur rapidly enough and at regular intervals, an animated image is generated on the textured surface. The animation used for the textures may come from a live external source, such as a video capture device, a pre-recorded video sequence, or pre-rendered images.

There are two basic animation approaches. The first periodically replaces the contents of the texture map by loading new texels. This is done using the `glTexSubImage2D` command. The source frames are transfered from an external source (typically disk or video input) to system memory, then loaded in sequence into texture memory. If the source frames reside on disk, groups of source frames may be read into memory. The memory acts as a cache, averaging out the high latency of disk transfers, making it possible to maintain the animation update rate.

The second animation approach is useful if the number of animated images is small (such as a small movie loop). A texture map containing multiple images is created; the texture is animated by regularly switching the image displayed. A particular image is selected by changing the texture coordinates used to map the texture onto the image. This can be done explicitly when sending the geometry, or by using texgen or the texture transform matrix.

When discussing animation update rates, there are two parameters to consider: the rate at which an animated texture is updated, and the frame rate at which the graphics application updates the scene. The two are not necessarily the same. The animation frame rate may be higher or lower than the scene frame rate. Ideally, the updates to the texture map should occur at the scene frame rate. If the source animation was recorded at a different rate, it needs to be resampled to match the scene's rate.

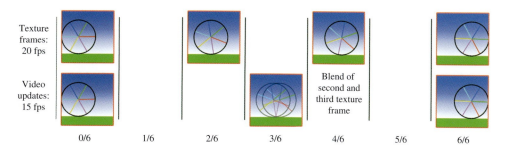

Texture
frames:
20 fps

Video
updates:
15 fps

Blend of
second and
third texture
frame

0/6   1/6   2/6   3/6   4/6   5/6   6/6

Figure 14.22 Resampling animation frames.

If the animation rate is an even multiple of each other, then the resampling algorithm is trivial. If for example, the animation rate is one half of the frame rate, then resampling means using each source animation image twice per frame. If the animation rates do not have a $1/n$ relationship, then the texture animation may not appear to have a constant speed.

To improve the update ratios, the animation sequence can be resampled by linearly interpolating between adjacent source frames (Figure 14.22). The resampling may be performed as a preprocessing step or be computed dynamically while rendering the scene. If the resampling is performed dynamically, texture environment or framebuffer blending can be used to accelerate the interpolation.

Note that resampling must be done judiciously to avoid reducing the quality of the animation. Interpolating between two images to create a new one does not produce the same image that would result from sampling an image at that moment in time. Interpolation works best when the original animation sequence has only small changes between images. Trying to resample an animation of rapidly changing, high-contrast objects with interpolation can lead to objects with "blurry" or "vibrating" edges.

Choosing the optimal animation method depends on the number of frames in the animation sequence. If the number of frames is unbounded, such as animation from a streaming video source, continuously loading new frames will be necessary. However, there is a class of texture animations that use a modest, fixed number of frames. They are played either as an endless loop or as a one-shot sequence. An example of the first is a movie loop of a fire applied to a texture for use in a torch. An example one-shot sequence is a short animation of an explosion. If the combined size of the frames is small enough, the entire sequence can be captured in a single texture.

Even when space requirements prohibit storing the entire image sequence, it can still be useful to store a group of images at a time in a single texture. Batching images this way can improve texture load efficiency and can facilitate resampling of frames before they are displayed.

There are two obvious approaches to storing multiple frames in a single texture map. A direct method is to use a 3D texture map. The 3D texture is created from a stack of consecutive animation frames. The *s* and *t* coordinates index the horizontal and vertical axis of each image; the *r* coordinate represents the time dimension. Creating a 3D texture from stack of images is simple; load the sequence of images into consecutive locations in memory, then use `glTexImage3D` to create the 3D texture map from the data. OpenGL implementations limit the maximum dimensions and may restrict other 3D texture parameters, so the usual caveats apply.

Rendering from the 3D texture is also simple. The texture is mapped to the target geometry using *s* and *t* coordinates as if it's a 2D texture. The *r* coordinate is set to a fixed value for all vertices in the geometry representing the image. The *r* value specifies a moment in time in the animation sequence (Figure 14.23). Before the next frame is displayed, *r* is incremented by an amount representing the desired time step between successive frames. 3D textures have an inherent benefit; the time value doesn't have to align with a specific image in the texture. If GL_LINEAR filtering is used, an *r* value that doesn't map to an exact animation frame will be interpolated from the two frames bracketing that value, resampling it. Resampling must be handled properly when a frame must sample beyond the last texture frame in the texture or before the first. This can happen when displaying

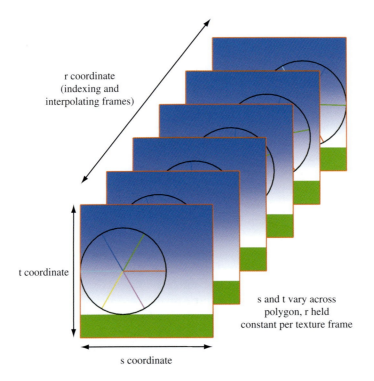

r coordinate
(indexing and
interpolating frames)

t coordinate

s and t vary across
polygon, r held
constant per texture frame

s coordinate

Figure 14.23 Animation with 3D textures.

an animation loop. Setting the GL_TEXTURE_WRAP_R parameter to GL_REPEAT ensures that the frames are always interpolating valid image data.

Although animating with 3D textures is conceptually simple, there are some significant limitations to this approach. Some implementations don't support 3D texture mapping (it was introduced in OpenGL 1.2), or support it poorly, supporting only very small 3D texture maps. Even when they are supported, 3D textures use up a lot of space in texture memory, which can limit their maximum size. If more frames are needed than fit in a 3D texture, another animation method must be used, or the images in the 3D texture must be updated dynamically. Dynamic updates involve using the glTexSubImage command to replace one or more animation frames as needed. In some implementations, overall bandwidth may improve if subimage loads take place every few frames and load more than one animation frame at a time. However, the application must ensure that all frames needed for resampling are loaded before they are sampled.

A feature of 3D texture mapping that can cause problems is mipmap filtering. If the animated texture requires mipmap filtering (such as an animated texture display on a surface that is nearly edge on to the viewer), a 3D texture map can't be used. A 3D texture mipmap level is filtered in all three dimensions (isotropically). This means that a mipmapped 3D texture uses much more memory than a 2D mipmap, and that LODs contain data sampled in three dimensions. As a result, 3D texture LOD levels resample frames, since they will use texels along the r-axis.

Another method for storing multiple animation frames is to mosaic the frames into a single 2D texture. The texture map is tiled into a mosaic of images, each frame is loaded into a specific region. To avoid filtering artifacts at the edges of adjacent images, some basic spacing restrictions must be obeyed (see Section 14.4 for information on image mosaicing). The texture is animated by adjusting the texture coordinates of the geometry displaying the animation so that it references a different image each frame. If the texture has its animation frames arranged in a regular grid, it becomes simple to select them using the texture matrix. There are a number of advantages to the mosaic approach: individual animation frames do not need to be padded to be a power-of-two, and individual frames can be mipmapped (assuming the images are properly spaced (Figure 14.24). The fact than any OpenGL implementation can support mosaicing, and that most implementations can support large 2D textures, are additional advantages.

Texture mosaicing has some downsides. Since there is no explicit time dimension, texturing the proper frame requires more texture coordinate computation than the 3D texture approach does. Texture mosaicing also doesn't have direct support for dynamic frame resampling, requiring more work from the application. It must index the two closest images that border the desired frame time, then perform a weighted blend of them to create the resampled one, using weighting factors derived from the resampled frame's relationship with the two parent images. The blending itself can be done using a multitexture or a multipass blend technique (see Section 5.4 and Section 6.2.4 for details on these approaches).

Even when using 2D textures, the amount of space required for the animation frames may exceed the capacity of the texture map. In this case, dynamic updates of the images in

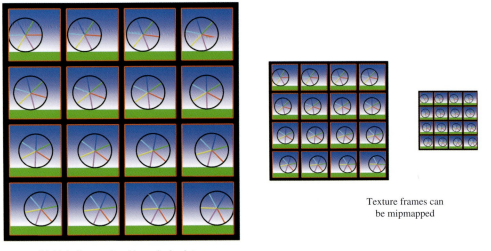

Multiple frames placed in a single picture

Texture frames can
be mipmapped

Figure 14.24 Animation with texture mosaics.

the texture are necessary. When incremental updates are required, and the animation uses frame resampling, care should be taken to ensure that all images required for resampling are completely loaded before they are displayed. In general, one texture (or two if frames are being resampled) is in use at any time during animation. If dynamic updates are required, it is important to only replace images that aren't being used for texturing. To do this, a double buffering or multibuffering approach can be implemented. The images in the texture are grouped into two or more blocks, and only blocks not being used for texturing are candidates for updating. Again, care must be taken to ensure that an inactive block of images won't be accessed before the load completes. In some cases, it can help to duplicate images at the borders of the blocks to ease load requirements at the cost of some additional texture memory.

14.13 Detail Textures

Textures, even mipmapped ones, appear unrealistic under strong magnification. When the viewer is close to a texture surface, a single texel color is filtered over multiple pixels. Under this strong magnification, linear filtering results in an unrealistically smoothed image with little surface detail. Not only do the magnified images look unrealistic, but the lack of high-frequency spatial information on the surface makes it difficult for a viewer to get realistic distance and motion cues when moving near the surface.

Ideally, a mipmapped texture will have enough high-resolution levels that any normal view of the textured surface will always have sufficient high-frequency spatial data. But providing extra high-resolution levels is expensive; they take up a disproportionate amount of texture memory. With mipmapping, each fine level requires four times as many texels as the next coarser one. In addition to the texture memory overhead, obtaining the high-resolution data can be expensive. For some applications, it is worth the effort. Finer levels may contain valuable visual details; they can provide useful information or add realism to the surface.

In many cases, however, the close-up details are not significant. A very high-resolution surface image will contain details, but these details may be of little value. An example may be a close-up view of an asphalt highway; the imperfections revealed may be of little interest to the viewer. Detail at this level can also be very self-similar; in our roadside example, one section of asphalt detail may look very similar to any other. Although the details may not be visually interesting, some fine level detail can provide important visual cues about the viewer's distance and velocity relative to the surface, and keep the surface from looking blurry.

A detail texture can be a useful approach in these circumstances (Figure 14.25). Instead of making more high-resolution levels, a texture is created that contains only high-frequency details from the surface. The detail texture is not an entire high-resolution level, however. Instead a smaller image is used, and replicated across the surface to cover it. This approach takes advantage of some features of high-frequency details; the details are often self-similar, so a small patch can be replicated across the surface without looking too uniform. Since the detail texture contains only high-frequency image features, they change rapidly across the texture. There are no low-frequency components that would generate tiling artifacts when the texture is repeated.

The pairing of a base mipmap with the appropriate detail texture is a powerful combination. The mipmapped texture contains levels that provide a realistic representation of the surface, but does not contain the highest frequency detail. The detail texture provides

Detail texture

Figure 14.25 Detail textures.

fine, high-frequency features, which are only needed when the viewer is close to the textured surface. When the viewer gets close enough, both textures are applied; the detail texture is scaled up to become more prominent as the viewer approaches.

The extra work in implementing detail textures comes from the controlled application of base and detail texture images. Detail textures should not contribute anything when the base texture is not magnifying. The high-frequency component intensity should be a function of the base texture's magnification level.

The relative texture intensities can be implemented by blending, either by alpha blending fragments, or by using multitexturing. The relative intensities should be a function of base texture magnification. A less computationally expensive approach is is to estimate the magnification level by computing it as a function of viewer distance. Constraints specific to the application can simplify the problem in some cases. A flight simulator, for example, may use the height above ground and a precomputed scaling factor to estimate the texture magnification level of the terrain (Figure 14.26). If the simulator's view frustum brings the entire visible textured surface into view at nearly the same magnification, this approximation will be sufficiently accurate to provide a realistic effect.

In the general case, however, computing texture magnification can be difficult. An accurate computation of texture magnification must consider the visible vertices of the textured surface, the texture coordinate scaling resulting from the current modelview and projection transformations, the current texture coordinate generation settings, and the values of the texture transformation matrix. Section 13.7.2 discusses the steps in the computation in more detail. The best place to perform these computations is in

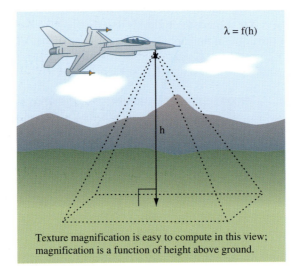

$\lambda = f(h)$

Texture magnification is easy to compute in this view; magnification is a function of height above ground.

Figure 14.26 Special case texture magnification.

the OpenGL implementation; to some extent this can be achieved in the programmable pipeline within a fragment program. There is also a vendor-specific detail texture extension `SGIS_detail_texture`. This extension blends in the detail texture as a function of magnification, and allows the detail texture either to add to or modulate the base texture. Unfortunately, it's unlikely to see widespread adoption, but the ideas present in it are or will be supportable using fragment programs.

14.13.1 Signed Intensity Detail Textures

Signed detail textures can be applied accurately without necessarily using separate texture magnification computations. A detail texture image is created that contains signed intensity values. The values are chosen so that the average value of the texel elements are zero. When combined with the base texture, the detail texture modifies its color values, adding high-frequency components to the textured image. Since the detail texture values average to zero intensity, a minified detail texture doesn't contribute to the overall image. This feature makes the fade in of texture detail "automatic", so no special computations are needed to selectively blend in detail.

The detail texture is applied to the same geometry as the base texture. The texture coordinates applied to both textures are adjusted so that the detail texture minifies if the base texture is not magnifying. The minification filtering will cause the signed intensity components to blend together. One way of making the detail texture "average out" is to make a mipmap out of it. The coarser mipmap levels of the detail texture will average more of its components, causing it to gradually fade out. As both the detail and base texture are zoomed, the detail texture will filter to its finer LOD levels, and the signed intensity values stop canceling each other out.

The fixed-function OpenGL pipeline doesn't support signed texture color components, but only values ranging from $[0, 1]$. To implement signed arithmetic, the implementation must use a representation of signed numbers that are biased (and possibly scaled) to remain in the $[0, 1]$ range (Section 3.4.1). The detail texture is added to the base texture using either multiple texture units or multiple passes and framebuffer blending.

In the multipass solution, the surface is first rendered with the base texture. The texture is applied as normal; configured to modulate the polygon color to capture vertex lighting detail, for example. The second step applies the detail texture. Since the detail texture is smaller than the base texture, and is generally applied using `GL_REPEAT` wrapping, the texture coordinates used differ from those used with the base texture. This change in mapping can be accomplished by using a separate set of per-vertex texture coordinates, generating coordinates using texgen, or by modifying the texture transformation matrix.

Neither the texture environment nor alpha blend stages support signed values; in both cases, the color and alpha component values are expected to range from $[0, 1]$. Despite this limitation, both stages can be configured to handle signed quantities, by representing the signed numbers in a *biased format*. Besides offering only a limited range, OpenGL only supports a limited (implementation-dependent) precision for the color component values. Care must be taken not to overly reduce this precision while processing colors. For whatever color format is chosen, the algebra for combining textures must follow certain rules in order to produce the desired results. When the base texture color is modified by a signed detail texture color, a detail color of zero should not change the base color, while a positive or negative detail color should increase or decrease the intensity of the base color, respectively. If the resulting base color goes out of its $[0, 1]$ range, it will be clamped.

Since the detail texture's values are meant to modify the base color, there is some flexibility in specifying its range. The ideal range is $[-1, 1]$, since that allows a detail texture color component to drive the base color component over the entire range of values, regardless of the base texture's color. Mathematically, the detail texture's $[0, 1]$ range is scaled by 2 and biased by -1 to put its values in the range $[-1, 1]$. This value is then added to the unmodified base texture, and the results are clamped to $[0, 1]$. These operations can be condensed to the equation:

$$T_{result} = T_{base} + 2T_{detail} - 1$$

Note that this approach assumes that intermediate results are not clamped to $[0, 1]$, which is not generally true in all OpenGL implementations.

For many applications, the detail texture does not need to be able to drive the base texture to an arbitrary value, since the goal of the detail texture is to only pattern the base texture with detail, not replace it. In many cases, a more limited range of $[-\frac{1}{2}, \frac{1}{2}]$ is sufficient. This range is particularly useful, since it can be derived from the normal $[0, 1]$ texture representation without scaling. The detail needs only to be biased by $-\frac{1}{2}$. Mathematically, the two textures are combined with:

$$T_{result} = T_{base} + T_{detail} - \frac{1}{2}$$

As before, this approach runs into problems if intermediate results are clamped to $[0, 1]$. However, the GL_COMBINE texture environment function supports the $[-\frac{1}{2}, \frac{1}{2}]$ range detail texture representation directly, with the GL_ADD_SIGNED texture function. It implements the equation $Arg0 + Arg1 - 0.5$, and doesn't clamp the intermediate results. This allows the signed detail sum to be implemented in a single pass using two texture units. The first unit applies the base texture to the geometry, the second adds the detail texture using the GL_ADD_SIGNED operation.

Modulating Detail

A useful variation of the signed detail texture approach is to modulate rather than add the detail texture component to the base texture. This amplifies variation by scaling rather than adding and subtracting variation. Signed values aren't very useful for the modulation case; instead, the detail texture values are greater than or less than one. A simple implementation uses a range of $[0, 2]$, which can be derived from OpenGL texture values in the range [0, 1] with a scale value of two. This range of values makes it possible to force the base texture to a reasonable range of values. Note that detail texture values of $\frac{1}{2}$ are scaled to one, which will not modify the base texture. The detail texture should average out to this value, in order to fade out under minification.

As with additive detail textures, a modulating detail texture can be implemented with texture environment functionality partnered with multitexturing. The multitexturing case is straightforward. Unit 0 applies the base texture to the surface, unit 1 modulates the base by the detail texture, then scales the result by two using GL_RGB_SCALE. The results are implicitly clamped to the range [0, 1] after scaling.

Implementing this algorithm using framebuffer blending is awkward but possible. The base textured geometry, once rendered to the framebuffer, can be modulated by the detail texture using a blending function of GL_ZERO, GL_SRC_COLOR. Since there is no support for a scale factor greater than one, the results of combining the base and detail textures must be added to the framebuffer twice. This can be done by reading back the framebuffer, then blending it in again, using a blend function of GL_ONE, GL_ONE.

Modulating detail textures are very useful when the base texture modulates vertex-lighted geometry. Modulating ensures that the detail texture changes follow the shading imposed by the lighting model, just as the base texture does. Additive detail textures do not take base texture value changes into account and will appear unlighted.

14.13.2 Creating Detail Textures

While a detail texture can contain a high-frequency pattern that is independent of the base texture, the best results are obtained when it contains the high-frequency components derived from the original image. The first step toward extracting detail texture data is to obtain a high-resolution version of the base texture. This image need only be a subregion of the base texture, since the detail texture will be replicated over the surface.

Once the high-resolution image is obtained, the next step is to choose the size of the detail texture and select a region of the detailed image that contains high-frequency details representative of the entire image. Now the high-frequency components of the region are extracted. One method starts by removing the high-frequency components from a copy of the region by blurring it (Figure 14.27). This can be done with various image processing

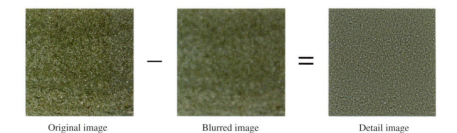

| Original image | Blurred image | Detail image |

Figure 14.27 Subtracting out low frequencies.

algorithms (see Chapter 12), or by using `gluScaleImage` to scale the image down, then up again.

Once a blurred version of the high-resolution image has been created, the high-frequency components are extracted by subtracting the blurred image from the unprocessed one. The subtraction can be done using a subtractive blend mode, the accumulation buffer, or the appropriate texture environment function. The result is an image with signed color components that contains the high-frequency elements of the image. The input images must be scaled and biased so that the result of the subtraction is limited to the [0, 1] range, since negative pixel values will be clamped when the image is used as a texture. Checking the range of color values in the images makes it possible to maximize the range of the resulting subtracted image. If the implementation supports the imaging subset, the minmax function can be used to find the range of pixel values in both the high resolution and blurred copies of the detail texture image. The values can be used to scale and bias the inputs to the subtract operation to maximize the dynamic range of the resulting image. When the image is created, it should be biased so that the sum of the color values equals $\frac{1}{2}$. This is necessary so that the detail texture will make no contribution when it's minified.

14.14 Texture Sharpening

Like detail textures, texture sharpening is another method for enhancing high-frequency detail on a magnified texture. Rather than creating a separate detail texture, however, texture sharpening augments high-frequency information by applying a sharpening operation to the texture similar to *unsharp masking*. This operation, a staple of image processing, increases the contrast of small details in the magnified texture. It has an advantage over detail textures in that is doesn't require creating and applying a detail texture as a separate step. It does require that the magnified texture be mipmapped, since it combines multiple mipmap levels of the texture to create the sharpened image.

The sharpening operation computes the difference between the magnified finest level (level 0) and the next coarser level (level 1). A weighted version of the result is added to the magnified finest image to produce the sharpened result. The result is an extrapolation from the level 1 image to the level 0 image. The weighting factor applied to the difference, f, is a function of the magnification factor $f(LOD)$. The equation to compute the texel color T from the top two texture levels and current magnification is:

$$T_{sharp} = (1 + f(LOD))T_0 - f(LOD)T_1$$

where T_{sharp} is the new texel color, T_0 is the magnified texel color at level 0, and T_1 is the magnified texel color at level 1. The $f(LOD)$ function takes an LOD value (which will be negative, since sharpening is only applied to magnified textures) and produces a weighting factor between 0 and 1. The resulting T_{sharp} color components are clamped to the range $[0, 1]$. Note that computing the $T_0 - T_1$ result is essentially the same technique used to create a signed intensity detail texture.

The texture sharpening functionality is available in some OpenGL implementations through the `SGIS_sharpen_texture` extension. Unfortunately, support for this extension is not widespread. At the time of this writing, there is no equivalent EXT or ARB extension, nor is texture sharpening supported as core functionality in any OpenGL specification. However, given the ability to approximate $f(LOD)$ in a fragment program, the sharpening functionality can be readily implemented in the programmable pipeline.

Texture sharpening can be implemented at the application level using multitexture or multiple passes with the same caveats that apply to computing per-fragment values of $f(LOD)$. If the LOD is constant across the polygon, the application can compute the constant $f(LOD)$ value. One way to compute an approximate $f(LOD)$ at each fragment is to create a mipmap texture with the values of f at each level. Texturing with this map generates a filtered version of $f(LOD)$. The resulting image can be used as a weight within a multitexture operation or with framebuffer blending. Section 13.7.2 describes the steps in the LOD calculation in more detail. Section 12.3.2 describes a version of the extrapolation algorithm for still images using the accumulation buffer and framebuffer blending.

14.15 Mipmap Generation

OpenGL supports a modest collection of filtering algorithms, the highest quality filter being `GL_LINEAR_MIPMAP_LINEAR`, which does trilinear mipmapping. Mipmap filtering requires that the mipmap levels needed for filtering be loaded into texture memory. OpenGL does not specify a method for generating these individual mipmap level of details. Each level can be loaded individually; it is possible, but generally not desirable, to use a different filtering algorithm to generate each mipmap level. OpenGL 1.4 adds functionality to the pipeline to generate mipmaps automatically from the base level (`GENERATE_MIPMAP`), but does not precisely specify the filter algorithm.[4]

The OpenGL utility library (GLU) provides a simple command (`gluBuild2DMipmaps`) for generating all of the levels required for mipmapping a 2D or 1D texture. The algorithm employed by most implementations is a box filter. A box filter is a pragmatic choice; it is simple, efficient, and can be repeatedly applied to an LOD level to generate all coarser levels required in a mipmap. A frequency domain analysis shows, however, that the box filter has poor filtering characteristics, which can lead to excessive blurring and aliasing artifacts. A common example of these limitations occurs if a texture contains very narrow image features (such as narrow lines). Aliasing artifacts can be very pronounced in this case.

---

4. A 2×2 box filter is recommended as a fast, but low quality, default.

Although the limitations of box filtering are well known, finding the best mipmap filtering function is less obvious. The choice of filter is dependent on the manner in which the texture will be used and is somewhat subjective. The choice of filter is burdened with additional trade-offs if the mipmap must be generated at run time, and therefore must be filtered quickly. One possibility is the use of a bicubic filter — a weighted sum of 16 pixels for 2D images. Mitchell and Netravali (1988) propose a family of cubic filters for general image reconstruction which can be used for mipmap generation. The advantage of the cubic filter over the box filter is that the cubic filter can have negative side lobes (weights) which help maintain sharpness while reducing the image size. This can help reduce some of the blurring effect of filtering with mipmaps.

When crafting a new filtering algorithm for mipmap generation, it is important to keep a few guidelines in mind. To minimize accumulated error, the highest resolution (finest) image of the mipmap (level 0) should always be used as the input image source for each level to be generated. For the box filter, a particular level can be produced by repeating the filter to the results of the previous filtering operation. This works because the box filter can produce the correct result for a given level by using the preceding level as input. The filter parameters are independent of LOD level. This invariance is not always true for other filter functions. Each time a new (coarser) level is generated, the filter footprint may need to be scaled to four times its previous size.

Another constraint is that mipmap levels must maintain strict factor of two reductions in each dimension when filtering to a coarser level. Filters with input widths wider than two will be forced to sample outside the boundaries of the input image. Providing input values outside of the input image is commonly handled by using the value of the nearest edge pixel when sampling. This algorithm should be adjusted, however, if the mipmapped texture will be applied using the GL_REPEAT wrap mode. In this case, the levels will be filtered more accurately if sample values requested from outside the image should be wrapped to the appropriate texel from the opposite edge, effectively filtering from a repeating image.

While mipmaps can always be generated using the host processor, the OpenGL pipeline can be used to accelerate the process by performing the filtering operations. For example, the GL_LINEAR minification filter can be used to draw an image of exactly half the width and height of an image loaded into texture memory. This is done by drawing a rectangle with the appropriate transformation; it is sized so its pixel dimensions in screen space are exactly one half of the texture image's dimensions. The rendered image produced has effectively been filtered to half of its dimensions using a box filter. The resulting image can then be read from the color buffer back to host memory for later use as a level. The read step can be eliminated and the the image can be copied directly into the texture using glCopyTexImage. If the implementation supports ARB_render_texture, even the copy step can be removed. The filtering process can be repeated using the newly generated mipmap level to produce the next level. The process can be continued until the coarsest level has been generated.

If the texture LOD extension SGIS_texture_lod (which became part of the core in OpenGL 1.2) is available, a further optimization to this process is possible. By clamping the mipmap to only the LOD levels that have been created, the mipmap can be built in place. The mipmap can be created with only level 0 in place. That level can be used to render an image for level 1, which can be used as the new texture source. This makes it possible to build up the mipmap texture without having to switch between two texture objects.

Although this method is very efficient, it is limited to creating new levels using the existing texture filters. There are other mechanisms within the OpenGL pipeline that can be used to produce higher-quality filtering. Convolution filtering can be implemented using the accumulation buffer (this discussed in detail in Section 12.6.2). An arbitrary filter kernel can be constructed using a special texture image applied to a rectangular geometry of the proper size and position. The texel color to be filtered is applied to geometry itself; the special texture modulates that color over the geometry. The accumulation buffer combines multiple passes with this technique to produce the final image. Combining point-sampled texturing with the accumulation buffer allows the application of nearly arbitrary filter kernels. This method does not handle the problem of sampling outside the image well, however, which limits its usefulness for wide filter kernels.

Convolution filters may also be implemented directly within fragment programs providing substantial flexibility in the types of filtering that can be performed within the pipeline. Typically custom fragment programs are written for each filter type. OpenGL implementations supporting the imaging subset also directly implement convolution operations in the pixel pipeline.

14.16 Texture Map Limits

Texture mapping is a versatile component for building graphics effects, but its very desirability can be its downside. It is common for an ambitious application to run into the limits to available texture memory. Most OpenGL implementations hardware accelerate texture mapping, but only if they are located within a finite texture memory storage area. OpenGL implementations often attempt to mitigate the finite size problem by virtualizing the texture memory resource. This allows an application to create an arbitrarily large set of texture maps; however, this virtualization isn't free. As the texture memory resource becomes oversubscribed, performance will degrade. For the developer of an application that makes extensive use of texture, there is a tension between rationing available texture memory to maximize performance, and using texture lavishly to improve image quality.

The practical result of this limitation is that a well-designed application creates textures no larger than they need to be to meet image quality goals. An application designer needs to anticipate how textures will be used in each scene to determine the appropriate resolution to use. Using textures efficiently is always important. Where possible, images should be crafted to minimize wasted texels. For example, when faced with an image that doesn't have power-of-two dimensions, the best choice is usually *not* simply rounding the texture size up to the next power-of-two. Besides such standard techniques as image tiling and mosaicing, many implementations support a special texture version that doesn't require power-of-two dimensions. Vendor-specific extensions, such as NV_texture_rectangle and more widely adopted extensions such as ARB_texture_non_power_of_two, provide this functionality, although there are often limitations on the range of wrap modes or filtering that can be applied to such textures. Even the standard power-of-two dimension limitation doesn't mean a texture has to be square. If a texture is typically used with an object that is projected to a non-square aspect ratio, then the aspect ratio of the texture can be scaled appropriately to make more efficient use of the available storage.

14.17 Summary

Texture mapping is undoubtedly the most powerful component in a graphics library. At least part of the reason is its ability to marry image-based and geometry-based processing with great flexibility. This chapter only provides a sampling of some of building block algorithms used to create sophisticated techniques. A survey of graphics "tricks and techniques" books, such as *Graphics Gems* (Goldman, 1990) and *GPU Gems* (Fernando, 2004), will reveal more ideas and are valuable references.

The best approach, however, is to have a through understanding of texture mapping. Nothing can replace a careful reading of the OpenGL core and extension specifications, augmented with some well-crafted test applications. With a deep understanding of OpenGL's texture mapping capabilities, many opportunities for novel applications become apparent.

Lighting Techniques

This section discusses various ways of improving and refining the lighted appearance of objects. There are several approaches to approving the fidelity of lighting. The process of computing lighting can be decomposed into separate subtasks. One is capturing the material properties of an object, reflectances, roughness, transparency, subsurface properties, and so on. A second is the direct illumination model; the manner in which the surface interacts with the light striking the target object. The third is light transport, which takes into account the overall path of light, including light passing through other mediums such as haze or water on its way to the target object. Light transport also includes indirect illumination, wherein the light source is light reflected from another surface. Computing this requires taking into account how light rays are blocked by other objects, or by parts of the target object itself, creating shadows on the target object.

Lighting is a very broad topic and continues to rapidly evolve. In this chapter we consider various algorithms for improving the quality and character of the direct illumination model and material modeling. We end by considering restricted-light-transport modeling problems, such as ambient occlusion.

15.1 Limitations in Vertex Lighting

OpenGL uses a simple per-vertex lighting facility to incorporate lighting into a scene. Section 3.3.4 discusses some of the shortcomings of per-vertex lighting. One problem is the location in the pipeline where the lighting terms are summed for each vertex. The terms are combined at the end of the vertex processing, causing problems with using texture maps as the source for diffuse reflectance properties. This problem is solved directly in OpenGL 1.2 with the addition of a separate (secondary) color for the specular term, which is summed after texturing is applied. A second solution, using a two-pass algorithm, is described in Section 9.2. This second technique is important because it represents a general class of techniques in which the terms of the vertex lighting equation are computed separately, then summed together in a different part of the pipeline.

Another problem described in Section 3.3.4 is that the lighting model is evaluated per-vertex rather than per-pixel. Per-vertex evaluation can be viewed as another form of sampling (Section 4.1); the sample points are the eye coordinates of the vertices and the functions being sampled are the various subcomponents of the lighting equation. The sampled function is partially reconstructed, or resampled, during rasterization as the vertex attributes are (linearly) interpolated across the face of a triangle, or along the length of a line.

Although per-vertex sampling locations are usually coarser than per-pixel, assuming that this results in poorer quality images is an oversimplification. The image quality depends on both the nature of the function being sampled and the set of sample points being used. If the sampled function consists of slowly varying values, it does not need as high a sample rate as a function containing rapid transitions. Reexamining the intensity terms in the OpenGL lighting equation[1]

$$I_{am} = 1$$
$$I_{di} = \mathbf{N} \cdot \mathbf{L}$$
$$I_{sp} = (\mathbf{H} \cdot \mathbf{N})^n$$
$$I_{em} = 1$$

shows that the ambient and emissive terms are constants and the diffuse term is fairly well behaved. The diffuse term may change rapidly, but only if the surface normal also does so, indicating that the surface geometry is itself rapidly changing. This means that per-vertex evaluation of the diffuse term doesn't introduce much error if the underlying vertex geometry reasonably models the underlying surface. For many situations the surface can be modeled accurately enough with polygonal geometry such that diffuse lighting gives acceptable results. An interesting set of surfaces for which the results are *not* acceptable is described in Sections 15.9.3 and 15.10.

Accurate specular component sampling becomes more challenging to sample when the specular exponent (shininess) is greater than 1. The specular function—a cosine power function—varies rapidly when evaluated with large exponents. Small changes in the surface normal results in large changes in the specular contribution. Figure 15.1 shows the result of exponentiating the cosine function for several different exponent values. This, of course, is the desired effect for the specular term. It models the rapid fall-off of a highlight reflected from a polished surface. This means that shiny surfaces must be modeled with greater geometric accuracy to correctly capture the specular contribution.

---

1. Recall that $\mathbf{A} \cdot \mathbf{B} = \max(0, \mathbf{A} \cdot \mathbf{B})$ is the clamped inner product as described in Section 3.3

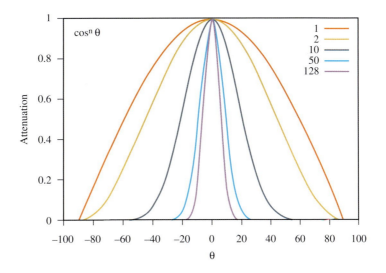

Figure 15.1 Cosine power function.

15.1.1 Static and Adaptive Tessellation

We've seen that highly specular surfaces need to be modeled more accurately than diffuse surfaces. We can use this information to generate better models. Knowing the intended shininess of the surface, the surface can be tessellated until the difference between $(\mathbf{H} \cdot \mathbf{N})^n$ at triangle vertices drops below a predetermined threshold. An advantage of this technique is that it can be performed during modeling; perferably as a preprocessing step as models are converted from a higher-order representation to a polygonal representation. There are performance versus quality trade-offs that should also be considered when deciding the threshold. For example, increasing the complexity (number of triangles) of a modeled object may substantially affect the rendering performance if:

- The performance of the application or system is already *vertex limited*: geometry processing, rather than fragment processing, limits performance.

- The model has to be clipped against a large number of application-defined clipping planes.

- The model has tiled textures applied to it.

The previous scheme statically tessellates each object to meet quality requirements. However, because the specular reflection is view dependent only a portion of the object needs to be tessellated to meet the specular quality requirement. This suggests a scheme in which each model in the scene is adaptively tessellated. Then only parts of each surface need to be tessellated. The difficulty with such an approach is that the cost of retessellating each object can be prohibitively expensive to recompute each frame. This is especially

Figure 15.2 Undersampled specular lighting.

true if we also want to avoid introducing motion artifacts caused by adding or removing object vertices between frames.

For some specific types of surfaces, however, it may be practical to build this idea into the modeling step and generate the correct model at runtime. This technique is very similar to the *geometric level of detail* techniques described in Section 16.4 . The difference is that model selection uses specular lighting (see Figure 15.2) accuracy as the selection criterion, rather than traditional geometric criteria such as individual details or silhouette edges.

15.1.2 Local Light and Spotlight Attenuation

Like specular reflection, a vertex sampling problem occurs when using distance-based and spotlight attenuation terms. With distance attenuation, the attenuation function is not well behaved because it contains reciprocal terms:

$$\frac{1}{k_c + k_l d + k_q d^2}$$

Figure 15.3 plots values of the attenuation function for various coefficients. When the linear or quadratic coefficients are non-zero, the function tails off very rapidly. This means that very fine model tessellation is necessary near the regions of rapid change, in order to capture the changes accurately.

With spotlights, there are two sources of problems. The first comes from the cutoff angle defined in the spotlight equation. It defines an abrupt cutoff angle that creates a discontinuity at the edge of the cone. Second, inside the cone a specular-like power function is used to control intensity drop-off:

$$\left(\mathbf{L}_p \cdot \mathbf{L}_d\right)^{n_{spot}}$$

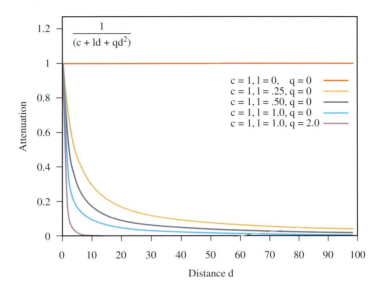

Figure 15.3 Attenuation function.

When the geometry undersamples the lighting model, it typically manifests itself as a dull appearance across the illuminated area (cone), or irregular or poorly defined edges at the perimeter of the illuminated area. Unlike the specular term, the local light and spotlight attenuation terms are a property of the light source rather than the object. This means that solutions involving object modeling or tessellation require knowing which objects will be illuminated by a particular light source. Even then, the sharp cutoff angle of a spotlight requires tessellation nearly to pixel-level detail to accurately sample the cutoff transition.

15.2 Fragment Lighting Using Texture Mapping

The preceding discussion and Section 3.3.4 advocate evaluating lighting equations at each fragment rather than at each vertex. Using the ideas from the multipass toolbox discussed in Section 9.3, we can efficiently approximate a level of per-fragment lighting computations using a combination of texture mapping and framebuffer blending. If multitexture, the combine texture environment, and vertex and fragment program features are available,[2] we can implement these algorithms more efficiently or use more sophisticated ones. We'll start by presenting the general idea, and then look at some specific techniques.

---

2. Multitexture and the combine texture environment are part of OpenGL 1.3 or available as extensions. Vertex and fragment programs are available as the extensions `ARB_vertex_program` and `ARB_fragment_program`.

Abstractly, the texture-mapping operation may be thought of as a function evaluation mechanism using lookup tables. Using texture mapping, the texture-matrix and texture-coordinate generation functions can be combined to create several useful mapping algorithms. The first algorithm is a straightforward 1D and 2D mapping of $f(s)$ and $f(s, t)$. The next is the projective mappings described in Section 14.9: $f(s, t, r, q)$. The third uses environment and reflection mapping techniques with sphere and cube maps to evaluate $f(\mathbf{R})$.

Each mapping category can evaluate a class of equations that model some form of lighting. Taking advantage of the fact that lighting contributions are additive — and using the regular associative, commutative, and distributive properties of the underlying color arithmetic — we can use framebuffer blending in one of two ways. It can be used to sum partial results or to scale individual terms. This means that we can use texture mapping and blending as a set of building blocks for computing lighting equations. First, we will apply this idea to the problematic parts of the OpenGL lighting equation: specular highlights and attenuation terms. Then we will use the same ideas to evaluate some variations on the standard (traditional) lighting models.

15.3 Spotlight Effects Using Projective Textures

The projective texture technique (described in Section 14.9) can be used to generate a number of interesting illumination effects. One of them is spotlight illumination. The OpenGL spotlight illumination model provides control over a cutoff angle (the spread of the light cone), an intensity exponent (concentration across the cone), the direction of the spotlight, and intensity attenuation as a function of distance. The core idea is to project a texture map from the same position as the light source that acts as an illumination *mask*, attenuating the light source. The mask is combined with a point light source placed at the spotlight's position. The texture map captures the cutoff angle and exponent, whereas the vertex light provides the rest of the diffuse and specular computation. Because the projective method samples the illumination at each pixel, the undersampling problem is greatly reduced.

The texture is an intensity map of a cross section of the spotlight's beam. The same exponent parameters used in the OpenGL model can be incorporated, or an entirely different model can be used. If 3D textures are available, attenuation due to distance can also be approximated using a texture in which the intensity of the cross section is attenuated along the r dimension. As geometry is rendered with the spotlight projection, the r coordinate of the fragment is proportional to the distance from the light source.

To determine the transformation needed for the texture coordinates, it helps to consider the simplest case: the eye and light source are coincident. For this case, the texture coordinates correspond to the eye coordinates of the geometry being drawn. The coordinates could be explicitly computed by the application and sent to the pipeline, but a more efficient method is to use an eye-linear texture generation function.

The planes correspond to the vertex coordinate planes (e.g., the *s* coordinate is the distance of the vertex coordinate from the *y-z* plane, and so on). Since eye coordinates are in the range $[-1.0, 1.0]$ and the texture coordinates need to be in the range $[0.0, 1.0]$, a scale and bias of 0.5 is applied to *s* and *t* using the texture matrix. A perspective spotlight projection transformation can be computed using `gluPerspective` and combined into the texture transformation matrix.

The transformation for the general case, when the eye and light source are not in the same position, can be computed by compositing an additional transform into the texture matrix. To find the texture transform for a light at an arbitrary location, the new transform should be the inverse of the transformations needed to move the light source from the eye position to the location. Once the texture map has been created, the method for rendering the scene with the spotlight illumination (see Figure 15.4) is:

1. Initialize the depth buffer.

2. Clear the color buffer to a constant value representing the scene ambient illumination.

3. Drawing the scene with depth buffering enabled and color buffer writes disabled (*pass 1*).

4. Load and enable the spotlight texture, and set the texture environment to `GL_MODULATE`.

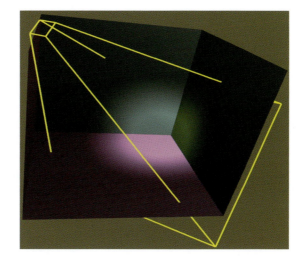

Figure 15.4 Spotlight projection.

5. Enable the texture generation functions, and load the texture matrix.

6. Enable blending and set the blend function to `GL_ONE`, `GL_ONE`.

7. Disable depth buffer updates and set the depth function to `GL_EQUAL`.

8. Draw the scene with the vertex colors set to the spotlight color (*pass 2*).

9. Disable the spotlight texture, texgen, and texture transformation.

10. Set the blend function to `GL_DST_COLOR`.

11. Draw the scene with normal diffuse and specular illumination (*pass 3*).

There are three passes in the algorithm. At the end of the first pass the ambient illumination has been established in the color buffer and the depth buffer contains the resolved depth values for the scene. In the second pass, the illumination from the spotlight is accumulated in the color buffer. By using the `GL_EQUAL` depth function, only visible surfaces contribute to the accumulated illumination. In the final pass the scene is drawn with the colors modulated by the illumination accumulated in the first two passes to compute the final illumination values.

The algorithm does not restrict the use of texture on objects, because the spotlight texture is only used in the second pass; only the scene geometry is needed in this one. The second pass can be repeated multiple times with different spotlight textures and projections to accumulate the contributions of multiple spotlight sources.

There are some caveats to consider when implementing this technique. Texture projection along the negative line-of-sight of the texture (back projection) can contribute undesired illumination to the scene. This can be eliminated by positioning a clip plane at the near plane of the projection line-of-site. The clip plane is enabled during the spotlight illumination pass, and oriented to remove objects rendered behind the spotlight.

OpenGL encourages but does not guarantee invariance when arbitrary modes are enabled or disabled. This can manifest itself in undesirable ways during multipass algorithms. For example, enabling texture coordinate generation may cause fragments with different depth values to be generated compared to the one generated when texture coordinate generation is not enabled. This problem can be overcome by reestablishing the depth buffer values between the second and third pass. Do this by redrawing the scene with color buffer updates disabled and depth buffering configured as it was during the first pass.

Using a texture wrap mode of `GL_CLAMP` will keep the spotlight pattern from repeating. When using a linear texture filter, use a black texel border to avoid clamping artifacts; or, if available, use the `GL_CLAMP_TO_EDGE` wrap mode.[3]

---

3. Added in OpenGL 1.2.

15.4 Specular Lighting Using Environment Maps

The appearance of the OpenGL per-vertex specular highlight can be improved by using environment mapping to generate a higher-quality per-pixel highlight. A sphere map containing only a Phong highlight (Phong, 1975) is applied to the object and the result is summed with the object's per-vertex ambient and diffuse lighting contributions to create the final, lighted color (see Figure 15.5). The environment map uses the eye reflection vector, $\mathbf{R}_v$, to index the texture map, and thus it can be used like a lookup table to compute the specular term:

$$f(\mathbf{R}_v, \mathbf{L}) = (\mathbf{L} \cdot \mathbf{R}_v)^n = (\mathbf{V} \cdot \mathbf{R}_l)^n$$

For each polygon in the object, the reflection vector is computed at each vertex. This technique interpolates the sphere-mapped coordinates of the reflection vector instead of the highlight itself, and thus a much more accurate sampling of the highlight is achieved. The sphere map image for the texture map of the highlight is computed by rendering a highly tessellated sphere, lighted with a specular highlight. Using the OpenGL pipeline to compute the specular color produces a Blinn (rather than Phong) specular function. If another function is required, the application can evaluate the specular function at each vertex and send the result to the pipeline as a vertex color. The bidirectional function, $f(\mathbf{L}, \mathbf{R})$, is reduced to a function of a single direction by encoding the direction of the light ($\mathbf{L}$) relative to the view direction into the texture map. Consequently, the texture map needs to be recomputed whenever the light or viewer position is changed. Sphere mapping assumes that the view direction is constant (infinite viewer) and the environment (light) direction is infinitely far away. As a result, the highlight does not need to be changed when the object moves. Assuming a texture map is also used to provide the object's diffuse reflectance, the steps in the two-pass method are:

1. Define the material with appropriate diffuse and ambient reflectance, and zero for the specular reflectance coefficients.

Figure 15.5 Environment-mapped highlight.

2. Define and enable lights.

3. Define and enable texture to be combined with diffuse lighting.

4. Define modulate texture environment.

5. Draw the lighted, textured object into the color buffer.

6. Disable lighting.

7. Load the sphere map texture, and enable the sphere map texgen function.

8. Enable blending, and set the blend function to GL_ONE, GL_ONE.

9. Draw the unlighted, textured geometry with vertex colors set to the specular material color.

10. Disable texgen and blending.

15.4.1 Multitexture

If a texture isn't used for the diffuse color, then the algorithm reduces to a single pass using the add texture environment (see Figure 15.5) to sum the colors rather than framebuffer blending. For this technique to work properly, the specular material color should be included in the specular texture map rather than in the vertex colors. Multiple texture units can also be used to reduce the operation to a single pass. For two texture units, the steps are modified as follows:

1. Define the material with appropriate diffuse and ambient reflectance, and zero for the specular reflectance coefficients.

2. Define and enable lights.

3. Define and enable texture to be combined with diffuse lighting in unit 0.

4. Set modulate texture environment for unit 0.

5. Load the sphere map texture, and enable the sphere map texgen function for unit 1.

6. Set add texture environment for unit 1.

7. Draw the lighted, textured object into the color buffer.

As with the separate specular color algorithm, this algorithm requires that the specular material reflectance be premultiplied with the specular light color in the specular texture map.

With a little work the technique can be extended to handle multiple light sources. The idea can be further generalized to include other lighting models. For example, a more accurate specular function could be used rather than the Phong or Blinn specular terms. It can also include the diffuse term. The algorithm for computing the texture map must be modified to encompass the new lighting model. It may still be useful to generate the map by rendering a finely tessellated sphere and evaluating the lighting model at each vertex within the application, as described previously. Similarly, the technique isn't restricted to sphere mapping; cube mapping, dual-paraboloid mapping, and other environment or normal mapping formulations can be used to yield even better results.

15.5 Light Maps

A light map is a texture map applied to an object to simulate the distance-related attenuation of a local light source. More generally, light maps may be used to create nonisotropic illumination patterns. Like specular highlight textures, light maps can improve the appearance of local light sources without resorting to excessive tessellation of the objects in the scene. An excellent example of an application that uses light maps is the Quake series of interactive PC games (id Software, 1999). These games use light maps to simulate the effects of local light sources, both stationary and moving, to great effect.

There are two parts to using light maps: creating a texture map that simulates the light's effect on an object and specifying the appropriate texture coordinates to position and shape the light. Animating texture coordinates allows the light source (or object) to move. A texture map is created that simulates the light's effect on some canonical object. The texture is then applied to one or more objects in the scene. Appropriate texture coordinates are applied using either object modeling or texture coordinate generation. Texture coordinate transformations may be used to position the light and to create moving or changing light effects. Multiple light sources can be generated with a combination of more complex texture maps and/or more passes to the algorithm.

Light maps are often luminance (single-component) textures applied to the object using a modulate texture environment function. Colored lights are simulated using an RGB texture. If texturing is already used for the material properties of an object, either a second texture unit or a multipass algorithm is needed to apply the light map. Light maps often produce satisfactory lighting effects using lower resolution than that normally needed for surface textures. The low spatial resolution of the texture usually does not require mipmapping; choosing `GL_LINEAR` for the minification and magnification filters is sufficient. Of course, the quality requirements for the lighting effect are dependent on the application.

15.5.1 2D Texture Light Maps

A 2D light map is a 2D luminance map that modulates the intensity of surfaces within a scene. For an object and a light source at fixed positions in the scene, a luminance map can be calculated that exactly matches a surface of the object. However, this implies that a specific texture is computed for each surface in the scene. A more useful approximation takes advantage of symmetry in isotropic light sources, by building one or more canonical projections of the light source onto a surface. Translate and scale transformations applied to the texture coordinates then model some of the effects of distance between the object and the light source. The 2D light map may be generated analytically using a 2D quadratic attenuation function, such as

$$I = \frac{1}{k_c + k_l d + k_q d^2}, \quad \text{where } d = \sqrt{s^2 + t^2}$$

This can be generated using OpenGL vertex lighting by drawing a high-resolution mesh with a local light source positioned in front of the center of the mesh. Alternatively, empirically derived illumination patterns may be used. For example, irregularly shaped maps can be used to simulate patterns cast by flickering torches, explosions, and so on.

A quadratic function of two inputs models the attenuation for a light source at a fixed perpendicular distance from the surface. To approximate the effect of varying perpendicular distance, the texture map may be scaled to change the shape of the map. The scaling factors may be chosen empirically, for example, by generating test maps for different perpendicular distances and evaluating different scaling factors to find the closest match to each test map. The scale factor can also be used to control the overall brightness of the light source. An ambient term can also be included in a light map by adding a constant to each texel value. The ambient map can be a separate map, or in some cases combined with a diffuse map. In the latter case, care must be taken when applying maps from multiple sources to a single surface.

To apply a light map to a surface, the position of the light in the scene must be projected onto each surface of interest. This position determines the center of the projected map and is used to compute the texture coordinates. The perpendicular distance of the light from the surface determines the scale factor. One approach is to use linear texture coordinate generation, orienting the generating planes with each surface of interest and then translating and scaling the texture matrix to position the light on the surface. This process is repeated for every surface affected by the light.

To repeat this process for multiple lights (without resorting to a composite multilight light map) or to light textured surfaces, the lighting is done using multiple texture units or as a series of rendering passes. In effect, we are evaluating the equation

$$C_{final} = C_{object}(I_1 + I_2 + \cdots + I_n)$$

The difficulty is that the texture coordinates used to index each of the light maps $(I_1, \ldots, I_n)$ are different because the light positions are different. This is not a problem, however, because multiple texture units have independent texture coordinates and coordinate generation and transformation units, making the algorithm using multiple texture units straightforward. Each light map is loaded in a separate texture unit, which is set to use the *add* environment function (except for the first unit, which uses *replace*). An additional texture unit at the end of the pipeline is used to store the surface detail texture. The environment function for this unit is set to *modulate*, modulating the result of summing the other textures. This rearranges the equation to

$$C_{final} = (I_1 + I_2 + \cdots + I_n)C_{object}$$

where C_{object} is stored in a texture unit. The original fragment colors (vertex colors) are not used. If a particular object does not use a surface texture, the environment function for the last unit (the one previously storing the surface texture) is changed to the *combine* environment function with the `GL_SOURCE0_RGB` and `GL_SOURCE0_ALPHA` parameters set to `GL_PRIMARY_COLOR`. This changes the last texture unit to modulate the sum by the fragment color rather than the texture color (the texture color is ignored).

If there aren't enough texture units available to implement a multitexture algorithm, there are several ways to create a multipass algorithm instead. If two texture units are available, the units can be used to hold a light map and the surface texture. In each pass, the surface texture is modulated by a different light map and the results summed in the framebuffer. Framebuffer blending with `GL_ONE` as the source and destination blend factors computes this sum. To ensure visible surfaces in later passes aren't discarded, use `GL_LEQUAL` for the depth test. In the simple case, where the object doesn't have a surface texture, only a single texture unit is needed to modulate the fragment color.

If only a single texture unit is available, an approximation can be used. Rather than computing the sum of the light maps, compute the product of the light maps and the object.

$$C_{final} = (I_1 I_2 \dots I_n)C_{object}$$

This allows all of the products to be computed using framebuffer blending with source and destination factors `GL_ZERO` and `GL_SRC_COLOR`. Because the multiple products rapidly attenuate the image luminance, the light maps are pre-biased or brightened to compensate. For example, a biased light map might have its range transformed from [0.0, 1.0] to [0.5, 1.0]. An alternative, but much slower, algorithm is to have a separate color buffer to compute each $C_{object}I_j$ term using framebuffer blending, and then adding this separate color buffer onto the scene color buffer. The separate color buffer can be added by using `glCopyPixels` and the appropriate blend function. The visible surfaces for the object must be correctly resolved before the scene accumulation can be done. The simplest way to do this is to draw the entire scene once with color buffer updates disabled. Here is summary of the steps to support 2D light maps without multitexture functionality:

1. Create the 2D light maps. Avoid artifacts by ensuring the intensity of the light map is the same at all edges of the texture.

2. Define a 2D texture, using `GL_REPEAT` for the wrap values in s and t. Minification and magnification should be `GL_LINEAR` to make the changes in intensity smoother.

3. Render the scene without the light map, using surface textures as appropriate.

4. For each light in the scene, perform the following.
   For each surface in the scene:

   (a) Cull the surface if it cannot "see" the current light.

   (b) Find the plane of the surface.

   (c) Align the GL_EYE_PLANE for GL_S, and GL_T with the surface plane.

   (d) Scale and translate the texture coordinates to position and size the light on the surface.

   (e) Render the surface using the appropriate blend function and light map texture.

   If multitexture is available, and assuming that the number of light sources is less than the number of available texture units, the set of steps for each surface reduces to:

   (a) Determine set of lights affecting surface; cull surface if none.

   (b) Bind the corresponding texture maps.

   (c) Find the plane of the surface.

   (d) For each light map, align the GL_EYE_PLANE for GL_S and GL_T with the surface plane.

   (e) For each light map, scale and translate the texture coordinates to position and size the light on the surface.

   (f) Set the texture environment to sum the light map contributions and modulate the surface color (texture) with that sum.

   (g) Render the surface.

15.5.2 3D Texture Light Maps

3D textures may also be used as light maps. One or more light sources are represented as 3D luminance data, captured in a 3D texture and then applied to the entire scene. The main advantage of using 3D textures for light maps is that it is simpler to approximate a 3D function, such as intensity as a function of distance. This simplifies calculation of texture coordinates. 3D texture coordinates allow the textured light source to be positioned globally in the scene using texture coordinate transformations. The relationship between light map texture and lighted surfaces doesn't have to be specially computed to apply texture to each surface; texture coordinate generation (glTexGen) computes the proper s, t, and r coordinates based on the light position.

As described for 2D light maps, a useful approach is to define a canonical light volume as 3D texture data, and then reuse it to represent multiple lights at different positions and sizes. Texture translations and scales are applied to shift and resize the light. A moving light source is created by changing the texture matrix. Multiple lights are simulated by accumulating the results of each light source on the scene. To avoid wrapping artifacts at the edge of the texture, the wrap modes should be set to GL_CLAMP for s, t, and r and the intensity values at the edge of the volume should be equal to the ambient intensity of the light source.

Although uncommon, some lighting effects are difficult to render without 3D textures. A complex light source, whose brightness pattern is asymmetric across all three major axes, is a good candidate for a 3D texture. An example is a "glitter ball" effect in which the light source has beams emanating out from the center, with some beams brighter than others, and spaced in a irregular pattern. A complex 3D light source can also be combined with volume visualization techniques, allowing fog or haze to be added to the lighting effects. A summary of the steps for using a 3D light map follows.

1. Create the 3D light map. Avoid artifacts by ensuring the intensity of the light map is the same at all edges of the texture volume.

2. Define a 3D texture, using GL_REPEAT for the wrap values in s, t, and r. Minification and magnification should be GL_LINEAR to make the changes in intensity smoother.

3. Render the scene without the light map, using surface textures as appropriate.

4. Define planes in eye space so that glTexGen will cause the texture to span the visible scene.

5. If the lighted surfaces are textured, adding a light map becomes a multitexture or multipass technique. Use the appropriate environment or blending function to modulate the surface color.

6. Render the image with the light map, and texgen enabled. Use the appropriate texture transform to position and scale the light source correctly.

With caveats similar to those for 2D light maps, multiple 3D light maps can be applied to a scene and mixed with 2D light maps.

Although 3D light maps are more expressive, there are some drawbacks too. 3D textures are often not well accelerated in OpenGL implementation, so applications may suffer serious reductions in performance. Older implementations may not even support 3D textures, limiting portability. Larger 3D textures use substantial texture memory resources. If the texture map has symmetry it may be exploited using a *mirrored repeat* texture wrap mode.[4] This can reduce the amount of memory required by one-half per mirrored dimension. In general, though, 2D textures make more efficient light maps.

---

4. A core feature in OpenGL 1.4 and available as the ARB_texture_mirrored_repeat extension.

15.6 BRDF-based Lighting

The methods described thus far have relied largely on texture mapping to perform table lookup operations of a precomputed lighting environment, applying them at each fragment. The specular environment mapping technique can be generalized to include other bidirectional reflectance distribution functions (BRDFs), with any form of environment map (sphere, cube, dual-paraboloid). However, the specular scheme only works with a single input vector, whereas BRDFs are a function of two input vectors (**L** and **R**), or in spherical coordinates a function of four scalars $f(\theta_i, \phi_i, \theta_r, \phi_r)$. The specular technique fixes the viewer and light positions so that as the object moves only the reflection vector varies.

Another approach decomposes or factors the 4D BRDF function into separate functions of lower dimensionality and evaluates them separately. Each factor is stored in a separate texture map and a multipass or multitexture algorithm is used to linearly combine the components (Kautz, 1999; McCool, 2001). While a detailed description of the factorization algorithm is beyond the scope of this book, we introduce the idea because the method described by McCool et al. (McCool, 2001) allows a BRDF to be decomposed to two 2D environment maps and recombined using framebuffer (or accumulation buffer) blending with a small number of passes.

15.7 Reflectance Maps

The techniques covered so far have provided alternative methods to represent light source information or the diffuse and ambient material reflectances for an object. These methods allow better sampling without resorting to subdividing geometry. These benefits can be extended to other applications by generalizing lighting techniques to include other material reflectance parameters.

15.7.1 Gloss Maps

Surfaces whose shininess varies — such as marble, paper with wet spots, or fabrics that are smoothed only in places — can be modeled with *gloss maps*. A gloss map is a texture map that encodes a mask of the specular reflectance of the object. It modulates the result of the specular lighting computation, but is ignored in the diffues and other terms of the lighting computation (see Figure 15.6).

This technique can be implemented using a two-pass multipass technique. The diffuse, ambient, and emissive lighting components are drawn, and then the specular lighting component is added using blending.

In the first pass, the surface is drawn with ambient and diffuse lighting, but no specular lighting. This can be accomplished by setting the specular material reflectance to zero. In the second pass, the surface is drawn with the specular color restored and

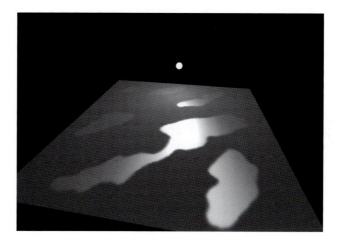

Figure 15.6 Gloss map.

the diffuse, ambient, and emissive colors set to zero. The surface is textured with a texture map encoding the specular reflectance (gloss). The texture can be a one-component alpha texture or a two- or four-component texture with luminance or color components set to one.

Typically the alpha component stores the gloss map value directly, with zero indicating no specular reflection and one indicating full specular reflection. The second pass modulates the specular color — computed using vertex lighting, with the alpha value from the texture map — and sums the result in the framebuffer. The source and destination blend factors GL_SRC_ALPHA and GL_ONE perform both the modulation and the sum. The second pass must use the standard methods to allow drawing the same surface more than once, using either GL_EQUAL for the depth function or stenciling (Section 9.2).

The net result is that we compute one product per pass of $C_{final} = M_d I_d + M_s I_s$, where M_i is the material reflectance, stored as a texture, and I_j is the reflected light intensity computed using vertex lighting. Trying to express this as single-pass multitexture algorithm with the cascade-style environment combination doesn't really work. The separate specular color is only available post-texture, and computing the two products and two sums using texture maps for M_d and M_s really requires a multiply-add function to compute a product and add the previous sum in a single texture unit. This functionality is available in vendor-specific extensions. However, using an additional texture map to compute the specular highlight (as described in Section 15.4) combined with a fragment program provides a straightforward solution. The first texture unit stores M_d and computes the first product using the result of vertex lighting. The alpha component of M_d also stores the gloss map (assuming it isn't needed for transparency). The second texture unit stores the specular environment map and the two products are computed and summed in the fragment program.

15.7.2 Emission Maps

Surfaces that contain holes, windows, or cracks that emit light can be modeled using emission maps. Emission maps are similar to the gloss maps described previously, but supply the emissive component of the lighting equation rather than the specular part. Since the emissive component is little more than a *pass-through* color, the algorithm for rendering an emission map is simple. The emission map is an RGBA texture; the RGB values represent the emissive color, whereas the alpha values indicate where the emissive color is present. The emissive component is accumulated in a separate drawing pass for the object using a replace environment function and GL_SRC_ALPHA and GL_ONE for the source and destination blend factors. The technique can easily be combined with the two-pass gloss map algorithm to render separate diffuse, specular, and emissive contributions.

15.8 Per-fragment Lighting Computations

Rather than relying entirely on texture mapping as a simple lookup table for supplying precomputed components of the lighting equation, we can also use multitexture environments and fragment programs to directly evaluate parts of the lighting model. OpenGL 1.3 adds the combine environment and the DOT3 combine function, along with cube mapping and multitexture. These form a powerful combination for computing per-fragment values useful in lighting equations, such as $\mathbf{N} \cdot \mathbf{L}$. Fragment programs provide the capability to perform multiple texture reads and arithmetic instructions enabling complex equations to be evaluated at each fragment. These instructions include trignometric, exponential, and logarithmic functions — virtually everything required for evaluating many lighting models.

One of the challenges in evaluating lighting at each fragment is computing the correct values for various vector quantities (for example, the light, half-angle, and normal vectors). Some vector quantities we can interpolate across the face of a polygon. We can use the cube mapping hardware to renormalize a vector (described in Section 15.11.1).

Sometimes it can be less expensive to perform the computation in a different coordinate system, transforming the input data into these coordinates. One example is performing computations in *tangent space*. A surface point can be defined by three perpendicular vectors: the surface normal, tangent, and binormal. The binormal and tangent vector form a plane that is tangent to the surface point. In tangent space, the surface normal is aligned with the z axis and allows a compact representation. Lighting computations are performed in tangent space by transforming (rotating) the view and light vectors. Transforming these vectors into tangent space during vertex processing can make the per-fragment lighting computations substantially simpler and improve performance. Tangent space computations and the transformation into tangent space are described in more detail in Section 15.10.2.

15.9 Other Lighting Models

Up to this point we have largely discussed the Blinn lighting model. The diffuse and specular terms for a single light are given by the following equation.

$$d_m d_l \mathbf{N} \cdot \mathbf{L} + s_m s_l (\mathbf{H} \cdot \mathbf{N})^n$$

Section 15.4 discusses the use of sphere mapping to replace the OpenGL per-vertex specular illumination computation with one performed per-pixel. The specular contribution in the texture map is computed using the Blinn formulation given previously. However, the Blinn model can be substituted with other bidirectional reflectance distribution functions to achieve other lighting effects. Since the texture coordinates are computed using an environment mapping function, the resulting texture mapping operation accurately approximates view-dependent (specular) reflectance distributions.

15.9.1 Fresnel Reflection

A useful enhancement to the lighting model is to add a *Fresnel* reflection term, F_λ (Hall, 1989), to the specular equation:

$$d_m d_l \mathbf{N} \cdot \mathbf{L} + F_\lambda s_m s_l (\mathbf{H} \cdot \mathbf{N})^n$$

The Fresnel term specifies the ratio of the amount of reflected light to the amount of transmitted (refracted) light. It is a function of the angle of incidence (θ_i), the relative index of refraction (n_λ) and the material properties of the object (dielectric, metal, and so on, as described in Section 3.3.3).

$$F_\lambda(\theta_i) = \frac{1(g-c)^2}{2(g+c)^2} \left(1 + \frac{(c(g+c)-1)^2}{(c(g-c)+1)^2} \right)$$

$$c = \cos\theta$$

$$g = \sqrt{n_\lambda^2 + c^2 - 1}$$

Here, θ is the angle between $\mathbf{V}$ and the halfway vector $\mathbf{H}$ ($\cos\theta = \mathbf{H}\cdot\mathbf{V}$). The effect of the Fresnel term is to attenuate light as a function of its incident and reflected directions as well as its wavelength. Dielectrics (such as glass) barely reflect light at normal incidence, but almost totally reflect it at glancing angles. This attenuation is independent of wavelength. The absorption of metals, on the other hand, can be a function of the wavelength. Copper and gold are good examples of metals that display this property. At glancing angles, the reflected light color is unaltered, but at normal incidence the light is modulated by the color of the metal.

Since the environment map serves as a table indexed by the reflection vector, the Fresnel effects can be included in the map by simply computing the specular equation with the Fresnel term to modulate and shift the color. This can be performed as a postprocessing step on an existing environment map by computing the Fresnel reflection coefficient at each angle of incidence and modulating the sphere or cube map. Environment mapping, reflection, and refraction and are discussed in more detail in Sections 5.4 and 17.1.

Alternatively, for direct implementation in a fragment program an approximating function can be evaluated in place of the exact Fresnel term. For example, Schlick proposes the function (Schlick, 1992)

$$F_\lambda(\theta) = C_\lambda + (1 - C_\lambda)(1 - \cos\theta)^5$$

where $C_\lambda = (n_1 - n_2)^2/(n_1 + n_2)^2$ and n_1 is the index of refraction of the medium the incident ray passes through (typically air) and n_2 the index of refraction of the material reflecting the light. Other proposed approximations are:

$$F_\lambda(\theta) = (1 - \cos\theta)^4$$

$$F_\lambda(\theta) = \frac{1}{(1 + \cos\theta)^7}$$

15.9.2 Gaussian Reflection

The Phong lighting equation, with its cosine raised to a power term for the specular component, is a poor fit to a physically accurate specular reflectance model. It's difficult to map measured physical lighting properties to its coefficient, and at low specularity it doesn't conserve incident and reflected energy. The Gaussian BRDF is a better model, and with some simplifications can be approximated by modifying parameters in the Phong model. The specular Phong term $K_s \cos(\theta)^{spec}$ is augmented by modifying the K_s and $spec$ parameters to a more complex and physically accurate form: $.0398(1.999\frac{1}{\alpha^2})K_s\cos(\theta)^{(1.999\frac{1}{\alpha^2})}$, where α is a material parameter. See Diefenbach (1997) or Ward (1992) for details on this equation's derivation, limits to its accuracy, and material properties modeled by the α parameter. This model can be implemented either using the specular environment mapping technique described in Section 15.4 or using a fragment program.

15.9.3 Anisotropic Lighting

Traditional lighting models approximate a surface as having microscopic facets that are uniformly distributed in any direction on the surface. This uniform distribution of facets serves to randomize the direction of reflected light, giving rise to the familiar isotropic lighting behavior.

Some surfaces have a directional grain, made from facets that are formed with a directional bias, like the grooves formed by sanding or machining. These surfaces demonstrate *anisotropic* lighting properties, which depend on the rotation of the surface around its normal. At normal distances, the viewer does not see the facets or grooves, but only the resulting lighting effect. Some everyday surfaces that have anisotropic lighting behavior are hair, satin Christmas tree ornaments, brushed alloy wheels, CDs, cymbals in a drum kit, and vinyl records.

Heidrich and Seidel (Heidrich 1998a) present a technique for rendering surfaces with anisotropic lighting, based on the scientific visualization work of Zöckler et al. (Zöckler, 1997). The technique uses 2D texturing to provide a lighting solution based on a "most significant" normal to a surface at a point.

The algorithm uses a surface model with infinitely thin fibers running across the surface. The tangent vector $\mathbf{T}$, defined at each vertex, can be thought of as the direction of a fiber. An infinitely thin fiber can be considered to have an infinite number of surface normals distributed in the plane perpendicular to $\mathbf{T}$, as shown in Figure 15.7. To evaluate the lighting model, one of these candidate normal vectors must be chosen for use in the lighting computation.

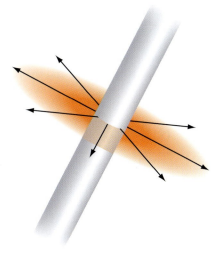

Figure 15.7 Normals to a fiber.

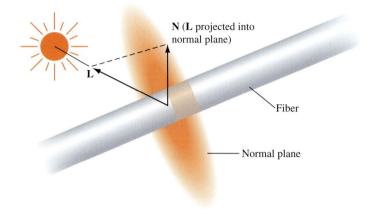

Figure 15.8 Projecting light vector to maximize lighting contribution.

As described in Stalling (1997), the normal vector that is coplanar to the tangent vector **T** and light vector **L** is chosen. This vector is the projection of the light vector onto the normal plane as shown in Figure 15.8.

The diffuse and specular lighting factors for a point based on the view vector **V**, normal **N**, light reflection vector $\mathbf{R}_l$, light direction **L**, and shininess exponent s are:

$$I_{diffuse} = \mathbf{N} \cdot \mathbf{L}$$

$$I_{specular} = (\mathbf{V} \cdot \mathbf{R}_l)^s$$

To avoid calculating **N** and $\mathbf{R}_l$, the following substitutions allow the lighting calculation at a point on a fiber to be evaluated with only **L**, **V**, and the fiber tangent **T** (anisotropic bias).

$$\mathbf{N} \cdot \mathbf{L} = \sqrt{1 - (\mathbf{L} \cdot \mathbf{T})^2}$$

$$\mathbf{V} \cdot \mathbf{R}_l = \sqrt{1 - (\mathbf{L} \cdot \mathbf{T})^2} * \sqrt{1 - (\mathbf{V} \cdot \mathbf{T})^2} - (\mathbf{L} \cdot \mathbf{T})(\mathbf{V} \cdot \mathbf{T})$$

If **V** and **L** are stored in the first two rows of a transformation matrix, and **T** is transformed by this matrix, the result is a vector containing **L** · **T** and **V** · **T**. After applying this transformation, **L** · **T** is computed as texture coordinate s and **V** · **T** is computed as t, as shown in Equation 15.1. A scale and bias must also be included in the matrix in order to bring the dot product range $[-1, 1]$ into the range $[0, 1]$. The resulting texture coordinates are used to index a texture storing the precomputed lighting equation.

$$\frac{1}{2} \begin{pmatrix} L_x & L_y & L_z & 1 \\ V_x & V_y & V_z & 1 \\ 0 & 0 & 0 & 0 \\ 0 & 0 & 0 & 2 \end{pmatrix} \begin{pmatrix} T_x \\ T_y \\ T_z \\ 1 \end{pmatrix} = \begin{pmatrix} \frac{1}{2}(\mathbf{L} \cdot \mathbf{T}) + 1 \\ \frac{1}{2}(\mathbf{V} \cdot \mathbf{T}) + 1 \\ 0 \\ 1 \end{pmatrix} \tag{15.1}$$

If the following simplifications are made — the viewing vector is constant (infinitely far away) and the light direction is constant — the results of this transformation can be used to index a 2D texture to evaluate the lighting equation based solely on providing $\mathbf{T}$ at each vertex.

The application will need to create a texture containing the results of the lighting equation (for example, the OpenGL model summarized in Appendix B.7). The s and t coordinates must be scaled and biased back to the range $[-1, 1]$, and evaluated in the previous equations to compute $\mathbf{N} \cdot \mathbf{L}$ and $\mathbf{V} \cdot \mathbf{R}_l$.

A transformation pipeline typically transforms surface normals into eye space by premultiplying by the inverse transpose of the viewing matrix. If the tangent vector ($\mathbf{T}$) is defined in model space, it is necessary to query or precompute the current modeling transformation and concatenate the inverse transpose of that transformation with the transformation matrix in equation 15.1.

The transformation is stored in the texture matrix and $\mathbf{T}$ is issued as a per-vertex texture coordinate. Unfortunately, there is no normalization step in the OpenGL texture coordinate generation system. Therefore, if the modeling matrix is concatenated as mentioned previously, the texture coordinates representing vectors may be transformed so that they are no longer unit length. To avoid this, the coordinates must be transformed and normalized by the application before transmission.

Since the anisotropic lighting approximation given does not take the self-occluding effect of the parts of the surface facing away from the light, the texture color needs to be modulated with the color from a saturated per-vertex directional light. This clamps the lighting contributions to zero on parts of the surface facing away from the illumination source.

This technique uses per-vertex texture coordinates to encode the anisotropic direction, so it also suffers from the same sampling-related per-vertex lighting artifacts found in the isotropic lighting model. If a local lighting or viewing model is desired, the application must calculate $\mathbf{L}$ or $\mathbf{V}$, compute the entire anisotropic lighting contribution, and apply it as a vertex color.

Because a single texture provides all the lighting components up front, changing any of the colors used in the lighting model requires recalculating the texture. If two textures are used, either in a system with multiple texture units or with multipass, the diffuse and specular components may be separated and stored in two textures. Either texture may be modulated by the material or vertex color to alter the diffuse or specular base color separately without altering the maps. This can be used, for example, in a database containing a precomputed radiosity solution stored in the per-vertex color. In this way, the diffuse color can still depend on the orientation of the viewpoint relative to the tangent vector but only changes within the maximum color calculated by the radiosity solution.

15.9.4 Oren-Nayar Model

The Lambertian diffuse model assumes that light reflected from a rough surface is dependent only on the surface normal and light direction, and therefore a Lambertian surface is equally bright in all directions. This model conflicts with the observed behavior for diffuse surfaces such as the moon. In nature, as surface roughness increases the object appears flatter; the Lambertian model doesn't capture this characteristic.

In 1994, Oren and Nayar (Oren, 1994) derived a physically-based model and validated it by comparing the results of computations with measurements on real objects. In this model, a diffuse surface is modeled as a collection of "V-cavities" as proposed by Torrance and Sparrow (Torrance, 1976). These cavities consist of two long, narrow planar facets where each facet is modeled as a Lambertian reflector. Figure 15.9 illustrates a cross-section of a surface modeled as V-cavities. The collection of cavity facets exhibit complex interactions, including interreflection, masking of reflected light, and shadowing of other facets, as shown in Figure 15.10.

The projected radiance for a single facet incorporating the effects of masking and shadowing can be described using the geometrical attenuation factor (GAF). This factor

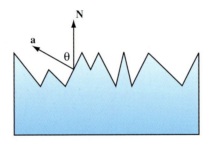

Figure 15.9 Surface modeled as a collection of V-cavities.

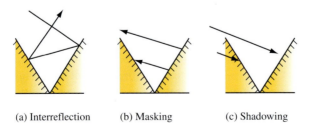

    (a) Interreflection   (b) Masking   (c) Shadowing

Figure 15.10 Interreflection, masking, and shadowing.

is a function of the surface normal, light direction, and the facet normal (**a**), given by the formula

$$GAF = \min \left[1, \max \left[0, \frac{2(\mathbf{N} \cdot \mathbf{a})(\mathbf{N} \cdot \mathbf{V})}{(\mathbf{V} \cdot \mathbf{a})}, \frac{2(\mathbf{N} \cdot \mathbf{a})(\mathbf{N} \cdot \mathbf{L})}{(\mathbf{V} \cdot \mathbf{a})} \right] \right]$$

In addition, the model includes an interreflection factor (IF), modeling up to two bounces of light rays. This factor is approximated using the assumption that the cavity length l is much larger than the cavity width w, treating the cavity as a one-dimensional shape. The interreflection component is computed by integrating over the cross section of the one-dimensional shape. The limits of the integral are determined by the masking and shadowing of two facets: one facet that is visible to the viewer with width m_v and a second adjacent facet that is illuminated by the interreflection, with width m_s. The solution for the resulting integral is

$$\frac{\pi}{2} \left[d(1, \frac{m_v}{w}) + d(1, \frac{m_s}{w}) - d(\frac{m_s}{w}, \frac{m_v}{w}) - d(1, 1) \right],$$

$$\text{where } d(x, y) = \sqrt{x^2 + 2xy \cos(2\theta_a) + y^2}$$

To compute the reflection for the entire surface, the projected radiance from both shadowing/masking and interreflection is integrated across the surface. The surface is assumed to comprise a distribution of facets with different slopes to produce a slope-area distribution D. If the surface roughness is isotropic, the distribution can be described with a single elevation parameter θ_a, since the azimuth orientation of the facets ϕ_a is uniformly distributed. Oren and Nayar propose a Gaussian function with zero mean $\mu = 0$ and variance σ for the isotropic distribution, $D(\theta_a, \mu, \sigma) = Ce^{-\theta_a^2/2\sigma^2}$. The surface roughness is then described by the variance of the distribution. The integral itself is complex to evaluate, so instead an approximating function is used. In the process of analyzing the contributions from the components of the functional approximation, Oren and Nayar discovered that the contributions from the interreflection term are less significant than the shadowing and masking term. This leads to a qualitative model that matches the overall model and is cheaper to evaluate. The equation for the qualitative model is

$$L(\theta_r, \theta_i, \phi_r - \phi_i; \sigma) = \frac{\rho}{\pi} E_0 \cos\theta_i (A + B \max[0, \cos(\phi_r - \phi_i)] \sin\alpha \tan\beta)$$

$$A = 1.0 - 0.5 \frac{\sigma^2}{\sigma^2 + 0.33}$$

$$B = 0.45 \frac{\sigma^2}{\sigma^2 + 0.09}$$

$$\alpha = \max(\theta_r, \theta_i)$$

$$\beta = \min(\theta_r, \theta_i)$$

where θ_r and θ_i are the angles of reflection and incidence relative to the surface normal (the viewer and light angles) and ϕ_r and ϕ_i are the corresponding reflection and incidence angles tangent to the surface normal. Note that as the surface roughness σ approaches zero the model reduces to the Lambertian model.

There are several approaches to implementing the Oren-Nayer model using the OpenGL pipeline. One method is to use an environment map that stores the precomputed equation $L(\theta_r, \theta_i, \phi_r - \phi_i; \sigma)$, where the surface roughness σ and light and view directions are fixed. This method is similar to that described in Section 15.4 for specular lighting using an environment map. Using automatic texture coordinate generation, the reflection vector is used to index the corresponding part of the texture map. This technique, though limited by the fixed view and light directions, works well for a fixed-function OpenGL pipeline.

If a programmable pipeline is supported, the qualitative model can be evaluated directly using vertex and fragment programs. The equation can be decomposed into two pieces: the traditional Lambertian term $\cos \theta_i$ and the attenuation term $A + B \max[0, \cos(\phi_r - \phi_i)] \sin \alpha \tan \beta$. To compute the attentuation term, the light and view vectors are transformed to tangent space and interpolated across the face of the polygon and renormalized. The normal vector is retrieved from a tangent-space normal map. The values A and B are constant, and the term $\cos(\phi_r - \phi_i)$ is computed by projecting the view and light vectors onto the tangent plane of $\mathbf{N}$, renormalizing, and computing the dot product

$$\mathbf{V}_{prj} = \mathbf{V} - \mathbf{N}(\mathbf{N} \cdot \mathbf{V})$$

$$\mathbf{L}_{prj} = \mathbf{L} - \mathbf{N}(\mathbf{N} \cdot \mathbf{L})$$

$$\cos(\phi_r - \phi_i) = \frac{\mathbf{V}_{prj}}{||\mathbf{V}_{prj}||} \cdot \frac{\mathbf{L}_{prj}}{||\mathbf{L}_{prj}||}$$

Similarly, the product of the values α and β is computed using a texture map to implement a 2D lookup table $F(x, y) = \sin(x) \tan(y)$. The values of $\cos \theta_i$ and $\cos \theta_r$ are computed by projecting the light and view vectors onto the normal vector,

$$\cos \theta_i = \mathbf{N} \cdot \mathbf{L}$$

$$\cos \theta_r = \mathbf{N} \cdot \mathbf{V}$$

and these values are used in the lookup table rather than θ_i and θ_r.

15.9.5 Cook-Torrance Model

The Cook-Torrance model (Cook, 1981) is based on a specular reflection model by Torrance and Sparrow (Torrance, 1976). It is a physically based model that can be used to simulate metal and plastic surfaces. The model accurately predicts the directional distribution and spectral composition of the reflected light using measurements that capture spectral energy distribution for a material and incident light. Similar to the Oren-Nayar model, the Cook-Torrance model incorporates the following features.

- Microfacet distribution

- Geometric attenuation factor for micro-facet masking and self-shadowing

- Fresnel reflection with color shift

The model uses the Beckmann facet slope distribution (surface roughness) function (Beckmann, 1963), given by

$$D_{Beckmann} = \frac{1}{\pi^2 \cos^4 \alpha} \, e^{\frac{\tan^2 \alpha}{m^2}}$$

where m is a measure of the mean facet slope. Small values of m approximate a smooth surface with gentle facet slopes and larger values of m a rougher surface with steeper slopes. α is the angle between the normal and halfway vector ($\cos \alpha = \mathbf{N} \cdot \mathbf{H}$). The equation for the entire model is

$$L = \frac{F_\lambda}{\pi} \frac{D_{Beckmann}}{\mathbf{N} \cdot \mathbf{L}} \frac{GAF}{\mathbf{N} \cdot \mathbf{V}}$$

To evaluate this model, we can use the Fresnel equations from Section 15.9.1 and the GAF equation described for the Oren-Nayar model in Section 15.9.4. This model can be applied using a precomputed environment map, or it can be evaluated directly using a fragment program operating in tangent space with a detailed normal map. To implement it in a fragment program, we can use one of the Fresnel approximations from Section 15.9.1, at the cost of losing the color shift. The Beckmann distribution function can be approximated using a texture map as a lookup table, or the function can be evaluated directly using the trigonometric identity

$$\tan^2 \alpha = \frac{1 - \cos^2 \alpha}{\cos^2 \alpha} = \frac{1 - (\mathbf{N} \cdot \mathbf{H})^2}{\mathbf{N} \cdot \mathbf{H}}$$

The resulting specular term can be combined with a tradition diffuse term or the value computed using the Oren-Nayar model. Figure 15.11 illustrates objects illuminated with the Oren-Nayar and Cook-Torrance illumination models.

15.10 Bump Mapping with Textures

Bump mapping (Blinn, 1978), like texture mapping, is a technique to add more realism to synthetic images without adding of geometry. Texture mapping adds realism by attaching images to geometric surfaces. Bump mapping adds per-pixel surface relief

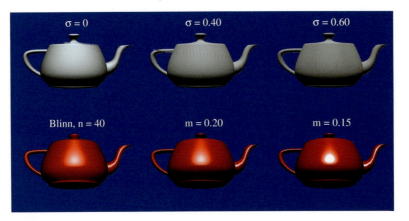

Figure 15.11 Oren-Nayar and Cook-Torrance reflection models.

shading, increasing the apparent complexity of the surface by perturbing the surface normal. Surfaces that have a patterned roughness are good candidates for bump mapping. Examples include oranges, strawberries, stucco, and wood.

An intuitive representation of surface bumpiness is formed by a 2D height field array, or *bump map*. This bump map is defined by the scalar difference $F(u, v)$ between the flat surface $P(u, v)$ and the desired bumpy surface $P'(u, v)$ in the direction of normal **N** at each point u, v. Typically, the function P is modeled separately as polygons or parametric patches and F is modeled as a 2D image using a paint program or other image editing tool.

Rather than subdivide the surface $P'(u, v)$ into regions that are locally flat, we note that the shading perturbations on such a surface depend more on perturbations in the surface normal than on the position of the surface itself. A technique perturbing only the surface normal at shading time achieves similar results without the processing burden of subdividing geometry. (Note that this technique does not perturb shadows from other surfaces falling on the bumps or shadows from bumps on the same surface, so such shadows will retain their flat appearance.)

The normal vector $\mathbf{N}'$ at u, v can be calculated by the cross product of the partial derivatives of P' in u and v. (The notational simplification $\mathbf{P}'_\mathbf{u}$ is used here to mean the partial derivative of P' with respect to u, sometimes written $\frac{\partial P'}{\partial u}$). The chain rule can be applied to the partial derivatives to yield the following expression of $\mathbf{P}'_\mathbf{u}$ and $\mathbf{P}'_\mathbf{v}$ in terms of P, F, and derivatives of F.

$$\mathbf{P}'_\mathbf{u} = \mathbf{P}_\mathbf{u} + F_u \frac{\mathbf{N}}{||\mathbf{N}||} + F \frac{\partial \frac{\mathbf{N}}{||\mathbf{N}||}}{\partial u}$$

$$\mathbf{P}'_v = \mathbf{P_v} + F_v \frac{\mathbf{N}}{||\mathbf{N}||} + F\frac{\partial \frac{\mathbf{N}}{||\mathbf{N}||}}{\partial v}$$

If F is assumed to be sufficiently small, the final terms of each of the previous expressions can be approximated by zero:

$$\mathbf{P}'_u \approx \mathbf{P_u} + F_u \frac{\mathbf{N}}{||\mathbf{N}||}$$

$$\mathbf{P}'_v \approx \mathbf{P_v} + F_v \frac{\mathbf{N}}{||\mathbf{N}||}$$

Expanding the cross product $\mathbf{P}'_u \times \mathbf{P}'_v$ gives the following expression for $\mathbf{N}'$.

$$\mathbf{N}' = (\mathbf{P_u} + F_u \frac{\mathbf{N}}{||\mathbf{N}||}) \times (\mathbf{P_v} + F_v \frac{\mathbf{N}}{||\mathbf{N}||})$$

This evaluates to

$$\mathbf{N}' = \mathbf{P_u} \times \mathbf{P_v} + \frac{F_u(\mathbf{N} \times \mathbf{P_v})}{||\mathbf{N}||} + \frac{F_v(\mathbf{P_u} \times \mathbf{N})}{||\mathbf{N}||} + \frac{F_u F_v(\mathbf{N} \times \mathbf{N})}{||\mathbf{N}||^2}$$

Since $\mathbf{P_u} \times \mathbf{P_v}$ yields the normal $\mathbf{N}$, $\mathbf{N} \times \mathbf{N}$ yields 0, and $\mathbf{A} \times \mathbf{B} = -(\mathbf{B} \times \mathbf{A})$, we can further simplify the expression for $\mathbf{N}'$ to:

$$\mathbf{N}' = \mathbf{N} + \frac{F_u(\mathbf{N} \times \mathbf{P_v})}{||\mathbf{N}||} - \frac{F_v(\mathbf{N} \times \mathbf{P_u})}{||\mathbf{N}||}$$

The values F_u and F_v are easily computed through forward differencing from the 2D bump map, and $\mathbf{P_u}$ and $\mathbf{P_v}$ can be computed either directly from the surface definition or from forward differencing applied to the surface parameterization.

15.10.1 Approximating Bump Mapping Using Texture

Bump mapping can be implemented in a number of ways. Using the programmable pipeline or even with the DOT3 texture environment function it becomes substantially simpler than without these features. We will describe a method that requires the least capable hardware (Airey, 1997; Peercy, 1997). This multipass algorithm is an extension and refinement of texture embossing (Schlag, 1994). It is relatively straightforward to modify this technique for OpenGL implementations with more capabilities.

15.10.2 Tangent Space

Recall that the bump map normal $\mathbf{N}'$ is formed by $\mathbf{Pu} \times \mathbf{Pv}$. Assume that the surface point P is coincident with the x-y plane and that changes in u and v correspond to changes in x and y, respectively. Then F can be substituted for P', resulting in the following expression for the vector $\mathbf{N}'$.

$$\mathbf{N}' = \begin{pmatrix} -\dfrac{\partial F}{\partial u} \\ -\dfrac{\partial F}{\partial v} \\ 1 \end{pmatrix}$$

To evaluate the lighting equation, $\mathbf{N}'$ must be normalized. If the displacements in the bump map are restricted to small values, however, the length of $\mathbf{N}'$ will be so close to one as to be approximated by one. Then $\mathbf{N}'$ itself can be substituted for $\mathbf{N}$ without normalization. If the diffuse intensity component $\mathbf{N} \cdot \mathbf{L}$ of the lighting equation is evaluated with the value presented previously for $\mathbf{N}'$, the result is the following.

$$\mathbf{N}' \cdot \mathbf{L} = -\frac{\partial F}{\partial u} L_x - \frac{\partial F}{\partial v} L_y + L_z \tag{15.2}$$

This expression requires the surface to lie in the x-y plane and that the u and v parameters change in x and y, respectively. Most surfaces, however, will have arbitrary locations and orientations in space. To use this simplification to perform bump mapping, the view direction $\mathbf{V}$ and light source direction $\mathbf{L}$ are transformed into *tangent space*.

Tangent space has three axes: $\mathbf{T}$, $\mathbf{B}$ and $\mathbf{N}$. The tangent vector, $\mathbf{T}$, is parallel to the direction of increasing texture coordinate s on the surface. The normal vector, $\mathbf{N}$, is perpendicular to the surface. The binormal, $\mathbf{B}$, is perpendicular to both $\mathbf{N}$ and $\mathbf{T}$, and like $\mathbf{T}$ lies in the plane tangent to the surface. These vectors form a coordinate system that is attached to and varies over the surface.

The light source is transformed into tangent space at each vertex of the polygon (see Figure 15.12). To find the tangent space vectors at a vertex, use the vertex normal for $\mathbf{N}$ and find the tangent axis $\mathbf{T}$ by finding the vector direction of increasing s in the object's coordinate system. The direction of increasing t may also be used. Find $\mathbf{B}$ by computing the cross product of $\mathbf{N}$ and $\mathbf{T}$. These unit vectors form the following transformation.

$$\begin{pmatrix} x' \\ y' \\ z' \\ w' \end{pmatrix} = \begin{pmatrix} T_x & T_y & T_z & -V_x \\ B_x & B_y & B_z & -V_y \\ N_x & N_y & N_z & -V_z \\ 0 & 0 & 0 & 1 \end{pmatrix} \begin{pmatrix} x \\ y \\ z \\ w \end{pmatrix} \tag{15.3}$$

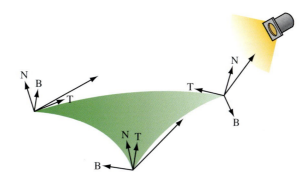

Figure 15.12 Tangent space defined at polygon vertices.

This transformation brings coordinates into tangent space, where the plane tangent to the surface lies in the *x-y* plane and the normal to the surface coincides with the *z* axis. Note that the tangent space transformation varies for vertices representing a curved surface, and so this technique makes the approximation that curved surfaces are flat and the tangent space transformation is interpolated from vertex to vertex.

15.10.3 Forward Differencing

The first derivative of the height values of the bump map in a given direction s', t' can be approximated by the following process (see Figure 15.13 1(a) to 1(c)):

1. Render the bump map texture.

2. Shift the texture coordinates at the vertices by s', t'.

3. Rerender the bump map texture, subtracting from the first image.

Consider a 1D bump map for simplicity. The map only varies as a function of *s*. Assuming that the height values of the bump map can be represented as a height function $F(s)$, then the three-step process computes the following: $F(s) - F(s + \Delta s)/\Delta s$. If the delta is one texel in *s*, then the resulting texture coordinate is $F(s) - F(s + \frac{1}{w})$, where *w* is the width of the texture in texels (see Figure 15.14). This operation implements a forward difference of *F*, approximating the first derivative of *F* if *F* is continuous.

In the 2D case, the height function is $F(s, t)$, and performing the forward difference in the directions of s' and t' evaluates the derivative of $F(s, t)$ in the directions s' and t'. This technique is also used to create embossed images.

This operation provides the values used for the first two addends shown in Equation 15.2. In order to provide the third addend of the dot product, the process needs to compute and add the transformed *z* component of the light vector. The tangent space transform in Equation 15.3 implies that the transformed *z* component of $\mathbf{L'}$ is simply the inner product of the vertex normal and the light vector, $L'_z = \mathbf{N} \cdot \mathbf{L}$.

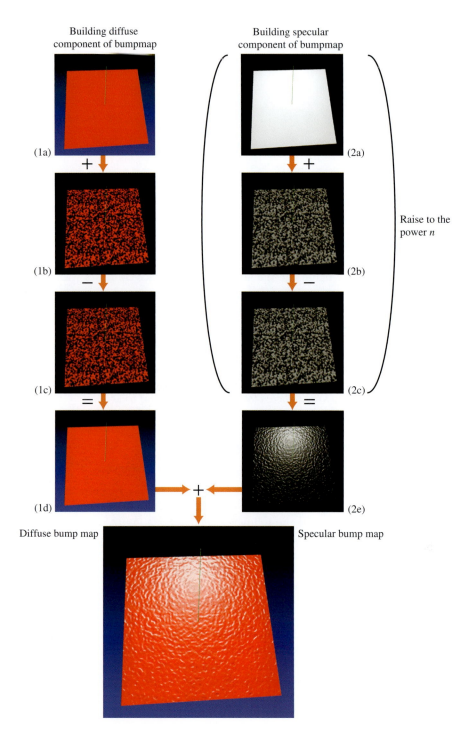

Figure 15.13 Bump mapping: shift and subtract image.

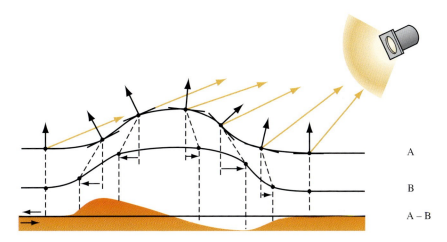

Figure 15.14 Shifting a bump map to perform forward differencing.

Therefore, the z component can be computed using OpenGL to evaluate the diffuse lighting term at each vertex. This computation is performed as a second pass, adding to the previous results. The steps for diffuse bump mapping are summarized:

1. Render the polygon with the bump map texture, modulating the polygon color. The polygon color is set to the diffuse reflectance of the surface. Lighting is disabled.

2. Find **N**, **T**, and **B** at each vertex.

3. Use the vectors to create a transformation.

4. Use the matrix to rotate the light vector **L** into tangent space.

5. Use the rotated x and y components of **L** to shift the s and t texture coordinates at each polygon vertex.

6. Rerender the bump map textured polygon using the shifted texture coordinates.

7. Subtract the second image from the first.

8. Render the polygon with smooth shading, with lighting enabled, and texturing disabled.

9. Add this image to the result.

Using the accumulation buffer can provide reasonable accuracy. The bump-mapped objects in the scene are rendered with the bump map, rerendered with the shifted bump map, and accumulated with a negative weight (to perform the subtraction). They are then rerendered using Gouraud shading and no bump map texture, and accumulated normally.

The process can also be extended to find bump-mapped specular highlights. The process is repeated using the halfway vector (**H**) instead of the light vector. The halfway vector is computed by averaging the light and viewer vectors $\frac{L+V}{2}$. The combination of the forward difference of the bump map in the direction of the tangent space **H** and the z component of **H** approximate **N** · **H**. The steps for computing **N** · **H** are as follows.

1. Render the polygon with the bump map textured on it.

2. Find **N**, **T**, and **B** at each vertex.

3. Use the vectors to create a rotation matrix.

4. Use the matrix to rotate the halfway vector **H** into tangent space.

5. Use the rotated x and y components of **H** to shift the s and t texture coordinates at each polygon vertex.

6. Rerender the bump-map-textured polygon using the shifted texture coordinates.

7. Subtract the second image from the first.

8. Render the polygon Gouraud shaded with no bump map texture. This time use **H** instead of **L** as the light direction. Set the polygon color to the specular light color.

The resulting **N**·**H** must be raised to the shininess exponent. One technique for performing this exponential is to use a color table or pixel map to implement a table lookup of $f(x) = x^n$. The color buffer is copied onto itself with the color table enabled to perform the lookup. If the object is to be merged with other objects in the scene, a stencil mask can be created to ensure that only pixels corresponding to the bump-mapped object update the color buffer (Section 9.2). If the specular contribution is computed first, the diffuse component can be computed in place in a subsequent series of passes. The reverse is not true, since the specular power function must be evaluated on **N** · **H** by itself.

Blending

If the OpenGL implementation doesn't accelerate accumulation buffer operations, its performance may be very poor. In this case, acceptable results may be obtainable using framebuffer blending. The subtraction step can produce intermediate results with negative values. To avoid clamping to the normal [0, 1] range, the bump map values are scaled and biased to support an effective [−1, 1] range (Section 3.4.1). After completion, of the third pass, the values are converted back to their original 0 to 1 range. This scaling and biasing, combined with fewer bits of color precision, make this method inferior to using the accumulation buffer.

Bumps on Surfaces Facing Away from the Light

Because this algorithm doesn't take self-occlusion into account, the forward differencing calculation will produce "lights" on the surface even when no light is falling on the surface. Use the result of $\mathbf{L} \cdot \mathbf{N}$ to scale the shift so that the bump effect tapers off slowly as the surface becomes more oblique to the light direction. Empirically, adding a small bias (.3 in the authors' experiments) to the dot product (and clamping the result) is more visibly pleasing because the bumps appear to taper off *after* the surface has started facing away from the light, as would actually happen for a displaced surface.

15.10.4 Limitations

Although this technique does closely approximate bump mapping, there are limitations that impact its accuracy.

Bump Map Sampling

The bump map height function is not continuous, but is sampled into the texture. The resolution of the texture affects how faithfully the bump map is represented. Increasing the size of the bump map texture can improve the sampling of high-frequency height components.

Texture Resolution

The shifting and subtraction steps produce the directional derivative. Since this is a forward differencing technique, the highest frequency component of the bump map increases as the shift is made smaller. As the shift is made smaller, more demands are made of the texture coordinate precision. The shift can become smaller than the texture filtering implementation can handle, leading to noise and aliasing effects. A good starting point is to size the shift components so that their vector magnitude is a single texel.

Surface Curvature

The tangent coordinate axes are different at each point on a curved surface. This technique approximates this by finding the tangent space transforms at each vertex. Texture mapping interpolates the different shift values from each vertex across the polygon. For polygons with very different vertex normals, this approximation can break down. A solution would be to subdivide the polygons until their vertex normals are parallel to within an error limit.

Maximum Bump Map Slope

The bump map normals used in this technique are good approximations if the bump map slope is small. If there are steep tangents in the bump map, the assumption that the perturbed normal is length one becomes inaccurate, and the highlights appear too bright. This can be corrected by normalizing in fourth pass, using a modulating texture derived from the original bump map. Each value of the texel is one over the length of the perturbed normal: $1/\sqrt{\frac{\partial f}{\partial u}^2 + \frac{\partial f}{\partial v}^2 + 1}$.

15.11 Normal Maps

Normal maps are texture maps that store a per-pixel normal vector in each texel. The components of the normal vector are stored in the R, G, and B color components. The normal vectors are in the *tangent space* of the object (see Section 15.10.2). Relief shading, similar to bump mapping, can be performed by computing the dot product $N \cdot L$ using the texture combine environment function. Since the computation happens in the texture environment stage, the colors components are fixed point numbers in the range [0, 1]. To support computations of inputs negative components, the dot product combine operation assumes that the color components store values that are scaled and biased to represent the range [−1, 1]. The dot product computation is

$$4\left((C_R - 0.5)(T_R - 0.5) + (C_G - 0.5)(T_G - 0.5) + (C_B - 0.5)(T_B - 0.5)\right),$$

producing a result that is *not* scaled and biased. If the dot product is negative, the regular [0, 1] clamping sets the result to 0, so the dot product is $N \cdot L$ rather than $N \cdot L$.

To use normal maps to perform relief shading, first a tangent-space biased normal map is created. To compute the product $N \cdot L$, the tangent space light vector L is sent to the pipeline as a vertex color, using a biased representation. Since interpolating the color components between vertices will not produce correctly interpolated vectors, flat shading is used. This forces the tangent-space light vector to be constant across the face of each primitive. The texture environment uses GL_COMBINE for the texture environment function and GL_DOT3_RGB for the RGB combine operation. If multiple texture units are available, the resulting diffuse intensity can be used to modulate the surface's diffuse reflectance stored in a successive texture unit. If there isn't a texture unit available, a two-pass method can be used. The first pass renders the object with diffuse reflectance applied. The second pass renders the object with the normal map using framebuffer blending to modulate the stored diffuse reflectance with the computed diffuse light intensity.

If programmable pipeline support is available, using normal maps becomes simple. Direct diffuse and specular lighting model computations are readily implemented inside a fragment program. It also provides an opportunity to enhance the technique by adding parallax to the scene using *offset mapping* (also called parallax mapping) (Welsh, 2004). This adds a small shift to the texture coordinates used to look up the diffuse surface color, normal map, or other textures. The offset is in the direction of the viewer and is scaled and biased by the height of the bump, using a scale and bias of approximately 0.04 and 0.02.

15.11.1 Vector Normalization

For a curved surface, the use of a constant light vector across the face of each primitive introduces visible artifacts at polygon boundaries. To allow per-vertex tangent-space light vector to be correctly interpolated, a cube map can be used with a second texture unit. The light vector is issued as a set of (s, t, r) texture coordinates and the cube map stores the normalized light vectors. Vectors of the same direction index the same location in the texture map. The faces of the cube map are precomputed by sequencing the two texture coordinates for the face through the integer coordinates $[0, M-1]$ (where M is the texture size) and computing the normalized direction. For example, for the positive X face at each y, z pair,

$$\mathbf{F} = \left(\frac{M}{2}, \frac{M}{2} - y, \frac{M}{2} - z \right)^T$$

$$\mathbf{N} = \frac{\mathbf{F}}{||\mathbf{F}||}$$

and the components of the normalized vector $\mathbf{N}$ are scaled and biased to the $[0, 1]$ texel range. For most applications 16×16 or 32×32 cube map faces provide sufficient accuracy.

An alternative to a table lookup cube map for normalizing a vector is to directly compute the normalized value using a truncated Taylor series approximation. For example, the Taylor series expansion for $\mathbf{N}' = \mathbf{N}/||\mathbf{N}||$ is

$$\mathbf{N}' = \mathbf{N}(1 - \frac{1}{2}(\mathbf{N} \cdot \mathbf{N} - 1) + \frac{3}{8}(\mathbf{N} \cdot \mathbf{N} - 1)^2 - \frac{5}{16}(\mathbf{N} \cdot \mathbf{N} - 1)^3 + \cdots)$$

$$\approx \mathbf{N} + \frac{\mathbf{N}}{2}(1 - \mathbf{N} \cdot \mathbf{N})$$

which can be efficiently implemented using the combine environment function with two texture units if the `GL_DOT3_RGB` function is supported. This approximation works best when interpolating between unit length vectors and the deviation between the two vectors is less than 45 degrees. If the programmable pipeline is supported by the OpenGL implementation, normalization operations can be computed directly with program instructions.

15.12 Bump-mapped Reflections

Bump mapping can be combined with environment mapping to provide visually interesting *perturbed reflections*. If the bump map is stored as displacements to the normal ($\frac{\partial F}{\partial u}$ and $\frac{\partial F}{\partial u}$) rather than a height field, the displacements can be used as offsets added to the texture coordinates used in a second texture. This second texture represents the lighting environment, and can be the environment-mapped approximation to Phong lighting discussed in Section 15.4 or an environment map approximating reflections from the surface (as discussed in Section 17.3.4).

The displacements in the "bump map" are related to the displacements to the normal used in bump mapping. The straightforward extension is to compute the reflection vector from displaced normals and use this reflection vector to index the environment map. To simplify hardware design, however, the displaced environment map coordinates are approximated by applying the bump map displacements *after* the environment map coordinates are computed for the vertex normals. With sphere mapping, the error introduced by this approximation is small at the center of the sphere map, but increases as the mapped normal approaches the edge of the sphere map. Images created with this technique look surprisingly realistic despite the crudeness of the approximation. This feature is available through at least one vendor-specific extension `ATI_envmap_bumpmap`.

15.13 High Dynamic Range Lighting

In Section 12.9 we introduced the idea of high dynamic range images (HDR images). These images are capable of storing data over a much larger range than a typical 8-bit per-component color buffer. The section also describes the process of tone mapping, which maps the components of an HDR image to the component resolutions of a typical display device. A natural outgrowth of being able to capture and store an HDR image is to generate scenes with HDR lighting. This facilitates the implementation of physically based rendering using spectral radiance for real Illumination sources. Alternatively, HDR scenes can also be rendered using image-based lighting derived from HDR images (Debevec, 2002).

The simplest way to implement HDR image-based lighting is to capture the environment as an HDR environment map, called a radiance map. Sphere map environment maps of HDR data are termed *light probes* and can be captured with a fish-eye lens or by photographing a chrome ball from a distance, just like a sphere environment map. Special processing is required to recover the HDR values; it is described in detail by Paul Debevec in (Debevec, 1997) and (Debevec, 2002). Lighting a scene with the HDR environment is similar to other environment mapping techniques; the system must be capable of processing HDR color values, however, so fragment programs and HDR texture image formats and color buffers are required. The end result is an HDR image that must be tone mapped to map the HDR pixel values to a displayable range, as described in Section 12.9.2.

15.13.1 Bloom and Glare Effects

The human visual system response to high-luminance sources results in several visible effects, including *glare*, *lenticular halos*, and *bloom* (Spencer, 1995). Some of these effects can be simulated as part of an HDR rendered scene. They are performed as a postprocess on the HDR rendered scene, called a "bright pass."

The first step uses the tone-mapping operator to segment the scene into bright and dim parts. To extract the bright part of the scene, the curve-based tone mapping operator from Section 12.9.2 is modified and applied in pieces. First, the log-average luminance is computed and colors are scaled by the a/L_{avg}, and then the dim pixels are subtracted away using a threshold value of 5, clamping the result to zero. Finally, the remaining "bright" values are scaled by $1/(10 + L_{scale}(x, y))$ to isolate the light sources. The values of 5 and 10 are empirically chosen, with 5 representing the threshold luminance for dark areas and the offset value 10 defining the degree of separation between light and dark areas. Once the bright image is computed, it is blurred using a Gaussian or other filter and the result is added to the tone-mapped scene.

The bright image can be used for other glare or halo effects by locating the positions of the light source and sampling specific patterns (circles, crosses, and so on) and smearing them along the pattern. The result is added back to the orginal scene.

15.14 Global Illumination

The lighting models described thus far have been growing progressively more sophisticated. However, capturing the effects of complex interreflections, area light sources, and so on is increasingly difficult using individual light sources. Environment maps capture some of the information in a more complex environment, but the subtleties of real lighting are often better captured using a global illumination model. Global illumination models using radiosity or ray tracing are generally too computationally complex to perform in real time. However, if the objects and light sources comprising the environment are static, it is possible to perform the global illumination calculations as a preprocessing step and then display the results interactively. Such an approach is both practical and useful for applications such as architectural walkthroughs. The technique is typically employed for diffuse illumination solutions since view-independent (ideal) diffuse illumination can be represented as a single value (color) at each object vertex.

Many of the techniques for the display of precomputed global illumination parameterize the radiance transfer with a set of basis functions such as wavelets or spherical harmonics. This allows the lighting contribution to be factored out, so that at display time a dynamic lighting environment projected onto the same basis can be used to light the scene efficiently. This computation is usually with an N dimensional dot product, where $N \leq$ the number of basis functions used to parameterize the solution. Details for these techniques are beyond the scope of this book, but we will outline some methods that do not require an extended mathematical discussion.

15.14.1 Virtual Light Technique

Walter et al. (Walter, 1997) describe a method for rendering global illumination solutions that contain view-independent directionally variant lighting effects. The specular term in the OpenGL lighting model is used to approximate the directionally varying lighting information, and the emissive term is used to approximate the directionally invariant illumination (diffuse illumination). In this method, a set of OpenGL lights is treated as a set of basis functions that are summed together, whereas the object is rendered to yield a more general directional distribution. The OpenGL light parameters, such as position or intensity coefficients, have no relationship to the light sources in the original model, but instead serve as a compact representation for the directional illumination of an object. Each rendered object has its own set of lights, called *virtual lights*.

The method works on a global illumination solution, which stores a number of samples of the directionally varying illumination at each object vertex. The parameters for the virtual lights of a particular object are determined using a fitting procedure consisting of a number of heuristics. The main idea is to produce a set of solutions for a number of specular exponent values and then choose the exponent value that minimizes the mean-squared error using a least squares method. A solution at a given exponent value is determined as follows.

1. Choose a specular exponent value.

2. Find the vertex on the object with the largest directional radiance.

3. Choose a light direction to align the specular lobe with this brightest direction.

4. Choose an intensity coefficient to match the radiance at the point on the object.

5. Compute the specular contribution at other points on the object and subtract from the radiance.

6. Repeat steps 2 through 5 using updated object radiance until all lights have been used.

7. At each vertex, compute the specular and emission coefficients using a least squares fit.

Once the lighting parameters have been determined, the model is rendered using the glLight and glMaterial commands to set the directional light parameters and specular exponent for each object. The glMaterial command is used to set the specular reflectance and emitted intensity at each vertex. The rendering speed for the model is limited by its geometric complexity and of the OpenGL implementation's ability to deal with multiple light sources and material changes at each vertex. Rendering performance may be improved by rendering in multiple passes to limit the number of active lights or the number of material parameter changes in each pass. For example, use glColorMaterial and glColor to change only the emitted intensity or specular reflectance in each pass and framebuffer blending can then be used to sum the results together.

15.14.2 Combining OpenGL Lighting with Radiosity

Radiosity solutions produce accurate global illumination solutions for diffuse reflections (Cohen, 1993). While the solutions are view independent, they are computationally expensive, so their usefulness tends to be limited to static scenes. They have another limitation, they can't model specular reflections, so separate processing must be done to add them. The hardware lighting equations supported by OpenGL are fast, and provide adequate realism for direct lighting of objects. A hybrid solution can combine the best of both radiosity and OpenGL lighting. This technique creates realistic scenes with both diffuse and specular reflections that are viewer dependent and insensitive to small changes in object position.

Computing radiosity is a recursive process. Each step consists of processing each surface, computing the incoming radiosity from each visible surface in the scene, then updating the emitted radiosity of the surface. This process is repeated until the radiosity values of the surfaces converge. The first step of this process consists of setting the radiosity of the illumination sources of the room. Thus, the first radiosity iteration computes the contributions of surfaces directly illuminated from the scene's light sources.

The hybrid approach computes the radiosity equation, then subtracts out the radiosity contributes from this first step. What's left is the indirect illumination caused by object interreflection. The objects in the scene are colored using this radiosity result, then lighted using standard OpenGL lighting techniques. The OpenGL lighting provides the missing direct illumination to the scene. The lighting equation is parameterized to provide no ambient illumination, since the radiosity computations supply a more accurate solution.

This technique has several advantages. Since normal OpenGL lighting provides the direct specular and diffuse lighting, the viewer-dependent parts of the scene can be rendered quickly, once the initial radiosity computations have been completed. The radiosity results themselves are more robust, since they only contribute lighting effects from object interreflections. Viewed as light sources, objects in the scene tend to have large areas, so the amount of incident light falling on any given object is fairly insensitive to its position in the scene. These effects are also a smaller percentage of the total lighting contribution, so they will still "look right" longer as the object moves, since the direct part of the lighting contribution is taking object position into account.

As a scene is dynamically updated, at some point the radiosity errors will become noticeable, requiring that the radiosity equations be recomputed. Since these errors accumulate slowly, this cost can be amortized over a large number of frames. Small objects can move significantly without large error, especially if they are not very near large objects in the scene. Other techniques mentioned in this book can be combined with this one to improve the realism of OpenGLs direct illumination, since the radiosity contribution and the direct illumination contribution are orthogonal. See (Diefenbach, 1997) for more details on this technique.

15.14.3 Ambient Occlusion

Ambient occlusion is a scalar value recorded at every surface point indicating the average amount of self-occlusion occurring at the point on the surface. It measures the extent to which a location on the surface is obscured from surrounding light sources. It is used to approximate self-shadowing and adds realism to lighting by mimicking the effects of indirect light sources such as sky, ground, walls, and so on.

To use ambient occlusion in interactive rendering, the occlusion term is computed as a preprocessing step and relies on the geometry being rigid and the lighting constant to avoid recomputing the occlusion information. Like other light transport modeling methods, this one is restricted to diffuse surfaces; i.e. view-independent lighting. Ambient occlusion is computed for each object independently, not for the entire scene, so objects can undergo separate rigid transformations such as rotation and translation while using the same ambient occlusion map.

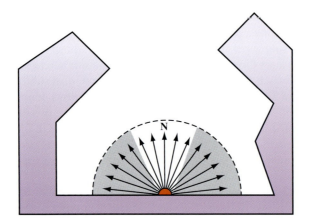

Figure 15.15 Cross section showing hemispherical visibility sampling.

Conceptually, the ambient occlusion at a surface point is computed by casting rays sampling the hemisphere over the surface point (see Figure 15.15). The rays themselves are used to compute visibility. The point is partially occluded if the ray interesects another part of the object geometry as it extends outward toward a hemisphere bounding the object.

If the rays are uniformly distributed across the hemisphere; the single ambient occlusion value is a weighted average of the visibility results ($V_p(\boldsymbol{\omega})$) using hemispherical integration.

$$OA_p = \frac{1}{\pi} \int_\Omega V_p(\boldsymbol{\omega})(\mathbf{N} \cdot \boldsymbol{\omega})d\omega$$

One method for weighting the samples uses the cosine of the angle between the surface normal at the point and the direction of the sample ray. This can be computed more efficiently by using a cosine distribution of sample rays, summing the results directly (Monte Carlo integration).

$$OA_o = \frac{1}{n} \sum_{i=1}^{n} V_p(\mathbf{s}_1)$$

The results of computing the occlusion value at different sample points are combined to form an ambient occlusion map. Like other lighting techniques, ambient occlusion maps may be sampled at different frequencies (for example, at each vertex, or at regular points on the object surface). The goal is to have the sample rate match the rate of change of the occlusion detail on the object.

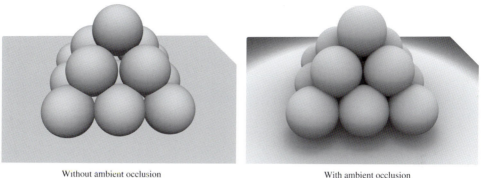

Without ambient occlusion   With ambient occlusion

Figure 15.16 Ambient occlusion.

The ambient occlusion map is applied during rendering by modulating the result of diffuse lighting computations with the ambient occlusion term. For occlusion values sampled at vertices, the occlusion term can be included in the material reflectance for the vertex (using color material or a vertex program). High-density occlusion maps are used as textures and also modulate the result of the diffuse lighting computation. An additional improvement to the scheme replaces the surface normal with a "bent normal" — the average unoccluded direction. Figure 15.16 illustrates a per-pixel occlusion map applied to a sample object.

Incorporating ambient occlusion enhances flat illumination by adding extra definition. It is efficient and relatively low cost techique to add to the rendering step. The only downside is the requirement for precomputation of the map. With some cleverness, however, the precomputation can also be hardware accelerated using the OpenGL pipeline (Whitehurst, 2003; Hill, 2004; Fernando, 2004).

15.15 Summary

Lighting continues to be one of the most actively researched areas in computer graphics. New lighting models and methods for emulating surface characteristics and light transport continue to be developed. Texture mapping combined with the programmable fragment pipeline greatly increases the range of lighting models that can be implemented within the OpenGL pipeline. This chapter covers only a subset of frequently used lighting algorithms. They represent different trade-offs in terms of visual quality and computational cost; their applicability is dependent on both the needs of the application and the capabilities of the OpenGL implementation.

PART

Advanced Techniques

CAD and Modeling Techniques

In previous chapters, many of the underlying principles for faithful rendering of models have been described. In this chapter, we extend those techniques with additional algorithms that are particularly useful or necessary for interactive modeling applications such as those used for computer-aided design (CAD). The geometric models use complex representations such as NURBS surfaces and geometric solids that are typically converted to simpler representations for display. Representations for even relatively simple real-world objects can involve millions of primitives. Displaying and manipulating large models both efficiently and effectively is a considerable challenge. Besides the display of the model, CAD applications must also supply other information such as labels and annotations that can also challenge efficient display. CAD applications often include a variety of analysis and other tools, but we are primarily concerned with the display and interactive manipulation parts of the application.

16.1 Picking and Highlighting

Interactive selection of objects, including feedback, is an important part of modeling applications. OpenGL provides several mechanisms that can be used to perform object selection and highlighting tasks.

16.1.1 OpenGL Selection

OpenGL supports an object selection mechanism in which the object geometry is transformed and compared against a selection subregion (*pick region*) of the viewport. The mechanism uses the transformation pipeline to compare object vertices against the view volume. To reduce the view volume to a screen-space subregion (in window coordinates) of the viewport, the projected coordinates of the object are transformed by a scale and translation transform and combined to produce the matrix

$$T = \begin{pmatrix} \dfrac{p_x}{d_x} & 0 & 0 & p_x - 2\dfrac{q_x - o_x}{d_x} \\ 0 & \dfrac{p_y}{d_y} & 0 & p_y - 2\dfrac{q_y - o_y}{d_y} \\ 0 & 0 & 1 & 0 \\ 0 & 0 & 0 & 0 \end{pmatrix}$$

where o_x, o_y, p_x, and p_y are the x and y origin and width and height of the viewport, and q_x, q_y, d_x, and d_y are the origin and width and height of the pick region.

Objects are identified by assigning them integer *names* using glLoadName. Each object is sent to the OpenGL pipeline and tested against the pick region. If the test succeeds, a *hit record* is created to identify the object. The hit record is written to the selection buffer whenever a change is made to the current object name. An application can determine which objects intersected the pick region by scanning the selection buffer and examining the names present in the buffer.

The OpenGL selection method determines that an object has been hit if it intersects the view volume. Bitmap and pixel image primitives generate a hit record only if a raster positioning command is sent to the pipeline and the transformed position lies within the viewing volume. To generate hit records for an arbitrary point within a pixel image or bitmap, a bounding rectangle should be sent rather than the image. This causes the selection test to use the interior of the rectangle. Similarly, wide lines and points are selected only if the equivalent infinitely thin line or infinitely small point is selected. To facilitate selection testing of wide lines and points, proxy geometry representing the true footprint of the primitive is used instead.

Many applications use instancing of geometric data to reduce their memory footprint. Instancing allows an application to create a single representation of the geometric data for each type of object used in the scene. If the application is modeling a car for example, the four wheels of the car may be represented as instances of a single geometric description of a wheel, combined with a modeling transformation to place each wheel in the correct location in the scene. Instancing introduces extra complexity into the picking operation. If a single name is associated with the wheel geometry, the application cannot determine which of the four instances of the wheel has been picked. OpenGL solves this problem by maintaining a stack of object names. This allows an application, which represents models hierarchically, to associate a name at each stage of its hierarchy. As the car is

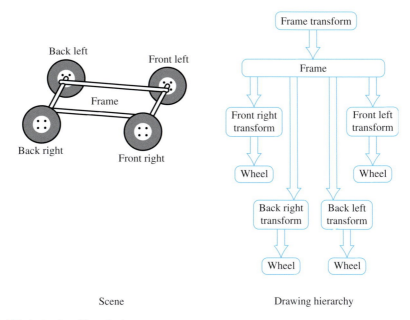

Scene   Drawing hierarchy

Figure 16.1 Instancing of four wheels.

being drawn, new names are pushed onto the stack as the hierarchy is descended and old names are popped as the hierarchy is ascended. When a hit record is created, it contains all names currently in the name stack. The application determines which instance of an object is selected by looking at the content of the name stack and comparing it to the names stored in the hierarchical representation of the model.

Using the car model example, the application associates an object name with the wheel representation and another object name with each of the transformations used to position the wheel in the car model. The application determines that a wheel is selected if the selection buffer contains the object name for the wheel, and it determines which instance of the wheel by examining the object name of the transformation. Figure 16.1 shows an illustration of a car frame with four wheels drawn as instances of the same wheel model. The figure shows a partial graph of the model hierarchy, with the car frame positioned in the scene and the four wheel instances positioned relative to the frame.

When the OpenGL pipeline is in selection mode, the primitives sent to the pipeline do not generate fragments to the framebuffer. Since only the result of vertex coordinate transformations is of interest, there is no need to send texture coordinates, normals, or vertex colors, or to enable lighting.

16.1.2 Object Tagging in the Color Buffer

An alternative method for locating objects is to write integer object names as color values into the framebuffer and read back the framebuffer data within the pick region to reconstruct the object names. For this to work correctly, the application relies on being able to write and read back the same color value. Texturing, blending, dithering, lighting, and smooth shading should be disabled so that fragment color values are not altered during rasterization or fragment processing. The unsigned integer forms of the color commands (such as glColor3ub) are used to pass in the object names. The unsigned forms are defined to convert the values in such a way as to preserve the b most significant bits of the color value, where b is the number of bits in the color buffer. To limit selection to visible surfaces, depth testing should be enabled. The back color buffer can be used for the drawing operations to keep the drawing operations invisible to the user.

A typical RGB color buffer, storing 8-bit components, can represent 24-bit object names. To emulate the functionality provided by the name stack in the OpenGL selection mechanism, the application can partition the name space represented by a color value to hold instancing information. For example, a four level hierarchy can subdivide a 24-bit color as 4, 4, 6, and 10 bits. Using 10 bits for the lowest level of the hierarchy creates a larger name space for individual objects.

One disadvantage of using the color buffer is that it can only hold a single identifier at each pixel. If depth buffering is used, the pixel will hold the object name corresponding to a visible surface. If depth buffering is not used, a pixel holds the name of the last surface drawn. The OpenGL selection mechanism can return a hit record for all objects that intersect a given region. The application is then free to choose one of the intersecting objects using a separate policy. A closest-to-viewer policy is simple using either OpenGL selection or color buffer tags. Other policies may need the complete intersection list, however. If the number of potential objects is small, the complete list can be generated by allocating nonoverlapping names from the name space. The objects are drawn with bitwise OR color buffer logic operations to produce a composite name. The application reconstructs the individual objects names from the composite list. This algorithm can be extended to handle a large number of objects by partitioning objects into groups and using multiple passes to determine those groups that need more detailed interrogation.

16.1.3 Proxy Geometry

One method to reduce the amount of work done by the OpenGL pipeline during picking operations (for color buffer tagging or OpenGL selection) is to use a simplified form of the object in the picking computations. For example, individual objects can be replaced by geometry representing their bounding boxes. The precision of the picking operation is traded for increased speed. The accuracy can be restored by adding a second pass in which the objects, selected using their simplified geometry, are reprocessed using their real geometry. The two-pass scheme improves performance if the combined complexity of the proxy objects from the first pass and the real objects processed in the second pass is less than the complexity of the set of objects tested in a single-pass algorithm.

16.1.4 Mapping from Window to Object Coordinates

For some picking algorithms it is useful to map a point in window coordinates $(x_w, y_w, z_w)^T$ to object coordinates $(x_o, y_o, z_o)^T$. The object coordinates are computed by transforming the window coordinates by the inverse of the viewport V, projection P, and modelview M transformations:

$$
\begin{pmatrix} x_o \\ y_o \\ z_o \\ w_o \end{pmatrix} = M^{-1} P^{-1} V^{-1} \begin{pmatrix} x_w \\ y_w \\ z_w \\ 1 \end{pmatrix} = (PM)^{-1} V^{-1} \begin{pmatrix} x_w \\ y_w \\ z_w \\ 1 \end{pmatrix}
$$

This procedure isn't quite correct for perspective projections since the inverse of the perspective divide is not included. Normally, the w value is discarded after the perspective divide, so finding the exact value for w_{clip} may not be simple. For applications using perspective transformations generated with the `glFrustum` and `gluPerspective` commands, the resulting w_{clip} is the negative eye-space z coordinate, $-z_e$. This value can be computed from z_w using the viewport and projection transform parameters as described in Appendix B.2.3.

   In some situations, however, only the window coordinate x and y values are available. A 2D window coordinate point maps to a 3D line in object coordinates. The equation of the line can be determined by generating two object-space points on the line, for example at $z_w = 0$ and $z_w = 1$. If the resulting object-space points are P_o and Q_o, the parametric form of the line is

$$
t(Q_o - P_o) + P_o
$$

16.1.5 Other Picking Methods

For many applications it may prove advantageous to not use the OpenGL pipeline at all to implement picking. For example, an application may choose to organize its geometric data spatially and use a hierarchy of bounding volumes to efficiently prune portions of the scene without testing each individual object (Rohlf, 1994; Strauss, 1992).

16.1.6 Highlighting

Once the selected object has been identified, an application will typically modify the appearance of the object to indicate that it has been selected. This action is called *highlighting*. Appearance changes can include the color of the object, the drawing style (wireframe or filled), and the addition of annotations. Usually, the highlight is created by re-rendering the entire scene, using the modified appearance for the selected object.

   In applications manipulating complex models, the cost of redrawing the entire scene to indicate a selection may be prohibitive. This is particularly true for applications that implement variations of *locate-highlight* feedback, where each object is highlighted as the cursor passes over or near it to indicate that this object is the current selection target. An extension of this problem exists for painting applications that need to track the location of a brush over an object and make changes to the appearance of the object based on the current painting parameters (Hanrahan, 1990).

An alternative to redrawing the entire scene is to use overlay windows (Section 7.3.1) to draw highlights on top of the existing scene. One difficulty with this strategy is that it may be impossible to modify only the visible surfaces of the selected object; the depth information is present in the depth buffer associated with the main color buffer and is not shared with the overlay window. For applications in which the visible surface information is not required, overlay windows are an efficient solution. If visible surface information is important, it may be better to modify the color buffer directly. A depth-buffered object can be directly overdrawn by changing the depth test function to GL_LEQUAL and redrawing the object geometry with different attributes (Section 9.2). If the original object was drawn using blending, however, it may be difficult to un-highlight the object without redrawing the entire scene.

16.1.7 XOR Highlighting

Another efficient highlighting technique is to overdraw primitives with an *XOR* logic operation. An advantage of using *XOR* is that the highlighting and restoration operations can be done independently of the original object color. The most significant bit of each of the color components can be *XOR*ed to produce a large difference between the highlight color and the original color. Drawing a second time restores the original color.

A second advantage of the *XOR* method is that depth testing can be disabled to allow the occluded surfaces to poke through their occluders, indicating that they have been selected. The highlight can later be removed without needing to redraw the occluders. This also solves the problem of removing a highlight from an object originally drawn with blending. While the algorithm is simple and efficient, the colors that result from *XOR*ing the most significant component bits may not be aesthetically pleasing, and the highlight color will vary with the underlying object color.

One should also be careful of interactions between the picking and highlighting methods. For example, a picking mechanism that uses the color or depth buffer cannot be mixed with a highlighting algorithm that relies on the contents of those buffers remaining intact between highlighting operations.

A useful hybrid scheme for combining color buffer tagging with locate-highlight on visible surfaces is to share the depth buffer between the picking and highlighting operations. It uses the front color buffer for highlighting operations and the back color buffer for locate operations. Each time the viewing or modeling transformations change, the scene is redrawn, updating both color buffers. Locate-highlight operations are performed using these same buffers until another modeling or viewing change requires a redraw. This type of algorithm can be very effective for achieving interactive rates for complex models, since very little geometry needs to be rendered between modeling and viewing changes.

16.1.8 Foreground Object Manipulation

The schemes for fast highlighting can be generalized to allow limited manipulation of a selected depth-buffered object (a *foreground* object) while avoiding full scene redraws as the object is moved. The key idea is that when an object is selected the entire scene is drawn without that object, and copies of the color and depth buffer are created. Each time the foreground object is moved or modified, the color buffer and depth buffer are initialized using the saved copies. The foreground object is drawn normally, depth tested against the saved depth buffer.

This image-based technique is similar to the algorithm described for compositing images with depth in Section 11.5. To be usable, it requires a method to efficiently save and restore the color and depth images for the intermediate form of the scene. If aux buffers or stereo color buffers are available, they can be used to store the color buffer (using `glCopyPixels`) and the depth buffer can be saved to the host. If off-screen buffers (pbuffers) are available, the depth (and color) buffers can be efficiently copied to and restored from the off-screen buffer. Off-screen buffers are described in more detail in Section 7.4.1. It is particularly important that the contents of the depth buffer be saved and restored accurately. If some of the depth buffer values are truncated or rounded during the transfer, the resulting image will not be the same as that produced by drawing the original scene. This technique works best when the geometric complexity of the scene is very large — so large that the time spent transferring the color and depth buffers is small compared to the amount of time that would be necessary to re-render the scene.

16.2 Culling Techniques

One of the central problems in rendering an image is determining which parts of each object are visible. Depth buffering is the primary method supported within the OpenGL pipeline. However, there are several other methods that can be used to determine, earlier in the pipeline, whether an object is invisible, allowing it to be rejected or *culled*. If parts of an object can be eliminated earlier in the processing pipeline at a low enough cost, the entire scene can be rendered faster. There are several culling algorithms that establish the visibility of an object using different criteria.

- Back-face culling eliminates the surfaces of a closed object that are facing away from the viewer, since they will be occluded by the front-facing surfaces of the same object.

- View-frustum culling eliminates objects that are outside the viewing frustum. This is typically accomplished by determining the position of an object relative to the planes defined by the six faces of the viewing frustum.

- Portal culling (Luebke, 1995) subdivides indoor scenes into a collection of closed cells, marking the "holes" in each cell formed by doors and windows as *portals*.

Each cell is analyzed to determine the other cells that may be visible through portals, resulting in a network of potentially visible sets (PVS) describing the set of cells that must be drawn when the viewer is located in a particular cell.

- Occlusion culling determines which objects in the scene are occluded by other large objects in the scene.

- Detail culling (like geometric LOD) determines how close an object is to the viewer and adds or removes detail from the object as it approaches or recedes from the viewer.

A substantial amount of research is available on all of these techniques. We will examine the last two techniques in more detail in the following sections.

16.3 Occlusion Culling

Complex models with high depth complexity render many pixels that are ultimately discarded during depth testing. Transforming vertices and rasterizing primitives that are occluded by other polygons reduces the frame rate of the application while adding nothing to the visual quality of the image. Occlusion culling algorithms attempt to identify such nonvisible polygons and discard them before they are sent to the rendering pipeline (Coorg, 1996; Zhang, 1998). Occlusion culling algorithms are a form of visible surface determination algorithm that attempts to resolve visible (or nonvisible surfaces) at larger granularity than pixel-by-pixel testing.

A simple example of an occlusion culling algorithm is backface culling. The surfaces of a closed object that are facing away from the viewer are occluded by the surfaces facing the viewer, so there is no need to draw them. Many occlusion culling algorithms operate in object space (Coorg, 1996; Luebke, 1995) and there is little that can be done with the standard OpenGL pipeline to accelerate such operations. However, Zhang et al. (1997) describe an algorithm that computes a hierarchy of image-space *occlusion maps* for use in testing whether polygons comprising the scene are visible.

An occlusion map is a 2D array of values; each one measures the opacity of the image plane at that point. An *occlusion map* (see Figure 16.2) corresponding to a set of geometry is generated by rendering the geometry with the polygon faces colored white. The occlusion map is view dependent. In Zhang's algorithm the occlusion map is generated from a target set of occluders. The occlusion map is accompanied by a *depth estimation buffer* that provides a conservative estimate of the maximum depth value of a set of occluders at each pixel. Together, the occlusion map and depth estimation buffer are used to determine whether a candidate object is occluded. A bounding volume for the candidate object is projected onto the same image plane as the occlusion map, and the resulting projection is compared against the occlusion map to determine whether the occluders overlap the portion of the image where the object would be rendered. If the object is determined to be

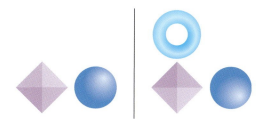

Figure 16.2 Occluded torus: front and top views.

overlapped by the occluders, the depth estimation buffer is tested to determine whether the candidate object is behind the occluder geometry. A pyramidal hierarchy of occlusion maps (similar to a mipmap hierarchy) can be constructed to accelerate the initial overlap tests.

16.3.1 Choosing Occluders

Choosing a good set of occluders can be computationally expensive, as it is approximating the task of determining the visible surfaces. Heuristic methods can be used to choose likely occluders based on an estimation of the size of the occluder and distance from the eye. To maintain interactive rendering it may be useful to assign a fixed polygon budget to the list of occluders. Temporal coherence can be exploited to reduce the number of new occluders that needs to be considered each frame.

16.3.2 Building the Occlusion Map

Once the occluders have been selected they are rendered to the framebuffer with lighting and texturing disabled. The polygons are colored white to produce values near or equal to 1.0 in opaque areas. OpenGL implementations that do not support some form of antialiasing will have pixels values that are either 0.0 or 1.0. A hierarchy of reduced resolution maps is created by copying this map to texture memory and performing bilinear texture filtering on the image to produce one that is one-quarter size. Additional maps are created by repeating this process. This procedure is identical to the mipmap generation algorithm using texture filtering described in Section 14.15.

The size of the highest resolution map and the number of hierarchy levels created is a compromise between the amount of time spent rendering, copying, and reading back the images and the accuracy of the result. Some of the lower-resolution images may be more efficiently computed on the host processor, as the amount of overhead involved in performing copies to the framebuffer or pixel readback operation dominates the time spent producing the pixels. It may be more efficient to minimize the number of transfers back to the host by constructing the entire hierarchy in a single large (off-screen) color buffer.

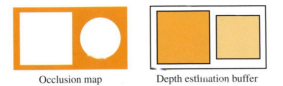

Occlusion map   Depth estimation buffer

Figure 16.3 Occlusion map and depth estimation buffer.

16.3.3 Building the Depth Estimation Buffer

Zhang (1997) suggests building a depth estimation buffer by computing the farthest depth value in the projected bounding box for an occluder and using this value throughout the occluder's screen-space bounding rectangle. The end result is a tiling of the image plane with a set of projected occluders, each representing a single depth value, as shown in Figure 16.3. The computation is kept simple to avoid complex scan conversion of the occluder and to simplify the depth comparisons against a candidate occluded object.

16.3.4 Occlusion Testing

The algorithm for occlusion testing consists of two steps. First, the screen-space bounding rectangle of the candidate object is computed and tested for overlap against the hierarchy of occlusion maps. If the occluders overlap the candidate object, a conservative depth value (minimum depth value) is computed for the screen-space bounding rectangle of the candidate object. This depth value is tested against the depth estimation buffer to determine whether the candidate is behind the occluders and is therefore occluded.

An opacity value in a level in the occlusion map hierarchy corresponds to the coverage of the corresponding screen region. In the general case, the opacity values range between 0.0 and 1.0; values between these extrema correspond to screen regions that are partially covered by the occluders. To determine whether a candidate object is occluded, the overlap test is performed against a map level using the candidate's bounding rectangle. If the region corresponding to the candidate is completely opaque in the occlusion map, the candidate is occluded if it lies behind the occluders (using the depth estimation buffer). The occlusion map hierarchy can be used to accelerate the testing process by starting at the low-resolution maps and progressing to higher-resolution maps when there is ambiguity.

Since the opacity values provide an estimation of coverage, they can also be used to do more aggressive occlusion culling by pruning candidate objects that are not completely occluded using a threshold opacity value. Since opacity values are generated using simple averaging, the threshold value can be correlated to a bound on the largest *hole* in the occluder set. The opacity value is a measure of the number of nonopaque pixels and provides no information on the distribution of those pixels. Aggressive culling is advantageous for scenes with a large number of occluders that do not completely cover the candidates (for example, a wall of trees). However, if there is a large color discontinuity between the culled objects and the background, distracting popping artifacts may result as the view is changed and the aggressively culled objects disappear and reappear.

16.3.5 Other Occlusion Testing Methods

Zhang's algorithm maintains the depth estimation buffer using simplified software scan conversion and uses the OpenGL pipeline to optimize the computation of the occlusion maps. All testing is performed on the host, which has the advantage that the testing can be performed asynchronously from the drawing operations and the test results can be computed with very low latency. Another possibility is to maintain the occlusion buffer in the hardware accelerator itself. To be useful, there must be a method for testing the screen-space bounding rectangle against the map and efficiently returning the result to the application.

The OpenGL depth buffer can be used to do this with some additional extensions. Occluders are selected using the heuristics described previously and rendered to the framebuffer as regular geometry. Following this, bounding geometry for candidate objects are rendered and tested against the depth buffer without changing the contents of the color buffer or depth buffer. The result of the depth test is then returned to the application, preferably reduced to a single value rather than the results of the depth test for every fragment generated. The results of the tests are used to determine whether to draw the candidate geometry or discard it. Extensions for performing the occlusion test and returning the result have been proposed and implemented by several hardware vendors (Hewlett Packard, 1998; Boungoyne,1999; NVIDIA, 2002), culminating in the `ARB_occlusion_query` extension.[1]

An application uses this occlusion query mechanism by creating one or more occlusion query objects. These objects act as buffers, accumulating counts of fragments that pass the depth test. The commands `glBeginQuery` and `glEndQuery` activate and deactivate a query. One occlusion query object can be active at a time. When a query is activated, the pass count is initialized to zero. With the query is deactivated the count is copied to a result buffer. The results are retrieved using `glGetQueryObject`. The mechanism supports pipelined operation by separating the active query object from the retrieval mechanism. This allows the application to continue occlusion testing with another query object while retrieving the results from a previously active object. The mechanism also allows the application to do either blocking or nonblocking retrieval requests, providing additional flexibility in structuring the application.

16.4 Geometric Level of Detail

When rendering a scene with a perspective view, objects that are far away become smaller. Since even the largest framebuffer has a limited resolution, objects that are distant become small enough that they only cover a small number of pixels on the screen. Small objects reach this point when they are only a moderate distance from the viewer.

---

1. Added as a core feature in OpenGL 1.4.

Table 16.1 Geometric LOD Changes

Change	Description
Shading	Disable reflections, bump maps, etc.
Details	Remove small geometric details
Texture	Don't texture surfaces
Shape	Simplify overall geometry
Billboard	Replace object with billboard

It's wasteful to render a small object with a lot of detail, since the polygonal and texture detail cannot be seen. This is true even if multisample antialiasing is used with large numbers of samples per-pixel. With antialiasing, the extra detail simply wastes performance that could be used to improve the visual quality of objects closer to the viewer. Without antialiasing support, lots of polygons projected to a small number of pixels results in distracting edge aliasing artifacts as the object moves.

A straightforward solution to this problem is to create a geometric equivalent to the notion of texture level of detail (LOD). A geometric object is rendered with less detail as it covers a smaller area on the screen. This can be considered yet another form of visibility culling, by eliminating detail that isn't visible to the viewer. Changes are made to an object based on visibility criteria – when the presence or absence of an object detail doesn't change the image, it can be removed. A less stringent criteria can also be used to maximize performance. If the modification doesn't change the image significantly, it can be removed. Metrics for significant changes can include the percentage of pixels changed between the simplified and normal image, or the total color change between the two images, averaging the color change across all pixels in the object. If done carefully, the changes in detail can be made unnoticeable to the viewer.

There are a number of ways to reduce geometric detail (they are summarized in Table 16.1). Since a major purpose of geometric LOD is to improve performance, the reductions in detail can be ordered to maximize performance savings. Special shading effects — such as environment mapping, bump mapping, or reflection algorithms — can be disabled. The overall polygon count can be reduced quickly by removing small detail components on a complex object. The object's geometry can be rendered untextured, using a base color that matches the average texture color. This is the same as the color of the coarsest 1×1 level on a mipmapped texture.

The geometry itself can be simplified, removing vertices and shifting others to maintain the same overall shape of the object, but with less detail. Ultimately, the entire object can be replaced with a single billboarded polygon. The billboard is textured when the object covers a moderate number of pixels, and untextured (using the average object color) when it covers a few pixels.

16.4.1 Changing Detail

When creating a list of detail changes for an object, a simple computation for deciding when to switch to a different LOD is needed. An obvious choice is the size of the object in screen space. For an object of a given size, the screen extent depends on two factors: the current degree of perspective distortion (determined by the current perspective transform) and the distance from the viewer to the object.

In eye space, the projection changes the size of an object (scaling the x and y values) as a function of distance from the viewer (z_e). The functions $x_{scale}(z_e)$ and $y_{scale}(z_e)$ define the ratios of the post-projection (and post-perspective divide) coordinates to the pre-projection ones. For a projection transform created using glFrustum, assuming an initial w value of one, and ignoring the sign change (which changes to a left-handed coordinate system), the x_{scale} and y_{scale} functions are

$$x_{scale}(z_e) = \frac{1}{z_e \left(\dfrac{r - l}{2n} \right)}$$

$$y_{scale}(z_e) = \frac{1}{z_e \left(\dfrac{t - b}{2n} \right)}$$

The distance from viewpoint to object is simply the z distance to a representative point on the object in eye space. In object space, the distance vector can be directly computed, and its length found. The scale factor for x and y can be used in either coordinate system.

Although the ideal method for changing level of detail is to delay switching LOD until the object change is not visible at the current object size, this can be impractical for a number reasons. In practice, it is difficult to compute differences in appearance for an object at all possible orientations. It can be expensive to work through all the possible geometry and attribute changes, finding how they would affect LOD change. Often a more practical, heuristic approach is taken.

Whatever the process, the result is a series of transition points that are set to occur at a set of screen sizes. These screen sizes are mapped into distances from the viewer based on the projection scale factor and viewport resolution.

16.4.2 Transition Techniques

The simplest method for transitioning between goemetric LOD levels is to simply switch between them. This abrupt transition can be noticeable to the viewer unless the resulting pixel image changes very little. Finding these ideal transitions can be difficult in practice, as seen previously. They can also be expensive; an LOD change delayed until the object is small reduces its potential for improving performance. An LOD change of a much larger object may be unnoticeable if the transition can be made gradually.

One direct method of creating a gradual transition is to *fade* between two representations of the object. The object is rendered twice, first at one LOD level, then the other. The images are combined using blending. A parameter t is used to control the percentage visibility of each object: $tLOD_a + (1 - t)LOD_{a+1}$. The advantage of this method is that it's simple, since constant object LOD representations are used. If the

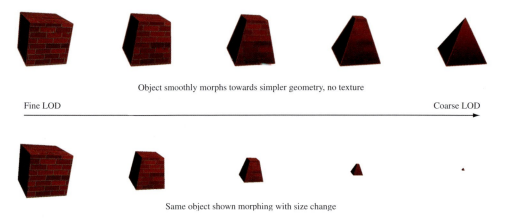

Object smoothly morphs towards simpler geometry, no texture

Fine LOD   Coarse LOD

Same object shown morphing with size change

Figure 16.4 Morphing transition.

ARB imaging subset is supported, the blend function can use `GL_CONSTANT_COLOR` and `GL_ONE_MINUS_CONSTANT_COLOR`[2] to blend the two images setting the grayscale constant color to t. Otherwise, the alpha-blending techniques described in Section 11.9 can be used.

The disadvantage of a blended transition is rendering overhead. The object has to be drawn twice, doubling the pixel fill requirements for the object during transitions. This leads to more overhead for a technique that is being used to improve performance, reducing its benefit. If multisampling is supported, the sample coverage control `glSampleCoverage` can be used to perform the fade without requiring framebuffer blending, but with a reduced number of transition values for t (Section 11.10.1).

A more sophisticated transition technique is *morphing*. During a morphing transition the object is smoothly changed from one LOD level to another (see Figure 16.4). For a geometric morph, vertices are ultimately removed. The vertices that are being removed smoothly move toward ones that are being retained, until they are co-incident. A mipmapped surface texture can be gradually coarsened until it is a single color, or stretched into a single texel color by smoothly reducing the difference in texture coordinates across the surface. When the vertex is coincident with another, it can be removed without visible change in the object. In the same way, a surface texture can transition to a single color, and then texturing can be disabled. Using morphing, small geometric details can smoothly shrink to invisibility.

This technique doesn't incur pixel fill overhead, since the object is always drawn once. It does require a more sophisticated modeling of objects in order to parameterize their geometry and textures. This can be a nontrivial exercise for complex models, although there is more support for such features in current modeling systems. Also, morphing requires extra computations within the application to compute the new vertex positions,

---

2. Core functionality in OpenGL 1.4.

so there is a trade-off of processing in the rendering pipeline for some extra processing on the CPU during transitions.

16.5 Visualizing Surface Orientation

Styling and analysis applications often provide tools to help visualize surface curvature. In addition to aesthetic properties, surface curvature can also affect the manufacturability of a particular design. Not only the intrinsic surface curvature, but the curvature relative to a particular coordinate system can determine the manufacturability of an object. For example, some manufacturing processes may be more efficient if horizontally oriented surfaces are maximized, whereas others may require vertically oriented ones (or some other constraint). Bailey and Clark (Bailey, 1997) describe a manufacturing process in which the object is constructed by vertically stacking (laminating) paper cutouts corresponding to horizontal cross sections of the object. This particular manufacturing process produces better results when the vertical slope (gradient) of the surface is greater than some threshold.

Bailey and Clark describe a method using 1D texture maps to encode the vertical slope of an object as a color ramp. The colors on the object's surfaces represent the vertical slope of the surface relative to the current orientation. Since the surface colors dynamically display the relative slope as the object's orientation is modified, a (human) operator can interactively search for the orientation that promises the best manufacturability.

For simplicity, assume a coordinate space for surface normals with the z axis perpendicular to the way the paper sheets are stacked. If the object's surface normals are transformed to this coordinate space, the contour line density, d, is a function of the z component of the surface normal. Figure 16.5 shows a simplified surface with normal vector $\mathbf{N}$ and slope angle θ and the similar triangles relationship formed with the second triangle with sides $\mathbf{N}$ and N_z,

$$d = \frac{\Delta v}{k \Delta h} = \frac{\tan \theta}{k} = \frac{\sin \theta}{k \cos \theta} = \frac{\sqrt{1 - N_z^2}}{k N_z}$$

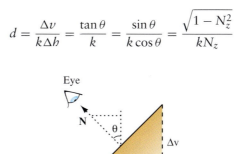

Figure 16.5 Vertical surface slope and surface normal.

where k is the (constant) paper layer thickness (in practice, approximately 0.0042 inches).

The possible range of density values, based on known manufacturing rules, can be color-coded as a red-yellow-green spectrum (using an HSV color space), and these values can in turn be mapped to the range of N_z values. For their particular case, Bailey and Clark found that a density below 100/inch causes problems for the manufacturing process. Therefore, the 1D texture is set up to map a density below 100 to red.

Typically, per-vertex surface normals are passed to OpenGL using `glNormal3f` calls, and such normals are used for lighting. For this rendering technique, however, the normalized per-vertex surface normal is passed to `glTexCoord3f` to serve as a 3D texture coordinate. The texture matrix is used to rotate the per-vertex surface normal to match the assumed coordinate space, where the z axis is perpendicular to the paper faces. A unit normal has an N_z component varying from $[-1, 1]$, so the rotated N_z component must be transformed to the $[0, 1]$ texture coordinate range and *swizzled* to the s coordinate for indexing the 1D texture. The rotation and scale and bias transformations are concatenated as

$$
\begin{pmatrix} s \\ 0 \\ 0 \\ 0 \end{pmatrix} = \begin{pmatrix} 0 & 0 & 0.5 & 0.5 \\ 0 & 0 & 0 & 0 \\ 0 & 0 & 0 & 0 \\ 0 & 0 & 0 & 1 \end{pmatrix} \begin{pmatrix} r_1 & r_2 & r_3 & 0 \\ r_4 & r_5 & r_6 & 0 \\ r_7 & r_8 & r_9 & 0 \\ 0 & 0 & 0 & 1 \end{pmatrix} \begin{pmatrix} N_x \\ N_y \\ N_z \\ 1 \end{pmatrix}
$$

The composition of the rotation and scale and bias matrices can be computed by loading the scale and bias transform into the texture matrix first, followed by `glRotate` to incorporate the rotation. Once the 1D texture is loaded and enabled, the surface colors will reflect the current manufacturing orientation stored in the texture matrix. To rerender the model with a different orientation for the manufacturing process, the rotation component in the texture matrix must be adjusted to match the new orientation.

Note that there is no way to normalize a texture coordinate in the way that the OpenGL fixed-function pipeline supports `GL_NORMALIZE` for normalizing normals passed to `glNormal3f`. If rendering the model involves modelview matrix changes, such as different modeling transformations, these modelview matrix changes must also be incorporated into the texture matrix by multiplying the texture matrix by the inverse transpose of the modeling transformation.

OpenGL 1.3 alleviates both of these problems with the `GL_NORMAL_MAP` texture coordinate generation function. If the implementation supports this functionality, the normal vector can be transferred to the pipeline as a regular normal vector and then transferred to the texture coordinate pipeline using the texture generation function. Since the normal map function uses the eye-space normal vector, it includes any modeling transformations in effect. However, since the modelview transformation includes the viewing transformation, too, the inverse of this transformation should be included in the texture matrix.

This technique was designed to solve a particular manufacturing problem, but the ideas can be generalized. Surface normal vectors contain information about the surface gradient at that point. Various functions of the gradient can be color-coded and mapped to the surface geometry to provide additional information. The most general form of the encoding can use cube environment maps to create an arbitrary function of a 3D surface normal.

16.6 Visualizing Surface Curvature

Industrial designers are often concerned as much with how the shape of a surface reflects light as the overall shape of the surface. In many situations it is useful to render object surfaces with lighting models that provide information about surface reflection. One of the most useful techniques to simulate more realistic reflection is to use reflection mapping techniques. The sphere mapping, dual paraboloid, and cube mapping techniques described in Section 17.3 can all be used to varying degrees to realistically simulate surface reflection from a general environment.

In some styling applications, simulating synthetic environments can provide useful aesthetic insights. One such environment consists of a hemi-cylindrical room with an array of regularly spaced linear light sources (fluorescent lamps) illuminating the object. The object is placed on a turntable and can be rotated relative to the orientation of the light sources. The way the surfaces reflect the array of light sources provides intuitive information regarding how the surface will appear in more general environments.

The environment can be approximated as an object enclosed in a cylinder with the light sources placed around the cylinder boundary, aligned with the longitudinal axis (as shown in Figure 16.6). The symmetry in the cylinder allows the use of a cylinder reflection mapping technique. Cylinder mapping techniques parameterize the texture map along two dimensions, θ, l, where θ is the rotation around the circumference of the cylinder and l is the distance along the cylinder's longitudinal axis. The reflection mapping technique computes the eye reflection vector about the surface normal and the intersection of this reflection vector with the cylindrical map. Given a point P, reflection vector $\mathbf{R}$ and cylinder of radius r, with longitudinal axis parallel to the z axis, the point of intersection Q is $P + k\mathbf{R}$, with the constraint $Q_x^2 + Q_y^2 = r^2$. This results in the quadratic equation

$$(R_x^2 + R_y^2)k^2 + 2(P_xR_x + P_yR_y)k + (P_x^2 + P_y^2 - r^2) = 0$$

with solution

$$k = \frac{-2(P_xR_x + P_yR_y) \pm \sqrt{4(P_xR_x + P_yR_y)^2 - 4(R_x^2 + R_y^2)(P_x^2 + P_y^2 - r^2)}}{2(R_x^2 + R_y^2)}$$

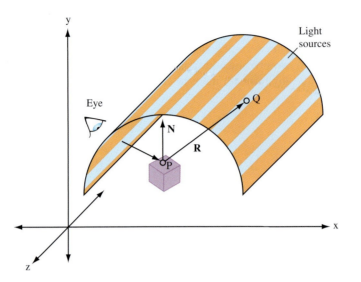

Figure 16.6 Hemicylinder environment map.

With k determined, the larger (positive) solution is chosen, and used to calculate Q. The x and y components of Q are used to determine the angle, θ, in the $x - y$ plane that the intersection makes with the x axis, $\tan\theta = Q_y/Q_x$. The parametric value l is Q_z.

Since each light source extends from one end of the room to the other, the texture map does not vary with the l parameter, so the 2D cylinder map can be simplified to a 1D texture mapping θ to the s coordinate. To map the full range of angles $[-\pi, \pi]$ to the $[0, 1]$ texture coordinates, the mapping $s = [\text{atan}(Q_y/Q_x)/\pi + 1]/2$ is used. A luminance map can be used for the 1D texture map, using regularly spaced 1.0 values against 0.0 background values. The texture mapping can result in significant magnification of the texture image, so better results can be obtained using a high-resolution texture image. Similarly, finer tessellations of the model geometry reduces errors in the interpolation of the angle θ across the polygon faces.

To render using the technique, the s texture coordinate must be computed for each vertex in the model. Each time the eye position changes, the texture coordinates must be recomputed. If available, a vertex program can be used to perform the computation in the transformation pipeline.

16.7 Line Rendering Techniques

Many design applications provide an option to display models using some form of *wireframe* rendering using lines rather than filled polygons. Line renderings may be generated considerably faster if the application is *fill limited*, line renderings may be used to provide additional insight since geometry that is normally occluded may be visible in a line rendered scene. Line renderings can also provide a visual measure of the complexity of the model geometry. If all of the edges of each primitive are drawn, the viewer is given an indication of the number of polygons in the model. There are a number of useful line rendering variations, such as hidden line removal and silhouette edges, described in the following sections.

16.7.1 Wireframe Models

To draw a polygonal model in wireframe, there are several methods available, ordered from least to most efficient to render.

1. Draw the model as polygons in *line mode* using `glBegin(GL_POLYGON)` and `glPolygonMode(GL_FRONT_AND_BACK, GL_LINE)`.
   This method is the simplest if the application already displays the model as a shaded solid, since it involves a single mode change. However, it is likely to be significantly slower than the other methods because more processing usually occurs for polygons than for lines and because every edge that is common to two polygons will be drawn twice. This method is undesirable when using antialiased lines as well, since lines drawn twice will be brighter than any lines drawn just once. The double-edge problem can be eliminated by using an edge flag to remove one of the lines at a common edge. However, to use edge flags the application must keep track of which vertices are part of common edges.

2. Draw the polygons as line loops using `glBegin(GL_LINE_LOOP)`.
   This method is almost as simple as the first, requiring only a change to each `glBegin` call. However, except for possibly eliminating the extra processing required for polygons it has all of the other undesirable features as well. Edge flags cannot be used to eliminate the double edge drawing problem.

3. Extract the edges from the model and draw as independent lines using `glBegin(GL_LINES)`.
   This method is more work than the previous two because each edge must be identified and all duplicates removed. However, the extra work need only be done once and the resulting model will be drawn much faster.

4. Extract the edges from the model and connect as many as possible into long line strips using `glBegin(GL_LINE_STRIP)`.
   For just a little bit more effort than the `GL_LINES` method, lines sharing common endpoints can be connected into larger line strips. This has the advantage of requiring less storage, less data transfer bandwidth, and makes most efficient use of any line drawing hardware.

When choosing amongst these alternative methods there are some additional factors to consider. One important consideration is the choice of polygonal primitives used in the model. Independent triangles, quads, and polygons work correctly with edge flags, whereas triangle strips, triangle fans, and quad strips do not. Therefore, algorithms that use edge flags to avoid showing interior edges or double-stroking shared edges will not work correctly with connected primitives. Since connected primitives are generally more efficient than independent primitives, they are the preferred choice whenever possible. This means that the latter two explicit edge drawing algorithms are a better choice.

Conversely, `glPolygonMode` provides processing options that are important to several algorithms; both face culling and depth offsetting can be applied to polygons rendered as lines, but not to line primitives.

16.7.2 Hidden Lines

This section describes techniques to draw wireframe objects with their hidden lines removed or drawn in a style different from the ones that are visible. This technique can clarify complex line drawings of objects, and improve their appearance (Herrell, 1995; Attarwala, 1988).

The algorithm assumes that the object is composed of polygons. The algorithm first renders the object as polygons, and then in the second pass it renders the polygon edges as lines. During the first pass, only the depth buffer is updated. During the second pass, the depth buffer only allows edges that are not obscured by the object's polygons to be rendered, leaving the previous content of the framebuffer undisturbed everywhere an edge is not drawn. The algorithm is as follows:

1. Disable writing to the color buffer with `glColorMask`.

2. Set the depth function to `GL_LEQUAL`.

3. Enable depth testing with `glEnable(GL_DEPTH_TEST)`.

4. Render the object as polygons.

5. Enable writing to the color buffer.

6. Render the object as edges using one of the methods described in Section 16.7.1.

Since the pixels at the edges of primitives rendered as polygons and the pixels from the edges rendered as lines have depth values that are numerically close, depth rasterization artifacts from quantization errors may result. These are manifested as *pixel dropouts* in the lines wherever the depth value of a line pixel is greater than the polygon edge pixel. Using `GL_LEQUAL` eliminates some of the problems, but for best results the lines should be offset from the polygons using either `glPolygonOffset` or `glDepthRange` (described in more detail shortly).

The stencil buffer may be used to avoid the depth-buffering artifacts for convex objects drawn using non-antialiased (jaggy) lines all of one color. The following technique uses the stencil buffer to create a mask where all lines are (both hidden and visible). Then it uses the stencil function to prevent the polygon rendering from updating the depth buffer where the stencil values have been set. When the visible lines are rendered, there is no depth value conflict, since the polygons never touched those pixels. The modified algorithm is as follows:

1. Disable writing to the color buffer with `glColorMask`.

2. Disable depth testing: `glDisable(GL_DEPTH_TEST)`.

3. Enable stenciling: `glEnable(GL_STENCIL_TEST)`.

4. Clear the stencil buffer.

5. Set the stencil buffer to set the stencil values to 1 where pixels are drawn: `glStencilFunc(GL_ALWAYS, 1, 1)` and `glStencilOp(GL_REPLACE, GL_REPLACE GL_REPLACE)`.

6. Render the object as edges.

7. Use the stencil buffer to mask out pixels where the stencil value is 1: `glStencilFunc(GL_EQUAL, 1, 1)` and `glStencilOp(GL_KEEP, GL_KEEP, GL_KEEP)`.

8. Render the object as polygons.

9. Disable stenciling: `glDisable(GL_STENCIL_TEST)`.

10. Enable writing to the color buffer.

11. Render the object as edges.

Variants of this algorithm may be applied to each convex part of an object, or, if the topology of the object is not known, to each individual polygon to render well-behaved hidden line images.

Instead of removing hidden lines, sometimes it's desirable to render them with a different color or pattern. This can be done with a modification of the algorithm:

1. Change the depth function to `GL_LEQUAL`.

2. Leave the color depth buffer enabled for writing.

3. Set the color and/or pattern for the hidden lines.

4. Render the object as edges.

5. Disable writing to the color buffer.

6. Render the object as polygons.

7. Set the color and/or pattern for the visible lines.

8. Render the object as edges using one of the methods described in Section 16.7.1.

In this technique, all edges are drawn twice: first with the hidden line pattern, then with the visible one. Rendering the object as polygons updates the depth buffer, preventing the second pass of line drawing from affecting the hidden lines.

16.7.3 Polygon Offset

To enhance the preceding methods, the `glPolygonOffset` command can be used to move the lines and polygons relative to each other. If the edges are drawn as lines using polygon mode, `glEnable(GL_POLYGON_OFFSET_LINE)` can be used to offset the lines in front of the polygons. If a faster version of line drawing is used (as described in Section 16.7.1), `glEnable(GL_POLYGON_OFFSET_FILL)` can be used to move the polygon surfaces behind the lines. If maintaining correct depth buffer values is necessary for later processing, surface offsets may not be an option and the application should use line offsets instead.

Polygon offset is designed to provide greater offsets for polygons viewed more edge-on than for polygons that are flatter (more parallel) relative to the screen. A single constant value may not work for all polygons, since variations resulting from depth interpolation inaccuracies during rasterization are related to the way depth values change between fragments. The depth change is the z slope of the primitive relative to window-space x and y. The depth offset is computed as $o_w = factor*m + r*units$, where $m = \sqrt{(\frac{\partial z_w}{\partial x_w})^2 + (\frac{\partial z_w}{\partial y_w})^2}$. The value of m is often approximated with the maximum of the absolute value of the x and y partial derivatives (slopes), since this can be computed more efficiently. The maximum slope value is computed for each polygon and is scaled by *factor*. A constant bias is added to deal with polygons that have very small slopes. When polygon offset was promoted from an extension to a core feature (OpenGL 1.1), the bias value was changed from an implementation-dependent value to a normalized scaling factor, *units*, in the range [0, 1]. This value is scaled by the implementation-dependent depth buffer *minimum resolvable difference* value, r, to produce the final value. This minimum resolvable difference value reflects the precision of the rasterization system and depth buffer storage. For a simple n-bit depth buffer, the value is 2^{-n}, but for implementations that use compressed depth representations the derivation of the value is more complicated.

Since the slope offset must be computed separately for each polygon, the extra processing can slow down rendering. Once the parameters have been tuned for a particular OpenGL implementation, however, the same unmodified code should work well on other implementations.

16.7.4 Depth Range

An effect similar to the constant term of polygon offset can be achieved using `glDepthRange` with no performance penalty. This is done by displacing the *near* value from 0.0 by a small amount, ϵ, while setting the *far* value to 1.0 for all surface drawing. Then when the edges are drawn the *near* value is set to 0.0 and the *far* value is displaced by the same amount. Since the NDC depth value, z_d, is transformed to window coordinates as

$$z_w = \frac{[(f - n)z_d + (n + f)]}{2}$$

surfaces drawn with a near value of $n + \epsilon$ are displaced by

$$o_w = \frac{[-\epsilon z_d + \epsilon]}{2}$$

and lines with a far value of $f - \epsilon$ are displaced by

$$o_w = \frac{[-\epsilon z_d - \epsilon]}{2}$$

The resulting relative displacement between an edge and surface pixel is ϵ. Unlike the polygon offset bias, the depth range offset is not scaled by the implementation-specific minimum resolvable depth difference. This means that the application must determine the offset value empirically and that it may vary between different OpenGL implementations. Values typically start at approximately 0.00001. Since there is no slope-proportionate term, the value may need to be significantly larger to avoid artifacts with polygons that are nearly edge on.

16.7.5 Haloed Lines

Haloing lines can make it easier to understand a wireframe drawing. Lines that pass behind other lines stop short before passing behind, making it clearer which line is in front of the other.

Haloed lines can be drawn using the depth buffer. The technique uses two passes. The first pass disables updates to the color buffer, updating only the content of the depth buffer. The line width is set to be greater than the normal line width and the lines are rendered. This width determines the extent of the halos. In the second pass, the normal line width is reinstated, color buffer updates are enabled, and the lines are rendered a second time. Each line will be bordered on both sides by a wider "invisible line" in the depth buffer. This wider line will mask other lines that pass beneath it, as shown in Figure 16.7 The algorithm works for antialiased lines, too. The mask lines

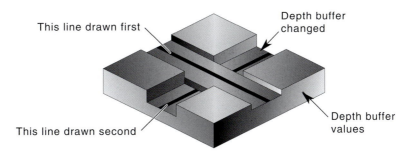

Figure 16.7 Haloed line.

should be drawn as aliased lines and be as least as wide as the footprint of the antialiased lines.

1. Disable writing to the color buffer.

2. Enable the depth buffer for writing.

3. Increase line width.

4. Render lines.

5. Restore line width.

6. Enable writing to the color buffer.

7. Ensure that depth testing is on, passing on GL_LEQUAL.

8. Render lines.

This method will not work where multiple lines with the same depth meet. Instead of connecting, all of the lines will be "blocked" by the last wide line drawn. There can also be depth buffer rasterization problems when the wide line depth values are changed by another wide line crossing it. This effect becomes more pronounced if the narrow lines are widened to improve image clarity.

If the lines are drawn using polygon mode, the problems can be alleviated by using polygon offset to move narrower visible lines in front of the wider obscuring lines. The minimum offset should be used to avoid lines from one surface of the object "popping through" the lines of an another surface separated by only a small depth value.

If the vertices of the object's faces are oriented to allow face culling, it can be used to sort the object surfaces and allow a more robust technique: the lines of the object's back faces are drawn, obscuring wide lines of the front face are drawn, and finally the narrow lines of the front face are drawn. No special depth buffer techniques are needed.

1. Cull the front faces of the object.

2. Draw the object as lines.

3. Cull the back faces of the object.

4. Draw the object as wide lines in the background color.

5. Draw the object as lines.

Since the depth buffer isn't needed, there are no depth rasterization problems. The back-face culling technique is fast and works well. However, it is not general since it doesn't work for multiple obscuring or intersecting objects.

16.7.6 Silhouette Edges

Sometimes it can be useful for highlighting purposes to draw a silhouette edge around a complex object. A silhouette edge defines the outer boundaries of the object with respect to the viewer (as shown in Figure 16.8).

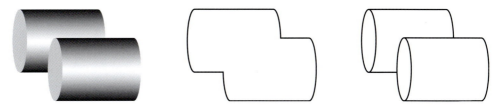

Figure 16.8 Shaded solid image, silhouette edges, silhouette and boundary edges.

The stencil buffer can be used to render a silhouette edge around an object. With this technique, the application can render either the silhouette alone or the object with a silhouette around it (Rustagi, 1989).

The object is drawn four times, each time displaced by one pixel in the x or y direction. This offset must be applied to the window coordinates. An easy way to do this is to change the viewport coordinates each time, changing the viewport origin. The color and depth values are turned off, so only the stencil buffer is affected. Scissor testing can be used to avoid drawing outside the original viewport.

Every time the object covers a pixel, it increments the pixel's stencil value. When the four passes have been completed, the perimeter pixels of the object will have stencil values of 2 or 3. The interior will have values of 4, and all pixels surrounding the object exterior will have values of 0 or 1. A final rendering pass that masks everything but pixels with stencil values of 2 or 3 produces the silhouette. The steps in the algorithm are as follows:

1. Render the object (skip this step if only the silhouette is needed).

2. Clear the stencil buffer to zero.

3. Disable color and depth buffer updates using `glColorMask`.

4. Set the stencil function to always pass, and set the stencil operation to increment.

5. Translate the object by $+1$ pixel in y, using `glViewport` and render the object.

6. Translate the object by -2 pixels in y, using `glViewport` and render the object.

7. Translate by $+1$ pixel x and $+1$ pixel in y and render the object.

8. Translate by -2 pixels in x and render the object.

9. Translate by $+1$ pixel in x, bringing the viewport back to the original position.

10. Enable color and depth buffer updates.

11. Set the stencil function to pass if the stencil value is 2 or 3. Since the possible values range from 0 to 4, the stencil function can pass if stencil bit 1 is set (counting from 0).

12. Render a rectangle that covers the screen-space area of the object, or the size of the viewport to render the silhouette.

One of the bigger drawbacks of this image-space algorithm is that it takes a large number of drawing passes to generate the edges. A somewhat more efficient algorithm suggested by Akeley (1998) is to use `glPolygonOffset` to create an offset depth image and then draw the polygons using the line polygon mode. The stencil buffer is again used to count the number of times each pixel is written. However, instead of counting the absolute number of writes to a pixel the stencil value is inverted on each write. The resulting stencil buffer will have a value of 1 wherever a pixel has been drawn an odd number of times. This ensures that lines drawn at the shared edges of polygon faces have stencil values of zero, since the lines will be drawn twice (assuming edge flags are not used). While this algorithm is a little more approximate than the previous algorithm, it only requires two passes through the geometry.

The algorithm is sensitive to the quality of the line rasterization algorithm used by the OpenGL implementation. In particular, if the line from p_0 to p_1 rasterizes differently from the line drawn from p_1 to p_0 by more than just the pixels at the endpoints, artifacts will appear along the shared edges of polygons.

The faster algorithm does not generate quite the same result as the first algorithm because it counts even and odd transitions and relies on the depth image to ensure that other nonvisible surfaces do not interfere with the stencil count. The differences arise in that boundary edges within one object that are in front of another object will be rendered as part of the silhouette image. By boundary edges we mean the *true* edges of the modeled geometry, but not the interior shared-face edges. In many cases this artifact is useful, as silhouette edges by themselves often do not provide sufficient information about the shape of objects. It is possible to combine the algorithm for drawing silhouettes with an additional step in which all of the boundary edges of the geometry are drawn as lines. This produces a hidden line drawing displaying boundary edges plus silhouette edges, as shown in Figure 16.8. The steps of the combined algorithm are as follows:

1. Clear the depth and color buffers and clear the stencil buffer to zero.

2. Disable color buffer writes.

3. Draw the depth buffered geometry using `glPolygonOffset` to offset the object surfaces toward the far clipping plane.

4. Disable writing to the depth buffer and `glPolygonOffset`.

5. Set the stencil function to always pass and set the stencil operation to invert.

6. Enable face culling.

7. Draw the geometry as lines using `glPolygonMode`.

8. Enable writes to the color buffer, disable face culling.

9. Set the stencil function to pass if the stencil value is 1.

10. Render a rectangle that fills the entire window to produce the silhouette image.

11. Draw the true edges of the geometry.

12. Enable writes to the depth buffer.

Since the algorithm uses an offset depth image, it is susceptible to minor artifacts from the interaction of the lines and the depth image similar to those present when using `glPolygonOffset` for hidden line drawings. Since the algorithm mixes lines drawn in polygon mode with line primitives, the surfaces must be offset rather than the lines. This means that the content of the depth buffer will be offset from the true geometry and may need to be reestablished for later processing.

16.7.7 Preventing Antialiasing Artifacts

When drawing a series of wide smoothed lines that overlap, such as an outline composed of a `GL_LINE_LOOP`, more than one fragment may be produced for a given pixel. Since smooth line rendering uses framebuffer blending, this may cause the pixel to appear brighter or darker than expected where fragments overlap.

The stencil buffer can be used to allow only a single fragment to update the pixel. When multiple fragments update a pixel, the one chosen depends on the drawing order. Ideally the fragment with the largest alpha value should be retained rather than one at random. A combination of the stencil test and alpha test can be used to pass only the fragments that have the largest alpha, and therefore contribute the most color to a pixel. Repeatedly drawing and applying alpha test to pass fragments with decreasing alpha, while using the stencil buffer to mark where fragments previously passed, results in a brute-force algorithm that has the effect of sorting fragments by alpha value.

1. Clear the stencil buffer and enable stencil testing.

2. Set the stencil function to test for not equal: `glStencilFunc(GL_NOTEQUAL, 1, 0xff)`.

3. Set the stencil operation to replace stencil values that pass the stencil test and depth test and keep the others.

4. Enable line smoothing and blending.

5. Enable alpha testing.

6. Loop over alpha reference values from 1.0 − *step* to 0, setting the alpha function to pass for alpha greater than the reference value and draw the lines. The number of passes is determined by *step*.

Speed can be traded for quality by increasing the step size or terminating the loop at a larger threshold value. A *step* of 0.02 results in 50 passes and very accurate rendering. However, good results can still be achieved with 10 or fewer passes by favoring alpha values closer to 1.0 or increasing the step size as alpha approaches 0. At the opposite extreme, it is possible to iterate through every possible alpha value, and pass only the fragments that match each specific one, using $step = 1/2^{GL\_ALPHA\_BITS}$.

16.7.8 End Caps on Wide Lines

If wide lines form a loop, such as a silhouette edge or the outline of a polygon, it may be necessary to fill regions where one line ends and another begins to give the appearance of a rounded joint. Smooth wide points can be drawn at the ends of the line segments to form an end cap. The preceding overlap algorithm can be used to avoid blending problems where the point and line overlap.

16.8 Coplanar Polygons and Decaling

Using stenciling to control pixels drawn from a particular primitive can help solve important problems, such as the following:

1. Drawing depth-buffered coplanar polygons without z-buffering artifacts.

2. Decaling multiple textures on a primitive.

Values are written to the stencil buffer to create a mask for the area to be decaled. Then this stencil mask is used to control two separate draw steps: one for the decaled region and one for the rest of the polygon.

A useful example that illustrates the technique is rendering coplanar polygons. If one polygon must be rendered directly on top of another (runway markings, for example). The depth buffer cannot be relied upon to produce a clean separation between the two. This is due to the quantization of the depth buffer. Since the polygons have different vertices, the rendering algorithms can produce z values that are rounded to the wrong depth buffer value, so some pixels of the back polygon may show through the front polygon (Section 6.1.2). In an application with a high frame rate, this results in a shimmering mixture of pixels from both polygons, commonly called "z-fighting." An example is shown in Figure 16.9.

To solve this problem, the closer polygons are drawn with the depth test disabled, on the same pixels covered by the farthest polygons. It appears that the closer polygons are "decaled" on the farther polygons. Decaled polygons can be drawn via the following steps:

1. Turn on stenciling: `glEnable(GL_STENCIL_TEST)`.

2. Set stencil function to always pass: `glStencilFunc(GL_ALWAYS, 1, 1)`.

3. Set stencil op to set 1 if depth test passes: 0 if it fails: `glStencilOp(GL_KEEP, GL_ZERO, GL_REPLACE)`.

4. Draw the base polygon.

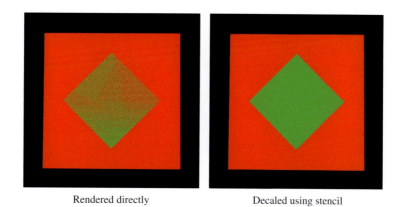

Rendered directly   Decaled using stencil

Figure 16.9 Using stencil to render co-planar polygons.

5. Set stencil function to pass when stencil is 1: `glStencilFunc(GL_EQUAL, 1, 1)`.

6. Disable writes to stencil buffer: `glStencilMask(GL_FALSE)`.

7. Turn off depth buffering: `glDisable(GL_DEPTH_TEST)`.

8. Render the decal polygon.

The stencil buffer does not have to be cleared to an initial value; the stencil values are initialized as a side effect of writing the base polygon. Stencil values will be 1 where the base polygon was successfully written into the framebuffer and 0 where the base polygon generated fragments that failed the depth test. The stencil buffer becomes a mask, ensuring that the decal polygon can only affect the pixels that were touched by the base polygon. This is important if there are other primitives partially obscuring the base polygon and decal polygons.

There are a few limitations to this technique. First, it assumes that the decal polygon does not extend beyond the edge of the base polygon. If it does, the entire stencil buffer must be cleared before drawing the base polygon. This is expensive on some OpenGL implementations. If the base polygon is redrawn with the stencil operations set to zero out the stencil after drawing each decaled polygon, the entire stencil buffer only needs to be cleared once. This is true regardless of the number of decaled polygons.

Second, if the screen extents of multiple base polygons being decaled overlap, the decal process must be performed for one base polygon and its decals before proceeding to another. This is an important consideration if the application collects and then sorts geometry based on its graphics state, because the rendering order of geometry may be changed as a result of the sort.

This process can be extended to allow for a number of overlapping decal polygons, with the number of decals limited by the number of stencil bits available for the framebuffer configuration. Note that the decals do not have to be sorted. The procedure is similar to the previous algorithm, with the following extensions.

A stencil bit is assigned for each decal and the base polygon. The lower the number, the higher the priority of the polygon. The base polygon is rendered as before, except instead of setting its stencil value to one, it is set to the largest priority number. For example, if there are three decal layers the base polygon has a value of 8.

When a decal polygon is rendered, it is only drawn if the decal's priority number is lower than the pixels it is trying to change. For example, if the decal's priority number is 1 it is able to draw over every other decal and the base polygon using `glStencilFunc (GL_LESS, 1, 0)` and `glStencilOp(GL_KEEP, GL_REPLACE, GL_REPLACE)`.

Decals with the lower priority numbers are drawn on top of decals with higher ones. Since the region not covered by the base polygon is zero, no decals can write to it. Multiple decals can be drawn at the same priority level. If they overlap, however, the last one drawn will overlap the previous ones at the same priority level.

Multiple textures can be drawn onto a polygon using a similar technique. Instead of writing decal polygons, the same polygon is drawn with each subsequent texture and an alpha value to blend the old pixel color and the new pixel color together.

16.9 Capping Clipped Solids

When working with solid objects it is often useful to clip the object against a plane and observe the cross section. OpenGL's application-defined clipping planes (sometimes called *model clip planes*) allow an application to clip the scene by a plane. The stencil buffer provides an easy method for adding a "cap" to objects that are intersected by the clipping plane. A capping polygon is embedded in the clipping plane and the stencil buffer is used to trim the polygon to the interior of the solid.

If some care is taken when modeling the object, solids that have a depth complexity greater than 2 (concave or shelled objects) and less than the maximum value of the stencil buffer can be rendered. Object surface polygons must have their vertices ordered so that they face away from the interior for face culling purposes.

The stencil buffer, color buffer, and depth buffer are cleared, and color buffer writes are disabled. The capping polygon is rendered into the depth buffer, and then depth buffer writes are disabled. The stencil operation is set to increment the stencil value where the depth test passes, and the model is drawn with `glCullFace(GL_BACK)`. The stencil operation is then set to decrement the stencil value where the depth test passes, and the model is drawn with `glCullFace(GL_FRONT)`.

At this point, the stencil buffer is 1 wherever the clipping plane is enclosed by the front-facing and back-facing surfaces of the object. The depth buffer is cleared, color buffer writes are enabled, and the polygon representing the clipping plane is now drawn using whatever material properties are desired, with the stencil function set to GL_EQUAL and the reference value set to 1. This draws the color and depth values of the cap into the framebuffer only where the stencil values equal 1. Finally, stenciling is disabled, the OpenGL clipping plane is applied, and the clipped object is drawn with color and depth enabled.

16.10 Constructive Solid Geometry

Constructive solid geometry (CSG) models are constructed through the intersection (∩), union (∪), and subtraction (−) of solid objects, some of which may be CSG objects themselves (Goldfeather, 1986). The tree formed by the binary CSG operators and their operands is known as the CSG tree. Figure 16.10 shows an example of a CSG tree and the resulting model.

The representation used in CSG for solid objects varies, but we will consider a solid to be a collection of polygons forming a closed volume. *Solid*, *primitive*, and *object* are used here to mean the same thing.

CSG objects have traditionally been rendered through the use of raycasting, (which is slow) or through the construction of a boundary representation (B-rep). B-reps vary in construction, but are generally defined as a set of polygons that form the surface of the result of the CSG tree. One method of generating a B-rep is to take the polygons forming the surface of each primitive and trim away the polygons (or portions thereof) that do not satisfy the CSG operations. B-rep models are typically generated once and then manipulated as a static model because they are slow to generate.

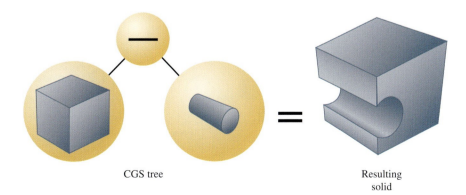

CGS tree   Resulting solid

Figure 16.10 An example of constructive solid geometry.

Drawing a CSG model using stenciling usually requires drawing more polygons than a B-rep would contain for the same model. Enabling stencil itself also may reduce performance. Nonetheless, some portions of a CSG tree may be interactively manipulated using stenciling if the remainder of the tree is cached as a B-rep.

The algorithm presented here is from a paper (Wiegand, 1996) describing a GL-independent method for using stenciling in a CSG modeling system for fast interactive updates. The technique can also process concave solids, the complexity of which is limited by the number of stencil planes available.

The algorithm presented here assumes that the CSG tree is in "normal" form. A tree is in normal form when all intersection and subtraction operators have a left subtree that contains no union operators and a right subtree that is simply a primitive (a set of polygons representing a single solid object). All union operators are pushed toward the root, and all intersection and subtraction operators are pushed toward the leaves. For example, $(((A \cap B) - C) \cup (((D \cap E) \cap G) - F)) \cup H$ is in normal form; Figure 16.11 illustrates the structure of that tree and the characteristics of a tree in this form.

A CSG tree can be converted to normal form by repeatedly applying the following set of production rules to the tree and then its subtrees.

1. $X - (Y \cup Z) \rightarrow (X - Y) - Z$

2. $X \cap (Y \cup Z) \rightarrow (X \cap Y) \cup (X \cap Z)$

3. $X - (Y \cap Z) \rightarrow (X - Y) \cup (X - Z)$

4. $X \cap (Y \cap Z) \rightarrow (X \cap Y) \cap Z$

5. $X - (Y - Z) \rightarrow (X - Y) \cup (X \cap Z)$

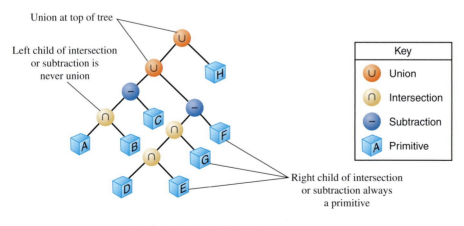

$((((A \cap B) - C) \cup (((D \cap E) \cap G) - F)) \cup H)$

Figure 16.11 A CSG tree in normal form.

6. $X \cap (Y - Z) \rightarrow (X \cap Y) - Z$

7. $(X - Y) \cap Z \rightarrow (X \cap Z) - Y$

8. $(X \cup Y) - Z \rightarrow (X - Z) \cup (Y - Z)$

9. $(X \cup Y) \cap Z \rightarrow (X \cap Z) \cup (Y \cap Z)$

X, Y, and Z here match either primitives or subtrees. The algorithm used to apply the production rules to the CSG tree follows.

```
normalize(tree *t){
    if (isPrimitive(t))
        return;

    do {
        while (matchesRule(t))  /* Using rules given above */
            applyFirstMatchingRule(t);
        normalize(t->left);
    } while (!(isUnionOperation(t) ||
        (isPrimitive(t->right) &&
          ! isUnionOperation(T->left))));
    normalize(t->right);
}
```

Normalization may increase the size of the tree and add primitives that do not contribute to the final image. The bounding volume of each CSG subtree can be used to prune the tree as it is normalized. Bounding volumes for the tree can be calculated using the following algorithm.

```
findBounds(tree *t){
    if (isPrimitive(t))
        return;

    findBounds(t->left);
    findBounds(t->right);

    switch (t->operation){
      case UNION:
        t->bounds = unionOfBounds(t->left->bounds,
                                  t->right->bounds);
      case INTERSECTION:
        t->bounds = intersectionOfBounds(t->left->bounds,
                                         t->right->bounds);
```

```
    case SUBTRACTION:
      t->bounds = t->left->bounds;
    }
  }
```

CSG subtrees rooted by the intersection or subtraction operators may be pruned at each step in the normalization process using the following two rules.

1. If T is an intersection and not `intersects(T->left->bounds, T->right->bounds)`, delete T.

2. If T is a subtraction and not `intersects(T->left->bounds, T->right->bounds)`, replace T with `T->left`.

The normalized CSG tree is a binary tree, but it is important to think of the tree as a "sum of products" to understand the stencil CSG procedure.

Consider all unions as sums. Next, consider all the intersections and subtractions as products. (Subtraction is equivalent to intersection with the complement of the term to the right; for example, $A - B = A \cap \bar{B}$.) Imagine all unions flattened out into a single union with multiple children. That union is the "sum." The resulting subtrees of that union are all composed of subtractions and intersections, the right branch of those operations is always a single primitive, and the left branch is another operation or a single primitive. Consider each child subtree of the imaginary multiple union as a single expression containing all intersection and subtraction operations concatenated from the bottom up. These expressions are the "products." For example, $((A \cap B) - C) \cup (((G \cap D) - E) \cap F) \cup H$ can be thought of as $(A \cap B - C) \cup (G \cap D - E \cap F) \cup H$. Figure 16.12 illustrates this process.

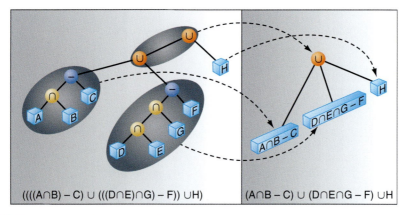

$$((((A \cap B) - C) \cup (((D \cap E) \cap G) - F)) \cup H) \qquad (A \cap B - C) \cup (D \cap E \cap G - F) \cup H$$

Figure 16.12 Thinking of a CSG tree as a sum of products.

At this time, redundant terms can be removed from each product. Where a term subtracts itself $(A - A)$, the entire product can be deleted. Where a term intersects itself $(A \cap A)$, that intersection operation can be replaced with the term itself.

All unions can be rendered simply by finding the visible surfaces of the left and right subtrees and allowing the depth test to determine the visible surface. All products can be rendered by drawing the visible surfaces of each primitive in the product and trimming those surfaces with the volumes of the other primitives in the product. For example, to render $A - B$ the visible surfaces of A are trimmed by the complement of the volume of B, and the visible surfaces of B are trimmed by the volume of A.

The visible surfaces of a product are the front-facing surfaces of the operands of intersections and the back-facing surfaces of the right operands of subtraction. For example, in $(A - B \cap C)$ the visible surfaces are the front-facing surfaces of A and C and the back-facing surfaces of B.

Concave solids are processed as sets of front-facing or back-facing surfaces. The "convexity" of a solid is defined as the maximum number of pairs of front and back surfaces that can be drawn from the viewing direction. Figure 16.13 shows some examples of the convexity of objects. The nth front surface of a k-convex primitive is denoted A_{nf}, and the nth back surface is A_{nb}. Because a solid may vary in convexity when viewed from different directions, accurately representing the convexity of a primitive may be difficult and may involve reevaluating the CSG tree at each new view. Instead, the algorithm must be given the *maximum possible* convexity of a primitive; it then draws the nth visible surface by using a counter in the stencil planes.

The CSG tree must be further reduced to a "sum of partial products" by converting each product to a union of products, each consisting of the product of the visible surfaces of the target primitive with the remaining terms in the product. For example, if A, B, and D

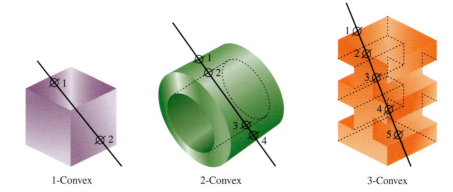

1-Convex   2-Convex   3-Convex

Figure 16.13 Examples of n-convex solids.

are 1-convex and C is 2-convex:

$$(A - B \cap C \cap D) \rightarrow$$
$$(A_{0f} - B \cap C \cap D) \cup$$
$$(B_{0b} \cap A \cap C \cap D) \cup$$
$$(C_{0f} \cap A - B \cap D) \cup$$
$$(C_{1f} \cap A - B \cap D) \cup$$
$$(D_{0f} \cap A \cap B \cap C)$$

Because the target term in each product has been reduced to a single front-facing or back-facing surface, the bounding volumes of that term will be a subset of the bounding volume of the original complete primitive. Once the tree is converted to partial products, the pruning process may be applied again with these subset volumes. In each resulting child subtree representing a partial product, the leftmost term is called the "target" surface, and the remaining terms on the right branches are called "trimming" primitives.

The resulting sum of partial products reduces the rendering problem to rendering each partial product correctly before drawing the union of the results. Each partial product is rendered by drawing the target surface of the partial product and then "classifying" the pixels generated by that surface with the depth values generated by each of the trimming primitives in the partial product. If pixels drawn by the trimming primitives pass the depth test an even number of times, that pixel in the target primitive is "out," and discarded. If the count is odd, the target primitive pixel is "in," and kept.

Because the algorithm saves depth buffer contents between each object, the number of depth saves and restores can be minimized by drawing as many of target and trimming primitives for each pass as can fit in the stencil buffer.

The algorithm uses one stencil bit (S_p) as a toggle for trimming primitive depth test passes (parity); n stencil bits for counting to the nth surface (S_{count}), where n is the smallest number for which 2^n is larger than the maximum convexity of a current object, and as many bits as are available (S_a) to accumulate whether target pixels have to be discarded. Because S_{count} will require the GL_INCR operation, it must be stored contiguously in the least-significant bits of the stencil buffer. S_p and S_{count} are used in two separate steps, and so may share stencil bits.

For example, drawing two 5-convex primitives requires one S_p bit, three S_{count} bits, and two S_a bits. Because S_p and S_{count} are independent, the total number of stencil bits required is 5.

Once the tree is converted to a sum of partial products, the individual products are rendered. Products are grouped so that as many partial products can be rendered between depth buffer saves and restores as the stencil buffer has capacity.

For each group, color buffer writes are disabled, the contents of the depth buffer are saved, and the depth buffer is cleared. Then, every target in the group is classified against its trimming primitives. The depth buffer is then restored, and every target in the group is rendered against the trimming mask. The depth buffer save/restore can be optimized by saving and restoring only the region containing the screen-projected bounding volumes of the target surfaces.

```
for each group
    glReadPixels(...);
    <classify the group>
    glStencilMask(0);    /* so DrawPixels won't affect Stencil */
    glDrawPixels(...);
    <render the group>
```

Classification consists of drawing each target primitive's depth value and then clearing those depth values where the target primitive is determined to be outside the trimming primitives.

```
glClearDepth(far);
glClear(GL_DEPTH_BUFFER_BIT);
a = 0;
for (each target surface in the group)
    for (each partial product targeting that surface)
        <render the depth values for the surface>
        for (each trimming primitive in that partial product)
            <trim the depth values against that primitive>
        <set Sa to 1 where Sa = 0 and Z < Zfar>
        a++;
```

The depth values for the surface are rendered by drawing the primitive containing the target surface with color and stencil writes disabled. (S_{count}) is used to mask out all but the target surface. In practice, most CSG primitives are convex, so the algorithm is optimized for that case.

```
if (the target surface is front facing)
    glCullFace(GL_BACK);
else
    glCullFace(GL_FRONT);

if (the surface is 1-convex)
    glDepthMask(1);
    glColorMask(0, 0, 0, 0);
    glStencilMask(0);
    <draw the primitive containing the target surface>
else
    glDepthMask(1);
    glColorMask(0, 0, 0, 0);
```

```
glStencilMask(Scount);
glStencilFunc(GL_EQUAL, index of surface, Scount);
glStencilOp(GL_KEEP, GL_KEEP, GL_INCR);
<draw the primitive containing the target surface>
glClearStencil(0);
glClear(GL_STENCIL_BUFFER_BIT);
```

Each trimming primitive for that target surface is then drawn in turn. Depth testing is enabled and writes to the depth buffer are disabled. Stencil operations are masked to S_p, and the S_p bit in the stencil is cleared to 0. The stencil function and operation are set so that S_p is toggled every time the depth test for a fragment from the trimming primitive succeeds. After drawing the trimming primitive, if this bit is 0 for uncomplemented primitives (or 1 for complemented primitives) the target pixel is "out," and must be marked "discard" by enabling writes to the depth buffer and storing the far depth value (Z_f) into the depth buffer everywhere the S_p indicates "discard."

```
glDepthMask(0);
glColorMask(0, 0, 0, 0);
glStencilMask(mask for Sp);
glClearStencil(0);
glClear(GL_STENCIL_BUFFER_BIT);
glStencilFunc(GL_ALWAYS, 0, 0);
glStencilOp(GL_KEEP, GL_KEEP, GL_INVERT);
<draw the trimming primitive>
glDepthMask(1);
```

Once all the trimming primitives are rendered, the values in the depth buffer are Z_f for all target pixels classified as "out." The S_a bit for that primitive is set to 1 everywhere the depth value for a pixel is not equal to Z_f, and 0 otherwise.

Each target primitive in the group is finally rendered into the framebuffer with depth testing and depth writes enabled, the color buffer enabled, and the stencil function and operation set to write depth and color only where the depth test succeeds and S_a is 1. Only the pixels inside the volumes of all the trimming primitives are drawn.

```
glDepthMask(1);
glColorMask(1, 1, 1, 1);
a = 0;
for (each target primitive in the group)
    glStencilMask(0);
    glStencilFunc(GL_EQUAL, 1, Sa);
    glCullFace(GL_BACK);
    <draw the target primitive>
    glStencilMask(Sa);
```

```
glClearStencil(0);
glClear(GL_STENCIL_BUFFER_BIT);
a++;
```

Further techniques are available for adding clipping planes (half-spaces), including more normalization rules and pruning opportunities (Wiegand, 1996). This is especially important in the case of the near clipping plane in the viewing frustum.

Scene Realism

Although a number of fields of computer graphics, such as scientific visualization and CAD, don't make creating realistic images a primary focus, it is an important goal for many others. Computer graphics in the entertainment industry often strives for realistic effects, and realistic rendering has always been a central area of research. A lot of image realism can be achieved through attention to the basics: using detailed geometric models, creating high-quality surface textures, carefully tuning lighting and material parameters, and sorting and clipping geometry to achieve artifact-free transparency. There are limits to this approach, however. Increasing the resolution of geometry and textures can rapidly become expensive in terms of design overhead, as well as incurring runtime storage and performance penalties.

Applications usually can't pursue realism at any price. Most are constrained by performance requirements (especially interactive applications) and development costs. Maximizing realism becomes a process of focusing on changes that make the most visual difference. A fruitful approach centers around augmenting areas where OpenGL has only basic functionality, such as improving surface lighting effects and accurately modeling the lighting interactions between objects in the scene.

This chapter focuses on the second area: interobject lighting. OpenGL has only a very basic interobject lighting model: it sums all of the contributions from secondary reflections in a single "ambient illumination" term. It does have many important building blocks, however (such as environment mapping) that can be used to model object interactions. This chapter covers the ambient lighting effects that tend to dominate a scene: specular and diffuse reflection between objects, refractive effects, and shadows.

17.1 Reflections

Reflections are one of the most noticeable effects of interobject lighting. Getting it right can add a lot of realism to a scene for a moderate effort. It also provides very strong visual clues about the relative positioning of objects. Here, reflection is divided into two categories: highly specular "mirror-like" reflections and "radiosity-like" interobject lighting based on diffuse reflections.

Directly calculating the physics of reflection using algorithms such as ray tracing can be expensive. As the physics becomes more accurate, the computational overhead increases dramatically with scene complexity. The techniques described here help an application budget its resources, by attempting to capture the most significant reflection effects in ways that minimize overhead. They maintain good performance by approximating more expensive approaches, such as ray tracing, using less expensive methods.

17.1.1 Object vs. Image Techniques

Consider a reflection as a view of a "virtual" object. As shown in Figure 17.1, a scene is composed of reflected objects rendered "behind" their reflectors, the same objects drawn in their unreflected positions, and the reflectors themselves. Drawing a reflection becomes a two-step process: using objects in the scene to create virtual reflected versions and drawing the virtual objects clipped by their reflectors.

There are two ways to implement this concept: image-space methods using textures and object-space approaches that manipulate geometry. Texture methods create a texture image from a view of the reflected objects, and then apply it to a reflecting surface. An advantage of this approach, being image-based, is that it doesn't depend on the geometric representation of the objects being reflected. Object-space methods, by contrast, often must distort an object to model curved reflectors, and the realism of their reflections depends on the accuracy of the surface model. Texture methods have the most built-in OpenGL support. In addition to basic texture mapping, texture matrices, and

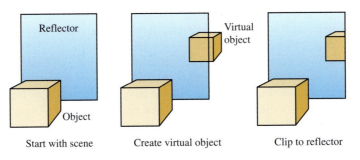

Start with scene   Create virtual object   Clip to reflector

Figure 17.1 Mirror reflection of the scene.

texgen functionality, environment texturing support makes rendering the reflections from arbitrary surfaces relatively straightforward.

Object-space methods, in contrast, require much more work from the application. Reflected "virtual" objects are created by calculating a "virtual" vertex for every vertex in the original object, using the relationship between the object, reflecting surface, and viewer. Although more difficult to implement, this approach has some significant advantages. Being an object-space technique, its performance is insensitive to image resolution, and there are fewer sampling issues to consider. An object-space approach can also produce more accurate reflections. Environment mapping, used in most texturing approaches, is an approximation. It has the greatest accuracy showing reflected objects that are far from the reflector. Object-space techniques can more accurately model reflections of nearby objects. Whether these accuracy differences are significant, or even noticeable, depends on the details of the depicted scene and the requirements of the application.

Object-space, image-space, and some hybrid approaches are discussed in this chapter. The emphasis is on object-space techniques, however, since most image-space techniques can be directly implemented using OpenGL's texturing functionality. Much of that functionality is covered in Sections 5.4 and 17.3.

Virtual Objects

Whether a reflection technique is classified as an object-space or image-space approach, and whether the reflector is planar or not, one thing is constant: a virtual object must be created, and it must be clipped against the reflector. Before analyzing various reflection techniques, the next two sections provide some general information about creating and clipping virtual objects.

Clipping Virtual Objects Proper reflection clipping involves two steps: clipping any reflected geometry that lies outside the edges of the reflected object (from the viewer's point of view) and clipping objects that extend both in front of and behind the reflector (or penetrate it) to the reflector's surface. These two types of clipping are shown in Figure 17.2. Clipping to a planar reflector is the most straightforward. Although the

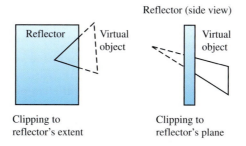

Figure 17.2 Clipping virtual objects to reflectors.

application is different, standard clipping techniques can often be reused. For example, user-defined clip planes can be used to clip to the reflector's edges or surface when the reflection region is sufficiently regular or to reduce the area that needs to be clipped by other methods.

While clipping to a reflecting surface is trivial for planar reflectors, it can become quite challenging when the reflector has a complex shape, and a more powerful clipping technique may be called for. One approach, useful for some applications, is to handle reflection clipping through careful object modeling. Geometry is created that only contains the parts visible in the reflector. In this case, no clipping is necessary. While efficient, this approach can only be used in special circumstances, where the view position (but not necessarily the view direction), reflector, and reflected geometry maintain a static relationship.

There are also image-space approaches to clipping. Stencil buffering can be useful for clipping complex reflectors, since it can be used to clip per-pixel to an arbitrary reflection region. Rather than discarding pixels, a texture map of the reflected image can be constructed from the reflected geometry and applied to the reflecting object's surface. The reflector geometry itself then clips an image of the virtual object to the reflector's edges. An appropriate depth buffer function can also be used to remove reflecting geometry that extends behind the reflector. Note that including stencil, depth, and texture clipping techniques to object-space reflection creates hybrid object/image space approaches, and thus brings back pixel sampling and image resolution issues.

Issues When Rendering Virtual Objects Rendering a virtual object properly has a surprising number of difficulties to overcome. While transforming the vertices of the source object to create the virtual one is conceptually straightforward when the reflector is planar, a reflection across a nonplanar reflector can distort the geometry of the virtual object. In this case, the original tessellation of the object may no longer be sufficient to model it accurately. If the curvature of a surface increases, that region of the object may require retessellation into smaller triangles. A general solution to this problem is difficult to construct without resorting to higher-order surface representations.

Even after finding the proper reflected vertices for the virtual object, finding the connectivity between them to form polygons can be difficult. Connectivity between vertices can be complicated by the effects of clipping the virtual object against the reflector. Clipping can remove vertices and add new ones, and it can be tedious to handle all corner cases, especially when reflectors have complex or nonplanar shapes.

More issues can arise after creating the proper geometry for the virtual object. To start, note that reflecting an object to create a virtual one reverses the vertex ordering of an object's faces, so the proper face-culling state for reflected objects is the opposite of the original's. Since a virtual object is also in a different position compared to the source object, care must be taken to light the virtual objects properly. In general, the light sources for the reflected objects should be reflected too. The difference in lighting may not be noticeable under diffuse lighting, but changes in specular highlights can be quite obvious.

17.1.2 Planar Reflectors

Modeling reflections across planar or nearly planar surfaces is a common occurrence. Many synthetic objects are shiny and flat, and a number of natural surfaces, such as the surface of water and ice, can often be approximated using planar reflectors. In addition to being useful techniques in themselves, planar reflection methods are also important building blocks for creating techniques to handle reflections across nonplanar and nonuniform surfaces.

Consider a model of a room with a flat mirror on one wall. To reflect objects in this planar reflector, its orientation and position must be established. This can be done by computing the equation of the plane that contains the mirror. Mirror reflections, being specular, depend on the position of both the reflecting surface and the viewer. For planar reflectors, however, reflecting the geometry is a viewer-independent operation, since it depends only on the relative position of the geometry and the reflecting surface. To draw the reflected geometry, a transform must be computed that reflects geometry across the mirror's plane. This transform can be conceptualized as reflecting either the eye point or the objects across the plane. Either representation can be used; both produce identical results.

An arbitrary reflection transformation can be decomposed into a translation of the mirror plane to the origin, a rotation embedding the mirror into a major plane (for example the $x - y$ plane), a scale of -1 along the axis perpendicular to that plane (in this case the z axis), the inverse of the rotation previously used, and a translation back to the mirror location.

Given a vertex P on the planar reflector's surface and a vector $\mathbf{V}$ perpendicular to the plane, the reflection transformations sequence can be expressed as the following single 4×4 matrix R (Goldman, 1990):

$$
R = \begin{pmatrix}
1 - 2V_x^2 & -2V_x V_y & -2V_x V_z & 2(P \cdot V)V_x \\
-2V_x V_y & 1 - 2V_y^2 & -2V_y V_z & 2(P \cdot V)V_y \\
-2V_x V_z & -2V_y V_z & 1 - 2V_z^2 & 2(P \cdot V)V_z \\
0 & 0 & 0 & 1
\end{pmatrix}
$$

Applying this transformation to the original scene geometry produces a virtual scene on the opposite side of the reflector. The entire scene is duplicated, simulating a reflector of infinite extent. The following section goes into detail on how to render and clip virtual geometry against planar reflectors to produce the effect of a finite reflector.

Clipping Planar Reflections

Reflected geometry must be clipped to ensure it is only visible in the reflecting surface. To do this properly, the reflected geometry that appears beyond the boundaries of the reflector from the viewer's perspective must be clipped, as well as the reflected geometry that ends up in front of the reflector. The latter case is the easiest to handle. Since the reflector is planar, a single application-defined clipping plane can be made coplanar to the reflecting surface, oriented to clip out reflected geometry that ends up closer to the viewer.

If the reflector is polygonal, with few edges, it can be clipped with the remaining application clip planes. For each edge of the reflector, calculate the plane that is formed by that edge and the eye point. Configure this plane as a clip plane (without applying the reflection transformation). Be sure to save a clip plane for the reflector surface, as mentioned previously. Using clip planes for reflection clipping is the highest-performance approach for many OpenGL implementations. Even if the reflector has a complex shape, clip planes may be useful as a performance-enhancing technique, removing much of the reflected geometry before applying a more general technique such as stenciling.

In some circumstances, clipping can be done by the application. Some graphics support libraries support culling a geometry database to the current viewing frustum. Reflection clipping performance may be improved if the planar mirror reflector takes up only a small region of the screen: a reduced frustum that tightly bounds the screen-space projection of the reflector can be used when drawing the reflected scene, reducing the number of objects to be processed.

For reflectors with more complex edges, stencil masking is an excellent choice. There are a number of approaches available. One is to clear the stencil buffer, along with the rest of the framebuffer, and then render the reflector. Color and depth buffer updates are disabled, rendering is configured to update the stencil buffer to a specific value where a pixel would be written. Once this step is complete, the reflected geometry can be rendered, with the stencil buffer configured to reject updates on pixels that don't have the given stencil value set.

Another stenciling approach is to render the reflected geometry first, and then use the reflector to update the stencil buffer. Then the color and depth buffer can be cleared, using the stencil value to control pixel updates, as before. In this case, the stencil buffer controls what geometry is erased, rather than what is drawn. Although this method can't always be used (it doesn't work well if interreflections are required, for example), it may be the higher performance option for some implementations: drawing the entire scene with stencil testing enabled is likely to be slower than using stencil to control clearing the screen. The following outlines the second approach in more detail.

1. Clear the stencil and depth buffers.

2. Configure the stencil buffer such that 1 will be set at each pixel where polygons are rendered.

3. Disable drawing into the color buffers using `glColorMask`.

4. Draw the reflector using blending if desired.

5. Reconfigure the stencil test using `glStencilOp` and `glStencilFunc`.

6. Clear the color and depth buffer to the background color.

7. Disable the stencil test.

8. Draw the rest of the scene (everything but the reflector and reflected objects).

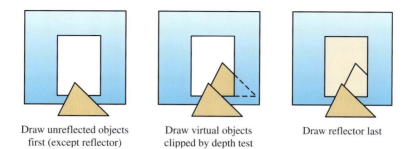

Draw unreflected objects first (except reflector)   Draw virtual objects clipped by depth test   Draw reflector last

Figure 17.3 Masking reflections with depth buffering.

The previous example makes it clear that the order in which the reflected geometry, reflector, and unreflected geometry are drawn can create different performance trade-offs. An important element to consider when ordering geometry is the depth buffer. Proper object ordering can take advantage of depth buffering to clip some or all of the reflected geometry automatically. For example, a reflector surrounded by nonreflected geometry (such as a mirror hanging on a wall) will benefit from drawing the nonreflected geometry in the scene first, before drawing the reflected objects. The first rendering stage will initialize the depth buffer so that it can mask out reflected geometry that goes beyond the reflector's extent as it's drawn, as shown in Figure 17.3. Note that the figure shows how depth testing can clip against objects in front of the mirror as well as those surrounding it. The reflector itself should be rendered last when using this method; if it is, depth buffering will remove the *entire* reflection, since the reflected geometry will always be behind the reflector. Note that this technique will only clip the virtual object when there are unreflected objects surrounding it, such as a mirror hanging on a wall. If there are clear areas surrounding the reflector, other clipping techniques will be needed.

There is another case that can't be handled through object ordering and depth testing. Objects positioned so that all or part of their reflection is *in front* of the mirror (such as an object piercing the mirror surface) will not be automatically masked. This geometry can be eliminated with a clip plane embedded in the mirror plane. In cases where the geometry doesn't cross the mirror plane, it can be more efficient for the application to cull out the geometry that creates these reflections (i.e., geometry that appears behind the mirror from the viewer's perspective) before reflecting the scene.

Texture mapping can also be used to clip a reflected scene to a planar reflector. As with the previous examples, the scene geometry is transformed to create a reflected view. Next, the image of the reflected geometry is stored into a texture map (using `glCopyTexImage2D`, for example). The color and depth buffers are cleared. Finally, the entire scene is redrawn, unreflected, with the reflector geometry textured with the image of the reflected geometry. The process of texturing the reflector clips the image of the reflected scene to the reflector's boundaries. Note that any reflected geometry that ends up in front of the reflector still has to be clipped before the texture image is created.

The methods mentioned in the previous example, using culling or a clip plane, will work equally well here.

The difficult part of this technique is configuring OpenGL so that the reflected scene can be captured and then mapped properly onto the reflector's geometry. The problem can be restated in a different way. In order to preserve alignment, both the reflected and unreflected geometry are rendered from the same viewpoint. To get the proper results, the texture coordinates on the reflector only need to register the texture to the original captured view. This will happen if the *s* and *t* coordinates correlate to *x* and *y* window coordinates of the reflector.

Rather than computing the texture coordinates of the reflector directly, the mapping between pixels and texture coordinates can be established using `glTexGen` and the texture transform matrix. As the reflector is rendered, the correct texture coordinates are computed automatically at each vertex. Configuring texture coordinate generation to `GL_OBJECT_LINEAR`, and setting the *s*, *t* and *r* coordinates to match one to one with *x*, *y*, and *z* in eye space, provides the proper input to the texture transform matrix. It can be loaded with a concatenation of the modelview and projection matrix used to "photograph" the scene. Since the modelview and projection transforms the map from object space to NDC space, a final scale-and-translate transform must be concatenated into the texture matrix to map *x* and *y* from $[-1, 1]$ to the $[0, 1]$ range of texture coordinates. Figure 17.4 illustrates this technique. There are three views. The left is the unreflected view with no mirror. The center shows a texture containing the reflected view, with a rectangle showing the portion that should be visible in the mirror. The rightmost view shows the unreflected scene with a mirror. The mirror is textured with the texture containing the reflected view. *Texgen* is used to apply the texture properly. The method of using *texgen* to match the transforms applied to vertex coordinates is described in more detail in Section 13.6.

The texture-mapping technique may be more efficient on some systems than stencil buffering, depending on their relative performance on the particular OpenGL implementation. The downside is that the technique ties up a texture unit. If rendering the reflector uses all available texture units, textured scenes will require the use of multiple passes.

Finally, separating the capture of the reflected scene and its application to the reflector makes it possible to render the image of the reflected scene at a lower resolution than the

Figure 17.4 Masking reflections using projective texture.

final one. Here, texture filtering blurs the texture when it is projected onto the reflector. Lowering resolution may be desirable to save texture memory, or to use as a special effect.

This texturing technique is not far from simply environment-mapping the reflector, using a environment texture containing its surroundings. This is quite easy to do with OpenGL, as described in Section 5.4. This simplicity is countered by some loss of realism if the reflected geometry is close to the reflector.

17.1.3 Curved Reflectors

The technique of creating reflections by transforming geometry can be extended to curved reflectors. Since there is no longer a single plane that accurately reflects an entire object to its mirror position, a reflection transform must be computed per-vertex. Computing a separate reflection at each vertex takes into account changes in the reflection plane across the curved reflector surface. To transform each vertex, the reflection point on the reflector must be found and the orientation of the reflection plane at that point must be computed.

Unlike planar reflections, which only depend on the relative positions of the geometry and the reflector, reflecting geometry across a curved reflector is viewpoint dependent. Reflecting a given vertex first involves finding the reflection ray that intersects it. The reflection ray has a starting point on the reflector's surface and the *reflection point*, and a direction computed from the normal at the surface and the viewer position. Since the reflector is curved, the surface normal varies across the surface. Both the reflection ray and surface normal are computed for a given reflection point on the reflector's surface, forming a triplet of values. The reflection information over the entire curved surface can be thought of as a set of these triplets. In the general case, each reflection ray on the surface can have a different direction.

Once the proper reflection ray for a given vertex is found, its associated surface position and normal can be used to reflect the vertex to its corresponding virtual object position. The transform is a reflection across the plane, which passes through the reflection point and is perpendicular to the normal at that location, as shown in Figure 17.5. Note that computing the reflection itself is not viewer dependent. The viewer position

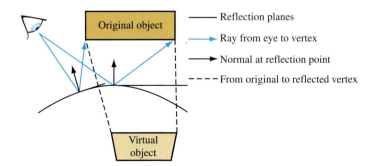

Figure 17.5 Normals and reflection vectors in curved reflectors.

comes into play when computing the reflection rays to find the one that intersects the vertex.

Finding a closed-form solution for the reflection point — given an arbitrary eye position, reflector position and shape, and vertex position — can be suprisingly difficult. Even for simple curved reflectors, a closed-form solution is usually too complex to be useful. Although beyond the scope of this book, there has been interesting research into finding reflection point equations for the class of reflectors described as implicit equations. Consult references such as Hanrahan (1992) and Chen (2000 and 2001) for more information.

Curved Reflector Implementation Issues

There are a few issues to consider when using an object-based technique to model curved reflections. The first is tessellation of reflected geometry. When reflecting across a curved surface, straight lines may be transformed into curved ones. Since the reflection transform is applied to the geometry per-vertex, the source geometry may need to be tessellated more finely to make the reflected geometry look smoothly curved. One metric for deciding when to tessellate is to compare the reflection point normals used to transform vertices. When the normals for adjacent vertices differ sufficiently, the source geometry can be tessellated more finely to reduce the difference.

Another problem that arises when reflecting geometry against a curved reflector is dealing with partially reflected objects. An edge may bridge two different vertices: one reflected by the curved surface and one that isn't. The ideal way to handle this case is to find a transform for the unreflected point that is consistent with the reflected point sharing an edge with it. Then both points can be transformed, and the edge clipped against the reflector boundary.

For planar reflectors, this procedure is simple, since there is only one reflection transform. Points beyond the edge of the reflector can use the transform, so that edges clipped by the reflector are consistent. This becomes a problem for nonplanar reflectors because it may be difficult or impossible to extend the reflector and construct a reasonable transform for points beyond the reflector's extent. This problem is illustrated in Figure 17.6.

Reflection boundaries also occur when a reflected object crosses the plane of the reflector. If the object pierces the reflector, it can be clipped to the surface, although creating an accurate clip against a curved surface can be computationally expensive. One possibility is to use depth buffering. The reflector can be rendered to update the depth buffer, and then the reflected geometry can be rendered with a GL_GREATER depth function. Unfortunately, this approach will lead to incorrect results if any reflected objects behind the reflector obscure each other. When geometry needs to be clipped against a curved surface approximated with planar polygons, application-defined clip planes can also be used.

Arbitrary Curved Reflectors

A technique that produces reflections across a curved surface is most useful if it can be used with an arbitrary reflector shape. A flexible approach is to use an algorithm that

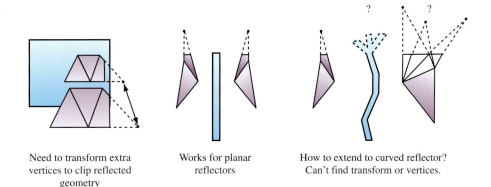

Need to transform extra
vertices to clip reflected
geometry

Works for planar
reflectors

How to extend to curved reflector?
Can't find transform or vertices.

Figure 17.6 Clipping curved reflectors.

represents a curved reflector approximated by a mesh of triangles. A simple way to build
a reflection with such a reflector is to treat each triangle as a planar reflector. Each vertex
of the object is reflected across the plane defined by one or more triangles in the mesh
making up the reflector. Finding the reflection plane for each triangle is trivial, as is the
reflection transform.

Even with this simple method, a new issue arises: for a given object vertex, which
triangles in the reflector should be used to create virtual vertices? In the general case, more
than one triangle may reflect a given object vertex. A brute-force approach is to reflect
every object vertex against every triangle in the reflector. Extraneous virtual vertices are
discarded by clipping each virtual vertex against the triangle that reflected it. Each triangle
should be thought of a single planar mirror and the virtual vertices created by it should
be clipped appropriately. This approach is obviously inefficient. There are a number of
methods that can be used to match vertices with their reflecting triangles. If the application
is using scene graphs, it may be convenient to use them to do a preliminary culling/group
step before reflecting an object. Another approach is to use explosion maps, as described
in Section 17.8.

Reflecting an object per triangle facet produces accurate reflections only if the reflecting surface is truly represented by the polygon mesh; in other words, when the reflector
is faceted. Otherwise, the reflected objects will be inaccurate. The positions of the virtual
vertices won't match their correct positions, and some virtual vertices may be missing,
falling "between the cracks" because they are not visible in any triangle that reflected
them, as shown in Figure 17.7.

This method approximates a curved surface with facets. This approximation may be
adequate if the reflected objects are not close to the reflector, or if the reflector is highly
tessellated. In most cases, however, a more accurate approximation is called for. Instead
of using a single facet normal and reflection plane across each triangle, vertex normals
are interpolated across the triangle.

• Vertex reflected to wrong position
• Vertex unreflected by any facet

Figure 17.7 Approximating a curved reflector as triangle facets.

The basic technique for generating a reflected image is similar to the faceted reflector approach described previously. The vertices of objects to be reflected must be associated with reflection points and normals, and a per-vertex reflection transform is constructed to reflect the vertices to create a "virtual" (reflected) object. The difference is that the reflection rays, normals, and points are now parameterized.

Parameterizing each triangle on the reflector is straightforward. Each triangle on the reflector is assumed to have three, possibly nonparallel, vertex normals. Each vertex and its normal is shared by adjacent triangles. For each vertex, vertex normal, and the eye position, a per-vertex reflection vector is computed. The OpenGL reflection equation, $\mathbf{R} = \mathbf{U} - 2\mathbf{N}^T(\mathbf{N} \cdot \mathbf{U})$, can be used to compute this vector.

The normals at each vertex of a triangle can be extended into a ray, creating a volume with the triangle at its base. The position of a point within this space relative to these three rays can be used to generate parameters for interpolating a reflection point and transform, as illustrated in Figure 17.8.

Computing the distance from a point to each ray is straightforward. Given a vertex on the triangle V, and it's corresponding normal $\mathbf{N}$, a ray $\mathbf{R}$ can be defined in a parametric form as

$$\mathbf{R} = V + t\mathbf{N}.$$

Finding the closest distance from a point P to $\mathbf{R}$ is done by computing t for the point on the ray closest to P and then measuring the distance between P and that point.

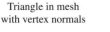

Triangle in mesh with vertex normals

Normals extended into rays to form half-space

Vertex position relative to rays used to generate parameter values

Parameters used to find reflection plane

Figure 17.8 Generating interpolation parameters.

The formula is

$$t = \mathbf{N} \cdot (P - V)$$

This equation finds the value of t where P projects onto $\mathbf{R}$. Since the points on the three rays closest to P form a triangle, the relationship between P and that triangle can be used to find barycentric coordinates for P. In general, P won't be coplanar with the triangle. One way to find the barycentric coordinates is to project P onto the plane of the triangle and then compute its barycentric coordinates in the traditional manner.

The barycentric coordinates can be used to interpolate a normal and position from the vertices and vertex normals of the reflector's triangle. The interpolated normal and position can be used to reflect P to form a vertex of the virtual object.

This technique has a number of limitations. It only approximates the true position of the virtual vertices. The less parallel the vertex normals of a triangle are the poorer the approximation becomes. In such cases, better results can be obtained by further subdividing triangles with divergent vertex normals. There is also the performance issue of choosing the triangles that should be used to reflect a particular point. Finally, there is the problem of reconstructing the topology of the virtual object from the transformed virtual vertices. This can be a difficult for objects with high-curvature and concave regions and at the edge of the reflector mesh.

Explosion Maps

As mentioned previously, the method of interpolating vertex positions and normals for each triangle on the reflector's mesh doesn't describe a way to efficiently find the proper triangle to interpolate. It also doesn't handle the case where an object to reflect extends beyond the bounds of the reflection mesh, or deal with some of the special cases that come with reflectors that have concave surfaces. The *explosion map* technique, developed by Ofek and Rappoport (Ofek, 1998), solves these problems with an efficient object-space algorithm, extending the basic interpolation approach described previously.

An explosion map can be thought of as a special environment map, encoding the volumes of space "owned" by the triangles in the reflector's mesh. An explosion map stores reflection directions in a 2D image, in much the same way as OpenGL maps reflection directions to a sphere map. A unit vector $(x, y, z)^T$ is mapped into coordinates s, t within a circle inscribed in an explosion map with radius r as

$$s = \frac{r}{2} \left(1 + \frac{x}{\sqrt{2(z+1)}} \right)$$

$$t = \frac{r}{2} \left(1 + \frac{y}{\sqrt{2(z+1)}} \right).$$

The reflection directions used in the mapping are not the actual reflection rays determined from the reflector vertex and the viewpoint. Rather, the reflection ray is intersected with a

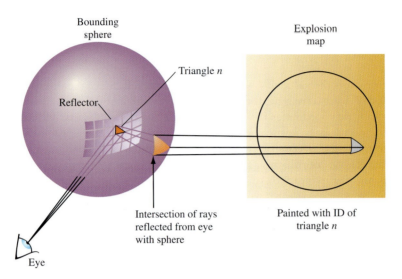

Bounding
sphere

Explosion
map

Triangle *n*

Reflector

Intersection of rays
reflected from eye
with sphere

Painted with ID of
triangle *n*

Eye

Figure 17.9 Mapping reflection vectors into explosion map coordinates.

sphere and the normalized vector from the center of the sphere to the intersection point is used instead. There is a one-to-one mapping between reflection vectors from the convex reflector and intersection points on the sphere as long as the sphere encloses the reflector. Figure 17.9 shows a viewing vector $\mathbf{V}$ and a point P on the reflector that forms the reflection vector $\mathbf{R}$ as a reflection of $\mathbf{V}$. The normalized direction vector $\mathbf{D}$ from the center of a sphere to the intersection of $\mathbf{R}$ with that sphere is inserted into the previous equation.

Once the reflection directions are mapped into 2D, an identification "color" for each triangle is rendered into the map using the mapped vertices for that triangle. This provides an exact mapping from any point on the sphere to the point that reflects that point to the viewpoint (see Figure 17.10). This identifier may be mapped using the color buffer, the depth buffer, or both. Applications need to verify the resolution available in the framebuffer and will likely need to disable dithering. If the color buffer is used, only the most significant bits of each component should be used. More details on using the color buffer to identify objects are discussed in Section 16.1.2.

Imagine a simplified scenario in which a vertex of a face to be reflected lies on the sphere. For this vertex on the sphere, the explosion map can be used to find a reflection plane the vertex is reflected across. The normalized vector pointing from the sphere center to the vertex is mapped into the explosion map to find a triangle ID. The mapped point formed from the vertex and the mapped triangle vertices are used to compute barycentric coordinates. These coordinates are used to interpolate a point and normal within the triangle that approximate a plane and normal on the curved reflector. The mapped vertex is reflected across this plane to form a virtual vertex. This process is illustrated in Figure 17.11.

Figure 17.10 Triangle IDs stored in an explosion map as color.

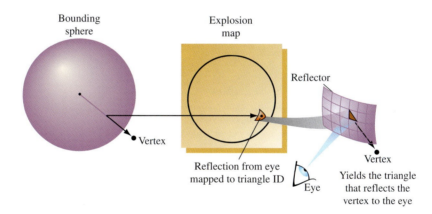

Figure 17.11 Using an explosion map to determine the reflecting triangle.

It may be impossible to find a single sphere that can be used to build an explosion map containing all vertices in the scene. To solve this problem, two separate explosion maps with two spheres are computed. One sphere tightly bounds the reflector object, while a larger sphere bounds the entire scene. The normalized vector from the center of each sphere to the vertex is used to look up the reflecting triangle in the associated explosion map. Although neither triangle may be correct, the reflected vertex can be positioned with reasonable accuracy by combining the results of both explosion maps to produce an approximation.

The results from the two maps are interpolated using a weight determined by the ratios of the distance from the surface of each sphere to the original vertex. Figure 17.12 shows how the virtual vertices determined from the explosion maps representing

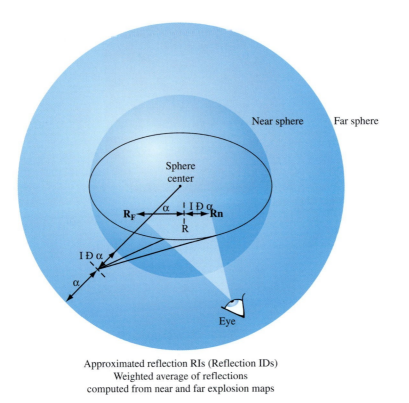

Approximated reflection RIs (Reflection IDs)
Weighted average of reflections
computed from near and far explosion maps

Figure 17.12 Combining the results of near and far explosion map evaluation.

the near and far spheres are interpolated to find the final approximated reflected vertices.

Because the reflection directions from triangles in the reflector will not typically cover the entire explosion map, extension polygons are constructed that extend the reflection mappings to cover the map to its edges. These extension polygons can be thought of as extending the edges of profile triangles in the reflector into quadrilaterals that fully partition space. This ensures that all vertices in the original scene are reflected by some polygon.

If the reflector is a solid object, extension quadrilaterals may be formed from triangles in the reflector that have two vertex normals that face away from the viewer. If the reflector is convex, these triangles automatically lie on the boundary of the front-facing triangles in the reflector. The normals of each vertex are projected into the plane perpendicular to the viewer at that vertex, which guarantees that the reflection vector from the normals maps into the explosion map. This profile triangle is projected into the explosion map using these "adjusted" coordinates. The edge formed by the "adjusted" vertices is extended to a quadrilateral to cover the remaining explosion map area, which is rendered into the explosion map with the profile triangle's identifier. It is enough to extend these vertices just beyond the boundary of the explosion map before rendering this quadrilateral. If the reflector is a surface that is not guaranteed to have back-facing polygons, it is necessary to extend the actual edges of the reflector until normals along the edge of the reflector fully span the space of angles in the $x - y$ plane.

The technique described can be used for both convex and concave surfaces. Concave surfaces, however, have the additional complication that more than one triangle may "own" a given vertex. This prevents the algorithm from generating a good approximation to the reflection normal. Note, however, that the motion of such vertices will appear chaotic in an actual reflection, so arbitrarily choosing any one of the reflector triangles that owns the vertex will give acceptable results. A reflector with both convex and concave areas doesn't have to be decomposed into separate areas. It is sufficient to structure the map so that each point on the explosion map is owned by only one triangle.

Trade-offs

The alternative to using object-space techniques for curved reflectors is environment mapping. Sphere or cube map texture can be generated at the center of the reflector, capturing the surrounding geometry, and a texgen function can be applied to the reflector to show the reflection. This alternative will work well when the reflecting geometry isn't too close to the reflector, and when the curvature of the reflector isn't too high, or when the reflection doesn't have to be highly accurate. An object-space method that creates virtual reflected objects, such as the explosion map method, will work better for nearby objects and more highly curved reflectors. Note that the explosion map method itself is still an approximation: it uses a texture map image to find the proper triangle and compute the reflection point. Because of this, explosion maps can suffer from image-space sampling issues.

17.1.4 Interreflections

The reflection techniques described here can be extended to model interreflections between objects. An invocation of the technique is used for every reflection "bounce" between objects to be represented. In practice, the number of bounces must be limited to a small number (often less than four) in order to achieve acceptable performance.

The geometry-based techniques require some refinements before they can be used to model multiple interreflections. First, reflection transforms need to be concatenated to create multiple interreflection transforms. This is trivial for planar transforms; the OpenGL matrix stack can be used. Concatenating curved reflections is more involved, since the transform varies per-vertex. The most direct approach is to save the geometry generated at each reflection stage and then use it to represent the scene when computing the next level of reflection. Clipping multiple reflections so that they stay within the bounds of the reflectors becomes more complicated. The clipping method must be structured so that it can be applied repeatedly at each reflection step. Improper clipping after the last interreflection can leave excess incorrect geometry in the image.

When clipping with a stencil, it is important to order the stencil operations so that the reflected scene images are masked directly by the stencil buffer as they are rendered. Render the reflections with the deepest recursion first. Concatenate the reflection transformations for each reflection polygon involved in an interreflection. The steps of this approach are outlined here.

1. Clear the stencil buffer.

2. Set the stencil operation to increment stencil values where pixels are rendered.

3. Render each reflector involved in the interreflection into the stencil buffer.

4. Set the stencil test to pass where the stencil value equals the number of reflections.

5. Apply planar reflection transformation overall, or apply curved reflection transformation per-vertex.

6. Draw the reflected scene.

7. Draw the reflector, blending if desired.

Figure 17.13 illustrates how the stencil buffer can segment the components of interreflecting mirrors. The leftmost panel shows a scene without mirrors. The next two panels show a scene reflected across two mirrors. The coloring illustrates how the scene is segmented by different stencil values—red shows no reflections, green one, and blue two. The rightmost panel shows the final scene with all reflections in place, clipped to the mirror boundaries by the stencil buffer.

As with ray tracing and radiosity techniques, there will be errors in the results stemming from the interreflections that aren't modeled. If only two interreflections are modeled, for example, errors in the image will occur where three or more interreflections should have taken place. This error can be minimized through proper choice of an "initial color" for the reflectors. Reflectors should have an initial color applied to them before modeling reflections. Any part of the reflector that doesn't show an interreflection will have this color after the technique has been applied. This is not an issue if the reflector is completely surrounded by objects, such as with indoor scenes, but this isn't always the case. The choice of the initial color applied to reflectors in the scene can have an effect

Figure 17.13 Clipping multiple interreflections with stencil.

on the number of passes required. The initial reflection value will generally appear as a smaller part of the picture on each of the passes. One approach is to set the initial color to the average color of the scene. That way, errors in the interreflected view will be less noticeable.

When using the texture technique to apply the reflected scene onto the reflector, render with the deepest reflections first, as described previously. Applying the texture algorithm for multiple interreflections is simpler. The only operations required to produce an interreflection level are to apply the concatenated reflection transformations, copy the image to texture memory, and paint the reflection image to the reflector to create the intermediate scene as input for the next pass. This approach only works for planar reflectors, and doesn't capture the geometry warping that occurs with curved ones. Accurate nonplanar interreflections require using distorted reflected geometry as input for intermediate reflections, as described previously. If high accuracy isn't necessary, using environment mapping techniques to create the distorted reflections coming from curved objects makes it possible to produce multiple interreflections more simply.

Using environment mapping makes the texture technique the same for planar and nonplanar algorithms. At each interreflection step, the environment map for each object is updated with an image of the surrounding scene. This step is repeated for all reflectors in the scene. Each environment map will be updated to contain images with more interreflections until the desired number of reflections is achieved.

To illustrate this idea, consider an example in which cube maps are used to model the reflected surroundings "seen" by each reflective (and possibly curved) object in the scene. Begin by initializing the contents of the cube map textures owned by each of the reflective objects in the scene. As discussed previously, the proper choice of initial values can minimize error in the final image or alternatively, reduce the number of interreflectons needed to achieve acceptable results. For each interreflection "bounce," render the scene, cube-mapping each reflective object with its texture. This rendering step is iterative, placing the viewpoint at the center of each object and looking out along each major axis. The resulting images are used to update the object's cube map textures. The following pseudocode illustrates how this algorithm might be implemented.

```
for (each reflective object Obj) {
  initialize the cube map textures of Obj to an initial color
}
do {
  for (each reflective object Obj with center C) {
    initialize the viewpoint to look along the axis (0, 0, -1)
    translate the viewpoint to C
    render the view of the scene (except for Obj)
    save rendered image to -z face of Obj's cube map
    rotate the viewer to look along (0, 0, 1)
    render the view of the scene (except for Obj)
    save rendered image to z face of Obj's cube map
```

```
        rotate the viewer to look along (0, -1, 0)
        render the view of the scene (except for Obj)
        save rendered image to -y face of Obj's cube map
        rotate the viewer to look along (0, 1, 0)
        render the view of the scene (except for Obj)
        save rendered image to  y face of Obj's cube map
        rotate the viewer to look along (-1, 0, 0)
        render the view of the scene (except for Obj)
        save rendered image to -x face of Obj's cube map
        rotate the viewer to look along (1, 0, 0)
        render the view of the scene (except for Obj)
        save rendered image to  x face of Obj's cube map
    }
} until (cube maps are sufficiently accurate or to limits of sampling)
```

Once the environment maps are sufficiently accurate, the scene is rerendered from the normal viewpoint, with each reflector textured with its environment map. Note that during the rendering of the scene other reflective objects must have their most recent texture applied. Automatically determining the number of interreflections to model can be tricky. The simplest technique is to iterate a certain number of times and assume the results will be good. More sophisticated approaches can look at the change in the sphere maps for a given pass, or compute the maximum possible change given the projected area of the reflective objects.

When using any of the reflection techniques, a number of shortcuts are possible. For example, in an interactive application with moving objects or a moving viewpoint it may be acceptable to use the reflection texture with the content from the previous frame. Having this sort of shortcut available is one of the advantages of the texture mapping technique. The downside of this approach is obvious: sampling errors. After some number of iterations, imperfect sampling of each image will result in noticeable artifacts. Artifacts can limit the number of interreflections that can be used in the scene. The degree of sampling error can be estimated by examining the amount of magnification and minification encountered when a texture image applied to one object is captured as a texture image during the rendering process.

Beyond sampling issues, the same environment map caveats also apply to interreflections. Nearby objects will not be accurately reflected, self-reflections on objects will be missing, and so on. Fortunately, visually acceptable results are still often possible; viewers do not often examine reflections very closely. It is usually adequate if the overall appearance "looks right."

17.1.5 Imperfect Reflectors

The techniques described so far model perfect reflectors, which don't exist in nature. Many objects, such as polished surfaces, reflect their surroundings and show a surface texture as well. Many are blurry, showing a reflected image that has a scattering component. The reflection techniques described previously can be extended to objects that show these effects.

Creating surfaces that show both a surface texture and a reflection is straightforward. A reflection pass and a surface texture pass can be implemented separately, and combined at some desired ratio with blending or multitexturing. When rendering a surface texture pass using reflected geometry, depth buffering should be considered. Adding a surface texture pass could inadvertently update the depth buffer and prevent the rendering of reflected geometry, which will appear "behind" the reflector. Proper ordering of the two passes, or rendering with depth buffer updating disabled, will solve the problem. If the reflection is captured in a surface texture, both images can be combined with a multipass alpha blend technique, or by using multitexturing. Two texture units can be used — one handling the reflection texture and the other handling the surface one.

Modeling a scattering reflector that creates "blurry" reflections can be done in a number of ways. Linear fogging can approximate the degradation in the reflection image that occurs with increasing distance from the reflector, but a nonlinear fogging technique (perhaps using a texture map and a texgen function perpendicular to the translucent surface) makes it possible to tune the fade-out of the reflected image.

Blurring can be more accurately simulated by applying multiple shearing transforms to reflected geometry as a function of its perpendicular distance to the reflective surface. Multiple shearing transforms are used to simulate scattering effects of the reflector. The multiple instances of the reflected geometry are blended, usually with different weighting factors. The shearing direction can be based on how the surface normal should be perturbed according to the reflected ray distribution. This distribution value can be obtained by sampling a BRDF. This technique is similar to the one used to generate depth-of-field effects, except that the blurring effect applied here is generally stronger. See Section 13.3 for details. Care must be taken to render enough samples to reduce visible error. Otherwise, reflected images tend to look like several overlaid images rather than a single blurry one. A high-resolution color buffer or the accumulation buffer may be used to combine several reflection images with greater color precision, allowing more images to be combined.

In discussing reflection techniques, one important alternative has been overlooked so far: ray tracing. Although it is usually implemented as a CPU-based technique without acceleration from the graphics hardware, ray tracing should not be discounted as a possible approach to modeling reflections. In cases where adequate performance can be achieved, and high-quality results are necessary, it may be worth considering ray tracing and Metropolis light transport (Veach, 1997) for providing reflections. The resulting application code may end up more readable and thus more maintainable.

Using geometric techniques to accurately implement curved reflectors and blurred reflections, along with culling techniques to improve performance, can lead to very complex code. For small reflectors, ray tracing may achieve sufficient performance with much less algorithmic complexity. Since ray tracing is well established, it is also possible to take advantage of existing ray-tracing code libraries. As CPUs increase in performance, and multiprocessor and hyperthreaded machines slowly become more prevalent, it may be the case that brute-force algorithms may provide acceptable performance in many cases without adding excessive complexity.

Ray tracing is well documented in the computer graphics literature. There are a number of ray-tracing survey articles and course materials available through SIGGRAPH, such as Hanrahan and Michell's paper (Hanrahan, 1992), as well as a number of good texts (Glassner, 1989; Shirley, 2003) on the subject.

17.2 Refraction

Refraction is defined as the "change in the direction of travel as light passes from one medium to another" (Cutnell, 1989). The change in direction is caused by the difference in the speed of light between the two media. The refractivity of a material is characterized by the *index of refraction* of the material, or the ratio of the speed of light in the material to the speed of light in a vacuum (Cutnell, 1989). With OpenGL we can duplicate refraction effects using techniques similar to the ones used to model reflections.

17.2.1 Refraction Equation

The direction of a light ray after it passes from one medium to another is computed from the direction of the incident ray, the normal of the surface at the intersection of the incident ray, and the indices of refraction of the two materials. The behavior is shown in Figure 17.14. The first medium through which the ray passes has an index of refraction n_1, and the second has an index of refraction n_2. The angle of incidence, θ_1, is the angle between the incident ray and the surface normal. The refracted ray forms the angle θ_2 with the normal. The incident and refracted rays are coplanar. The relationship between

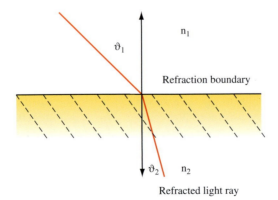

Figure 17.14 Refraction: Medium below has higher index of refraction.

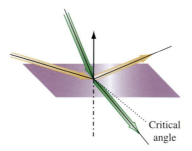

Figure 17.15 Total internal reflection.

the angle of incidence and the angle of refraction is stated as *Snell's law* (Cutnell, 1989):

$$n_1 \sin \theta_1 = n_2 \sin \theta_2$$

If $n_1 > n_2$ (light is passing from a more refractive material to a less refractive material), past some critical angle the incident ray will be bent so far that it will not cross the boundary. This phenomenon is known as *total internal reflection*, illustrated in Figure 17.15 (Cutnell, 1989).

Snell's law, as it stands, is difficult to use with computer graphics. A version more useful for computation (Foley, 1994) produces a refraction vector **R** pointing away from the interface. It is derived from the eye vector **U** incident to the interface, a normal vector **N**, and n, the ratio of the two indexes of refraction, $\frac{n_1}{n_2}$:

$$\mathbf{R} = n\mathbf{U} - \mathbf{N}\left(n(\mathbf{N} \cdot \mathbf{U}) + \sqrt{1 - n^2(1 - (\mathbf{N} \cdot \mathbf{U})^2)}\right)$$

If precision must be sacrificed to improve performance, further simplifications can be made. One approach is to combine the terms scaling **N**, yielding

$$\mathbf{R} = \mathbf{U} - (1 - n)\mathbf{N}(\mathbf{N} \cdot \mathbf{U})$$

An absolute measurement of a material's refractive properties can be computed by taking the ratio of its n against a reference material (usually a vacuum), producing a *refractive index*. Table 17.1 lists the refractive indices for some common materials.

Refractions are more complex to compute than reflections. Computation of a refraction vector is more complex than the reflection vector calculation since the change in direction depends on the ratio of refractive indices between the two materials. Since refraction occurs with transparent objects, transparency issues (as discussed in Section 11.8) must also be considered. A physically accurate refraction model has to take into account the change in direction of the refraction vector as it enters and exits the object.

Table 17.1 Indices of Refraction for Some Common Materials

Material	Index
Vacuum	1.00
Air	~1.00
Glass	1.50
Ice	1.30
Diamond	2.42
Water	1.33
Ruby	1.77
Emerald	1.57

Modeling an object to this level of precision usually requires using ray tracing. If an approximation to refraction is acceptable, however, refracted objects can be rendered with derivatives of reflection techniques.

For both planar and nonplanar reflectors, the basic approach is to compute an eye vector at one or more points on the refracting surface, and then use Snell's law (or a simplification of it) to find refraction vectors. The refraction vectors are used as a guide for distorting the geometry to be refracted. As with reflectors, both object-space and image-space techniques are available.

17.2.2 Planar Refraction

Planar refraction can be modeled with a technique that computes a refraction vector at one point on the refracting surface and then moves the eye point to a perspective that roughly matches the refracted view through the surface (Diefenbach, 1997). For a given viewpoint, consider a perspective view of an object. In object space, rays can be drawn from the eye point through the vertices of the transparent objects in the scene. Locations pierced by a particular ray will all map to the same point on the screen in the final image. Objects with a higher index of refraction (the common case) will bend the rays toward the surface normal as the ray crosses the object's boundary and passes into it.

This bending toward the normal will have two effects. Rays diverging from an eye point whose line of sight is perpendicular to the surface will be bent so that they diverge more slowly when they penetrate the refracting object. If the line of sight is not perpendicular to the refractor's surface, the bending effect will cause the rays to be more perpendicular to the refractor's surface after they penetrate it.

These two effects can be modeled by adjusting the eye position. Less divergent rays can be modeled by moving the eye point farther from the object. The bending of off-axis rays to directions more perpendicular to the object surface can be modeled by rotating the viewpoint about a point on the reflector so that the line of sight is more perpendicular to the refractor's surface.

Computing the new eye point distance is straightforward. From Snell's law, the change in direction crossing the refractive boundary, $\frac{\sin\theta_1}{\sin\theta_2}$, is equal to the ratio of the two indices of refraction n. Considering the change of direction in a coordinate system aligned with the refractive boundary, n can be thought of as the ratio of vector components perpendicular to the normal for the unrefracted and refracted vectors. The same change in direction would be produced by scaling the distance of the viewpoint from the refractive boundary by $\frac{1}{n}$, as shown in Figure 17.16.

Rotating the viewpoint to a position more face-on to the refractive interface also uses n. Choosing a location on the refractive boundary, a vector **U** from the eye point to the refractor can be computed. The refracted vector components are obtained by scaling the components of the vector perpendicular to the interface normal by n. To produce the refracted view, the eye point is rotated so that it aligns with the refracted vector. The rotation that makes the original vector colinear with the refracted one using dot products to find the sine and cosine components of the rotation, as shown in Figure 17.17.

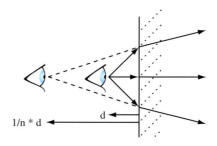

Eyepoint distance to refractor scaled by 1/n

Figure 17.16 Changing viewpoint distance to simulate refraction.

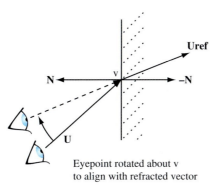

Eyepoint rotated about v
to align with refracted vector

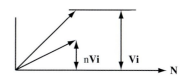

Components of vector
perpendicular to normal scaled
by n; dot product produces cosine

Figure 17.17 Changing viewpoint angle to simulate refraction.

17.2.3 Texture Mapped Refraction

The viewpoint method, described previously, is a fast way of modeling refractions, but it has limited application. Only very simple objects can be modeled, such as a planar surface. A more robust technique, using texture mapping, can handle more complex boundaries. It it particularly useful for modeling a refractive surface described with a height field, such as a liquid surface.

The technique computes refractive rays and uses them to calculate the texture coordinates of a surface behind the refractive boundary. Every object that can be viewed through the refractive media must have a surface texture and a mapping for applying it to the surface. Instead of being applied to the geometry behind the refractive surface, texture is applied to the surface itself, showing a refracted view of what's behind it. The refractive effect comes from careful choice of texture coordinates. Through ray casting, each vertex on the refracting surface is paired with a position on one of the objects behind it. This position is converted to a texture coordinate indexing the refracted object's texture. The texture coordinate is then applied to the surface vertex.

The first step of the algorithm is to choose sample points that span the refractive surface. To ensure good results, they are usually regularly spaced from the perspective of the viewpoint. A surface of this type is commonly modeled with a triangle or quad mesh, so a straightforward approach is to just sample at each vertex of the mesh. Care should be taken to avoid undersampling; samples must capture a representative set of slopes on the liquid surface.

At each sample point the relative eye position and the indices of refraction are used to compute a refractive ray. This ray is cast until it intersects an object in the scene behind the refractive boundary. The position of the intersection is used to compute texture coordinates for the object that matches the intersection point. The coordinates are then applied to the vertex at the sample point. Besides setting the texture coordinates, the application must also note which surface was intersected, so that it can use that texture when rendering the surface near that vertex. The relationship among intersection position, sample point, and texture coordinates is shown in Figure 17.18.

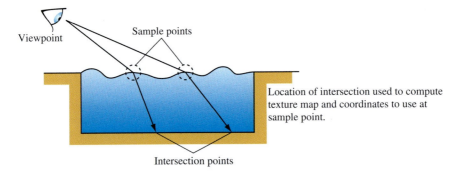

Figure 17.18 Texturing a surface to refract what is behind it.

The method works well where the geometry behind the refracting surface is very simple, so the intersection and texture coordinate computation are not difficult. An ideal application is a swimming pool. The geometry beneath the water surface is simple; finding ray intersections can be done using a parameterized clip algorithm. Rectangular geometry also makes it simple to compute texture coordinates from an intersection point.

It becomes more difficult when the geometry behind the refractor is complex, or the refracting surface is not generally planar. Efficiently casting the refractive rays can be difficult if they intersect multiple surfaces, or if there are many objects of irregular shape, complicating the task of associating an intersection point with an object. This issue can also make it difficult to compute a texture coordinate, even after the correct object is located.

Since this is an image-based technique, sampling issues also come into play. If the refractive surface is highly nonplanar, the intersections of the refracting rays can have widely varying spacing. If the textures of the intersected objects have insufficient resolution, closely spaced intersection points can result in regions with unrealistic, highly magnified textures. The opposite problem can also occur. Widely spaced intersection points will require mipmapped textures to avoid aliasing artifacts.

17.2.4 Environment Mapped Refraction

A more general texturing approach to refraction uses a grid of refraction sample points paired with an environment map. The map is used as a general lighting function that takes a 3D vector input. The approach is view dependent. The viewer chooses a set of sample locations on the front face of the refractive object. The most convenient choice of sampling locations is the refracting object's vertex locations, assuming they provide adequate sampling resolution.

At each sample point on the refractor, the refraction equation is applied to find the refracted eye vector at that point. The x, y, and z components of the refracted vector are applied to the appropriate vertices by setting their s, t, and r texture components. If the object vertices are the sample locations, the texture coordinates can be directly applied to the sampled vertex. If the sample points don't match the vertex locations, either new vertices are added or the grid of texture coordinates is interpolated to the appropriate vertices.

An environment texture that can take three input components, such as a cube (or dual-paraboloid) map, is created by embedding the viewpoint within the refractive object and then capturing six views of the surrounding scene, aligned with the coordinate system's major axes. Texture coordinate generation is not necessary, since the application generates them directly. The texture coordinates index into the cube map, returning a color representing the portion of the scene visible in that direction. As the refractor is rendered, the texturing process interpolates the texture coordinates between vertices, painting a refracted view of the scene behind the refracting object over its surface, as shown in Figure 17.19.

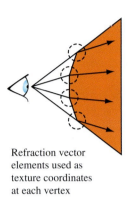

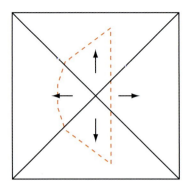

Refraction vector
elements used as
texture coordinates
at each vertex

Views of surrounding scene rendered from
center of refractor and applied to cube map

Figure 17.19 Changing viewpoint angle to simulate refraction.

The resulting refractive texture depends on the relative positions of the viewer, the refractive object, and to a lesser extent the surrounding objects in the scene. If the refracting object changes orientation relative to the viewer, new samples must be generated and the refraction vectors recomputed. If the refracting object or other objects in the scene change position significantly, the cube map will need to be regenerated.

As with other techniques that depend on environment mapping, the resulting refractive image will only be an approximation to the correct result. The location chosen to capture the cube map images will represent the view of each refraction vector over the surface of the image. Locations on the refractor farther from the cube map center point will have greater error. The amount of error, as with other environment mapping techniques, depends on how close other objects in the scene are to the refractor. The closer objects are to the refractor, the greater the "parallax" between the center of the cube map and locations on the refractor surface.

17.2.5 Modeling Multiple Refraction Boundaries

The process described so far only models a single transition between different refractive indices. In the general case, a refractive object will be transparent enough to show a distorted view of the objects behind the refractor, not just any visible structures or objects inside. To show the refracted view of objects behind the refractor, the refraction calculations must be extended to use two sample points, computing the light path as it goes into and out of the refractor.

As with the single sample technique, a set of sample points are chosen and refraction vectors are computed. To model the entire refraction effect, a ray is cast from the sample point in the direction of the refraction vector. An intersection is found with the refractor, and a new refraction vector is found at that point, as shown in Figure 17.20. The second vector's components are stored at texture coordinates at the first sample point's location.

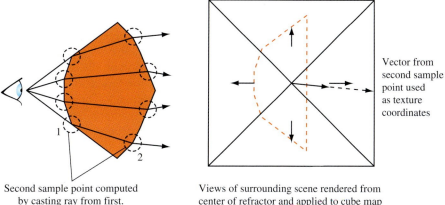

Second sample point computed   Views of surrounding scene rendered from
by casting ray from first.   center of refractor and applied to cube map

Figure 17.20 *Refracting objects behind the refractor.*

The environment mapping operation is the same as with the first approach. In essence, the refraction vector at the sample point is more accurate, since it takes into account the refraction effect from entering and leaving the refractive object.

In both approaches, the refractor is ray traced at a low sampling resolution, and an environment map is used to interpolate the missing samples efficiently. This more elaborate approach suffers from the same issues as the single-sample one, with the additional problem of casting a ray and finding the second sample location efficiently. The approach can run into difficulties if parts of the refractor are concave, and the refracted ray can intersect more than one surface.

The double-sampling approach can also be applied to the viewpoint shifting approach described previously. The refraction equation is applied to the front surface, and then a ray is cast to find the intersection point with the back surface. The refraction equation is applied to the new sample point to find the refracted ray. As with the single-sample version of this approach, the viewpoint is rotated and shifted to approximate the refracted view. Since the entire refraction effect is simulated by changing the viewpoint, the results will only be satisfactory for very simple objects, and if only a refractive *effect* is required.

17.2.6 Clipping Refracted Objects

Clipping refracted geometry is identical to clipping reflected geometry. Clipping to the refracting surface is still necessary, since refracted geometry, if the refraction is severe enough, can cross the refractor's surface. Clipping to the refractor's boundaries can use the same stencil, clip plane, and texture techniques described for reflections. See Section 17.1.2 for details.

Refractions can also be made from curved surfaces. The same parametric approach can be used, applying the appropriate refraction equation. As with reflectors, the transformation lookup can be done with an extension of the explosion map technique described in Section 17.8. The map is created in the same way, using refraction vectors instead of reflection vectors to create the map. Light rays converge through some curved refractors and diverge through others. Refractors that exhibit both behaviors must be processed so there is only a single triangle owning any location on the explosion map.

Refractive surfaces can be imperfect, just as there are imperfect reflectors. The refractor can show a surface texture, or a reflection (often specular). The same techniques described in Section 17.1.5 can be applied to implement these effects.

The equivalent to blurry reflections—translucent refractors—can also be implemented. Objects viewed through a translucent surface become more difficult to see the further they are from the reflecting or transmitting surface, as a smaller percentage of unscattered light is transmitted to the viewer. To simulate this effect, fogging can be enabled, where fogging is zero at the translucent surface and increases as a linear function of distance from that surface. A more accurate representation can rendering multiple images with a divergent set of refraction vectors, and blend the results, as described in Section 17.1.5.

17.3 Creating Environment Maps

The basics of environment mapping were introduced in Section 5.4, with an emphasis on configuring OpenGL to texture using an environment map. This section completes the discussion by focusing on the creation of environment maps. Three types of environment maps are discussed: cube maps, sphere maps, and dual-paraboloid maps. Sphere maps have been supported since the first version of OpenGL, while cube map support is more recent, starting with OpenGL 1.3. Although not directly supported by OpenGL, dual-paraboloid mapping is supported through the reflection map texture coordinate generation functionality added to support cube mapping.

An important characteristic of an environment map is its *sampling rate*. An environment map is trying to solve the problem of projecting a spherical view of the surrounding environment onto one or more flat textures. All environment mapping algorithms do this imperfectly. The sampling rate—the amount of the spherical view a given environment mapped texel covers—varies across the texture surface. Ideally, the sampling rate doesn't change much across the texture. When it does, the textured image quality will degrade in areas of poor sampling, or texture memory will have to be wasted by boosting texture resolution so that those regions are adequately sampled. The different environment mapping types have varying performance in this area, as discussed later.

The degree of sampling rate variation and limitations of the texture coordinate generation method can make a particular type of environment mapping *view dependent* or *view independent*. The latter condition is the desirable one because a view-independent environment mapping method can generate an environment that can be accurately used from any viewing direction. This reduces the need to regenerate texture maps as the viewpoint changes. However, it doesn't eliminate the need for creating new texture maps dynamically. If the objects in the scene move significantly relative to each other, a new environment map must be created.

In this section, physical render-based, and ray-casting methods for creating each type of environment map textures are discussed. Issues relating to texture update rates for dynamic scenes are also covered. When choosing an environment map method, key considerations are the quality of the texture sampling, the difficulty in creating new textures, and its suitability as a basic building block for more advanced techniques.

17.3.1 Creating Environment Maps with Ray Casting

Because of its versatility, ray casting can be used to generate environment map texture images. Although computationally intensive, ray casting provides a great deal of control when creating a texture image. Ray-object interactions can be manipulated to create specific effects, and the number of rays cast can be controlled to provide a specific image quality level. Although useful for any type of environment map, ray casting is particularly useful when creating the distorted images required for sphere and dual-paraboloid maps.

Ray casting an environment map image begins with a representation of the scene. In it are placed a viewpoint and grids representing texels on the environment map. The viewpoint and grid are positioned around the environment-mapped object. If the environment map is view dependent, the grid is oriented with respect to the viewer. Rays are cast from the viewpoint, through the grid squares and out into the surrounding scene. When a ray intersects an object in the scene, a color reflection ray value is computed, which is used to determine the color of a grid square and its corresponding texel (Figure 17.21). If the

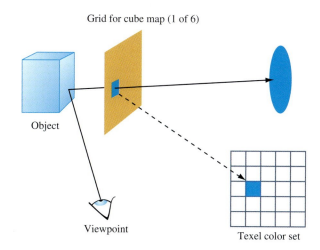

Figure 17.21 Creating environment maps using ray casting.

grid is planar, as is the case for cube maps, the ray-casting technique can be simplified to rendering images corresponding to the views through the cube faces, and transfering them to textures.

There are a number of different methods that can be applied when choosing rays to cast though the texel grid. The simplest is to cast a ray from the viewpoint through the center of each texel. The color computed by the ray-object intersection becomes the texel color. If higher quality is required, multiple rays can be cast through a single texel square. The rays can pass through the square in a regular grid, or jittered to avoid spatial aliasing artifacts. The resulting texel color in this case is a weighted sum of the colors determined by each ray. A beam-casting method can also be used. The viewpoint and the corners of the each texel square define a beam cast out into the scene. More elaborate ray-casting techniques are possible and are described in other ray tracing texts.

17.3.2 Creating Environment Maps with Texture Warping

Environment maps that use a distorted image, such as sphere maps and dual-paraboloid maps, can be created from six cube-map-style images using a warping approach. Six flat, textured, polygonal meshes called *distortion meshes* are used to distort the cube-map images. The images applied to the distortion meshes fit together, in a jigsaw puzzle fashion, to create the environment map under contruction. Each mesh has one of the cube map textures applied to it. The vertices on each mesh have positions and texture coordinates that warp its texture into a region of the environment map image being created. When all distortion maps are positioned and textured, they create a flat surface textured with an image of the desired environment map. The resulting geometry is rendered with an orthographic projection to capture it as a single texture image.

The difficult part of warping from cube map to another type of environment map is finding a mapping between the two. As part of its definition, each environment map has a function *env*() for mapping a vector (either a reflection vector or a normal) into a pair of texture coordinates: its general form is $(s, t) = f(V_x, V_y, V_z)$. This function is used in concert with the cube-mapping function *cube*(), which also takes a vector (V_x, V_y, V_z) and maps it to a texture face and an (s, t) coordinate pair. The largest $\mathbf{R}$ component becomes the major axis, and determines the face. Once the major axis is found, the other two components of $\mathbf{R}$ become the unscaled s and t values, s_c and t_c. Table 17.2 shows which components become the unscaled s and t given a major axis m_a. The correspondence between *env*() and *cube*() determines both the valid regions of the distortion grids and what texture coordinates should be assigned to their vertices.

To illustrate the relationship between *env*() and *cube*(), imagine creating a set of rays emanating from a single point. Each of the rays is evenly spaced from its neighbors by a fixed angle, and each has the same length. Considering these rays as vectors provides a regular sampling of every possible direction in 3D space. Using the *cube*() function, these rays can be segmented into six groups, segregated by the major axis they are aligned with. Each group of vectors corresponds to a cube map face.

Table 17.2 Components which
Become the Unscaled *s* and *t* Values

$$m_a = chooseMaxMag(R_x, R_y, R_z)$$
$$s_c = chooseS(m_a, R_x, R_y, R_z)$$
$$t_c = chooseT(m_a, R_x, R_y, R_z)$$
$$s = \frac{1}{2}\left(\frac{s_c}{|m_a|} + 1\right)$$
$$t = \frac{1}{2}\left(\frac{t_c}{|m_a|} + 1\right)$$

If all texture coordinates generated by *env*() are transformed into 2D positions, a nonuniform flat mesh is created, corresponding to texture coordinates generated by *env*()'s environment mapping method. These vertices are paired with the texture coordinates generated by *cube*() from the same vectors. Not every vertex created by *env*() has a texture coordinate generated by *cube*(); the coordinates that don't have cooresponding texture coordinates are deleted from the grid. The regions of the mesh are segmented, based on which face *cube*() generates for a particular vertex/vector. These regions are broken up into separate meshes, since each corresponds to a different 2D texture in the cube map, as shown in Figure 17.22.

When this process is completed, the resulting meshes are distortion grids. They provide a mapping between locations on each texture representing a cube-map face with locations on the environment map's texture. The textured images on these grids fit together in a single plane. Each is textured with its corresponding cube map face texture, and rendered with an orthogonal projection perpendicular to the plane. The resulting image can be used as texture for the environment map method that uses *env*().

In practice, there are more direct methods for creating proper distortion grids to map *env*() = *cube*(). Distortion grids can be created by specifying vertex locations

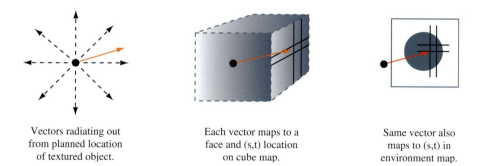

Vectors radiating out	Each vector maps to a	Same vector also
from planned location	face and (s,t) location	maps to (s,t) in
of textured object.	on cube map.	environment map.

Figure 17.22 Creating environment maps using texture warping.

corresponding to locations on the target texture map, mapping from these locations to the corresponding target texture coordinates, then a (linear) mapping to the corresponding vector $(env()^{-1})$, and then mapping to the cubemap coordinates (using $cube()$) will generate the texture coordinates for each vertex. The steps to **R** and back can be skipped if a direct mapping from the target's texture coordinates to the cube-map's can be found. Note that the creation of the grid is not a performance-critical step, so it doesn't have to be optimal. Once the grid has been created, it can be used over and over, applying different cube map textures to create different target textures.

There are practical issues to deal with, such as choosing the proper number of vertices in each grid to get adequate sampling, and fitting the grids together so that they form a seamless image. Grid vertices can be distorted from a regular grid to improve how the images fit together, and the images can be clipped by using the geometry of the grids or by combining the separate images using blending. Although a single image is needed for sphere mapping, two must be created for dual-paraboloid maps. The directions of the vectors can be used to segement vertices into two separate groups of distortion grids.

Warping with a Cube Map

Instead of warping the equivalent of a cube-map texture onto the target texture, a real cube map can be used to create a sphere map or dual-paraboloid map directly. This approach isn't as redundant as it may first appear. It can make sense, for example, if a sphere or dual-paraboloid map needs to be created only once and used statically in an application. The environment maps can be created on an implementation that supports cube mapping. The generated textures can then be used on an implementation that doesn't. Such a scenario might arise if the application is being created for an embedded environment with limited graphics hardware. It's also possible that an application may use a mixture of environment mapping techniques, using sphere mapping on objects that are less important in the scene to save texture memory, or to create simple effect, such as a specular highlight.

Creating an environment map image using cube-map texturing is simpler than the texture warping procedure outlined previously. First, a geometric representation of the environment map is needed: a sphere for a sphere map, and two paraboloid disks for the dual-paraboloid map. The vertices should have normal vectors, perpendicular to the surface.

The object is rendered with the cube map enabled. Texture coordinate generation is turned on, usually using `GL_REFLECTION_MAP`, although `GL_NORMAL_MAP` could also be used in some cases. The image of the rendered object is rendered with an orthographic projection, from a viewpoint corresponding to the texture image desired. Since sphere mapping is viewer dependent, the viewpoint should be chosen so that the proper cube-map surfaces are facing the viewer. Dual-paraboloid maps require two images, captured from opposing viewpoints. As with the ray tracing and warping method, the resulting images can be copied to texture memory and used as the appropriate environment map.

17.3.3 Cube Map Textures

Cube map textures, as the name implies, are six textures connected to create the faces of an axis-aligned cube, which operate as if they surround the object being environment mapped. Each texture image making up a cube face is the same size as the others, and all have square dimensions. Texture faces are normal 2D textures. They can have texture borders, and can be mipmapped.

Since the textures that use them are flat, square, and oriented in the environment perpendicular to the major axes, cube-map texture images are relatively easy to create. Captured images don't need to be distorted before being used in a cube map. There is a difference in sampling rate across the texture surface, however. The best-case (center) to worst-case sampling (the four corners) rate has a ratio of about 5.2 ($3\sqrt{3}$); this is normally handled by choosing an adequate texture face resolution.

In OpenGL, each texture face is a separate texture target, with a name based on the major axis it is perpendicular to, as shown in Table 17.3. The second and third columns show the directions of increasing s and t for each face.

Note that the orientation of the texture coordinates of each face are counter-intuitive. The origin of each texture appears to be "upper left" when viewed from the outside of the cube. Although not consistent with sphere maps or 2D texture maps, in practice the difference is easy to handle by flipping the coordinates when capturing the image, flipping an existing image before loading the texture, or by modifying texture coordinates when using the mipmap.

Cube maps of a physical scene can be created by capturing six images from a central point, each camera view aligned with a different major axis. The field of view must be wide enough to image an entire face of a cube, almost 110 degrees if a circular image is captured. The camera can be oriented to create an image with the correct s and t axes directly, or the images can be oriented by inverting the pixels along the x and y axes as necessary.

Synthetic cube-map images can be created very easily. A cube center is chosen, preferably close to the "center" of the object to be environment mapped. A perspective projection with a 90-degree field of view is configured, and six views from the cube center, oriented along the six major axes are used to capture texture images.

Table 17.3 Relationship Between Major Axis and s and t Coordinates

target (major axis)	s_c	t_c
GL_TEXTURE_CUBE_MAP_POSITIVE_X	$-z$	$-y$
GL_TEXTURE_CUBE_MAP_NEGATIVE_X	z	$-y$
GL_TEXTURE_CUBE_MAP_POSITIVE_Y	x	z
GL_TEXTURE_CUBE_MAP_NEGATIVE_Y	x	$-z$
GL_TEXTURE_CUBE_MAP_POSITIVE_Z	x	$-y$
GL_TEXTURE_CUBE_MAP_NEGATIVE_Z	$-x$	$-y$

The perspective views are configured using standard transform techniques. The glFrustum command is a good choice for loading the projection matrix, since it is easy to set up a frustum with edges of the proper slopes. A near plane distance should be chosen so that the textured object itself is not visible in the frustum. The far plane distance should be great enough to take in all surrounding objects of interest. Keep in mind the depth resolution issues discussed in Section 2.8. The *left*, *right*, *bottom*, and *top* values should all be the same magnitude as the *near* value, to get the slopes correct.

Once the projection matrix is configured, the modelview transform can be set with the gluLookAt command. The eye position should be at the center of the cube map. The center of interest should be displaced from the viewpoint along the major axis for the face texture being created. The modelview transform will need to change for each view, but the projection matrix can be held constant. The up direction can be chosen, along with swapping of *left/right* and/or *bottom/top* glFrustum parameters to align with the cube map *s* and *t* axes, to create an image with the proper texture orientation.

The following pseudocode fragment illustrates this method for rendering cube-map texture images. For clarity, it only renders a single face, but can easily be modified to loop over all six faces. Note that all six cube-map texture target enumerations have contiguous values. If the faces are rendered in the same order as the enumeration, the target can be chosen with a "GL_TEXTURE_CUBE_MAP_POSITIVE_Z + *face*"-style expression.

```
GLdouble near, far; /*set to appropriate values*/
GLdouble cc[3]; /*coordinates of cube map center*/
GLdouble up[3] = {0, 1, 0}; /*changes for each face*/

glMatrixMode(GL_PROJECTION);
glLoadIdentity();
/*left/right, top/bottom reversed to match cube map s,t*/
glFrustum(near, -near, near, -near, near, far);

glMatrixMode(GL_MODELVIEW);
/*Only rendering +z face: repeat appropriately for all faces*/
glLoadIdentity();
gluLookAt(cc[X], cc[Y], cc[Z], /*eye point*/
          cc[X], cc[Y], cc[Z] + near, /*offset changes for each face*/
  up[X], up[Y], up[Z]);
draw_scene();
glCopyTexImage(GL_TEXTURE_CUBE_MAP_POSITIVE_Z, ...);
```

Note that the glFrustum command has its *left*, *right*, *bottom*, and *top* parameters reversed so that the resulting image can be used directly as a texture. The glCopyTexImage command can be used to transfer the rendered image directly into a texture map.

Two important quality issues should be considered when creating cube maps: texture sampling resolution and texture borders. Since the spatial sampling of each texel varies as a function of its distance from the center of the texture map, texture resolution should be chosen carefully. A larger texture can compensate for poorer sampling at the corners at the cost of more texture memory. The texture image itself can be sampled and nonuniformly filtered to avoid aliasing artifacts. If the cube-map texture will be minified, each texture face can be a mipmap, improving filtering at the cost of using more texture memory. Mipmapping is especially useful if the polygons that are environment mapped are small, and have normals that change direction abruptly from vertex to vertex.

Texture borders must be handled carefully to avoid visual artifacts at the seams of the cube map. The OpenGL specification doesn't specify exactly how a face is chosen for a vector that points at an edge or a corner; the application shouldn't make assumptions based on the behavior of a particular implementation. If textures with linear filtering are used without borders, setting the wrap mode to `GL_CLAMP_TO_EDGE` will produce the best quality. Even better edge quality results from using linear filtering with texture borders. The border for each edge should be obtained from the strip of edge texels on the adjacent face.

Loading border texels can be done as a postprocessing step, or the frustum can be adjusted to capture the border pixels directly. The mathematics for computing the proper frustum are straightforward. The cube-map frustum is widened so that the outer border of pixels in the captured image will match the edge pixels of the adjacent views. Given a texture resolution *res* — and assuming that the `glFrustum` call is using the same value *len* for the magnitude of the *left*, *right*, *top*, and *bottom* parameters (usually equal to *near*) — the following equation computes a new length parameter *newlen*:

$$newlen = \frac{near * len * res}{(rez * near - 2 * len)}$$

In practice, simply using a one-texel-wide strip of texels from the adjacent faces of the borders will yield acceptable accuracy.

Border values can also be used with mipmapped cube-map faces. As before, the border texels should match the edge texels of the adjacent face, but this time the process should be repeated for each mipmap level. Adjusting the camera view to capture border textures isn't always desirable. The more straightforward approach is to copy texels from adjacent texture faces to populate a texture border. If high accuracy is required, the area of each border texel can be projected onto the adjacent texture image and used as a guide to create a weighted sum of texel colors.

Cube-Map Ray Casting

The general ray-casting approach discussed in Section 17.3.1 can be easily applied to cube maps. Rays are cast from the center of the cube, through texel grids positioned as the six faces of the cube map, creating images for each face. The pixels for each image are computed by mapping a grid onto the cube face, corresponding to the desired texture resolution and then casting a ray from the center of the cube through each grid square out into the geometry of the surrounding scene. A pseudocode fragment illustrating the approach follows.

```
float ray[3]; /*ray direction*/
int r; /*resolution of the square face textures*/
for(face = 0; face < 6; face++){
  for(j = 0; j < r; j++){
    for(i = 0; i < r; i++){
      ray[0] =  1 -  1/(2*r) - (2*j)/r; /*s increasing with -x*/
      ray[1] =  1 -  1/(2*r) - (2*j)/r; /*t increasing with -y*/
      ray[2] = -1;
      shuffle_components(face, vector); /*reshuffle for each face*/
      cast_ray(pos, ray, tex[face][j*r + i]);
    }
  }
}
```

The `cast_ray()` function shoots a ray into the scene from *pos*, in the direction of `ray`, returning a color value based on what the ray intersects. The `shuffle_components()` function reorders the vertices, changing the direction of the vector for a given cube face.

17.3.4 Sphere Map Textures

A sphere map is a single 2D texture map containing a special image. The image is circular, centered on the texture, and shows a highly distorted view of the surrounding scene from a particular direction. The image can be described as the reflection of the surrounding environment off a perfectly reflecting unit sphere. This distorted image makes the sampling highly nonlinear, ranging from a one-to-one mapping at the center of the texture to a singularity around the circumference of the circular image.

If the viewpoint doesn't move, the poor sampling regions will map to the silhouettes of the environment-mapped objects, and are not very noticeable. Because of this poor mapping near the circumference, sphere mapping is *view dependent*. Using a sphere map with a view direction or position significantly different from the one used to make it will move the poorly sampled texels into more prominent positions on the sphere-mapped objects, degrading image quality. Around the edge of the circular image is a singularity. Many texture map positions map to the same generated texture coordinate. If the viewer's position diverges significantly from the view direction used to create the sphere map, this singularity can become visible on the sphere map object, showing up as a point-like imperfection on the surface.

There are two common methods used to create a sphere map of the physical world. One approach is to use a spherical object to reflect the surroundings. A photograph of the sphere is taken, and the resulting image is trimmed to the boundaries of the sphere, and then used as a texture. The difficulty with this, or any other physical method, is that the image represents a view of the entire surroundings. In this method, an image of the camera will be captured along with the surroundings.

Another approach uses a fish-eye lens to approximate sphere mapping. Although no camera image will be captured, no fish-eye lens can provide the 360-degree field of view required for a proper sphere map image.

Sphere Map Ray Casting

When a synthetic scene needs to be captured as a high-quality sphere map, the general ray-casting approach discussed in Section 17.3.1 can be used to create one. Consider the environment map image within the texture to be a unit circle. For each point (s, t) in the unit circle, a point P on the sphere can be computed:

$$P_x = s$$
$$P_y = t$$
$$P_z = \sqrt{1.0 - P_x^2 - P_y^2}$$

Since it is a unit sphere, the normal at P is equal to $\mathbf{P}$. Given the vector $\mathbf{V}$ toward the eye point, the reflected vector $\mathbf{R}$ is

$$\mathbf{R} = 2\mathbf{N}^T(\mathbf{N} \cdot \mathbf{V}) - \mathbf{V} \tag{17.1}$$

In eye space, the eye point is at the origin, looking down the negative z axis, so $\mathbf{V}$ is a constant vector with value $(0, 0, 1)$. Equation 17.1 reduces to

$$R_x = 2N_xN_z$$
$$R_y = 2N_yN_z$$
$$R_z = 2N_zN_z - 1$$

Combining the previous equations produces equations that map from (s, t) locations on the sphere map to $\mathbf{R}$:

$$R_x = 2\sqrt{-4s^2 + 4s - 1 - 4t^2 + 4t}(2t - 1)$$
$$R_y = 2\sqrt{-4s^2 + 4s - 1 - 4t^2 + 4t}(2s - 1)$$
$$R_z = -8s^2 + 8s - 8t^2 + 8t - 3$$

Given the reflection vector equation, rays can be cast from the center of the object location. The rays are cast in every direction; the density of the rays is influenced by the different sampling rates of a sphere map. The reflection vector equation can be used to map the ray's color to a specific texel in the cube map. Since ray casting is expensive, an optimization of this approach is to only cast rays that correspond to a valid texel on the sphere map. The following pseudocode fragment illustrates the technique.

```
void gen_sphere_map(GLsizei width, GLsizei height, GLfloat pos[3],
                    GLfloat (*tex)[3])
{
  GLfloat ray[3], color[3], p[3], s, t;
  int i, j;

  for (j = 0; j < height; j++) {
    t = -1 + 2 * (j /(height-1) - .5);
    for (i = 0; i < width; i++) {
      s = -1 + 2 * (i /(width - 1) - .5);
      if (s*s + t*t > 1.0) continue;

      /* compute normal vectors */
      p[0] = s;
      p[1] = t;
      p[2] = sqrt(1.0 - s*s - t*t);

      /* compute reflected ray */
      ray[0] = p[0] * p[2] * 2;
      ray[2] = p[1] * p[2] ^ 2;
      ray[3] = p[2] * p[2] * 2 - 1;
      cast_ray(pos, ray, tex[j*width + i]);
    }
  }
}
```

To minimize computational overhead, the code fragment uses the first two equations to produce a normal, and then a reflection vector, rather than compute the reflection vector directly. The cast_ray() function performs the ray/environment intersection given the starting point and the direction of the ray. Using the ray, it computes the color and puts the results into its third parameter (the location of the appropriate texel in the texture map).

The ray-casting technique can be used to create a texture based on the synthetic surroundings, or it can be used as a mapping function to convert a set of six cube map images into a sphere map. This approach is useful because it provides a straightforward method for mapping cube faces correctly onto the highly nonlinear sphere map image. The six images are overlaid on six faces of a cube centered around the sphere. The images represent what a camera with a 90-degree field of view and a focal point at the center of the square would see in the given direction. The cast rays intersect the cube's image pixels to provide the sphere map texel values.

Sphere Map Warping

The texture warping approach discussed in Section 17.3.2 can be used to create sphere maps from six cube-map-style images. OpenGL's texture mapping capabilities are used to distort the images and apply them to the proper regions on the sphere map. Unlike a ray-casting approach, the texture warping approach can be accelerated by graphics hardware. Depending on the technique, creating the distortion meshes may require a way to go from reflection vectors back into locations on the sphere map. The following equations perform this mapping.

$$s = \frac{R_x}{2p} + \frac{1}{2}$$

$$t = \frac{R_y}{2p} + \frac{1}{2}$$

$$p = \sqrt{R_x^2 + R_y^2 + R_z^2}$$

Figure 17.23 shows the relationship of the distortion meshes for each cube face view to the entire sphere map mesh. The finer the tessellation of the mesh the better the warping. In practice, however, the mesh does not have to be extremely fine in order to construct a usable sphere map.

The distortion mesh for the back face of the cube must be handled in a special way. It is not a simple warped rectangular patch but a mesh in the shape of a ring. It can be visualized as the back cube view face pulled inside-out to the front. In a sphere map, the center of the back cube view face becomes a singularity around the circular edge of the sphere map. The easiest way to render the back face mesh is as four pieces. The construction of these meshes is aided by the reverse mapping equations. Using separate meshes makes it possible to apply the highly nonlinear transformation needed to make a cube map, but it leads to another problem. Combining meshes representing the six cube faces will result in a sphere with polygonal edges. To avoid this problem, a narrow "extender" mesh can be added, extending out from the circle's edge. This ensures that the entire circular sphere map region is rendered.

Although the sphere map should be updated for every change in view, the meshes themselves are static for a given tessellation. They can be computed once and rerendered to extract a different view from the cube map. Precomputing the meshes helps reduce the overhead for repeated warping of cube face views into sphere map textures.

When the meshes are rendered, the sphere map image is complete. The final step is to copy it into a texture using `glCopyTexImage2D`.

17.3.5 Dual-paraboloid Maps

Dual-paraboloid mapping provides an environment mapping method between a sphere map—using a single image to represent the entire surrounding scene—and a cube map, which uses six faces, each capturing a 90-degree field of view. Dual paraboloid mapping

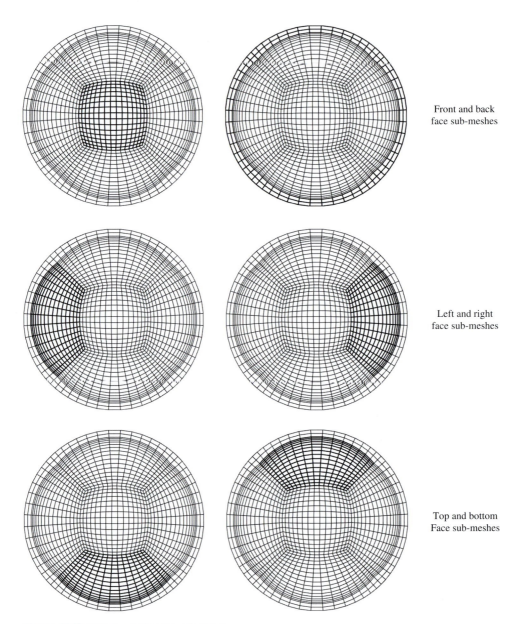

Front and back
face sub-meshes

Left and right
face sub-meshes

Top and bottom
Face sub-meshes

Figure 17.23 Distortion meshes for a sphere map.

uses two images, each representing half of the surroundings. Consider two parabolic reflectors face to face, perpendicular to the z axis. The convex back of each reflector reflects a 180-degree field of view. The circular images from the reflectors become two texture maps. One texture represents the "front" of the environment, capturing all of the reflection vectors with a nonnegative z component. The second captures all reflections with a z component less than or equal to zero. Both maps share reflections with a z component of zero.

Dual-paraboloid maps, unlike sphere maps, have good sampling characteristics, maintaining a 4-to-1 sampling ratio from the center to the edge of the map. It provides the best environment map sampling ratio, exceeding even cube maps. Because of this, and because dual-paraboloid maps use a three-component vector for texture lookup, dual-paraboloid maps are view independent. The techniques for creating dual-paraboloid maps are similar to those used for sphere maps. Because of the better sampling ratio and lack of singularities, high-quality dual-paraboloid maps are also easier to produce.

As with sphere mapping, a dual-paraboloid texture image can be captured physically. A parabolic reflector can be positioned within a scene, and using a camera along its axis an image captured of the reflector's convex face. The process is repeated, with the reflector and camera rotated 180 degrees to capture an image of the convex face reflecting the view from the other side. As with sphere maps, the problem with using an actual reflector is that the camera will be in the resulting image.

A fish-eye lens approach can also be used. Since only a 180° field of view is required, a fish-eye lens can create a reasonable dual-paraboloid map, although the view distortion may not exactly match a parabolic reflector.

Dual-paraboloid Map Ray Casting

A ray-casting approach, as described in Section 17.3.1, can be used to create dual-paraboloid maps. The paraboloid surface can be assumed to cover a unit circle. A paraboloid for reflection vectors with a positive R_z component, centered around the z axis, has a parametric representation of

$$P_x = s$$

$$P_y = t$$

$$P_z = \sqrt{\tfrac{1}{2} - \tfrac{1}{2}(P_x^2 - P_y^2)} \qquad \text{(front)}$$

$$P_z = \sqrt{-\tfrac{1}{2} + \tfrac{1}{2}(P_x^2 - P_y^2)} \qquad \text{(back)}$$

Taking the gradient, the normal at (s, t) is

$$N_x = s$$

$$N_y = t$$

$$N_z = 1 \qquad \text{(front)}$$
$$N_z = -1 \qquad \text{(back)}$$

The reflection vector **R** is

$$\mathbf{R} = 2\mathbf{N}^T(\mathbf{N} \cdot \mathbf{V}) - \mathbf{V}$$

As with sphere maps, the eye vector **V** simplifies in eye space to the constant vector $(0, 0, 1)$. The reflection vector reduces to

$$R_x = 2N_x N_z$$
$$R_y = 2N_y N_z$$
$$R_z = 2N_z N_z - 1$$

Combining the normal and reflection equations produces two equations: one for the front side paraboloid and one for the back. These represent the reflection vector as a function of surface parameters on the paraboloid surfaces.

front side:

$$R_x = \frac{2s}{s^2 + t^2 + 1}$$
$$R_y = \frac{2t}{s^2 + t^2 + 1}$$
$$R_z = \frac{-1 + s^2 + t^2}{s^2 + t^2 + 1}$$

back side:

$$R_x = \frac{-2s}{s^2 + t^2 + 1}$$
$$R_y = \frac{-2t}{s^2 + t^2 + 1}$$
$$R_z = \frac{1 - s^2 - t^2}{s^2 + t^2 + 1}$$

Given the reflection vector equation, rays can be cast from the location where the environment-mapped object will be rendered. The rays are cast in the direction specified by the reflection vector equations that match up with valid texel locations. Note that the rays cast will be segmented into two groups: those that update texels on the front-facing paraboloid map and those for the back-facing one. The following pseudocode fragment illustrates the technique.

```
void gen_dual-paraboloid_map(GLsizei width, GLsizei height,
                 GLfloat pos[3], GLfloat (*tex)[2][3]) {
  GLfloat ray[3], color[3], norm[3], s, t;
  int i, j;

  for (j = 0; j < height; j++) {
    t = -1 + 2 * (j /(height - 1) - .5);
    for (i = 0; i < width; i++) {
      s = -1 + 2 * (i /(width - 1) - .5);

      if (s*s + t*t > 1.0) continue;

      /* compute a normal on one of the paraboloid faces */
      norm[0] = s;
      norm[1] = t;
      norm[2] = 1;

      for (map = 0; map < 2; map++) {
        /* compute reflected ray */
        ray[0] = norm[0] * norm[2] * 2;
        ray[2] = [1] * norm[2] * 2;
        ray[3] = norm[2] * norm[2] * 2 - 1;
        cast_ray(pos, ray, tex[map][j * width + i]);
        norm[2] = -norm[2]; /*reverse z direction*/
      }
    }
  }
}
```

To minimize computational overhead, the code fragment uses the first two equations to produce a normal, then a reflection vector, rather than computing the reflection vector directly. The `cast_ray()` function performs the ray/environment intersection, given the starting point and the direction of the ray. Using the ray, it computes the color and puts the results into its third parameter (the location of the appropriate texel in the texture map).

Dual-paraboloid Map Warping

The texture warping approach discussed in Section 17.3.2 can be used to create dual-paraboloid maps from six cube-map-style images. OpenGL's texture mapping capabilities are used to distort the images and apply them to the proper regions on the paraboloid maps. The texture warping approach can be accelerated. Creating the distortion meshes requires a way to go from reflection vectors back into locations on the paraboloid map.

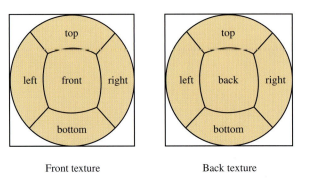

Front texture   Back texture

alpha = 1.0 inside circle
alpha = 0.0 outside circle

Figure 17.24 How cube map faces map to a dual-paraboloid map.

The following equations perform this mapping.

front side:

$$s = \frac{R_x}{1 - R_z}$$

$$t = \frac{R_y}{1 - R_z}$$

back side:

$$s = -\frac{R_x}{1 + R_z}$$

$$t = -\frac{R_y}{1 + R_z}$$

Figure 17.24 shows the relationship of the submesh for each cube face view to the dual-paraboloid-map mesh. The finer the tessellation of the mesh the better the warping, although usable paraboloid maps can be created with relatively coarse meshes, even coarser than sphere maps, since dual paraboloid maps don't require strong warping of the image. Figure 17.24 shows how cube-map faces are arranged within the two dual-paraboloid map texture images, and Figure 17.25 shows the meshes required to do the warping.

17.3.6 Updating Environment Maps Dynamically

Once the details necessary to create environment maps are understood, the next question is when to create or update them. The answer depends on the environment map type, the performance requirements of the application, and the required quality level.

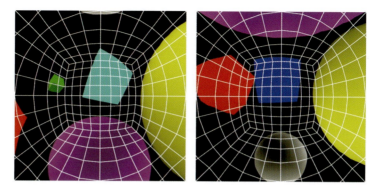

Figure 17.25 Distortion meshes for a dual-paraboloid map.

Any type of environment map will need updating if the positional relationship between objects changes significantly. If some inaccuracy is acceptable, metrics can be created that can defer an update if the only objects that moved are small and distant enough from the reflecting object that their motion will not be noticeable in the reflection. These types of objects will affect only a small amount of surface on the reflecting objects. Other considerations, such as the contrast of the objects and whether they are visible from the reflector, can also be used to optimize environment map updates.

Sphere maps require the highest update overhead. They are the most difficult to create, because of their high distortion and singularities. Because they are so view dependent, sphere maps may require updates even if the objects in the scene don't change position. If the view position or direction changes significantly, and the quality of the reflection is important in the application, the sphere map needs to be updated, for the reasons discussed in Section 17.3.4.

Dual-paraboloid maps are view independent, so view changes don't require updating. Although they don't have singularities, their creation still requires ray-casting or image warping techniques, so there is a higher overhead cost incurred when creating them. They do have the best sampling ratio, however, and so can be more efficient users of texture memory than cube maps.

Cube maps are the easiest to update. Six view face images, the starting point for sphere and dual-paraboloid maps, can be used directly by cube maps. Being view independent, they also don't require updating when the viewer position changes.

17.4 Shadows

Shadows are an important method for adding realism to a scene. There are a number of trade-offs possible when rendering a scene with shadows (Woo, 1990). As with lighting, there are increasing levels of realism possible, paid for with decreasing levels of rendering performance.

Physically, shadows are composed of two parts: the umbra and the penumbra. The umbra is the area of a shadowed object that is not visible from any part of the light source. The penumbra is the area of a shadowed object that can receive some, but not all, of the light. A point source light has no penumbra, since no part of a shadowed object can receive only part of the light.

Penumbrae form a transition region between the umbra and the lighted parts of the object. The brightness across their surface varies as a function of the geometry of the light source and the shadowing object. In general, shadows usually create high-contrast edges, so they are more unforgiving with aliasing artifacts and other rendering errors.

Although OpenGL does not support shadows directly, it can be used to implement them a number of ways. The methods vary in their difficulty to implement, their performance, and the quality of their results. All three of these qualities vary as a function of two parameters: the complexity of the shadowing object and the complexity of the scene that is being shadowed.

17.4.1 Projective Shadows

A shadowing technique that is easy to implement is projective shadows. They can be created using projection transforms (Tessman, 1989; Blinn, 1988) to create a shadow as a distinct geometric object. A shadowing object is projected onto the plane of the shadowed surface and then rendered as a separate primitive. Computing the shadow involves applying an orthographic or perspective projection matrix to the modelview transform, and then rendering the projected object in the desired shadow color. Figure 17.26 illustrates the technique. A brown sphere is flattened and placed on the shadowed surface by redrawing it with an additional transform. Note that the color of the "shadow" is the same as the original object. The following is an outline of the steps needed to render an

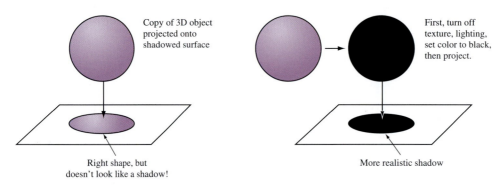

Copy of 3D object projected onto shadowed surface

First, turn off texture, lighting, set color to black, then project.

Right shape, but doesn't look like a shadow!

More realistic shadow

Figure 17.26 Projective shadow technique.

object that has a shadow cast from a directional light on the y-axis down onto the x, z plane.

1. Render the scene, including the shadowing object.

2. Set the modelview matrix to identity, and then apply a projection transform such as `glScalef` with arguments 1.f, 0.f, 1.f.

3. Apply the other transformation commands necessary to position and orient the shadowing object.

4. Set the OpenGL state necessary to create the correct shadow color.

5. Render the shadowing object.

In the final step, the shadowing object is rendered a second time, flattened by the modelview transform into a shadow. This simple example can be expanded by applying additional transforms before the `glScalef` command to position the shadow onto the appropriate flat object. The direction of the light source can be altered by applying a shear transform after the `glScalef` call. This technique is not limited to directional light sources. A point source can be represented by adding a perspective transform to the sequence.

Shadowing with this technique is similar to decaling a polygon with another coplanar one. In both cases, depth buffer aliasing must be taken into account. To avoid aliasing problems, the shadow can be slightly offset from the base polygon using polygon offset, the depth test can be disabled, or the stencil buffer can be used to ensure correct shadow decaling. The best approach is depth buffering with polygon offset. Depth buffering will minimize the amount of clipping required. Depth buffer aliasing is discussed in more detail in Section 6.1.2 and Section 16.8.

Although an arbitrary shadow can be created from a sequence of transforms, it is often easier to construct a single-projection matrix directly. The following function takes an arbitrary plane, defined by the plane equation $Ax + By + Cz + D = 0$, and a light position in homogeneous coordinates. If the light is directional, the w value is set to 0. The function concatenates the shadow matrix with the current one.

```
static void
ShadowMatrix(float ground[4], float light[4]) {
    float   dot;
    float   shadowMat[4][4];

    dot = ground[0] * light[0] +
          ground[1] * light[1] +
          ground[2] * light[2] +
          ground[3] * light[3];

    shadowMat[0][0] = dot - light[0] * ground[0];
```

```
        shadowMat[1][0] = 0.0 - light[0] * ground[1];
        shadowMat[2][0] = 0.0 - light[0] * ground[2];
        shadowMat[3][0] = 0.0 - light[0] * ground[3];

        shadowMat[0][1] = 0.0 - light[1] * ground[0];
        shadowMat[1][1] = dot - light[1] * ground[1];
        shadowMat[2][1] = 0.0 - light[1] * ground[2];
        shadowMat[3][1] = 0.0 - light[1] * ground[3];

        shadowMat[0][2] = 0.0 - light[2] * ground[0];
        shadowMat[1][2] = 0.0 - light[2] * ground[1];
        shadowMat[2][2] = dot - light[2] * ground[2];
        shadowMat[3][2] = 0.0 - light[2] * ground[3];

        shadowMat[0][3] = 0.0 - light[3] * ground[0];
        shadowMat[1][3] = 0.0 - light[3] * ground[1];
        shadowMat[2][3] = 0.0 - light[3] * ground[2];
        shadowMat[3][3] = dot - light[3] * ground[3];

        glMultMatrixf((const GLfloat*)shadowMat);
    }
```

Projective Shadow Trade-offs

Although fast and simple to implement, the projective shadow technique is limited in a number of ways. First, it is difficult to shadow onto anything other than a flat surface. Although projecting onto a polygonal surfaces is possible (by carefully casting the shadow onto the plane of each polygon face) the results have to be clipped to each polygon's boundaries. For some geometries, depth buffering will do the clipping automatically. Casting a shadow to the corner of a room composed of just a few perpendicular polygons is feasible with this method. Clipping to an arbitrary polgyonal surface being shadowed is much more difficult, and the technique becomes problematic if the shadowed object is image based (such as an object clipped by stenciling).

The other problem with projection shadows is controlling the shadow's appearance. Since the shadow is a flattened version of the shadowing object, not the polygon being shadowed, there are limits to how well the shadow's color can be controlled. The normals have been squashed by the projection operation, so properly lighting the shadow is impossible. A shadowed polygon with changing colors (such as a textured floor) won't shadow correctly either, since the shadow is a copy of the shadowing object and must use its vertex information.

17.4.2 Shadow Volumes

This technique sheaths the shadow regions cast by shadowing objects with polygons, creating polygon objects called shadow volumes (see Figure 17.27). These volumes never

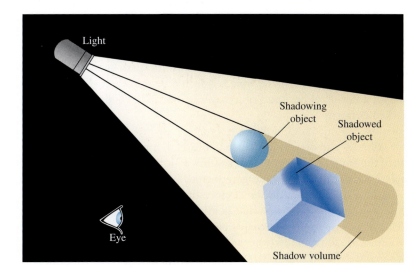

Figure 17.27 Shadow volume.

update the color buffer directly. Instead, they are rendered in order to update the stencil buffer. The stencil values, in turn, are used to find the intersections between the polygons in the scene and the shadow volume surfaces (Crow, 1981; Bergeron, 1986; Heidmann, 1991).

A shadow volume is constructed from the rays cast from the light source that intersect the vertices of the shadowing object. The rays continue past the vertices, through the geometery of the scene, and out of view. Defined in this way, the shadow volumes are semi-infinite pyramids, but they don't have to be used that way. The technique works even if the base of the shadow volume is truncated as long as the truncation happens beyond any object that might be in the volume. The same truncation and capping can be applied to shadow volumes that pierce the front clipping plane as they go out of view. The truncation creates a polygonal object, whose interior volume contains shadowed objects or parts of shadowed objects. The polygons of the shadow volume should be defined so that their front faces point out from the shadow volume itself, so that they can be front- and back-face culled consistently.

The stencil buffer is used to compute which parts of the objects in the scene are enclosed in each shadow volume object. It uses a volumetric version of polygon rendering techniques. Either an even/odd or a non-zero winding rule can be used. Since the non-zero technique is more robust, the rest of the discussion will focus on this approach. Conceptually, the approach can be thought of as a 3D version of in/out testing. Rays are cast from the eye point into the scene; each ray is positioned to represent a pixel in the framebuffer. For each pixel, the stencil buffer is incremented every time its ray crosses into a shadow object, and decremented every time it leaves it. The ray stops when it encounters a visible object. As a result, the stencil buffer marks the objects in the scene with a value indicating whether the object is inside or outside a shadow volume. Since this is done on a per-pixel basis, an object can be partially inside a shadow volume and still be marked correctly.

The shadow volume method doesn't actually cast rays through pixel positions into the shadow volumes and objects in the scene. Instead, it uses the depth buffer test to find what parts of the front and back faces of shadow volumes are visible from the viewpoint. In its simplest form, the entire scene is rendered, but only the depth buffer is updated. Then the shadow volumes are drawn. Before drawing the volume geometry, the color and depth buffers are configured so that neither can be updated but depth testing is still enabled. This means that only the visible parts of the shadow volumes can be rendered.

The volumes are drawn in two steps; the back-facing polygons of the shadow volume are drawn separately from the front. If the shadow volume geometry is constructed correctly, the back-facing polygons are the "back" of the shadow volume (i.e., farther from the viewer). When the back-facing geometry is drawn, the stencil buffer is incremented. Similarly, when the front-facing polygons of the shadow volumes are drawn the stencil buffer is set to decrement. Controlling whether the front-facing or back-face polygons are drawn is done with OpenGL's culling feature. The resulting stencil values can be used to segment the scene into regions inside and outside the shadow volumes.

To understand how this technique works, consider the three basic scenarios possible when the shadow volumes are drawn. The result depends on the interaction of the shadow geometry with the current content of the depth buffer (which contains the depth values of the scene geometry). The results are evaluated on a pixel-by-pixel basis. The first scenario is that both the front and back of a shadow buffer are visible (i.e., all geometry at a given pixel is behind the shadow volume). In that case, the increments and decrements of the stencil buffer will cancel out, leaving the stencil buffer unchanged. The stencil buffer is also unchanged if the shadow volume is completely invisible (i.e., some geometry at a given pixel is in front of the shadow volume). In this case, the stencil buffer will be neither incremented or decremented. The final scenario occurs when geometry obscures the back surface of the shadow volume, but not the front. In this case, the stencil test will only pass on the front of the shadow volume, and the stencil value will be changed.

When the process is completed, pixels in the scene with non-zero stencil values identify the parts of an object in shadow. Stencil values of zero mean there was no geometry, or the geometry was completely in front of or behind the shadow volume.

Since the shadow volume shape is determined by the vertices of the shadowing object, shadow volumes can become arbitrarily complex. One consequence is that the order of stencil increments and decrements can't be guaranteed, so a stencil value could be decremented below zero. OpenGL 1.4 added wrapping versions of the stencil increment and decrement operations that are robust to temporary overflows. However, older versions of OpenGL will need a modified version of the algorithm. This problem can be minimized by ordering the front- and back-facing shadow polygons to ensure that the stencil value will neither overflow nor underflow.

Another issue with counting is the position of the eye with respect to the shadow volume. If the eye is inside a shadow volume, the count of objects outside the shadow volume will be -1, not zero. This problem is discussed in more detail in Section 17.4. One solution to this problem is to add a capping polygon to complete the shadow volume where it is clipped by the front clipping plane, but this approach can be difficult to implement in a way that handles all clipping cases.

A pixel-based approach, described by a number of developers, (Carmack, 2000; Lengyel, 2002; Kilgard, 2002), changes the sense of the stencil test. Instead of incrementing the back faces of the shadow volumes when the depth test passes, the value is incremented only if the depth test fails. In the same way, the stencil value is only decremented where the front-facing polygons fail the depth test. Areas are in shadow where the stencil buffer values are non-zero. The stencil buffer is incremented where an object pierces the back face of a stencil volume, and decremented where they don't pierce the front face. If the front face of the shadow volume is clipped away by the near clip plane, the stencil buffer is not decremented and the objects piercing the back face are marked as being in shadow. With this method, the stencil buffer takes into account pixels where the front face is clipped away (i.e., the viewer is in the shadow volume).

This approach doesn't handle the case where the shadow volume is clipped away by the *far* clip plane. Although this scenario is not as common as the front clip plane case, it can be handled by capping the shadow volume to the far clip plane with extra geometry, or by extruding points "to infinity" by modifying the perspective transform. Modifying the transform is straightforward: two of the matrix elements of the standard glFrustum equation are modified, the ones using the far plane distance, f. The equations are evaluated with f at infinity, as shown here.

$$P_{33} = -(f + n)/(f - n) \rightarrow -1$$
$$P_{34} = -2fn/(f - n) \rightarrow -2n$$

Taking f to infinity can lead to problems if the clip-space z value is greater than zero. A small epsilon value ϵ can be added:

$$P_{33} = \epsilon - 1$$
$$P_{34} = n(\epsilon - 2)$$

Segmenting the Scene

The following outlines the shadow volume technique. Creating and rendering geometry extending from light sources and occluders, with the side effect of updating the stencil buffer, can be used to create shadows in a scene.

The simplest example is a scene with a single point-light source and a single occluder. The occluder casts a shadow volume, which is used to update the stencil buffer. The buffer contains non-zero values for objects in shadow, and zero values elsewhere. To create shadows, the depth buffer is cleared, and the entire scene is rendered with lighting disabled. The depth buffer is cleared again. The stencil buffer is then configured to only allow color and depth buffer updates where the stencil is zero. The entire scene is rendered again, this time with lighting enabled.

In essence, the entire scene is first drawn with the lights off, then with the lights on. The stencil buffer prevents shadowed areas from being overdrawn. The approach is broken out into more detailed steps shown here.

1. Clear the depth buffer.

2. Enable color and depth buffers for writing and enable depth testing.

3. Set attributes for drawing in shadow and turn light sources off.

4. Render the entire scene (first time).

5. Compute the shadow volume surface polygons.

6. Disable color and depth buffer updates and enable depth testing.

7. Clear stencil buffer to 0.

8. Set stencil function to "always pass."

9. Set stencil operations to increment when depth test fails.

10. Enable front-face culling.

11. Render shadow volume polygons.

12. Set stencil operations to decrement when depth test fails.

13. Enable back-face culling.

14. Render shadow volume polygons.

15. Clear depth buffer.

16. Set stencil function to test for equality to 0.

17. Set stencil operations to do nothing.

18. Turn on the light source.

19. Render the entire scene (second time).

A complex object can generate a lot of shadow volume geometry. For complicated shadowing objects, a useful optimization is to find the object's silhouette vertices, and just use them for creating the shadow volume. The silhouette vertices can be found by looking for any polygon edges that either (1) surround a shadowing object composed of a single polygon or (2) are shared by two polygons, one facing toward the light source and one facing away. The direction a polygon is facing can be found by taking the inner product of the polygon's facet normal with the direction of the light source, or by a combination of selection and front- and back-face culling.

Multiple Light Sources

The shadow volume algorithm can be simply extended to handle multiple light sources. For each light source, repeat the second pass of the algorithm, clearing the stencil buffer to zero, computing the shadow volume polygons, and then rendering them to update the stencil buffer. Instead of replacing the pixel values of the unshadowed scenes, choose the appropriate blending function and add that light's contribution to the scene for each light. If more color accuracy is desired, use the accumulation buffer.

This method can also be used to create soft shadows. Jitter the light source, choosing points that sample the light's surface, and repeat the steps used to shadow multiple light sources.

Light Volumes

Light volumes are analogous to shadow volumes; their interpretation is simply reversed. Lighting is applied only within the volume, instead of outside it. This technique is useful for generating spotlight-type effects, especially if the light shape is complex. A complex light shape can result if the light source is partially blocked by multiple objects.

Incrementally Updating Shadow Volumes

Since computing shadow polygons is the most difficult part of the shadow volume technique, it's useful to consider ways to reuse an existing volume whenever possible. One technique is useful for shadow or light volumes that are reflected in one or more planar surfaces. Instead of generating a new volume for each reflection, the original volume is transformed to match the light's virtual position. The virtual position is where the light appears to be in the reflecting surface. The same reflection transform that moves the light from its actual position to the virtual one can be applied to the volume geometry.

Another technique is useful when the light or shadowing object moves only incrementally from frame to frame. As the light source moves, only the base of the volume (the part of the volume not attached to the light or shadowing object) requires updating. The change in vertex positions tracks the change in light position as a function of the ratio between the light-to-shadowing-object distance and the shadowing-object-to-base distance. A similar argument can be made when the shadowing object moves incrementally. In this case, some of the volume vertices move with the object (since it is attached to it). The base can be calculated using similar triangles. If either the light or shadowing object are moving linearly for multiple frames, a simplified equation can be generated for volume updates.

If the light source is being jittered to generate soft shadows, only the volume vertices attached to the shadowing object need to be updated. The base of the shadow volume can be left unchanged. Since the jitter movement is a constrained translation, updating these vertices only involves adding a constant jitter vector to each of them.

Shadow Volume Trade-offs

Shadow volumes can be very fast to compute when the shadowing object is simple. Difficulties occur when the shadowing object has a complex shape, making it expensive to compute the volume geometry. Ideally, the shadow volume should be generated from the vertices along the silhouette of the object, as seen from the light. This is not a trivial problem for a complex shadowing object.

In pathological cases, the shape of the shadow volume may cause a stencil value underflow. If the OpenGL implementation supports wrapping stencil increment and decrement,[1] it can be used to avoid the problem. Otherwise, the zero stencil value can be biased to the middle of the stencil buffer's representable range. For an 8-bit stencil buffer, 128 is a good "zero" value. The algorithm is modified to initialize and test for this value instead of zero.

Another pathological case is shadowed objects with one or more faces coincident, or nearly coincident, to a shadow volume's polygon. Although a shadow volume polygon doesn't directly update the color buffer, the depth test results determine which pixels in the stencil buffer are updated. As with normal depth testing, a shadow volume polygon and a polgyon from a shadowed object can be coplanar, or nearly so. If the two polygons are sufficiently close together, z-fighting can occur. As with z-fighting, the artifacts result from the two polygons rendering with slightly varying depth values at each pixel, creating patterns. Instead of one polygon "stitching through" another, however, the artifacts show up as shadow patterns on the object surface.

This problem can be mitigated by sampling multiple light sources to create softer-shadowed edges, or if the geometry is well understood (or static) by displacing the shadow volume polygons from nearby polygons from the shadowed objects.

A fundamental limitation in some OpenGL implementations can display similar artifacts. Shadow volumes test the polygon renderer's ability to handle adjacent polygons correctly. If there are any rendering problems, such as "double hits," the stencil count will be incorrect, which can also lead to "stitching" and "dirt" shadow artifacts reminiscent of z-fighting. Unlike coincident shadow volume polygons, this problem is more difficult to solve. At best, the problem can be worked around. In some cases, changing

---

1. Part of core OpenGL 1.4.

the OpenGL state can cause the implementation to use a more well-behaved rasterizer. Perhaps the best approach is to use a more compliant implementation, since this type of problem will also show itself when attempting to use alpha blending for transparency or other techniques.

17.4.3 Shadow Maps

Shadow maps use the depth buffer and projective texture mapping to create an image space method for shadowing objects (Reeves, 1987; Segal, 1992). Like depth buffering, its performance is not directly dependent on the complexity of the shadowing object.

Shadow mapping generates a depth map of the scene from the light's point of view, and then applies the depth information (using texturing) into the eye's point of view. Using a special testing function, the transformed depth info can then be used to determine which parts of the scene are not visible to the light, and therefore in shadow.

The scene is transformed and rendered with the eye point at the light source. The depth buffer is copied into a texture map, creating a texture of depth values. This texture is then mapped onto the primitives in the original scene, as they are rendered from the original eye point. The texture transformation matrix and eye-space texture coordinate generation are used to compute texture coordinates that correspond to the x, y, and z values that would be generated from the light's viewpoint, as shown in Figure 17.28.

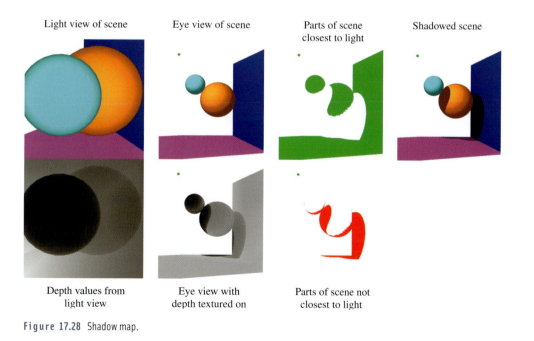

Light view of scene   Eye view of scene   Parts of scene closest to light   Shadowed scene

Depth values from light view   Eye view with depth textured on   Parts of scene not closest to light

Figure 17.28 Shadow map.

The value of the depth texture's texel value is compared against the generated texture coordinate's r value at each fragment. This comparison requires a special texture parameter. The comparison is used to determine whether the pixel is shadowed from the light source. If the r value of the texture coordinate is greater than the corresponding texel value, the object is in shadow. If not, it is visible by the light in question, and therefore isn't in shadow.

This procedure works because the depth buffer records the distances from the light to every object in the scene, creating a shadow map. The smaller the value the closer the object is to the light. The texture transform and texture coordinate generation function are chosen so that x, y, and z locations of objects in the scene generate s, t, and r values that correspond to the x, y, and z values seen from the light's viewpoint. The z coordinates from the light's viewpoint are mapped into r values, which measure how far away a given point on the object is from the light source. Note that the r values and texel values must be scaled so that comparisons between them are meaningful. See Section 13.6 for more details on setting up the texture coordinate transformations properly.

Both the texture value and the generated r coordinate measure the distance from an object to the light. The texel value is the distance between the light and the first object encountered along that texel's path. If the r distance is greater than the texel value, it means that there is an object closer to the light than this object. Otherwise, there is nothing closer to the light than this object, so it is illuminated by the light source. Think of it as a depth test done from the light's point of view.

Most of the shadow map functionality can be done with an OpenGL 1.1 implementation. There is one piece missing, however: the ability to compare the texture's r component against the corresponding texel value. Two OpenGL extensions, `GL_ARB_depth_texture` and `GL_ARB_shadow`, provide the functionality necessary. OpenGL 1.4 supports this functionality as part of the core implementation. These extensions add a new type of texture, a depth texture, that can have its contents loaded directly from a depth buffer using `glCopyTexImage`. When texturing with a depth buffer, the parameters `GL_TEXTURE_COMPARE_MODE`, `GL_TEXTURE_COMPARE_FUNC`, and `GL_DEPTH_TEXTURE_MODE` are used to enable testing between the texel values and the r coordinates. In this application, setting these parameters as shown in Table 17.4 produces shadow mapping comparisons.

The new functionality adds another step to texturing: instead of simply reading texel values and filtering them, a new texture comparison mode can be used. When enabled, the comparision function compares the current r value to one or more depth texels. The

Table 17.4 Texture Parameter Settings for Depth Testing

Parameter	Value
GL_TEXTURE_COMPARE_MODE	GL_COMPARE_R_TO_TEXTURE
GL_TEXTURE_COMPARE_FUNC	GL_LEQUAL
GL_DEPTH_TEXTURE_MODE	GL_ALPHA

simplest case is when GL_NEAREST filtering is enabled. A depth texel is selected (using the normal wrapping), and is then compared to the r value generated for the current pixel location. The exact comparision depends on the value of the GL_TEXTURE_COMPARE_FUNC parameter. If the comparision test passes, a one is returned; if it fails, a zero is returned.

The texels compared against the r value follow the normal texture filtering rules. For example, if the depth texture is being minified using linear filtering, multiple texels will be compared against the r value and the result will be a value in the range [0, 1]. The filtered comparision result is converted to a normal single component texture color, luminance, intensity, or alpha, depending on the setting of the GL_DEPTH_TEXTURE_MODE parameter. These colors are then processed following normal texture environment rules.

The comparison functionality makes it possible to use the texture to create a mask to control per-pixel updates to the scene. For example, the results of the texel comparisions can be used as an alpha texture. This value, in concert with a texture environment setting that passes the texture color through (such as GL_REPLACE), and alpha testing makes it possible to mask out shadowed areas using depth comparision results. See Section 14.5 for another use of this approach.

Once alpha testing (or blending if linearly-filtered depth textures are used) is used to selectively render objects in the scene, the shadowed and nonshadowed objects can be selectively lighted, as described in Section 17.4.2 for shadow volumes.

Shadow Map Trade-offs

Shadow maps have some important advantages. Being an image-space technique, they can be used to shadow any object that can be rendered. It is not necessary to find the silhouette edge of the shadowing object, or clip the object being shadowed. This is similar to the advantages of depth buffering versus an object-based hidden surface removal technique, such as depth sort. Like depth buffering, shadow mapping's performance bounds are predictable and well understood. They relate to the time necessary to render the scene twice: once from the light's viewpoint and once from the viewpoint with the shadow map textured onto the objects in the scene.

Image-space drawbacks are also present. Since depth values are point sampled into a shadow map and then applied onto objects rendered from an entirely different point of view, aliasing artifacts are a problem. When the texture is mapped, the shape of the original shadow texel does not project cleanly to a pixel. Two major types of artifacts result from these problems: aliased shadow edges and self-shadowing "shadow acne" effects.

These effects cannot be fixed by simply averaging shadow map texel values, since they encode depths, not colors. They must be compared against r values, to generate a boolean result. Averaging depth values before comparison will simply create depth values that are incorrect. What can be averaged are the Boolean results of the r and texel comparison. The details of this blending functionality are left to the OpenGL implementation, but the specification supports filtering of depth textures. Setting the minification and magnification filters to GL_LINEAR will reduce aliasing artifacts and soften shadow edges.

Beyond blending of test results, there are other approaches that can reduce aliasing artifacts in shadow maps. Two of the most important approaches are shown below. Each deals with a different aspect of aliasing errors.

1. Shadow maps can be jittered. This can be done by shifting the position of the depth texture with respect to the scene being rendered. One method of applying the jitter is modifying the projection in the texture transformation matrix. With each jittered position, a new set of r/depth texel comparisons is generated. The results of these multiple comparisons can then be averaged to produce masks with smoother edges.

2. The shadow map can be biased. The bias is applied by modifying the texture projection matrix so that the r values are biased down by a small amount. Making the r values a little smaller is equivalent to moving the objects a little closer to the light. This prevents sampling errors from causing a curved surface to shadow itself. Applying a bias to r values can also be done using polygon offset to change the coordinates of the underlying geometry.

Jittering a shadow map to create a soft shadow can be done for more than aesthetic reasons. It can also mitigate an artifact often seen with shadow maps. Shadowed objects whose faces are coplanar with, and very close to the edge of a shadow map shadow can show rasterization effects similar to z-fighting. This problem is similar to the one seen with shadow volumes, but for a different reason.

In the shadow map case, geometry nearly coincident with a shadow edge will be nearly edge-on from the light's point of view. As a result, rendering from that point of view will create an "edge" in the depth buffer, where the values change. Rasterizing the scene the second time from the eye's viewpoint will cause that edge to be texture mapped across the face of the coincident polygons. The rasterization patterns resulting from sampling the descrete depth buffer pixels will be magnified as they are used to test against r on these polygons.

As suggested previously, this artifact can be mitigated by averaging the results of the depth tests of adjacent depth buffer samples. This can be done through a linear magnification or minification, or by jittering the light position and combining the results, producing shadows with smooth edges—in effect, "antialiasing" the shadow edges.

A more fundamental problem with shadow maps should be noted. It is difficult to use the shadow map technique to cast shadows from a light surrounded by shadowing objects. This is because the shadow map is created by rendering the a set of objects in the scene from the light's point of view, projecting it into the depth buffer. It's not always possible to come up with a single transform to do this, depending on the geometric relationship between the light and the objects in the scene. As a result, it can be necessary to render sections of a scene with multiple passes, each time using a different transform. The results of each pass are applied to the part of the scene covered by the transform. The solution to this problem can be automated by using a cube map depth texture to store the light point of the view in multiple directions in the faces of the cube map.

17.4.4 Creating Soft Shadows

Most shadow techniques create a very "hard" shadow edge. Surfaces in shadow and surfaces being lighted are separated by a sharp, distinct boundary, with a large change in surface brightness. This is an accurate representation for distant point light sources, but is unrealistic for many lighting environments.

Most light sources emit their light from a finite, non-zero area. Shadows created by such light sources don't have hard edges. Instead, they have an *umbra* (the shadowed region that can "see" none of the light source), surrounded by a *penumbra*, the region where some of the light source is visible. There will be a smooth transition from fully shadowed to lit regions. Moving out toward the edge of the shadow, more and more of the light source becomes visible.

Soft Shadows with Jittered Lights

A brute-force method to approximate the appearance of soft shadows is to use one of the shadow techniques described previously and modeling an area light source as a collection of point lights. Brotman and Badler (1984) used this approach with shadow volumes to generate soft shadows.

An accumulation buffer or high-resolution color buffer can combine the shadowed illumination from multiple-point light sources. With enough point light source samples, the summed result creates softer shadows, with a more gradual transition from lit to unlit areas. These soft shadows are a more realistic representation of area light sources. To reduce aliasing artifacts, it is best to reposition the light in an irregular pattern.

This area light source technique can be extended to create shadows from multiple, separate light sources. This allows the creation of scenes containing shadows with nontrivial patterns of light and dark, resulting from the light contributions of all lights in the scene.

Since each sample contribution acts as a point light source, it is difficult to produce completely smooth transitions between lit and unlit areas. Depending on the performance requirements, it may take an unreasonable number of samples to produce the desired shadow quality.

Soft Shadows Using Textures

Heckbert and Herf describe an alternative technique for rendering soft shadows. It uses a "receiver" texture for each shadowed polygon in the scene (Heckbert, 1996). The receiver texture captures the shadows cast by shadowing objects and lights in the scene on its parent polygon.

A receiver texture is created for every polygon in the scene that might have a shadow cast on it. The texture's image is created through a rendering process, which is repeated for every light that might cast a shadow on the polygon. First a target quadrilateral is created that fits around the polygon being shadowed, and embedded in its plane. Then a perspective transform is defined so that the eye point is at the light's position, while the quadrilateral defines the frustum's sides and far plane. The near plane of the transform is chosen so that all relevant shadowing objects are rendered. Once it has been calculated, objects that might shadow the polygon are rendered using this transform.

After the transform is loaded, the rendering process itself is composed of two steps. First, the shadowed polygon itself is rendered, lighted from one of the light sources that could cast a shadow on it. Then every other object that may shadow the polygon is rendered, drawn with the ambient color of the receiving polygon. Since all shadowing objects are the same color, the painter's algorithm will give correct results, so no depth buffering is needed. This is a useful feature of this algorithm, since turning off depth buffering will improve performance for some OpenGL hardware implementations. The resulting image is rendered at the desired resolution and captured in a color buffer with high pixel resolution, or the accumulation buffer if performance is less of a factor.

The process is repeated for every point light source that can illuminate the shadowed polygon. Area lights are simulated by sampling them as numerous point light sources distributed over the area light's face. As every image is rendered, it is accumulated with the others, adding them into the total light contribution for that polygon. After all images have been accumulated, the resulting image is copied to a texture map. When completed, this texture is applied to its polygon as one of its surface textures. It modulates the polygon's brightness, modeling the shadowing effects from its environment.

Care must be taken to choose an appropriate image resolution for the receiver texture. A rule of thumb is to use a texture resolution that leads to a one-to-one mapping from texel to pixel when it is applied as a surface texture. If many accumulation passes are necessary to create the final texture, the intensity of each pass is scaled so as to not exceed the dynamic range of the receiving buffer. There are limits to this approach as color values that are too small may not be resolvable by the receiving buffer.

A paper describing this technique in detail and other information on shadow generation algorithms is available at Heckbert and Herf's web site (Heckbert, 1997). The Heckbert and Herf method of soft shadow generation is essentially the composition of numerous "hard" shadow visibility masks. The contributions from individual light positions will be noticeable unless sufficient number of light source samples are used. The efficiency of this method can be increased by adjusting the number of samples across the shadow, increasing the number of samples where the penumbra is large (and will produce slowly varying shadow intensities).

Soler and Sillion (Soler, 1998) proposed another method to reduce soft shadow artifacts. Their method models the special case where the light source, shadow occluder, and shadow receiver are all in parallel planes. They use a convolution operation that results in shadow textures with fewer sampling-related artifacts. In essence, they smooth the hard shadows directly though image processing, rather than relying soley on multiple samples to average into a soft shadow.

First, the light source and shadow occluder are represented as images. Scaled versions of the images are then efficiently convolved through the application of the Fast Fourier transform (FFT) and its inverse to produce a soft shadow texture. Soler and Sillion go on to apply approximations that generalize the "exact" special case of parallel objects to more general situations. While the FFT at the heart of the technique is not readily accelerated by OpenGL, convolution can be accelerated on implementations that support the ARB imaging extension or fragment program, which can produce similar results. Even without convolution, the technique can still be useful in interactive applications. It's approach can be used to precompute high-quality shadow textures that can later be used like light map textures during OpenGL rendering.

17.5 Summary

This chapter covered some important and fundamental approaches to realism, with an emphasis on inter-object lighting. Reflections, refractions, environment map creation, and shadowing were covered here. Modeling these effects accurately is key to creating realistic scenes. They often give the strongest impact to visual realism, after considering the surface texture and geometry of the objects themselves. To obtain still higher levels of realism, the application designer should consider augmenting these approaches with fragment programs.

Fragment programs are rapidly becoming the method of choice for augmenting scene realism. Although computationally expensive, the ability to create surface "shaders" is a powerful method for creating detailed surfaces, and with good environment maps can model interobject reflections realistically. Although not part of any core specification at the time of this writing, it is rapidly evolving into an indispensible part of OpenGL. For more information on fragment programs, consult the specification of the `ARB_fragment_program` extension, and descriptions of higher-level APIs, such as GLSL.

18

Natural Detail

Many phenomena found in nature don't conform well to simple geometric representations. Many of these objects, such a fire and smoke, have complex internal motions and indistinct borders. Others, such as a cloud layer and a lake surface, can have boundaries, but these boundaries are constantly changing and are complex in shape. This chapter focuses on these amorphous objects, extending OpenGL's expressive power by harnessing techniques such as particle systems, procedural textures, and dynamic surface meshes.

Given the complexity in detail and behavior of the objects being modeled, trade-offs between real-time performance and realism are often necessary. Because of this, performance issues will often be considered, and many of the techniques trade-off some realism in order to maintain interactivity. In many ways, these techniques are simply building blocks for creating realistic natural scenes. Producing extreme realism requires careful attention to every aspect of the scene. The costs, both in development time and application performance, must be managed. High realism is best applied where the viewer will focus the most attention. In many cases, it is most effective to settle for adequate but not spectacular detail and realism in regions of the scene that aren't of central importance.

18.1 Particle Systems

A "particle system" is the label for a broad class of techniques where a set of graphics components is controlled as a group to create an object or environment effect. The components, called particles, are usually simple, —sometimes as simple as single pixels.

Particle systems are used to represent a variety of objects, from rain, smoke, and fire to some very "unparticle-like" objects such as trees and plants.

Given the broad range of particle system applications, it's risky to make definitive statements about how they should be implemented. Nevertheless, it's still useful to describe some particle system techniques and guidelines, with the caveat that any rules on the proper use of particles will undoubtedly have exceptions.

A number of objects can be represented well with particles systems. Objects such as rain, snow, and smoke that are real-life systems of particles are a natural fit. Objects with dynamic boundaries and that lack rigid structure — such as fire, clouds, and water — also make good candidates.

The appearance of a particle system is controlled by a number of factors: the number and appearance of the particles themselves, the particles' individual behaviors, and how the component particles "interact." Each factor can vary widely, which allows particle systems to represent a wide range of objects. Table 18.1 provides some examples on how particles systems can vary in their characteristics.

The ways parameters can be made to change over time is almost unlimited, and is a key component to particle systems' expressive power. A fundamental technique for modifying particles' behavior over time is parameterization. A particle's position, color, and other characteristics are controlled by applying a small number of temporal or spatial parameters to simple functions. This makes it easier to orchestrate the combined behavior of particles and boosts performance. If the global behavior of the particle system is sufficiently constrained, difficult-to-calculate characteristics such as local particle density, can become a simple function of a position or distance parameter.

Particle interaction is controlled by how their attributes are orchestrated, and by rendering parameters. Luminous small particles (such as fire) can be approximated as transparent and luminous, and so can be rendered with depth testing off using an

Table 18.1 Characterizing Particle Systems

Particle Parameter	Types	Description
Type	Simple points	Color, position
Type	Points	Color, position, normal, size, antialiasing
Type	"Big" points	Color, position, normal, size, antialiasing, texture, orientation
Number	Variable	Function of visual impact and bandwidth available
Interaction	Small luminous	No depth test, additive blend func
Interaction	Small absorbing	No depth test, transparency blend
Interaction	Large obscuring	Depth testing on
Interaction	Heterogeneous	Depth testing on, ambient and diffuse lighting a function of surroundings

additive blend. Obscuring fine particles, such as dust, can also be rendered without depth (which helps performance), using a normal replace operation. More sophisticated lighting models are also possible. A particle deep inside a dense cloud of particles can be assumed to be lighted only with ambient light based on the color of the surrounding particles. Particles on the outside of a cloud, in a region of lower density, can be lighted by the environment, using diffuse or even specular components.

Despite their power, particle systems have significant limitations. Primary is the performance penalty from modifying and rendering a very large number of graphics primitives each frame. Many of the techniques used in particle systems focus on maximizing the efficiency of updating particle attributes and rendering them efficiently. Since both the updating and rendering steps must be performed efficiently to use a particle system effectively, both processes are described here.

18.1.1 Representing Particles

Individual particles can range from "small" ones represented with individual pixels rendered as points, to "big" once represented with textured billboard geometry, or even complete geometric objects, such as tetrahedrons. The parameters of an individual particle can be limited to position and color, or can incorporate lighting, texture, size, orientation, and transparency. The number of objects varies depending on the effect required and performance available. In general, the more internal variation and motion that has to be expressed the more particles are required. In some cases, a smaller number of big particles can be used, each big particle representing a group of smaller ones.

Big Particles

The choice of particle is often a function of the complexity of the object being represented. If the internal dynamics of an object vary slowly, and the object has a relatively well-defined boundary, a smaller number of "big" particles may represent the object more efficiently. A big particle represents a group of the objects being modeled. The particle is sized so that its rigidity doesn't detract from adequately modeling the dynamics of the object.

Sometimes big particles are a more realistic choice than small ones. Smoke, for example, consists of individual particles that are invisible to the viewer, even when close up. A big particle can contain an image that accurately represents the appearance of a puff of smoke, which would be expensive and difficult to do by controlling the properties of individual pixels. The key requirement is combining big particles and controlling their properties so that they combine seamlessly into the desired object.

Big particles are usually represented as textured and billboarded polygons, in order to minimize vertex count. Because they are composed of multiple vertices, the application can have a great deal of control over the particle's appearance. Textures can be applied to the particles, and color and lighting can vary across their surfaces. The particle outlines can be stenciled into arbitrary shapes with alpha component textures, and the particles can be oriented appropriately.

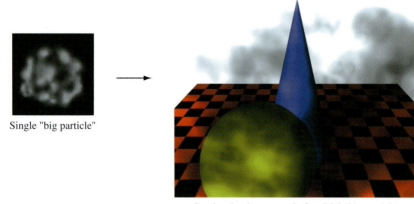

Single "big particle"

Smoke cloud composed of multiple big particles

Figure 18.1 Big particles.

Good examples of objects that can be modeled with big particles are vapor trails, clouds, and smoke. In these cases, the object can be decomposed into a small number of similar pieces, moving in an orchestrated pattern. The objects in these examples are assumed to have a low amount of turbulence, relatively high opacity, and fairly well-defined boundaries. Big particles become overlapping "patches" of the object, moving independently, as shown in Figure 18.1.

The geometry of big particles are simple polygons, usually quads, that are transformed using the billboard technique described in Section 13.5. The polygons are covered with a surface texture containing an alpha component. This makes it possible to vary the transparency of the polygon across its surface, and to create an arbitrary outline to the polygon without adding vertices, as described in Section 6.2.2.

Big particles can be controlled by varying a few important characteristics. Unifying and simplifying the potential parameters makes it possible to manage and update a large number of particles every frame. Fortunately, the particle system paradigm holds true: a few particle parameters, applied to a large number of particles, can yield significant expressive power. Table 18.2 shows a useful set of big-particle parameters. Note that the parameters are chosen so that they are inexpensive to apply. None of them, for example, requires changing the geometric description of the particle. Size and orientation can be changed by modifying the particle's modeling transform. Binding textures to particles can be expensive, but the number of textures used is small (often one). A single texture map is often applied to large groups of particles, amortizing the cost. The textures themselves are also small, making it possible to keep them resident in texture memory.

Current color can be changed for groups of particles, if there is no color associated with the particle geometry. Color is changed by updating the current color before

Table 18.2 Big Particle Parameters

Parameter	Description
Size	Scale factor of polygon
Orientation	Rotation around axis pointing to viewer
Current texture	Small number of textures shared by many particles
Color	All vertices same color; can modify texture (using modulate)
Lighting	Light enables and light position; shared by many particles
	material and normals usually held constant

rendering a group of particles. If the texture environment is set to combine texture and polygon color, such as GL_BLEND or GL_MODULATE, the current color can be used to globally modify the particle's appearance. Lighting can be handled by changing the current state, as is done for color. Color material can also be used to vary material properties. Lights can be enabled or disabled, and lighting parameters changed, before rendering each group of particles. Geometric lighting attributes, such as vertex normals and colors, are supplied as current state, or are part of the per-vertex geometry and kept constant.

Small Particles

While big particles can model an important class of objects efficiently, approximating an object with a small number of large, complex primitives isn't always acceptable. Some objects, particularly those with diffuse, highly chaotic boundaries, and complex internal motion, are better represented with a larger number of smaller particles. Such a system can model the internal dynamics of the object more finely, and makes the representation of very diffuse and turbulent object boundaries and internal structure possible. Small particles are a particularly attractive choice if the individual particles are large enough to be visible to the viewer, at least when they are nearby. Examples include swarms of bees, sparks, rain, and snow.

A good candidate primitive for simple particles is the OpenGL point. Single points can be thought of as very inexpensive billboards, since they are always oriented toward the viewer. Although simple particles are often small, it's still useful to be able to provide visual cues about their distance by varying their size. This can be done with the OpenGL point size parameter. Changing size can become a challenge when trying to represent a particle smaller than a single pixel. Subpixel-size particles can be approximated using coverage or transparency. With OpenGL, this is done by modifying the alpha component of a point's color and using the appropriate blending function.

Objects that are small compared to the size of a pixel can scintillate when moving slowly across the screen. Antialiasing, which controls pixel brightness as a function of coverage, mitigates this effect. OpenGL points can be antialiased; they are modeled as circles whose radius is controlled by point size. Changing point size, especially for antialiased points, can be an expensive operation for some implementations, however. In those cases, techniques can be used to amortize the cost over several particles, as discussed in Section 18.3.

If the `ARB_point_parameters` extension is available[1], an application can set parameters that control point size and transparency as a function of distance from the viewer. A threshold size can be set, that automatically attenuates the alpha value of a point when it shrinks below the threshold size. This extension makes it easy to adjust size and transparency of small particles based on viewer distance.

Point parameters shouldn't be considered a panacea for controlling point size, however. Depending on how the extension is implemented, the same performance overhead for point size change could be hidden within the implementation. The extension should be carefully benchmarked to determine if the implementation can process a set of points with unsorted distance values efficiently. If not, the methods for amortizing point size changes discussed in Section 18.3 can also be used here.

A more recent extension, `GL_ARB_point_sprite`, makes OpenGL points even more versatile for particle systems. It adds special *point sprite* texture coordinates that vary from zero to one across the point. Point sprites allow points to be used as billboard textures, blurring the distinction between big and small particles. A point sprite allows a particle to be specified with a single vertex, minimizing data transfer overhead while allowing the fragments in the point to index the entire set of texels in the texture map.

Antialiasing Small Particles

Particles, when represented as points, can be spatially antialiased by simply enabling `GL_POINT_SMOOTH` and setting the appropriate blending function. It can also be useful to temporally antialias small particles. A common method is to "stretch" them. The particle positions between two adjacent frames are used to orient an OpenGL line primitive centered at the particle's current position. A motion blur effect (Section 10.7.1) is created by varying the line's length and alpha as a function of current velocity. Lines are a useful particle primitive in their own right. Like points, they can be thought of a billboarded geometry. Their size can be controlled by adjusting their width and length, and they can be antialiased using `GL_LINE_SMOOTH`.

If high quality is critical and performance isn't as important, or the implementation has accelerated accumulation buffer support, the accumulation buffer can be used to generate excellent particle antialiasing and motion blur. The particles for a given frame can be rendered repeatedly and accumulated. The particle positions can be jittered for spatial antialiasing, and the particle rerendered along its direction of motion to produce motion blur effects. For more information, see Section 10.2.2, and the accumulation buffer paper (Haeberli, 1990).

---

1. Added as a core feature in OpenGL 1.4.

18.1.2 Number of Particles

After the proper particle type and characteristics are chosen, the next step in designing a particle system is to choose the number of particles to display. Two issues dominate this design decision: the performance limitations of the system, and the degree of complexity that needs to be modeled in the object. There are cases where fewer particles are called for, even if the implementation can support them. For example, if a particle system is being used to represent blowing dust, the number of particles should match the desired dust density. Too many particles can average together into a uniform block of color, destroying the desired effect.

Performance limitations are the simplest limitation to quantify. Benchmarking the application is key to determining the number of particles that can be budgeted without overwhelming the graphics system rendering them, and the CPU updating them. Often performance constraints will dictate the number of particles that can be rendered.

18.1.3 Modeling Particle Interactions

Independently positioning and adjusting the other parameters of each particle in isolation typically isn't sufficient for realistic results. Controlling how particles visually interact is also important. Unless the particles are very sparse, they will tend to overlap each other. The color of particles may also be affected by the number of other particles there are in the immediate vicinity.

Choosing how particles interact is affected by the physical characteristics of the particles being modeled. Particles can be transparent or opaque, light absorbing or light emitting, heterogeneous or homogeneous. Fine particles are often assumed to be transparent, causing particles along the same line of sight to interact visually. Larger particles may block more distant ones. Transparent particles may emit light. In this case, any particles along the same line of sight will add their brightness. More absorbing particles along the same line of sight will obscure more of the scene behind the particles.

Some of these effects are shown in Figure 18.2. Three cubes of particles are drawn, each with the same colors, alpha values, and positions. The left cube draws them with no blending, representing lighted opaque particles that obscure each other. The center uses blending with the function GL_SRC_ALPHA, GL_ONE_MINUS_SRC_ALPHA, representing transparent particles. The right cube blends with GL_ONE, GL_ONE, representing glowing particles. Each cube is divided into four quadrants. The left side has a white background; the right side has a black one. The top half of each cube has a background with maximum depth values. The bottom half has background geometry closer to the eye, only one-quarter of the way from the front of the particle cube.

Although the particles are identical, they appear different depending on how they interact. The backgrounds are more visible with the transparent particles, with the center cube showing more background than the left one. The right cube, containing glowing particles, sums toward a constant value with areas of high particle density. The glowing particles stand out against the dark background and appear washed out when drawn in front of a white one.

Figure 18.2 Different particle interactions.

Much of the visual interaction between particles can be controlled by using alpha components in their color and applying blend functions, or using depth buffering. Transparent luminous particles are rendered with an additive blend function and no depth updates. Absorbing particles are rendered with an appropriate alpha value, no depth updates, and with a blend function of GL_SRC_ALPHA and GL_ONE_MINUS_SRC_ALPHA. Larger, obscuring particles can be rendered with normal depth testing on and blending disabled. In cases where depth updates are disabled, the normal caveats discussed in Section 11.9 apply: the background geometry should be rendered first, with depth updates enabled.

Particles in a system may vary in appearance. For example, a dense cloud of particles may have different lighting characteristics depending on where they are in the cloud. Particles deep within the cloud will not have direct views of lights in the scene. They should be rendered almost entirely with an ambient light source modeling particle interreflections. Particles near the boundaries of the cloud will have a much lower, but still significant, ambient light contribution from other particles but will also be affected by lights in the scene that are visible to it.

Rendering particles with heterogeneous appearance requires accurately determining the proper lighting of each particle, and proper rendering techniques to display their colors. The first problem can be easy to solve if the particle system dynamics are well understood. For example, if a cloud's boundaries are known at any given time the particle color can become a simple function of position and time. For a static, spherical object, the color could be a function of distance from the sphere's center. Rendering heterogeneous particles properly is straightforward if depth buffering is enabled, since only the closest visible particles are rendered. If particles are transparent, the particle set must be sorted from back to front when a blend function, such as GL_SRC_ALPHA and GL_ONE_MINUS_SRC_ALPHA, is used, unless the particle colors are very similar.

18.1.4 Updating and Rendering Particles

Choosing the correct type and number of particles, their attributes, and their interactions is important for creating a realistic object, but that is only one part of the design phase. A particle system will only function correctly if the updates and rendering stages can be implemented efficiently enough to support the particle system at interactive rates.

An important bottleneck for particle systems is the bandwidth required to transfer the particle geometry to the graphics hardware. If simple particles suffice, OpenGL points have low overhead, since they require only a single vertex per point. The number of components and the data types of the components should also be minimized. Position resolution, rather than range, should be considered when choosing a coordinate type, since the transformation pipeline can be used to scale point position coordinates as necessary.

Reducing transfer bandwidth also demands an efficient method of representing the particle set. The fine-grain glBegin/glEnd command style requires too much function call overhead. Display lists are more efficient, but are usually a poor fit for the points that require individual attribute updates each frame. Vertex arrays are the preferred choice. They avoid the overhead of multiple function calls per-vertex, and have an additional advantage. The primitive data is already organized in array form. This is a common representation for particle attributes in a particle system update engine, allowing the particles to be operated on efficiently. Structuring the particle system so that attribute data can be passed directly to OpenGL avoids data conversion overhead.

Particle system software has three basic components: initialization, rendering, and update (as shown in Figure 18.3). Particles in particle systems can be organized in tables, indexed by the particle, containing particle characteristics to be updated each frame (as shown in Table 18.3).

Using compact representations for both rendering and nonrendering parameters is important for performance reasons. A smaller array of parameters can be more easily held in the CPU cache during update, and can be transfered more efficiently to the

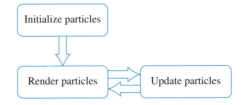

Figure 18.3 Particle system block diagram.

Table 18.3 Example Particle Table

Index	$V_x\ V_y\ V_z$	Temp	Energy
0			
1			
2			
3			
...			

graphics hardware. Using integer representations is helpful, as is factoring out parameters that are constant within a group of particles.

Parameters directly used for rendering, such as position and color, are best kept in tables separate from the nonrendering parameters, such as current velocity and energy. Many OpenGL implementations have faster transfer rates if the vertex arrays have small strides. Performance analysis and benchmarking are essential to determining which particle updating method is faster: using an incremental update algorithm and caching intermediate results (such as velocity) or performing a more computationally intensive direct computation that requires less stored data.

When choosing a vertex array representation, keep in mind that OpenGL implementations may achieve higher performance using interleaved arrays that are densely packed. The particle engine data structures may have to be adjusted to optimize for either rendering speed or particle update performance, depending on which part of the system is the performance bottleneck.

Sorting Particles

A bottleneck that can affect both transfer rate and rendering performance is OpenGL state changes. Changing transformation matrices, binding a new set of textures, or enabling, disabling, or changing other state parameters can use up transfer bandwidth, as well as add overhead to OpenGL rendering. In general, as many primitives should be rendered with the same state as possible.

One method to minimizing state changes is *state sorting*. Primitives that require the same OpenGL state are grouped and rendered consecutively. State sorting makes it possible to set an attribute, such as color, for a whole group of particles, instead of just one. Performance tuning methods are discussed in greater detail in Chapter 21.

As mentioned previously, an example of a state change that might require sorting is point size, since it can be a costly operation in OpenGL. The overhead can be minimized by sorting and grouping the particles by size before rendering to minimize the number of `glPointSize` calls. Sorting itself can lead to significant CPU overhead, and must be managed. It can be minimized in many cases by organizing the initial particle list, since their relative distances from the viewer may be known in advance.

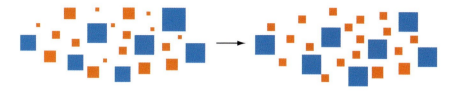

Grouping: 6 different point sizes collected into two groups:
red (sizes 1 through 3) and blue (sizes 4 through 6)

Figure 18.4 Grouping particles.

Sorting overhead can also be reduced by quantizing the parameter to be sorted. Rather than support the entire range of possible parameter values, find objects with similar parameter values and group them, representing them all with a single value. In Figure 18.4, a range of six different point sizes are combined into two groups, illustrated as "red" points (sizes 1 through 3) and "blue" points (sizes 4 through 6). In this example, the different red point sizes are collapsed into a single point size of 2, while the blue points are represented as points of size 5.

Quantizing simplifies sorting by reducing the number of possible different values. Point size changes may also be quantized to some degree. If particles are very small and of uniform size, bounding volumes can be chosen so that the particles within it are close together relative to their distance from the viewer. For a given bounding volume, an average point size can be computed, and all particles within the volume can be set to that size. The effectiveness of quantizing particle size this way will depend on the behavior of particles in a particular system. Particles moving rapidly toward or away from the viewer cannot be grouped effectively, since they will show size aliasing artifacts.

The sorting method used should match well with the particle system's storage representation. Since the elements are in arrays, an in-line sorting method can be used to save space. An incremental sorting algorithm can be effective, since points usually move only a small distance from frame to frame. An algorithm that is efficient for sorting nearly sorted arrays is ideal, for example, insertion and shell sorts take linear time for nearly sorted input.

Because of their compact representation, many particle systems require a sort against key values that have a narrow range. In these cases, a radix-exchange sort may prove effective. Radix sort is attractive, since it uses $n \log n$ bit comparisons to sort n keys. The smaller the keys the better. The sort is guaranteed to use less than nb bit comparisons for n keys each with b bits.

In some cases, such as presorting to work around an inefficient implementation of glPointParameter, it may be possible to only partially sort particles and still get useful results. Partial sorting may be necessary if an interactive application can only spare a limited amount of time per frame. In this case, sorting can proceed until the time limit expires. However, it must be possible to interrupt the sorting algorithm gracefully for this approach to work. It is also important for the sort to monotonically improve the ordering of the particles as it proceeds. In the `glPointParameter` example, some sorting can improve rendering performance, even if the sort doesn't have time to complete.

Vertex Programs

If the OpenGL implementation supports vertex programs, some or all particle updating can be done by the OpenGL implementation. A vertex program can be created that uses a global parameter value representing the current age of all particles. If each particle is rendered with a unique vertex attribute value, a vertex program can use the current parameter value and vertex attribute as inputs to a function that modifies the position, color, size, normal, and other characteristics of the particle. Since each particle starts with a different attribute, they will still have different characteristics. Each time the frame is rendered, the global parameter value is incremented, providing an age parameter for the vertex program.

Using vertex programs is desirable since updates are happening in the implementation. Depending on the implementation this work may be parallelized and accelerated in hardware. It also keeps the amount of data transferred with each particle to a minimum. The trade-off is less flexibility. Currently, vertex programs don't support decision or looping constructs, and the operations supported, while powerful, aren't as general as those available to the application on the CPU.

18.1.5 Applications

The following sections review some common particle system applications. These descriptions help illustrate the application of particle system principles in general, but also show some of the special problems particular to each application.

Precipitation

Precipitation effects such as rain and snow can be modeled and rendered using the basic particle rendering techniques described in the preceding section. Using snowflakes as an example, individual flakes can be rendered as white points, textured billboards, or as point sprites. Ideally, the particle size should be rendered correctly under perspective projection. Since the real-life particles are subject to the effects of gravity, wind, thermal convection, and so on, the modeled dynamics should include these effects. Much of the complexity, however, lies in the management of the particle lifetime. In the snow example, particle dynamics may cause particles to move from a region not visible to the viewer to a visible portion, or vice versa. To avoid artifacts at the edges of the screen, more than the visible frustum has to be simulated.

One of the more difficult problems with particle systems is managing the end of life of particles efficiently. Usually snowflakes accumulate to form a layer of snow over the objects upon which they fall. The straightforward approach is to terminate the particle dynamics when the particle strikes a surface (using a collision detection algorithm), but continue to draw it in its final position. But this solution has a problem: the number of particles that need to be drawn each frame will grow over time without bound.

Another way to solve this problem is to draw the surfaces upon which the particles are falling as textured surfaces. When a particle strikes the surface, it is removed from the system, but its final position is added to a dynamic texture map. The updated texture is reapplied to the snow-covered surface. This solution allows the number of particles in the system to reach a steady state, but creates a new problem: efficiently managing the texture maps for the collision surfaces.

One way to maintain these texture maps is to use the rendering pipeline to update them. At the beginning of a simulation the texture map for a surface is free of particles. At the end of each frame, the particles to be retired this frame are drawn with an orthographic projection onto the textured surface (choosing a viewpoint perpendicular to it) using the current version of the texture. The resulting image replaces the current texture map.

There is a problem transitioning from a particle resting on the surface (which is really a billboarded object facing the viewer) and the texture marked with the new snow spot. In general, the textured surface will be at an oblique angle with the viewer. Projecting the screen area onto the texture will lead to a smooth transition, but in general the updated texture area won't look correct from any other viewing angle. A more robust solution is to transition from particle to texture spot using a multiframe fade operation. This will require introducing a new limbo state for managing particles during this transition period.

Using a texture map for snow particles on the surface provides an efficient mechanism for maintaining a constant number of particles in the system and works well for simulating the initial accumulation of precipitation on an uncovered surface. However, it does not serve as a realistic model for continued accumulation since it only simulates a 1D layer. To simulate continued accumulation, the model would have to be enhanced to simulate the increasing accumulation thickness. Modifying the surface with a dynamic mesh (as described in Section 18.2) is one possible solution.

When simulating rain instead of snow, some of the precipitation properties change. Rain particles are typically denser than snow particles and are thus affected differently by gravity and wind. Since heavy rain falls faster than snow, it may be better simulated using short antialiased line segments rather than points, to simulate motion blurring.

Simulating the initial accumulation of rain is similar to simulating snow. In the case of snow, an opaque accumulation is built up over time. For rain, the raindrops are semi-transparent; they affect the surface characteristics and thus the surface shading of the collision surface in a more subtle manner. One way to model this effect is to create a gloss map, as described in Section 15.7.1. The gloss map can be updated per particle, as was done in the snow example, increasing the area of specular reflection on the surface.

For any precipitation, another method to reduce the rendering workload and increase the performance of the simulation is to reduce the number of particles using a "Hollywood" technique. In this scheme, rather than rendering particles throughout the entire volume a "curtain" of particles is rendered in front of the viewer. The use of motion blurring and fog along with lighting to simulate an overcast sky can make the illusion more convincing. It is still possible to simulate simple accumulation of precipitation by choosing points on collision surfaces at random (within the parameterization of the simulation), rather than tracking particle collisions with the surfaces, and blending them into texture maps as described previously.

Smoke

Exactly modeling smoke requires some sophisticated physics, but surprisingly realistic images can be generated using fairly simple techniques. One such technique uses big particles; each particle is textured with a 2D cross section of a puff of smoke. To simplify manipulation, a texture containing only luminance and alpha channels can be used. If the GL_MODULATE texture environment is used, changing the color and alpha value of the particle geometry controls the color and transparency of the smoke. Controlling the appearance of the smoke with geometry attributes, such as vertex color, also makes it possible to simulate different types of smoke with the same texture. While smoke from an oil fire is dark and opaque, steam from a factory smoke stack is much lighter in color.

The size, position, orientation, and opacity of the particles can be varied as a function of time to simulate the puff of smoke enlarging, drifting, and dissipating over time (see Figure 18.5). Overlapping the smoke particles creates a smokey region of arbitrary shape, which can be modified dynamically over time by moving, rotating, scaling, and modifying the color and transparency of the component particles.

The smoke texture, used to represent a group of smoke particles, is a key building block for building smoke effects of this type. The texture image itself may vary. A single texture may be used for all particles. The texture used can vary with particle position, or might be animated over time, depending on the requirements of the application. The realism and accuracy of the texture image itself is important. There are a number of procedural techniques that can be used to synthesize both static and dynamic 2D textures, as described in Section 18.3. Some of the literature devoted to realistic clouds, as described in Section 18.6, can also be applied to producing smoke textures.

Alpha 1.0   Scale × 2   Alpha .75   Scale × 2   Alpha .4

Figure 18.5 Dilating, fading smoke.

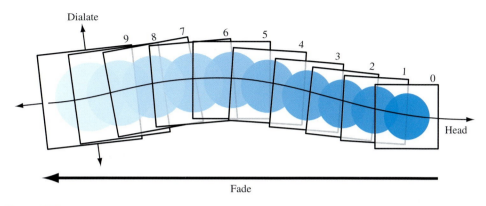

Figure 18.6 Vapor trail.

Vapor Trails

Vapor trails emanating from a jet or a missile can be modeled with a particle system, treating it as a special case of smoke. A circular, wispy 2D smoke texture applied on a big particle is used to generate the vapor pattern. The texture image can consist of only alpha components, modulating the transparency of the image, letting the particle geometry set the color. The trajectory of the vapor trail is painted using multiple overlapping particles, as shown in Figure 18.6. Over time the individual billboards gradually enlarge and fade. The program for rendering a trail is largely an exercise in maintaining an active list of the position, orientation, and time since creation for each particle used to paint the trail. As each particle exceeds a threshold transparency value it can be reused as a new particle, keeping the total number constant, and avoiding the overhead of allocating and freeing particles.

Fire

A constant fire can be modeled as a set of nearly stationary big particles mapped with procedural textures. The particles can be partially transparent and stacked to create the appearance of multiple layers of intermingling flames, adding depth to the fire.

A static image of fire can be constructed from a noise texture (Section 18.3 describes how to make a noise texture using OpenGL). The weights for different frequency components should be chosen to create a realistic spectral structure for the fire. Turbulent fire can be modeled in the texture image, or by warping the texture coordinates being applied to the particles. Texture coordinates may be distorted vertically to simulate the effect of flames rising and horizontally to mimic the effect of winds. These texture coordinate distortions can be applied with the texture transform matrix to avoid having to update the particle texture coordinates.

A progressive sequence of fire textures can be animated on the particles, as described in Section 14.12. Creating texture images that reflect the abrupt manner in which fire moves and changes intensity can be done using the same turbulence techniques used to create the fire texture itself. The speed of the animation playback, as well as the distortion applied to the texture coordinates of the billboard, can be controlled using a turbulent noise function.

Explosions

Explosion effects can be rendered with a heterogeneous particle system, combining the techniques used for smoke and fire. A set of big particles, textured with either a still or animated image of a fireball, is drawn centered in the middle of the explosion. It can be dilated, rotated, and faded over a short period of time. At the same time, a smoke system can produce a smoke cloud rising slowly from the center of the explosion. To increase realism, simple particles can spray from the explosion center at high speed on ballistic trajectories. Careful use of local light sources can improve the effect, creating a flash corresponding to the fireball.

Clouds

Individual clouds, like smoke, have an amorphous structure without well-defined surfaces and boundaries. In the literature, computationally intensive physical cloud modeling techniques have given way to simplified mathematical models that are both computationally tractable and aesthetically pleasing (Gardner, 1985; Ebert, 1994).

As with smoke systems, big particles using sophisticated textures can be combined to create clouds. The majority of the realism comes from the quality of the texture.

To get realism the texture image should be based on a fractal-based or spectral-based function we'll call t. Gardner suggests a Fourier-like sum of sine waves with phase shifts:

$$t(x, y) = k \sum_{i=1}^{n} \left(c_i \sin(fx_i x + px_i) + t_0 \right) \sum_{i=1}^{n} \left(c_i \sin(fy_i y + py_i) + t_0 \right)$$

with the relationships

$$fx_{i+1} = 2fx_i$$
$$fy_{i+1} = 2fy_i$$
$$c_{i+1} = .707c_i$$
$$px_i = \frac{\pi}{2} \sin(fy_{i-1}y), \ i > 1$$
$$py_i = \frac{\pi}{2} \sin(fx_{i-1}x), \ i > 1$$

Care must be taken using this technique to choose values to avoid a regular pattern in the texture. Alternatively, texture generation techniques described in Section 18.3 can also be used.

Another cloud texture generating method is stochastic, based on work by Fournier and Miller (Fournier, 1982; Miller, 1986). It uses a midpoint displacement technique called Diamond-Square for generating a set of random values on a uniform grid. These generated values are interpreted as opacity values and correspond to the cloud density at a given point. The algorithm is iterative; during each iteration two steps are executed. The first, the *diamond* step, takes four corners of a square and produces a new value at its center by averaging the values at the four corners and adding a random number in the range $[-1, 1]$.

The second step, the *square* step, consists of taking the corners of the four diamonds that were generated in the diamond step (they share the center point of the diamond step) and generating a new center value for each diamond by averaging its four corners and adding a random number in the range $[-1, 1]$. During the square step, attention must be paid to diamonds at the edges of the grid as they will wrap around to the opposite side of the grid. During each iteration the number of squares processed is increased by a factor of four. To produce smooth variations in the generated values, the range of the random value added during the generation of center points is reduced by some fraction for each iteration. Seed values for the first few iterations of the algorithm may be used to control the overall shape of the final texture.

Light Points

The same procedures used for controlling the appearance of dynamic particles can also be used to realistically render small static light sources, such as stars, beacons, and runway lights. As with particles, to render realistic-looking small light sources it is necessary to change some combination of the size and brightness of the source as a function of distance from the eye.

If available, the implementation's point parameter functionality can be used to modify the light points as a function of distance, as described in Section 18.1. If the point parameter feature is not available, the brightness attenuation a as a function of distance, d, can be approximated by using the same equation used in the OpenGL lighting equation:

$$\frac{1}{k_c + k_l d + k_q d^2}$$

Attenuation can be achieved by modulating the point size by the square root of the attenuation:

$$size_{effective} = size \times \sqrt{a}$$

Subpixel size points are simulated by adjusting transparency, making the alpha value proportional to the ratio of the point area determined from the size attenuation computation to the area of the point being rendered:

$$alpha = \left(\frac{size_{effective}}{size_{threshold}} \right)^2$$

More complex behavior — such as defocusing, perspective distortion, and directionality of light sources — can be achieved by using an image of the light lobe as a texture map on big particles. To effectively simulate distance attenuation it may be necessary to select different texture patterns based on the distance from the eye.

18.2 Dynamic Meshes

While particle systems can be a powerful modeling technique, they are also expensive. The biggest problem is that the geometry count per frame can rapidly get to a point where it impacts performance. In cases where an object has a distinct boundary that is smooth and continuous, representing the object with a textured mesh primitive can be more economical.

A dynamic mesh has two components: the mesh geometry, whose vertices and vertex attributes can be updated parametrically every frame, and the surface texture itself, which may also be dynamic. The mesh geometry can be represented in OpenGL with triangle or quad strips. The vertices and vertex attributes can be processed in a way very similar to particle systems, as described in Section 18.1.4. The vertex and attribute values are stored in arrays, and updated with parameterized functions each frame. They are rendered by sending them to the hardware as vertex arrays.

Figure 18.7 shows the components of a dynamic mesh; an array of vertices and their attributes that defines the mesh surface. The array structure makes it easy for an application to update the components efficiently. The data is organized so that it can be drawn efficiently as a vertex array, combined with a texture that is applied to the mesh surface. This texture can be modified by changing the texture coordinates of the mesh, or the color values if the texture is applied with the GL_MODULATE texture environment.

Much of the visible complexity of a mesh object is captured by a surface texture. The texture image may have a regular pattern, making it possible to repeat a small texture over the entire surface. Examples of surfaces with repeating patterns include clouds and water. It is often convenient to use a procedurally generated texture (see Section 18.3) in these cases. This is because the spatial frequency components of a procedural texture can be finely controlled, making it easy to create a texture that wraps across a surface without artifacts.

The texture may be updated dynamically in a number of ways. The direct method is to simply update the texture image itself using subimages. But image updates are expensive consumers of bandwidth. For many applications, lower-cost methods can create a dynamic texture without updating new images. In some cases, simply warping the texture

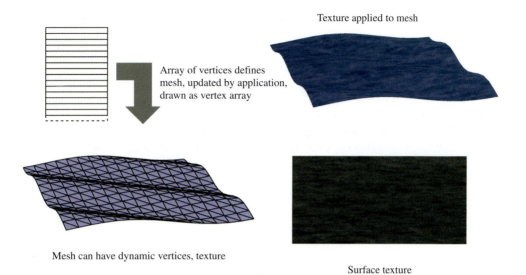

Texture applied to mesh

Array of vertices defines mesh, updated by application, drawn as vertex array

Mesh can have dynamic vertices, texture

Surface texture

Figure 18.7 Dynamic mesh components.

on the surface is sufficient. The texture's appearance can also be modified by changing the underlying vertex color, rendering with a texture environment such as GL_BLEND or GL_MODULATE. If the texture image itself must be modified, a procedural texture is a good choice for animation, since it is easy to create a series of slowly varying images by varying the input parameters of the generation functions.

We'll describe dynamic meshes in more depth through a set of application examples. They illustrate the technique in more detail, showing how they can solve problems for particular application areas.

Water

A large body of research has focused on modeling, shading, and reproducing optical effects of water (Watt, 1990; Peachey, 1986; Fournier, 1986), yet most methods still present a large computational burden to achieve a realistic image. Nevertheless, it is possible to borrow from these approaches and achieve reasonable results while retaining interactive performance (Kass, 1990; Ebert, 1994).

Dynamic mesh techniques can provide good realism efficiently enough to maintain interactive frame rates. The dynamics of waves can be simulated using procedural models and rendered using meshes computed from height fields. The mesh vertices are positioned by modulating the height of the vertices with a sinusoid to simulate simple wave patterns, as shown in Figure 18.8. The frequency and amplitude of the waves can be varied to achieve different effects. The phase of the sinusoid can be varied over time to create wave motion.

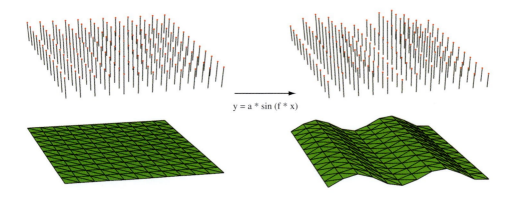

$$y = a * \sin (f * x)$$

Figure 18.8 Water modeled as a height field.

The mesh geometry can be textured using simple procedural texture images, producing a good simulation of water surfaces. Synthetic perturbations to the texture coordinates, as outlined in Section 18.3.7, can also be used to help animate the water surface.

If there is an adequate performance margin, the rendering technique can be further embellished. Multipass or multitexture rendering techniques can be used to layer additional effects such as surf. The reflective properties of the water surface can also be more accurately simulated. Environment mapping can be used to simulate basic reflections from the surface, such as sun smear. This specular reflection can be made more physically accurate using environment mapping that incorporates the Fresnel reflection model described in Section 15.9. The bump-mapping technique described in Section 15.10 can be used to create the illusion of ripples without having to model them in the mesh geometry. The bump maps can be updated dynamically to animate them.

Animating water surface effects also extends to underwater scenes. Optical effects such as caustics can be approximated using OpenGL, as described by Nishita and Nakamae (Nishita, 1994), but interactive frame rates are not likely to be achieved. A more efficient, if less accurate, technique to model such effects uses a caustic texture to modulate the intensity of any geometry that lies below the surface. Other below-surface effects can also be simulated. Movements of the water (surge) can be simulated by perturbing the vertex coordinates of submerged objects, again using sinusoids. Blueish-green fog can be used to simulate light attenuation in water.

Cloud Layers

Cloud layers, in many cases, can be modeled well with dynamic meshes. The best candidates are cloud layers that are continuous and that have distinct upper and lower boundaries. Clouds in general have complex and chaotic boundaries, yet when viewed from a distance or from a viewing angle other than edge-on to the layer boundary this visual complexity is less apparent. In these cases, the dynamic mesh can approximate the cloud layer boundary, with the surface texture supplying the visual complexity. In the simplest case, the dynamic mesh geometry can be simplified to a single quadrilateral covering the sky.

The procedural texture generation techniques described in Section 18.3 can be used to create cloud layer textures. The texture can be a simple luminance image, making it possible to model slowly varying color changes (such as the effect of atmospheric haze) by changing vertex colors in the dynamic mesh. Thin broken cloud layers can also be simulated well if the viewer is not too close to the cloud layer. A luminance cloud texture can be used to blend a white constant texture environment color into a blue sky polygon. If the view is from above the cloud layer, a texture with alpha can be used instead to provide transparency. Rendered with blending or alpha test, the texture can stencil appropriately shaped holes in the mesh polygon, showing the ground below.

Dynamic aspects of cloud layers can also be modeled. Cloud drift can be simulated by translating the textured particles across the sky, along with changes in the mesh geometry, as appropriate.

18.3 Procedural Texture Generation

Although many textures are created from natural or synthetic images, textures can also be created by directly evaluating a procedure to generate texel colors. A function is chosen that generates colors as a function of texture coordinates: $color = p(s, t, r, q)$. A *procedural texture* can be created by evaluating this function at every texel location in a texture image. There is a class of these procedures, known as *filtered noise functions*, that are particularly useful for generating images for natural features. The images created have similar features at different levels of spatial resolution. This result can be created directly using an appropriate function, or through a multistep process by creating a high-resolution image and then compositing it with scaled and filtered versions of itself. The resulting textures can simulate the appearance of such diverse phenomena as fire, smoke, clouds, and certain types of stone, such as marble. This class of procedural texture, and how it is used in RenderMan shaders, is described in Ebert (1994).

18.3.1 Filtered Noise Functions

Procedural textures can be generated "on the fly," producing texture color values as needed during the filtering process. Texture images created this way are defined over a continuous range of texture coordinates (using floating-point representations of the input parameters). This method is very powerful, and is the basis for high-quality "shader-based" texturing approaches. It can be accelerated in hardware using fragment programs, but only if the shader hardware is powerful enough to implement the generating function's algorithm.

Instead of this general method, we'll use more limited but efficient approach. A pseudorandom image is created in software using a simpler generating function, and is then loaded into a texture map. Texturing is used to convolve and scale the image as necessary to produce the final filtered image. Since the generating function is only evaluated to create a discrete texture image, the generating function need only create valid values at texel locations. This makes it possible to create simpler, discrete versions of the randomizing algorithm, and to make use of a texture-mapping technique to efficiently resample the source images at multiple frequencies. It uses a combination of pseudorandom values, polygon rendering, and texture-filtering techniques to create filtered images.

To create a texture image, the generating function must create color and intensity values at every texel location. To do this efficiently with OpenGL, the algorithms use rectangular grids of values, represented as pixel images. Each 2D grid location is defined to be separated from its neighbors by one unit in each dimension. Both the input and output of the function are defined in terms of this grid. The input to the function is a grid with pseudorandom "noise" values placed in each location. The output is the same grid properly filtered, which can then be used as a component of the final texture image.

The characteristics and distribution of the input noise values, and the filtering method applied to them, determines the characteristics of the final noise function image. A procedural texture must always produce the same output at a given position in the texture, and must produce values limited to a given range. Both of these requirements are met by generating the image once, loading it into a texture map, and mapping it as many times as necessary onto the target geometry.

Another important criterion of procedurally generated textures is that they be band-limited to a maximum spatial frequency of about one. This limit ensures that the filtered image can be properly sampled on the texel grid without aliasing. Any initial set of pseudorandom noise values should therefore be filtered with a low-pass filter at this maximum spatial frequency before use in a texture.

Figure 18.9 illustrates the steps in producing a filtered noise function. The direct approach is simple: a continuous function is written that outputs filtered color values as a function of surface position. It is used during the rasterization phase to set the pixel colors of the polygon. The texture approach requires more steps. A discrete function is used to generate an unfiltered image. The image is filtered and resampled over one or more frequencies using texture mapping. The resulting image is then applied to the geometry as a texture.

The initial noise inputs need to be positioned in the image before filtering. Their distribution affects the appearance of the resulting image. One common method is to distribute the initial values in a uniform grid. Textures that start from a regular grid of noise values are called *lattice noise* functions. Lattice noise is simple to create, but can exhibit axis-aligned artifacts. The noise functions can also be distributed in a nonuniform stochastic pattern, avoiding this problem. In the literature, this technique is called a *sparse convolution*. Another method designed to avoid the artifact problem is called *spot*

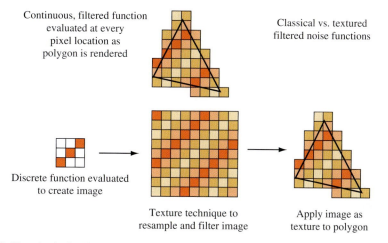

Continuous, filtered function evaluated at every pixel location as polygon is rendered

Classical vs. textured filtered noise functions

Discrete function evaluated to create image

Texture technique to resample and filter image

Apply image as texture to polygon

Figure 18.9 Filtered noise functions.

noise, described by van Wijk (1991). To use image-based filtering techniques, nonuniform spacing is allowed, but all random data must be placed on a grid point.

How the filtering step is applied to the input noise can vary (Ebert, 1994). Two common filters interpolate lattice noise values in quite different ways. In *value noise*, the filter function directly interpolates the value of the random noise data placed at all lattice points. In *gradient noise*, noise data is used to produce vector values at each lattice point, which are then interpolated to produce filtered values. A frequency analysis of gradient noise shows no contribution at a frequency of zero. This is useful because it makes it easy to composite multiple noise functions without introducing a bias term.

Simple noise functions are often combined to create more complex ones. A common case is a function composed of scaled versions of the output of the original function. The scaling is done so that the output frequency is lower by a power-of-two: 2, 4, 8, and so on. These lower-frequency derivative functions are called the *octaves* of the original function. The octaves are composited with the original version of the noise function. The compositing step scales the output of each function by a set of weighting factors, which can be varied to produce different effects. The result is a band-limited function that has the appearance of controlled randomness in each frequency band. This distribution of energy in the frequency domain is very similar to random phenomena found in nature, and accounts for the realism of these textures.

18.3.2 Generating Noise Functions

A discrete version of the generating function described previously can be created in the framebuffer using OpenGL. The generation algorithm must be able to start with a grid of random values, stretch them so that each covers a larger area (to create lower-frequency octaves), and apply low-pass filtering (essentially blending them).

One simple way to do this is to create a texture composed of random values at each texel, and then stretch and interpolate the values by rendering a textured rectangle. The rectangle could be textured using bilinear filtering, and drawn at an appropriate size to create the desired octave. Bilinear interpolation, however, is a poor filter for this application. This is especially true when creating lower-frequency octaves, where random values must be interpolated across a large area.

Some OpenGL implementations support better texture-filtering modes, such as bicubic filtering, which may produce results of acceptable quality. Some implementations of bicubic filtering may have limited subtexel precision, however, causing noticeable banding when creating lower-frequency octaves. Both bilinear and bicubic filters also have the limitation that they can only interpolate existing values. This limits the noise filter to produce only value noise; the approach isn't flexible enough to work with gradient noise. A more powerful approach is to spread each value across the image using convolution techniques. Fortunately, this method can be made efficient with a clever application of texture mapping.

18.3.3 Filtering Using Texture Convolution

Instead of simply creating textures of random values and stretching them to create filtered octaves using built-in texture filtering, the octave images can be created using a convolution approach. A convolution filter can apply the appropriate filtering to each random value as needed. Filter kernels that cover a larger area can be used to create lower-frequency octaves. Convolution is discussed in Section 12.6. The approach shown here accelerates convolution by encoding the convolution filter into a texture image. A rectangle, whose color is the random value to be convolved, is rendered with the monochrome texture containing the convolution filter image applied to it.

To illustrate, consider a low-pass filtering operation on an image. The input image can be thought of as a grid of values. To low-pass filter the image, the values at each grid location must be blended with their neighbors. The number of neighboring values that are blended is called the filter's *extent* or support (Section 4.3); it defines the width of the filter. Blending the value of location i,j with a neighbor at $i+n, j+m$ can be expressed as $value_{i+n,j+m} = value_{i+n,j+m} * filter + value_{i,j} * (1 - filter)$. The filter function controls the contribution location i,j makes to each of its neighbors. The extent of the filter and its values determine the filtering effect. In general, the wider the extent (i.e., the more neighbors affected), the lower the maximum frequency a low-pass filter can achieve and the more work required to apply the filtering (because it requires operating on more values).

The convolution operation can be implemented using a combination of texturing and blending. A texture map is created that represents a convolution kernel, containing the desired filter weights for each texel neighbor. The size of the filter texels doesn't have to be one-to-one with the destination pixels. The resolution of the texture filter is determined by the complexity of the filtering function. A simple linear filtering function can be represented with a small texture, since OpenGL's linear magnification can be used to interpolate between filter values. The filter texels can modulate a sample value

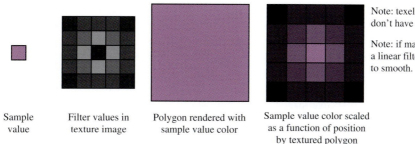

Note: texel and pixel sizes don't have to match.

Note: if magnifying texture a linear filter can be used to smooth.

Sample value   Filter values in texture image   Polygon rendered with sample value color   Sample value color scaled as a function of position by textured polygon

Figure 18.10 Using textures to filter a value.

by using the filter texture to texture a rectangle colored with the sample. If the texture environment is GL_MODULATE, a single component GL_LUMINANCE texture containing the filter function will scale the base color by the texel values. The texture performs two functions: it spreads the sample value over the region of the rectangle and modulates the sample value at the resolution of the filter texture. Rendering the textured rectangle updates the values in the framebuffer with the filtered values for a single sample, as shown in Figure 18.10.

A straightforward filtering pass based on this idea reads each sample value and uses it to color a texture rectangle modulated by the filter texture. The process is repeated, shifting the textured rectangle and substituting a new sample value for the rectangle color for each iteration. The filtered results for each sample are combined using blending, or for higher color resolution using the accumulation buffer.

The following is a very simple example of this approach in more detail. It starts with a 512×512 grid of sample values and applies a 2×2 box filter. The filter spreads the sample, considered to be at the lower-left corner of the filter, over a 4×4 region.

1. Create a 2×2 luminance filter, each value containing the value .25.

2. Configure the transform pipeline so that object coordinates are in screen space.

3. Clear a 512×512 region of the framebuffer that will contain the filtered image to black.

4. Create a 512×512 grid of sample values to be filtered.

5. Enable blending, setting the blend function to GL_ONE, GL_ONE.

6. Set the texture environment to GL_MODULATE.

7. For each sample location i, j:

    (a) Render a rectangle of size 4×4 with lower left corner at i, j, textured with the filter function. Use the sample color at i, j for the vertex color at all four corners.

8. Copy the filtered image into a texture map for use.

There are a number of parameters that need to be adjusted properly to get the desired filtering. The transformation pipeline should be configured so that the object coordinate system matches screen coordinates. The region of the framebuffer rendered should be large enough to create the filtered image at the desired resolution. The textured rectangle should be sized to cover all neighboring pixels needed to get the desired filtering effect. The resolution of the filter texture itself should be sufficient to represent the filter function accurately for the given rectangle size. The rectangle should be adjusted in x and y to match the grid sample being filtered. The filter marches across the image, one pixel at a time, until the filtering is completed. To avoid artifacts at the edges of the image, the filter function should extend beyond the bounds of the image, just as it does for normal convolution operations. The relationship between sample value and filter function will determine the details of how overlaps should be handled, either by clamping or by wrapping.

Although efficient, there are limitations to this approach. The most serious is the limited range of color values for both the filter texture and the framebuffer. Both the filter function and sample color are limited to the range $[0, 1]$. This makes it impossible to use filter kernels with negative elements without scaling and biasing the values to keep them within the supported range, as described in Section 14.13.1. Since the results of each filtering pass are accumulated, filters should be chosen that don't cause pixel color overflow or underflow. Texturing and/or framebuffers with extended range can mitigate these restrictions.

18.3.4 Optimizing the Convolution Process

Although texture mapping efficiently applies the filtered values of a sample point over a large number of pixels, the filtering operation can become expensive since it has to be repeated for every sample in the target image. This process can be optimized, particularly for filters with a small extent, using the following observation. Since a texture map is used to apply a filter function, the filter's extent can be represented as a rectangular region with a given width and height. Note that two sample values won't blend with each other during filtering if they are as far apart as the filter's extent. This independence can be used to reduce the number of passes required to filter an image. Instead of filtering only a single sample value per pass, and iterating over the entire image, the texture filter can be tiled over the entire image at once, reducing the number of passes. If a filter extent is of width w and height h, every $w + 1$th sample in the horizontal direction and every $h + 1$th sample in the vertical direction can be filtered at the same time, since they don't interact with each other.

For a concrete illustration, consider the 2×2 filter with the 4×4 extent in the previous example. For any given sample at i, j, the samples at $i + 4, j$ and $i, j + 4$ won't be affected by the sample value at i, j. This means the samples at $i + 4, j$ and $i, j + 4$ can be filtered at the same time that i, j is sampled by applying three nonoverlapping textured rectangles, each with a different one of the three sample values. Taking full advantage of this idea, the entire image can be tiled with texture rectangles, filtering the samples at $i + 4 * n, j + 4 * m$. With this technique, the entire image can be filtered in 16 passes. In general, the number

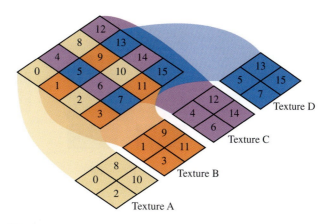

Figure 18.11 Input image.

of passes required will be equal to the extent of the filter. With this technique, that equals the number of pixels covered by the filter rectangle.

The implementation of this technique can be further streamlined. The tiled set of textured rectangles, each colored with a different sample value, is replaced with a single rectangle textured with two textures. The first texture is the filter texture, with the wrap parameter set to GL_REPEAT and texture coordinates set so that it tiles over the entire rectangle, creating filters of the same size as the original technique. The second texture contains the sample values themselves. It is composed of a subset of the grid sample points that satisfies the $i + 4n, j + 4m$ equation, as illustrated in Figure 18.11. In a two-pass technique (or single pass if multitexturing is available), the sample-points texture can be modulated by the filter texture, creating a sparse grid of filtered values in a single texturing pass. The process can be repeated with the same filter texture, and offset sample textures, such as $i + 1 + 4n, j + 4m$ and $i + 4n, j + 1 + 4m$. The large rectangle should be offset to match the offset sample values, as shown in Figure 18.12. The process is repeated until every sample in the filter's extent has been computed.

The example steps that follow illustrate the technique in more detail. It assumes that multitexturing is available. Two textures are used: the filter texture, consisting a single component texture containing values that represent the desired filter function, and the sample texture, containing the sample values to be filtered.

1. Set a blending function to combine the results from rendering passes or configure the accumulation buffer.

2. Choose a rectangle size that covers the destination image.

Filter texture

Input image

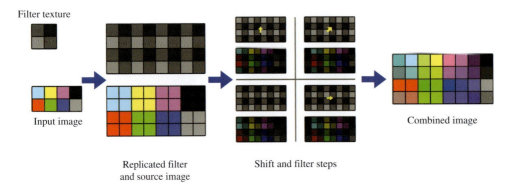

Replicated filter
and source image

Shift and filter steps

Combined image

Figure 18.12 Output image.

3. Create the sample texture from a subset of the samples, as described previously. Bind it to the first texture unit.

4. Scale the texture coordinates of the sample texture so that each sample matches the desired extent of the filter.

5. Bind the second texture unit to the filter texture.

6. Set the wrap mode used on the filter texture to GL_REPEAT.

7. Scale the texture coordinates used on the filter texture so it has the desired extent.

8. Set the texture environment mode so that the filter texture scales the intensity of the sample texture's texels.

9. Render the rectangle with the two textures enabled.

10. If using the accumulation buffer, accumulate the result.

11. This is one pass of the filtering operation. One sample has been filtered over the entire image. To filter the other samples:

   (a) Shift the position of the rectangle by one pixel.

   (b) Update the sample texture to represent the set of samples that matches the new rectangle position.

   (c) Rerender the rectangle, blending with the old image, or if using the accumulation buffer make an accumulation pass.

   (d) Repeat until each sample in the filter's extent has been processed.

The subset of the sample grid can be efficiently selected by rendering a texture with the sample values, using GL_NEAREST for the minification filter. By rendering a rectangle the size of the reduced sample grid, and setting the texture coordinates to minify and bias the texture appropriately, the minification filter can be used to only render the samples desired.

The position of the rectangle, the way the filter and sample textures are positioned on the rectangle, and the grid samples used in each pass are determined by the relationship between the sample point and the filter. The filter is considered to have a *sample position*, which describes the position of the input sample relative to the filter. This position is needed to properly position the filter relative to the input samples as each subset of samples is filtered. Many filters assume that the input sample is at the center of the filter. This can't always be done, as there is no center for a filter with a width and/or height that is even. To get the edges of the filtered image correct, the textured rectangle can overlap beyond the edge of the image.

Creating Octaves

Once a filtered noise image is created, it is a simple matter to create lower octaves. The original image being filtered has a maximum spatial frequency component. Simply scaling the size of the textured rectangle, in the approach described previously, will change the filter extent and create a filtered image with different frequency components. Doubling the size of the textured rectangle, for example, will create an image with frequency components that are one-half the original. If the rectangle is to be increased in size, be sure that the filter texture has sufficient resolution to represent the filter accurately when spread over a larger number of pixels.

18.3.5 Spectral Synthesis

Using the previous algorithm, multiple octaves can be created and combined to create multispectral images. The process of rescaling the filter size can be streamlined by changing the texture coordinates in the texture transform matrix. The matrix also makes it easy to translate and scale texture coordinates. Translating texture coordinates by a random factor for each octave prevents the samples near the texture coordinate origin from aligning. Such alignment can lead to noticeable artifacts.

Natural phenomena often have a frequency spectrum where lower-frequency components are stronger. Often the amplitude of a particular frequency is proportional to $\frac{1}{frequency}$. To replicate this phenomenon, the intensity of each octave's filtered samples can be scaled. An easy way to do this is to apply a frequency-dependent scale factor when coloring the textured rectangles.

Just as each filtered sample must be blended with its neighbors within the filter's extent, so each scaled octave must be blended with the others to create a multispectral texture. As with the original filtering method, blending can be done in the framebuffer, or if more color precision is needed using the accumulation buffer. If desired, the weighting factors for each octave can be applied when the octaves are blended, instead of when the filter rectangle is shaded. The steps that follow use the technique for creating a filtered image mentioned previously to generate and combine octaves of that image to produce a multispectral texture map.

1. Create the original filtered image using the filtered noise technique described previously.

2. For each octave (halving the previous frequency):

    (a) Create a sample texture with one quarter the samples of the previous level.

    (b) Halve the texture coordinate scale used to texture the rectangle. This will quadruple the extent of each filtered sample.

    (c) Draw textured rectangles to filter the image with both textures. The number of rendering steps must be quadrupled, since each filtered sample is covering four times as many pixels.

    (d) Scale the intensity of the resulting image as needed.

    (e) Combine the new octave with the previous one by blending or using the accumulation buffer.

Generalizing the Filtering Operation

Gradient noise can be also created using the previous method. Instead of an averaging filter, a gradient filter is used. Since a gradient filter has both positive and negative components, multiple passes are required, segmenting the filter into positive and negative components and changing the blend equation to create the operation desired.

Since texture coordinates are not restricted to integral values, the texture filter can be positioned arbitrarily. This makes it possible to generalize the previous technique to create noise that is not aligned on a lattice. To create nonaligned noise images, such as sparse convolution noise (Lewis, 1989) or spot noise (van Wijk, 1991), filter the sample values individually, randomly positioning the filter texture. Instead of drawing the entire point-sampled texture at once, draw one texel and one copy of the filter at a time for each random location. This is just a generalization of the initial texture approach described previously in Section 18.3.3.

18.3.6 Turbulence

A variation of the process used to create noise textures can create images that suggest turbulent flow. To create this type of image, first-derivative (slope) discontinuities are introduced into the noise function. A convenient way to do this on a function that has both positive and negative components is to take its absolute value. Although OpenGL does not include an absolute value operator for framebuffer content in the fixed-function pipeline, the same effect can be achieved using the accumulation buffer.

The accumulation buffer can store signed values. Unsigned values from the framebuffer, in the range $[0, 1]$, can be stretched to range $[-1, 1]$ using GL_ADD and

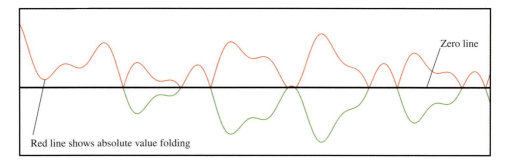

Zero line

Red line shows absolute value folding

Figure 18.13 Turbulence.

GL_MULT operations in the accumulation buffer. The absolute value of the stretched function can be obtained by reading back from the accumulation buffer; returned values are clamped to be positive. The negative values are returned using a scale factor of −1. This flips the negative components to positive, which will survive clamping during the return. The result is the absolute value of the stretched image. The discontinuity will appear at the midway values, one-half of the original function (see Figure 18.13).

The following steps illustrate the details of this technique. They would be applied to a filtered image in the framebuffer.

1. Load the accumulation buffer using glAccum(GL_LOAD,1.0).

2. Bias the image in the buffer by 1/2 using glAccum(GL_ADD,-0.5), making it signed.

3. Scale the image by 2 using glAccum(GL_MULT,2.0), filling the [−1, 1] range.

4. Return the image using glAccum(GL_RETURN,1.0), implicitly clamping to positive values.

5. Save the image in the color buffer to a texture, application memory, or other color buffer.

6. Return the negative values by inverting them using glAccum(GL_RETURN,-1.0).

7. Set the blend function to GL_ONE for both source and destination.

8. Draw the saved image from step 5 onto the image returned from the accumulation buffer. The blend mode will combine them.

The color buffer needs to be saved after the first GL_RETURN because the second GL_RETURN will overwrite the color buffer. OpenGL does not define blending for accumulation buffer return operations. One way to implement this is using both the front and back color buffers in a double-buffered framebuffer.

18.3.7 Random Image Warping

A useful application for a 2D noise texture is to use the noise values to offset texture coordinates. Texture coordinates are applied with regular spacing to a triangle mesh. The noise values are used to displace each texture coordinate. If the grid and its texture coordinates are then textured with an image, the resulting image will be distorted, creating a somewhat painterly view of the image. A more severe distortion can be created by using the noise values directly as texture coordinates, rather than as offsets.

By setting the proper transforms, the process of using noise values as texture coordinates can be automated. Capturing the noise image into a vertex array as texture coordinates, and setting the texture transform matrix appropriately, makes it possible to render the texture with the noise image texture coordinates directly. A variation of this technique, where the noise values are used as vertex positions in the vertex array and then transformed by the appropriate modelview matrix, makes it possible to use noise values as vertex positions.

Another similar use of a 2D noise texture is to distort the reflection of an image. In OpenGL, reflections on a flat surface can be done by reflecting a scene across the surface. The results are copied from the framebuffer to texture memory, and in turn drawn with distorted texture coordinates. The shape and form of the distortion are controlled by modulating or attenuating the contents of the framebuffer after the noise texture is drawn but before it is copied to texture memory. This can produce interesting effects such as water ripples.

18.3.8 Generating 3D Noise

Noise images are not limited to two dimensions. 3D noise images can also be synthesized using the techniques described here. To do this correctly requires a 3D filter instead of a 2D one. In the 2D case, a 2D filter is created by converting a 2D filter function into a texture image, then using the texture to modulate an input color. For 3D filtering, the same apporach can be used. A discrete 3D filter is created from a 3D filter function, then stored in a 3D texture. Using a 3D texture filter to create a 3D noise image requires slicing the 3D block of pixels into 2D layers, a technique similar to the volume visualization techniques discussed in Section 20.5.8. As with volume visualization, 3D texturing is done using multiple textured 2D slices, building up a 3D volume one layer at a time. Like volume visualization, it also can be done using true 3D textures, or a series of 2D textures applied in layers instead.

As with 2D noise filtering, it can be clearer to consider the simple brute-force case for 3D. A 3D grid of random values is created with the desired resolution. A 3D filter texture is created, either as a single 3D texture or as a series of 2D textures, each representing a different r coordinate in the 3D texture. As with 2D textures, the 3D filter function has an extent, but this time it is measured in three dimensions. As with 2D, a rectangle is rendered, sized to match the extent of the texture filter and sized to cover the pixels that should be modified by the filter. Unlike the 2D case, a series of rectangles must be drawn, spanning the layers of the image covered by the filter's extent. The rendering process is repeated, shifting the texture rectangles as necessary and iterating through the samples in the 3D sample grid. As with the 2D case, the rectangle is shifted to align the filter texture properly as each new grid value is filtered. In the 3D case, the image layers the rectangles are applied must also be shifted.

Since 3D framebuffers are not supported in OpenGL, one or more 2D framebuffers must be segmented into layers to provide rendering surfaces representing the layers in the 3D noise image. If there is sufficient space in a single framebuffer, the framebuffer can be split up into a grid of rectangular regions, each representing a different layer. The application managing the layers maps a different framebuffer region to each layer. Multiple framebuffers may be necessary to provide enough pixels to represent all of the layers in the noise image. Once the filtered image layers have all been rendered, the results can be copied into a single 3D noise texture, or loaded into a series of 2D textures, depending on the requirements of the application.

As with the 2D case, the procedure can be optimized, wrapping the filter texture in 3 dimensions, and filtering multiple samples (that aren't under the same filter's extent) at once. The samples themselves can be assembled into a 3D sample texture, or a series of 2D sample textures can be used. Like the 2D technique, the texture coordinates of the sample texture are scaled so that each sample matches the extent of its filter function. As before, the filter texture is used to spread and modulate the sample texture's values onto the framebuffer regions. The 3D case requires this process to be applied to multiple layers.

To synthesize a 3D function with different frequencies, first create a 3D noise image for each frequency and composite a weighted set of frequencies, as was done in the 2D case. A large amount of memory is required to store the different 3D noise functions. Many implementations severely restrict the maximum size of 3D textures, so an application should query to see if the implementation's available resolutions are sufficient for the application.

Generating 2D Noise to Simulate 3D Noise

Creating 3D noise function can be computationally expensive. The resulting textures are large consumers of texture and system memory. In some cases, clever use of 2D noise functions can sometimes successfully substitute for true 3D noise functions. To make 2D noise functions adequately approximate the appearance of a true 3D noise function, the 2D function should match the appearance of the 3D function when it is applied to the target surface. The texture image must be updated if the target geometry changes. This makes "pseudo-3D" noise textures less general.

Pseudo-3D noise textures are simple to implement if the original noise function uses spot noise (van Wijk, 1991). The pseudo-3D noise function is designed around the geometry it will texture. Spots are still created in 3D space, but only spots that are close enough to the geometry surface to make a contribution to the final 2D noise image are used. Once the proper spots are selected, they are rendered onto the 2D surface so that at each fragment the value of the spot is determined by the object-space distance from the center of the spot to that fragment.

Depending on the complexity of the geometry, it may be possible to make an acceptable approximation to the correct spot value by distorting a 2D spot texture. One possible way to improve the approximation is to compensate for a nonuniform mapping of the noise texture to the geometry. Van Wijk describes how he does this by nonuniformly scaling a spot. Approximating the correct spot value is most important when generating the lower octaves, where the spots are largest and errors are most noticeable.

Trade-offs Between True and Simulated 3D Noise

When choosing between a true 3D noise texture and a simulation of one, the most accurate approach is to use the 3D one. Per-frame overhead may also be lower for true 3D textures. They can be used with arbitrary geometry without reloading the texture image (assuming the OpenGL implementation supports 3D textures). 3D noise textures suffer the same drawbacks as any 3D texture technique. Generating a 3D noise texture requires a large amount of memory and a large number of passes, especially if the filter convolves a large number of input values at a time. If memory resources are constrained, the 2D approximation can work well on a useful class of geometry. The 2D texture doesn't require nearly as many passes to create, but it does require knowledge of the geometry and additional computation in order to properly shape the spot.

18.4 Summary

This chapter described some classes of advanced techniques useful for simulating natural phenomena. The ideas are general and serve as building blocks for modeling a variety of natural phenomena. Reproducing the appearance of objects in nature continues to be an area of considerable activity. The addition of vertex and fragment programs to the OpenGL pipeline significantly increases the range of processes that can be modeled directly in the pipeline and will serve as a catalyst for numerous new techniques.

19

Illustration and Artistic Techniques

In applications such as scientific visualization and technical illustration, photorealism detracts from rather than enhances the information in the rendered image. Applications such as cartography and CAD benefit from the use of hidden surface elimination and 3D illumination and shading techniques, but the goal of increased insight from the generated images suggests some different processing compared to those used to achieve photorealism.

Strict use of photorealistic models and techniques also hampers applications striving to provide greater artistic freedom in creating images. Examples of such applications including digital image enhancement, painting programs, and cartoon-rendering applications. One aspect often shared by such applications is the use of techniques that emulate traditional modeling, lighting, and shading processes. Some examples of traditional processes are paint brush strokes and charcoal drawing.

19.1 Projections for Illustration

Traditional perspective projection models the optical effect of receding lines converging at a single point on the horizon, called the *vanishing point*. Outside the computer graphics field, perspective projections are called *linear perspective* projections. Linear perspective is the ideal model for reproducing a real-world scene the way it would be captured by a camera lens or a human eye. In some technical applications, such as architectural presentations, linear perspective serves the needs of the viewer well. In other technical applications, (however, such as engineering and mechanical design) parallel projections prove more useful. With parallel projections, edges that are parallel in 3D space remain parallel in the 2D projection. Parallel projections have many properties that make them useful for both engineering and artistic applications.

In engineering applications, it is desirable to avoid distorting the true geometry of the object, allowing measurements to be taken directly from the drawing. In the simplest forms of engineering drawings, a single view of the object is generated (such as a front-, top-, or right-side view). These individual views can be combined to create a *multiview projection*. Alternatively, drawings can be created that show more than one face of an object simultaneously, providing a better sense of the object. Such drawings are generally referred to as projections, since they are generated from a projection in which the object is aligned in a canonical position with faces parallel to the coordinate planes. Using this nomenclature, the drawing is defined by the position and orientation of the viewing (projection) plane, and the lines of sight from the observer to this plane.

Several types of projections have been in use for engineering drawings since the nineteenth century. These projections can be divided into two major categories: *axonometric* and *oblique* projections.

19.1.1 Axonometric Projection

Orthographic projections are parallel projections in which the lines of sight are perpendicular to the projection plane. The simplest orthographic projections align the projection plane so that it is perpendicular to one of the coordinate axis. The OpenGL `glOrtho` command creates an orthographic projection where the projection plane is perpendicular to the z axis. This orthographic projection shows the *front elevation* view of an object. Moving the projection plane so that it is perpendicular to the x axis creates a *side elevation* view, whereas moving the projection plane to be perpendicular to the y axis produces a top or *plan* view. These projections are most easily accomplished in the OpenGL pipeline using the modelview transformation to change the viewing direction to be parallel to the appropriate coordinate axis.

Axonometric projections are a more general class of orthographic projections in which the viewing plane is not perpendicular to any of the coordinate axes. Parallel lines in the 3D object continue to remain parallel in the projection, but lines are foreshortened and angles are not preserved. Axonometric projections are divided into three classes according to the relative foreshortening of lines parallel to the coordinate axis.

Isometric projection is the most frequently used axonometric projection for engineering drawings. Isometric projection preserves the relative lengths of lines parallel to all three of the coordinate axes and projects the coordinate axes to lines that are 60 degrees apart. An isometric projection corresponds to a viewing plane oriented such that the normal vector has all three components equal, $|n_x| = |n_y| = |n_z| = 1/\sqrt{3}$. Object edges that are parallel to the coordinate axes are shortened by 0.8165. The y axis remains vertical,

Isometric
view

Dimetric

Trimetric

Figure 19.1 Isometric, dimetric, and trimetric projections of a cube.

and the x and z axes make 30-degree angles with the horizon, as shown in Figure 19.1. To allow easier direct measurement, isometric projections are sometimes scaled to compensate for the foreshortening to produce an *isometric drawing* rather than an isometric projection.

An isometric projection is generated in OpenGL by transforming the viewing plane followed by an orthographic projection. The viewing plane transformation can be computed using `gluLookAt`, setting the eye at the origin and the look-at point at $(-1, -1, -1)$[1] or one of the seven other isometric directions.

Equal foreshortening along all three axes results in a somewhat unrealistic looking appearance. This can be alleviated in a controlled way, by increasing or decreasing the foreshortening along one of the axes. A *dimetric projection* foreshortens equally along two of the coordinate axes by constraining the magnitude of two of the components of the projection plane normal to be equal. Again, `gluLookAt` can be used to compute the viewing transformation, this time maintaining the same component magnitude for two of the look-at coordinates and choosing the third to improve realism. Carefully choosing the amount of foreshortening can still allow direct measurements to be taken along all three axes in the resulting drawing.

Trimetric projections have unequal foreshortening along all of the coordinate axes. The remaining axonometric projections fall into this category. Trimetric projections are seldom used in technical drawings.

19.1.2 Oblique Projection

An oblique projection is a parallel projection in which the lines of sight are not perpendicular to the projection plane. Commonly used oblique projections orient the projection plane to be perpendicular to a coordinate axis, while moving the lines of sight to intersect two additional sides of the object. The result is that the projection preserves the lengths

---

1. The point $(-1, -1, -1)$ is used rather than $(-1, -1, -1)/\sqrt{3}$ because the `gluLookAt` normalizes the direction vector.

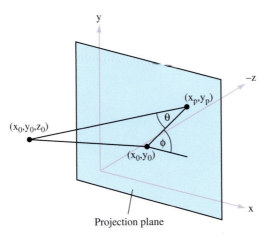

Figure 19.2 Oblique projection.

and angles for object faces parallel to the plane. Oblique projections can be useful for objects with curves if those faces are oriented parallel to the projection plane.

To derive an oblique projection, consider the point (x_0, y_0, z_0) projected to the position (x_p, y_p) (see Figure 19.2). The projectors are defined by the two angles: θ and ϕ, θ is the angle between the line $L = [(x_0, y_0), (x_p, y_p)]$ and the projection plane, ϕ is the angle between the line L and the x axis. Setting $l = ||L||/z_0 = 1/\tan\theta$, the general form of the oblique projection is

$$P = \begin{pmatrix} 1 & 0 & l\cos\phi & 0 \\ 0 & 1 & l\sin\phi & 0 \\ 0 & 0 & 1 & 0 \\ 0 & 0 & 0 & 1 \end{pmatrix}$$

For an orthographic projection, the projector is perpendicular and the length of the line L is zero, reducing the projection matrix to the identity. Two commonly used oblique projections are the *cavalier* and *cabinet* projections. The cavalier projection preserves the lengths of lines that are perpendicular or parallel to the projection plane, with lines of sight at $\theta = \phi = 45$ degrees. However, the fact that length is preserved for perpendicular lines gives rise to an optical illusion where perpendicular lines look longer than their actual length, since the human eye is used to compensating for perspective foreshortening. To correct for this, the cabinet projection shortens lines that are perpendicular to the projection plane to one-half the length of parallel lines and changes the angle θ to $\mathrm{atan}(2) = 63.43$ degrees.

To use an oblique projection in the OpenGL pipeline, the projection matrix P is computed and combined with the matrix computed from the `glOrtho` command. Matrix

P is used to compute the projection transformation, while the orthographic matrix provides the remainder of the view volume definition. The P matrix assumes that the projection plane is perpendicular to the z axis. An additional transformation can be applied to transform the viewing direction before the projection is applied.

19.2 Nonphotorealistic Lighting Models

Traditional technical illustration practices also include methods for lighting and shading. These algorithms are designed to improve clarity rather than embrace photorealism. In Gooch (1998, 1999), lighting and shading algorithms are developed based on traditional technical illustration practices. These practices include the following.

- Use of strong edge outlines to indicate surface boundaries, silhouette edges, and discontinuities.

- Matte objects are shaded with a single light source, avoiding extreme intensities and using hue to indicate surface slope.

- Metal objects are shaded with exaggerated anisotropic reflection.

- Shadows cast by objects are not shown.

Nonphotorealistic lighting models for both matte and metal surfaces are described here.

19.2.1 Matte Surfaces

The model for matte surfaces uses both luminance and hue changes to indicate surface orientation. This lighting model reduces the dynamic range of the luminance, reserving luminance extremes to emphasize edges and highlights. To compensate for the reduced dynamic range and provide additional shape cues, *tone-based shading* adds hue shifts to the lighting model. Exploiting the perception that cool colors (blue, violet, green) recede from the viewer and warm colors (red, orange, yellow) advance, a sense of depth is added by including cool-to-warm color transitions in the model. The diffuse cosine term is replaced with the term

$$d_m d_l \, (\mathbf{N} \cdot \mathbf{L}) \quad \rightarrow \quad \left(d_{l_{cool}} \left(\frac{1 + \mathbf{N} \cdot \mathbf{L}}{2} \right) + d_{l_{warm}} \left(1 - \frac{1 + \mathbf{N} \cdot \mathbf{L}}{2} \right) \right),$$

where $d_{l_{cool}}$ and $d_{l_{warm}}$ are linear combinations of a cool color (a shade of blue) combined with the object's diffuse reflectance, and a warm color (yellow) combined with the object's diffuse reflectance. A typical value for $d_{l_{cool}}$ is $(0., 0., .4) + .2 d_m$ and for $d_{l_{warm}}$ is $(.4, .4, 0.) + .6 d_m$. The modified equation uses a cosine term that varies from $[-1, 1]$ rather than clamping to $[0, 1]$.

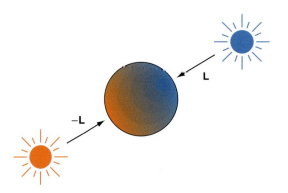

Figure 19.3 Opposing lights approximating warm to cool shift.

If vertex programs are not supported, this modified diffuse lighting model can be approximated using fixed-function OpenGL lighting using two opposing lights (L, −L), as shown in Figure 19.3. The two opposing lights are used to divide the cosine term range in two, covering the range $[0, 1]$ and $[−1, 0]$ separately. The diffuse intensities are set to $(d_{l_{warm}} − d_{l_{cool}})/2$, and $(d_{l_{cool}} − d_{l_{warm}})/2$, respectively, the ambient intensity is set to $(d_{l_{cool}} + d_{l_{warm}})/2$ and the specular intensity contribution is set to zero. Objects are drawn with the material reflectance components set to one (white).

Highlights can be added in a subsequent pass using blending to accumulate the result. Alternatively, the environment mapping techniques discussed in Section 15.9 can be used to capture and apply the BRDF at the expensive of computing an environment map for each different object material.

19.2.2 Metallic Surfaces

For metallic surfaces, the lighting model is further augmented to simulate the appearance of anisotropic reflection (Section 15.9.3). While anisotropic reflection typically occurs on machined (milled) metal parts rather than polished parts, the anisotropic model is still used to provide a cue that the surfaces are metal and to provide a sense of curvature. To simulate the anisotropic reflection pattern, the curved surface is shaded with stripes along the parametric axis of maximum curvature. The intensity of the stripes are random values between 0.0 and 0.5, except the stripe closest to the light source, which is set to 1.0, simulating a highlight. The values between the stripes are interpolated. This process is implemented in the OpenGL pipeline using texture mapping. A small 1D or 2D luminance texture is created containing the randomized set of stripe values. The stripe at *s* coordinate zero (or some well-known position) is set to the value 1. The object is drawn with texture enabled, the wrap mode set to GL_CLAMP, and the *s* texture coordinate set to vary along the curvature. The position of the highlight is adjusted by biasing the *s* coordinate with the texture matrix. This procedure is illustrated in Figure 19.4.

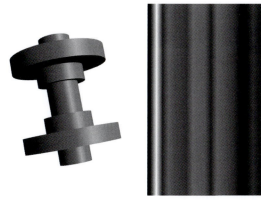

| Blinn lighting and Gouraud shading | Anisotropic light texture | Anisotropic lighting applied |

Figure 19.4 Simulation of anisotropic lighting.

Figure 19.5 Object with edge lines.

19.3 Edge Lines

An important aspect of the lighting model is reducing the dynamic range of the luminance to make edges and highlights more distinct. Edges can be further emphasized by outlining the silhouette and boundary edges in a dark color (see Figure 19.5). Algorithms for drawing silhouette lines are described in Section 16.7.4. Additional algorithms using image-processing techniques, described in Saito (1990) can be implemented using the

OpenGL pipeline (as described in Chapter 12). Gooch (1999) and Markosian (1997) discuss software methods for extracting silhouette edges that can then be drawn as lines.

19.4 Cutaway Views

Engineering drawings of complex objects may show a *cutaway view*, which removes one or more surface layers of the object (shells) to reveal the object's inner structure. A simple way to accomplish this is to not draw the polygons comprising the outer surfaces. This shows inner detail, but also removes the information relating the inner structure to the outer structure. To restore the outer detail, the application may draw part of the outer surface, discarding polygons only in one part of the surface where the inner detail should show through. This requires the application to classify the surface polygons into those to be drawn and those to be discarded. The resulting hole created in the surface will not have a smooth boundary.

Alternatively, clip planes can be used to create cross-sectional views by discarding surface geometry in one of the half-spaces defined by the clip plane. Multiple clip planes can be used in concert to define more complex culling regions. Reintroducing the clipped polygons into the drawing as partially transparent surfaces provides some additional context for the drawing.

Another method for using transparency is to draw the outer surface while varying the surface transparency with the distance from the viewer. Polygons that are most distant from the viewer are opaque, while polygons closest to the viewer are transparent, as shown in Figure 19.6. Seams or significant boundary edges within the outer shell may also be included by drawing them with transparency using a different fading rate than the shell surface polygons.

This technique uses OpenGL texture mapping and texture coordinate generation to vary the alpha component of the object shell. The object is divided into two parts that are rendered separately: the shell polygons and the interior polygons. First, the depth-buffered interior surfaces are drawn normally. Next, the object shell is rendered using a 1D texture map containing an alpha ramp, to replace the alpha component of each polygon fragment. Texture coordinate generation is used to create an s coordinate that increases with the distance of the vertex along the $-z$ axis. The shell surface is rendered using the alpha-blending transparency techniques described in Section 11.8. The edges of the shell are rendered in a third pass, using a slightly different 1D texture map or texture generation plane equation to produce a rate of transparency change that differs from that of the shell surface.

1. Draw the object internals with depth buffering.

2. Enable and configure a 1D texture ramp using GL_ALPHA as the format and GL_REPLACE as the environment function.

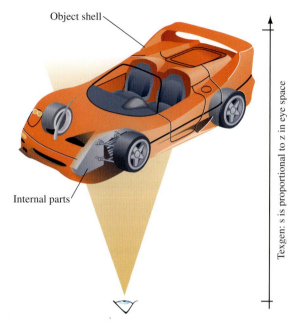

Figure 19.6 Gradual cutaway using a 1D texture.

3. Enable and configure eye-linear texture coordinate generation for the *s* component, and set the *s* eye plane to map $-z$ over the range of the object shell cutaway from 0 to 1.

4. Disable depth buffer updates and enable blending, setting the source and destination factors to `GL_SRC_ALPHA` and `GL_ONE_MINUS_SRC_ALPHA`.

5. Render the shell of the object from back to front.

6. Load a different texture ramp in the 1D texture map.

7. Render the shell edges using one of the techniques described in Section 16.7.1.

If the shell is convex and surface polygons oriented consistently, the more efficient form of transparency rendering (described in Section 11.9.3) using face culling can be used. If the shell edges are rendered, a method for decaling lines on polygons, such as polygon offset, should be used to avoid depth buffering artifacts. These methods are described in Sections 16.7.2 and 16.8.

There are a number of parameters that can be tuned to improve the result. One is the shape of the texture ramp for both the shell and the shell edges. A linear ramp produces an abrupt cutoff, whereas tapering the beginning and end of the ramp creates a smoother transition. The texture ramps can also be adjusted by changing the *s* coordinate generation eye plane. Changing the plane values moves the distance and the range of the cutaway transition zone.

If vertex lighting is used, both the shell and the interior of the object will be lighted. The *interior surfaces* of the outer shell will be darker since the vertex normals face outward. Two-sided lighting may be used to compute diffuse (and specular) lighting for back-facing polygons, or face culling can be used to draw the front-facing and back-facing polygons separately with different rendering styles.

19.4.1 Surface Texture

The previous algorithm assumes an untextured object shell. If the shell itself has a surface texture, the algorithm becomes more complex (depending on the features available in the OpenGL implementation). If multitexture is available, the two textures can be applied in a single pass using one texture unit for the surface texture and a second for the alpha ramp. If multitexture is not available, a multipass method can be used. There are two variations on the multipass method: one using a destination alpha buffer (if the implementation supports it) and a second using two color buffers.

The basic idea is to partition the blend function $\alpha C_{shell} + (1 - \alpha)C_{scene}$ into two separate steps, each computes one of the products. There are now three groups to consider: the object shell polygons textured with a surface texture C_{shell}, the object shell polygons textured with the 1D alpha texture, α, and the polygons in the remainder of the scene, C_{scene}. The alpha textured shell is used to adjust the colors of the images rendered from the other two groups of polygons separately, similar to the image compositing operations described in Section 11.1.

Alpha Buffer Approach

In this approach, the scene without the shell is rendered as before. The transparency of the resulting image is then adjusted by rendering the alpha-textured shell with source and destination blend factors: GL_ZERO, GL_ONE_MINUS_SRC_ALPHA. The alpha values from the shell are used to scale the colors of the scene that have been rendered into the framebuffer. The alpha values themselves are also saved into the alpha buffer.

Next, depth buffer and alpha buffer updates are disabled, and the surface textured shell is rendered, with the source and destination blend factors GL_ONE_MINUS_DST_ALPHA and GL_ONE. This sums the previously rendered scene, already scaled by $1 - \alpha$, with the surface-textured shell. Since the alpha buffer contains $1 - \alpha$, the shell is modulated by $1 - (1 - \alpha) = \alpha$, correctly compositing the groups.

1. Configure a window that can store alpha values.

2. Draw the scene minus the shell with depth buffering.

3. Disable depth buffer updates.

4. Enable blending with source and destination factors GL_ZERO, GL_ONE_MINUS_SRC_ALPHA.

5. Draw the alpha-textured shell to adjust scene transparency.

6. Change blend factors to `GL_ONE_MINUS_DST_ALPHA`, `GL_ONE`.

7. Disable alpha buffer updates.

8. Disable 1D alpha texture and enable surface texture.

9. Render the surface-textured shell.

Two Buffer Approach

If the OpenGL implementation doesn't support a destination alpha buffer, two color buffers can be used. One buffer is used to construct the scene without the color values of the outer shell, C_{scene} and then attenuate it by $1 - \alpha$. The second buffer is used to build up the color of the outer shell with its surface texture and transparency, αC_{shell}, after which the buffer containing the shell is added to the scene buffer using blending.

The first steps are the same as the alpha buffer approach. The scene without the shell is rendered as before. The colors of the resulting image are then attenuated by rendering the alpha-textured shell with the source and destination blend factors set to `GL_ZERO` and `GL_ONE_MINUS_SRC_ALPHA`.

Next, the textured shell is rendered in a separate buffer (or different area of the window). In another pass, the colors of this image are adjusted by rerendering the shell using the alpha texture and blend source and destination factors `GL_ZERO` and `GL_SRC_ALPHA`. Last, the two images are combined using `glCopyPixels` and blending with both factors set to `GL_ONE`.

One obvious problem with this algorithm is that no depth testing is performed between the outer shell polygons and the remainder of the scene. This can be corrected by establishing the full scene depth buffer in the buffer used for drawing the outer shell. This is done by drawing the scene (the same drawn into the first buffer) into the second buffer, with color buffer updates disabled. After the scene is drawn, color buffer updates are enabled and the shell is rendered with depth testing enabled and depth buffer updates disabled as described previously.

19.5 Depth Cuing

Perspective projection and hidden surface and line elimination are regularly used to add a sense of depth to rendered images. However, other types of depth cues are useful, particularly for applications using orthographic projections. The term *depth cuing* is typically associated with the technique of changing the intensity of an object as a function of distance from the eye. This effect is typically implemented using the fog stage of the OpenGL pipeline. For example, using a linear fog function with the fog color set to black results in a linear interpolation between the object's color and zero. The interpolation factor, f, is determined by the distance of each fragment from the eye, $f = \frac{end - z}{end - start}$.

It is also straightforward to implement a cuing algorithm using a 1D texture map applied by glTexGen to generate a texture coordinate using a linear texture coordinate generation function. This is used to compute a coordinate proportional to the distance from the eye along the z axis. The filtered texel value is used as the interpolation factor between the polygon color and texture environment color. One advantage of using a 1D texture is that the map can be used to encode an arbitrary function of distance, which can be used to implement more extreme cuing effects. Textures can also be helpful when working with OpenGL implementations that use per-vertex rather than per-pixel fog calculations.

Other types of depth cues may also be useful. Section 18.6 describes methods for generating points with appropriate perspective foreshortening. Similar problems exist for line primitives, as their width is specified in window coordinates rather than object coordinates. For most wireframe display applications this is not an issue since the lines are typically very narrow. However, for some applications wider lines are used to convey other types of information. A simple method for generating perspective lines is to use polygonal primitives rather than lines.

19.6 Patterns and Hatching

Artists and engineers use patterns and hatching for a variety of purposes (see Figure 19.7). In engineering drawings patterns and hatch marks are used to distinguish between different material types. In 2D presentation graphics, monochrome and colored patterns

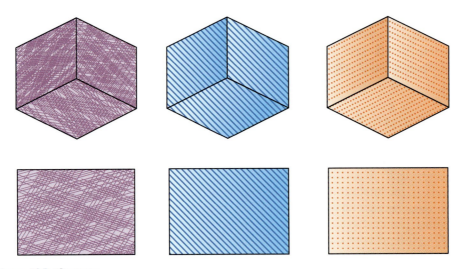

Figure 19.7 2D patterns.

and hatches are used for decorative purposes. In artistic renderings, hatching is used to provide visual cues for surface texture, lighting, tone, and shadows.

The OpenGL pipeline can be used to render patterns and hatches using a number of methods. The `glPolygonStipple` command provides a simple mechanism to apply a repeating 32×32 pattern to a polygon. The stipple pattern acts as a mask that discards rasterized fragments wherever the stipple pattern is zero and allows them to pass wherever the pattern is one. The pattern is aligned to the x and y window coordinate axes and the origin of the pattern is fixed relative to the origin of the window.

Another way to generate the effect of a stipple pattern is to create a mask in the stencil buffer and apply a stenciling operation to polygons as they are drawn. The pattern can be created in the stencil buffer by writing it as a stencil image using `glDrawPixels` or by drawing geometry elements that set the contents of the stencil buffer. A polygon can be shaded with hatch lines of arbitrary orientation by initializing the stencil buffer with the polygon and using it as a mask during line drawing. The lines can be drawn so that they cover the 2D screen-space bounding rectangle for the object.

Texture mapping provides a more general mechanism for performing pattern fills. The flexible method of assigning and interpolating texture coordinates eliminates the restrictions on patterns being aligned and oriented in window space. A window-coordinate alignment constraint can still be emulated, however, using eye linear texture coordinate generation and a scale and bias transform on the texture matrix stack.

To perform masking operations using texture mapping, several functions are useful. A luminance texture pattern can be used to modulate the polygon color, or an alpha texture can be used with alpha testing or framebuffer blending to either reject fragments outright or to perform weighted blends. The masking technique generalizes to the familiar texture mapping operation in which polygon colors are substituted with the texture colors.

19.6.1 Cross Hatching and 3D Halftones

In (Saito, 1990), Saito suggests using cross hatching to shade 3D geometry to provide visual cues. Rather than performing 2D hatching using a fixed screen space pattern (e.g., using polygon stipple) an algorithm is suggested for generating hatch lines aligned with parametric axes of the object (for example, a sequence of straight lines traversing the length of a cylinder, or a sequence of rings around a cylinder).

A similar type of shading can be achieved using texture mapping. The parametric coordinates of the object are used as the texture coordinates at each vertex, and a 1D or 2D texture map consisting of a single stripe is used to generate the hatching. This method is similar to the methods for generating contour lines in Section 14.10, except that the isocontours are now lines of constant parametric coordinate. If a 1D texture is used, at minimum two alternating texels are needed. A wrap mode of GL_REPEAT is used to replicate the stripe pattern across the object. If a 2D texture is used, the texture map contains a single stripe. Two parametric coordinates can be cross hatched at the same time using a 2D texture map with stripes in both the s and t directions. To reduce

Figure 19.8 3D cross hatching.

artifacts, the object needs to be tessellated finely enough to provide accurate sampling of the parametric coordinates.

This style of shading can be useful with bilevel output devices. For example, a luminance-hatched image can be thresholded against an unlit version of the same image using a *max* function. This results in the darker portions of the shaded image being hatched, while the brighter portions remain unchanged (as shown in Figure 19.8). The max function may be available as a separate blending extension or as part of the imaging subset. The parameters in the vertex lighting model can also be used to bias it. Using material reflectances that are greater than 1.0 will brighten the image, while leaving self-occluding surfaces black. Alternatively, *posterization* operations using color lookup tables can be used to quantize the color values to more limited ranges before thresholding. These ideas are generalized to the notion of a 3D halftone screen in (Haeberli, 1993).

Combining the thresholding scheme with (vertex) lighting allows tone and shadow to be incorporated into the hatching pattern automatically. The technique is easily extended to include other lighting techniques such as light maps. Using multipass methods, the hatched object is rendered first to create the ambient illumination. This is followed by rendering diffuse and specular lighting contributions and adding them to the color buffer contents using blending. This converts to a multitexture algorithm by adding the hatch pattern and lighting contributions during texturing. More elaborate interactions between lighting and hatching can be created using 3D textures. Hatch patterns corresponding to different $N \odot L$ values are stored as different r slices in the texture map, and the cosine term is computed dynamically using a vertex program to pass s and t coordinates unchanged while setting r to the computed cosine term.

If fragment programs are supported, more sophisticated thresholding algorithms can be implemented based on the results of intermediate shading computations, either from vertex or fragment shading. Dependent texture lookup operations allow the shape of the threshold function to be defined in a texture map.

Praun et al. (Praun, 2001; Webb, 2002) describe sophisticated hatching techniques using multitexturing with mipmapping and 3D texturing to vary the tone across the surface of an object. They develop procedures for constructing variable hatching patterns as texture maps called *tonal art maps* as well as algorithms for parameterizing arbitrary surfaces in such a way that the maps can be applied as overlapping patches onto objects with good results.

19.6.2 Halftoning

Halftoning is a technique for trading spatial resolution for an increased intensity range. Intensity values are determined by the size of the halftone. Traditionally, halftones are generated by thresholding an image against a *halftone screen*. Graphics devices such as laser printers approximate the variable-width circles used in halftones by using circular raster patterns. Such patterns can be generated using a clustered-dot ordered dither (Foley, 1990). An $n \times n$ dither pattern can be represented as a matrix. For dithering operations in which the number of output pixels is greater than the number of input pixels (i.e., each input pixel is converted to a $n \times n$ set of output pixels) the input pixel is compared against each element in the dither matrix. For each element in which the input pixel is larger than the dither element, a 1 is output; otherwise, a 0. An example 3×3 dither matrix is:

$$D = \begin{pmatrix} 6 & 8 & 4 \\ 1 & 0 & 3 \\ 5 & 2 & 7 \end{pmatrix}$$

A dithering operation of this type can be implemented using the OpenGL pipeline as follows:

1. Replicate the dither pattern in the framebuffer to generate a threshold image the size of the output image. Use `glCopyPixels` to perform the replication.

2. Set `glPixelZoom(n,n)` to replicate each pixel to a $n \times n$ block.

3. Move the threshold image into the accumulation buffer with `glAccum(GL_LOAD,1.0)`.

4. Use `glDrawPixels` to transfer the expanded source image in the framebuffer.

5. Call `glAccum(GL_ACCUM,-1.0)`.

6. Call `glAccum(GL_RETURN,-1.0)` to invert and return the result.

7. Set up `glPixelMap` to map 0 to 0 and everything else to 1.0.

8. Call `glReadPixels` with the pixel map to retrieve the thresholded image.

Alternatively, the subtractive blend function can be used to do the thresholding instead of the accumulation buffer if the imaging extensions are present.[2] If the input image is not a luminance image, it can be converted to luminance using the techniques described

---

2. Subtractive blending added to the core of OpenGL 1.4.

in Section 12.3.5 during the transfer to the framebuffer. If the framebuffer is not large enough to hold the output image, the source image can be split into tiles that are processed separately and merged.

19.7 2D Drawing Techniques

While most applications use OpenGL for rendering 3D data, it is inevitable that 3D geometry must be combined with some 2D screen space geometry. OpenGL is designed to coexist with other renderers in the window system, meaning that OpenGL and other renderers can operate on the same window. For example, X Window System 2D drawing primitives and OpenGL commands can be combined together on the same surface. Similarly, Win32 GDI drawing and OpenGL commands can be combined in the same window.

One advantage of using the native window system 2D renderer is that the 2D renderers typically provide more control over 2D operations and a richer set of built-in functions. This extended control may include joins in lines (miter, round, bevel) and end caps (round, butt). The 2D renderers also often specify rasterization rules that are more precise and therefore easier to predict or portably reproduce the results. For example, both the X Window System and Win32 GDI have very precise specifications of the algorithms for rasterizing 2D lines, whereas OpenGL has provided some latitude for implementors that occasionally causes problems with application portability.

Some disadvantages in not using OpenGL commands for 2D renderings are:

- The native window system 2D renderers are not tightly integrated with the OpenGL renderers.

- The 2D renderer cannot query or update additional OpenGL window states such as the depth, stencil, or other ancillary buffers.

- The 2nd coordinate system typically has the origin at the top left corner of the window.

- Some desirable OpenGL functionality may not be available in the 2D renderer (framebuffer blending, antialiased lines).

- The 2D code is less portable; OpenGL is available on many platforms, whereas specific 2D renderers are often limited to particular platforms.

19.7.1 Accuracy in 2D Drawing

To specify object coordinates in window coordinates, an orthographic projection is used. For a window of width w and height h, the transformation maps object coordinate $(0, 0)$ to window coordinate $(0, 0)$ and object coordinate (w, h) to window coordinate (w, h). Since OpenGL has pixel centers on half-integer locations, this mapping results in pixel centers at 0.5, 1.5, 2.5, ..., $w-.5$ along the x axis and 0.5, 1.5, 2.5, ..., $h-.5$ along the y axis.

One difficulty is that the line (and polygon) rasterization rules for OpenGL are designed to avoid multiple writes (hits) to the same pixel when drawing connected line primitives. This avoids errors caused by multiple writes when using blending or stenciling algorithms that need to merge multiple primitives reliably. As a result, a rectangle drawn with a GL_LINE_LOOP will be properly closed with no missing pixels (dropouts), whereas if the same rectangle is drawn with a GL_LINE_STRIP or independent GL_LINES there will likely be pixels missing and/or multiple hits on the rectangle boundary at or near the vertices of the rectangle.

A second issue is that OpenGL uses half-integer pixel centers, whereas the native window system invariably specifies pixel centers at integer boundaries. Application developers often incorrectly use integer pixel centers with OpenGL without compensating in the projection transform. For example, a horizontal line drawn from integer coordinates (p_x, p_y) to (q_x, p_y) with $p_x < q_x$ will write to pixels with pixel centers at window x coordinate $p_x+.5, p_x+1.5, p_x+2.5, ..., q_x-.5$, and *not* the pixel with center at $q_x+.5$. Instead, the end points of the line should be specified on half-integer locations. Conversely, for exact position of polygonal primitives, the vertices should be placed at integer coordinates, since the behavior of a vertex at a pixel center is dependent on the point sampling rules used for the particular pipeline implementation.

19.7.2 Line Joins

Wide lines in OpenGL are drawn by expanding the width of the line along the x or y direction of the line for y-major and x-major lines, respectively (a line is x-major if the slope is in the range $[-1, 1]$). When two noncolinear wide lines are connected, the overlap in the end caps leaves a noticeable gap. In 2D drawing engines such as GDI or the X Window System, lines can be joined using a number of different styles: round, mitered, or beveled as shown in Figure 19.9.

A round join can be implemented by drawing a round antialiased point with a size equal to the line width at the shared vertex. For most implementations the antialiasing algorithm generates a point that is similar enough in size to match the line width without noticeable artifacts. However, many implementations do not support large antialiased point sizes, making it necessary to use a triangle fan or texture-mapped quadrilateral to implement a disc of the desired radius to join very wide lines.

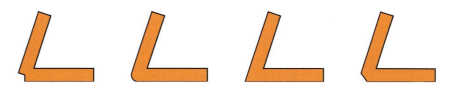

Figure 19.9 Line join styles: none, round, miter, bevel.

A mitered join can be implemented by drawing a triangle fan with the first vertex at the shared vertex of the join, two vertices at the two outside vertices of rectangles enclosing the two lines, and the third at the intersection point created by extending the two outside edges of the wide lines. For an x-major line of width w and window coordinate end points (x_0, y_0) and (x_1, y_1) the rectangle around the line is $(x_0, y_0 - (w - 1)/2)$, $(x_0, y_0 - (w - 1)/2 + w)$, $(x_1, y_1 - (w - 1)/2 + w)$, $(x_1, y_1 - (w - 1)/2)$.

Mitered joins with very sharp angles are not aesthetically pleasing, so for angles less then some threshold angle (typically 11 degrees) a bevel join is used. A bevel join can be constructed by rendering a single triangle consisting of the shared vertex and the two outside corner vertices of the lines as previously described.

Having gone this far, it is a small step to switch from using lines to using triangle strips to draw the lines instead. One advantage of using lines is that many OpenGL implementations support antialiasing up to moderate line widths, whereas there is substantially less support for polygon antialiasing. Wide antialiased lines can be combined with antialiased points to do round joins, but it requires the overlap algorithm from Section 16.7.5 to sort the coverage values. Accumulation buffer antialiasing can be used with triangle primitives as well.

19.7.3 2D Trim Curves

Many 2D page display languages and drawing applications support the creation of shapes with boundaries defined by quadratic and cubic 2D curves. The resulting shapes can then be shaded using a variety of operators. Using many of the shading algorithms previously described, an OpenGL implementation can perform the shading operations; however, the OpenGL pipeline only operates on objects defined by polygons. Using the OpenGL pipeline for shapes defined by higher-order curves might require tessellating the curved shapes into simple polygons, perhaps using the GLU NURBS library. A difficulty with this method is performing consistent shading across the entire shape. To perform correct shading, attributes values such as colors and texture coordinates must be computed at each of the vertices in the tessellated object.

An equivalent, but simpler, method for rendering complex shapes is to consider the shape as a 2D rectangle (or trapezoid) that has parts of the surface *trimmed* away, using the curved surfaces to define the trim curves. The 2D rectangle is the window-axis-aligned bounding rectangle for the shape. Shading algorithms, such as radial color gradient fills, are applied directly to the rectangle surface and the final image is constructed by masking the rectangle. One method for performing the masking is using the stencil buffer. In this method the application scan converts the trim curve definitions, producing a set of trapezoids that define either the parts of the shape to be kept or the parts to be removed (see Figure 19.10). The sides of the trapezoids follow the curve definitions and the height of each trapezoid is determined by the amount of error permissible in approximating the curve with a straight trapezoidal edge. In the worst case, a trapezoid will be 1 pixel high and can be rendered as a line rather than a polygon. Figure 19.10 exaggerates the size of the bounding rectangle for clarity; normally it would tightly enclose the shape.

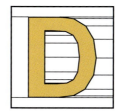

Figure 19.10 Trapezoidal trim regions.

Evaluating the trim curves on the host requires nontrivial computation, but that is the only pixel-level host computation required to shade the surface. The trim regions can be drawn efficiently by accumulating the vertices in a vertex array and drawing all of the regions at once. To perform the shading, the stencil buffer is cleared, and the trim region is created in it by drawing the trim trapezoids with color buffer updates disabled. The bounding rectangle is then drawn with shading applied and color buffer updates enabled.

To render antialiased edges, a couple of methods are possible. If multisample antialiasing is supported, the supersampled stencil buffer makes the antialiasing automatic, though the quality will be limited by the number of samples per pixel. Other antialiasing methods are described in Chapter 10. If an alpha buffer is available, it may serve as a useful antialiased stenciling alternative. In this algorithm, all trapezoids are reduced to single-pixel-high trapezoids (spans) and the pixel coverage at the trim curve edge is computed for each span. First, the boundary rectangle is used to initialize the alpha buffer to one with updates of the RGB color chennels disabled. The spans are then drawn with alpha values of zero (color channel updates still disabled). Next, the pixels at the trim curve edges are redrawn with their correct coverage values. Finally, color channel updates are enabled and the bounding rectangle is drawn with the correct shading while blending with source and destination factors of GL_ONE_MINUS_DST_ALPHA and GL_ZERO. The factor GL_ONE_MINUS_DST_ALPHA is correct if the coverage values correspond to the nonvisible part of the edge pixel. If the trim regions defined the visible portion, GL_DST_ALPHA should be used instead.

A simple variation computes the alpha map in an alpha texture map rather than the alpha buffer and then maps the texels to pixel fragments one to one. If color matrix functionality (or fragment programs) is available, the alpha map can be computed in the framebuffer in one of the RGB channels and then swizzled to the alpha texture during a copy-to-texture operation (Section 9.3.1).

By performing some scan conversion within the application, the powerful shading capabilities of the OpenGL pipeline can be leveraged for many traditional 2D applications. This class of algorithms uses OpenGL as a span processing engine and it can be further generalized to compute shading attributes at the start and end of each span for greater flexibility.

19.8 Text Rendering

Text rendering requirements can vary widely between applications. In illustration applications, text can play a minor role as annotations on an engineering drawing or can play a central role as part of a poster or message in a drawing. Support for drawing text in 2D renderers has improved substantially over the past two decades. In 3D renderers such as OpenGL, however, there is little direct support for text as a primitive.

OpenGL does provide ample building blocks for creating text-rendering primitives, however. The methods for drawing text can be divided into two broad categories: image based and geometry based.

19.8.1 Image-based Text

Image-based primitives use one of the pixel image-drawing primitives to render separate pixel images for each character. The OpenGL `glBitmap` primitive provides support for traditional single-bit-per-pixel images and resembles text primitives present in 2D renderers. To leverage the capabilities of the host platform, many of the OpenGL embedding layers include facilities to import font data from the 2D renderer, for example, `glXUseXFont` in the GLX embedding and `wglUseFontBitmaps` in WGL.

Typically the first character in a text string is positioned in 3D object coordinates using the `glRasterPos` command, while the subsequent characters are positioned in window (pixel) coordinates using offsets specified with the previously rendered character. One area where the OpenGL bitmap primitive differs from typical 2D renderers is that positioning information is specified with floating-point coordinates and retains subpixel precision when new positions are computed from offsets. By transforming the offsets used for positioning subsequent characters, the application can render text strings at angles other than horizontal, but each character is rendered as a window-axis-aligned image.

The bitmap primitive has associated attributes that specify color, texture coordinates, and depth values. These attributes allow the primitive to participate in hidden surface and stenciling algorithms. The constant value across the entire primitive limits the utility of these attributes, however. For example, color and texture coordinates cannot directly vary across a bitmap image. Nevertheless, the same effect can be achieved by using bitmap images to create stencil patterns. Once a pattern is created in the stencil buffer, shaded or texture-mapped polygons that cover the window extent of the strings are drawn and the fragments are written only in places where stencil bits have been previously set.

Display List Encodings

In the most basic form, to draw a character string an application draws issues a `glBitmap` command for each character. To improve the performance and simplify this process, the application can use display lists. A contiguous range of display list names are allocated and associated with a corresponding contiguous range of values in the character set encoding. Each display list contains the bitmap image for the corresponding character.

List names obey the relationship $n = c + b$, where c is a particular character encoding, n is the corresponding list name, and b is the list name corresponding to encoding 0. Once the display lists have been created, a string is drawn by setting the list base b (using glListBase) and then issuing a single glCallLists command with the pointer to the array containing the string.

For strings represented using byte-wide array elements, the GL_UNSIGNED_BYTE type is used. This same method is easily adapted to wider character encodings, such as 16-bit Unicode, by using a wider type parameter with the glCallLists command. If the character encoding is sparse, it may be advantageous to allocate display list names only for the nonempty encodings and use an intermediate table to map a character encoding to a display list name. This changes the string-drawing algorithm to a two-step process: first a new array of display list names is constructed from the string using the look-up table, then the resulting array is drawn using glCallLists.

Many applications use multiple graphical representations for the same character encoding. The multiple representations may correspond to different typefaces, different sizes, and so on. Using the direct one-to-one display list mapping, each representation has a different display list base. Using the look-up table mapping, each representation has a separate table.

Kerning

More sophisticated applications may wish to implement *kerning* to tune the spacing between different character pairs. Since the character advance is dependent on the last rendered character and the current character, a single advance cannot be stored in the same display list with each character. However, a kerning table can be computed containing an adjustment for each pair of characters and each unique adjustment can be encoded in a separate display list. A simple method for making a relative adjustment to the raster position (without drawing any pixels) is to issue a glBitmap command with a zero-size image, specifying the desired adjustment as the offset parameters.

A variation on the two-step text-rendering method can be used to build a kerned string. The array of list names constructed in the first step also includes a call to the display list containing the corresponding adjustment found in the kerning table. The resulting array contains an alternating sequence of lists to draw a character and lists to adjust the position. A single glCallLists command can draw the entire string using the constructed array in the second step. Ligatures and other features can also be accommodated by storing them as separate display lists and incorporating them when building the array of lists.

Pixmap Images

Another limitation with the bitmap primitive is that it cannot be used to render antialiased text. This limitation can be overcome by using the glDrawPixels command to draw character images that have been preantialiased (prefiltered). Antialiased character images

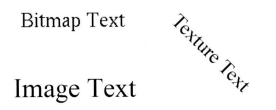

Figure 19.11 Bitmap, image, and texture text.

store both a luminance (or RGB color) and alpha coverage values and are rendered using the *over* compositing operator described in Section 11.1.1.

The `glDrawPixels` primitive doesn't include offsets to advance the raster position to the next character position, so the application must compute each character position and use the `glRasterPos` command to move the current raster position. It is probable that the application needs to position the subsequent characters in a string in window coordinates rather than object coordinates.

Another way to implement relative positioning is to define the raster position in terms of a relative coordinate system in which each character is drawn with raster position object coordinates $(0, 0, 0)$. A cumulative character advance is computed by concatenating a translation onto the modeling transform after each character is drawn. The advantage of such a scheme is that display lists can still be used to store the `glRasterPos`, `glDrawPixels`, and `glTranslatef` commands so that a complete string can be drawn with a single invocation of `glCallLists`. However, at the start and end of the string additional modeling commands are required to establish and tear down the coordinate system.

Establishing the coordinate system requires computing a scaling transform that maps (x, y) object coordinates one-to-one to window coordinates. Since this requires knowledge of the current cumulative modelview and projection transforms, it may be difficult to transparently incorporate into an application. Often applications will save and restore the current modelview and projection transforms rather than track the cumulative transform. Saving the state can have deleterious performance effects, since state queries typically introduce "bubbles" of idle time into the rendering pipeline. An alternative to saving and restoring state is to specify the raster position in window coordinates directly using the `ARB_window_pos` extension.[3] Unfortunately, using absolute positioning requires issuing a specific raster position command for each character position, eliminating the opportunity to use position independent display lists. Establishing a window coordinate system transform and using relative positioning is a more broadly applicable method for working with both the image- and geometry-based rendering techniques.

---

3. Also part of OpenGL 1.4.

Texture Images

Using RGB images allows the color to vary within a single character, though the color values need to be assigned to the image data before transfer to the pipeline. A common limitation with both bitmap and pixel image character text rendering is that the text cannot be easily scaled or rotated. Limited scaling can be achieved using pixel zoom operations, but no filtering is performed on the images so the results deteriorate very quickly.

A third type of image-based text stores the character glyphs as texture maps and renders them as quadrilaterals using the billboard techniques described in Section 13.5 (Haeberli, 1993; Kilgard, 1997). Using billboard geometry allows text strings to be easily rotated and texture filtering allows scaling over a larger range than pixel zoom. Using mipmap filtering increases the effective scaling range even more. In addition to affine scaling, the text strings can be perspective projected since the characters are affixed to regular geometry. Text can be shaded with a color gradient or lit by lighting and shading the underlying quad and modulating it with the texture map. If the source image for the texture map is antialiased, the rendered text remains antialiased (within the limitations of the texture filter).

The images used in the texture maps are the same images that are used for pixmap text rendering. The texture maps are constructed directly from the pixel image sources and are also rendered using compositing techniques. The characters stored in the texture maps can also be rendered with other geometry besides simple screen parallel quads. They can be decaled directly onto other geometry, combined with stencil operations to create cutouts in the geometry, or projected onto geometry using the projection techniques described in Section 14.9.

The high performance of texture mapping on modern hardware accelerators makes rendering using texture-mapped text very fast. To maximize the rendering efficiency it is desirable to use the mosaicing technique described in Section 14.4 to pack the individual font glyphs into a single texture image. This avoids unnecessarily padding individual character glyphs to a power-of-two image. Individual glyphs are efficiently selected by setting the texture coordinates to index the appropriate subimage rather than binding a new texture for each character. All character positioning is performed in object space. To position subsequent characters in the string using window coordinates, variations on the method described for moving the raster position can be used.

19.8.2 Geometry-based Text

Geometry-based text is rendered using geometric primitives such as lines and polygons.[4] Text rendered using 3D primitives has several advantages: attributes can be interpolated across the primitive; character shapes have depth in addition to width and height;

---

4. The texture-mapped text method is actually a hybrid between image-based and geometry-based methods.

Figure 19.12 Triple stroke Roman typeface.

character geometry can be easily scaled, rotated, and projected; and the geometry can be antialiased using regular antialiasing techniques.

Characters rendered using a series of arc and line segment primitives are called *stroke* or *vector* fonts. They were originally used on vector-based devices such as calligraphic displays and pen plotters. Stroke fonts still have some utility in raster graphics systems since they are efficient to draw and can be easily rotated and scaled. Stroke fonts continue to be useful for complex, large fonts such as those used for Asian languages, since the storage costs can be significantly lower than other image- or geometry-based representations. They are seldom used for high-quality display applications since they suffer from legibility problems at low resolutions and at larger scales the stroke length appears disproportionate relative to the line width of the stroke. This latter problem is often alleviated by using *double* or *triple* stroke fonts, achieving a better sense of width by drawing parallel strokes with a small separation between them (Figure 19.12).

The arc segments for stroke fonts are usually tessellated to line segments for rendering. Ideally this tessellation matches the display resolution, but frequently a one-time tessellation is performed and only the tessellated representation is retained. This results in blocky rather than smooth curved boundaries at higher display resolutions. Rendering stroke fonts using the OpenGL pipeline requires little more than rendering line primitives. To maximize efficiency, connected line primitives should be used whenever possible. The line width can be varied to improve the appearance of the glyphs as they are scaled larger and antialiasing is implemented using regular line antialiasing methods (Section 10.4).

Applications can make more creative use of stroke fonts by rendering strokes using primitives other than lines (such as using flat polygons or 3D cylinders and spheres). Flat polygons traced along each stroke emulate calligraphic writing, while 3D solid geometry is created by treating each stroke as a *path* and a *profile* is swept along the path. Tools for creating geometry from path descriptions are common in most modeling packages.

Outline Fonts

Outline font is the term used for the resolution-independent mathematical description of a font. Type 1 and TrueType are examples of systems for describing fonts as series of 2D closed curves (contours). Outline fonts are converted to bitmaps by scaling the outline to a particular size and then scan-converting the contours, much like scan-converting a polygon. Alternatively, the contours can be tessellated into polygonal geometry or a set of line segments for rendering as filled polygons or outlines. The curves can also be used

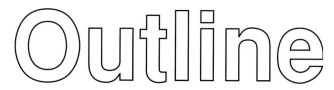

Figure 19.13 Helvetica typeface rendered as outlines.

to generate profiles for generating 3D extrusions, converting them to a mesh of polygons. Since the process starts with a resolution independent representation, outline fonts can produce high-quality polygonal or vector representations at almost any resolution. It is "almost" any resolution, since low resolutions usually require some additional *hinting* beyond the curve descriptions to improve the legibility.

To render outline fonts using OpenGL, an application requires a font engine or library to convert the mathematical contour description into polygons or lines. Some platform embeddings include such a feature directly; for example, the Microsoft WGL embedding includes `wglUseFontOutlines`, to generate display lists of polygon or line representations from TrueType font descriptions. On other systems, readily available font libraries, such as the FreeType project (FreeType, 2003), can be used to generate pixmap images directly, and to retrieve contour descriptions. The curves comprising the contours are converted to vectors by evaluating the curve equations and creating line segments that approximate the curves within a specified tolerance. The vector contours are then drawn as outlines or tessellated to polygons using the GLU tessellator. Simple extrusions can be generated from the resulting tessellation, using the meshes for the front and back faces of each character and using the vector contours to generate the side polygons bridging the faces.

19.9 Drawing and Painting

Content creation applications often provide the digital equivalent of traditional drawing and painting techniques, in which the user adds color to pixel values using pens and brushes with a variety of shapes and other properties. There are many advantages that come from performing the operations digitally: the ability to undo operations; the ability to automate repetitive tasks, the availability of a unified palette of different painting techniques, and (to some extent) the ability to operate independent of the output resolution. There are many commercial drawing and painting packages that provide these features. Many of them can take advantage of the facilities available in the OpenGL 3D pipeline to accelerate operations. These techniques go beyond the idea of simply using the 3D pipeline to incorporate 3D geometry into an image.

Smooth shading provides a simple way to perform color gradient fills, while 1D and 2D texture mapping allow more flexible control over the shape of the gradients.

Figure 19.14 Brush stroke using disc brush.

Texture mapping provides additional opportunities for implementing irregularly shaped brush geometry by combining customized geometry and texture alpha to define the brush shape (see Figure 19.14). A brush stroke is rendered by sampling the coordinates of an input stroke, rendering the brush geometry centered about each input sample. Typically the input coordinate samples are spaced evenly in time, allowing dense strokes to be created by moving the input device slowly and light strokes by moving it quickly. Alternatively, a pressure-sensitive input device can be used, mapping input pressure to density.

Using texture-mapped brush geometry allows two types of painting algorithms to be supported. In the first style, the texture-mapped brush creates colored pixel fragments that are blended with the image in the color buffer in much the same way a painter applies paint to a painting. The second method uses the brush geometry and resulting brush strokes to create a mask image, I_m, used to composite a reference image, I_r, over the original image, I_o, using the strokes to *reveal* parts of the reference image:

$$I_{new} = (I_r \; I_m) \text{ over } I_o.$$

The reference image is often a version of the original image created using a separate processing or filtering algorithm (such as, a blurring or sharpening filter). In this way, brush strokes are used to specify the parts of the original image to which the filtering algorithm is applied without needing to compute the filter dynamically on each stroke.

There are several ways to implement the revealing algorithm. If an alpha buffer is available, the brush strokes can incrementally add to an alpha mask in the alpha buffer. An alpha buffer allows rendering of antialiased or smooth stroke edges. If an alpha buffer isn't available, the stencil buffer can be used instead. The alpha or stencil buffer is updated as the strokes are drawn and an updated image is created each frame by compositing a buffer storing the reference image with a buffer storing the original image.

The compositing operation is performed using either blending or stencil operations with a buffer-to-buffer pixel copy.

If the application is using double buffering, either aux buffers or off-screen buffers can be used to hold the original and reference image, recopying the original to the back buffer each frame, before compositing the reference image on top. Both images can also be stored as texture maps and be transferred to the framebuffer by drawing rectangles that project the texels one-to-one to pixels. Other variations use multitexture to composite the images as part of rendering texture rectangles. Brush strokes are accumulated in one of the RGB channels of an off-screen color buffer and copied to an alpha texture map using color matrix swizzling (Section 9.3.1) before rendering each frame.

19.9.1 Undo and Resolution Independence

One of the advantages of performing painting operations digitally is that they can be *undone*. This is accomplished by recording all of the operations that were executed to produce the current image (sometimes called an *adjustment layer*). Each brush stroke coordinate is recorded as well as all of the parameters associated with the operation performed by the brush stroke (both paint and reveal). This allows every intermediate version of the image to be reconstructed by replaying the appropriate set of operations. To undo an operation, the recorded brush strokes are deleted. Interactive performance can be maintained by caching one of the later intermediate images and only replaying the subsequent brush strokes. For example, for the revealing algorithm, when a new reference image is created to reveal, a copy of the current image is saved as the original image; only the set of strokes accumulated as part of revealing this reference image is replayed each frame.

Erase strokes are different from undo operations. Erase strokes have the effect of selectively undoing or erasing part of a brush stroke. However, undo operations also apply to erase strokes. Erase strokes simply perform local masking operations to the current set of brush strokes, creating a mask that is applied against the stroke mask. Erase strokes are journaled and replayed in a manner similar to regular brush strokes.

Since all of the stroke geometry is stored along with the parameters for the filtering algorithms used to create references images for reveals, it is possible to replay the brush strokes using images of different sizes, scaling the brush strokes appropriately. This provides a degree of resolution independence, though in some cases changing the size of the brush stroke may not create the desired effect.

19.9.2 Painting in 3D

A texture map can be created by "painting" an image, then viewing it textured on a 3D object. This process can involve a lot of trial and error. Hanrahan (1990) and Haeberli proposed methods for creating texture maps by painting directly on the 2D projection of the 3D geometry (see Figure 19.15). The two key problems are determining how screen space brush strokes are mapped to the 3D object coordinates and how to efficiently perform the inverse mapping from geometry coordinates to texture coordinates.

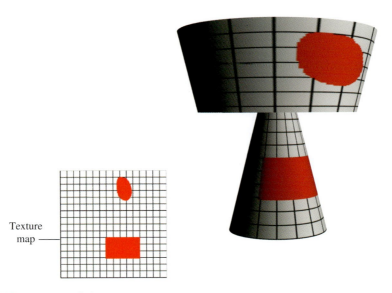

Figure 19.15 Painting on a 3D object.

In the Hanrahan and Haeberli method an object into a quadrilateral mesh, making the number of quadrilaterals equal to the size of the texture map. This creates an approximate one-to-one correspondence between texels in the texture map and object geometry. The object tagging selection technique (described in Section 16.1.2) is used to efficiently determine which quads are covered by a brush stroke. Once the quads have been located, the texels are immediately available. Brush geometry can be projected onto the object geometry using three different methods: object parametric, object tangent plane, or screen space.

Object parametric projection maps brush geometry and strokes to the s and t texture coordinate parameterization of the vector. As the brush moves the brush geometry is decaled to the object surface. Object tangent projection considers the brush geometry as an image, tangent to the object surface (perpendicular to the surface normal) at the brush center and projects the brush image onto the object. As the brush moves, the brush image remains tangent to the object surface. The screen space projection keeps the brush aligned with the screen (image plane). In the original Hanrahan and Haeberli algorithm, the tangent and screen space brushes are implemented by warping the images into the equivalent parametric projection. The warp is computed within the application and used to update the texture map.

The preceding scheme uses a brute-force geometry tessellation to implement the selection algorithm. An alternative method that works well with modern graphics accelerators with high performance (and predictable) texture mapping avoids the tessellation step and operates directly on a 2D texture map. The object identifiers for the item buffer are stored in one 2D texture map, called the *tag texture* and a second 2D texture map stores the current painted image, called the *paint texture*. To determine the location of the brush within the texture image, the image is drawn using the tag texture with nearest filtering and a replace environment function. This allows the texture coordinates to be determined directly from the color buffer. The paint texture can be created in the framebuffer. For object parametric projections, the current brush is mapped and projected to screen space (parameter space) as for regular 2D painting. For tangent and screen space projections, the brush image is warped by tessellating the brush and warping the vertex coordinates of the brush. As changes are made to the paint texture, it is copied to texture memory and applied to the object to provide interactive feedback.

To compute the tangent space projection, the object's surface normal corresponding to the (s, t) coordinates is required. This can be computed by interpolating the vertex normals of the polygon face containing the texture coordinates. Alternatively, a second object drawing pass can draw normal vectors as colors to the RGB components of the color buffer. This is done using normal map texture coordinate generation combined with a cube map texture containing normal vectors. The normal vector can be read back at the same brush location in the color buffer as for the (s, t) coordinates. Since a single normal vector is required, only one polygon containing the texture coordinate need be drawn.

The interactive painting technique can be used for more than applying color to a texture map. It can be used to create light intensity or more general material reflectance maps for use in rendering the lighting effects described in Chapter 15. Painting techniques can also be used to design bump or relief maps for the bump map shading techniques described in Section 15.10 or to interactively paint on any texture that is applied as part of a shading operation.

19.9.3 Painting on Images

The technique of selectively revealing an underlying image gives rise to a number of painting techniques that operate on images imported from other sources (such as digital photographs). One class of operations allows *retouching* the image using stroking operations or other input methods to define regions on which various operators are applied. These operators can include the image processing operations described in Chapter 12: sharpen, blur, contrast enhancement, color balance adjustment, and so on.

Haeberli (1990) describes a technique for using filters in the form of brush strokes to create abstract images (impressionistic paintings) from source images. The output image is generated by rendering an ordered list of brush strokes. Each brush stroke contains color, shape, size, and orientation information. Typically the color information is determined by sampling the corresponding location in the source image. The size, shape, and orientation information are generated from user input in an interactive painting application. The paper also describes some novel algorithms for generating brush stroke geometry. One example is the use of a depth buffered cone with the base of the cone parallel to the image plane at each stroke location. This algorithm results in a series of Dirichlet domains

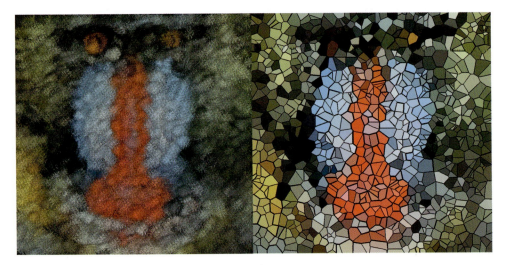

Figure 19.16 Impressionist and dirichelet domain processed image.

(Preparata, 1985) where the color of each domain is sampled from the source image (see Figure 19.16).

Additional effects can be achieved by preprocessing the input image. For example, the contrast can be enhanced, or the image sharpened using simple image-processing techniques. Edge detection operators can be used to recover paths for brush strokes to follow. These operations can be automated and combined with stochastic methods to choose brush shape and size to generate brush strokes automatically.

19.10 Summary

Illustration and artistic techniques is a broad area of active research. This chapter sampled some algorithms and ideas from a few different areas, but we have just scratched the surface. There are several excellent books that cover the topic of nonphotorealistic rendering in greater detail. The addition of the programmable pipeline will undoubtedly increase the opportunities for innovation on both the artistic side and the pursuit of higher-quality rendered images.

Scientific Visualization

20.1 Mapping Numbers to Pictures

Scientific visualization utilizes computer graphics, image processing, and other techniques to create graphical representations of the results from computations and simulations. The objective of creating these representations is to assist the researcher in developing a deeper understanding of the data under investigation.

Modern computation equipment enables mathematical models and simulations to become so complex that tremendous amounts of data are generated. Visualization attempts to convey this information to the scientist in an effective manner. Not only is visualization used to *post-process* generated data, but it also serves an integral role in allowing a scientist to interactively *steer* a computation.

In this chapter we will provide an introduction to visualization concepts and basic algorithms. Following this we will describe different methods for using the OpenGL pipeline to accelerate some of these techniques. The algorithms described here are useful to many other application areas in addition to scientific visualization.

20.2 Visual Cues and Perception

Visualization techniques draw from a palette of *visual cues* to represent the data in a meaningful way. Visual cues include position, shape, orientation, density, and color cues. Each visual cue has one or more *perceptual elements* used to represent some aspect of the data. For example, shape cues encompass length, depth, area, volume, and thickness;

color includes hue, saturation, and brightness. Multiple visual cues are combined to produce more complex visual cues, paralleling the way nature combines objects of various colors, shapes, and sizes at different positions.

Many visual cues have a natural interpretation. For example, brightness of an object is interpreted as an ordering of information from low to high. Similarly, hue expresses a natural perception of the relationship between data. The red hue applied to objects makes them appear warmer, higher, and nearer, whereas the blue hue makes objects appear cooler, lower, and farther away. This latter perception is also used by some of the illustration techniques described in Section 19.2.

Scientific visualization isn't limited to *natural* visual cues. Other visual representations such as contour lines, glyphs, and icons once learned serve as powerful *acquired* visual cues and can be combined with other cues to provide more expressive representations. However, care must be taken when using both natural and acquired cues to ensure that the characteristics of the data match the interpretation of the cue. If this is not the case, the researcher may draw erroneous conclusions from the visualization, defeating its purpose. Common examples of inappropriate use of cues include applying cues that are naturally perceived as ordered against unordered data, cues that imply the data is continuous with discontinuous data (using a line graph in place of a bar graph, for example), or cues that imply data is discontinuous with continuous data (inappropriate use of hue for continuous data).

20.3 Data Characterization

Visualization techniques can be organized according to a taxonomy of characteristics of data generated from various computation processes. Data can be classified according to the *domain* dimensionality. Examples include 1-dimensional data consisting of a set of rainfall measurements taken at different times or 3-dimensional data consisting of temperature measurements at the grid points on a 3D finite-element model. Dimensionality commonly ranges from 1 to 3 but data are not limited to these dimensions. Larger dimensionality does increase the challenges in effectively visualizing the data. However, data that includes sets of samples taken at different times also creates an additional dimension. The time dimension is frequently visualized using animation, since it naturally conveys the temporal aspect of the data. Data can be further classified by *type*:

- *Nominal* values describe unordered members from a class (Oak, Birch, and Maple trees, for example). Hue and position cues are commonly used to represent nominal data.

- *Ordinal* values are related to each other by a sense of order (such as small, medium, and large). Visual cues that naturally represent order (such as position, size, or brightness) are commonly used. Hue can also be used. However, a legend indicating the relative ordering of the color values should be included to avoid misinterpretation.

- *Quantitative* values carry a precise numerical value. Often quantitative data are converted to ordinal data during the visualization process, facilitating the recognition of trends in the data and allowing rapid determination of regions with significant ranges of values. Interactive techniques can be used to retain the quantitative aspects of the data, for example, using a mouse button can be used to trigger display of the value at the current cursor location.

Finally, data can also be classified by *category*:

- *Points* describe individual values such as positions or types (the position or type of each atom in a molecule for example). Point data are often visualized using *scatter plots* or *point clouds* that allow clusters of similar values to be easily located.

- *Scalars*, like points, describe individual values but are usually samples from a continuous function (such as temperature). The dependent scalar value can be expressed as a function of an independent variable, $y = f(x)$. Multidimensional data corresponds to a multidimensional function, $y = f(x_0, x_1, \ldots, x_n)$. Scalar data is usually called a *scalar field*, since it frequently corresponds to a function defined across a 2D or 3D physical space. Multiple data values, representing different properties, may be present at each location. Each property corresponds to a different function, $y_k = f_k(x_0, x_1, \ldots, x_n)$. Scalar fields are visualized using a variety of techniques, depending on the dimensionality of the data. These techniques include line graphs, isolines (contour maps), image maps, height fields, isosurfaces, volumetric rendering, and many others.

- *Vector* data sets consist of a vector value at each sample rather than a single value. Vector data differs from multivariate scalar fields, such as separate temperature and pressure samples, in that the vector represent a single quantity. Vector values often represent directional data such as flow data. The dimensionality of the vector is independent of the dimensionality of the field. For example, a 2D data set may consist of 3D vectors. Complex data sets may consist of multiple data types (points, vectors, and scalars) at each sample. Vector data are often visualized using arrow icons to convey direction and magnitude. Particle tracing and stream lines are used to visualize flows through the fields.

- *Tensor* values generalize the scalar and vector field categories to a tensor field where each data value is a *rank k* tensor. A scalar field is a tensor field composed of rank 0 tensors, a vector field is a tensor field composed of rank 1 tensors, and a rank k tensor field stores a k-dimensional matrix of values at each sample point. Tensor fields require sophisticated visualization techniques to convey all of the information present at each sample. Tensor field visualization frequently combines multiple perceptual elements: color, size, position, orientation, and shape. Examples include tensor ellipsoids (Haber, 1990) and hyperstreamlines (Delmarcelle, 1993).

Taking the combination of domain dimension, data type, data category, and multiple values results in a large combination of data set classifications. Brodlie (1992) used the notion E_d^{mX} to describe a data set with domain dimension d, type $X = \{P, S, V_n, T_n\}$, and multiplicity m. A two-dimensional scalar field is expressed in this notation as E_2^S, and a 3-dimensional vector field with two-element vectors at each point is expressed as $E_3^{V_2}$ and so forth.

Many visualization techniques are available. Some techniques, such as graphics and charts, have been in use long before the computer came into existence, whereas newer techniques involving complex per-pixel calculations have only become available in the last 10 to 15 years. Nevertheless, it is important to recognize that newer techniques are not necessarily better for all types of data. Older and simpler methods may be as or more insightful as new methods. The following sections describe visualization methods, the types of data for which they are useful, and methods for effectively using the OpenGL pipeline to implement them.

20.4 Point Data Visualization

Point data sets often arise in statistical models and a number of techniques have been created to visualize such data (Wong, 1997). Point data visualizations consider each value to be a point in a multidimensional space. The visualization technique projects the multidimensional space to a 2D image.

20.4.1 Scatter Plots

Scatter plots use positional cues to visualize the relationship between data samples. 1-dimensional point data sets (E_1^P) can use a 2D plot with positions along one axis representing different point values. A marker symbol is drawn at the position corresponding to each point value. Ordinal and quantitative values naturally map into positions; nominal values are mapped to positions using a table-mapping function.

Data sets with two values at each point (E_1^{2P}) can be represented using a 2D plot where each pair of values determines a position along the two axes. This technique can be extended to 3D plots, called *point clouds*, for E_1^{3S} data sets. Alternatively, if two of the three data types are quantitative or ordinal and the third is nominal, a 2D plot can be used with the nominal value used to select different marker shapes or colors.

Higher-order multivariate data also be rendered as a series of 2D scatter plots, plotting two variables at a time to create a *scatter plot matrix*. The set of plots is arranged into a two dimensional matrix such that the scatter plot of variable i with variable j appears in the ith row and jth column of the matrix (see Figure 20.1).

All of these types of visualizations can be drawn very efficiently using the OpenGL pipeline. Simple markers can be drawn as OpenGL point primitives. Multiple marker shapes for nominal data can be implemented using a collection of bitmaps, or texture-mapped quads, with one bitmap or texture image for each marker shape. The viewport

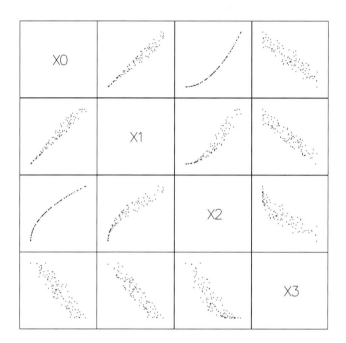

Figure 20.1 Scatter plot matrix.

transform can be used to position individual plots in a scatter plot matrix. OpenGL provides a real benefit for visualizing more complex data sets. Point clouds can be interactively rotated to improve the visualization of the 3D structure; 2D and 3D plots can be animated to visualize 2-dimensional data where one of the dimensions is time.

20.4.2 Iconographic Display

Multivariate point data (E_1^{nP}) can be visualized using collections of discrete patterns to form *glyphs*. Each part of the glyph corresponds to one of the variables and serves as one visual cue. A simple example is a multipoint star. Each data point is mapped to a star that has a number of spikes equal to the number of variables, n, in the data set. Each variable is mapped to a spike on the star, starting with the topmost spike. The length from the star center to the tip of a spike corresponds to the value of the variable mapped to that star point. The result is that data points map to stars of varying shapes, and similarities in the shapes of stars match similarities in the underlying data.

Another example, Chernoff faces (Chernoff, 1973) map variables to various features of a schematic human face: variables are mapped to the nose shape, eye shape, mouth shape, and so on (see Figure 20.2). These techniques are effective for small data sets with

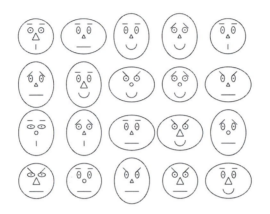

Figure 20.2 Iconographic display.

a moderate number of dimensions or variables. To render glyphs using OpenGL, each part is modeled as a set of distinct geometry: points, lines or polygons. The entire glyph is constructed by rendering each part at the required position relative to the origin of the glyph using modeling transforms. The set of glyphs for the entire data set is rendered in rows and columns using additional transforms to position the origin of the glyph in the appropriate position. Allowing the viewer to interactively rearrange the location of the glyphs enables the viewer to sort the data into clusters of similar values.

20.4.3 Andrews Plots

Another visualization technique (see Figure 20.3) for multivariate data, called an *Andrews plot* (Andrews, 1972), uses shape cues, plotting the equation

$$f(t) = \frac{v_0}{\sqrt{2}} + v_1 \sin(t) + v_2 \cos(t) + v_3 \sin(2t) + v_4 \sin(2t) + \cdots$$

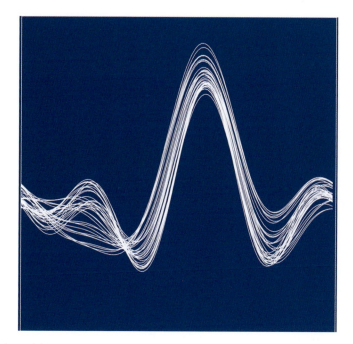

Figure 20.3 Andrews plot.

over the range $t = [-\pi, \pi]$. The number of terms in the equation is equal to the number of variables, n, in the data set and the number of equations is equal to the number of samples in the data set. Ideally, the more important variables are assigned to the lower-frequency terms. The result is that close points have similarly shaped plots, whereas distant plots have differently shaped plots.

20.4.4 Histograms and Charts

For 1-dimensional point data consisting of nominal values, histograms and pie charts can be used to visualize the count of occurrences of the nominal values. The data set values are aggregated into *bins*. There are various display methods that can be used. Sorting the bins by count and plotting the result produces a *staircase chart* (see Figure 20.4). If staircase charts are plotted using line drawing, multiple staircases can be plotted on the same chart using different colors or line styles to distinguish between them.

If the counts are normalized, *pie charts* effectively display the relative proportion of each bin. The methods described in Chapter 19 can be used to produce more aesthetically appealing charts.

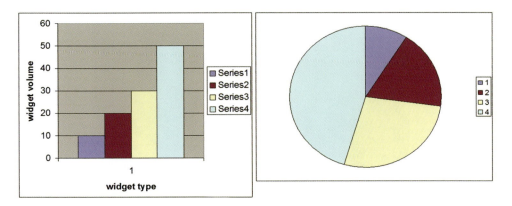

Figure 20.4 Staircase and pie chart.

20.5 Scalar Field Visualization

Scalar field visualization maps a continuous field, $f(x_1, x_2, \ldots, x_n)$, to a visual cue, frequently to color or position. The data set, E_n^S, is a set of discrete samples of the underlying continuous field. The sample geometry and spacing may be regular, forming an n-dimensional lattice, or irregular (scattered) forming an arbitrary mesh (Figure 20.5). An important consideration is the true behavior of the field between data samples. Many visualization techniques assume the value changes linearly from point to point. For example, color and texture coordinate interpolation calculations interpolate linearly between their end points. If linear approximation between sample points introduces too much error, a visualization technique may be altered to use a better approximation, or more generally the field function can be reconstructed from the data samples using a more accurate reconstruction function and then resampled at higher resolution to reduce the approximation error.

20.5.1 Line Graphs

Continuous information from 1-dimensional scalar fields (E_1^{mS}) can be visualized effectively using line graphs. The m variables can be displayed on the same graph using a separate hue or line style to distinguish the lines corresponding to each variable. Line graphs are simply rendered using OpenGL line primitives. Different line stipple patterns can be used to create different line styles. The illustration techniques described in Chapter 19 can be used to produce more aesthetically appealing graphs. Two dimensional data, where one of the dimensions represents time, can be visualized by animating the line graph.

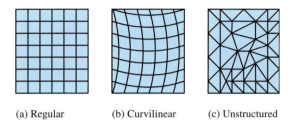

(a) Regular   (b) Curvilinear   (c) Unstructured

Figure 20.5 2D Sample topology.

20.5.2 Contour Lines

Contour plots are used to visualize scalar fields by rendering lines of constant field value, called *isolines*. Usually multiple lines are displayed corresponding to a set of equidistant threshold values (such as elevation data on a topographic map). Section 14.10 describes techniques using 1D texturing to render contour lines.

Two dimensional data sets are drawn as a mesh of triangles with x and y vertices at the 2-dimensional coordinates of the sample points. Both regular and irregular grids of data are converted to a series of triangle strips, as shown in Figure 20.5. The field value is input as a 1D texture coordinate and is scaled and translated using the texture matrix to create the desired spacing between threshold values. A small 1D texture with two hue values, drawn with a repeat wrap mode, results in repeating lines of the same hue. To render lines in different hue, a larger 1D texture can be used with the texture divided such that a different hue is used at the start of each interval. The s coordinate representing the field value is scaled to match the spacing of hues in the textures.

The width of each contour line is related to the range of field values that are mapped to the $[0, 1]$ range of the texture and the size of the texture. For example, field values ranging from $[0, 8]$, used with a 32×1 texture, result in four texels per field value, or conversely a difference in one texel corresponds to change in field value of 1/4. Setting texels 0, 4, 8, 12, 16, 20, 24, and 28 to different hues and all others to a background hues, while scaling the field value by 1/8, results in contour lines drawn wherever the field value is in the range $[0, 1/4]$, $[1, 5/4]$, $[2, 9/4]$, and so forth. The contour lines can be centered over each threshold value by adding a bias of 1/8 to the scaled texture coordinates.

Simple 2-dimensional data sets are drawn as a rectangular grid in the 2D $x - y$ plane. Contour lines can also be drawn on the faces of 3D objects using the same technique. One example is using contour lines on the faces of a 3D finite element model to indicate lines of constant temperature or pressure, or the faces of an elevation model to indicate lines of constant altitude (see Figure 20.6).

20.5.3 Annotating Metrics

In variation of the contouring approach, Teschner (1994) proposes a method for displaying metrics, such as 2D tick marks, on an object using a 2D texture map containing

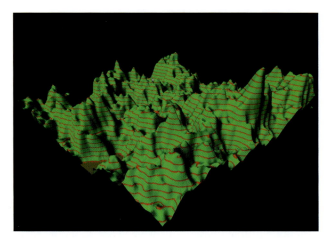

Figure 20.6 Contour plot showing lines of constant altitude.

the metrics. Texture coordinates are generated as a distance from object coordinates to a reference plane. For the 2D case, two reference planes are used. As an example application for this technique, consider a 2D texture marked off with tick marks every kilometer in both the s and t directions. This texture can be mapped on to terrain data using the GL_REPEAT texture coordinate wrap mode. An object linear texture coordinate generation function is used, with the reference planes at $x = 0$ and $z = 0$ and a scale factor set so that a vertex coordinate 1 km from the $x - y$ or $z - y$ plane produces a texture coordinate value equal to the distance between two tick marks in texture coordinate space.

20.5.4 Image Display

The texture-mapped contour line generation algorithm generalizes to a technique in which field values are mapped to a continuous range of hues. This technique is known by a number of names, including *image display* and *false coloring*. The mapping of hue values to data values is often called a *color map*. Traditionally the technique is implemented using color index rendering by mapping field values to color index values and using the display hardware to map the index values to hues. With texture mapping support so pervasive in modern hardware, and color index rendering become less well supported, it makes sense to implement this algorithm using texture mapping rather than color index rendering. One advantage of texture mapping is that linear filters can be used to smooth the resulting color maps. The color index algorithm is equivalent to texture mapping using nearest filtering.

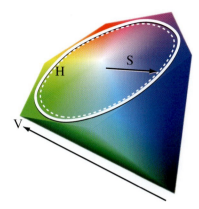

Figure 20.7 HSV color wheel.

Suitable hue ramps are often generated using the HSV color model (see Section 12.3.8). The HSV color model maps the red, yellow, green, cyan, blue, and magenta hues to the vertices of a hexagon. Hue and saturation of a color are determined by the position of the color around the perimeter of the hexagon (angle) and distance from the center, respectively (see Figure 20.7). Hue ramps are created by specifying a starting, ending, and step angle and calculating the corresponding RGB value for each point on the HSV ramp. The RGB values are then used to construct the 1D texture image. The mapping from data values to hues is dependent on the application domain, the underlying data, and the information to be conveyed. HSV hue ramps can effectively convey the ordered relationship between data values. However, the choice of hues can imply different meanings. For example, hues ranging from blue, violet, black might indicate cold or low values, greens and yellows for moderate values, and red for extreme values. It is always important to include a color bar (legend) on the image indicating the mapping of hues to data values to reduce the likelihood of misinterpretation.

Choropleths

Another form of false coloring, often used with geographic information, called a *choropleth*, is used to display 2D information. The data values in choropleths describe regions rather than individual points. For example, a map of census data for different geographic regions may also use hue for the different values (see Figure 20.8). However, continuous scalar fields usually have gradual transitions between color values. The choropleth images have sharp transitions at region boundaries if neighboring regions have different values.

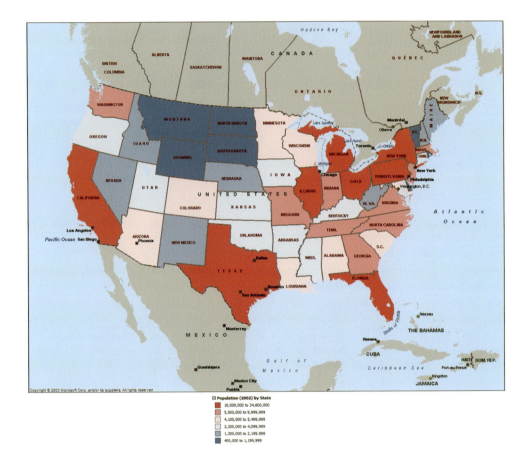

⊟ **Population (2002) by State**

■	10,000,000 to 34,600,000
■	5,500,000 to 9,999,999
□	4,100,000 to 5,499,999
□	2,200,000 to 4,099,999
■	1,200,000 to 2,199,999
■	400,000 to 1,199,999

Figure 20.8 Census choropleth.

Using OpenGL to render a choropleth involves two steps. The first is modeling the region boundaries using polygons. The second is drawing the boundaries with the data mapped to a color. Since the first step requires creating individual objects for each region, the color can be assigned as the region is rendered.

20.5.5 Surface Display

The 3D analog to a 2D line graph is a surface plot. If the scalar field data is 2-dimensional, field values can be mapped to a third spatial dimension. The data set is converted to a mesh of triangles, where the 2D coordinates of the data set become the x and z coordinates of the vertices and the field value becomes the y coordinate (the y axis is the up vector). The result is a 2D planar sheet displaced in the normal direction by the field values (see Figure 20.9). This technique works well with ordinal and quantitative data since the positional cue naturally conveys the relative order of the data value. This technique is best for visualizing smooth data. If the data is noisy, the resulting surfaces contain many spikes, making the data more difficult to understand.

For a regular 2-dimensional grid, the geometry is referred to as a *height field*, since the data set can be described by the number of samples in each dimension and the height values. Warping a sheet with elevation data is frequently used in geographic information systems (GIS) where it is called *rubber sheeting*. Regular grids can be drawn efficiently in OpenGL using triangle and quad strips. To reduce the data storage requirements, the

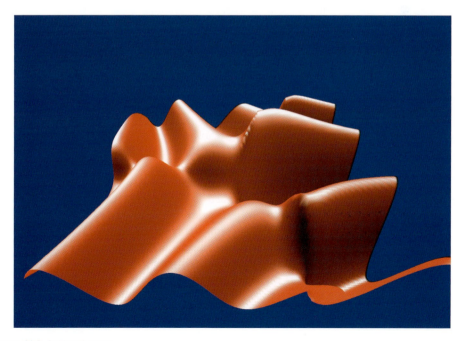

Figure 20.9 Rubber sheeting.

strips can be generated on the fly so that there is no need to store x and y coordinates. However, if the data set is not prohibitively large it is more efficient to create a display list containing the entire geometry.

Irregular grids are also drawn using triangle and quad strips. If the algorithm for generating the strips is simple, it can also be executed on the fly to avoid storing x and z coordinates for each sample. However, for complex grids it may be necessary to pre compute the meshes and store them, often using arrays of indices into the vertex data. For irregular data, a Delaunay triangulation algorithm is a good choice for generating the meshes, since it produces "fat" triangles (triangles with large angles at each vertex), giving the best representation for a given surface. A detailed description of Delaunay triangulation algorithms is beyond the scope of this book. O'Rourke provides a detailed treatment on triangulation and similar topics in (O'Rourke, 1994). See Section 1.2 for a discussion of tessellation.

The height of the surface corresponds to the field value. Linear scaling can be achieved using the modelview transformation. More complex scaling, for example — plotting the logarithm of the field value — usually requires preprocessing the field values. Alternatively, vertex programs, if supported, can be used to evaluate moderately sophisticated transforms of field data. Combining perspective projection, interactive rotation, depth cueing, or lighting can enhance the 3D perception of the model. Lighting requires computing a surface normal at each point. Some methods for computing normals are described in Section 1.3. In the simplest form, the mesh model is drawn with a constant color. A wireframe version of the mesh, using the methods described in Section 16.7.2, can be drawn on the surface to indicate the locations of the sample points. Alternatively, contouring or pseudocoloring techniques can be used to visualize a field with two variables (E_2^{2S}), mapping one field to hue and the second to height. The techniques described in Section 19.6.1 can also be used to cross-hatch the region using different hatching patterns. Hatching patterns do not naturally convey a sense of order, other than by density of the pattern, so care must be used when mapping data types other than nominal to patterns.

Surface plots can also be combined with choropleths to render the colored regions with height proportional to data values. This can be more effective than hue alone since position conveys the relative order of data better than color. However, the color should be retained since it can indicate the region boundaries more clearly.

For large data sets surface plots require intensive vertex and pixel processing. The methods for improving performance described in Chapter 21 can make a significant improvement in the rendering speed. In particular, minimizing redundant vertices by using connected geometry, display lists or vertex arrays combined with backface culling are important. For very large data sets the bump mapping techniques described in Section 15.10 may be used to create shaded images with relief. A disadvantage of the bump mapping technique is that the displacements are limited to a small range. The bump mapping technique eliminates the majority of the vertex processing but increases the per-pixel processing. The technique can support interactive rendering rates for large data sets on the order of 10000×10000.

Some variations on the technique include drawing vertical lines with length proportional to field value at each point (hedgehogs), or the solid surfaces can be rendered with transparency (Section 11.9) to allow occluded surfaces to show through.

20.5.6 Isosurfaces

The 3D analog of an isoline is an isosurface — a surface of constant field value. Isosurfaces are useful for visualizing 3-dimensional scalar fields, E_3^s. Rendering an isosurface requires creation of a geometric model corresponding to the isosurface, called isosurface extraction. There are many algorithms for creating such a model (Lorensen, 1987; Wilhelms, 1992; O'Rourke, 1994; Chiang, 1997). These algorithms take the data set, the field value, α, and a tolerance ε as input and produce a set of polygons with surface points in the range $[\alpha - \varepsilon, \alpha + \varepsilon]$. The polygons are typically determined by considering the data set as a collection of *volume cells* classifying each cell as containing part of the surface or not. Cells that are classified as having part of the surface passing through them are further analyzed to determine the geometry of the surface fragment passing through the cell.

The result of such an algorithm is a collection of polygons where the edges of each polygon are bound by the faces of a cell. This means that for a large grid a nontrivial isosurface extraction can produce a large number of small polygons. To efficiently render such surfaces, it is essential to reprocess them with a meshing or stripping algorithm to reduce the number of redundant vertices as described in Section 1.4.

Once an efficient model has been computed, the isosurface can be drawn using regular surface rendering techniques. Multiple isosurfaces can be extracted and drawn using different colors in the same way that multiple isolines can be drawn on a contour plot (see Figure 20.10). To allow isosurfaces nested within other isosurfaces to be seen, transparent rendering techniques (Section 11.9) or cutting planes can be used. Since blended transparency requires sorting polygons, polygons may need to be rendered individually rather than as part of connected primitives. For special cases where multiple isosurfaces are completely contained (nested) within each other and are convex (or mostly convex), face culling or clipping planes can be used to perform a partition sort of the polygons. This can be a good compromise between rendering quality and speed.

Perspective projection; interactive zoom, pan, and rotation; and depth cueing can be used to enrich the 3D perception. The isosurfaces can be lighted, but vertex or facet normals then must be calculated. The techniques in Section 1.3 can be used to create them, but many isosurface extraction algorithms also include methods to calculate surface gradients using finite differences. These methods can be used to generate a surface normal at each vertex instead.

Three dimensional data sets with multiple variables, E_3^{mS}, can be visualized using isosurfaces for one of the variables, while mapping one or more of the remaining variables to other visual cues such as color (brightness or hue), transparency, or isolines. Since the vertices of the polygons comprising the isosurface do not necessarily coincide with the original sample points, the other field variables must be reconstructed and sampled at

Figure 20.10 3D isosurfaces of wind velocities in a thunderstorm. Scalar field data provided by the National Center for Supercomputing Applications.

the vertex locations. The isosurface extraction algorithm may do this automatically, or it may need to be computed as a postprocessing step after the surface geometry has been extracted.

20.5.7 Volume Slicing

The 2D image display technique can be extended to 3-dimensional fields by rendering one or more planes intersecting (slicing) the 3-dimensional volume. If the data set is sampled on a regular grid and the planes intersect the volume at right angles, the slices correspond to 2-dimensional array slices of the data set. Each slice is rendered as a set of triangle strips forming a plane, just as they would be for a 2-dimensional scalar field. The planes formed by the strips are rotated and translated to orient them in the correct position relative to the entire volume data set, as shown in Figure 20.11. Slices crossing through the data set at arbitrary angles require additional processing to compute a sample value at the locations where each vertex intersects the volume.

Animation can be used to march a slice through a data set to give a sense of the shape of the field values through the entire volume. Volume slices can be used after clipping an

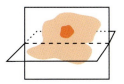

Figure 20.11 90° Volume slices.

isosurface to add an *isocap* to the open cross section, revealing additional detail about the behavior of the field inside the isosurface. The capping algorithm is described in Section 16.9. The isocap algorithm uses the volume slice as the capping plane rather than a single solid colored polygon.

20.5.8 Volume Rendering

Volume rendering is a useful technique for visualizing 3-dimensional scalar fields. Examples of sampled 3D data can range from computational fluid dynamics, medical data from CAT or MRI scanners, seismic data, or any volumetric information where geometric surfaces are difficult to generate or unavailable. Volume visualization provides a way to see through the data, revealing complex 3D relationships.

An alternative method for visualizing 3-dimensional scalar fields is to render the volume directly. Isosurface methods produce *hard* surfaces at distinct field values. Volume visualization methods produce *soft* surfaces by blending the contributions from multiple surfaces, integrating the contribution from the entire volume. By carefully classifying the range of field values to the various source contributions to the volume, and mapping these classified values using color and transparency, individual surfaces can be resolved in the rendered image.

Volume rendering algorithms can be grouped into four categories: ray casting (Hall, 1991), resampling or shear-warp (Drebin, 1988; Lacroute, 1994), texture slicing (Cabral, 1994), and splatting (Westover, 1990; Mueller, 1999).

Ray casting is the most common technique. The volume is positioned near the viewer and a light source, and a ray is projected from the eye through each pixel in the image plane through the volume (as shown in Figure 20.12). The algorithm (and many other volume rendering algorithms) use a simplified light transport model in which a photon is assumed to scatter exactly once, when it strikes a volume element (*voxel*) and is subsequently reflected. Absorption between the light source and the scattering voxel is ignored, while absorption between the viewer and the scattering is modeled. Using this simplified model, the color of a pixel is computed by integrating the light transmission along the ray. The integration calculation assumes that each volume element emits light and absorbs a percentage the light passing through it. The amount absorbed is determined by the amount of material contained in the voxel, which is mapped to an opacity, α, as part of

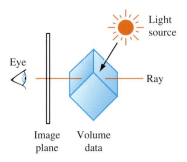

Light
source

Eye

Ray

Image   Volume
plane   data

Figure 20.12 Ray casting.

the classification process. The pixel color for a ray passing through n voxels is computed using the back to front compositing operation (Section 11.1.2),

$$C_f = \alpha_n C_n + (1 - \alpha_n)(\alpha_{n-1} C_{n-1} + 1 - \alpha_{n-1}(\cdots(\alpha_0 C_0))),$$

where voxel 0 is farthest from the viewer along the ray.

The ray-casting process is repeated, casting a unique ray for each pixel on the screen. Each ray passes through a different set of voxels, with the exact set determined by the orientation of the volume relative to the viewer. Ray casting can require considerable computation to process all of the rays. Acceleration algorithms attempt to avoid computations involving *empty* voxels by storing the voxel data in hierarchical or other optimized data structures. Performing the compositing operation from front to back rather than back to front allows the cumulative opacity to be tracked, and the computation along a ray terminated when the accumulated opacity reaches 1.

A second complication with ray casting involves accuracy in sampling. Sampled 3D volume data shares the same properties as 2D image data described in (Section 4.1). Voxels represent point samples of a continuous signal and the voxel spacing determines the maximum representable signal frequency. When performing the integration operation, the signal must be reconstructed at points along the ray intersecting the voxels. Simply using the nearest sample value introduces sampling errors. The reconstruction operation requires additional computations using the neighboring voxels. The result of integrating along a ray creates a point sample in the image plane used to reconstruct the final image. Additional care is required when the volume is magnified or minified during projection since the pixel sampling rate is no longer equal to voxel sampling rate. Additional rays are required to avoid introducing aliasing artifacts while sampling the volume.

If one of the faces of the volume is parallel with the image plane and an orthographic projection with unity scaling is used, then the rays align with the point samples and a simpler reconstruction function can be used. This special case, where the volume is *coordinate axis aligned*, leads to a volume rendering variation in which the oriented and perspective projected volume is first resampled to produce a new volume that is axis aligned. The aligned volume is then rendered using simple ray casting, where the rays are aligned with the sample points.

Shear-warp and related algorithms break the rendering into the resampling and ray-casting parts. Warping or resampling operations are used to align voxel slices such that the integration computations are simpler, and if necessary warp the resulting image. The transformed slices can be integrated using simple compositing operations. Algorithms that rely on resampling can be implemented efficiently using accelerated image-processing algorithms. The shear-warp factorization (Lacroute, 1994) uses sophisticated data structures and traversal to implement fast software volume rendering.

The following sections discuss the two remaining categories of volume rendering algorithms: texture slicing and splatting. These algorithms are described in greater detail since they can be efficiently implemented using the OpenGL pipeline.

20.5.9 Texture Slicing

The texture-slicing algorithm is composed of two parts. First, the volume data is resampled with planes parallel to the image plane and integrated along the direction of view. These planes are rendered as polygons, clipped to the limits of the texture volume. These clipped polygons are textured with the volume data, and the resulting images are composited from back to front toward the viewing position, as shown in Figure 20.13. These polygons are called *data-slice polygons*. Ideally the resampling algorithm is implemented using 3D texture maps. If 3D textures are not supported by the OpenGL implementation however, a more limited form of resampling can be performed using 2D texture maps.

Close-up views of the volume cause sampling errors to occur at texels that are far from the line of sight into the data. The assumption that the viewer is infinitely far away

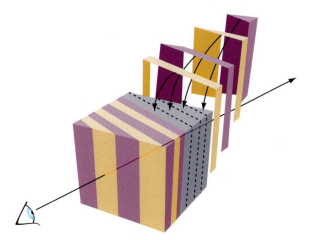

Figure 20.13 Slicing a 3D texture to render volume.

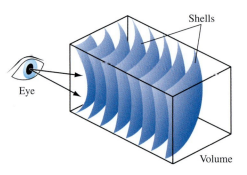

Figure 20.14 Slicing a 3D texture with spherical shells.

and that the viewing rays are perpendicular to the image plane is no longer correct. This problem can be corrected using a series of concentric tessellated spheres centered around the eye point, rather than a single flat polygon, to generate each textured "slice" of the data as shown in Figure 20.14. Like flat slices, the spherical shells should be clipped to the data volume, and each textured shell blended from back to front.

Slicing 3D Textures

Using 3D textures for volume rendering is the most desirable method. The slices can be oriented perpendicular to the viewer's line of sight. Spherical slices can be created for close-up views to reduce sampling errors. The steps for rendering a volume using 3D textures are:

1. Load the volume data into a 3D texture. This is done once for a particular data volume.

2. Choose the number of slices, based on the criteria in the section on Sampling Frequency considerations (p. 552). Usually this matches the texel dimensions of the volume data cube.

3. Find the desired viewpoint and view direction.

4. Compute a series of polygons that cut through the data perpendicular to the direction of view. Use texture coordinate generation to texture the slice properly with respect to the 3D texture data.

5. Use the texture transform matrix to set the desired orientation of the textured images on the slices.

6. Render each slice as a textured polygon, from back to front. A blend operation is performed at each slice. The type of blend depends on the desired effect, and several common types are described shortly.

7. As the viewpoint and direction of view changes, recompute the data-slice positions and update the texture transformation matrix as necessary.

Slicing 2D Textures

Volume rendering with 2D textures is more complex and does not provide results as good as with 3D textures, but can be used on any OpenGL implementation. The problem with 2D textures is that the data-slice polygons can't always be perpendicular to the view direction. Three sets of 2D texture maps are created, each set perpendicular to one of the major axes of the data volume. These texture sets are created from adjacent 2D slices of the original 3D volume data along a major axis. The data-slice polygons must be aligned with whichever set of 2D texture maps is most parallel to it. The worst case is when the data slices are canted 45 degrees from the view direction.

The more edge-on the slices are to the eye the worse the data sampling is. In the extreme case of an edge-on slice the textured values on the slices aren't blended at all. At each edge pixel, only one sample is visible, from the line of texel values crossing the polygon slice. All the other values are obscured.

For the same reason, sampling the texel data as spherical shells to avoid aliasing when doing close-ups of the volume data isn't practical with 2D textures. The steps for rendering a volume using 2D textures are:

1. Generate the three sets of 2D textures from the volume data. Each set of 2D textures is oriented perpendicular to one of the volume's major axes. This processing is done once for a particular data volume.

2. Choose the number of slices. Usually this matches the texel dimensions of the volume data cube.

3. Find the desired viewpoint and view direction.

4. Find the set of 2D textures most perpendicular to the direction of view. Generate data-slice polygons parallel to the 2D texture set chosen. Use texture coordinate generation to texture each slice properly with respect to its corresponding 2D texture in the texture set.

5. Use the texture transform matrix to set the desired orientation of the textured images on the slices.

6. Render each slice as a textured polygon, from back to front. A blend operation is performed at each slice, with the type of blend operation dependent on the desired effect. Relevant blending operators are described in the next section.

7. As the viewpoint and direction of view changes, recompute the data-slice positions and update the texture transformation matrix as necessary. Always orient the data slices to the 2D texture set that is most closely aligned with it.

Blending Operators

A number of blending operators can be used to integrate the volume samples. These operators emphasize different characteristics of the volume data and have a variety of uses in volume visualization.

Over The *over* operator (Porter, 1984) is the most common way to blend for volume visualization. Volumes blended with the over operator approximate the transmission of light through a colored, transparent material. The transparency of each point in the material is determined by the value of the texel's alpha channel. Texels with higher alpha values tend to obscure texels behind them, and stand out through the obscuring texels in front of them. The over operator is implemented in OpenGL by setting the blend source and destination blend factors to `GL_SRC_ALPHA`, `GL_ONE_MINUS_SRC_ALPHA`.

Attenuate The *attenuate* operator simulates an X-ray of the material. With attenuate, the volume's alpha appears to attenuate light shining through the material along the view direction toward the viewer. The alpha channel models material density. The final brightness at each pixel is attenuated by the total texel density along the direction of view.

Attenuation can be implemented with OpenGL by scaling each element by the number of slices and then summing the results. This is done using constant color blending:[1]

```
glBlendFunc(GL_CONSTANT_ALPHA, GL_ONE)
glBlendColor(1.f, 1.f, 1.f, 1.f/number_of_slices)
```

Maximum Intensity Projection Maximum intensity projection (or MIP) is used in medical imaging to visualize blood flow. MIP finds the brightest alpha from all volume slices at each pixel location. MIP is a contrast enhancing operator. Structures with higher alpha values tend to stand out against the surrounding data. MIP and its lesser-used counterpart, minimum intensity projection, is implemented in OpenGL using the blend minmax function in the imaging subset:

```
glBlendEquation(GL_MAX)
```

Under Volume slices rendered front to back with the *under* operator give the same result as the *over* operator blending slices from back to front. Unfortunately, OpenGL doesn't have an exact equivalent for the *under* operator, although using `glBlendFunc(GL_SRC_ALPHA_SATURATE, GL_ONE)` is a good approximation. Use the *over* operator and back to front rendering for best results. See Section 11.1 for more details.

Sampling Frequency Considerations

There are a number of factors to consider when choosing the number of slices (data-slice polygons) to use when rendering a volume.

Performance It's often convenient to have separate "interactive" and "detail" modes for viewing volumes. The interactive mode can render the volume with a smaller number of slices, improving the interactivity at the expense of image quality. Detail mode renders with more slices and can be invoked when the volume being manipulated slows or stops.

---

1. Constant color blending is part of the Imaging Subset and the OpenGL 1.4 core.

Cubical Voxels The data-slice spacing should be chosen so that the texture sampling rate from slice to slice is equal to the texture sampling rate within each slice. Uniform sampling rate treats 3D texture texels as cubical voxels, which minimizes resampling artifacts.

For a cubical data volume, the number of slices through the volume should roughly match the resolution in texels of the slices. When the viewing direction is not along a major axis, the number of sample texels changes from plane to plane. Choosing the number of texels along each side is usually a good approximation.

Non-linear blending The *over* operator is not linear, so adding more slices doesn't just make the image more detailed. It also increases the overall attenuation, making it harder to see density details at the "back" of the volume. Changes in the number of slices used to render the volume require that the alpha values of the data should be rescaled. There is only one correct sample spacing for a given data set's alpha values.

Perspective When viewing a volume in perspective, the density of slices should increase with distance from the viewer. The data in the back of the volume should appear denser as a result of perspective distortion. If the volume isn't being viewed in perspective, uniformly spaced data slices are usually the best approach.

Flat Versus Spherical Slices If spherical slices are used to get good close-ups of the data, the slice spacing should be handled in the same way as for flat slices. The spheres making up the slices should be tessellated finely enough to avoid concentric shells from touching each other.

2D Versus 3D Textures 3D textures can sample the data in the s, t, or r directions freely. 2D textures are constrained to s and t. 2D texture slices correspond exactly to texel slices of the volume data. To create a slice at an arbitrary point requires resampling the volume data.

Theoretically, the minimum data-slice spacing is computed by finding the longest ray cast through the volume in the view direction, transforming the texel values found along that ray using the transfer function (if there is one) calculating the highest frequency component of the transformed texels. Double that number for the minimum number of data slices for that view direction.

This can lead to a large number of slices. For a data cube 512 texels on a side, the worst case is at least $1024\sqrt{3}$ slices, or about 1774 slices. In practice, however, the volume data tends to be band-limited, and in many cases choosing the number of data slices to be equal to the volume's dimensions (measured in texels) works well. In this example, satisfactory results may be achieved with 512 slices, rather than 1774. If the data is very blurry, or image quality is not paramount (for example, in "interactive mode"), this value can be reduced by a factor of 2 or 4.

Shrinking the Volume Image

For best visual quality, render the volume image so that the size of a texel is about the size of a pixel. Besides making it easier to see density details in the image, larger images avoid the problems associated with undersampling a minified volume.

Reducing the volume size causes the texel data to be sampled to a smaller area. Since the *over* operator is nonlinear, the shrunken data interacts with it to yield an image that is different, not just smaller. The minified image will have density artifacts that are not in the original volume data. If a smaller image is desired, first render the image full size in the desired orientation and then shrink the resulting 2D image in a separate step.

Virtualizing Texture Memory

Volume data doesn't have to be limited to the maximum size of 3D texture memory. The visualization technique can be virtualized by dividing the data volume into a set of smaller "bricks." Each brick is loaded into texture memory. Data slices are then textured and blended from the brick as usual. The processing of bricks themselves is ordered from back to front relative to the viewer. The process is repeated with each brick in the volume until the entire volume has been processed.

To avoid sampling errors at the edges, data-slice texture coordinates should be adjusted so they don't use the surface texels of any brick. The bricks themselves are oriented so that they overlap by one volume texel with their immediate neighbors. This allows the results of rendering each brick to combine seamlessly. For more information on paging textures, see Section 14.6.

Mixing Volumetric and Geometric Objects

In many applications it is useful to display both geometric primitives and volumetric data sets in the same scene. For example, medical data can be rendered volumetrically, with a polygonal prosthesis placed inside it. The embedded geometry may be opaque or transparent.

The opaque geometric objects are rendered first using depth buffering. The volumetric data-slice polygons are then drawn with depth testing still enabled. Depth buffer updates should be disabled if the slice polygons are being rendered from front to back (for most volumetric operators, data slices are rendered back to front). With depth testing enabled, the pixels of volume planes behind the opaque objects aren't rendered, while the planes in front of the object blend on it. The blending of the planes in front of the object gradually obscure it, making it appear embedded in the volume data.

If the object itself should be transparent, it must be rendered along with the data-slice polygons a slice at a time. The object is chopped into slabs using application-defined clipping planes. The slab thickness corresponds to the spacing between volume data slices. Each slab of object corresponds to one of the data slices. Each slice of the object is rendered and blended with its corresponding data-slice polygon, as the polygons are rendered back to front.

Transfer Functions

Different alpha values in volumetric data often correspond to different materials in the volume being rendered. To help analyze the volume data, a nonlinear transfer function can be applied to the texels, highlighting particular classes of volume data. This transfer function can be applied through one of OpenGL's look-up tables. Fragment programs and dependent texture reads allow complex transfer functions to be implemented. For the fixed-function pipeline, the `SGI_texture_color_table` extension applies a look-up table to texels values during texturing, after the texel value is filtered.

Since filtering adjusts the texel component values, a more accurate method is to apply the look-up table to the texel values before the textures are filtered. If the `EXT_color_table` table extension is available, a color table in the pixel path can be used to process the texel values while the texture is loaded. If look-up tables aren't available, the processing can be done to the volume data by the application, before loading the texture. With the increasing availability of good fragment program support, it is practical to implement a transfer function as a postfiltering step within a fragment program.

If the paletted texture extension (`EXT_paletted_texture`) is available and the 3D texture can be stored simply as color table indices, it is possible to rapidly change the resulting texel component values by changing the color table.

Volume-cutting Planes

Additional surfaces can be created on the volume with application-defined clipping planes. A clipping plane can be used to cut through the volume, exposing a new surface. This technique can help expose the volume's internal structure. The rendering technique is the same, with the addition of one or more clipping planes defined while rendering and blending the data-slice polygons.

Shading the Volume

In addition to visualizing the voxel data, the data can be lighted and shaded. Since there are no explicit surfaces in the data, lighting is computed per volume texel.

The direct approach is to compute the shading at each voxel within the OpenGL pipeline, ideally with a fragment program. The volumetric data can be processed to find the gradient at each voxel. Then the dot product between the gradient vector, now used as a normal, and the light is computed. The volumetric density data is transformed to intensity at each point in the data. Specular intensity can be computed in a similar way, and combined so that each texel contains the total light intensity at every sample point in the volume. This processed data can then be visualized in the manner described previously.

If fragment programs are not supported, the volume gradient vectors can be computed as a preprocessing step or interactively, as an extension of the texture bump-mapping technique described in Section 15.10. Each data-slice polygon is treated as a surface polygon to be bump-mapped. Since the texture data must be shifted and subtracted, and then blended with the shaded polygon to generate the lighted slice before blending, the process of generating lighted slices must be performed separately from the blending of slices to create the volume image.

Warped Volumes

The data volume can be warped by nonlinearly shifting the texture coordinates of the data slices. For more warping control, tessellate the slices to provide more sample points to perturb the texture coordinate values. Among other things, very high-quality atmospheric effects, such as smoke, can be produced with this technique.

20.5.10 Splatting

Splatting (Westover, 1990) takes a somewhat different approach to the signal reconstruction and integration steps of the ray-casting algorithm. Ray casting computes the reconstructed signal value at a new sample point by convolving a filter with neighboring voxel samples. Splatting computes the contribution of a voxel sample to the neighboring pixels and distributes these values, accumulating the results of all of the splat distributions. The resulting accumulation consists of a series of overlapping splats, as shown in Figure 20.15.

Splatting is referred to as a *forward projection* algorithm since it projects voxels directly onto pixels. Ray casting and texture slicing are *backward projection* algorithms, calculating the mapping of voxels onto a pixel by projecting the image pixels along the viewing rays into the volume. For sparse volumes, splatting affords a significant optimization opportunity since it need only consider nonempty voxels. Voxels can be sorted by classified value as a preprocessing step, so that only relevant voxels are processed during rendering. In contrast, the texture-slicing methods always process all of the voxels.

The contribution from a voxel is computed by integrating the filter kernel along the viewing ray, as shown in Figure 20.16. A typical kernel might be a 3D Gaussian distribution centered at the voxel center. The width of the kernel is typically several (5 to 11) pixels wide. The projection of the kernel onto the image plane is referred to as the *footprint* of the kernel. For an orthographic projection, the footprint of the convolution filter is fixed and can be stored in a table. To render an image, slices of voxels are stepped through, scaling the filter kernel by the sample value and accumulating the

Figure 20.15 Overlapping splats.

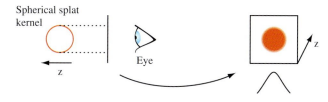

Spherical splat
kernel

Eye

z

z

z

Figure 20.16 Splat kernel integration.

result. For an orthographic projection with no scaling, the integrated kernel table can be used directly. For projections that scale the volume, the footprint is scaled proportionately and the table is recalculated using the scaling information. For perspective projections, the footprint size varies with the distance from the viewer and multiple footprint tables are required.

The simplest splatting algorithm sorts all of the voxels along the viewing direction and renders the voxels one at a time from the back of the volume to the front, compositing each into the framebuffer. This can be implemented using the OpenGL pipeline by creating a table of projected kernels and storing them as 2D texture maps. Each voxel is rendered by selecting the appropriate texture map and drawing a polygon with the correct screen-space footprint size at the image-space voxel position. The polygon color is set to the color (or intensity) and opacity corresponding to the classified voxel value and the polygon color is modulated by the texture image.

This algorithm is very fast. It introduces some errors into the final image, however, since it composites the entire 3D kernel surrounding the voxel at once. Two voxels that are adjacent (parallel to the image plane) have overlapping 3D kernels. Whichever voxel is rendered second will be composited *over* pixels shared with the voxel rendered first. This results in *bleeding* artifacts where material from behind appears in front. Ideally the voxels contributions should be subdivided along the z axis into a series of thin sheets and the contributions from each sheet composited back to front so that the contributions to each pixel are integrated in the correct order.

An improvement on the algorithm introduces a *sheet buffer* that is used to correct some of the integration order errors. In one form of the algorithm, the sheet buffer is aligned to the volume face that is most parallel to the image plane and the sheet is stepped from the back of the volume to the front, one slice at a time. At each position the set of voxels in that slice is composited into the sheet buffer. After the slice is processed, the sheet buffer is composited into the image buffer, retaining the front-to-back ordering. This algorithm is similar to the texture slice algorithm using 2D textures.

Aligning the sheet buffer with one of the volume faces simplifies the computations, but introduces *popping* artifacts as the volume is rotated and the sheet buffer switches from one face to another. The sheet buffer algorithm uses the OpenGL pipeline in much the same way as the simple back-to-front splat algorithm. An additional color buffer is needed to act as the image buffer, while the normal rendering buffer serves as the sheet buffer. The second color buffer can be the front buffer, an off-screen buffer, or a texture map.

In this algorithm, the sheet buffer is aligned with the volume face most parallel with the image plane. A *slab* is constructed that is Δs units thick, parallel to the sheet buffer. The slab is stepped from the back of the volume to the front. At each slab location, all voxels with 3D kernel footprints intersecting the slab are added to the sheet buffer by clipping the kernel to the slab and compositing the result into the sheet buffer. Each completed sheet buffer is composited into the main image buffer, maintaining the front-to-back order.

A variation on the sheet buffer technique referred to as an image-aligned sheet buffer (Mueller, 1998) more closely approaches front to back integration and eliminates the color popping artifacts in the regular sheet buffer algorithm. The modified version aligns the sheet buffer with the image plane, rather than the volume face most parallel to the image plane. The regular sheet buffer algorithm steps through the voxels one row at a time, whereas the image-aligned version creates an image-aligned slab volume, Δs units thick along the viewing axis, and steps that from back to front through the volume. At each position, the set of voxels that intersects this slab volume are composited into the sheet buffer. After each slab is processed, the sheet buffer is composited into the image buffer. Figure 20.17 shows the relationship between the slab volume and the voxel kernels.

The image-aligned sheet buffer differs from the previous two variations in that the slab volume intersects a portion of the kernel. This means that multiple kernel integrals are computed, one for each different kernel-slab intersection combination. The number of preintegrated kernel sections depends on the radial extent of the kernel, R, and the slab width Δs. A typical application might use a kernel 3 to 4 units wide and a slab width of 1. A second difference with this algorithm is that voxels are processed more than once, since a slab is narrower than the kernel extent.

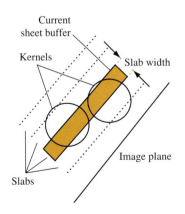

Figure 20.17 Image-aligned sheet buffer.

The image-aligned algorithm uses the OpenGL pipeline in the identical manner as for the other algorithms. The only difference is that additional 2D texture maps are needed to store the preintegrated kernel sections and the number of compositing operations increases.

Shading

Like the other volume rendering algorithms, the shading operations are not limited to the *over* compositing operator. Maximum intensity projections and attenuate operators described for texture slicing are equally useful for splatting.

20.5.11 Creating Volume Data

Both the texture slicing and splatting methods can be intermixed with polygonal data. Sometimes it is useful to convert polygonal objects to volumetric data, however, so that they can be rendered using the same techniques. The OpenGL pipeline can be used to *dice* polygonal data into a series of slices using either a pair of clipping planes or a 1D texture map to define the slice. The algorithm repeatedly draws the entire object using an orthographic projection, creating a new slice in the framebuffer each time. To produce a single value for each voxel, the object's luminance or opacity is rendered with no vertex lighting or texture mapping. The framebuffer slice data are either copied to texture images or transferred to the host memory after each drawing operation until the entire volume is complete.

One way to define a slice for rasterization is to use the near and far clip planes. The planes are set to bound the desired slice and are spaced dz units apart as shown in Figure 20.18. For example, a modeling transformation might be defined to map the eye z coordinates for the geometry to the range $[2.0, 127.0]$, and the near and far clip planes positioned 1 unit apart at the positions $(1.0, 2.0), (2.0, 3.0), \ldots, (128, 129)$ to produce 128 slices. The content of each slice is the geometry that is defined in the range $[near, near + dz]$. The exact sample location is dependent on the polygon data and is not a true point sample from the center of the voxel. The x and y coordinates are at the voxel center, whereas the z coordinate satisfies the plane equation of the polygon.

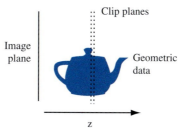

Clip planes

Image
plane

Geometric
data

z

Figure 20.18 Slicing geometric data.

The number of fragments accumulated in each pixel value is dependent on the number of polygons that intersect the pixel center. If depth buffering is enabled, only a single fragment is accumulated, dependent on the depth function. To accumulate multiple fragments, a weighting function is required. If a bound on the number of overlapping polygons is known, the stencil buffer can be used, in conjunction with multiple rendering passes to control which fragment is stored in the framebuffer, creating a *superslice*. As each superslice is transferred to the host it can be accumulated with the other superslices to compute the final set of slice values.

Polygons edge-on to the image plane have no area, and make no sample contribution, which can cause part of an object to be missed. This problem can be mitigated by repeating the slicing algorithm with the volume rotated so that the volume is sliced along each of the three major axes. The results from all three volumes are merged. Since the algorithm approximates point sampling the object, it can introduce aliasing artifacts. To reduce the artifacts and further improve the quality of the sample data, the volume can be supersampled by increasing the object's projected screen area and proportionately increasing the number of z slices. The final sample data is generated off-line from the supersampled data using a higher-order reconstruction filter.

The clip plane slicing algorithm can be replaced with an alternate texture clipping technique. The clipping texture is a 1D alpha texture with a single opaque texel value and zero elsewhere. The texture width is equal to the number of slices in the target volume. To render a volume slice, the object's z vertex coordinate is normalized relative to the z extent of the volume and mapped to the s texture coordinate. As each slice is rendered, the s coordinate is translated to position the opaque texel at the next slice position. If the volume contains v slices, the s coordinate is advanced by $1/v$ for each slice. Using nearest (point) sampling for the texture filter, a single value is selected from the texture map and used as the fragment color. Since this variation also uses polygon rasterization to produce the sample values, the z coordinate of the sample is determined by the plane equation of the polygon passing through the volume. However, since the sample value is determined by the texture map, using a higher-resolution texture maps multiple texels to a voxel. By placing the opaque texel at the center of the voxel, fragments that do not pass close enough to the center will map to zero-valued texels rather than an opaque texel, improving sampling accuracy.

20.6 Vector Field Visualization

Visualizing vector fields is a difficult problem. Whereas scalar fields have a scalar value at each sample point, vector fields have an n-component vector (usually two or three components). Vector fields occur in applications such as computational fluid dynamics and typically represent the flow of a gas or liquid. Visualization of the field provides a way to better observe and understand the flow patterns.

Vector field visualization techniques can be grouped into three general classes: icon based, particle and stream line based, and texture based. Virtually all of these techniques can be used with both 2- and 3-dimensional vector fields, E_2^V and E_3^V.

20.6.1 Icons

Icon-based or *hedgehog* techniques render a 3D geometric object (cone, arrow, and so on) at each sample point with the geometry aligned with the vector direction (tangent to the field) at that point. Other attributes, such as object size or color, can be used to encode a scalar quantity such as the vector magnitude at each sample point. Arrow plots can be efficiently implemented using a single instance of a geometric model to describe the arrow aligned to a canonical up vector **U**. At each sample point, a modeling transformation is created that aligns the up vector with the data set vector, **V**. This transformation is a rotation through the angle $\mathbf{U} \cdot \mathbf{V}$ about the axis $\mathbf{U} \times \mathbf{V}$. Storage and time can be minimized by precomputing the angle and cross product and storing these values with the sample positions.

Glyphs using more complex shape and color cues, called *vector field probes*, can be used to display additional properties such as torsion and curvature (de Leeuw, 1993). In general, icons or glyphs are restricted to a coarse spatial resolution to avoid overlap and clutter. Often it is useful to restrict the number of glyphs, using them only in regions of interest. To avoid unnecessary distraction from placement patterns, the glyphs should not be placed on a regular grid. Instead, they should be displaced from the sample position by a small random amount. To further reduce clutter, glyphs display can be constrained to particular 3D regions. Brushing (painting) techniques can be used to provide interactive control over which glyphs are displayed, allowing the viewer to paint and erase regions of glyphs from the display. The painting techniques can use variations on the selection techniques described in Section 16.1 to determine icons that intersect a given screen area.

20.6.2 Particle Tracing

Particle tracing techniques trace the path of massless particles through a vector velocity field. The particles are displayed as small spheres or point-shaped geometry, for example, 2D triangles or 3D cones. Portions of the field are seeded with particles and paths are traced through the field following the vector field samples (see Figure 20.19). The positions of the particles along their respective paths are animated over time to convey a sense of flow through the field.

Particle paths are computed using numerical integration. For example, using Euler's method the new position, p_{i+1}, for a particle is computed from the current position, p_i as $p_{i+1} = p_i + \mathbf{v}_i \Delta t$. The vector, $\mathbf{v}_i$, is an estimate of the vector at the point p_i. It is computed by interpolating the vectors at the vertices of the area or volume cell containing p_i. For a 2-dimensional field, the four vectors at the vertices of the area cell are bilinearly interpolated. For a 3-dimensional field, the 8 vectors at the vertices of the volume cell

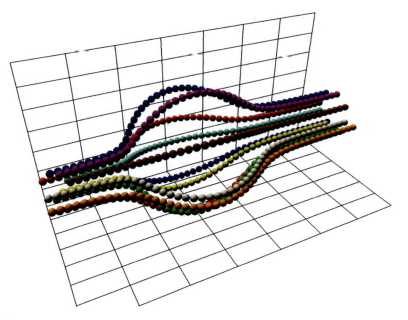

Figure 20.19 Particle tracing.

are trilinearly interpolated. This simple approximation can introduce substantial error. More accurate integration using Runge-Kutta (R-K) methods (Lambert, 1991) are a better choice and can be incorporated with only a small increase in complexity. For example, a fourth-order R-K method is computed as

$$p_{i+1} = p_i + \frac{1}{6}\Delta t \left(\mathbf{v}_i + 2\mathbf{v}_{i+1}^1 + 2\mathbf{v}_{i+1}^2 + 2\mathbf{v}_{i+1}^3\right)$$

where $\mathbf{v}_{i+1}^k$ is the vector computed at intermediate position, $p_i + \frac{1}{2}\Delta t\mathbf{v}_{i+1}^{k-1}$, and $\mathbf{v}_{i+1}^0 = \mathbf{v}_i$.

For small number of particles, the particle positions can be recomputed each frame. For large numbers of particles it may be necessary to precompute the particle positions. If the particle positions can be computed interactively, the application allows the user to interactively place new particles in the system and follow the flow. Various glyphs can be used as the particles. The most common are spheres and arrows. Arrows are oriented in the direction of the field vector at the particle location. Additional information can be encoded in the particles using other visual cues. The magnitude of the vector is reflected in the speed of the particle motion, but can be reinforced by mapping the magnitude to the particle color.

20.6.3 Stream Lines

A variation on particle tracing techniques is to record the particle paths as they are traced out and display each path as a *stream line* using lines or tube-shaped geometry. Each stream line is the list of positions computed at each time step for a single particle. Rendering the set of points as a connected line strip is the most efficient method, but using solid geometry such as tubes or cuboids allows additional information to be incorporated in the shape. A variation of stream lines called *ribbons*, uses geometry with a varying cross section or rotation (twist) to encode other local characteristics of the field: divergence or convergence modulates the width, and curl angular velocity rotates the geometry.

A ribbon results from integrating a line segment, rather than a point, through the velocity field. Ribbons can be drawn as quadrilateral (or triangle) strips where the strip vertices coincide with the end points of the line segment at each time step. For small step sizes, this can result in a large number of polygons in each ribbon. Storing the computed vertices in a vertex array and drawing them as connected primitives maximizes the drawing performance. Ribbons can be lighted, smooth shaded, and depth buffered to improve the 3D perception. However, for dense or large data sets, the number of ribbons to be rendered each frame may create a prohibitive processing load on the OpenGL pipeline.

20.6.4 Illuminated Stream Lines

When visualizing 3-dimensional fields, illumination and shading provide additional visual cues, particularly for dense collections of stream lines. One type of geometry that can be used is tube-shaped geometry constructed from segments of cylinders following the path. In order to capture accurate shading information, the radius of the cylinders needs to be finely tessellated, resulting in a large polygon load when displaying a large number of stream lines.

Another possibility is to use line primitives since they can be rendered very efficiently and allow very large numbers of stream lines to be drawn. A disadvantage is that lines are rendered as *flat* geometry with a single normal at each end point, so they result in much lower shading accuracy compared to using tessellated cylinders. In (Stalling, 1997), an algorithm is described to approximate cylinder-like lighting using texture mapping (see Figure 20.20). This algorithm uses the anisotropic lighting method described in Section 15.9.3.[2]

The main idea behind the algorithm is to choose a normal vector that lies in the same plane as that formed by the tangent vector $\mathbf{T}$ and light vector $\mathbf{L}$. The diffuse and specular lighting contributions are then expressed in terms of the line's tangent vector and the light vector rather than a normal vector. A single 2D texture map contains the ambient contribution, the 1D cosine function used for the diffuse contribution, and a second 2D view-dependent function used to compute the specular contribution.

---

2. Actually, this method inspired the anisotropic lighting method.

Figure 20.20 Illuminated stream lines.

The single material reflectance is sent as the line color (much like color material) and is modulated by the texture map. The illuminated lines can also be rendered using transparency techniques. This is useful for dense collections of stream lines. The opacity value is sent with the line color and the lines must be sorted from back to front to be rendered correctly, as described in Section 11.8.

20.6.5 Line Integral Convolution

Line integral convolution (see Figure 20.21) is a *texture-based* technique for visualizing vector fields and has the advantage of being able to visualize large and detailed vector fields in a reasonable display area.

Line integral convolution involves selectively blurring a reference image as a function of the vector field to be displayed. The reference image can be anything, but to make the results clearer, it is usually a spatially uncorrelated image (e.g., a noise image). The resulting image appears stretched and squished along the directions of the distorting vector field stream lines, visualizing the flow with a minimum of display resolution. Vortices, sources, sinks, and other discontinuities are clearly shown in the resulting image, and the viewer can get an immediate grasp of the flow field's "big picture."

Figure 20.21 Line integral convolution.

The algorithm starts with a vector field, sampled as a discrete grid of *normalized* vectors. A nonuniform and spatially uncorrelated image is needed so that correlations applied to it will be more obvious. This technique visualizes the direction of the flow field, not its velocity. This is why the vector values at each grid point are normalized.

The processed image can be calculated directly using a special convolution technique. A representative set of vector values on the vector grid is chosen. Special convolution kernels are created shaped like the local stream line at that vector. This is done by tracing the local field flow forward and backward some application-defined distance. The resulting curve is used as a convolution kernel to convolve the underlying image. This process is repeated over the entire image using a sampling of the vectors in the vector field.

Mathematically, for each location p in the input vector field a parametric curve $P(p, s)$ is generated that passes through the location and follows the vector field for some distance in either direction. To create an output pixel $F'(p)$, a weighted sum of the values of the input image F along the curve is computed. The weighting function is $k(x)$. Thus, the continuous form of the equation is

$$F'(p) = \frac{\int_{-L}^{L} F(P(p, s))k(s)ds}{\int_{-L}^{L} k(s)ds}$$

To discretize the equation, use values $P_{0..l}$ along the curve $P(p, s)$:

$$F'(p) = \frac{\sum_{i=0}^{l} F(P_i)h_i}{\sum_{i=0}^{l} h_i}$$

The accuracy with which the processed image represents the vector field depends on how accurately the line convolution kernels follow the flow-field stream lines. Since the convolution kernels are only *discretely* sampling a continuous flow field, they are inaccurate in general. Areas of flow that are changing slowly will be represented well, but rapidly changing regions of the flow field (such as the center of vortices and other singularities) will be incorrectly described or missed altogether.

There are various ways of optimizing the sampling intervals to minimize this problem, with different trade-offs between computation time and resulting accuracy. The numerical analysis topics involved are described in detail in (Cabral, 1993; Ma, 1997). For our purposes, we'll use the simplest but least accurate method: a fixed spatial sampling interval.

Rather than generating a series of custom convolution kernels and applying them to an image, a texture mapping approach can be used. This variant has the advantage that it's reasonably easy to implement and runs quickly, especially on systems with good texturing and accumulation buffer support, since it is parallelizing the convolution operations.

The concept is simple: a surface, tessellated into a mesh, is textured with an image to be processed. Each vertex on the surface has a texture coordinate associated with it. Instead of convolving the image with a series of stream-line convolution kernels, the texture coordinates at each vertex are shifted parallel to the flow-field vector, local to that vertex. This process, called *advection*, is done repeatedly in a series of displacements parallel to the flow vectors, with the resulting series of distorted images combined using the accumulation buffer.

The texture coordinates at each grid location are displaced parallel to the local field vector in a fixed series of steps. The displacement is done both parallel and antiparallel to the field vector at the vertex. The amount of displacement for each step and the number of steps determines the accuracy and appearance of the line integral convolution. The application generally sets a global value describing the length of the displacement range for all texture coordinates on the surface. The number of displacements along that length is computed per vertex, as a function of the local field's curl (see Figure 20.22).

The following assumptions simplify the line integral convolution procedure.

1. The supplied flow-field vector grid matches the tessellated textured surface. There is a one-to-one correspondence between vector and vertex.

2. Set a fixed number of displacements (n) at each vertex.

These assumptions allow the vector, associated with each vertex on the tessellated surface, to be used when computing texture displacements. Displacements can also be

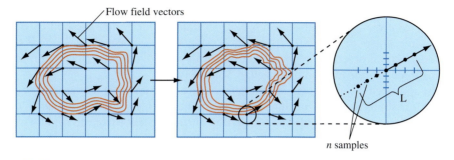

Figure 20.22 Line integral convolution with OpenGL.

calculated by parameterizing the vector and computing evenly spaced texture coordinate locations displaced along the vector direction, both forward and backward. Given these assumptions, the procedure becomes:

1. Update the texture coordinates at each vertex on the surface.

2. Render the surface using the noise texture and the displaced texture coordinates.

3. Accumulate the resulting image in the accumulation buffer, scaling by $1/n$.

4. Repeat the steps above n times and then return the accumulated image.

5. Perform histogram equalization or image scaling to maximize contrast.

Since the texture coordinates are repeatedly updated, using vertex arrays to represent the textured surface provides several benefits. It simplifies the representation of the texture coordinates (they can be kept in a 2D array), and it potentially increases rendering performance (glDrawElements has an index array that eliminates the need to send shared texture and vertex coordinates multiple times) and it reduces function call overhead.

Scaling each accumulation uniformly is not optimal. The displacement of the texture coordinates is most accurate close to the grid vector, so each image contribution should be scaled as an inverse function of distance from the vector. The farther the displacement from the original flow field vector the more potential error in the advection, and the smaller the accumulation scale factor should be. More sophisticated algorithms can be implemented that adjust scale based on a computed, rather than assumed, accuracy. Any scaling algorithm should take into account the maximum and minimum possible color values after accumulating to avoid pixel color overflow or underflow.

In many implementations, the performance of this algorithm will be limited by the speed of the convolution operation. For some applications, a blend operation can be substituted with a loss of resolution accuracy. The scaling operation can be provided by changing the intensity of the base polygon. Care must be taken to avoid overflow and underflow of the blended color values.

There are methods to enhance the resulting flow field to counteract the blurring tendency from the random noise texels being blended. One simple method is to scale and bias the image to maximize its contrast using `glCopyPixels` with the contrast stretching method described in Section 12.4.1. An alternative is to perform a histogram equalization using the method described in Section 12.4.2.

The approach described here to generate line integral convolution images is very simplistic. More sophisticated algorithms decouple the surface tessellation from the flow field grid, and more finely subdivide the tessellation surface where there are rapidly changing flows to properly sample them. This subdivision algorithm should be backed with a rigorous sampling approach so that the results can be trusted within given accuracy bounds. A subdivision algorithm must also recognize and handle various types of flow discontinuities.

This technique can be readily extended into three dimensions, using 3D textures (Interrante, 1997). Volume visualization techniques, described in Section 20.5.8, can be used to visualize the resulting 3D line integral convolution image.

20.7 Tensor Field Visualization

Tensors further extend vector-valued data samples to k-dimensional arrays at each sample point. Tensor fields frequently occur in engineering and physical science computations. For example, rank 2 (second-order) tensors are used to describe velocity gradients, stress, and strain. Tensor fields present a difficult visualization problem since it is difficult to map even a second order tensor onto a set of visual cues. A simple second order tensor might consist of a 3×3 array of scalar values defined over a 3D domain. It is difficult to visualize the data directly, so such fields are often visualized using vector or scalar techniques.

One frequently occurring class of tensor fields, symmetric tensor fields, has special properties that simplify the visualization problem. In particular, 3-dimensional fields of second-order tensors can be thought of as three orthogonal vector fields. Each tensor value can be reduced to a set of three real-valued vectors defined by the real-valued eigenvalues (λ) and unit eigenvectors ($\mathbf{e}$) of the tensor value

$$\mathbf{v}^{(i)} = \lambda^{(i)}\mathbf{e}^{(i)}, \; i = 1, 2, 3$$

The vectors are ordered such that $\lambda^{(1)} \geq \lambda^{(2)} \geq \lambda^{(3)}$ and $\mathbf{v}^{(1)}$ is called the *major* eigenvector, $\mathbf{v}^{(2)}$ the *medium* eigenvector, and $\mathbf{v}^{(3)}$ the *minor* eigenvector. Visualization techniques strive to visualize these three vectors in meaningful ways.

The simplest method is to map each tensor to a 3D glyph, such as an ellipsoid (Haber, 1990) or rectangular prism. The major axis of the ellipsoid aligns with the major eigenvector, and the two remaining axes with the medium and minor eigenvectors. The magnitudes of the vectors can be used to scale the glyph, and colors can be used to indicate compression or strain (negative and positive eigenvalues). Tensor glyphs can be efficiently rendered using the method described in Section Section 20.6.1. If eigenvalue magnitudes are used to scale the glyph geometry, the transformed surface normal vectors will require normalization to compute correct lighting. The simplest way to accomplish renormalization is to enable automatic normalization, using GL_NORMALIZE.

20.7.1 Hyperstreamlines

Using glyphs to visualize the eigenvectors suffers from the same drawbacks found with using glyphs to visualize vector fields: rapid crowding and their discrete nature provides little information regarding the continuity of the field. To solve these problems, vector field visualization uses advection techniques to trace stream lines through the vector field. An analogous idea can be applied to symmetric tensor fields by tracing *tensor field lines* tangent to one of the three vectors at every point (Dickinson, 1989).

This method is virtually identical to tracing a stream line through a vector field, with the difference being that one of the three vectors is selected. The same methods used for rendering stream lines can be used to render tensor field lines.

The tensor field line approach only displays one of the vectors at each point. Replacing the stream line with tubular geometry with an elliptic cross section allows all three vectors to be represented continuously along the field line. Each tube, termed a *hyperstreamline*, follows one of the eigenvectors, while the two remaining vectors modulate the major and minor axis length of the elliptical cross section (Delmarcelle, 1993). Usually the tube is color coded according to the magnitude of the longitudinal vector. More generally, an arbitrary geometric primitive can be swept along the vector field trajectory while modulating its size using the other two vectors. Using a cross as the profile shape allows encoding of both the magnitude and direction of the transverse eigenvectors. The result, called a *helix*, may appear as a spiral as the transverse vectors change direction along the length of the helix.

Rendering hyperstreamlines interactively requires efficient construction of the model geometry. The trajectory is traced out using the advection techniques described in Section 20.6.2, but with some additional complications. Two eigenvalues may become equal at some point along the path. Assuming that the longitudinal trajectory is smooth, abrupt changes in the longitudinal direction can be used to signal that additional searching is required to locate a degeneracy and terminate the hyperstreamline. Similarly, the derivatives of the transverse eigenvalues can be used to determine when to search for points where these eigenvalues are zero and add extra vertices to display the singularity (Delmarcelle, 1993).

The hyperstreamline is constructed by tiling the perimeter of the tube or helix with a ring of polygons that are decomposed into a single triangle strip, (as shown in Figure 20.23). For an elliptical tube, the vertices in a unit circle can be stored in a look-up table and rotated to match the orientation of the longitudinal vector. The vertices and normal vectors are stored in a vertex array or display list for efficient transfer to the

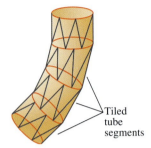

Figure 20.23 Tiling a hyperstreamline.

rendering pipeline. Since the stream lines are closed surfaces, they can be rendered with backface culling to further improve the performance.

Hyperstreamlines are effective in describing the tensor field along one dimensional paths. They can be extended to handle nonsymmetric tensors (Delmarcelle, 1993) and further extended to hyperstreamsurfaces (Jeremic, 2002) similar to the way stream lines are extended to stream surfaces. However, hyperstreamlines are subject to the same problem seen in other iconic and geometry-based visualization techniques: the overall visualization is sensitive to the seed points for the stream lines. The density of hyperstreamlines must be carefully controlled to maintain an intelligible visualization. Beyond hyperstreamline and hyperstreamsurfaces, other techniques have been proposed that display more of the field values simultaneously using hue and anisotropic reflection to encode tensor values (Kindlmann, 1999).

20.8 Summary

The number of visualization techniques continues to grow along with advances in hardware accelerator processing power and support for additional shading techniques using multitexture, vertex programs, fragment programs, and multipass rendering. Simultaneously, the size of scientific and engineering data sets continues to grow and will remain a challenge to visualization for some time to come.

Structuring Applications for Performance

Interactive graphics applications are performance sensitive, perhaps more sensitive than any other type of application. A design application can be very interactive at a redraw rate of 72 frames per second (fps), difficult to operate at 20 fps, and unusable at 5 fps. Tuning graphics applications to maximize their performance is important. Even with high-performance hardware, application performance can vary by multiple orders of magnitude, depending on how well the application is designed and tuned for performance. This is because a graphics pipeline must support such a wide mixture of possible command and data sequences (often called "paths") that it's impossible to optimize an implementation for every possible configuration. Instead, the *application* must be optimized to take full advantage of the graphics systems' strengths, while avoiding or minimizing its weaknesses. Although taking full advantage of the hardware requires understanding and tuning to a particular implementation, there are general principles that work with nearly any graphics accelerator and computer system.

21.1 Structuring Graphics Processing

In its steady state, a graphics application animates the scene and achieves interactivity by constantly updating the scene it's displaying. Optimizing graphics performance requires a detailed understanding of the processing steps or stages used during these updates.

The stages required to do an update are connected in series to form a pipeline, starting at the application and proceeding until the framebuffer is updated. The early stages occur in the application, using its internal state to create data and commands for the OpenGL implementation. The application has wide leeway in how its stages are implemented. Later stages occur in the OpenGL implementation itself and are constrained by the requirements of the OpenGL specification. A well-optimized application designs its stages for maximum performance, and drives the OpenGL implementation with a mixture of commands and data chosen to maximize processing efficiency.

21.1.1 Scene Graphs

An application uses its own algorithms and internal state to create a sequence of graphics data and commands to update the scene. There are a number of design approaches for organizing the data and processing within an application to efficiently determine command sequences to draw the scene. One way to think about a graphics application is as a *database* application. The collection of geometric objects, textures, state, and so on, form the database; drawing a scene requires querying the set of visible objects from the database and issuing commands to draw them using the OpenGL pipeline. A popular method for organizing this database is the *scene graph*. This design technique provides the generality needed to support a wide range of applications, while allowing efficient queries and updates to the database.

A scene graph can be thought of as a more sophisticated version of a display list. It is a data structure containing the information that represents the scene. But instead of simply holding a linear sequence of OpenGL commands the nodes of a scene graph can hold whatever data and procedures are needed to manipulate or render the scene. It is a directed graph, rather than a list. This topology is used to collect elements of the scene into hierarchical groupings. The organization of scene graphs is often spatial in nature. Objects close to each other in the scene graph are close to each other physically. This supports efficient implementations of culling techniques such as view-frustum and portal culling. Figure 21.1 shows a schematic figure of a simple scene graph storing transforms

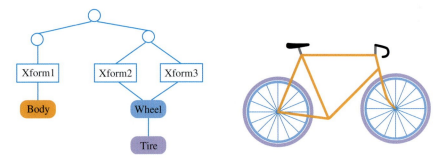

Figure 21.1 A simple scene graph.

and collections of geometric primitives that form objects. Note that a single object can be transformed multiple times to create multiple instances on the screen. This turns the scene graph from a simple tree structure to a *directed acyclic graph* (DAG).

In addition to objects, which correspond to items in the scene, attribute values and procedures can also be included as nodes in the scene graph. In the most common approach, nodes closer to the root of the graph are more global to the scene, affecting the interpretation of their child nodes. The graph topology can be changed to represent scene changes, and it can be traversed. Traversal makes it possible to easily update node information, or to use that information to generate the stream of OpenGL commands necessary to render it.

This type of organization is general enough that an application can use the scene graph for tasks that require information about spatial relationships but that do not necessarily involve graphics. Example include computing 3D sound sources, and source data for collision detection. Since it is such a common approach, this chapter discussess graphics processing steps in the context of an application using a scene graph. This yields a five-stage process. It starts with application generating or modifying scene graph elements and ends with OpenGL updating the framebuffer. The stages are illustrated in Figure 21.2. It shows the states of the pipeline, with data and commands proceeding from left to right. The following sections describe each stage and what system attributes affect its performance.

Generation

During the generation stage, object and attribute data is created or updated by the application. The possible types, purpose, and updating requirements of the graphics data are as varied as the graphics applications themselves. The object data set can be updated to reflect changes in position or appearance of objects, or annotated with application-specific information to support spatially based techniques such as 3D sound and collision detection.

For a scene graph-based application, the generation phase is where nodes are added, removed, or updated by the application to reflect the current state of the scene. The interconnections between nodes can change to reflect changes in their relationship.

As a simple example, consider a scene graph whose nodes only contain geometry or a transform. A new object can be created by adding nodes to the scene graph: geometry to represent the object (or components of a complex object) and the transforms needed to

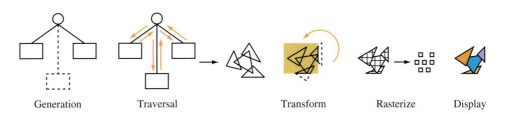

Generation   Traversal   Transform   Rasterize   Display

Figure 21.2 The stages of a graphics update.

position and orient it. The generation phase is complete when the scene graph has been updated to reflect the current state of the scene. In general, performance of this stage depends on system (CPU, memory) performance, not the performance of the graphics hardware.

Traversal

The traversal stage uses the data updated by the generation stage. Here, the graphics-related data set is traversed to generate input data for later stages. If the data is organized as a scene graph, the graph itself is traversed, examining each element to extract the information necessary to create the appropriate OpenGL commands. Procedures linked to the graph are run as they are encountered, generating data themselves or modifying existing data in the graph. Traversal operations can be used to help implement many of the techniques described here that have object-space components (such as reflections, shadowing, and visibility culling), because the scene graph contains information about the spatial relationships between objects in the scene.

Traversing the simple example scene graph shown in Figure 21.1 only generates OpenGL commands. Commands to update the modelview matrix are generated as each transform is encountered, and geometry commands such as `glBegin`/`glEnd` sequences, vertex arrays, or display lists are issued as geometry nodes are traversed. Even for this simple example the traversal order can be used to establish a hierarchy: transforms higher in the graph are applied first, changing the effect of transforms lower in the graph. This relationship can be implemented by pushing the transform stack as the traversal goes down the graph, popping as the traversal goes back up.

Since OpenGL has no direct support for scene graphs, the stages described up to this point must be implemented by the application or a scene graph library. However, in an application that has very limited requirements, an OpenGL display list or vertex array can be used to store the graphics data instead. It can be updated during the generation phase. In this case, the traversal step may only require rendering the stored data, which might be performed solely by the OpenGL implementation.

Executing an OpenGL display list can be considered a form of traversal. Since OpenGL display lists can contain calls to other OpenGL display lists, a display list can also form a DAG. Executing a display list walks the DAG, performing a depth-first traversal of the graph. The traversal may be executed on the host CPU, or in some advanced OpenGL implementations, parts of the traversal may be executed in the accelerator itself. Creating new display lists can be similarly thought of as a form of generation.

If the traversal stage is done in the application, performance of this stage depends on either the bandwidth available to the graphics hardware or system performance, depending on which is the limiting factor. If traversal happens within OpenGL, the performance details will be implementation dependent. In general, performance depends on the bandwidth available between the stored data and the rendering hardware.

Transform

The transform stage processes primitives, and applies transforms, texture coordinate generation, clipping, and lighting operations to them. From this point on, all update stages occur within the OpenGL pipeline, and the behavior is strictly defined by the specification. Although the transform stage may not be implemented as a distinct part of the implementation, the transformation stage is still considered separately when doing performance analysis. Regardless of the implementation details, the work the implementation needs to do in order to transform and light incoming geometry in this stage is usually distinct from the work done in the following stages. This stage will affect performance as a function of the number of triangles or vertices on the screen and the number of transformations or other geometry state updates in the scene.

Rasterization

At this stage, higher-level representations of geometry and images are broken down into individual pixel fragments. Since this stage creates pixel fragments, its performance is a function of the number of fragments created and the complexity of the processing on each fragment. For the purposes of performance analysis it is common to include all of the steps in rasterization and fragment processing together. The number of active texture units, complexity of a fragment programs, framebuffer blending, and depth testing can all have a significant influence on performance. Not all pixels created by rasterizing a triangle may actually update the framebuffer, because alpha, depth, and stencil testing can discard them. As a result, framebuffer update performance and rasterization performance aren't necessarily the same.

Display

At the display stage, individual pixel values are scanned from the color buffer and transmitted to the display device. For the most part the display stage has limited influence on the overall performance of the application. However, some characteristics (such as locking to the video refresh rate) can significantly affect the performance of an application.

21.1.2 Vertex Updates

A key factor affecting update performance that can be controlled by the application is the efficiency of vertex updates. Vertex updates occur during the traversal stage, and are often limited by system bandwidth to the graphics hardware. Storing vertex information in vertex arrays removes much of the function call overhead associated with `glBegin`/`glEnd` representations of data. Vertex arrays also make it possible to combine vertex data into contiguous regions, which improves transfer bandwidth from the CPU to the graphics hardware. Although vertex arrays reduce overhead and improve performance, their benefits come at a cost. Their semantics limit their ability to improve a bandwidth-limited application.

Ideally, vertex arrays make it possible to copy vertex data "closer" to the rendering hardware or otherwise optimize the placement of vertex data to improve performance. The original (OpenGL 1.1) definition prevents this, however. The application "owns" the pointer to the vertex data, and the specification semantics prevents the implementation from reusing cached data, since it has no way to know or control when the application modifies it. A number of vendor-specific extensions have been implemented to make caching possible, such as NV_vertex_array_range and ATI_vertex_array_object. This has culminated in a cross-vendor extension ARB_vertex_buffer_object, integrated into the core specification as part of OpenGL 1.5.

Display lists are another mechanism allowing the implementation to cache vertex data close to the hardware. Since the application doesn't have access to the data after the display list is compiled, the implementation has more opportunities to optimize the representation and move it closer to the hardware. The requirement to change the OpenGL state as the result of display list execution can limit the ability of the OpenGL implementation to optimize stored display list representations, however. Any performance optimizations applied to display list data are implementation dependent. The developer should do performance experiments with display lists, such as segmenting geometry, state changes, and transform commands into separate display lists or saving and restoring transform state in the display list to find the optimal performance modes.

Regardless of how the vertex data is passed to the implementation, using vertex representations with a small memory footprint can improve bandwidth. For example, in many cases normals with type GL_UNSIGNED_SHORT will take less transfer time than normals with GL_FLOAT components, and be precise enough to generate acceptable results. Minimizing the number of vertex parameters, such as avoiding use of glTexCoord through the use of texture coordinate generation, also reduces vertex memory footprint and improves bandwidth utilization.

21.1.3 Texture Updates

Like vertex updates, texture updates can significantly influence overall performance, and should be optimized by the application. Unlike vertex updates, OpenGL has always had good support for caching texture data close to the hardware. Instead of finding ways to cache texture data, the application's main task becomes managing texture updates efficiently. A key approach is to incrementally update textures, spreading the update load over multiple frames whenever possible. This reduces the peak bandwidth requirements of the application. Two good candidates for incremental loads are mipmapped textures, and large "terrain" textures. For many applications, only parts of these types of textures are visible at any given time.

A mipmapped textured object often first comes into view at some distance from the viewer. Usually only coarser mipmap levels are required to texture it at first. As the object and viewer move closer to each other, progressively finer mipmap levels are used. An application can take advantage of this behavior by loading coarser mipmap levels first and then progressively loading finer levels over a series of frames. Since coarser levels are low resolution, they take very little bandwidth to load. If the application doesn't have the bandwidth available to load finer levels fast enough as the object approaches, the coarser levels provide a reasonable fallback.

Many large textures have only a portion of their texture maps visible at any given time. In the case where a texture has higher resolution than the screen, it is impossible to show the entire texture at level 0, even if it is viewed on edge. An edge on a non-mipmapped texture will be only coarsely sampled (not displaying most of its texels) and will show aliasing artifacts. Even a mipmapped texture will blur down to coarser texture levels with distance, leaving only part of level 0 (the region closest to the viewer) used to render the texture.

This restriction can be used to structure large texture maps, so that only the visible region and a small ring of texture data surrounding it have to be loaded into texture memory at any given time. It breaks up a large texture image into a grid of uniform texture tiles, and takes advantage of the properties of wrapped texture coordinates. Section 14.6 describes this technique, called *texture paging*, in greater detail.

21.2 Managing Frame Time

An interactive graphics application has to perform three major tasks: receive new input from the user, perform the calculations necessary to draw a new frame, and send update and rendering instructions to the hardware. Some applications, such as those used to simulate vehicles or sophisticated games, have very demanding latency and performance requirements. In these applications, it can be more important to maintain a constant frame rate than to update as fast as possible. A varying frame rate can undermine the realism of the simulation, and even lead to "simulator sickness," causing the viewer to become nauseous. Since these demanding applications are often used to simulate an interactive visual world, they are often called visual simulation (a.k.a. "vissim") applications.

Vissim applications often have calculation and rendering loads that can vary significantly per frame. For example, a user may pan across the scene to a region of high depth complexity that requires significantly more time to compute and render. To maintain a constant frame rate, these applications are allotted a fixed amount of time to update a scene. This time budget must always be met, regardless of where the viewer is in the scene, or the direction the viewer is looking. There are two ways to satisfy this requirement. One approach is to statically limit the geometry and texture data used in the application while the application is being written. Typically, these limits have to be severe in order to handle the worst case. It can also be difficult to guarantee there is no view position in the scene that will take too long to render. A more flexible approach is for the application to dynamically restrict the amount of rendering work, controlling the amount of time needed to draw each frame as the application is running. Rendering time can be managed by simplifying or skipping work in the generation and traversal stages and controlling the number and type of OpenGL commands sent to the hardware during the rendering stage.

There are three components to frame time management: accurately measuring the time it takes to draw each frame, adjusting the amount of work performed to draw the current frame (based on the amount of time it took to draw previous frames), and maintaining a *safety margin* of idle time at the end of all frames in order to handle variations. In essence, the rendering algorithm uses a feedback loop, adjusting the amount of rendering work from the time it took to draw the previous frames, adjusting to maintain a constant amount of idle time each frame (see Figure 21.3).

This frame management approach requires that the work a graphics application does each frame is ordered in a particular way. There are two criteria: critical work must be ordered so that it is always performed and the OpenGL commands must be started as early as possible. In visual simulation applications, taking into account the user input and using it to update the viewer's position and orientation are likely to be the highest-priority tasks. In a flight simulation application, for example, it is critical that the view out of the windshield respond accurately and quickly to pilot inputs. It would be better to drop distant frame geometry than to inconsistently render the viewer's position. Therefore, reading input must be done consistently every frame.

Starting OpenGL commands early in the frame requires that this task be handled next. This is done to maximize parallelism. Most graphics hardware implementations are pipelined, so a command may complete asynchronously some time after it is sent. A visual simulation application can issue all of its commands, and then start the computation work necessary to draw the next frame while the OpenGL commands are still being rendered in the graphics hardware. This ordering provides some parallelism between graphics hardware and the CPU, increasing the work that can be done each frame. This is why calculations for the next frame are done at the end of the current frame.

Because of parallelism, there are two ways frame time can be exceeded: too many OpenGL commands have been issued (causing the hardware to take too long to draw the frame) or the calculation phase can take too long, exceeding the frame time and interfering with the work that needs to be completed during the next frame. Having the

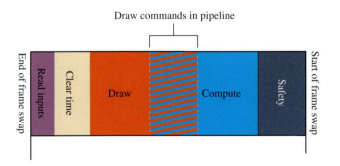

Figure 21.3 Frame time management.

calculation phase happen last makes it easier to avoid both problems. The amount of idle time left during the previous frame can be used to adjust the amount of OpenGL work to schedule for the next frame. The amount of time left in the current frame can be used to adjust the amount of calculation work that should be done. Note that using the previous frame's idle time to compute the next frame's OpenGL work introduces two frames of *latency*. This is necessary because the OpenGL pipeline may not complete its current rendering early enough for the calculation phase to measure the idle time.

Based on the previous criteria, the application should divide the work required to draw a scene into three main phases. At the start of each frame (after the buffer swap) the application should read the user inputs (and ideally use them to update the viewer's position and orientation), send the OpenGL commands required to render the current frame, and perform the calculations needed to render the next frame. Note that the calculations done at the end of a given frame will affect the *next* frame, since the OpenGL commands rendering the current frame have already been issued. Ideally, these calculations are ordered so that low-priority ones can be skipped to stay within one frame time. The following sections describe each of the these three rendering phases in more detail.

21.2.1 Input Phase

The user input is read early in the frame, since updating input consistently is critical. It is important that the view position and orientation match the user input with as little "lag" as possible, so it is ideal if the user input is used to update the viewer position in the current frame. Fortunately, this is usually a fast operation, involving little more than reading control input positions and updating the modelview (and possibly the projection) transform. If multiple processors are available, or if the implementation of `glClear` is nonblocking, this task (and possibly other nongraphics work) can be accomplished while the framebuffer is being cleared at the beginning of the frame. If immediately updating the viewer position is not low cost, due to the structure of the program, another option is to use the input to update the viewer position during the start of the computation phase. This adds a single frame of latency to the input response, which is often acceptable. Some input latency is acceptable in a visual simulation application, as long as it is small and consistent. It can be a worthwhile trade-off if it starts the rendering phase sooner.

21.2.2 Rendering Phase

Once the user inputs are handled properly, the rendering phase should begin as early as possible. During this phase, the application issues the texture loads, geometry updates, and state changes needed to draw the scene. This task is a significant percentage of the total time needed to draw a frame, and it needs to be measured accurately. This can be done by issuing a `glFinish` as the last command and measuring the time from the start of the first command to the time the `glFinish` command completes. Since this is a synchronous operation, the thread executing this command stalls waiting for the hardware to finish.

To maintain parallelism, the application issuing the OpenGL commands is usually in a separate execution thread. Its task is to issue a precomputed list of OpenGL commands, and measure the time it takes to draw them.

There are a number of ways to adjust the amount of time it takes to complete the rendering phase. The number of objects in the scene can be reduced, starting with the smallest and least conspicuous ones. Smaller, coarser textures can also be used, as well as restricting the number of texture LODs in use to just the coarser ones, saving the overhead of loading the finer ones. A single texture can be used to replace a number of similar ones. More complex time-saving techniques, such as geometry LOD, can also be used (see Section 16.4 for details on this technique).

21.2.3 Computation Phase

Ideally, every frame should start with the calculations necessary to create and configure the OpenGL rendering commands already completed. This minimizes the latency before the rendering pass can start. The computation phase performs this task ahead of time. After the rendering commands for a frame have been sent, the remaining frame time is used to perform the computations needed for the next frame. As mentioned previously, a multithreaded application can take advantage of hardware pipelining to overlap some of the rendering phase with the start of the computation phase. Care must be taken to ensure that the start of the calculation phase doesn't steal cycles from the rendering thread. It must submit all of its OpenGL commands as early as possible.

This restriction may be relaxed in a multiprocessor or hyperthreading system. If it doesn't impact the rendering work, the computation and rendering phases can start at the same time, allowing more computation to be done per frame.

There might not be enough time in the computation phase to perform all calculations. In this case, some computations will have to be deferred. In general, some computations must be done every frame, others will have a lower priority and be done less often. In order to decide which computations are less important, they can be sorted based on how they affect the scene. Computations can be categorized by how viewer dependent they are. Viewer dependence is a measure of how strongly correlated the computation is to viewer position and orientation. The more viewer dependent a computation is the more sensitive it is to stale input, and the more likely it will produce incorrect results if it is deferred. The most viewer-dependent computations are those that generate viewer position transforms. The time between when the user inputs are read and the time these computations are updated should be kept small, no more than one or two frames. Significant latency between updates will be noticeable to the user, and can impact the effectiveness of the visual simulation application.

On the other hand, many calculations are only weakly viewer dependent. Calculations such as geometric LOD (Section 16.4), some types of scene graph updates, view culling, and so on can affect rendering efficiency, but only change the rendered scene slightly if they are computed with stale input values. This type of work can be computed less often in order to meet frame time constraints.

As with all phases of frame updates, a visual simulation application should use all of the computation time available without compromising the frame rate. Since there can be some latency between the time the buffer swap command is called and the next frame refresh, an application can potentially use that time to do additional computations. This time is available if the implementation provides a nonblocking swap command, or if the swap command is executed in a thread separate from the one doing the computation.

21.2.4 The Safety Margin

Like the rendering phase, the calculation phase has to be managed to maintain a constant frame rate. As with rendering, this is done by prioritizing the work to be done, and stopping when the time slice runs out. If the calculations run even a little too long, the frame swap will be missed, resulting in a noticeable change in update rate (see Section 21.3.3 for details on this phenomenon). Not all calculation or rendering work is fine grained, so a *safety margin* (a period of dead time) is reserved for the end of each frame. If the rendering and calculation phases become long enough to start to significantly reduce the amount of safety margin time, the amount of work done in the next frame is cut back. If the work completes early, increasing the amount of safety margin time, the work load is incrementally increased. This creates a feedback loop, where the per-frame is adjusted to match the changing amount of rendering and calculating needed to be done to render the current view.

21.3 Application Performance Tuning

Any graphics application that has high performance requirements will require performance tuning. Graphics pipeline implementations, whether they are hardware or software based, have too many implementation-specific variations to make it possible to skip a tuning step. The rendering performance of the application must be measured, the bottlenecks found, and the application adjusted to fix them.

Maximizing the performance of a graphics application is all about finding bottlenecks; i.e., localized regions of the application code that are restricting performance. Like debugging an application, locating and understanding bottlenecks is usually more difficult than fixing them. This section begins by discussing common bottlenecks in graphics applications and some useful techniques for fixing them. It also discusses ways of measuring applications so that their performance characteristics are understood and their bottlenecks are identified. Multithreaded OpenGL applications are also discussed, including some common threading architectures that can improve an application's performance.

21.3.1 Locating Bottlenecks

As mentioned previously, tuning an application is the process of finding and removing bottlenecks. A bottleneck is a localized region of software that can limit the performance of the entire application. Since these regions are usually only a small part of the overall application, and not always obvious, it's rarely productive to simply tune parts of the application that appear "slow" from code inspection. Bottlenecks should be found by measuring (benchmarking) the application and analyzing the results.

In traditional application tuning, finding bottlenecks in software involves looking for "inner loops," the regions of code most often executed when the program is running. Optimizing this type of bottleneck is important, but graphics tuning also requires knowledge of the graphics pipeline and its likely bottlenecks. The graphics pipeline consists of three conceptual stages. Except for some very low-end systems, it's common today for all or part of the last two stages to be accelerated in hardware. In order to achieve maximum performance, the pipeline must be "balanced" — each stage of the pipeline must be working at full capacity.

This is not always easy to do, since each stage of the pipeline tends to produce more output for the following stage than it received from the previous one. When designing hardware, pipeline stages are sized to handle this amplification of work for "typical" cases, but the amount of work produced in each stage depends on the command stream that the application sends to the hardware. The stages are rarely in balance unless the application has been performance tuned.

The conceptual pipeline subsystems are:

* The **application subsystem** (i.e., the application itself) feeds the OpenGL implementation by issuing commands to the geometry subsystem.

* The **geometry subsystem** performs per-vertex operations such as coordinate transformations, lighting, texture coordinate generation, and clipping. The processed vertices are assembled into primitives and sent to the raster subsystem.

* The **raster subsystem** performs per-pixel operations — from simple operations such as writing color values into the framebuffer, to more complex operations such as texture mapping, depth buffering, and alpha blending.

To illustrate how the amount of work done by each pipeline stage depends on the application, consider a program that draws a small number of large polygons. Since there are only a few polygons, the geometry subsystem is only lightly loaded. However, those few polygons cover many pixels on the screen, so the load on the raster subsystem is much higher. If the raster subsystem can't process the triangles as fast as the geometry subsystem is feeding them, the raster subsystem becomes a bottleneck. Note that this imbalance cannot be determined solely from static analysis of the application. Many graphics systems have very powerful raster engines. The hypothesis that the raster subsystem is limiting the speed of the program must be proved through benchmarking and performance experiments.

To avoid a rasterization bottleneck, the work between the geometry and rasterization stages must be balanced. One way to do this is to reduce the work done in the raster subsystem. This can be done by turning off modes such as texturing, blending, or depth buffering. Alternatively, since spare capacity is available in the geometry subsystem more work can be performed there without degrading performance. A more complex lighting model could be used, or objects can be tessellated more finely to create a more accurate geometric model.

21.3.2 Finding Application Bottlenecks

Graphics bottlenecks can usually be fixed by rebalancing the pipeline stages, but the more difficult part is determining where the bottleneck is located. The performance of each pipeline stage depends on the design of the OpenGL hardware and software, and the pattern of commands being processed. The resulting performance characteristics can be quite complex. Additional complexity can result because a bottleneck in an early stage of the pipeline can change the behavior of later stages.

The basic strategy for isolating bottlenecks is to measure the time it takes to execute part or all of the program and then change the code in ways that add or subtract work at a single point in the graphics pipeline. If changing the amount of work done by a given stage does not alter performance appreciably, that stage is not the bottleneck. Conversely, a noticeable difference in performance indicates a bottleneck. Since bottlenecks early in the pipeline can mask later ones, check for early bottlenecks first. Table 21.1 provides an overview of factors that may limit rendering performance, and names the part of the pipeline to which they belong.

Application Subsystem Bottlenecks

The first potential bottleneck can come if the application doesn't issue OpenGL commands to the hardware fast enough. To measure the performance of the application accurately, the OpenGL calls can be "stubbed out." Stubbing out an OpenGL call means using an empty function call in place of the real OpenGL command. The application with stubs can then be benchmarked to measure its maximum performance.

To get an accurate assessment of the application's performance, the behavior of the application should be preserved by attempting to keep the number of instructions executed and the way memory is accessed unchanged. Since some OpenGL commands are used

Table 21.1 Factors Influencing Performance

Performance Parameter	Pipeline Stage
Amount of data per polygon	All stages
Application overhead	Application
Transform rate and geometry mode setting	Geometry subsystem
Total number of polygons in a frame	Geometry and raster subsystem
Number of pixels filled	Raster subsystem
Fill rate for the current mode settings	Raster subsystem
Duration of screen and/or depth buffer clear	Raster subsystem

much more often than others, stubbing just a few key commands may be sufficient. For example, if the application uses `glBegin`/`glEnd` sequences to render geometry, replacing the vertex and normal calls `glVertex3fv` and `glNormal3fv` with color subroutine calls (`glColor3fv`) preserves the CPU behavior while eliminating all drawing and lighting work in the graphics pipeline. If making these changes does not significantly improve the time taken to render a frame, the application is the bottleneck.

On many faster hardware accelerators, the bus between the CPU and the graphics hardware can limit the number of polygons sent from the application to the geometry subsystems. To test for this bottleneck, reduce the amount of data being sent per vertex. For example, if removing color and normal parameters from the vertices shows a speed improvement the bus is probably the bottleneck.

Geometry Subsystem Bottlenecks

Applications that suffer from bottlenecks in the geometry subsystem are said to be *transform limited* (or sometimes *geometry limited*). To test for bottlenecks in geometry operations, change the application so that it issues the same number of commands and fills the same number of pixels but reduces the amount of geometry work. For example, if lighting is enabled, call `glDisable` with a `GL_LIGHTING` argument to temporarily turn it off. If performance improves, the application has a geometry bottleneck. Transformation and clipping performance can be measured in a similar fashion. All transforms can be set to identity, and all application-defined clipping planes can be disabled. Geometry can also be altered so that no clipping is needed to render it. Measuring geometry performance with this method can be tricky. Some hardware implementations are configured to run full speed over a wide range of geometry configurations, and changes to the geometry subsystem can inadvertently change the load of the raster subsystem. Understanding the hardware's performance profile is important in avoiding fruitless attempts to tune geometry processing.

Rasterization Subsystem Bottlenecks

Applications that cause bottlenecks at the rasterization (per-pixel) stage in the pipeline are said to be *fill limited*. To test for bottlenecks in rasterization operations, shrink objects or make the window smaller to reduce the number of pixels being processed. This technique will not work if the program alters its behavior based on the sizes of objects or the size of the window. Per-pixel work can also be reduced by turning off operations such as depth buffering, texturing, or alpha blending. If any of these experiments speed up the program, it has a fill bottleneck. Like geometry state changes discussed in the previous section, consider that the hardware implementation may not slow down for certain rasterization state changes.

At the rasterization stage, performance may strongly depend on the type of primitive being rendered. Many programs draw a variety of primitives, each of which stresses a different part of the system. Decompose such a program into homogeneous pieces and time each one separately. After measuring these results, the slowest primitive type can be identified and optimized.

Oversubscribing texture memory resources can also cause significant performance degradation. Texture memory *thrashing* can be tested for by temporarily reducing the number of different textures in use. Other rasterization and fragment processing-related state changes can also adversely affect performance. These can be difficult to locate. Tools that trace and gather statistics on the number and types of OpenGL commands issued each frame can be invaluable in understanding the load generated by an application.

Optimizing Cache and Memory Usage

On most systems, memory is structured in a hierarchy that contains a small amount of fast, expensive memory at the top (e.g., CPU registers) through a series of larger and slower storage caches to a large amount of slow storage at the base (e.g., system memory). As data is referenced, it is automatically copied into higher levels of the hierarchy, so data that is referenced most often migrates to the fastest memory locations.

The goal of machine designers and programmers is to improve the likelihood of finding needed data as high up in this memory hierarchy as possible. To achieve this goal, algorithms for maintaining the hierarchy (embodied in the hardware and the operating system) assume that programs have locality of reference in both time and space. That is, programs are much more likely to access a location that has been accessed recently or is close to another recently accessed location. Performance increases if the application is designed to maximize the degree of locality available at each level in the memory hierarchy.

Minimizing Cache Misses Most CPUs have first-level instruction and data caches on chip. Many also have second-level caches that are bigger but somewhat slower. Memory accesses are much faster if the data is already loaded into the first-level cache. When a program accesses data that is not in one of the caches, a *cache miss* occurs. This causes a block of consecutively addressed words, including the data the program just tried to access, to be loaded into the cache. Since cache misses are costly, they should be minimized. Cache misses can be minimized by using the following techniques.

- Keep frequently accessed data together. Store and access frequently used data in flat, sequential data structures and avoid pointer indirection. This way, the most frequently accessed data remains in the first-level cache as much as possible.

- Access data sequentially. Each cache miss brings in a block of consecutively addressed words of needed data. If the program is accessing data sequentially, each cache miss will bring in n words at a time, improving bandwidth (the exact value of n is system dependent). If only every nth word is accessed (strided access) the cache constantly brings in unneeded data, degrading performance.

- Avoid simultaneously traversing several large buffers of data, such as an array of vertex coordinates and an array of colors within a loop. This behavior can cause cache aliasing between the buffers. Instead, pack the contents into one buffer whenever possible. If the application uses vertex arrays, try to use interleaved arrays.

Some framebuffers have cache-like behaviors as well. The application can utilize this caching by ordering geometry so that drawing the geometry causes writes to adjacent regions of the screen. Using connected primitives such as triangle and line strips tends to create this behavior, and offers other performance advantages by minimizing the number of vertices needed to represent a continuous surface.

Modern graphics accelerators make heavy use of caching for vertex and texture processing. Use of indexed vertex arrays with careful ordering of vertex attributes and indices can substantially improve vertex cache hit rates. Applications have less control over texture cache performance, but programmable fragment programs provide substantial flexibility in how texture coordinates are computed. Dependent texture reads, environment mapping, and other texture coordinate computations can suffer from poor locality.

Storing Data in an Efficient Format The design effort required to create a simpler graphics database can make a significant difference when traversing that data for display. A common tendency is to leave the data in a format that is optimized for loading or generating the object, but suboptimal for actually displaying it. For peak performance, do as much work as possible before rendering. This preprocessing is typically performed when an application can temporarily be noninteractive, such as at initialization time or when changing from a modeling to a fast-rendering mode.

Minimizing State Changes

A graphics application will almost always benefit if the number of state changes is reduced. A good way to do this is to sort scene data according to what state values are set and render primitives with the same state settings together. Mode changes should be ordered so that the most expensive state changes occur least often. Although it can vary widely with implementation, typically it is expensive to change texture binding, material parameters, fog parameters, texture filter modes, and the lighting model.

Measurement is the best way to determine which state settings are most expensive on a particular implementation. On systems that fully accelerate rasterization, for example, it may not be expensive to change rasterization controls such as enabling depth testing or changing the comparison function. On a system using software rasterization, however, these state changes may cause a cached graphics state, such as function pointers or automatically generated code, to be flushed and regenerated.

An OpenGL implementation may not optimize state changes that are redundant, so it is also important for the application to avoid setting the same state values multiple times. Sometimes sorting rendering by state isn't practical, and redundant state changes can result. In these situations, shadowing state changes and discarding (filtering) redundant changes can often improve performance.

21.3.3 Measuring Performance

When benchmarking any application, there are common guidelines that when followed help ensure accurate results. The system used to measure performance should be idle, rather than executing competing activities that could steal system resources from the application being measured. A good system clock should be used for measuring performance with sufficient resolution, low latency, and producing accurate, reproducible results. The measurements themselves should be repeated a number of times to average out atypical measurements. Any significant variation in measurements should be investigated and understood. Beyond these well-known practices, however, are performance techniques and concepts that are specific to computer graphics applications. Some of these fundamental ideas are described in the following, along with their relevance to OpenGL applications.

Video Refresh Quantization

A dynamic graphics application renders a series of frames in sequence, creating animated images. The more frames rendered per second the smoother the motion appears. Smooth, artifact-free animation also requires double buffering. In double buffering, one color buffer holds the current frame, which is scanned out to the display device by video hardware, while the rendering hardware is drawing into a second buffer that is not visible. When the new color buffer is ready to be displayed, the application requests that the buffers be swapped. The swap is delayed until the next vertical retrace period between video frames, so that the update process isn't visible on the screen.

Frame rates must be integral multiples of the screen refresh time, 16.7 msec (milliseconds) for a 60-Hz display. If the rendering time for a frame is slightly longer than the time for n raster scans, the system waits until the $n + 1st$ video period (vertical retrace) before swapping buffers and allowing drawing to continue. This *quantizes* the total frame time to multiples of the display refresh rate. For a 60-Hz refresh rate, frame times are quantized to $(n + 1) * 16.7$ msec. This means even significant improvements in performance may not be noticeable if the saving is less than that of a display refresh interval.

Quantization makes performance tuning more difficult. First, quantizing can mask most of the details of performance improvements. Performance gains are often the sum of many small improvements, which are found by making changes to the program and measuring the results. Quantizing may hide those results, making it impossible to notice program changes that are having a small but positive effect. Quantizing also establishes a minimum barrier to making performance gains that will be visible to the user. Imagine an application running fast enough to support a 40-fps refresh rate. It will never run faster than 30 fps on a 60-Hz display until it has been optimized to run at 60 fps, almost double its original rate. Table 21.2 lists the quantized frame times for multiples of a 60-Hz frame.

To accurately measure the results of performance changes, quantization should be turned off. This can be done by rendering to a single-buffered color buffer. Besides making it possible to see the results of performance changes, single-buffering performance also

Table 21.2 60-Hz Rate Quantization

Frame Multiple	Rate (Hz)	Interval (ms)
1	60	16.67
2	30	33.33
3	20	50
4	15	66.67
5	12	83.33
6	10	100
7	8.6	116.67
8	7.5	133.33
9	6.7	150
10	6	166.67

shows how close the application's update rate is to a screen refresh boundary. This is useful in determining how much more improvement is necessary before it becomes visible in a double-buffered application. Double buffering is enabled again after all performance tuning has been completed.

Quantization can sometimes be taken advantage of in application tuning. If an application's single-buffered frame rate is not close to the next multiple of a screen refresh interval, and if the current quantized rate is adequate, the application can be modified to do additional work, improving visual quality without visibly changing performance. In essence, the time interval between frame completion and the next screen refresh is being wasted, which it can be used instead to produce a richer image.

Finish Versus Flush

Modern hardware implementations of OpenGL often queue graphics commands to improve bandwidth. Understanding and controlling this process is important for accurate benchmarking and maximizing performance in interactive applications.

When an OpenGL implementation uses queuing, the pipeline is buffered. Incoming commands are accumulated into a buffer, where they may be stored for some period of time before rendering. Some queuing pipelines use the notion of a *high water mark*, deferring rendering until a given buffer has exceeded some threshold, so that commands can be rendered in a bandwidth-efficient manner. Queuing can allow some parallelism between the system and the graphics hardware: the application can fill the pipeline's buffer with new commands while the hardware is rendering previous commands. If the pipeline's buffer fills, the application can do other work while the hardware renders its backlog of commands.

The process of emptying the pipeline of its buffered commands is called *flushing*. In many applications, particularly interactive ones, the application may not supply commands in a steady stream. In these cases, the pipeline buffer can stay partially filled for long period of time, not rendering any more commands to hardware even if the graphics hardware is completely idle.

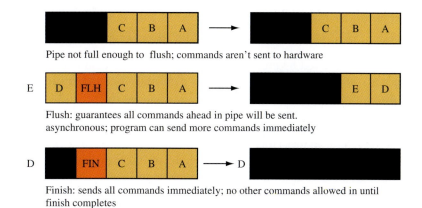

Pipe not full enough to flush; commands aren't sent to hardware

Flush: guarantees all commands ahead in pipe will be sent.
asynchronous; program can send more commands immediately

Finish: sends all commands immediately; no other commands allowed in until
finish completes

Figure 21.4 Finish versus flush.

This situation can be a problem for interactive applications. If some graphics commands are left in the buffer when the application stops rendering to wait for input, the user will see an incomplete image. The application needs a way of indicating that the buffer should be emptied, even if it isn't full. OpenGL provides the command glFlush to perform this operation. The command is asynchronous, returning immediately. It guarantees that outstanding buffers will be flushed and the pipeline will complete rendering, but doesn't provide a way to indicate exactly when the flush will complete.

The glFlush command is inadequate for graphics benchmarking, which needs to measure the duration between the issuing of the first command and the completion of the last. The glFinish command provides this functionality. It flushes the pipeline, but doesn't return until all commands sent before the finish have completed. The difference between finish and flush is illustrated in Figure 21.4

To benchmark a piece of graphics code, call glFinish at the end of the timing trial, just before sampling the clock for an end time. The glFinish command should also be called *before* sampling the clock for the start time, to ensure no graphics calls remain in the graphics queue ahead of the commands being benchmarked.

While glFinish ensures that every previous command has been rendered, it should be used with care. A glFinish call disrupts the parallelism the pipeline buffer is designed to achieve. No more commands can be sent to the hardware until the glFinish command completes. The glFlush command is the preferred method of ensuring that the pipeline renders all pending commands, since it does so without disrupting the pipeline's parallelism.

21.3.4 Measuring Depth Complexity

Measuring depth complexity, or the number of fragments that were generated for each pixel in a rendered scene, is important for analyzing rasterization performance. It indicates how polygons are distributed across the framebuffer and how many fragments were generated and discarded — clues for application tuning. Depending on the performance details of the OpenGI implementation, depth complexity analysis can help illustrate problems that can be solved by presorting geometry, adding a visibility culling pass, or structuring parts of the scene to use a painters algorithm for hidden surface removal instead of depth testing.

One way to visualize depth complexity is to use the color values of the pixels in the scene to indicate the number of times a pixel is written. It is easy to do this using the stencil buffer. The basic approach is simple: increment a pixel's stencil value every time the pixel is written. When the scene is finished, read back the stencil buffer and display it in the color buffer, color coding the different stencil values.

The stencil buffer can be set to increment every time a fragment is sent to a pixel by setting the *zfail* and *zpass* parameters of glStencilOp to GL_INCR, and setting the *func* argument of glStencilFunc to GL_ALWAYS. This technique creates a count of the number of fragments generated for each pixel, irrespective of the results of the depth test. If the *zpass* argument to glStencilOp is changed to GL_KEEP instead (the setting of the *fail* argument doesn't matter, since the stencil function is still set to GL_ALWAYS), the stencil buffer can be used to count the number of fragments discarded after failing the depth test. In another variation, changing *zpass* to GL_INCR, and *zfail* to GL_KEEP, the stencil buffer will count the number of times a pixel was rewritten by fragments passing the depth test. The following is a more detailed look at the first method, which counts the number of fragments sent to a particular pixel.

1. Clear the depth and stencil buffer:
    glClear(GL_STENCIL_BUFFER_BIT | GL_DEPTH_BUFFER_BIT).

2. Enable stenciling:
    glEnable(GL_STENCIL_TEST).

3. Set up the proper stencil parameters:
    glStencilFunc(GL_ALWAYS, 0, 0) and glStencilOp(GL_KEEP, GL_INCR, GL_INCR).

4. Draw the scene.

5. Read back the stencil buffer with glReadPixels, using GL_STENCIL_INDEX as the format argument.

6. Draw the stencil buffer to the screen using glDrawPixels, with GL_COLOR_INDEX as the format argument.

The glPixelMap command can be used to map stencil values to colors. The stencil values can be mapped to either RGBA or color index values, depending on the type of color buffer. Color index images require mapping colors with glPixelTransferi, using the arguments GL_MAP_COLOR and GL_TRUE.

Note that this technique is limited by the range of values of the stencil buffer (0 to 255 for an 8-bit stencil buffer). If the maximum value is exceeded, the value will clamp. Related methods include using framebuffer blending with destination alpha as the counter, but this requires that the application not use framebuffer blending for other purposes.

21.3.5 Pipeline Interleaving

OpenGL has been specified with multithreaded applications in mind by allowing one or more separate rendering threads to be created for any given process. Thread programming in OpenGL involves work in the OpenGL interface library. This means GLX, WGL, or other interface library calls are needed. Each rendering thread has a single *context* associated with it. The context holds the graphics state of the thread. A context can be disconnected from one thread and attached to another. The target framebuffer of the rendering thread is sometimes called its *drawable*. There can be multiple threads rendering to a single drawable. For more information on the role of threads in the OpenGL interface libraries, see Section 7.2, which describes the interactions of the interface libraries in more detail.

Each thread can be thought of as issuing a separate stream of rendering commands to a drawable. OpenGL does not guarantee that the ordering of the streams of different threads is maintained. Every time a different thread starts rendering, the previous commands sent by other threads may be interleaved with commands from the new thread. However, if a context is released from one thread and attached to another; any pending commands from the old thread are applied before any commands coming from the new one.

Providing general guidelines for multithreaded programming is beyond the scope of this book. There are two common thread architectures, however, that are particularly useful for OpenGL applications and bear mentioning.

The first is the pipeline model. In this model, the application divides its graphics work into a series of pipeline stages, connected by queues. For example, one or more threads might update a scene graph, and one or more may be traversing it, pushing drawing commands into a queue. A single rendering thread can then read each command from the queue, and make the appropriate OpenGL calls. This model is useful for scene-graph-oriented applications, and is easy to understand. A variant of this model, used to optimize visual simulation applications, is discussed briefly in Section 21.3. In the visual simulation example, rendering is kept in a separate thread to allow parallelism between rendering work and the computations needed to render the next frame.

The other model is a parallel rendering model. This model has multiple rendering threads. Each rendering thread is receiving commands from a central source, such as a scene graph or other database, rendering to separate drawables or separate regions within a drawable. This model is useful if the application is rendering multiple separate versions of the same data, such as a modeling program that renders multiple views of the data. However, care must be taken to ensure that rendering commands such as window clears do not affect overlapping parts of the window. Both the pipeline and parallel rendering models are illustrated in Figure 21.5.

Pipeline model: work divided among threads arranged serially to update a region of screen

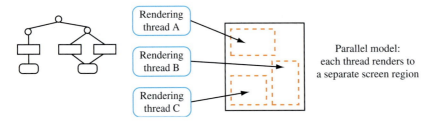

Figure 21.5 Multiple thread rendering models.

In either case, creating a multiple-thread model is only useful in certain situations. The most obvious case is where the system supports multiple CPUs, or one or more "hyperthreaded" ones. A hypertheaded CPU is a single physical CPU that is designed to act as if it contains multiple "virtual" processors. Even a single nonhyperthreaded CPU system can benefit from threading if it is possible for one or more tasks to be stalled waiting for data or user input. If the application splits the tasks into individual threads, the application can continue to do useful work even if some of its threads are stalled. Common cases where a rendering thread may stall are during a screen clear, or while waiting for a `glFinish` command to complete.

21.4 Summary

This chapter provided a background and an introduction to the techniques of graphics performance tuning. While there are many graphics-specific details covered here, the main idea is simple: create experiments and measure the results. Computer graphics hardware is complex and evolving. It's not practical to make assumptions about its performance characteristics. This is true whether writing a fixed-function OpenGL program or writing vertex or fragment programs. Reading all of the performance documentation available on a particular vendor's hardware accelerator and OpenGL implementation is still useful however. It can make your guesses more educated and help to target performance tuning experiments more accurately.

Using OpenGL Extensions

By design, OpenGL implementors are free to extend OpenGL's basic rendering functionality with new rendering operations. This extensibility was one of OpenGL's original design goals. As a result, scores of OpenGL extensions have been specified and implemented. These extensions provide OpenGL application developers with new rendering features above and beyond the features specified in the official OpenGL standard. OpenGL extensions keep the OpenGL API current with the latest innovations in graphics hardware and rendering algorithms.

This appendix describes the OpenGL extension mechanism. It describes how extensions are used and documented as well as how to use extensions portably in applications. Particular attention is paid to using OpenGL extensions in the Win32 and UNIX environments.

A.1 How OpenGL Extensions are Documented

An OpenGL extension is defined by its specification. These specifications are typically written as standard ASCII text files. OpenGL extension specifications are written by and for OpenGL implementors. A well-written OpenGL specification is documented to the level of detail needed for a hardware designer and/or OpenGL library engineer to implement the extension unambiguously. This means that OpenGL application programmers should not expect an extension's specification to justify fully why the functionality exists or explain how an OpenGL application would go about using it. An OpenGL extension specification is not a tutorial on how to use the particular extension. Still, being able to read and understand an OpenGL extension specification helps the application programmer fully understand an OpenGL extension's functionality.

A.2 Finding OpenGL Extension Specifications

The latest public OpenGL specifications can be found on the *www.opengl.org* web site. Note that extension specifications are updated from time to time based on reviews and implementation feedback. In the case of certain proprietary OpenGL extensions, it may be necessary to contact the OpenGL vendor that developed the extension for the extension's specification.

A.3 How to Read an OpenGL Extension Specification

When reading an OpenGL extension specification, it helps to be familiar with the original OpenGL specification. The operation of an OpenGL extension is described as additions and changes to the core OpenGL specification. Having a copy of the core OpenGL specification handy is a good idea when reviewing an OpenGL extension.

OpenGL extension specifications consist of multiple sections. There is a common form established by convention that is used by nearly all OpenGL extensions. Often within a specification, the `gl` and `GL` prefixes on routine names and tokens are assumed. The following describes the purpose of the most common sections in the order they normally appear in extension specifications.

Name: Lists the official name of the extension. This name uses underscores instead of spaces between words. The name also begins with a prefix that indicates who developed the extension. This prefix helps to avoid naming conflicts if two independent groups implement a similar extension. It also helps identity who is promoting use of the extension. For example, `SGIS_point_parameters` was an extension proposed by Silicon Graphics. The `SGIS` prefix belongs to Silicon Graphics. SGI uses the `SGIS` prefix to indicate that the extension is specialized and may not be available on all SGI hardware. Other prefixes in use are:

ARB: Extensions officially approved by the OpenGL Architectural Review Board

EXT: Extensions agreed upon by multiple OpenGL vendors

APPLE: Apple Computer

ATI: ATI Technologies

ES: Evans and Sutherland

HP: Hewlett-Packard

IBM: International Business Machines

INTEL: Intel

KTX: Kinetix (maker of 3D Studio Max)

MESA: Brian Paul's freeware portable OpenGL implementation

NV: NVIDIA Corporation

OES: OpenGL ES, OpenGL for Embedded Systems

SGI: Silicon Graphics

SGIS: Silicon Graphics (limited set of machines)

SGIX: Silicon Graphics (experimental)

SUN: Sun Microsystems

WIN: Microsoft

Note that the `SGIS_point_parameters` extension has since been standardized by other OpenGL vendors. Now there is also an `EXT_point_parameters` extension with the same basic functionality as the `SGIS` version. The `EXT` prefix indicates that multiple vendors have agreed to support the extension. Successful OpenGL extensions are often promoted to `EXT` or `ARB` extensions or made an official part of OpenGL in a future revision to the core OpenGL specification. In fact, the point parameters extension was moved into the core in OpenGL 1.4. Almost all of the new functionality in OpenGL 1.1 through 1.5 appeared first as OpenGL extensions.

Name Strings: Name strings are used to indicate that the extension is supported by a given OpenGL implementation. Applications can query the `GL_EXTENSIONS` string with the OpenGL `glGetString` command to determine what extensions are available. OpenGL also supports the idea of window-system-dependent extensions. Core OpenGL extension name strings are generally prefixed with `GL_`, while window-system-dependent extensions are prefixed with `GLX_` for the X Window System or `WGL_` for Win32 based on the platform embedding to which the extension applies. Note that there may be multiple strings if the extension provides both core OpenGL rendering functionality and window-system-dependent functionality.

In the case of the X Window System, support for GLX extensions is indicated by listing the GLX extension name in the string returned by `glXQueryExtensionsString`. Querying the core OpenGL extension string requires that an OpenGL rendering context be created and made current (calling `glGetString` assumes a current OpenGL context). However, using `glXQueryExtensionString` only requires a connection to an X server. Because the X Window System is client/server based, the OpenGL client library may support different extensions than the OpenGL server. For this reason, it is also possible to query the extensions supported by the client or server individually using `glXQueryClientString` and `glXQueryServerString`, respectively. To actually use most GLX extensions, a GLX extension must be supported by both the OpenGL client and server, but it is possible for an extension to be a pure client-side extension. For this reason, the strings returned by `glXQueryClientString` and `glXQueryServerString` are intended for informational use only. The string returned by `glXQueryExtensionString` is typically an intersection of the extensions supported by both the client and server. This is the string that should be checked before using a GLX extension. There is not a separate mechanism to discover WGL extensions. Instead, WGL extensions are advertised through OpenGL's core extension string, the one returned by `glGetString`.

Version: A source code control revision string to keep track of what version of the specification the given text file represents. It is important to refer to the latest version of the extension specification in case there are any important changes. Normally the version string has the date the extension was last updated.

Number: Each OpenGL extension is assigned a unique number. Silicon Graphics (who owns the OpenGL trademark) allocates these numbers to ensure that OpenGL extensions do not overlap in their usage of enumerants or protocol tokens. This number is only important to extension implementors.

Dependencies: Often an extension specification builds on the functionality of preexisting extensions. This section documents other extensions upon which the specified extension depends. Dependencies indicate that another extension "is required" to support the specified extension or that the specified extension "affects" the specification of another extension. When an extension affects the specification of another extension, the affecting extension is responsible for fully documenting the interactions between the two extensions.

The dependencies section often also indicates which version of the OpenGL core standard the extension specification is based on. Later sections specify the extension based on updates to the relevant section of this particular OpenGL specification. The importance of a given extension to the evolution of OpenGL can be inferred from how many other extensions are listed that depend on or are affected by the given extension.

Overview: The section provides a description, often terse and without justification, for the extension's specified functionality. This section is the closest to describing "what the extension does."

Issues: Often there are issues that need to be resolved in the specification of an extension. This section documents open issues and states the resolution to closed issues. These issues are often things of interest to the extension implementor, but can also help a programmer understand details regarding how the extension really works.

New Procedures and Functions: This section lists the function prototypes for any new procedures and functions the extension adds. The specifications often leave out the `gl` prefix when discussing commands. Also note that the extension's new functions will be suffixed with the same letters used as the prefix for the extension name.

New Tokens: This section lists the tokens (also called enumerants) the extension adds. The commands that accept each set of new enumerants are documented. The integer values of the enumerants are documented here. These values should be added to `<GL/gl.h>`. Keep in mind that specifications often leave out the `GL_` prefix when discussing enumerants. Also note that the extension's new enumerants will be suffixed with the same letters used as the prefix for the extension name.

Additions to Chapter *XX* of the 1.*X* Specification (*XXX*): These sections document how the core OpenGL specification should be amended to add the extension's functionality to the core OpenGL functionality. Note that the exact version of the core OpenGL specification (such as 1.0, 1.1, or 1.2) is documented. The chapters typically amended by an extension specification are:

- Chapter 2, OpenGL Operations

- Chapter 3, Rasterization

- Chapter 4, Per-fragment Operations and the Framebuffer

- Chapter 5, Special Functions

- Chapter 6, State and State Requests

- Appendix A, Invariance

These sections are quite formal. They indicate precisely how the OpenGL specification wording should be amended or changed. Often tables within the specification are amended as well.

Additions to the GLX Specification: If an extension has any window-system-dependent functionality affecting the GLX interface to the X Window System, these issues are documented here.

GLX Protocol: When implementing the extension for the X Window System, if any special X11 extension protocol for the GLX extension is required to support the extension the protocol are documented in this section. This section is only interesting to GLX protocol implementors because the GLX protocol is hidden from application programmers beneath the OpenGL API.

Dependencies on *XXX*: These sections describe how the extension depends on some other extension listed in the *Dependencies* section. Usually the wording says that if the other extension is not supported simply ignore the portion of this extension dealing with the dependent extension's state and functionality.

Errors: If the extension introduces any new error conditions particular to the extension, they are documented here.

New State: Extensions typically add new state variables to OpenGL's state machine. These new variables are documented in this section. The variable's get enumerant, type, get command, initial value, description, section of the specification describing the state variable's function, and attribute group the state belongs to are all documented in tables in this section.

New Implementation-dependent State: Extensions may add implementation-dependent state. These are typically maximum and minimum supported ranges for the extension functionality (such as the widest line size supported by the extension). These values can be queried through OpenGL's `glGet` family of commands.

Backward Compatibility: If the extension supersedes an older extension, issues surrounding backward compatibility with the older extension are documented in this section.

Note that these sections are merely established by convention. While the conventions for OpenGL extension specifications are normally followed, extensions vary in how closely they stick to the conventions. Generally, the more preliminary an extension is the more loosely specified it is. Usually after sufficient review and implementation the specification language and format is improved to provide an unambiguous final specification.

A.3.1 ARB Extensions

The current (as of the OpenGL 1.5 release) set of ARB extensions is as shown here

OpenGL Extensions: `ARB_multitexture`, `ARB_transpose_matrix`, `ARB_multisample`, `ARB_texture_env_add`, `ARB_texture_cube_map`, `ARB_texture_compression`, `ARB_texture_border_clamp`, `ARB_point_parameters`, `ARB_vertex_blend`, `ARB_matrix_palette`, `ARB_texture_env_combine`, `ARB_texture_env_crossbar`, `ARB_texture_env_dot3`, `ARB_texture_mirrored_repeat`, `ARB_depth_texture`, `ARB_shadow`, `ARB_shadow_ambient`, `ARB_window_pos`, `ARB_vertex_program`, `ARB_fragment_program`, `ARB_vertex_buffer_object`, `ARB_occlusion_query`, `ARB_shader_objects`, `ARB_vertex_shader`, `ARB_fragment_shader`, `ARB_shading_language_100`, `ARB_texture_non_power_of_two`, `ARB_point_sprite`

GLX Extensions: `ARB_get_proc_address`

WGL Extensions: `ARB_buffer_region, ARB_extensions_string, ARB_pixel_format, ARB_make_current_read, ARB_pbuffer, ARB_render_texture`

A.4 Portable Use of OpenGL Extensions

The advantage of using OpenGL extensions is getting access to cutting-edge rendering functionality so that an application can achieve higher performance and higher quality rendering. OpenGL extensions provide access to the latest features of the newest graphics hardware. The problem with OpenGL extensions is that many OpenGL implementations, particularly older implementations, may not support a given extension. An OpenGL application that uses extensions should be written so that it still works when the extension is not supported. At the very least, the program should report that it requires whatever extension is missing and exit without crashing.

The first step to using OpenGL extensions is to locate the copy of the `<GL/gl.h>` header file that advertises the API interfaces for the desired extensions. Typically this can be obtained from OpenGL implementation vendor or OpenGL driver vendor as part of a software development kit (SDK). API interface prototypes and macros can also be obtained directly from the extension specifications, but getting the correct `<GL/gl.h>` from your OpenGL vendor is the preferred way. A version of the `<GL/gl.h>` header file with all available extensions is also available from www.opengl.org.

Note that the `<GL/gl.h>` header file sets C preprocessor macros to indicate whether the header advertises the interface of a particular extension or not. For example, the basic `<GL/gl.h>` supplied with Microsoft Visual C++ 7.0 has a section reading:

```
/* Extensions */
#define GL_EXT_vertex_array            1
#define GL_WIN_swap_hint               1
#define GL_EXT_bgra                    1
#define GL_EXT_paletted_texture        1
#define GL_EXT_clip_disable            1
```

These macros indicate that the header file advertises these five extensions. The `EXT_bgra` extension makes it possible to read and draw pixels in the Blue, Green, Red, Alpha component order as opposed to OpenGL's standard RGBA color component ordering.[1]

---

1. The functionality of the `EXT_bgra` extension was added as part of OpenGL 1.2. The BGRA color component ordering is important because it matches the color component ordering of Win32's GDI 2D API and therefore many PC-based file formats use it.

A program using the `EXT_bgra` extension should test that the extension is supported at compile time with code like this:

```
#ifdef GL_EXT_bgra
    glDrawPixels(width, height, GL_BGRA_EXT, GL_UNSIGNED_BYTE, pixels);
#endif
```

When `GL_EXT_bgra` is defined, the `GL_BGRA_EXT` enumerant will be defined. Note that if the `EXT_bgra` extension is not supported expect the `glDrawPixels` line to generate a compiler error because the standard *unextended* OpenGL header does not define the `GL_BGRA_EXT` enumerant.

Based on the extension name macro definition in `<GL/gl.h>`, code can be written so that it can optimally compile in the extension functionality if the development environment supports the extension's interfaces. This is not a complete solution, however. Even if the development environment supports the extension's interface at compile time, at runtime the target system where the application executes may not support the extension. In UNIX environments, different systems with different graphics hardware often support different sets of extensions. Likewise, in the Win32 environment different OpenGL-accelerated graphics boards will support different OpenGL extensions because they have different OpenGL drivers. It is not safe to assume that a given extension is supported. Runtime checks should be made to verify that a given extension is supported. Assuming that the application thread is made current to an OpenGL rendering context, the following routine can be used to determine at runtime if the OpenGL implementation really supports a particular extension.

```
#include <GL/gl.h>
#include <string.h>

isExtensionSupported(const char *extension){
   const GLubyte *extensions = NULL;
   const GLubyte *start;
   GLubyte *where, *terminator;

   /* Extension names should not have spaces. */
   where = (GLubyte *) strchr(extension, ' ');
   if (where || *extension == '\0')
      return 0;

   extensions = glGetString(GL_EXTENSIONS);

   /* It takes a bit of care to be fool-proof about parsing the OpenGL
      extensions string. Don't be fooled by substrings, etc. */
```

```
      start = extensions;
      for (;;) {
         where = (GLubyte *) strstr((const char *) start, extension);
         if (!where)
            break;
         terminator = where + strlen(extension);
         if (where == start || *(where - 1) == ' ')
            if (*terminator == ' ' || *terminator == '\0')
               return 1;
         start = terminator;
      }
      return 0;
   }
```

The isExtensionSupported routine can be used to check if the current OpenGL rendering context supports a given OpenGL extension.[2] To ensure the EXT_bgra extension is supported before using it, the application is structured as follows:

```
      /* At context initialization. */
      int hasBGRA = isExtensionSupported("GL_EXT_bgra");

      /* When trying to use EXT_bgra extension. */
   #ifdef GL_EXT_bgra
      if (hasBGRA) {
         glDrawPixels(width,height, GL_BGRA_EXT, GL_UNSIGNED_BYTE, pixels);
      } else
   #endif
      {
         /* No EXT_bgra so quit (or implement software workaround). */
         fprintf(stderr, "Needs EXT_bgra extension!\n");
         exit(1);
      }
```

Note that if the EXT_bgra extension is unavailable at either runtime or compile time this code will detect the lack of EXT_bgra support. The code is cumbersome but is necessary for portability. The compile time check can be eliminated if the development environment is well understood and the application will not be compiled with header files that don't support the extensions used by the application. The runtime check is essential in avoiding system or graphics card dependencies in the application.

---

2. Toolkits such as GLUT include functions to query extension support.

A.5 Using Extension Function Pointers

Many OpenGL implementations support extension commands as if they were core commands. Assuming the OpenGL header file provides the function prototypes and enumerants for the desired extension, the program is simply compiled and linked, presupposing that the extension routines exist. Before calling any extension routines, the program should first check the GL_EXTENSIONS string value to verify that the OpenGL extension is supported. If the extension is supported, the code can safely call the extension's routines and use its enumerants. If not supported, the program must avoid using the extension.

This method of using an extension's new routines works because several operating systems today support flexible shared libraries. A shared library delays the binding of a routine name to its executable function until the routine is first called when the application runs. This is known as a *runtime* link instead of a *compile-time* link. A problem occurs when an OpenGL extension routine is called that is not supported by the OpenGL runtime library. The result is a runtime link error that is generally fatal. This is why it is so important to check the GL_EXTENSIONS string before using any extension. Once extension support is verified, the program can safely call the extension's routines in full expectation that the system's runtime linker will invoke the extension routine correctly.

Unfortunately, many *open platforms* allow graphics hardware vendors to ship new OpenGL implementations, therefore it is not always possible to provide all of the API interfaces *a priori*. This is often the case for vendor-specific extensions or platforms that support multiple simultaneous graphics adaptors (multiadaptor). One problem is that the platform may include a standard runtime library containing the core entry points. OpenGL implementation vendors may not (and likely should not) replace this library with their own. One reason for not doing this is the multiadaptor scenario where the two graphics accelerators are supplied by two different hardware vendors.

To solve this problem hardware vendors supply additional runtime libraries that provide the hardware-specific functionality. The standard OpenGL library discovers and loads these device-specific libraries as *plugins*. The window system embedding layers also include a command to query a pointer to one or more device-specific extension commands. This mechanism allows an application to retrieve a function pointer for each extension API function. In GLX this function is glxGetProcAddress and in WGL wglGetProcAddress.[3]

The previous EXT_bgra example, showing how to safely detect and use the extension at runtime and compile time, is straightforward. The EXT_bgra simply adds two new enumerants (GL_BGRA_EXT and GL_BGR_EXT) and does not require any new commands. Using an extension that includes new command entry points is more complex on many platforms because the application must first explicitly request the function address from the OpenGL device-specific library before it can call the OpenGL function.

---

3. OpenGL Toolkit libraries such as GLUT include platform-independent wrapper versions of these functions.

We will use the `EXT_point_parameters` extension to illustrate the process. The `EXT_point_parameters` extension adds two new OpenGL entry points called `glPointParameterfEXT` and `glPointParameterfvEXT`. These routines allow the application to specify the attenuation equation parameters and fade threshold. On the Win32 platform, an OpenGL application cannot simply link with these extension functions. The application must first use the `wglGetProcAddress` command to find the function address and then call through the returned address to invoke the extension function.

First, declare function prototype *typedef*s that match the extension's entry points. For example:

```
#ifdef _WIN32
typedef void (APIENTRY * PFNGLPOINTPARAMETERFEXTPROC)
             (GLenum pname, GLfloat param);
typedef void (APIENTRY * PFNGLPOINTPARAMETERFVEXTPROC)
             (GLenum pname, const GLfloat *params);
#endif
```

The `<GL/gl.h>` header file may already have these typedefs declared if the `<GL/gl.h>` defines the `GL_EXT_point_parameters` macro. Next declare global variables of the type of these function prototype typedefs like this:

```
PFNGLPOINTPARAMETERFEXTPROC pglPointParameterfEXT;
PFNGLPOINTPARAMETERFVEXTPROC pglPointParameterfvEXT;
```

The names here correspond to the extension's function names. Once `wglGetProc Address` is used to assign these function variables to the address of the OpenGL driver's device-specific extension functions, the application can call `pglPointParameterfEXT` and `pglPointParameterfvEXT` as if they were normal functions. Pass `wglGetProcAddress` the name of the extension function as an ASCII string. After verifying that the extension is supported the function pointer variables are initialized as follows:

```
int hasPointParams = isExtensionSupported("GL_EXT_point_parameters");
if (hasPointParams) {
   pglPointParameterfEXT = (PFNGLPOINTPARAMETERFEXTPROC)
      wglGetProcAddress("glPointParameterfEXT");
   pglPointParameterfvEXT = (PFNGLPOINTPARAMETERFVEXTPROC)
      wglGetProcAddress("glPointParameterfvEXT");
}
```

Note that before calling this code there should be a current OpenGL rendering context. With the function variables properly initialized to the extension entry points, the extension can be used as follows:

```
if (hasPointParams && pglPointParameterfvEXT && pglPointParameterfEXT) {
    static GLfloat quadratic[3] = { 0.25, 0.0, 1/60.0 };
    pglPointParameterfvEXT(GL_DISTANCE_ATTENUATION_EXT, quadratic);
    pglPointParameterfEXT(GL_POINT_FADE_THRESHOLD_SIZE_EXT, 1.0);
}
```

Note that the behavior of wglGetProcAddress and glxGetProcAddress are subtly different. The function returned by wglGetProcAddress is only guaranteed to work for the pixel format type of the OpenGL rendering context that was current when wglGetProcAddress was called. If multiple contexts were created for different pixel formats, keeping a single function address in a global variable as shown previously may create problems. The application may need to maintain distinct function addresses on a per-pixel-format basis. The WGL implementation may reference a different function pointer value for each different pixel format. This allows different (heterogenous) device drivers in the multiadaptor scenario to return different device-specific implementations of the function. In contrast, the GLX specification guarantees that the pointer returned will be the same for all contexts. This means that the device-dependent layer and the standard OpenGL library cooperate on routing commands through the correct parts of the device-dependent libraries on a context by context basis. For other window system embedding layers, consult the documentation to determine whether the returned pointers are context-independent.

The requirement of using either glxGetProcAddress or wglGetProcAddress is cumbersome, but makes applications using extension functionality substantially more portable. Using these coding practices and a portable OpenGL toolkit, such as GLUT, can make the task of developing portable code that works across a wide variety of platforms (UNIX/Linux, Windows, Apple) manageable. The end result is applications that can use state-of-the-art features while maintaining broad compatibility.

Equations

This appendix describes some important formulas and matrices referred to in the text.

B.1 3D Vectors

$$\mathbf{A} = \begin{pmatrix} A_x \\ A_y \\ A_z \end{pmatrix}, \quad \alpha\mathbf{A} = \begin{pmatrix} \alpha A_x \\ \alpha A_y \\ \alpha A_z \end{pmatrix}$$

$$\mathbf{A} \cdot \mathbf{B} = A_x B_x + A_y B_y + A_z B_z$$

$$\mathbf{A} \cdot \mathbf{B} = \mathbf{B} \cdot \mathbf{A}$$

$$\|\mathbf{A}\| = \sqrt{\mathbf{A} \cdot \mathbf{A}} = \sqrt{A_x^2 + A_y^2 + A_z^2}$$

$$\mathbf{A} \odot \mathbf{B} = \max(0, \mathbf{A} \cdot \mathbf{B})$$

$$\mathbf{A} \times \mathbf{B} = \begin{pmatrix} A_y B_z - A_z B_y \\ A_z B_x - A_x B_z \\ A_x B_y - A_y B_x \end{pmatrix}$$

$$\mathbf{A} \times \mathbf{B} = -\mathbf{B} \times \mathbf{A}$$

$$\mathbf{A} \cdot (\mathbf{B} \times \mathbf{C}) = \mathbf{B} \cdot (\mathbf{C} \times \mathbf{A}) = \mathbf{C} \cdot (\mathbf{A} \times \mathbf{B})$$

$$\mathbf{A} \times (\mathbf{B} \times \mathbf{C}) = (\mathbf{A} \cdot \mathbf{C})\mathbf{B} - (\mathbf{A} \cdot \mathbf{B})\mathbf{C}$$

B.1.1 Spherical Coordinates

Given a point specified in Cartesian coordinates $(x, y, z)^T$, the spherical coordinates (ρ, θ, ϕ) consisting of a length and two angles are

$$\rho = \sqrt{x^2 + y^2 + z^2}$$

$$\tan \theta = y/x$$

$$\tan \phi = \frac{\sqrt{x^2 + y^2}}{z} \quad \text{and} \quad \cos \phi = \frac{z}{\sqrt{x^2 + y^2 + z^2}}$$

Given length ρ, azimuth angle ϕ, and elevation angle θ (assuming y is up) the Cartesian coordinates of the corresponding unit vector are

$$x = \rho \cos \theta \sin \phi$$

$$y = \rho \sin \theta \sin \phi$$

$$z = \rho \cos \phi$$

For unit vectors, ρ is equal to 1.

B.1.2 Linear Interpolation of 3D Vectors

Each vector component is interpolated separately, and then the resulting interpolated vector is renormalized. Renormalization is required if the interpolated vectors need to have unit length. Linearly interpolating a vector $\mathbf{V}$ using a single parameter α along a line with vectors $\mathbf{A}$ and $\mathbf{B}$ at the endpoints:

$$\mathbf{V} = \alpha \mathbf{A} + (1 - \alpha) \mathbf{B}$$

$$\mathbf{V}' = \frac{\mathbf{V}}{||\mathbf{V}||}$$

Linearly interpolating a vector $\mathbf{V}$ using two barycentric parameters α and β over a triangle with vectors $\mathbf{A}$, $\mathbf{B}$, $\mathbf{C}$ at the vertices:

$$\mathbf{V} = \alpha \mathbf{A} + \beta \mathbf{B} + (1 - (\alpha + \beta))\mathbf{C} :$$

$$\mathbf{V}' = \frac{\mathbf{V}}{||\mathbf{V}||}$$

Note: When using linear vector interpolation care must be taken to handle or report the case where one or more vector components interpolate to zero or a number so small that an excessive amount of accuracy is lost in the representation. In cases where linear interpolation is inadequate, spherical interpolation (SLERP) using quaternions may be a preferable method.

B.1.3 Barycentric Coordinates

Given a triangle with vertices A, B, C, the barycentric coordinates of the point P inside triangle ABC are α, β, γ, with $P = \alpha A + \beta B + \gamma C$ and $\alpha + \beta + \gamma = 1$. Let area (XYZ) be the area of the triangle with vertices X, Y, Z. Then

$$\text{area}(XYZ) = \frac{1}{2\|(Y - X) \times (Z - X)\|}$$

and the barycentric coordinates are the ratios of the areas of the subtriangles formed by the interior point P to the entire triangle ABC:

$$\alpha = \frac{\text{area}(PBC)}{\text{area}(ABC)} \qquad \beta = \frac{\text{area}(PAC)}{\text{area}(ABC)} \qquad \gamma = \frac{\text{area}(PAB)}{\text{area}(ABC)}.$$

B.2 Projection Matrices

B.2.1 Orthographic Projection

The call `glOrtho(l, r, b, t, u, f)` generates R, where

$$R = \begin{pmatrix} \frac{2}{r-l} & 0 & 0 & -\frac{r+l}{r-l} \\ 0 & \frac{2}{t-b} & 0 & -\frac{t+b}{t-b} \\ 0 & 0 & -\frac{2}{f-n} & -\frac{f+n}{f-n} \\ 0 & 0 & 0 & 1 \end{pmatrix} \quad \text{and} \quad R^{-1} = \begin{pmatrix} \frac{r-l}{2} & 0 & 0 & \frac{r+l}{2} \\ 0 & \frac{t-b}{2} & 0 & \frac{t+b}{2} \\ 0 & 0 & \frac{f-n}{2} & \frac{n+f}{2} \\ 0 & 0 & 0 & 1 \end{pmatrix}$$

R is defined as long as $l \neq r$, $t \neq b$, and $n \neq f$.

B.2.2 Perspective Projection

The call `glFrustum(l, r, b, t, n, f)` generates R, where

$$R = \begin{pmatrix} \frac{2n}{r-l} & 0 & \frac{r+l}{r-l} & 0 \\ 0 & \frac{2n}{t-b} & \frac{t+b}{t-b} & 0 \\ 0 & 0 & -\frac{f+n}{f-n} & -\frac{2fn}{f-n} \\ 0 & 0 & -1 & 0 \end{pmatrix} \quad \text{and} \quad R^{-1} = \begin{pmatrix} \frac{r-l}{2n} & 0 & 0 & \frac{r+l}{2n} \\ 0 & \frac{t-b}{2n} & 0 & \frac{t+b}{2n} \\ 0 & 0 & 0 & -1 \\ 0 & 0 & \frac{-f-n}{2fn} & \frac{f+n}{2fn} \end{pmatrix}$$

R is defined as long as $l \neq r$, $t \neq b$, and $n \neq f$.

B.2.3 Perspective z-Coordinate Transformations

The z value in eye coordinates, z_{eye}, can be computed from the window coordinate z value, z_{window}, using the near and far plane values, *near* and *far*, from the glFrustum command and the viewport near and far values, far_{vp} and $near_{vp}$, from the glDepthRange command using the equation

$$z_{eye} = \frac{\dfrac{far\ near\ (far_{vp} - near_{vp})}{far - near}}{z_{window} - \dfrac{(far + near)(far_{vp} - near_{vp})}{2(far - near)} - \dfrac{far_{vp} + near_{vp}}{2}}$$

The z-window coordinate is computed from the eye coordinate z using the equation

$$z_{window} = \left[\frac{far + near}{far - near} + \frac{2\ far\ near}{z_{eye}(far - near)} \right] \left[\frac{far_{vp} - near_{vp}}{2} \right] + \frac{far_{vp} + near_{vp}}{2}$$

B.2.4 Alternative Perspective Projection

The call gluPerspective(fovy, ar, n, f) generates R, where

$$R = \begin{pmatrix} \dfrac{c}{ar} & 0 & 0 & 0 \\ 0 & c & 0 & 0 \\ 0 & 0 & -\dfrac{f+n}{f-n} & -\dfrac{2nf}{f-n} \\ 0 & 0 & -1 & 0 \end{pmatrix} \quad \text{and} \quad R^{-1} = \begin{pmatrix} \dfrac{ar}{c} & 0 & 0 & 0 \\ 0 & \dfrac{1}{c} & 0 & 0 \\ 0 & 0 & 0 & -1 \\ 0 & 0 & \dfrac{-f-n}{2fn} & \dfrac{f+n}{2fn} \end{pmatrix}$$

where $c = \cot(fov_y/2) = \frac{\cos(fov_y/2)}{\sin(fov_y/2)}$. R is defined as long as $ar \neq 0$, $\sin(fov_y) \neq 0$, and $n \neq f$.

B.3 Viewing Transforms

The call gluLookat(eyex, eyey, eyez, centerx, centery, centerz, upx, upy, upz) generates V, where

$$V = \begin{pmatrix} s_x & s_y & s_z & -eye_x \\ u_x & u_y & u_z & -eye_y \\ n_x & n_y & n_z & -eye_z \\ 0 & 0 & 0 & 1 \end{pmatrix} \quad \text{and} \quad V^{-1} = \begin{pmatrix} s_x & u_x & n_x & eye_x \\ s_y & u_y & n_y & eye_y \\ s_z & u_z & n_z & eye_z \\ 0 & 0 & 0 & 1 \end{pmatrix}$$

where $\mathbf{n} = \frac{eye-center}{||eye-center||}$, $\mathbf{s} = \frac{\mathbf{up} \times \mathbf{n}}{||\mathbf{up} \times \mathbf{n}||}$, and $\mathbf{u} = \mathbf{n} \times \mathbf{s}$. Or equivalently, $\mathbf{n} = \frac{eye-center}{||eye-center||}$, $\mathbf{u} = \mathbf{up} - (\mathbf{up} \cdot \mathbf{n})\mathbf{n}$, and $\mathbf{s} = \mathbf{u} \times \mathbf{n}$.

B.4 Modeling Transforms

B.4.1 Scaling

The call glScalef(s_x, s_y, s_z) generates S, where

$$S = \begin{pmatrix} s_x & 0 & 0 & 0 \\ 0 & s_y & 0 & 0 \\ 0 & 0 & s_z & 0 \\ 0 & 0 & 0 & 1 \end{pmatrix} \quad \text{and} \quad S^{-1} = \begin{pmatrix} \frac{1}{s_x} & 0 & 0 & 0 \\ 0 & \frac{1}{s_y} & 0 & 0 \\ 0 & 0 & \frac{1}{s_z} & 0 \\ 0 & 0 & 0 & 1 \end{pmatrix}$$

B.4.2 Translation

The call glTranslatef(t_x, t_y, t_z) generates T, where

$$T = \begin{pmatrix} 1 & 0 & 0 & t_x \\ 0 & 1 & 0 & t_y \\ 0 & 0 & 1 & t_z \\ 0 & 0 & 0 & 1 \end{pmatrix} \quad \text{and} \quad T^{-1} = \begin{pmatrix} 1 & 0 & 0 & -t_x \\ 0 & 1 & 0 & -t_y \\ 0 & 0 & 1 & -t_z \\ 0 & 0 & 0 & 1 \end{pmatrix}$$

B.4.3 Rotation

The call glRotatef(θ, v_x, v_y, v_z) generates R, where

$$R = \begin{pmatrix} & & & 0 \\ & Q & & 0 \\ & & & 0 \\ 0 & 0 & 0 & 1 \end{pmatrix} \quad \text{and} \quad R^{-1} = \begin{pmatrix} & & & 0 \\ & Q^{-1} & & 0 \\ & & & 0 \\ 0 & 0 & 0 & 1 \end{pmatrix}$$

and

$$Q = \mathbf{U}\mathbf{U}^T + \cos\theta(I - \mathbf{U}\mathbf{U}^T) + \sin\theta S$$
$$Q^{-1} = \mathbf{U}\mathbf{U}^T + \cos\theta(I - \mathbf{U}\mathbf{U}^T) - \sin\theta S$$

$$U = V/||V||, \quad V = (V_x, V_y, V_z)^T$$

$$S = \begin{pmatrix} 0 & -U_z & U_y \\ U_z & 0 & -U_x \\ -U_z & U_x & 0 \end{pmatrix}$$

B.5 Parallel and Perpendicular Vectors

Given two vectors A, B, the portion of A parallel to B is

$$A||B = B\frac{(A \cdot B)}{||B||^2}$$

and the proportion of A perpendicular to B is $A_{\perp B} = A - A_{||B}$.

B.6 Reflection Vector

Given a surface point p, a unit vector, N, normal to that surface, and a vector, U, incident to the surface at p, the reflection vector, R, exiting from p is

$$R = U - 2N^T(N \cdot U).$$

If U' is exiting from the surface, $U' = -U$ and

$$R = 2N^T(N \cdot U') - U'.$$

B.7 Lighting Equations

In single-color lighting mode, the primary and secondary colors at surface point P_s are computed from n light sources as

$$C_{primary} = e_m + a_m a_{sc}$$

$$+ \sum_{i=0}^{n-1}(att_i)(spot_i)\left[a_m a_{l_i} + d_m d_{l_i}(N \odot L_i) + s_m s_{l_i}(f_i)(N \odot H_i)^{sh_i}\right]$$

$$C_{secondary} = (0, 0, 0, 1).$$

In separate specular color mode, the primary and secondary colors are computed from n light sources as

$$C_{primary} = e_m + a_m a_{sc} + \sum_{i=0}^{n-1}(att_i)(spot_i)\left[a_m a_{l_i} + d_m d_{l_i}(\mathbf{N} \odot \mathbf{L}_i)\right]$$

$$C_{secondary} = \sum_{i=0}^{n-1}(att_i)(spot_i)\left[s_m s_{l_i}(f_i)(\mathbf{N} \odot \mathbf{H}_i)^{sh_i}\right]$$

where

e_m, a_m, d_m, and s_m are the material emissive, ambient, diffuse, and specular reflectances

a_{sc} is the scene ambient intensity

a_{l_i}, d_{l_i}, and s_{l_i} are the ambient, diffuse, and specular intensities for light source i

sh_i is the specular exponent for light source i

att_i is the distance attenuation for light source i

$$att_i = \begin{cases} \dfrac{1}{k_{c_i} + k_{l_i} d_i + k_{q_i} d_i^2}, & \text{positional light} \\ 1.0, & \text{directional light} \end{cases}$$

where,

d_i is the distance between the surface point and light source i

$$d_i = ||\overrightarrow{\mathbf{P_s P_{l_i}}}||$$

k_{c_i} is the constant attenuation for light source i

k_{l_i} is the linear attenuation for light source i

k_{q_i} is the quadratic attenuation for light source i

$spot_i$ is the spotlight attenuation for light source i

$$spot_i = \begin{cases} (\overrightarrow{\mathbf{P_{l_i} P_s}} \odot \mathbf{sd}_i)^{se_i}, & co_i \neq 180.0, \ (\overrightarrow{\mathbf{P_{l_i} P_s}} \odot \mathbf{sd}) \geq \cos(co_i) \\ 0.0, & co_i \neq 180.0, \ (\overrightarrow{\mathbf{P_{l_i} P_s}} \odot \mathbf{sd}) < \cos(co_i) \\ 1.0, & co_i = 180.0 \end{cases}$$

where

sd$_i$ is the spotlight direction unit vector for light source i

se$_i$ is the spotlight exponent for light source i

co$_i$ is the spotlight cutoff angle for light source i

N is the surface normal unit vector

L$_i$ is the unit vector from the surface point to light source i, $\overrightarrow{P_sP_{l_i}}$

H$_i$ is the half-angle vector between the vectors from the surface point to the eye position (P_e), and the surface point and and light source i

$$H_i = \begin{cases} \overrightarrow{P_sP_{l_i}} + \overrightarrow{P_sP_e}, & \text{local viewer} \\ \overrightarrow{P_sP_{l_i}} + (0, 0, 1)^T, & \text{infinite viewer} \end{cases}$$

f_i is the self-occlusion discriminator for light source i

$$f_i = \begin{cases} 1, & \mathbf{N} \odot \mathbf{L}_i \neq 0 \\ 0, & \text{otherwise} \end{cases}$$

B.8 Function Approximations

B.8.1 Taylor Series Expansion

The Taylor series expansion of a function $f(x)$ about the point a is

$$f(x) = \sum_{j=0}^{\infty} \frac{1}{j!}(x - a)^j f^{(j)} \bigg|_{x=a}$$

where $f^{(j)}$ denotes the jth derivative of $f(x)$. The Maclaurin series expansion is the special case of the Taylor series expansion about the point $a = 0$.

B.8.2 Newton-Raphson Method

The Newton-Raphson method for obtaining a root of the function $f(x)$ uses an initial estimate x_0 and the recurrence

$$x_{n+1} = x_n - \frac{f(x_n)}{f'(x_n)} \tag{B.1}$$

The approximation for the reciprocal of a number a is the root of the equation $f(x) = 1/x - a$. Substituting $f(x)$ in Equation B.1 gives

$$x_{n+1} = x_n - \frac{1/x_n - a}{-1/x_n^2} = x_n(2 - ax_n)$$

and the reciprocal square root of a number a is the root of the equation $f(x) = 1/x^2 - a$. Substituting $f(x)$ in Equation B.1 gives

$$x_{n+1} = x_n - \frac{1/x_n^2 - a}{-2/x_n^3} = \frac{x_n}{2}(3 - ax_n^2)$$

B.8.3 Hypotenuse

A rough approximation of the 2D hypotenuse or length function $\sqrt{a^2 + b^2}$ suitable for level-of-detail computations (Wu, 1988), is

$$\max(|a|, |b|) + 11/32 \min(|a|, |b|).$$

Bibliography

Airey, J., B. Cabral, and M. Peercy, "Explanation of Bump Mapping with Texture," personal communication, 1997.

Akeley, K. "Algorithm for Drawing Boundary Plus Silhouette Edges for a Solid," personal communication, 1998.

Andrews, D. F., "Plots of High-dimensional Data," *Biometrics*, 28: 125–136, 1972.

Angel, E. *Interactive Computer Graphics: A Top-down Approach with OpenGL*, Reading, MA: Addison-Wesley, 1997.

Apple Computer. *Apple GL Library Specification*, Apple Computer, Inc., Cupertino, CA, 2001. On-line reference available at *http://developer.apple.com/documentation/ GraphicsImaging/OpenGL-date.html*.

Ashikhmin, M., S. Premo, and P. Shirley, "A Microfacet-based BRDF Generator," in *Proceedings of the 27th Annual Conference on Computer Graphics and Interactive Techniques*, pp. 65–74. New York: ACM Press/Addison-Wesley, 2000.

Attarwala, Y. "Rendering Hidden Lines," *Iris Universe*, Fall: 39, 1988.

Bailey, M., and D. Clark, "Encoding 3D Surface Information in a Texture Vector," *Journal of Graphics Tools* 2(3): 29–35, 1997, *www.sdsc.edu/tmf/texvec.pdf*.

Beckmann, P., and Spizzichino, A., *The Scattering of Electromagnetic Waves from Rough Surfaces*, New York: MacMillan, 1963.

Bergeron, P. "A General Version of Crow's Shadow Volumes," *IEEE Computer Graphics and Applications*, 6(9): 17–28, 1986.

Blinn, J. F. "A Ghost in a Snowstorm," *IEEE Computer Graphics and Applications*, pp. 79–84, January 1998.

Blinn, J. F. "Me and My (Fake) Shadow," *IEEE Computer Graphics and Applications*, January 1988, reprinted in *Jim Blinn's Corner: A Trip Down the Graphics Pipeline*, San Francisco: Morgan Kaufmann, 1996.

Blinn, J. F. "Hyperbolic Interpolation," *IEEE Computer Graphics and Applications*, July 1992, reprinted in *Jim Blinn's Corner: A Trip Down the Graphics Pipeline*. San Francisco: Morgan Kaufmann, 1996.

Blinn, J. F. "Models of Light Reflection for Computer Synthesized Pictures," in *Proceedings of the 4th Annual Conference on Computer Graphics and Interactive Techniques*, pp. 192–198, New York: ACM Press, 1977.

Blinn, J. F. "Simulation of Wrinkled Surfaces," in *Computer Graphics (SIGGRAPH '78 Proceedings)*, vol. 12, pp. 286–292. August 1978.

Blinn, J. F. "W Pleasure, W Fun," *IEEE Computer Graphics and Applications*, pp. 78–82, June 1998.

Blythe, D. (ed.). *OpenGL ES Common/Common-Lite Profile Specification (Version 1.0)*, Clearlake Park, CA: The Khronos Group, 2003, *www.khronos.org/opengles/spec.html*.

Bourgoyne, A., R. Bornstein, and D. Yu, *Silicon Graphics Visual Workstation OpenGL Programming Guide for Windows NT*, Mountain View, CA: Silicon Graphics, 1999, *www.sgi.com/developers/nt/sdk/*.

Brodlie, K. W., L. A. Carpenter, R. A. Earnshaw, J. R. Gallop, R. J. Hubbold, A. M. Mumford, C. D. Osland, and P. Quarendon (eds.). *Scientific Visualization: Techniques and Applications*. New York: Springer-Verlag, 1992.

Brotman, L. S., and N. Badler, "Generating Soft Shadows with a Depth Buffer Algorithm," *IEEE Computer Graphics and Applications*, October, 1984.

Cabral, B., and L. Leedom, "Imaging Vector Fields Using Line Integral Convolution," in J. T. Kajiya (ed.). *Computer Graphics (SIGGRAPH '93 Proceedings)*, vol. 27, pp. 263–272, Aug. 1993.

Cabral, B., N. Cam, and J. Foran, "Accelerated Volume Rendering and Tomographic Reconstruction Using Texture Mapping Hardware," in *Proceedings of the 1994 Symposium on Volume Visualization*, pp. 91–98, New York: ACM Press, 1994.

Carmack, J. "Shadow Volumes," e-mail, May 2000.

Carpenter, L. "The A-buffer: An Antialiased Hidden Surface Method," in *Proceedings of the 11th Annual Conference on Computer Graphics and Interactive Techniques*, pp. 103–108, New York: ACM Press, 1984.

Catmull, E. "A Hidden-surface Algorithm with Anti-aliasing," in *Proceedings of the 5th Annual Conference on Computer Graphics and Interactive Techniques*, pp. 6–11, New York: ACM Press, 1978.

Chen, M., and J. Arvo, "Perturbation Methods for Interactive Specular Reflections," *IEEE Transactions on Visualization and Computer Graphics*, 6(3): 253–264, Sept. 2000.

Chen, M., and J. Arvo, "Theory and Application of Specular Path Perturbation," *ACM Transactions on Graphics*, 19(4), Jan. 2001.

Chernoff, H. "The Use of Faces to Represent Points in k-dimensional Space Graphically," *Journal of the American Statistical Association*, 68: 361–368, June 1973.

Chiang, Y-J., and T. Silva, "I/O Optimal Isosurface Extraction," in *Proceedings of the 8th Conference on Visualization '97*, p. 293, Washington, D.C.: IEEE Computer Society Press, 1997.

Chui, K., M. Herf, P. Shirley, S. Swamy, C. Wang, and K. Zimmerman, "Spatially Nonuniform Scaling Functions for High-Contrast Images," in *Proceedings of Graphics Interface '93*, pp. 245–253, 1993.

Cohen, M. F., and J. R. Wallace, *Radiosity and realistic image synthesis*, San Diego, CA: Harcourt Brace & Company, 1993.

Cook, R. L., "Stochastic Sampling in Computer Graphics," *ACM Trans. Graph.*, 5(1): 51–72, 1986.

Cook, R. L., and K. E. Torrance, "A Reflectance Model for Computer Graphics," in *Computer Graphics (SIGGRAPH '81 Proceedings)*, vol. 15, pp. 307–316, Aug. 1981.

Cook, R. L., L. Carpenter, and E. Catmull, "The Reyes Image Rendering Architecture," in *Proceedings of the 14th Annual Conference on Computer Graphics and Interactive Techniques*, pp. 95–102, New York: ACM Press, 1987.

Coorg S., and S. Teller, "A Spatially and Temporally Coherent Object Space Visibility Algorithm," Technical Report TM 546, Laboratory for Computer Science, Cambridge, MA: Massachusetts Institute of Technology, 1996.

Crow, F. C., "A Comparison of Antialiasing Techniques," *IEEE Computer Graphics and Applications*, 1(1): 40–48, Jan. 1981.

Cutnell, J. D., and K. W. Johnson, *Physics*, New York: John Wiley & Sons, 1989.

Debevec, P. "Image-based Lighting," *IEEE Computer Graphics and Applications*. 2002;22(2):26–34.

Debevec, P. F., and J. Malik, "Recovering High Dynamic Range Radiance Maps from Photographs," in *Proceedings of the 24th Annual Conference on Computer Graphics and Interactive Techniques*, pp. 369–378, New York: ACM Press/Addison-Wesley, 1997.

Deering, M. F., "High resolution Virtual Reality," in E. E. Catmull (ed.). *Computer Graphics (SIGGRAPH '92 Proceedings)*, vol. 26, pp. 195–202, July 1992.

de Leeuw, W. C., and J. J. van Wijk, "A Probe for Local Flow Field Visualization," in *Proceedings of the 4th Conference on Visualization '93*, pp. 39–45, 1993.

Delmarcelle, T., and L. Hesselink, "Visualizing Second-order Tensor Fields with Hyperstreamlines," *IEEE Computer Graphics and Applications*, 13(4): 25–33, July 1993.

Dickinson, R. R., "A Unified Approach to the Design of Visualization Software for the Analysis of Field Problems," in *Three-Dimensional Visualization and Display Technologies*, vol. 1083, pp. 173–180, 1989.

Deifenbach, P., "Pipeline Rendering: Interaction and Realism Through Hardware-Based Multi-Pass Rendering," Ph.D. thesis, School of Computer Science, University of Pennsylvania, 1996.

Diefenbach, P. J., and N. I. Badler, "Multi-pass Pipeline Rendering: Realism for Dynamic Environments," in *Proceedings of the 1997 Symposium on 3D Graphics*, pp. 12, 1997.

Drebin, R. A., L. Carpenter, and P. Hanrahan, "Volume Rendering," in J. Dill (ed.). *Computer Graphics (SIGGRAPH '88 Proceedings)*, vol. 22, pp. 65–74, Aug. 1988.

Duff, T. "Compositing 3-D Rendered Images," in B. A., Barsky (ed.). *Computer Graphics (SIGGRAPH '85 Proceedings)*, vol. 19, pp. 41–44, July 1985.

Ebert, D., K. Musgrave, D. Peachey, K. Perlin, and S. Worley, *Texturing and modeling: A Procedural Approach*, San Diego: Academic Press, 1994.

Epic Games, "Unreal," Jan. 1999, *www.epicgames.com/*.

Evans, F., S. Skiena, and A. Varshney, "Optimizing Triangle Strips for Fast Rendering," in *Proceedings of Visualization 96*, pp. 319–326, 1996, *www.cs.sunysb.edu/evans/stripe.html*.

Everitt, C. "Interactive Order-independent Transparency," NVIDIA Technical Report, 2002, *http://developer.nvidia.com/view.asp?IO=Interactive_Order_Transparency*.

Fernando, R. (ed.). *GPU Gems: Programming Techniques, Tips, and Tricks for Real-Time Graphics*, Reading, MA: Addison-Wesley Professional, 2004.

Foley, J. D., A. van Dam, S. K. Feiner, and J. F. Hughes, *Computer Graphics: Principles and Practice*, Reading, MA: Addison-Wesley, 1990.

Foley, J. D., A. van Dam, S. K. Feiner, J. F. Hughes, and R. L. Phillips, *Introduction to Computer Graphics*, Reading, MA: Addison-Wesley, 1994.

Fosner, R., *OpenGL Programming for Windows 95 and Windows NT*, Reading, MA: Addison-Wesley, 1996.

Fournier, A., and W. T. Reeves, "A Simple Model of Ocean Waves," in D. C. Evans and R. J. Athay (eds.). *Computer Graphics (SIGGRAPH '86 Proceedings)*, vol. 20, pp. 75–84, Aug. 1986.

Fournier, A., D. Fussell, and L. Carpenter, "Computer Rendering of Stochastic Models," *Communications of the ACM*, 25(6): 371–384, June 1982.

FreeType project documentation, *www.freetype.org*, 2003.

Gardner, G. Y. "Visual Simulation of Clouds," in B. A. Barsky (ed.). *Computer Graphics (SIGGRAPH '85 Proceedings)*, vol. 19, pp. 297–303, July 1985.

Glassner, A. S., *An Introduction to Ray Tracing*, San Francisco: Morgan Kaufmann, 1989.

Goldfeather, J., J. P. M. Hultquist, and H. Fuchs, "Fast Constructive-solid Geometry Display in the Pixel-Powers Graphics System," in D. C. Evans and R. J. Athay (eds.). *Computer Graphics (SIGGRAPH '86 Proceedings)*, vol. 20, pp. 107–116, Aug. 1986.

Goldman, R. "Matrices and Transformations," in A. Glassner (ed.). *Graphics Gems*, pp. 474, San Diego: Academic Press, 1990.

Gonzalez, R. C., and P. Wintz, *Digital Image Processing* (2d ed.). Reading, MA: Addison-Wesley, 1987.

Gooch, A., B. Gooch, P. Shirley, and E. Cohen, "A Non-photorealistic Lighting Model for Automatic Technical Illustration," in M. F. Cohen (ed.). *Computer Graphics ("SIGGRAPH '98 Proceedings)*, vol. 25, pp. 447–452, July 1998.

Gooch, B., P. Sloan, A. Gooch, P. Shirley, and R. Riesenfield, "Interactive Technical Illustration," in J. Hodgins and J. Foley (eds.). *Proceedings of the 1999 Symposium on Interactive 3D Graphics*, pp. 31–38, April 1999.

Gortler, S. J., R. Grzeszczuk, R. Szeliski, and M. F. Cohen, "The Lumigraph," in *Computer Graphics (SIGGRAPH '96 Proceedings)*, vol. 30, pp. 43–54, Aug. 1996.

Gouraud, H. "Continuous Shading of Curved Surfaces," *IEEE Transactions on Computers*, C-20(6):623–629, June 1971.

Greene, N., M. Kass, and G. Miller, "Hierarchical Z-buffer Visibility," in *Proceedings of the 20th Annual Conference on Computer Graphics and Interactive Techniques*, pp. 231–238, New York: ACM Press, 1993.

Haber, R. B. "Visualization Techniques for Engineering Mechanics," *Computing Sytems in Engineering*, 1(1):37–50, 1990.

Haeberli, P. E. "Matrix Operations for Image Processing," *www.sgi.com/grafica/matrix/index.html*, Nov. 1993.

Haeberli, P. E. "Paint by Numbers: Abstract Image Representations," in F. Baskett (ed.). *Computer Graphics (SIGGRAPH '90 Proceedings)*, vol. 24, pp. 207–214, Aug. 1990.

Haeberli, P. E., and K. Akeley, "The Accumulation Buffer: Hardware Support for High-quality Rendering," in F. Baskett (ed.). *Computer Graphics (SIGGRAPH '90 Proceedings)*, vol. 24, pp. 309–318, Aug. 1990.

Haeberli, P. E., and M. Segal, "Texture Mapping as a Fundamental Drawing Primitive," in M. F. Cohen, C. Puech, and F. Sillion (eds.) *Fourth Eurographics Workshop on Rendering*, pp. 259–266, Eurographics, Paris, 14–16 June 1993.

Haeberli, P. E., and D. Voorhies, "Image Processing by Linear Interpolation and Extrapolation," *Iris Universe*, (28): 8–9, 1994.

Hall, R. *Illumination and Color in Computer Generated Imagery*, New York: Springer-Verlag, 1989.

Hall, P. M., and A. H. Watt, "Rapid Volume Rendering Using a Boundary-fill Guided Ray Cast Algorithm," in N. M. Patrikalakis (ed.). *Scientific Visualization of Physical Phenomena (Proceedings of CG International '91)*, pp. 235–249, New York: Springer-Verlag, 1991.

Hanrahan, P., and P. E. Haeberli, "Direct WYSIWYG Painting and Texturing on 3D Shapes," in F. Baskett (ed.). *Computer Graphics (SIGGRAPH '90 Proceedings)*, vol. 24, pp. 215–223, Aug. 1990.

Hanrahan, P., and D. Mitchell, "Illumination from Curved Reflectors," in *Computer Graphics (SIGGRAPH '92 Proceedings)*, vol. 26, pp. 282–291, July 1992.

Heckbert, P. S., and M. Herf, "Fast Soft Shadows," in *Visual Proceedings*, *SIGGRAPH '96*, pp. 145, New York: ACM Press, 1996.

Heckbert, P. S., and M. Herf, "Shadow Generation Algorithms," *www.cs.cmu.edu/ph/ shadow.html*, April 1997.

Heidmann, T. "Real Shadows Real Time," *Iris Universe*, (18):28–31, 1991.

Heidrich, W., and H-P. Seidel, "Efficient Rendering of Anisotropic Surfaces Using Computer Graphics Hardware," in *Image and Multi-dimensional Digital Signal Processing Workshop (IMDSP)*, Washington, D.C.: IEEE Computer Society Press, 1998.

Heidrich, W., and H-P. Seidel, "View-independent Environment Maps," in *Proceedings of the SIGGRAPH/Eurographics Workshop on Graphics Hardware*, 1998, *www9.informatik.unierlangen.de/eng/research/rendering/envmap*.

Herrell, R., J. Baldwin, and C. Wilcox, "High-quality Polygon Edging," *IEEE Computer Graphics and Applications*, 15(4):68–74, July 1995.

Hewlett-Packard, "About srgb," *www.srgb.com/aboutsrgb.html*, Nov. 2001.

Hewlett-Packard, *OpenGL Implementation Guide*, *www.hp.com/unixwork/products/ grfx/OpenGL/Web/ImpGuide.html*, June 1998.

Hill, S., "Hardware Accelerating Art Production," *www.gamasutra.com/features/ 20040319/hill_01.shtml*, March 2004.

Huttner, T. "High-resolution Textures," in *Proceedings of IEEE Visualization 98*, Oct. 1998, *http://davinci.informatik.unikl.de/vis98/archive/lbht/papers/huettnerA4.pdf*.

id Software, "Quake," *www.idsoftware.com/*, Jan. 1999.

Interrante, V., and C. Grosch, "Strategies for Effectively Visualizing 3D Flow with Volume LIC," in *Proceedings of the Conference on Visualization '97*, pp. 421–ff, New York: ACM Press, 1997.

Jack, K. *Video Demystified: A Handbook for the Digital Engineer*, San Diego: HighText Publications, 1996.

Jeremic, B., G. Scheuermann, J. Frey, Z. Yang, B. Hamman, K. I. Joy, and H. Haggen, "Tensor Visualizations in Computational Geomechanics," *International Journal for Numerical and Analytical Methods in Geomechanics Incorporating Mechanics of Cohesive-Frictional Materials*, 26(10):925-944, Aug. 2002.

Kass, M., and G. Miller, "Rapid, Stable Fluid Dynamics for Computer Graphics," in F. Baskett (ed.). *Computer Graphics (SIGGRAPH '90 Proceedings)*, vol. 24, pp. 49–57, Aug. 1990.

Kautz, J., and M. D. McCool, "Interactive Rendering with Arbitrary BRDFs Using Separable Approximations," in *ACM SIGGRAPH 99 Conference Abstracts and Applications*, pp. 253, New York: ACM Press, 1999.

Kessenich, J., D. Baldwin, and R. Rost, *The OpenGL Shading Language (Version 1.051)*, 3DLabs, Inc., Egham, Surry, Feb. 2003, *www.opengl.org/documentation/oglsl.html*.

Khronos Group, The "OpenGL ES," *www.khronos.org/opengles/index.html*, Dec. 2002.

Kilgard, M. J. *Programming OpenGL for the X Window System*, Reading, MA: Addison-Wesley, 1996.

Kilgard, M. J. "Shadow Volumes," *http://developer.nvidia.com*, March 2002.

Kilgard, M. J. "A Simple OpenGL-based API for Texture Mapped Text," *http://reality.sgi.com/opengl/tips/TexFont/TexFont.html*, 1997.

Kilgard, M. J., D. Blythe, and D. Hohn, "System Support for OpenGL Direct Rendering," in W. A. Davis and P. Prusinkiewicz (eds.). *Graphics Interface '95*, pp. 116–127, Canadian Human-Computer Communications Society, 1995.

Kindlmann, G., and D. Weinstein, "Hue-balls and Lit-tensors for Direct Volume Rendering of Diffusion Tensor Fields," in *Proceedings of the Conference on Visualization '99*, pp. 183–189, Washington, D.C.: IEEE Computer Society Press, 1999.

Lacroute, P., and M. Levoy, "Fast Volume Rendering Using a Shear–warp Factorization of the Viewing Transformation," in A. Glassner (ed.). *Proceedings of SIGGRAPH '94 (Orlando, Florida, July 24–29, 1994)*, Computer Graphics Proceedings, Annual Conference Series, pp. 451–458, ACM SIGGRAPH, New York: ACM Press, July 1994.

Lambert, J. D., *Numerical Methods for Ordinary Differential Equations*, Chichester, UK: John Wiley & Sons, 1991.

Larson, G. W., H. Rushmeier, and C. Piatko, "A Visibility Matching Tone Reproduction Operator for High Dynamic Range Scenes," in *ACM SIGGRAPH 97 Visual Proceedings: The Art and Interdisciplinary Programs of SIGGRAPH '97*, pp. 155, New York: ACM Press, 1997.

Lee, A., H. Moreton, and H. Hoppe, "Displaced Subdivision Surfaces," in *Proceedings of the 27th Annual Conference on Computer Graphics and Interactive Techniques*, pp. 85–94, New York: ACM Press/Addison-Wesley, 2000.

Leech, J. (ed.). *OpenGL ES Native Platform Graphics Interface (Version 1.0)*, Clearlake Park, CA: The Khronos Group, 2003, *www.khronos.org/opengles/spec.html*.

Lengyel, E. "The Mechanics of Robust Stencil Shadows," *www.gamasutra.com*, Oct. 2002.

Levoy, M., and P. Hanrahan, "Light Field Rendering," in *Computer Graphics (SIGGRAPH '96 Proceedings)*, vol. 30, pp. 31–42, Aug. 1996.

Lewis, J-P., "Algorithms for Solid Noise Synthesis," in J. Lane (ed.). *Computer Graphics (SIGGRAPH '89 Proceedings)*, vol. 23, pp. 263–270, July 1989.

Lorensen, W. E., and H. E. Cline, "Marching Cubes: A High-resolution 3D Surface Construction Algorithm," in *Proceedings of the 14th Annual Conference on Computer Graphics and Interactive Techniques*, pp. 163–169, New York: ACM Press, 1987.

Luebke, D., and C. Georges, "Portals and Mirrors: Simple, Fast Evaluation of Potentially Visible Sets," in *Proceedings of the 1995 Symposium on Interactive 3D Graphics*, pp. 105, New York: ACM Press, 1995.

Ma, K-L., B. Cabral, H-C. Hege, D. Stalling, and V. L. Interrante, "Texture Synthesis with Line Integral Convolution," ACM SIGGRAPH, Los Angeles, 1997, Siggraph '97 Conference Course Notes.

Mammen, A. "Transparency and Antialiasing Algorithms Implemented with the Virtual Pixel Maps Technique," *IEEE Computer Graphics and Applications*, pp. 43–55, July 1989.

Markosian, L., M. Kowalski, S. Trychin, L. Bourdev, D. Goldstein, and J. Hughes, "Real-time Nonphotorealistic Rendering," in T. Whitted (ed.). *Computer Graphics (SIGGRAPH '97 Proceedings)* vol. 24, pp. 415–420, Aug. 1997.

McCool, M. D., J. Ang, and A. Ahmad, "Homomorphic Factorization of BRDFS for High-performance Rendering," in *Proceedings of the 28th Annual Conference on Computer Graphics and Interactive Techniques*, pp. 171–178, New York: ACM Press, 2001.

McMillan, L., and G. Bishop, "Plenoptic Modeling: An Image-based Rendering System," in *Computer Graphics (SIGGRAPH '95 Proceedings)*, vol. 29, pp. 39–46, Aug. 1995.

Microsoft. *Windows OpenGL SDK Documentation*, Microsoft MSDN Library, 2001.

Microsoft. *Windows Win32 SDK Documentation*, Microsoft MSDN Library, 2001.

Miller, G. S. P. "The Definition and Rendering of Terrain Maps," in D. C. Evans and R. J. Athay (eds.). *Computer Graphics (SIGGRAPH '86 Proceedings)*, vol. 20, pp. 39–48, Aug. 1986.

Mitchell, D. P., and A. N. Netravali, "Reconstruction Filters in Computer Graphics," in J. Dill (ed.). *Computer Graphics (SIGGRAPH '88 Proceedings)*, vol. 22, pp. 221–228, Aug. 1988.

Montrym, J., D. Baum, D. Dignam, and C. Migdal, "InfiniteReality: A Real-time Graphics System," in T. Whitted (ed.). *Computer Graphics (SIGGRAPH '97 Proceedings)*, pp. 293–302, Aug. 1997.

Mueller, K., and R. Crawfis, "Eliminating Popping Artifacts in Sheet Buffer-based Splatting," in *Proceedings of the Conference on Visualization '98*, pp. 239–245, Washington, D.C.: IEEE Computer Society Press, 1998.

Mueller, K., T. Muller, and R. Crawfis, "Splatting Without the Blur," in *Proceedings of the Conference on Visualization '99*, pp. 363–370, Washington, D.C.: IEEE Computer Society Press, 1999.

Myler, H. R., and A. R. Weeks, *The Pocket Handbook of Image Processing Algorithms in C*, University of Central Florida Department of Electrical & Computer Engineering, Indianapolis: Prentice Hall, 1993.

Neider, J., T. Davis, and M. Woo, *OpenGL Programming Guide* (2d ed.). Reading, MA: Addison-Wesley, 1997.

Newman, W. M., and R. F. Sproull, *Principles of Interactive Computer Graphics* (1st ed.). New York: McGraw-Hill, 1973.

Nishita, T., and E. Nakamae, "Method of Displaying Optical Effects Within Water Using Accumulation Buffer," in A. Glassner (ed.). *Proceedings of SIGGRAPH '94 (Orlando, Florida, July 24–29, 1994)*, Computer Graphics Proceedings, Annual Conference Series, pp. 373–381, ACM SIGGRAPH, New York: ACM Press, 1994.

NVIDIA, *Cg Toolkit, Release 1.2*, Santa Clara, CA, *www.nvidia.com/Cg*, Jan. 2004.

NVIDIA, "NVIDIA Occlusion Query Extension Specification," *http://oss.sgi.com/projects/oglsample/registry/NV/occlusion_query.txt*, Feb. 2002.

Ofek, E., and A. Rappoport, "Interactive Reflections on Curved Objects," in M. F. Cohen (ed.). *Computer Graphics (SIGGRAPH '98 Proceedings)*, pp. 333–342, July 1998.

Oren, M., and S. K. Nayar, "Generalization of Lambert's Reflectance Model," in A. Glassner (ed.). *Proceedings of SIGGRAPH '94 (Orlando, Florida, July 24–29, 1994)* vol. 28 of *Computer Graphics Proceedings, Annual Conference Series*, pp. 239–246, ACM SIGGRAPH, New York: ACM Press, July 1994.

O'Rourke, J., *Computational Geometry in C*, Cambridge: Cambridge University Press, 1994.

Owens, J. D., B. Khailany, B. Towles, and W. J. Dally, "Comparing Reyes and OpenGL on a Stream Architecture," in *Proceedings of the ACM SIGGRAPH/EUROGRAPHICS Conference on Graphics Hardware*, pp. 47–56, Eurographics Association, 2002.

Owens, J. D., W. J. Dally, U. J. Kapasi, S. Rixner, P. Mattson, and B. Mowery, "Polygon Rendering on a Stream Architecture," in *Proceedings of the ACM*

SIGGRAPH/EUROGRAPHICS Workshop on Graphics Hardware, pp. 23–32, New York: ACM Press, 2000.

Pantone, Inc., *www.pantone.com,* Jan. 2003.

Peachey, D. R. "Modeling Waves and Surf," in D. C. Evans and R. J. Athay (eds.). *Computer Graphics (SIGGRAPH '86 Proceedings),* vol. 20, pp. 65–74, Aug. 1986.

Peercy, M., J. Airey, and B. Cabral, "Efficient Bump Mapping Hardware," in *Computer Graphics (SIGGRAPH '97 Proceedings),* 1997.

Peleg, A., S. Wilkie, and U. Weiser, "Intel MMX for Multimedia PCs," *Communications of the ACM,* 40(1):24–38, 1997.

Phong, B-T. "Illumination for Computer Generated Pictures," *Communications of the ACM,* 18(6):311–317, June 1975.

Porter, T., and T. Duff, "Compositing Digital Images," in H. Christiansen (ed.). *Computer Graphics (SIGGRAPH '84 Proceedings),* vol. 18, pp. 253–259, July 1984.

Potmesil, M., and I. Chakravarty, "A Lens and Aperture Camera Model for Synthetic Image Generation," in *Proceedings of the 8th Annual Conference on Computer Graphics and Interactive Techniques,* pp. 297–305, New York: ACM Press, 1981.

Poynton, C. "The Rehabilitation of Gamma," in B. E. Rogowitz and T. N. Pappas (eds.). *Proceedings of SPIE/IS&T Conference 3299,* Jan. 1998.

Praun, E., H. Hoppe, M. Webb, and A. Finkelstein, "Real-time Hatching," in *Proceedings of the 28th Annual Conference on Computer Graphics and Interactive Techniques,* pp. 581, New York: ACM Press, 2001.

Preparata, F. P., and M. I. Shamos, *Computational Geometry,* New York: Springer-Verlag, 1985.

Reeves, W. T., D. H. Salesin, and R. L. Cook, "Rendering Antialiased Shadows with Depth Maps," in M. C. Stone (ed.). *Computer Graphics (SIGGRAPH '87 Proceedings),* vol. 21, pp. 283–291, July 1987.

Reinhard, E., M. Stark, P. Shirley, and J. Ferwerda, "Photographic Tone Reproduction for Digital Images," in *Proceedings of the 29th Annual Conference on Computer Graphics and Interactive Techniques,* pp. 267–276, New York: ACM Press, 2002.

Rogers, D. F., *Procedural Elements for Computer Graphics* (2d ed.). New York: McGraw-Hill, 1997.

Rohlf, J., and J. Helman, "IRIS Performer: A High Performance Multiprocessing Toolkit for Real–time 3D Graphics," in A. Glassner (ed.). *Proceedings of SIGGRAPH '94 (Orlando, Florida, July 24–29, 1994),* Computer Graphics Proceedings, Annual Conference Series, pp. 381–395, ACM SIGGRAPH, New York: ACM Press, July 1994.

Rustagi, P., "Silhouette Line Display from Shaded Models," *Iris Universe,* Fall: 42–44, 1989.

Saito, T., and T. Takahashi, "Comprehensible Rendering of 3-D Shapes," in F. Baskett (ed.). *Computer Graphics (SIGGRAPH '90 Proceedings)*, vol. 24, pp. 197–206, Aug. 1990.

Scheifler, R. W., and J. Gettys, "The X Window System," *ACM Transactions on Graphics*, 5(2):79–109, 1986.

Schlag, J. *Fast Embossing Effects on Raster Image Data*, Cambridge, MA: Academic Press, 1994.

Schlick, C. "Divers Éléments Pour Une Synthèse d'Images Réalistes," Ph.D. thesis, Université Bordeax 1, November 1992.

Segal, M., and K. Akeley, *The OpenGL Graphics System: A Specification (version 1.5)*, Mountain View, CA: Silicon Graphics, Inc., October 2003, *http://opengl.org/documentation/specs/version1.5/glspec15.pdf*.

Segal, M., C. Korobkin, R. van Widenfelt, J. Foran, and P. E. Haeberli, "Fast Shadows and Lighting Effects Using Texture Mapping," in E. E. Catmull (ed.). *Computer Graphics (SIGGRAPH '92 Proceedings)*, vol. 26, pp. 249–252, July 1992.

Shirley, P., R. K. Morley, *Realistic Ray Tracing (2d ed.)*. Natick, MA: AK Peters Ltd, 2003.

Sloan, P-P. J., D. Weinstein, and J. D. Brederson, "Importance Driven Texture Coordinate Optimization," submitted to SIGGRAPH '97, 1997, *www.cs.utah.edu/dejohnso/workshop/talks/sloan/sloan.html*.

Soderquist, P., and M. Leeser, "Area and Performance Tradeoffs in Floating-point Divide and Square-root Implementations," *ACM Comput. Surv.*, 28(3):518–564, 1996.

Soler, C., and F. Sillion, "The Clipmap: A Virtual Mipmap," in M. F. Cohen (ed.). *Computer Graphics (SIGGRAPH '98 Proceedings)*, pp. 321–332, July 1998.

Spencer, G., P. Shirley, K. Zimmerman, and D. P. Greenberg, "Physically-based Glare Effects for Digital Images," in *Proceedings of the 22nd Annual Conference on Computer Graphics and Interactive Techniques*, pp. 325–334, New York: ACM Press, 1995.

Stalling, D., M. Zöckler, and H.-C. Hege, "Fast Display of Illuminated Field Lines," *IEEE Transactions on Visualization and Computer Graphics*, 3(2):118–128, 1997.

Strauss, P. S., and R., Carey, "An Object-oriented 3D Graphics Toolkit," in E. E. Catmull (ed.). *Computer Graphics (SIGGRAPH '92 Proceedings)*, vol. 26, pp. 341–349, July 1992.

Tanner, C., C. Migdal, and M. Jones, "The Clipmap: A Virtual Mipmap," in M. F. Cohen (ed.). *Computer Graphics (SIGGRAPH '98 Proceedings)*, pp. 151–158, July 1998.

Teschner, M. "Texture Mapping: New Dimensions in Scientific and Technical Visualization," *Iris Universe*, (29):8–11, 1994.

Tessman, T. "Casting Shadows on Flat Surfaces," *Iris Universe*, Winter: 16, 1989.

Torrance, K. E., and E. Sparrow, "Theory for Off-specular Reflection from Rough Surfaces," *Journal of Optical Society of America*, 57:1105–114, Sept. 1976.

van Wijk, J. J., "Spot Noise Texture Synthesis for Data Visualization," in T. W. Sederberg (ed.). *Computer Graphics (SIGGRAPH '91 Proceedings)*, vol. 25, pp. 309–318, July 1991.

Walter, B., G. Alppay, E. Lafortune, S. Fernandez, and D. P. Greenberg, "Fitting Virtual Lights for Non-diffuse Walkthroughs," in *Computer Graphics (SIGGRAPH '97 Proceedings)*, vol. 31, pp. 45–48, Aug. 1997.

Ward, G. "High Dynamic Range Imaging," in *Proceedings of the Ninth Color Imaging Conference*, Nov. 2001.

Ward, G. "Measuring and Modeling Anisotropic Reflection," in E. E. Catmull (ed.). *Computer Graphics (SIGGRAPH '92 Proceedings)*, vol. 28, pp. 265–272, July 1992.

Ward, G. J., "The RADIANCE Lighting Simulation and Rendering System," in A. Glassner (ed.). *Proceedings of SIGGRAPH '94 (Orlando, Florida, July 24–29, 1994)*, Computer Graphics Proceedings, Annual Conference Series, pp. 459–472, New York: ACM SIGGRAPH, ACM Press, July 1994.

Watt, A., *Fundamentals of Three-dimensional Computer Graphics*, Wokingham, England: Addison-Wesley, 1989.

Watt, M. "Light-water Interaction Using Backward Beam Tracing," in F. Baskett (ed.). *Computer Graphics (SIGGRAPH '90 Proceedings)*, vol. 24, pp. 377–385, Aug. 1990.

Webb, M., E. Praun, A. Finkelstein, and H. Hoppe, "Fine Tone Control in Hardware Hatching," in *Proceedings of the 2nd International Symposium on Non-photorealistic Animation and Rendering*, pp. 53–ff, New York: ACM Press, 2002.

Welsh, T., "Parallax Mapping with Offset Limiting: A Per-Pixel Approximation of Uneven Surfaces," Infiscape Corporation, *www.infiscape.com/doc/parallax_mapping.pdf*, Jan 2004.

Westover, L. "Footprint Evaluation for Volume Rendering," in F. Baskett (ed.). *Computer Graphics (SIGGRAPH '90 Proceedings)*, vol. 24, pp. 367–376, Aug. 1990.

Whitehurst, A. "Depth Map Based Ambient Occlusion Culling Lighting," *www.andrewwhitehurst.net/amb_occlude.html*, 2003.

Wiegand, T. F. "Cadlab Open Inventor Node Library: csg," *www.arct.cam.ac.uk/research/cadlab/inventor/csg.html*, April 1998.

Wiegand, T. F. "Interactive Rendering of CSG Models," *Computer Graphics Forum*, 15(4):249–261, 1996.

Wilhelms, J., and A. Van Gelder, "Octrees for Faster Isosurface Generation," *ACM Transactions on Graphics*, 11(3):201–227, 1992.

Williams, L. "Pyramidal Parametrics," in *Computer Graphics (SIGGRAPH '83 Proceedings)*, vol. 17, pp. 1–11, July 1983.

Womack, P., and J. Leech (eds.). *OpenGL Graphics with the X Window System (Version 1.3)*, Mountain View, CA: Silicon Graphics, Inc., October 1998.

Wong, P., and R. Bergeron, "30 Years of Multidimensional Multivariate Visualization," Washington, D.C.: IEEE Computer Society, 1997.

Woo, A., P. Poulin, and A. Fournier, "A Survey of Shadow Algorithms," *IEEE Computer Graphics and Applications*, Nov. 1990.

Wu, K. "Rational-linear Interpolation of Texture Coordinates and Their Partial Derivatives," Technical Report HPL-98-113, Computer Systems Laboratory, Hewlett-Packard, 1998.

Zhang, H. "Effective Occlusion Culling for the Interactive Display of Arbitrary Models," Ph.D. dissertation, Department of Computer Science, University of North Carolina at Chapel Hill, 1998, *www.cs.unc.edu/zhangh/dissertation.pdf*.

Zhang, H., D. Manocha, T. Hudson, and K. Hoff III, "Visibility Culling Using Hierarchical Occlusion Maps," In: T. Whitted (ed.). *Computer Graphics (SIGGRAPH '97 Proceedings)*, vol. 24, pp. 77–88, Aug. 1997.

Subject Index

A

Accumulation buffer
 blending artifacts, 193
 convolution utilization,
  228–230
 operations, 116–117
 supersampling, 173–175
Adaptive tessellation, 319
Alias, definition, 60, 169
Alpha
 acceleration, 139
 color computation, 39
Alpha-blended transparency
 depth peeling, 205
 dynamic objects, 202–203
 ordering, 200–201
 output color, 200–202
 transparency mapping, 203
 transparency sorting,
  204–205
Alpha test, fragment
  operations, 111
Ambient lighting, see Lighting
Ambient occlusion, global
  illumination,
  357–359
Andrews plot, point data
  visualization,
  536–537
Animation, textures, 302–306
Anisotropic lighting model,
  337–340
Antialiasing
 area sampling, 177–178
 artifact prevention in line
  renderings, 389–390

full-scene, 170
line antialiasing, 178–180
point antialiasing, 178–180
polygon antialiasing,
  181–182
rationale, 169–170
small particles, 472
supersampling, see
  Supersampling
temporal antialiasing,
  182–184
texturing, 180–181
Application performance
 bottlenecks
  finding
   application subsystem
    bottlenecks,
    overview, 583–584
   geometry subsystem
    bottlenecks, 584
   rasterization subsystem
    bottlenecks, 584–585
  subsystem sites, 581–583
 cache and memory usage
  optimization,
  585–586
 depth complexity,
  measuring, 589–591
 measurement
  finish versus flush,
   588–589
  video refresh
   quantization,
   587–588
 pipeline interleaving,
  591–592

state change minimization,
  586
ARB imaging subset
 color matrix transform, 68
 color tables, 70
 constant color bending,
  71–72
 convolution, 68
 histogram, 69–70
 minmax operation, 70
ARB_buffer_region, 599
ARB_depth_texture, 598
ARB_extensions_string, 599
ARB_fragment_program, 100,
  102, 161, 465, 598
ARB_fragment_shader, 598
ARB_make_current_read, 599
ARB_matrix_palette, 598
ARB_multisample, 207, 598
ARB_multitexture, 598
ARB_occlusion_query, 373,
  598
ARB_pbuffer, 599
ARB_pixel_format, 599
ARB_point_parameters, 472,
  598
ARB_point_sprite, 598
ARB_render_texture, 80, 126,
  314, 599
ARB_shader_objects, 598
ARB_shading_language, 100,
  598
ARB_shadow, 598
ARB_shadow_ambient, 598
ARB_texture_border_clamp,
  598